lonely planet

PHRASEBOOK & DICTIONARY

Acknowledgments
Publisher Mina Patria
Associate Product Director Angela Tinson
Product Editor Martine Power
Series Designer James Hardy
Cover Image Researcher Naomi Parker

Thanks
Elin Berglund, Briohny Hooper, Elizabeth Jones, David Kemp, Chris Love, Wayne Murphy, Darren O'Connell, Branislava Vladisavljevic, Juan Winata

Published by Lonely Planet Publications Pty Ltd
ABN 36 005 607 983

2nd Edition – Sep 2014
ISBN 978 1 74179 480 9

Cover Image Taj Mahal, Agra, Gavin Hellier/Getty
Printed in China 10 9 8 7 6 5 4 3 2 1

Contact lonelyplanet.com/contact

acknowledgments

This book is based on existing editions of Lonely Planet's phrasebooks and was developed with the help of the following people:

- Shahara Ahmed for the Bengali chapter
- Madhu Thaker for the Gujarati chapter
- Richard Delacy for the Hindi chapter
- Hari Prasad Nadig for the Kannada chapter
- Omkar N Koul for the Kashmiri chapter
- Bert Naik for the Konkani chapter
- Amrit Parmar and Jatinder Singh for the Punjabi chapter
- Aruna Magier for the Telugu chapter
- Richard Delacy for the Urdu chapter
- PAEN Language Services for the Assamese, Malayalam, Marathi, Marwari (Rajasthani), Oriya and Tamil chapters, with special thanks to Dr Andreas Ernst, Managing Director

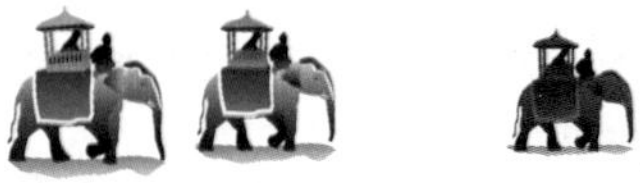

contents

CONTENTS

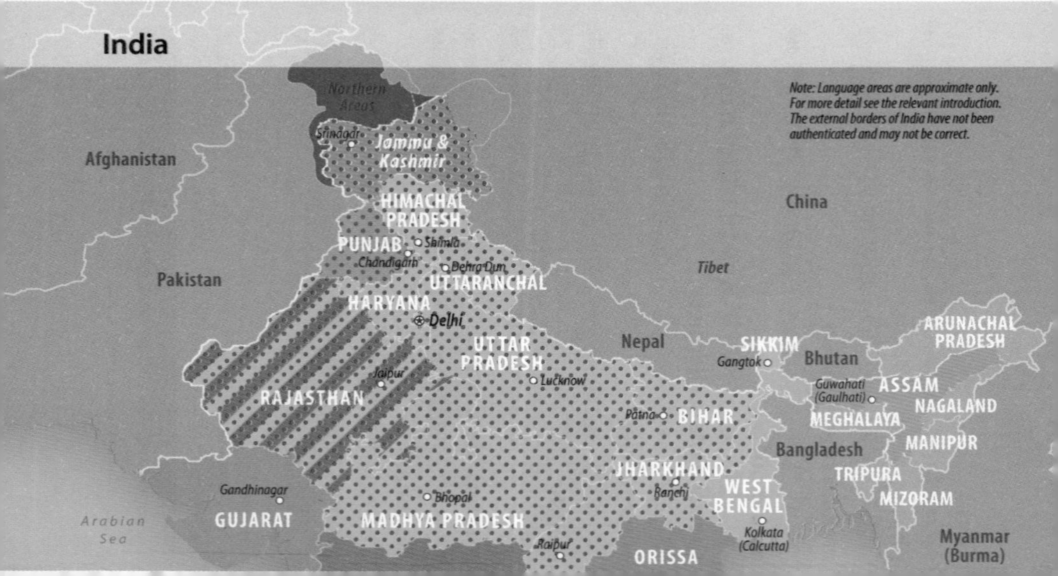
India
Note: Language areas are approximate only. For more detail see the relevant introduction. The external borders of India have not been authenticated and may not be correct.
Afghanistan
Pakistan
Northern Areas
Srinagar
Jammu & Kashmir
HIMACHAL PRADESH
PUNJAB
Shimla
Chandigarh
Dehra Dun
UTTARANCHAL
HARYANA
Delhi
UTTAR PRADESH
Lucknow
Jaipur
RAJASTHAN
China
Tibet
Nepal
SIKKIM
Gangtok
Bhutan
ARUNACHAL PRADESH
Guwahati (Gaulhati)
ASSAM
NAGALAND
MEGHALAYA
MANIPUR
Bangladesh
TRIPURA
MIZORAM
Patna
BIHAR
JHARKHAND
Ranchi
WEST BENGAL
Kolkata (Calcutta)
Myanmar (Burma)
Gandhinagar
GUJARAT
Bhopal
MADHYA PRADESH
Raipur
ORISSA
Arabian Sea

MAHARASHTRA
CHHATTISGARH
Bhubaneswar
Mumbai (Bombay)
Hyderabad
ANDHRA PRADESH
Bay of Bengal
Panaji (Panjim)
GOA
KARNATAKA
INDIAN OCEAN
Lakshadweep Islands (India)
Bengaluru (Bangalore)
Chennai (Madras)
Andaman Islands (India)
Andaman Sea
LAKSHADWEEP
TAMIL NADU
KERALA
0 500 km
0 250 mi
ANDAMAN & NICOBAR ISLANDS
Thiruvananthapuram (Trivandrum)
Sri Lanka
INDIAN OCEAN
Nicobar Islands (India)
Assamese
Bengali
Gujarati
Hindi
Kannada
Kashmiri
Konkani
Malayalam
Marathi
Marwari (Rajasthani)
Oriya
Punjabi
Tamil
Telugu
Urdu
Bengali also spoken in Bangladesh; Urdu also spoken in Pakistan

india – at a glance

In addition to its many other attractions, India offers incredible linguistic diversity. There is no one 'Indian' language as such, which is probably part of the reason why English is still widely spoken more than 50 years after the British left India and why it's still in official use. The Constitution recognises another 22 languages – apart from these, over 1600 minor languages and dialects are spoken throughout the country. Most of India's languages have their own script, but written English is also quite common. Except for Urdu, which is written in a modified version of the Arabic script, all other alphabets have developed from India's ancient Brahmi script.

The languages of India fall into two major groups: Indic (or Indo-Aryan) and Dravidian. The Indic languages are a branch of the Indo-European language family (to which English belongs) and they were brought to India by the peoples of Central Asia. Around 74% of the population, predominantly in the north, speak one of the Indic languages, with Hindi as the main representative. The Dravidian languages, such as Tamil, are believed to be native to India, although they have been influenced by Sanskrit and Hindi throughout history. The Dravidian languages are spoken by about 24% of the population, mainly in the south of India.

For many educated Indians, English is virtually their first language, and for the large number of Indians who speak more than one language, English is often their second tongue. Major efforts have been made to promote Hindi as the national language of India and to gradually phase out English. However, while Hindi is the predominant language of the north, it bears little relation to the Dravidian languages of the south – subsequently, very few people in the south speak Hindi and there is strong support for the retention of English.

did you know?

- Sanskrit is one of the oldest languages in the world (dating from around 1000 BC). The sacred Hindu texts, the Vedas, and classical literature such as the Mahabharata and the Ramayana, were written in this Indic language, which is now one of India's official languages.
- The most commonly used numeral system in the world, the positional decimal system, was developed in ancient India. The numerals used in English and other languages worldwide (ie 1, 2, 3 …) also originate from India – they developed from the Brahmi numerals which date back to the 3rd century BC.
- Unesco declared 21 February the International Mother Language Day, commemorating the day in 1952 when students from Dhaka University were shot dead by police as they campaigned for the recognition of Bengali as the official language of East Pakistan (now Bangladesh).

Assamese

alphabet

vowels				
অ a	আ aa	ই i	ঈ ee	উ u
ঊ oo	এ e	ঐ oy	ও o	ঔ ow

consonants				
ক ka	খ k'a	গ ga	ঘ g'a	ঙ un·ga
চ cha	ছ ch'a	জ ja	ঝ j'a	ঞ ni·ya
ট ta	ঠ t'a	ড da	ঢ d'a	ণ ṇa
ত ţa	থ ţ'a	দ đa	ধ đ'a	ন na
প pa	ফ p'a	ব ba	ভ b'a	ম ma
য ya	ৰ ra	ল la	ৱ wa	শ sha
ষ sa	স sa	হ ha	ক্ষ k'ya	ড় ṛa
ঢ় ṛ'a	ং nga	ঃ ħa	ঁ nya	

numerals									
0	1	2	3	4	5	6	7	8	9
০	১	২	৩	৪	৫	৬	৭	৮	৯

introduction

Despite being related to other languages of northern India, most closely to Bengali, Assamese (ak·so·mee·a অসমীয়া) sounds distinctly non-Indian: it has none of the peculiar 'r'-flavoured consonants of other Indian languages. This is due to past contact with unrelated languages in the surrounding areas of Southeast Asia. Assamese, spoken by around 13 million people in India (mostly in the state of Assam), is a member of the Indo-European family's Indo-Aryan branch, therefore distantly related to the languages of Europe. As one of the languages used to write the Charyapadas, the mysterious millennium-old palm-leaf manuscripts containing Buddhist songs, Assamese has a long literary tradition. It's written in Assamese script, which is similar to that of Bengali. The British forced the people of Assam to use Bengali in the colonial times of the early 1800s – however, due to fierce opposition from the locals, they reinstated Assamese as the main official language a half-century later. Try your hand (or rather tongue) at Assamese – this will surely endear you to its proud owners!

assamese

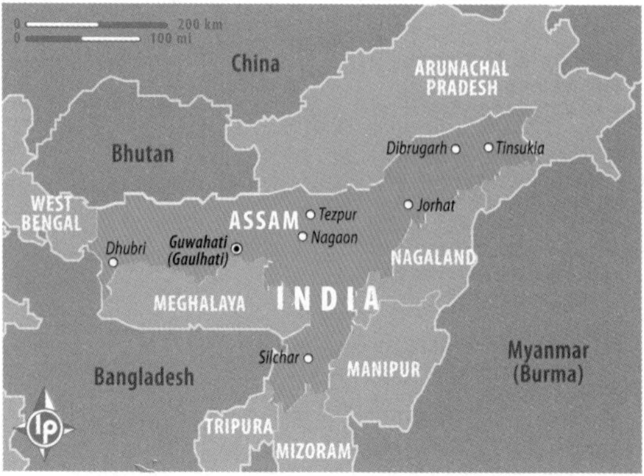

pronunciation

Vowels	
Symbol	**English sound**
a	run
aa	father
ai	aisle
e	bet
ee	see
ey	hey
i	hit
o	pot
oy	toy
oo	zoo
oh	note
ow	now
u	put

In this chapter, the Assamese pronunciation is given in blue after each phrase.

Aspirated consonants (pronounced with a puff of air after the sound) are represented with an apostrophe after the letter – b', ch', d', đ', g', j', k', p', ŗ', t' and ţ'. Retroflex consonants (pronounced with the tongue bent backwards) are included in this table.

Each syllable is separated by a dot. For example:

মই দুঃখিত। moy duk·k'i·ta

Consonants	
Symbol	**English sound**
b	bed
ch	cheat
d	dog
đ	retroflex d
g	go
h	hat
ħ	nasal h
j	jar
k	kit
l	lot
m	man
n	not
ņ	retroflex n
ny	canyon
ng	sing
p	pet
r	red
ŗ	retroflex r
s	sun
sh	shoot
t	top
ţ	retroflex t
w	win
y	yes
z	zero

essentials		
Yes./No.	হয় ।/নহয় ।	hoy/no·hoy
Please.	অনুগ্ৰহ কৰি ।	a·nu·gro·ha ko·ri
Thank you.	ধন্যবাদ ।	đ'on·yo·baađ
Excuse me.	ক্ষমা কৰিব ।	k'yo·ma ko·ri·bo
Sorry.	মই দুঃখিত ।	moy duk·k'i·ta

language difficulties

Do you speak English?
আপুনি ইংৰাজি ভাষা ক'ব পাৰেনে? — aa·pu·ni ing·ra·ji b'a·k'a ko·bo paa·re·ne

Do you understand?
আপুনি বুজি পায়নে? — aa·pu·ni bu·ji pai·ne

I understand.
মই বুজি পাওঁ । — moy bu·ji pow

I don't understand.
মই বুজি নাপাওঁ । — moy bu·ji na·pow

Could you please ...?	আপুনি অনুগ্ৰহ কৰি ...?	aa·pu·ni a·nu·gro·ha ko·ri ...
repeat that	আকৌ এবাৰ	a·kow e·bar
speak more slowly	লাহে লাহে কওঁক	laa·he laa·he ko·uk

numbers					
0	শূন্য	ksuyn·ya	20	বিশ	bees
1	এক	ek	30	ত্ৰিশ	tris
2	দুই	đuy	40	চল্লিছ	sol·lis
3	তিনি	ţi·ni	50	পঞ্চাছ	pon·saas
4	চাৰি	sa·ri	60	ষাঠি	ha·t'i
5	পাঁচ	paans	70	সত্তৰ	hot·ţor
6	ছয়	soy	80	আশী	aak·si
7	সাত	ksaat	90	নব্বই	nob·boy
8	আঠ	aat'	100	এশ	ek·so
9	ন	na	1000	এক হেজাৰ	ek he·zaar
10	দহ	đo·ha	1,000,000	এক লাখ	ek lakh

time & dates

What time is it?	এতিয়া কেইটা বাজিছে?	e·ţi·ya key·ta ba·ji·se
It's (two) o'clock.	এতিয়া (দুটা) বাজিছে।	e·ţi·ya (đu·ta) ba·ji·se
Quarter past (two).	(দুটা) পোন্ধৰ।	(đu·ta) pon·đ'a·ra
Half past two.	আঢ়ৈ।	aar·hoy
Quarter to (three).	(তিনিটালৈ) পোন্ধৰ মিনিট।	(ţi·ni·ta·loy) pon·đ'a·ra mi·nit
At what time ...?	কেইটা বজাত ...?	key·ta bo·jaţ ...
At ...	টা বজাত ...	ta bo·jat ...
It's (15 December).	আজি (১৫ ডিচেম্বৰ)।	aa·ji (pon·đ'a·ra đe·sem·ber)

yesterday	কালি	kaa·li
today	আজি	aa·ji
tomorrow	কালিলৈ	kaa·li·loy

Monday	সোমবাৰ	ksom·baar
Tuesday	মঙ্গলবাৰ	mon·gol·baar
Wednesday	বুধবাৰ	buđ'·baar
Thursday	বৃহস্পতিবাৰ	bri·hos·po·ti·baar
Friday	শুক্ৰবাৰ	ksu·kro·baar
Saturday	শনিবাৰ	kso·ni·baar
Sunday	দেওবাৰ	đe·o·baar

border crossing

I'm here ...	মই ইয়াত আছোঁ ...	moy e·yat a·su ...
in transit	ভ্ৰমণ কৰি থকা অৱস্থাত	b'ro·mon ko·ri t'o·ka o·bos·t'at
on business	ব্যৱসায়ৰ সংক্ৰান্তত	byo·wak·sai kson·kraan·tot
on holiday	বন্ধ উপভোগ কৰিবলৈ	bon·đha u·po·b'ug ko·ri·bo·loy

I'm here for ...	মই ইয়াত থাকিম ...	moy e·yat t'a·kim ...
(10) days	(১০) দিনৰ বাবে	(đo·ha) đi·nor baa·be
(three) weeks	(তিনি) সপ্তাহৰ বাবে	(ţi·ni) ksop·taa·hor baa·be
(two) months	(দুই) মাহৰ বাবে	(đuy) maa·hor baa·be

I'm going to (Guwahati).
মই (গুৱাহাটী)লৈ গৈ আছোঁ। — moy (gu·waa·ha·ti)·loy goy aa·su

I'm staying at the (Hotel Mayur).
মই (ময়ুৰ হোটেল)ত আছোঁ। — moy (mo·yur ho·tel)·ot aa·su

I have nothing to declare.
ঘোষণা কৰিবলৈ মোৰ হাতত একো নাই। — g'o·k'o·na ko·ri·bo·loy mur haa·tot e·ai·ku nai

I have this to declare.
মই এইটো ঘোষণা কৰিব বিচাৰিছোঁ। — moy ai·tu g'o·k'o·na ko·ri·bo bi·saa·ri·su

That's (not) mine.
এইটো মোৰ (নহয়)। — e·ai·tu mur (no·hoy)

tickets & luggage

Where can I buy a ticket?
মই টিকট ক'ত কিনিব পাৰিম? — moy ti·kat kot ki·ni·bo paa·rim

Do I need to book a seat?
মই আসন বুক কৰিব লাগিব নেকি? — moy aak·son buk ko·ri·bo·laa·gi·bo ne·ki

One … ticket (to Guwahati), please.	অনুগ্ৰহ কৰি (গুৱাহাটীৰ) বাবে এটা … টিকট দিয়ক।	a·nu·gro·ha ko·ri (gu·waa·ha·tir) baa·be e·a·ta … ti·kat đi·yok
one-way	যোৱাৰ	ju·waar
return	ঘূৰি অহাৰ	g'u·ri aa·har

I'd like to … my ticket, please.	অনুগ্ৰহ কৰি, টিকটটো … কৰিলেপালে ভাল পাম।	a·nu·gro·ha ko·ri ti·kat·tu … pa·le b'aal pam
cancel	বাতিল	ba·til
change	সলনি	ksa·lo·ni
collect	সংগ্ৰহ	kson·grah

I'd like a nonsmoking/smoking seat, please.
অনুগ্ৰহ কৰি মোক ধূমপান কৰিব নোৱাৰা/পৰা আসন এটা দিয়ক। — a·nu·gro·ha ko·ri muk đ'um·paan ko·ri·bo nu·waa·raa/po·ra aak·son e·a·ta di·yok

Is there a toilet?
শৌচালয় থকা হয় নে? — ksoh·saa·loy t'o·ka hoy ne

Is there air conditioning?
শীততাপ নিয়ন্ত্ৰণ থকা হয় নে? — ksit·tap ni·yon·tron t'o·ka hoy ne

How long does the trip take?
ভ্ৰমণ কৰোতে কিমান সময় ল'ব? — b'ro·mon ko·ru·te ki·man kso·moy lo·bo

Is it a direct route?
এইটো পোনপটীয়া বাট নেকি? — ai·tu pun·po·ti·ya baat ne·ki

My luggage has been …	মোৰ বয়বস্তুবোৰ …	mur boy·bos·đu·bur …
damaged	নষ্ট হ'ল	nos·to hol
lost	হেৰাল	he·ral
stolen	চুৰি হ'ল	su·ri hol

transport

Where does flight (IC-880) arrive?
(আই-চি-৮৮০) উৰাজাহাজ কৰ পৰা আহিব? — (ai·si·aat'·aat'·ksuyn·ya) u·ra·ja·haj kor po·raa a·hi·bo

Where does flight (IC-880) depart?
(আই-চি-৮৮০) উৰাজাহাজ কলৈ যাব? — (ai·si·aat'·aat'·ksuyn·ya) u·ra·ja·haj ko·loy ja·bo

Is this the … to (Guwahati)?	এইখন (গুৱাহাটী)লৈ … যাব নেকি?	ai·k'on (gu·waa·ha·ti)·loy … ja·bo ne·ki
boat	নাওঁ	now
bus	বাছ	bus
plane	উৰাজাহাজ	u·raa·ja·haj
train	ৰেলগাড়ী	rel·gaar·hi

What time's the … bus?	… বাছৰ সময় কি?	… bu·sor kso·moy ki
first	প্ৰথম	pro·t'om
last	শেষ	kseks
next	পিছৰ	pi·sot

How long will it be delayed?
কিমান পলম হ'ব? — ki·maan po·lom ho·bo

Please tell me when we get to (Shillong).
অনুগ্ৰহ কৰি (চিলং) কেতিয়া পামগৈ? — a·nu·gro·ha ko·ri (shil·long) ke·ti·ya paam·goy

That's my seat.
এইখন মোৰ আসন। — ey·k'on mur aak·son

I'd like a taxi …	মোক টেক্সি এখন লাগিব …	muk tak·si e·k'on laa·gi·bo …
at (9am)	(ৰাতি পুৱা ৯) বজাত	(raa·ti pu·wa na) bo·jaat
now	এতিয়া	e·ti·ya

How much is it to (Shillong)?
(চিলং) যাবলৈ কিমান খৰচ হ'ব? — (shil·long) ja·bo·loy ki·maan k'o·ros ho·bo

Please put the meter on.
মিটাৰ চলাওক। — me·ter so·la·wok

Please take me to (this address).
মোক (এই ঠিকনালৈ) লৈ যাওক। — muk (ey t'i·ko·na·loy) loy ja·wok

Please stop here.
অনুগ্ৰহ কৰি ইয়াত ৰ'ব। — a·nu·gro·ha ko·ri e·yat ro·bo

Please wait here.
অনুগ্ৰহ কৰি ইয়াত অপেক্ষা কৰক। — a·nu·gro·ha ko·ri e·yat a·pek·k'a ka·rak

I'd like to hire a car (with a driver).
মই এখন গাড়ী ভাড়া কৰিব বিচাৰিছো (চালকৰ সৈতে)। — moy e·k'on gar·hi b'a·ra ko·ri·ba bi·sa·ri·su (sa·lo·kor ksoy·te)

I'd like to hire a 4WD (with a driver).
মই এখন ৪ হুইলড্ৰাইভ ভাড়া কৰিব বিচাৰিছো (চালকৰ সৈতে)। — moy e·k'on sa·ri weel·đraiw b'a·ra ko·ri·ba bi·sa·ri·su (sa·lo·kor ksoy·te)

How much for daily/weekly hire?
দৈনিক/সাপ্তাহিক ভাড়া কিমান ল'ব? — đoy·nik/ksap·ta·hik b'aa·r'a ki·maan lo·ba

directions

Where's the ...?	... ক'ত আছে?	... kat aa·se
bank	বেঙ্ক	bank
foreign currency exchange	বিদেশী মুদ্ৰা বিনিময়	bi·đek·si muđ·ra bi·ni·moy
post office	ডাকঘৰ	đaak·g'or

Is this the road (to Shillong)?
এইটো (চিলঙলৈ) যোৱা ৰাস্তা নেকি? — ey·tu (shil·lon·go·loy) ju·wa raas·ta ne·ki

Can you show me (on the map)?
আপুনি (মানচিত্ৰত) দেখুৱাব পাৰিব নেকি? — aa·pu·ni (maan·chi·tra·ot) đe·k'u·wa·bo paa·ri·bo ne·ki

What's the address?
ঠিকনাটো কি? — t'i·ko·na·to ki

How far is it?
কিমান দূৰত? — ki·maan đu·rot

How do I get there?
মই তালৈ কেনেকৈ যাব পাৰিম? — moy ta·loy ke·ne·koy ja·bo paa·rim

Turn left/right.
সোঁ/বাওঁ ফালে। — kso/bow p'aa·le

It's …	এইটো …	ey·tu …
behind …	পিছফালে …	pis·p'aa·le …
in front of …	সন্মুখত …	kson·mu·k'ot …
near (to …)	ওচৰত …	u·so·rot …
on the corner	চুকত	su·kot
opposite …	বিপৰীত …	bi·po·rit …
straight ahead	পোনে পোনে	po·ne po·ne
there	তাত	taat

accommodation

Where's a guesthouse/hotel nearby?
ওচৰত গেষ্টহাউচ/হোটেল ক'ত আছে? — u·so·rot gest·hows/ho·tel ko·te aa·se

Can you recommend somewhere cheap/good?
আপুনি সস্তা/ভাল ঠাইৰ বিষয়ে পৰামৰ্শ দিবনে? — aa·pu·ni ksos·ta/b'aal t'air bik·soy·ey po·ra·mor·k'o đi·bo·ne

I'd like to book a room, please.
অনুগ্ৰহ কৰি, মোৰ বাবে কোঠা এটা বুক কৰকচোন। — a·nu·gro·ha ko·ri mo·re baa·be ko·t'aa e·ta buk ko·rok·sun

I have a reservation.
মোৰ আৰক্ষণ আছে। — mo·re aa·rok'·yan aa·se

Do you have a … room?	আপোনালোকৰ ওচৰত … কোঠা এটা আছে নে?	aa·pu·naa·lo·kar u·so·rot … ko·t'aa e·ta aa·se ne
single	এজনীয়া	e·a·jo·nya
double	দুজনীয়া	đu·jo·nya
twin	দ্বৈত	đoy·to

How much is it per night/person?
প্ৰতি ৰাতি/গাইপতি মূল্য কিমান? — pro·ti raa·ti/gai·po·ti mul·ya ki·maan

I'd like to stay for (two) nights.
মই (দুই) ৰাতি থাকিব বিচাৰিছো। — moy (đuy) raa·ti t'a·ki·bo bi·sa·ri·su

Can I have my key, please?
অনুগ্ৰহ কৰি মোৰ কোঠাৰ চাবিটো পামনে? — a·nu·gro·ha ko·ri mo·re ko·t'aar saa·bi·to paam·ne

Can I get another (blanket)?
মই আন এখন (কম্বল) পামনে? — moy aan e·k'on (kom·bol) paam·ne

The (air conditioning) doesn't work.
(শীততাপ নিয়ন্ত্ৰণে) কাম কৰা নাই। — (ksit·taap ni·yan·tra·ne) kaam ko·ra nai

Is there an elevator/a safe?
তাত লিফ্‌ট/আলমাৰী আছে নে? — taat lift/aal·maa·ri aa·se ne

What time is checkout?
এৰাৰ সময় কি? — e·rar kso·moy ki

Can I have my ..., please?	অনুগ্ৰহ কৰি ... মোৰটো পামনে?	a·nu·gro·ha ko·ri ... mor·tu paam·ne
deposit	জমা কৰা	jo·maa ko·ra
passport	পাচপ'ৰ্ট	paas·port
valuables	মূল্যবান সামগ্ৰী	mul·ya·baan ksa·mog·ri

banking & communications

Where's an ATM/a public phone?
এ টি এম/পাব্লিক ফোন ক'ত আছে? — a·ti·em/pub·lik p'on kot aa·se

I'd like to ...	মই কৰিবলৈ ভাল পাম ...	moy ko·ri·bo·loy b'aal paam ...
arrange a transfer	ট্ৰেঞ্চফাৰৰ ব্যৱস্থা	trans·fe·ror bya·bos·t'a
change a travellers cheque	ট্ৰেভেলাৰ্চ চেক ভাঙিবলৈ	tra·b'e·lars sek b'aan·gi·bo·loy
change money	টকা খুচুৰা কৰিবলৈ	to·ka k'u·su·raa ko·ri·bo·loy
withdraw money	টকা উলিয়াবলৈ	to·ka u·li·ya·bo·loy

What's the ...?	কি হ'ব ...?	ki ho·bo ...
charge for that	এইটোৰ মূল্য	ey·tur mul·ya
exchange rate	বিনিময় হাৰ	bi·no·moy haar

Where's the local internet café?
স্থানীয় ইন্টাৰনেট কাফে ক'ত আছে? — st'a·ni·ya in·tar·net ka·fe ko·te aa·se

How much is it per hour?
ঘন্টাত কিমান লয়? — g'on·taat ki·man loy

I'd like to ...	মই ভাল পাম ...	moy b'aal paam ...
get internet access	ইন্টাৰনেট ব্যৱহাৰ কৰিবলৈ	in·tar·net bya·bo·har ko·ri·bo·loy
use a printer/ scanner	প্ৰিন্টাৰ/স্কেনাৰ ব্যৱহাৰ কৰিবলৈ	prin·tar/ska·naar bya·bo·har ko·ri·bo·loy

I'd like a ...	মই বিচাৰো ...	moy bi·sa·ru ...
mobile/cell phone for hire	ম'বাইল/চেল ফোন ভাড়া কৰিবলৈ	mo·bail/sel p'on b'aa·raa ko·ri·bo·loy
SIM card for your network	আপোনালোকৰ নেটৱৰ্কৰ চিমকাৰ্ড	aa·pu·naa·lo·kar net·work·or sim·kaarđ

What are the rates?
মূল্যৰ হাৰ কি? — mul·yar haar ki

What's your phone number?
আপোনাৰ ফোনৰ নম্বৰ কি? — aa·pu·nar p'o·nor nom·bor ki

The number is ...
নম্বৰটো হ'ল ... — nom·bor·tu ho·le ...

I'd like to buy a phonecard.
মই ফোনকাৰ্ড এখন কিনিব বিচাৰিছো। — moy p'on·kaarđ e·k'on ki·ni·bo bi·sa·ri·su

I want to ...	মই বিচাৰিছো ...	moy bi·sa·ri·su ...
call (Canada)	কল ফোন কৰিবলৈ (কানাডা)	kol p'on ko·ri·bo·loy (ka·na·đa)
call collect	ফোন কলৰ মূল্য সংগ্ৰহ	p'on ko·lor mul·ya kson·grah

I want to send a fax/parcel.
মই এখন ফে'/পাৰ্চেল পঠিয়াব বিচাৰোঁ। — moy e·k'on p'aks/paar·sel po·t'i·ya·bo bi·sa·ri·su

I want to buy a stamp/an envelope.
মই এখন ডাকটিকট/লেফাফা কিনিব বিচাৰোঁ। — moy e·k'on đaak·ti·kot/le·p'a·p'a ki·ni·bo bi·sa·ru

Please send it (to Australia).
অনুগ্ৰহ কৰি পঠিয়াই দিয়ক (অস্ট্ৰেলিয়ালৈ)। — a·nu·gro·ha ko·ri po·t'i·yai đi·yok (as·tra·lya·loy)

sightseeing

fort	দুৰ্গ	đur·go
main square	মূখ্য চাৰিআলি	muk'·ya sa·ri·aa·li
mosque	মচজিদ	mos·jiđ
old city	পুৰণা নগৰ	pu·ro·na no·gor
palace	ৰাজপ্ৰসাদ	raaj·prok·sađ
ruins	ধ্বংসাৱশেষ	đ'nong·k'a·wak·sek'
temple	মন্দিৰ	mon·đir

sightseeing

What time does it open/close?
ই কেইটা বজাত খুলিব/বন্ধ হ'ব? — e key·taa bo·jat k'u·li·bo/bon·đ'o ho·bo

What's the admission charge?
প্ৰবেশ মূল্য কিমান? — pro·bek' mul·ya ki·maan

Is there a discount for students/children?
ছাত্ৰ/শিশুৰ বাবে ৰেহাই আছে নেকি? — sat·tro/ksik·sur baa·be re·hai aa·se ne·ki

I'd like to hire a guide.
মই এজন গাইড ভাড়াত ল'ব বিচাৰোঁ। — moy e·jon gaiđ b'aa·raat lo·bo bi·sa·ru

I'd like a catalogue/map.
মই এখন কেটলগ/মানচিত্ৰ ল'ব বিচাৰোঁ। — moy e·k'on ḱe·te·log/maan·sit·tro lo·bo bi·sa·ru

I'd like to go somewhere off the beaten track.
মই আগতে নোযোৱা পথেৰে ক'ৰবালৈ যাব বিচাৰো। — moy aa·go·te nu·ju·wa po·t'e·re ko·ro·ba·loy ja·bo bi·sa·ru

I'd like to see …	মই … চাবলৈ বিচাৰোঁ।	moy … sa·bo bi·sa·ru
What's that?	সেইটো কি?	ksey·tu ki
Can I take a photo?	মই ফটো এখন তোলোনে?	moy p'o·to e·k'on tu·lu·ne
When's the next tour?	পিছৰ যাত্ৰা কেতিয়া?	pi·sor jat·tra ke·ti·ya
How long is the tour?	ভ্ৰমণটো কিমান দিনৰ?	b'ro·mon ki·man đi·nor

Is … included?	… অন্তৰ্ভুক্তনে?	… on·tor·b'uk·to·ne
accommodation	থকা ঠাই	ţ'a·ka t'ai
admission	নাম লিখা	naam li·k'aa
food	আহাৰ	aa·haar
transport	পৰিবহণ	po·ri·bo·hon

shopping

Where's a … ?	ক'ত আছে …?	kot aa·se …
camera shop	কেমেৰাৰ দোকান	ke·me·raar đu·kaan
market	বজাৰ	bo·jaar
souvenir shop	স্মৰণীয় সামগ্ৰীৰ দোকান	sma·ra·ni·o bas·tur đu·kaan

I'm looking for …	মই বিচাৰিছো …	moy bi·saa·ru·su …

Can I look at it?
মই এইটো চাব পাৰোনে? — moy ey·tu sa·bo pa·ro·ne

Can I have it sent overseas?
মই এইটো বিদেশলৈ পঠিয়াব পাৰোনে? — moy ey·tu bi·đe·k'o·loy po·t'i·ya·bo paa·ru·ne

Can I have my (camera) repaired?
মোৰ (কেমেৰা) মেৰামতি হ'বনে? — mo·re (ke·me·raa) me·ra·mo·ti ho·bo·ne

It's faulty.
এইটো বেয়া হ'ল। — ey·tu be·ya ho·le

How much is it?
এইটোৰ দাম কিমান? — ey·tur đaam ki·maan

Can you write down the price?
আপুনি দামটো তলত লিখি দিব নেকি? — aa·pu·ni đaam to·lot li·k'i đi·bo ne·ki

That's too expensive.
সেইটো বৰ বেচি দাম। — ksey·tu bor be·si đaam

I'll give you (300 rupees).
মই তোমাক (৩০০ টকা) দিম। — moy to·mak (ţi·nik·sa to·ka) đim

There's a mistake in the bill.
বিলখনত এটা ভুল আছে। — bilk'·not e·ta b'ul aa·se

Do you accept ...?	আপুনি গ্ৰহণ কৰিবনে ...?	aa·pu·ni gro·hon ko·ri·bo·ne ...
credit cards	ক্ৰেডিট কাৰ্ড	kre·dit karđ
debit cards	ডেবিট কাৰ্ড	đe·bit karđ
travellers cheques	ট্ৰেভেলাৰ্চ চেক	tra·b'e·lars sek

I'd like (a) ..., please.	অনুগ্ৰহ কৰি, মোক দিয়ক ...	a·nu·gro·ha ko·ri mo·ke đi·yak ...
bag	এটা মোনা	e·ta mo·naa
my change	মোৰ খুচুৰা	mo·re k'u·su·ra
receipt	এখন ৰচিদ	e·k'on ro·siđ
refund	পইচা উভতাই দিয়া	poy·sa u·b'o·tai di·ya

Less.	কম।	kom
Enough.	যথেষ্ট।	jo·t'es·to
More.	বেচি।	be·si

photography

Can you ...?	আপুনি পাৰিবনে ... ?	aa·pu·ni paa·ri·bo·ne ...
burn a CD from my memory card/ stick	মোৰ স্মৃতি কাৰ্ড/ স্টিকৰ পৰা চিডি বাৰ্ন কৰিব বিচাৰো	mo·re smri·ti karđ/ stik·or po·ra si·đi burn ko·ri·bo bi·sa·ru
develop this film	এই ৰিলটো ডেভেলপ কৰক	ey ril·tu đe·b'e·lop ko·rok

I need a film for this camera.
মোক এই কেমেৰাটোৰ বাবে ৰিল লাগে। mo·ke ey ke·me·raa·tur baa·be ril laa·ge

When will it be ready?
কেতিয়া তৈয়াৰ হ'ব? ke·ti·ya toy·yaar ho·bo

making conversation

Hello./Goodbye.	নমস্কাৰ।/বিদায়।	no·mos·kaar/bi·đai
Good night.	শুভৰাত্ৰি।	kso·b'o·raat·tri
Mr/Mrs	মিঃ/মিচেচ	mis·ter/mi·siz
Miss/Ms	মিচ/মিজ	mis/miz
How are you?	আপুনি কেনে আছে?	aa·pu·ni ke·ne aa·se
Fine, thanks.	ভালে আছো, ধন্যবাদ।	b'aa·le aa·su đ'on·yo·baađ
And you?	আৰু আপুনি?	aa·ru aa·pu·ni
What's your name?	আপোনাৰ নাম কি?	aa·pu·naar naam ki
My name is ...	মোৰ নাম ...	mo·re naam ...
I'm pleased to meet you.	আপোনাক লগ পাই ভাল লাগিল।	aa·pu·naak lo·ge pai b'aal la·gil
This is my ...	এয়া মোৰ ...	e·ya mo·re ...
brother	ভাই	b'ai
daughter	জীয়েক	ji·yek
father	পিতা	pi·taa
friend	বন্ধু	bon·đ'u
husband	স্বামী	swa·mee
mother	মাঁ	ma
sister	ভনী	b'o·ni
son	পুত্ৰ	put·tra
wife	স্ত্ৰী	stree

Here's my (address).	মোৰ (ঠিকনা) এইটো।	mo·re (t'i·ko·na) ey·tu
What's your (email)?	আপোনাৰ (ইমেইল) কি?	aa·pu·naar (e·me·il) ki
Where are you from?	আপুনি ক'ৰ পৰা আহিছে?	aa·pu·ni ko·re po·ra aa·hi·se
I'm from …	মই আহিছোঁ …	moy aa·hi·su …
Australia	অস্ট্ৰেলিয়া	as·tra·lya
Canada	কানাডা	ka·na·đa
New Zealand	নিউজিলেন্ড	nyu·ji·land
the UK	ইংলেন্ড	ing·land
the USA	মাৰ্কিন যুক্তৰাষ্ট্ৰ	maar·kin juk·to·ras·tro
What's your occupation?	আপোনাৰ জীৱিকা কি?	aa·pu·naar ji·bi·kaa ki
I'm a/an …	মই এজন …	moy e·jon …
businessperson	ব্যৱসায়ী	byo·wak·saa·e
office worker	অফিচৰ কৰ্মচাৰী	a·p'i·sor kor·mo·sa·ri
tradesperson	বেপাৰী	be·pa·ri
Do you like …?	আপুনি ভাল পাইনে …?	aa·pu·ni b'aal pai·ne …
I like …	মই ভাল পাও …	moy b'aal pow …
I don't like …	মই ভাল নাপাও …	moy b'aal na·pow …
art	কলা	ko·la
movies	চিনেমা	si·ne·maa
music	সংগীত	ksong·git
reading	পঢ়া	por·haa
sport	খেলা	k'e·laa

eating out

I'd like (a/the) …, please.	অনুগ্ৰহ কৰি, মোক দিয়ক …	a·nu·gro·ha ko·ri muk đi·yok …
bill	বিল	bil
drink list	পানীয় তালিকা	paa·ni·yo taa·li·ka
local speciality	স্থানীয় বিশেষত্ব	st'a·ni·yo bik·sek·sot·ta
menu	মেনু	me·nu
(non)smoking section	ধূমপান (বৰ্জনীয়) ক্ষেত্ৰ	đ'um·paan (bor·jo·nya) k'set·tro
table for (four)	(চাৰি জনৰ) বাবে টেবুল	(sa·ri jo·nor) baa·be te·bul
that dish	সেই খাদ্যবিধ	ksey k'ađ·đya·biđ'

Can you recommend a …?	আপুনি পৰামৰ্শ দিবনে … ?	aa·pu·ni po·ra·mor·k'o đi·bo·ne …
bar	বাৰ	bar
dish	আহাৰ	aa·haar
place to eat	খোৱা ঠাই	k'o·wa t'ai

breakfast	ৰাতিপুৱাৰ জলপান	raa·ti·pu·war jol·paan
lunch	দিনৰ আহাৰ	đi·nor aa·haar
dinner	নৈশ আহাৰ	naik·sa aa·haar

(cup of) coffee …	… (একাপ) কফি	… (a·kaap) ko·p'i
(cup of) tea …	… (একাপ) চাহ	… (a·kaap) saah
with milk	গাখীৰ দিয়া	ga·k'eer đi·ya
without sugar	চেনী নিদিয়া	se·nee ni·đi·ya

(orange) juice	(কমলা) ৰস	(ko·mo·la) roks
lassi	লাচ্চি	laas·chi
soft drink	শীতল পানীয়	ksee·tol paa·nee·yo

I'll have boiled/mineral water.
মোৰ উতলোৱা/মিনাৰেল পানী আছে। — mo·re u·to·lu·wa/mi·ne·ral paa·nee aa·se

I'll buy you a drink.
মই আপোনাক খুৱাব বিচাৰিছোঁ। — moy aa·pu·naak k'u·wa·bo bi·sa·ri·su

What would you like?
আপুনি কি ভাল পাব? — aa·pu·ni ki b'aal pa·bo

a bottle/glass of beer	এবটল/এগিলাচ বিয়েৰ	a·bo·tol/a·gi·laas beer
a bottle/glass of wine	এবটল/এগিলাচ মদ	a·bo·tol/a·gi·laas mođ

special diets & allergies

Do you have … food?	আপোনাৰ খাদ্যবোৰ … ?	aa·pu·naar k'ađ·đyo·bur …
halal	হালাল	ha·lal
kosher	কোশ্বাৰ	ko·sher
vegetarian	নিৰামিষভোজী	ni·ra·mik'·b'o·ji

I'm allergic to …	মোৰ এলাৰ্জি হয় …	mo·re e·laar·ji hoy …
dairy products	ডায়েৰী সামগ্ৰী	đey·ri ksong·gro·ha
eggs	কণী	ko·ni
meat stock	মাংস	mang·k'o
nuts	বাদাম	ba·đaam
seafood	সাগৰীয়া খাদ্য	ksa·gor·ya k'ađ·ya

emergencies

Help!	সহায়!	kso·hai
Stop!	ৰ'ব!	ro·bo
Go away!	আঁতৰি যাওক!	aa·to·ri ja·wok
Thief!	চোৰ!	cho·re
Fire!	জুই!	juy
Watch out!	সাৱধান!	ksa·bo·đ'an

Call ...!	ফোন কৰক ...!	p'on ko·rok ...
an ambulance	এম্বুলেঞ্চ	am·bu·lans
a doctor	ডাক্তৰ	đaak·tor
the police	আৰক্ষী	aa·rok·k'i

Could you help me, please?
অনুগ্ৰহ কৰি, মোক সহায় কৰিবনে? — a·nu·gro·ha ko·ri mo·ke kso·hai ko·ri·bo·ne

I have to use the phone.
মই ফোন ব্যৱহাৰ কৰিব বিচাৰো। — moy p'on bya·bo·haar kor·bo bi·sa·ru

I'm lost.
মই হেৰাইছোঁ। — moy he·rai·su

Where are the toilets?
শৌচালয় ক'ত আছে? — ksoh·saa·loy ko·te aa·se

Where's the police station?
আৰক্ষী চকিটো ক'ত আছে? — aa·rok·k'i so·ki ko·te aa·se

I have insurance.
মোৰ বীমা আছে। — mo·re bi·ma aa·se

I want to contact my embassy.
মই মোৰ দূতাৱাসৰ সৈতে যোগাযোগ কৰিব বিচাৰো। — moy mo·re đu·ţa·wa·k'or ksoy·te jo·ga·jo·ge ko·ri·bo bi·sa·ru

I've been ...	মোক কৰা হৈছে ...	mo·ke ko·ra hoy·se ...
assaulted	মাৰপিট	maar·pit
raped	বলাৎকাৰ	bo·lat·kaar
robbed	ডকাইতি	đo·kai·ti

I've lost my ...	মোৰ হেৰাইছে ...	mo·re he·rai·se ...
My ... was stolen.	মোৰ চুৰি হৈছে ...	mo·re su·ri hoy·se ...
bag	মোনা	mo·naa
money	টকা	to·ka
passport	পাচপোৰ্ট	paas·port

health

Where's the nearest ...?	ক'ত আছে ...?	ko·te aa·se ...
dentist	দাঁতৰ ডাক্তৰ	đaa·tor đaak·tor
doctor	ডাক্তৰ	đaak·tor
hospital	চিকিৎসালয়	si·kit·sa·loy
pharmacist	ফাৰ্মাচিষ্ট	p'ar·maa·sist

I need a doctor (who speaks English).
মোক এজন ডাক্তৰৰ প্ৰয়োজন (ইংৰাজী কব পৰা)।
mo·ke e·jon đaak·to·ror pro·yo·jon (ing·ra·ji ko·bo po·ra)

Could I see a female doctor?
মই মহিলা ডাক্তৰ এগৰাকীক লগ পাব পাৰোনে?
moy mo·hi·la đaak·tor a·go·raa·kik log paa·bo paa·ru·ne

I've run out of my medication.
মোৰ ঔষধ শেষ হৈছে।
mo·re oh·k'ođ kseks hoy·se

It hurts here.
ইয়াত দুখ পাইছো।
e·yat đuk' pai·su

I have (a) ...	মোৰ আছে ...	mo·re aa·se ...
asthma	এজমা	ej·maa
constipation	শৌচ কচা	ksohs·ko·sa
diarrhoea	হাগনী	ha·go·ni
fever	জ্বৰ	jor
heart condition	হৃদৰোগ	hriđ·ro·ge
nausea	বমি ভাব	bo·mi b'aab

I'm allergic to ...	মোৰ তলত দিয়াবোৰৰ পৰা এলাৰ্জি হয় ...	mo·re to·lot đi·ya·bo·rar po·ra e·laar·ji hoy ...
antibiotics	এন্টিবায়টিক	an·ti·bi·o·tik
anti-inflammatories	এন্টি-ইনফ্লেমেটৰী	an·ti·in·fla·ma·to·ri
aspirin	এচপিৰিন	as·pi·rin
bees	বীজ	bij
codeine	কোডেইন	ko·đe·in

responsible travel

I'd like to learn some Assamese.
মই অলপ অসমীয়া ভাষা শিকিব বিচাৰিছোঁ। — moy a·lop ak·so·mee·a b'a·k'a ksi·ki·bo bi·sa·ri·su

What's this called in Assamese?
অসমীয়া ভাষাত ইয়াক কি বুলি কোৱা হয়? — ak·so·mee·a b'a·k'a·te e·yak ki bu·li ko·wa hoy

Would you like me to teach you some English?
মই বাৰু আপোনাক ইংৰাজী অলপ শিকাব পাৰোনে? — moy baa·ru aa·pu·naak ing·ra·ji a·lop ksi·ka·bo aa·ru·ne

I didn't mean to do/say anything wrong.
মই দুঃখ দিয়াকৈ একো কৰিবলৈ/ কব বিচৰা নাছিলো। — moy đuk' đi·ya·koy e·ku ko·ri·bo·loy/ ko·bo bi·so·ra aa·si·lu

Is this a local or national custom?
এইটো স্থানীয় নে ৰাষ্ট্ৰীয় ৰীতি? — ey·tu st'a·ni·yo ne raas·tri·yo ri·ti

I'd like to stay at a locally run hotel.
মই স্থানীয় ভাবে পৰিচালিত হোটেলত থাকিব বিচাৰিছোঁ। — moy st'a·ni·yo b'a·be po·ri·sa·li·to ho·te·lot t'a·ki·bo bi·sa·ri·su

Where can I buy locally produced goods?
মই স্থানীয় ভাবে উৎপাদিত সামগ্ৰী কʼত কিনিব পাৰিম? — moy st'a·ni·yo b'a·be ut·paa·đi·to ksaa·mog·ri ko·te kin·bo paa·rim

Where can I buy locally produced souvenirs?
মই স্থানীয় ভাবে উৎপাদিত স্মৰণীয় বস্তু কʼত কিনিব পাৰিম? — moy st'a·ni·yo b'a·be ut·paa·đi·to sma·ro·ni·ya bos·tu ko·te kin·bo paa·rim

What's this made from?
ইয়াক কিহেৰে বনোৱা হৈছে? — e·yaak ki·he·re bo·nu·wa hoy·se

Does your company have responsible tourism policies?
আপোনালোকৰ কোম্পানীৰ দায়িত্বশীল পৰ্যটন আঁচনি আছেনে? — aa·pu·na·lo·kaar kom·pa·nir đa·yit·tok·seel por·jo·ton aa·so·ni aa·se·ne

I'd like to do some volunteer work (for your organisation).
মই (আপোনালোকৰ অনুষ্ঠানত) কিছুমান কাম স্বেচ্ছাই কৰিবলৈ ভাল পাম। — moy (aa·pu·na·lo·kar a·nus·t'a·not) ki·su·maan kaam ses·sai ko·ri·bo·loy paam

I'm (an English teacher). Can I volunteer my skills?
মই (এজন ইংৰাজী ভাষাৰ শিক্ষক)। মই মোৰ দক্ষতা আগবঢ়াব পাৰোনে? — moy (e·jon ing·ra·ji b'a·k'ar ksik·sok) moy mo·re đok·k'o·ta aag·bor·ha·bo paa·ru·ne

english–assamese dictionary

Words in this dictionary are marked as n (noun), a (adjective), v (verb), sg (singular), pl (plural), inf (informal) and pol (polite) where necessary.

A

accident দুৰ্ঘটনা dur·g'a·ta·na
accommodation থকা ঠাই ţ'a·ka t'ai
adaptor অভিযোজন কৰোঁতা a·b'i·jon ka·ro·ţa
address n ঠিকনা t'i·ko·na
after পিছত pi·saţ
air-conditioned বাতানুকূল ba·ţa·nu·kul
airplane উৰা-জাহাজ u·raa·ja·haj
airport বিমান-বন্দৰ bi·man·ban·dar
alcohol মদ mod
all সকলো kso·ko·lu
allergy এলাৰ্জি e·laar·ji
ambulance এম্বুলেঞ্চ am·bu·lans
and আৰু a·ru
ankle সৰু গাঁঠি ksa·ru g'a·t'i
antibiotics এন্টিবায়'টিক an·ti·bi·o·tik
arm বাহু ba·hu
ATM এ টি এম a·ti·am

B

baby কেঁচুবা ke·su·a
back (of body) পিঠি pi·t'i
backpack পিঠিত কঢ়িওৱাঁ মোনা pi·t'iţ ka·di·wa·wa mo·naa
bad বেয়া be·ya
bag মোনা mo·naa
baggage claim যাত্ৰীৰ-বস্তু দাবী jat·rir bas·tu da·bi
bank বেঙ্ক bank
bar বাৰ baar
bathroom স্নানাগাৰ sna·na·gar
battery বেটাৰী ba·te·ri
beautiful ধুনীয়া d'u·nya
bed বিছনা bi·sa·na
before আগত aa·gaţ
behind পিছত pi·soţ
bicycle চাইকেল sai·kel
big ডাঙৰ dang·or
bill বিল bil
blanket কম্বল kam·bol
blood group ৰক্ত বৰ্গ rak·ta bar·ga
boat নাওঁ now
book (make a reservation) v বুক কৰা buk ko·ra
bottle বটল bo·tol
boy ল'ৰা lo·ra
brakes (car) ব্ৰেক breyk
breakfast ৰাতিপুৱাৰ জলপান raa·ti·pu·war jol·paan
broken (faulty) বেয়া be·ya
bus বাছ bus
business ব্যৱসায় be·wak·say
buy v কিনা ki·na

C

camera কেমেৰা ke·me·raa
cancel বাতিল ba·til
car গাড়ী gar·hi
cash n নগদ ধন na·gađ đ'an
cash (a cheque) v চেক ভঙোৱা se·ka b'an·ga·wa
cell phone ছে'ল ফোন sel p'on
centre n কেন্দ্ৰ kan·đra
change (money) v খুচুৰা পইচা k'u·su·ra poy·sa
cheap সস্তা ksas·ta
check (bill) বিল bil
check-in n নাম লিখা nam li·k'a
chest (body) বুকু bu·ku
child শিশু ksik·su
cigarette চিগাৰেট si·ga·ra·te
city মহানগৰ ma·ha·na·gar
clean a পৰিষ্কাৰ pa·riş·kar
closed বন্ধ bon·đ'a
cold a শীতল ksi·ţol
collect call কল সংগ্ৰহ ka·la ksan·gra·ha
come আহক aa·hak
computer কম্পিউটাৰ kam·pu·ter
condom কনড'ম kan·dom
contact lenses কন্টেক্ট লেঞ্চ kan·takt le·ni·yach'
cook v ৰান্ধক ran·đ'ak
cost n মূল্য mul·ya
credit card ক্ৰেডিত কাৰ্ড kre·dit karđ
currency exchange মুদ্ৰা বিনিময় কেন্দ্ৰ mudˈ·ra bi·ni·moy ken·đra
customs (immigration) কাষ্টম kas·tom

D

dangerous বিপদজ্জনক bi·pađ·ja·nak
date (time) তাৰিখ ţa·rik'
day দিন din
delay n পলম po·lom
dentist দাঁতৰ ডাক্তৰ đaa·tor đaak·tor
depart বিদায় bi·đay
diaper ডাইপাৰ dai·par
dinner নৈশ আহাৰ naik·sa aa·har

direct a প্ৰত্যক্ষ praṭ·ya·k'a
dirty মলিয়ন ma·li·yan
disabled অক্ষম ak'·yam
discount n ৰেহাই re·hai
doctor ডাক্তৰ đaak·tor
double bed দুজনীয়া বিছনা đu·jo·nya bi·sa·na
double room দুজনীয়া কোঠা đu·jo·nya ko·t'aa
drink n পানীয় pa·ni·yo
drive v গাড়ী চলা ga·ṛi so·la
drivers licence চালকৰ লাইচেঞ্চ sa·lo·kor lai·sen·ze
drug (illicit) মাদক দ্ৰব্য ma·đak đrab·ya

E

ear কাণ kan
east পূব pub
eat খোৱা k'a·ho·a
economy class সাধাৰণ শ্ৰেণী ksa·đ'a·ron shre·ni
electricity বিদ্যুৎ biđ·yot
elevator লিফ্‌ট lift
email ইমেইল e·me·il
embassy দূতাবাস đu·ṭa·waks
emergency জৰুৰী ja·ru·ri
English (language) ইংৰাজী ভাষা ing·ra·ji b'a·k'a
evening গধূলী ga·đ'u·li
exit n প্ৰস্থান pros·t'aan
expensive দামী đa·mi
eye চকু sa·ku

F

far দূৰ đur
fast দ্ৰুত đru·ta
father পিতা pi·taa
film (camera) ৰিল ril
finger আঙুলি an·gu·li
first-aid kit প্ৰাথমিক-চিকিৎসাৰ বাকচ praď·mik si·kiđ·sar ba·kos
first class প্ৰথম শ্ৰেণী pra·đ'am shre·ni
fish n মাছ maas
food আহাৰ aa·haar
foot ভৰি b'a·ri
free (of charge) মুকলি muk·li
friend বন্ধু bon·đu
fruit ফল p'al
full সম্পূৰ্ণ ksam·pur·na

G

gift উপহাৰ u·pa·haar
girl ছোৱালী su·a·li
glass (drinking) গিলাছ gi·laas
glasses আইনা ai·na
go যোৱা ju·wa
good ভাল b'al
guide n গাইড gaiđ

H

half n আধা ađ·ha
hand হাত hat
happy সুখী ksu·k'i
have আছে aa·se
he তেওঁ te·o
head n মুৰ mur
heart হৃদয় hri·đoy
heavy গধুৰ gođ·hur
help v সহায় kso·hay
here ইয়াত i·yat
high উচ্চ us·ch'a
highway প্ৰধান পথ pro·đan pot'
hike v দীঘলীয়াকৈ খোজ কঢ়া কাৰ্য đi·go·lya·koy k'oj k'o·ra kar·jo
holiday ছুটী বা বন্ধৰ দিন su·ti ba bon·đor đin
homosexual n&a সমকামী ksa·ma·ka·mi
hospital চিকিৎসালয় si·kit·sa·loy
hot উত্তপ্ত u·tap·ta
hotel হোটেল ho·tel
hungry ভোকাতুৰ b'u·ka·đur
husband স্বামী swa·mee

I

I মই moy
identification (card) চিনাক্তকৰণ কাৰ্ড si·nak·đa·ka·ran karđ
ill অসুস্থ ak·sus·t'a
important গুৰুত্বপূৰ্ণ gu·ru·tađ·pur·na
injury আঘাত aa·g'at
insurance বীমা bi·ma
internet ইন্টাৰনেট in·tar·net
interpreter দোভাষী đo·vak·si

J

jewellery গহণা ga·ha·đa
job কাম kaam

K

key চাবি saa·bi
kilogram কিলোগ্ৰাম ki·lo·gram
kitchen পাকঘৰ paak·g'ar
knife কটাৰী ko·ta·ri

L

laundry (place) কাপোৰ ধোৱা দোকান kaa·por d'o·a đu·kaan
lawyer উকিল u·kil
left (direction) বাওঁ ফাল bow p'al
leg (body) ভৰি b'o·ri
lesbian n সমকামী মহিলা ksa·ma·ka·mi ma·hi·la
less কম kom
letter (mail) চিঠি si·t'i
light n পোহৰ pu·hor
like v নিচিনা ni·si·na
lock n তলা বন্ধ taa·la bon·đ'o
long দীঘল đi·g'al
lost হেৰুৱা he·ru·waa
love v প্ৰেম prem
luggage বয়বস্তু boy·bos·đu
lunch দিনৰ আহাৰ đi·nor aa·har

M

mail n ডাক daak
man মানুহ ma·nuh
map মানচিত্ৰ maan·sit·tro
market বজাৰ bo·jaar
matches জুইশলা juyk·sa·la
meat মাংস mang·kso
medicine ঔষধ oh·kođ'
message বাৰ্তা bar·đa
milk গাখীৰ ga·k'eer
minute মিনিট mi·nit
mobile phone ছে'ল ফোন sel p'on
money টকা to·ka
month মাহ ma·ha
morning ৰাতিপুৱা ra·đip·wa
mother মা ma
motorcycle মটৰ চাইকেল mo·tor sai·kel
mouth মুখ mu·k'a

N

name নাম naam
near ওচৰত o·sa·rađ
neck n ডিঙি din·gi
new নতুন na·tun
newspaper বাতৰি কাকত ba·đo·ri kaa·kođ
night ৰাতি ra·đi
no নহয় no·hoy
noisy কোলাহলপূৰ্ণ ko·laa·hol·pur·na
nonsmoking ধুমপান বৰ্জনীয় đ'um·paan bor·jo·nya
north উত্তৰ u·đar
nose নাক naa·ka
now এতিয়া e·ti·ya
number নম্বৰ nom·bor

O

old পুৰণা pu·ro·na
one-way ticket যোৱা টিকট ju·a ti·kat
open a খোলা k'a·o·la
outside বাহিৰ baa·hir

P

passport পাচপোৰ্ট paas·port
pay v পৰিশোধ po·rik·sođ
pharmacy ফাৰ্মেচি p'ar·maa·si
phonecard ফোনকাৰ্ড p'on·kaarđ
photo ফোটো p'o·to
police আৰক্ষী aa·rok·k'i
postcard পোস্টকাৰ্ড post·kaarđ
post office ডাকঘৰ đaak·g'or
pregnant গৰ্ভৱতী gar·b'a·ba·đi
price n দাম đaam

Q

quiet a নিৰব ni·rab

R

rain n বৰষুণ bark·sun
razor ৰেজৰ re·jor
receipt n ৰচিদ ro·sid
refund n পইচা উভতাই দিয়া poy·sa u·b'o·tai di·ya
registered mail ৰেজিস্টাৰ্ড চিঠি ra·jis·tarđ si·t'i
rent v ভাড়া b'a·đa
repair v মেৰামতি me·ra·mo·đi
reservation আৰক্ষণ a·rak'·yan
restaurant ৰেস্টুৰেন্ট res·tu·rant
return v উভতি অহা ub'·đi o·ha
return ticket উভতি অহা টিকট ub'·đi o·ha ti·kat
right (direction) সোঁ ফালে su p'a·le
road ৰাস্তা ras·đa
room n কোঠা ko·t'aa

S

safe a নিৰাপদ ni·raa·pađ
sanitary napkin চেনিটেৰী নেপকিন sa·ni·ta·ri nap·kin
seat n আসন aak·son
send পঠাওক po·t'a·ok
sex যৌন সম্পৰ্কীয় yow·no ksom·por·ki·o
shampoo চেম্পু sam·poo
share (a dorm) ভাগ বটোৱাৰ b'ag bo·to·ar

she (younger/older) তাই/তেখেত tai/te·k'et
sheet (bed) বিচনা ছাদৰ bi·sa·na sa·đor
shirt চোলা so·la
shoes জোতা jo·ta
shop n দোকান đu·kaan
short চুটি su·ti
shower n চাৱাৰ saa·war
single room এজনীয়া কোঠা e·jo·nya ko·t'aa
skin n ছাল sal
skirt n স্কাৰ্ট skaart
sleep v টোপনি to·pa·ni
slowly লাহে লাহে la·he la·he
small সৰু ksa·ru
soap চাবুন sa·bun
some কিছুমান ki·su·maan
soon সোনকালে kson·ka·le
south দক্ষিণ đak'·yaiđ
souvenir shop স্মৰণীয় বস্তুৰ দোকান
sma·ra·ni·o bas·tur đu·kaan
stamp টিকট ti·kat
stand-by ticket ষ্টেণ্ডবাই টিকট stand·bai ti·kat
station (train) ষ্টেচন sta·son
stomach পেট pet
stop v ৰ'ব rab'
stop (bus) n বাচ ষ্টপ bus stop
street পথ pađ'
student ছাত্ৰ-ছাত্ৰী sat·ro·sat·ri
sun বেলি be·li
sunscreen চানস্ক্ৰীন san·skreen
swim v সাঁতোৰা ksa·đa·ro

T

tampons টেম্পন tam·pon
teeth দাঁত đađ
telephone n টেলিফোন te·le·p'on
temperature (weather) তাপমান đaa·pa·maan
that (one) সেইটো ksey·to
they সিহঁত ksi·hat
thirsty পিয়াহ pi·ah
this (one) এইটো ey·to
throat ডিঙি đin·gi
ticket টিকট ti·kat
time সময় kso·moy
tired ভাগৰুৱা b'ag·ru·a
tissues টিচু ti·su
today আজি a·ji
toilet শৌচালয় ksoh·saa·loy
tomorrow কালিলৈ kaa·li·loy
tonight আজি ৰাতি a·ji ra·đi
toothbrush টুথব্ৰাচ toođ'·brus
toothpaste টুথপেষ্ট toođ'·peyst
torch (flashlight) টৰ্চ tors
tour n পৰ্যটন par·ya·tan
tourist office পৰ্যটন কাৰ্যলয় par·ya·tan kar·ya·loy
towel টাৱেল tow·el
train n ৰেলগাড়ী rel·gaar·hi
translate অনুবাদ a·nu·baađ
travel agency ট্ৰেভেল এজেঞ্চি tra·b'el a·jen·si
travellers cheque ট্ৰেভেলাৰ্চ চেক tra·b'e·lars sek
trousers পেন্ট pent
twin beds দুজনীয়া বিচনা đu·jo·nya bi·sa·na

U

underwear পানীৰ তলত pa·nir đo·lođ
urgent জৰুৰী ja·ro·ri

V

vacant খালি k'a·li
vegetable n পাচলি paa·so·li
vegetarian a নিৰামিষভোজী ni·ra·mik'·b'o·ji
visa ভিচা b'i·sa

W

walk v খোজ কৰা k'owj ko·ra
wallet ৱালেট waa·let
wash (something) ধোৱা đ'a·wa
watch n দৃষ্টি đris·ti
water n পানী paa·nee
we আমি a·mi
weekend সপ্তাহ শেষ ksap·đa·ha kseks
west পশ্চিম pash·sim
wheelchair চকা লগোৱা চকি so·ka la·gow·a so·ki
when কেতিয়া ke·tya
where ক'ত ko·te
who কোন kun
why কিয় ki·o
wife স্ত্ৰী stree
window খিৰিকি k'i·ri·ki
with সৈতে ksoy·te
without অবিহনে a·bi·ho·ne
woman মহিলা ma·hi·laa
write লিখক li·k'a·ok

Y

yes হয় hoy
yesterday কালি kaa·li
you sg pol/inf আপুনি/তুমি aa·pu·ni/tu·mi
you pl pol/inf আপোনালোক/তোমালোক
aa·pu·na·luk/tu·ma·luk

Bengali

alphabet

vowels

অ	আ	ই	ঈ	উ	উ	ঋ	এ	ঐ	ও	ঔ
o	a	i	i	u	u	ri	e	*oh*·i	oh	*oh*·u

consonants

ক ko	খ k'o	গ go	ঘ g'o	ঙ *u*·mong	চ cho	ছ ch'o	জ jo	ঝ j'o
ঞ *ee*·o	ট to	ঠ t'o	ড đo	ঢ đ'o	ণ no	ত ţo	থ ţ'o	দ do
ধ d'o	ন no	প po	ফ fo	ব bo	ভ b'o	ম mo	য jo	র ro
ল lo	শ sho	ষ sho	স sho	হ ho				

numerals

0	1	2	3	4	5	6	7	8	9
০	১	২	৩	৪	৫	৬	৭	৮	৯

BENGALI

বাংলা

introduction

Bengali (*baang*·la বাংলা) is spoken by approximately 220 million people, ranking it as the fourth most spoken language in the world. As well as being the official language of Bangladesh and the Indian states of Tripura and West Bengal, it's also spoken by large communities in North America and parts of Europe and the Middle East. Bengali belongs to the Indic group of the Indo-European language family, with Sanskrit, Hindi, Assamese and Oriya as close relatives. Old Bengali, with its distinctive Brahmi script, had developed by about AD1000 and was strongly flavoured with Prakrit and Sanskrit words, to be spiced up with Persian, Arabic and Turkish vocabulary when Bengal was conquered by Muslims in the 12th century AD. Today's Bengali has two literary forms – *sha*·d'u·b'a·sha সাধুভাষা (lit: elegant language), the traditional literary style of 16th-century Middle Bengali, and *chohl*·ṭi·b'a·sha চলতি ভাষা (lit: running language), a more colloquial form based on the Bengali spoken in Kolkata. The best-known Bengali author is Rabindranath Tagore, the winner of the Nobel Prize for Literature in 1913 and writer of the national anthems of both India and Bangladesh.

bengali

pronunciation

Vowels		Consonants	
Symbol	**English sound**	**Symbol**	**English sound**
a	run	b	bed
ae	act	ch	cheat
aa	father	d	dog
ai	aisle	đ	retroflex d
ay	say	f	fun
e	bet	g	go
ee	see	h	hat
i	hit	j	joke
o	pot	k	kit
oh	note	l	lot
oy	toy	m	man
u	put	n	not
ui	quick	ng	ring
		p	pet
		r	run
		ŗ	retroflex r
		s	sun
		sh	shut
		t	top
		ţ	retroflex t
		v	very
		w	win
		y	yes
		z	zero

In this chapter, the Bengali pronunciation is given in blue after each phrase.

Aspirated consonants (pronounced with a puff of air after the sound) are represented with an apostrophe after the letter – b', ch', d', đ', g', j', k', p', t' and ţ'. Retroflex consonants (pronounced with the tongue bent backwards) are included in this table.

Each syllable is separated by a dot, and the syllable stressed in each word is italicised. For example:

শুনুন। *shu*·nun

essentials

Yes./No.	হ্যাঁ।/না।	hạng/naa
Please.	প্লিজ।	pleez
Thank you.	ধন্যবাদ।	*d'oh*·noh·baad
Excuse me. (to get past)	একটু দেখি।	*ek*·tu *de*·k'i
Excuse me. (to get attention)	শুনুন।	*shu*·nun
Sorry.	সরি।	*so*·ri

language difficulties

Do you speak English?
আপনি কি ইংরেজি বলতে পারেন? — *aap*·ni ki ing·*re*·ji *bohl*·ţe *paa*·ren

Do you understand?
আপনি কি বুঝতে পারছেন? — *aap*·ni ki *buj'*·ţe *paar*·ch'en

I understand.
আমি বুঝতে পারছি। — *aa*·mi *buj'*·ţe *paar*·ch'i

I don't understand.
আমি বুঝতে পারছি না। — *aa*·mi *buj'*·ţe *paar*·ch'i na

Could you please ...?	... প্লিজ?	... pleez
repeat that	আবার বলেন	*aa*·bar *boh*·len
speak more slowly	আরো ধিরে বলেন	*aa*·roh *d'i*·re *boh*·len

numbers

0	শূন্য	*shun*·noh	**20**	বিশ	beesh
1	এক	aek	**30**	তিরিশ	*ţi*·rish
2	দুই	dui	**40**	চল্লিশ	*chohl*·lish
3	তিন	ţeen	**50**	পঞ্চাশ	*pon*·chaash
4	চার	chaar	**60**	ষাট	shaat
5	পাচ	paach	**70**	সত্তুর	*shohţ*·ţur
6	ছয়	ch'oy	**80**	আশি	*aa*·shi
7	সাত	shaaţ	**90**	নব্বই	*nohb*·boh·i
8	আট	aat	**100**	এক শ	aek shoh
9	নয়	noy	**1,000**	এক হাজার	aek *haa*·jaar
10	দশ	dosh	**100,000**	এক লাখ	aek laak'

time & dates

What time is it?	কয়টা বাজে?	*koy*·ta *baa*·je
It's (ten) o'clock.	(দশটা) বাজে।	(*dosh*·ta) *baa*·je
Quarter past (ten).	সোয়া (দশটা)।	*shoh*·aa (*dosh*·ta)
Half past (ten).	সাড়ে (দশটা)।	*shaa*·ŗe (*dosh*·ta)
Quarter to (ten).	পৌনে (দশটা)।	*poh*·ne (*dosh*·ta)
At what time ...?	কটার সময় ...?	*ko*·tar *sho*·moy ...
At (seven) am/pm.	সকাল/রাত (সাতটায়)।	*sho*·kaal/raaţ (*shaţ*·ta·e)
It's (18 October).	আজ (আঠারই অক্টোবার)।	aaj (*aa*·t'aa·roh·i *ok*·toh·baar)
yesterday	গতকাল	*go*·ţoh·kaal
today	আজকে	*aaj*·ke
tomorrow	আগামিকাল	*aa*·ga·mi·kaal
Monday	সোমবার	*shohm*·baar
Tuesday	মঙ্গলবার	*mohng*·gohl·baar
Wednesday	বুধবার	*bud'*·baar
Thursday	বৃহস্পতিবার	*bri*·hohsh·poh·ţi·baar
Friday	শুক্রবার	*shuk*·roh·baar
Saturday	শনিবার	*shoh*·ni·baar
Sunday	রবিবার	*roh*·bi·baar

border crossing

I'm ...	আমি ...	*aa*·mi ...
in transit	ট্রান্জিটে আছি	*traan*·zee·te *aa*·ch'i
on business	ব্যবসার কাজে এসেছি	*baeb*·shaar *kaa*·je *e*·she·ch'i
on holiday	ছুটিতে আছি	*ch'u*·ti·ţe *aa*·ch'i
I'm here for (two) ...	আমি এখানে (দুই) ... আছি।	*aa*·mi e·k'a·ne (dui) ... *aa*·ch'i
days	দিন	din
weeks	সপ্তাহ	*shop*·ţaa·hoh
months	মাস	maash

I'm going to (Tangail).
আমি (টাঙ্গাইল) যাচ্ছি। *aa*·mi (*taang*·ail) *jaach*·ch'i

I'm staying at the (Parjatan Motel).
আমি (পর্যটন মোটেলে) আছি। *aa*·mi (*por*·joh·ton *moh*·te·le) *aa*·ch'i

I have nothing to declare.
আমার ডিকলিয়ার করার কিছু নাই। *aa*·mar *đik*·li·aar *ko*·rar *ki*·ch'u nai

I have something to declare.
আমার কিছু ডিকলিয়ার করতে হবে। *aa*·mar *ki*·ch'u *đik*·li·aar *kohr*·ţe *ho*·be

That's (not) mine.
ওটা আমার (না)। *oh*·ta *aa*·mar (na)

tickets & luggage

Where do I buy a ticket?
কোথায় টিকেট কিনবো? *koh*·ţ'ay *ti*·ket *kin*·boh

Do I need to book well in advance?
এ্যাডভান্স বুকিং লাগবে কি? *aeđ*·vaans *bu*·king *laag*·be ki

A ... ticket (to Dhaka).	(ঢাকার) জন্য একটা ... টিকেট।	(*đ'aa*·kaar) *john*·noh *aek*·ta ... *ti*·ket
one-way	ওয়ানওয়ে	*wan*·way
return	রিটার্ন	*ri*·tarn

I'd like to ... my ticket, please.	আমার টিকেট ... করতে চাই।	*aa*·mar *ti*·ket ... *kohr*·ţe chai
cancel	ক্যান্সেল	*kaen*·sel
change	বদলাতে	*bod*·la·ţe
confirm	কনফার্ম	*kon*·farm

I'd like a (non)smoking seat.
আমাকে একটা ধুমপান (নিষেধ) এলাকায় সিট দেন। *aa*·ma·ke *aek*·ta *d'um*·paan (*ni*·shed') e·la·ka·e seet den

Is there a toilet/air conditioning?
টয়লেট/এয়ারকন্ডিশনার আছে কি? *toy*·let/*e*·aar·kon·di·shoh·nar *aa*·ch'e ki

How long does the trip take?
যেতে কতক্ষন লাগবে? *je*·ţe *ko*·tohk·k'ohn *laag*·be

Is it a direct route?
এটা কি ডাইরেক্ট রাস্তা? e·ta ki *đai*·rekt *raas*·ţa

My luggage has been ...	আমার লাগেজ ...	*aa*·mar *laa*·gej ...
damaged	ড্যামেজ হয়েছে	*đae*·mej *hoh*·e·ch'e
lost	হারিয়ে গেছে	*haa*·ri·ye *gae*·ch'e
stolen	চুরি হয়েছে	*chu*·ri *hoh*·e·ch'e

transport

Where does flight (BG007) arrive?		
ফ্লাইট (বিজি ০০৭) কোন গেটে আসবে?		flait (*bi*·ji *shun*·noh *shun*·noh shaaţ) kohn *ge*·te *aash*·be
Where does flight (BG007) depart?		
ফ্লাইট (বিজি ০০৭) কোন গেটে থেকে যাবে?		flait (*bi*·ji *shun*·noh *shun*·noh shaaţ) kohn *ge*·te *t'e*·ke *jaa*·be

Is this the … to (Chittagong)?	এই … কি (চিটাগাঙের)?	ay … ki (*chi*·ta·gang·er)
boat	নৌকা	*noh*·u·ka
bus	বাস	bas
plane	প্লেন	plen
train	ট্রেন	tren

When's the … (bus)?	… (বাস) কখন?	… (bas) *ko*·k'ohn
first	প্রথম	*proh*·t'ohm
last	শেষ	shesh
next	পরের	*po*·rer

How long will it be delayed?		
কত দেরি হবে?		*ko*·toh *de*·ri *ho*·be
Please tell me when we get to (Sylhet).		
(সিলেট) আসলে আমাকে বলবেন, প্লিজ।		(*si*·let) *aash*·le *aa*·maa·ke *bohl*·ben pleez

I'd like a taxi …	আমার … ট্যাক্সি লাগবে।	*aa*·mar … *tak*·si *laag*·be
at (9am)	সকাল (নটায়)	*sho*·kal (*noy*·ta)
now	এখন	*ae*·k'ohn

How much is it to …?		
… যেতে কত লাগবে?		… *je*·ţe *ko*·toh *laag*·be
Please put the meter on.		
প্লিজ মিটার লাগান।		pleez *mee*·tar *laa*·gan
Please take me to this address.		
আমাকে এই ঠিকানায় নিয়ে যান।		*aa*·ma·ke ay *t'i*·kaa·na·e *ni*·ye jaan
Please stop here.		
এখানে থামেন।		e·k'aa·ne *ţ'aa*·men
Please wait here.		
এখানে অপেক্ষা করেন।		e·k'aa·ne o·*pek*·k'a *koh*·ren

I'd like to hire a car/4WD (with a driver).
আমি একটা গাড়ি/ফোর হুয়িল ড্রাইভ (ড্রাইভার সহ) ভাড়া করতে চাই।
aa·mi *aek*·ta *gaa*·ṛi/fohr weel đraiv (*đrai*·var *sho*·hoh) *b'a*·ṛa *kohr*·te chai

How much for daily/weekly hire?
দৈনিক/সাপ্তাহিক ভাড়া করতে কত লাগবে?
doh·i·nik/*shap*·ţa·hik *b'a*·ṛa *kohr*·ţe *ko*·ţoh *laag*·be

directions

Where's the ...?	... কোথায়?	... *koh*·ţ'a·e
bank	ব্যাংক	baenk
foreign currency exchange	ফরেন এক্সচেঞ্জ অফিস	*fo*·ren eks·*chenj o*·fish
post office	পোস্ট অফিস	pohst *o*·fish

Is this the road to (Rangamati)?
এটা কি (রাঙ্গামাটি) যাওয়ার রাস্তা?
e·ta ki (*raang*·a·maa·ti) *ja*·waar *raa*·sţa

Can you show me (on the map)?
আমাকে (ম্যাপে) দেখাতে পারেন?
aa·ma·ke (*mae*·pe) *dae*·k'a·ţe *paa*·ren

What's the address?
ঠিকানা কি?
ţ'i·kaa·na ki

How far is it?
এটা কত দুর?
e·ta *ko*·ţoh dur

How do I get there?
ওখানে কি ভাবে যাব?
oh·k'a·ne ki *b'a*·be *ja*·boh

Turn left/right.
বামে/ডানে টার্ন করবেন
baa·me/*daa*·ne taarn *kohr*·ben

It's ...	এটা ...	*e*·ta ...
behind ...	...এর পিছনে	...·er *pi*·ch'oh·ne
in front of ...	...এর সামনে	...·er *shaam*·ne
near ...	...এর কাছে	...·er *ka*·ch'e
on the corner	কর্নারে	*koŗ*·na·re
opposite ...	...এর উল্টো দিকে	...·er *ul*·toh *di*·ke
straight ahead	সোজা	*shoh*·ja
there	ঐ যে	*oh*·i je

accommodation

Where's a guesthouse/hotel?
গেষ্টহাউস/হোটেল কোথায়? — gest·*ha*·us/*hoh*·tel *koh*·ţ'ay

Can you recommend somewhere cheap/good?
বলতে পারেন কোনো সস্তা/ভাল যায়গা কোথায়? — *bohl*·ţe *paa*·ren *koh*·noh *shos*·ţa/*b'a*·loh *ja*·e·gaa *koh*·ţ'ay

I'd like to book a room, please.
আমি একটা রুম বুক করতে চাই, প্লিজ। — *aa*·mi *aek*·ta rum buk *kohr*·ţe chai pleez

I have a reservation.
আমার একটা বুকিং আছে। — *aa*·mar *aek*·ta *bu*·king *aa*·ch'e

Do you have a ... room?	আপনার কি ... রুম আছে?	*aap*·nar ki ... rum *aa*·ch'e
single	সিঙ্গেল	*sin*·gel
double	ডবল	*đo*·bohl
twin	টুইন	*tu*·in

How much is it per night/person?
প্রতি রাতে/জনে কত? — *proh*·ţi *raa*·ţe/*jo*·ne *ko*·ţoh

For (three) nights.
(তিন) রাতের জন্য। — (ţeen) *raa*·ţer *john*·noh

Can I have my key, please?
আমাকে আমার চাবি দিতে পারেন, প্লিজ? — *aa*·ma·ke *aa*·mar *cha*·bi *di*·ţe *paa*·ren pleez

Can I get another (blanket)?
আমাকে একটা এক্সট্রা (কম্বল) দিতে পারেন? — *aa*·ma·ke *aek*·ta *ek*·stra (*kom*·bohl) *di*·ţe *paa*·ren

The (air conditioning) doesn't work.
(এয়ারকন্ডিশনার) কাজ করে না। — (*e*·aar·kon·đi·shoh·nar) kaaj *koh*·re na

Is there an elevator/a safe?
আপনার কি লিফ্ট/লকার আছে? — *aap*·nar ki lift/*lo*·kar *aa*·che

What time is checkout?
চেক আউট ক'টার সময়? — chek *aa*·ut *ko*·tar *sho*·moy

Can I have my ..., please?	আমার ... দেবেন, প্লিজ?	*aa*·mar ... *de*·ben pleez
deposit	ডিপোজিট	*đi*·poh·zit
passport	পাসপোর্ট	*pas*·pohrt

banking & communications

Where's an ATM/a public phone?
এ-টি-এম/ পাবলিক ফোন কোথায়? — *e*·ti·em/ *pab*·lik fohn *koh*·ţ'ay

I'd like to …	আমি … চাই।	*aa*·mi … chai
arrange a transfer	ট্রান্সফার করতে	*trans*·faar *kohr*·ţe
change a travellers cheque	একটা ট্র্যাভেলার্স চেক ভাঙ্গাতে	*aek*·ta *trae*·ve·lars chek *b'ang*·ga·ţe
change money	টাকা ভাঙ্গাতে	*ta*·ka *b'ang*·ga·ţe
withdraw money	টাকা তুলতে	*ta*·ka *ţul*·ţe

What's the …?	… কি?	… ki
charge for that	ওটার জন্য চার্জ	*oh*·tar *john*·noh charj
exchange rate	এক্সচেঞ্জ রেট	eks·*chenj* rayt

Where's the local internet café?
কাছাকাছি ইন্টারনেট ক্যাফে কোথায়? — *ka*·ch'a·ka·ch'i *in*·tar·net *kae*·fe *koh*·ţ'ay

How much is it per hour?
প্রতি ঘন্টায় কত? — *proh*·ţi *g'on*·ta·e *ko*·ţoh

I'd like to …	আমি … চাই।	*aa*·mi … chai
get internet access	ইন্টারনেট এ্যাকসেস	*in*·tar·net *aek*·ses
use a printer/ scanner	প্রিন্টার/স্ক্যানার ব্যবহার করতে	*prin*·tar/*skae*·nar *bae*·boh·har *kohr*·ţe

I'd like a …	… চাই।	… chai
mobile/cell phone for hire	একটা মোবাইল ফোন ভাড়া করতে	*aek*·ta *moh*·bail fohn *b'a*·ŗa *kohr*·ţe
SIM card for your network	আপনার নেটওয়ার্কের জন্য সিম কার্ড	*aap*·nar *net*·wark·er *john*·noh sim kard

What are the rates?
রেট কি? — rayt ki

What's your phone number?
আপনার ফোন নম্বর কি? — *aap*·nar fohn *nom*·bohr ki

The number is …
নম্বরটা হচ্চে … *nom*·bohr·ta *hohch*·ch'e …

I'd like to buy a phonecard.
আমি একটা ফোনকার্ড কিনতে চাই। *aa*·mi *aek*·ta *fohn*·kard *kin*·ţe chai

I want to …	আমি … চাই।	*aa*·mi … chai
call (Canada)	(ক্যানাডা) কল করতে	(*kae*·na·da) kol *kohr*·ţe
call collect	চার্জটা রিভার্স করতে	*charj*·ta *ri*·vars *kohr*·ţe

I want to send a fax/parcel.
আমি একটা ফ্যাক্স/পার্সেল পাঠাতে চাই। *aa*·mi *aek*·ta faeks/*par*·sel *pa*·ţ'a·ţe chai

I want to buy a stamp/an envelope.
আমি একটা স্ট্যাম্প/এনভেলাপ কিনতে চাই। *aa*·mi *aek*·ta staemp/*en*·ve·lap *kin*·ţe chai

Please send it to (Australia).
এটা প্লিজ (অস্ট্রেলিয়া) পাঠান। *e*·ta pleez (*o*·stre·li·a) *pa*·ţ'an

sightseeing

What time does it open/close?
এটা কখন খুলে/বন্ধ হয়? *e*·ta *ko*·k'ohn *k'u*·le/*bon*·d'oh hoy

What's the admission charge?
টিকেট কত? *ti*·ket *ko*·ţoh

Is there a discount for students/children?
ছাত্রদের/বাচ্চাদের জন্য কোন কনসেশন আছে? *ch'aţ*·ţroh·der/*baach*·cha·der *john*·noh *koh*·noh *kon*·se·shohn *aa*·ch'e

I'd like to hire a guide.
আমি একটা গাইড চাই। *aa*·mi *aek*·ta gaid chai

I'd like a catalogue/map.
আমি একটা ক্যাটালগ/ম্যাপ চাই। *aa*·mi *aek*·ta *kae*·ta·log/maep chai

I'd like to see …
আমি … দেখতে চাই। *aa*·mi … *dek'*·ţe chai

What's that?
ওটা কি? *oh*·ta ki

Can I take a photo?
আমি একটা ছবি নিতে পারি? *aa*·mi *aek*·ta *ch'o*·bi *ni*·ţe *paa*·ri

I'd like to go somewhere off the beaten track.
আমি অসাধারন কোথাও যেতে চাই — *aa*·mi *o*·sha·d'a·rohn *koh*·ţ'ao *je*·ţe chai

When's the next tour?
এর পরের ট্যুর কখন? — er *poh*·rer tur *ko*·k'ohn

How long is the tour?
ট্যুরটা কতক্ষন? — *tur*·ta *ko*·tohk·k'ohn

Is ... included?	এটা কি ... সহ?	*e*·ta ki ... *sho*·hoh
accommodation	থাকার ব্যবস্থা	*ţ'a*·kar *bae*·boh·sţ'a
admission	ভর্তি ফি	b'ohr·ţi fee
food	খাবার	*k'a*·bar
transport	যানবাহন	*jan*·ba·hohn

sightseeing		
fort	কেল্লা	*kel*·la
mosque	মসজিদ	*mos*·jid
palace	রাজ প্রাসাদ	raj *pra*·shad
ruins	ধ্বংসস্তুপ	*d'ong*·shoh·sţup
temple	মন্দির	*mon*·dir

shopping

Where's a ...?	... কোথায়?	... *koh*·ţ'ai
camera shop	ক্যামেরার দোকান	*kae*·me·rar *doh*·kan
market	বাজার	*ba*·jar
souvenir shop	সুভেনিয়ারের দোকান	*su*·ve·ni·e·rer *doh*·kan

I'd like to buy ...
একটা ... কিনতে চাই। — *aek*·ta ... *kin*·ţe chai

Can I look at it?
এটা দেখতে পারি? — e·ta *dek'*·ţe *paa*·ri

Can I have it sent overseas?
এটা কি বিদেশে পাঠাতে পারি? — e·ta ki *bi*·de·she *pa*·ţ'a·ţe *paa*·ri

Can I have my (camera) repaired?
আমার (ক্যামেরা) কি মেরামত করাতে পারি? — *aa*·mar (*kae*·me·ra) ki *me*·ra·moţ *ko*·ra·ţe *paa*·ri

It's faulty.
এটা নষ্ট। — e·ta *nosh*·toh

How much is it?
এটার দাম কত? — e·tar dam *ko*·ţoh

Can you write down the price?
দামটা কি লিখে দিতে পারেন? — *dam*·ta ki *li*·k'e *di*·ţe *paa*·ren

That's too expensive.
বেশী দাম। — *be*·shi dam

I'll give you (30 taka).
আমি (তিরিশ টাকা) দিব। — *aa*·mi (*ţi*·rish *ta*·ka) *di*·boh

There's a mistake in the bill.
বিলে ভুল আছে। — *bi*·le b'ul *aa*·ch'e

Do you accept ...?	আপনি কি ... নেন?	*aap*·ni ki ... nen
credit cards	ক্রেডিট কার্ড	*kre*·đit kar đ
debit cards	ডেবিট কার্ড	*đe*·bit kar đ
travellers cheques	ট্র্যাভেলার্স চেক	*trae*·ve·lars chek

I'd like (a) ..., please.	আমি ... চাই, প্লিজ।	*aa*·mi ... chai pleez
bag	ব্যাগ	baeg
my change	আমার ভাঙ্গতি	*aa*·mar *b'ang*·ţi
receipt	রিসিট	ri·*seet*
refund	পয়সা ফেরত	*poy*·sha *fe*·rohţ

Less.	কম।	kom
Enough.	যথেষ্ঠ।	jo·*ţ'esh*·toh
More.	আরেকটু।	*a*·rek·tu

photography

Can you transfer photos from my camera to CD?
আমার ক্যামেরা থেকে ছবি সি-ডিতে তুলতে পারেন? — *aa*·mar *kae*·me·ra *ţ'e*·ke *ch'oh*·bi *si*·đi·ţe *ţul*·ţe *paa*·ren

Can you develop this film?
এই ফিল্মটা ডেভেলাপ করতে পারেন? — e·i *film*·ta *đe*·ve·lap *kohr*·ţe *paa*·ren

I need a film for this camera.
এই ক্যামেরার জন্য আমার ফিল্ম লাগবে। — e·i *kae*·me·rar *john*·noh *aa*·mar film *laag*·be

When will it be ready?
এটা কখন রেডি হবে? — e·ta *ko*·k'ohn *re*·di *ho*·be

making conversation

Hello. (Hindu)	নমস্কার।	*no*·mohsh·kar
Hello. (Muslim greeting)	আস্‌সালাম ওয়ালাইকুম।	as·*sa*·lam wa·*lai*·kum
Hello. (Muslim response)	ওয়ালাইকুম আস্‌সালাম।	wa·*lai*·kum as·*sa*·lam
Goodbye./Good night. (Hindu)	নমস্কার।	*no*·mosh·kar
Goodbye./Good night. (Muslim)	আল্লাহ হাফেজ।	*al*·laa *ha*·fez

Mr/Mrs	মিস্টার/মিসেস	*mis*·tar/*mi*·ses
Ms/Miss	মিজ/মিস	miz/mis

How are you?	কেমন আছেন?	*kae*·mohn *aa*·ch'en
Fine, and you?	ভাল, আপনি?	*b'a*·loh *aap*·ni
What's your name?	আপনার নাম কি?	*aap*·nar naam ki
My name is ...	আমার নাম ...	*aa*·mar naam ...
I'm pleased to meet you.	আপনার সাথে পরিচিত হয়ে খুশি হয়েছি।	*aap*·nar *sha*·ţ'e *poh*·ri·chi·toh *hoh*·e *k'u*·shi *hoh*·e·ch'i

This is my ...	এটা আমার ...	e·ta *aa*·mar ...
brother	ভাই	b'ai
daughter	মেয়ে	*me*·e
father	বাবা	*ba*·ba
friend	বন্ধু	*bohn*·d'u
husband	স্বামী	*sha*·mi
mother	মা	maa
sister	বোন	bohn
son	ছেলে	*ch'e*·le
wife	স্ত্রী	sţree

Here's my (address).	এই যে আমার (ঠিকানা)।	e·i je *aa*·mar (*ţ'i*·ka·na)
What's your (email)?	আপনার (ইমেইল) কি?	*aap*·nar (*ee*·mayl) ki
Where are you from?	আপনি কোথা থেকে এসেছেন?	*aap*·ni *koh*·ţay *ţ'e*·ke *e*·she·ch'en

I'm from ...	আমি ... থেকে এসেছি।	*aa*·mi ... *ţ'e*·ke *e*·she·ch'i
Australia	অস্ট্রেলিয়া	*o*·stre·li·a
Canada	ক্যানাডা	*kae*·na·da
New Zealand	নিউ জিল্যান্ড	nyu *zi*·laend
the UK	ইংল্যান্ড	*ing*·laend
the USA	আমেরিকা	*ae*·me·ri·ka

What's your occupation?	আপনি কি করেন?	*aap*·ni ki *ko*·ren
I'm a …	আমি …	*aa*·mi …
businessperson	ব্যাবসায়ি m&f	*baeb*·shai
teacher	শিক্ষক/শিক্ষীকা m/f	*shik*·k'ohk/*shik*·k'i·ka
journalist	সাংবাদিক m&f	*shang*·ba·dik
Do you like …?	আপনি কি … পছন্দ করেন?	*aap*·ni ki … *po*·ch'ohn·doh *koh*·ren
I (don't) like …	আমি … পছন্দ করি (না)।	*aa*·mi … *po*·ch'ohn·doh *koh*·ri (na)
art	শিল্পকলা	*shil*·poh·ko·la
movies	ছবি দেখতে	*ch'o*·bi *dek'*·ţe
music	মিউজিক	mi·*u*·zik
reading	বই পড়তে	*boh*·i *pohṛ*·ţe
sport	খেলাধুলা	*k'ae*·la·d'u·la

eating out

Can you recommend a …?	একটা ভাল … কোথায় হবে বলেন তো?	*aek*·ta *b'a*·loh … *koh*·ţ'ai *ho*·be *boh*·len *ţoh*
bar	বার	baar
dish	ডিশ	dish
place to eat	রেস্তোরা	*res*·ţoh·ra
I'd like a/the …, please.	আমি … চাই, প্লিজ।	*aa*·mi … chai pleez
bill	বিলটা	*bil*·ta
drink list	ড্রিঙ্কের লিস্টটা	*đrin*·ker *list*·ta
menu	ম্যেনুটা	*me*·nu·ta
(non)smoking section	(নন) স্মোকিং সেকশন	(non) *smoh*·king *sek*·shohn

I'd like to reserve a table for (two) people.
আমি (দুই) জনের জন্য একটা টেবিল রিজার্ভ করতে চাই। — *aa*·mi (dui) *joh*·ner *john*·no *aek*·ta *te*·bil *ri*·zarv *kohr*·ţe chai

What's the local speciality?
এখানকার বিশেষ খাবার কি? — e·k'an·kar *bi*·shesh *k'a*·bar ki

breakfast	নাস্তা	*naash*·ţa
lunch	দুপুরের খাওয়া	*du*·pu·rer k'a·wa
dinner	রাতের খাওয়া	*raa*·ţer k'a·wa

(cup of) coffee/tea …	(কাপ) কফি/চা …	(kap) *ko*·fi/cha …
with milk	দুধ সহ	dud' *sho*·hoh
without sugar	চিনি ছাড়া	*chi*·ni *ch'a*·ṛa
(orange) juice	(অরেঞ্জ) জুস	(orenj) jus
lassi	লাচ্ছি	*las*·si
soft drink	কোল্ড ড্রিন্ক	kold dreenk
boiled water	সিদ্ধ পানি	*shid*·d'oh *pa*·ni
mineral water	মিনেরাল ওয়াটার	mi·*ne*·ral *wa*·tar

I'll have that.
আমি ওটা নিব। *aa*·mi *oh*·ta *ni*·boh

I'll buy you a drink.
আপনাকে আমি ড্রিংন্ক খাওয়াবো। *aap*·na·ke *aa*·mi dreenk *k'a*·wa·boh

What would you like?
আপনাকে কি দিতে পারি? *aap*·na·ke ki *di*·ţe *pa*·ri

a bottle/glass of beer	এক বোতল/গ্লাস বিয়ার	aek *boh*·ţohl/glash *bi*·ar
a bottle/glass of	এক বোতল/গ্লাস	aek *bo*·tohl/glash
… wine	… ওয়াইন	… wain
red	রেড	red
white	ওয়াইট	wait

special diets & allergies

Do you have …	আপনার কাছে কি …	*aap*·nar *ka*·ch'e ki …
food?	খাবার আছে?	*k'a*·bar *aa*·ch'e
halal	হালাল	*ha*·lal
vegetarian	ভেজিটেরিয়ান	*ve*·ji·te·ri·an
Could you prepare a meal without …?	আপনি কি … ছাড়া খাবার তৈরী করতে পারেন?	*aap*·ni ki … *ch'a*·ṛa *k'a*·bar *ţoh*·i·ri *kohr*·ţe *paa*·ren
I'm allergic to …	আমার …এ এ্যালার্জি আছে।	*aa*·mar …·e *ae*·lar·ji *aa*·ch'e
dairy produce	দুধ জাতিয় খাবার	dud' *ja*·ţi·o *k'a*·bar
eggs	ডিম	đim
meat	মাংস	*maang*·shoh
nuts	বাদাম	*baa*·dam
shellfish	চিংড়ি মাছ	*ching*·ṛi maach'

emergencies

Help!	বাচান!	*ba*·chan
Stop!	থামুন!	*ţ'a*·mun
Go away!	চলে যান!	*choh*·le jan
Thief!	চোর!	chohr
Fire!	আগুন!	*aa*·gun
Watch out!	দেখুন!	*de*·k'un

Call …!	… ডাকেন।	… *da*·ken
a doctor	ডাক্তার	*đak*·ţar
an ambulance	এ্যাম্বুলেন্স	*aem*·bu·lens
the police	পুলিশ	*pu*·lish

Could you please help?
একটু সাহায্য করতে পারেন? — *ek*·tu *sha*·haj·joh *kohr*·ţe *paa*·ren

Can I use your phone?
আপনার ফোন ব্যাবহার করতে পারি কি? — *aap*·nar fohn *bae*·boh·har *kohr*·ţe *pa*·ri ki

I'm lost.
আমি হারিয়ে গেছি। — *aa*·mi *ha*·ri·ye *gae*·ch'i

Where are the toilets?
টয়লেট কোথায়? — *toy*·let *koh*·ţ'ay

Where's the police station?
পুলিশ স্টেশন কোথায়? — *pu*·lish *ste*·shohn *koh*·ţ'ay

I have insurance.
আমার ইন্সুরেন্স আছে — *aa*·mar *in*·shu·rens *aa*·ch'e

I want to contact my embassy.
আমি আমার এ্যাম্বাসির সাথে যোগাযোগ করতে চাই। — *aa*·mi *aa*·mar *em*·bae·sir *sha*·ţ'e *johg*·a·johg *kohr*·ţe chai

I've been …	আমাকে …	*aa*·ma·ke …
raped	ধর্শন করেছে	*d'or*·shon *koh*·re·ch'e
robbed	ছিনতাই করেছে	*ch'in*·ţai *koh*·re·ch'e

I've lost my …	আমার … হারিয়ে গেছে।	*aa*·mar … *ha*·ri·ye *gae*·ch'e
bag	ব্যাগ	baeg
credit card	ক্রেডিট কার্ড	*kre*·đit karđ
money	টাকা	*ta*·ka
passport	পাসপোর্ট	*pas*·pohrt
travellers cheques	ট্র্যাভেলার্স চেক	*trae*·ve·lars chek

health

Where's the nearest ...?	কাছাকাছি ... কোথায়?	*ka*·ch'a·ka·ch'i ... *koh*·ţay
dentist	ডেন্টিষ্ট	*đen*·tist
doctor	ডাক্তার	*đak*·ţar
hospital	হাসপাতাল	*hash*·pa·ţal
pharmacist	ঔষধের দোকান	*oh*·shud'·er *doh*·kan

I need a doctor (who speaks English).
আমার একজন ডাক্তার লাগবে (যিনি ইংরেজিতে কথা বলতে পারেন)।
aa·mar *aek*·john *đak*·ţar *laag*·be (*ji*·ni *ing*·re·ji·ţe *ko*·ţ'a *bohl*·ţe *paa*·ren)

Could I see a female doctor?
আমি কি মহিলা ডাক্তার দেখাতে পারি?
aa·mi ki *moh*·hi·la *đak*·ţar *dae*·k'a·ţe *paa*·ri

I've run out of my medication.
আমার ঔষুধ শেষ হয়ে গেছে।
aa·mar *oh*·shud shesh *hoh*·e *gae*·ch'e

It hurts here.
এখানে ব্যাথা করছে।
e·k'a·ne *bae*·ţ'a *kohr*·ch'e

I have (a) ...	আমার ... আছে।	*aa*·mar ... *aa*·che
asthma	এ্যাজমা	*aez*·ma
constipation	কন্সটিপেশন	*kons*·ti·pe·shohn
diarrhoea	ডাইরিয়া	*đai*·ri·a
fever	জ্বর	jor
heart condition	হার্ট কন্ডিশন	hart *kon*·đi·shohn
nausea	বমি ভাব	*boh*·mi b'ab

I'm allergic to ...	আমার ...-এ এল্যার্জি আছে।	*aa*·mar ...·e *ae*·lar·ji *aa*·ch'e
antibiotics	এ্যান্টিবায়োটিক	*aen*·ti·bai·o·tik
anti-inflammatories	ব্যাথার ঔষুধ	*bae*·ţ'ar *oh*·shud'
aspirin	এ্যাসপিরিন	*aes*·pi·rin
bees	মৌমাছির কামোড়	*mo*·u·ma·ch'ir *ka*·mohŗ
codeine	কোডিন	*koh*·đin

responsible travel

I'd like to learn some Bengali.
আমি কিছু বাংলা শিখতে চাই। — *aa*·mi *ki*·ch'u *baang*·la *shik'*·ţe chai

What's this called in Bengali?
এটা বাংলায় কি হবে? — e·ta *baang*·lay ki *ho*·be

Would you like me to teach you some English?
আপনি কি আমার কাছে কিছু ইংরেজি শিখতে চান? — *aap*·ni ki *aa*·mar *ka*·ch'e *ki*·ch'u *ing*·re·ji *shik'*·ţe chan

I didn't mean to do/say anything wrong.
আমি খারাপ কিছু করতে/বলতে চাই নাই। — *aa*·mi *k'a*·rap *ki*·ch'u *kohr*·ţe/*bohl*·ţe chai nai

Is this a local or national custom?
এই চর্চা কি আঞ্চলিক না জাতীয়? — ay *chor*·cha ki *aan*·choh·lik na *ja*·ţi·o

I'd like to stay at a locally run hotel.
আমি স্থানীয় হোটেলে থাকতে চাই। — *aa*·mi *sţ'a*·ni·oh *ho*·te·le *ţ'ak*·ţe chai

Where can I buy locally produced goods/souvenirs?
আমি স্থানীয় তৈরী সুভেনিয়ার কিনতে চাই? — *aa*·mi *st'a*·ni·oh *ţohy*·ri *su*·ve·ni·er *kin*·ţe chai

What's this made from?
এটা কি দিয়ে তৈরী? — e·ta ki *di*·ye *ţohy*·ri

I'd like to do some volunteer work (for your organisation).
আমি (আপনার সংঘটনে) ভলানটারি কাজ করতে চাই। — *aa*·mi (*aap*·nar *shong*·g'o·to·ne) *vo*·laan·t'a·ri kaaj *kohr*·ţe chai

I'm (an English teacher). Can I volunteer my skills?
আমি (একজন ইংরেজি টিচার)। আমি ভলানটিয়ার হিসাবে কাজ করতে পারি? — *aa*·mi (*aek*·john *ing*·re·ji *ti*·char) *aa*·mi *vo*·laan·ti·ar *hi*·sha·be kaaj *kohr*·te *paa*·ri

বাংলা – responsible travel

52

english–bengali dictionary

Words in this dictionary are marked as n (noun), a (adjective), v (verb), sg (singular), pl (plural), inf (informal) and pol (polite) where necessary.

A

accident দূর্ঘটনা *dur*·g'o·toh·na
accommodation থাকার ব্যবস্থা *ţ'a*·kar *bae*·bohs·ţ'a
adaptor এ্যাডাপ্টার *ae*·đap·tar
address n ঠিকানা *t'i*·ka·na
after পরে *po*·re
air conditioner এয়ারকন্ডিশনার *e*·ar·kon·đi·shoh·nar
airplane প্লেন plen
airport এয়ারপোর্ট *e*·ar·pohrt
alcohol মদ mod
all সব shob
allergy এ্যালার্জি *ae*·lar·ji
ambulance এ্যামবুলেন্স *aem*·bu·lens
and এবং *e*·bohng
ankle গোড়ালি *goh*·ŗa·li
antibiotics এ্যান্টিবায়োটিক *aen*·ti·bai·o·tik
arm বাহু *ba*·hu'
ATM এটিএম *e*·ti·em

B

baby বাচ্চা *baach*·cha
back (body) পিঠ peeţ'
backpack ব্যাক প্যাক baek paek
bad খারাপ *k'a*·rap
bag ব্যাগ baeg
baggage claim ব্যাগেজ ক্লেইম *bae*·gej klaym
bank ব্যাংক baenk
bar বার baar
bathroom গোসল খানা *goh*·sohl *k'a*·na
battery ব্যাটারি *bae*·ta·ri
beautiful সুন্দর *shun*·dohr
bed বিছানা *bi*·ch'a·na
before আগে *aa*·ge
behind পিছন *pi*·ch'ohn
bicycle সাইকেল *sai*·kel
big বড় *bo*·ŗoh
bill বিল bil
blanket কম্বল *kom*·bohl
blood group ব্লাড গ্রুপ blad grup
boat নৌকা *noh*·u·ka
book (make a reservation) v বুকিং *bu*·king
bottle বোতল *boh*·ţohl
boy ছেলে *ch'e*·le
brakes (car) ব্রেক brek
breakfast নাস্তা *nash*·ţa
broken (faulty) ভাঙ্গা *b'ang*·a
bus বাস bas
business ব্যবসা *baeb*·sha
buy কেনা *ke*·na

C

camera ক্যামেরা *kae*·me·ra
cancel ক্যান্সেল *kaen*·sel
car গাড়ি *ga*·ŗi
cash n ক্যাশ kaesh
cash (a cheque) v চেক ভাঙ্গানো chek *b'ang*·ga·noh
cell phone মোবাইল ফোন *moh*·bail fohn
centre মাঝখানে *maj'*·k'a·ne
change (money) v ভাঙ্গানো *b'ang*·ga·noh
cheap সস্তা *sho*·sţa
check (bill) বিল bil
check-in n চেক-ইন *chek*·in
chest (body) বুক buk
child বাচ্চা *baach*·cha
cigarette সিগারেট *si*·ga·ret
city শহর *sho*·hohr
clean a পরিষ্কার *poh*·rish·kar
closed বন্ধ *bon*·d'oh
cold a ঠান্ডা *t'an*·đa
collect call কালেক্ট কল *ka*·lekt kol
come আসুন *aa*·shun
computer কম্পিউটার *kom*·pyu·tar
condom কন্ডম *kon*·dohm
contact lenses কন্টাক্ট লেন্স *kon*·takt lens
cook n বাবুর্চি *ba*·bur·chi
cost n খরচ *k'o*·rohch
credit card ক্রেডিট কার্ড *kre*·đit karđ
currency exchange টাকা ভাঙ্গানো
ta·ka *b'ang*·ga·noh
customs (immigration) কাস্টম্‌স *kas*·tohms

D

dangerous বিপদজনক *bi*·pod·jo·nohk
date (time) তারিখ *ţa*·rik'
day দিন din
delay n দেরি *de*·ri
dentist ডেন্টিষ্ট *đen*·tist
depart গমন *go*·mohn
diaper ডাইপার *đai*·par
dinner রাতের খাবার *ra*·ţer *k'a*·bar

direct a ডাইরেক্ট *đai*·rekt
dirty ময়লা *moy*·la
disabled পঙ্গু *pohng*·gu
discount n ডিসকাউন্ট *đis*·ka·unt
doctor ডাক্তার *đak*·ţar
double bed ডবল বেড *đo*·bohl beđ
double room ডবল রুম *đo*·bohl rum
drink n পানিয় *pa*·ni·o
drive v ড্রাইভ đraiv
drivers licence ড্রাইভারস লাইসেন্স *đrai*·vars *lai*·sens
drug (illicit) ড্রাগ đrag

E

ear কান kaan
east পূর্ব *pur*·boh
eat খাওয়া *k'a*·wa
economy class ইকোনমি ক্লাস *ee*·ko·no·mi klas
electricity ইলেকট্রিসিটি *ee*·lek·tri·si·ti
elevator লিফট্ lift
email ইমেইল *ee*·mayl
embassy দূতাবাস *du*·ţa·bash
emergency এমার্জেন্সি *e*·mar·jen·si
English (language) ইংরেজি *ing*·re·ji
evening সন্ধ্যা *shohn*·d'a
exit v বাহির *ba*·hir
expensive দামি *da*·mi
eye চোখ chohk'

F

far দূর dur
fast জোরে *joh*·re
father বাবা *ba*·ba
film (camera) ফিল্ম film
finger আঙ্গুল *ang*·gul
first-aid kit ফার্স্ট এইড বক্স farst ayđ boks
first class ফার্স্ট ক্লাস farst klas
fish n মাছ maach'
food খাবার *k'a*·bar
foot পায়ের পাতা *pa*·yer *pa*·ţa
free (of charge) নির্দোষ *nir*·dohsh
friend বন্ধু *bohn*·d'u
fruit ফল p'ol
full ভরা *b'o*·ra

G

gift উপহার *u*·poh·har
girl মেয়ে *me*·e
glass (drinking) গ্লাস glash
glasses চশমা *chosh*·ma
go যান jan
good a ভাল *b'a*·loh
guide n গাইড gaiđ

H

half n অর্ধেক *or*·d'ek
hand হাত haat'
happy সুখী *shu*·k'i
have আছে *aa*·ch'e
he pol/inf উভন/ও *u*·ni/ oh
head n মাথা *ma*·ţ'a
heart হার্ট hart
heavy ভারি *b'a*·ri
help v সাহায্য *sha*·haj·joh
here এখানে *e*·k'a·ne
high উচা *u*·cha
highway মহাসড়ক *mo*·ha·sho·ŗok
hike v পায়ে হাটা *pa*·e *ha*·ta
holiday ছুটি *ch'u*·ti
hospital হাসপাতাল *hash*·pa·ţal
hot গরম *go*·rohm
hotel হোটেল *hoh*·tel
hungry ক্ষুধার্ত *k'u*·d'ar·ţoh
husband স্বামি *shaa*·mi

I

I আভম *aa*·mi
identification (card) আইডেন্টিটি কার্ড *ai*·đen·ti·ti karđ
ill অসুস্থ *o*·shu·sţ'oh
important গুরুত্বপূর্ন *gu*·ruţ·ţoh·pur·noh
injury হত *ho*·ţoh
insurance ইন্সুরেন্স *in*·shu·rens
internet ইন্টারনেট *in*·tar·net
interpreter দোভাষী *doh*·b'a·shi

J

jewellery গহনা *go*·hoh·na
job কাজ kaj

K

key চাবি *cha*·bi
kilogram কিলো *ki*·loh
kitchen রান্না ঘর *ran*·na g'or
knife ছুরি *ch'u*·ri

L

laundry (place) লন্ড্রি *lon*·đri
lawyer উকিল *u*·kil
left (direction) বামে *baa*·me
leg (body) পা pa
less কম kom
letter (mail) চিঠি *chi*·ţ'i
light n বাতি *ba*·ţi
like v পছন্দ *po*·ch'ohn·doh
lock n তালা *ţa*·la
long লম্বা *lom*·ba
lost হারিয়ে গেছে *ha*·ri·ye *gae*·ch'e
love n ভালবাসা *b'a*·loh·ba·sha
luggage মালপত্র *mal*·poţ·roh
lunch দুপুরের খাওয়া *du*·pu·rer *k'a*·wa

M

mail n পোস্ট pohst
man পুরুষ লোক *pu*·rush lohk
map ম্যাপ maep
market বাজার *ba*·jar
matches দেশলাই *desh*·lai
meat মাংস *mang*·shoh
medicine ঔষধ *oh*·shud'
message সংবাদ *shong*·bad
milk দুধ dud'
minute মিনিট *mi*·nit
mobile phone মোবাইল ফোন *moh*·bail fohn
money টাকা-পয়সা *ta*·ka·poy·sha
month মাস mash
morning সকাল *sho*·kal
mother মা maa
motorcycle মটরসাইকেল *mo*·tohr·sai·kel
mouth মুখ muk'

N

name নাম nam
near কাছে *ka*·ch'e
neck n গলা *go*·lah
new নতুন *noh*·tun
newspaper খবরের কাগজ *k'o*·boh·rer *ka*·gohz
night রাত raaţ
no না na
noisy হৈচৈ *hoi*·choi
nonsmoking ধুমপান নিষেধ *d'um*·pan *ni*·shed'
north উত্তর *uţ*·ţohr
nose নাক nak
now এখন *ae*·k'ohn
number নম্বর *nom*·bohr

O

old (person) বৃদ্ধ *brid*·d'oh
old (thing) পুরানো *pu*·ra·noh
one-way ticket ওয়ান-ওয়ে টিকেট *wan*·way *ti*·ket
open a খোলা *k'oh*·la
outside বাইরে *bai*·re

P

passport পাসপোর্ট *pas*·pohrt
pay v দাম দেওয়া dam *dae*·wa
pharmacy ঔষধের দোকান *oh*·shu·d'er *doh*·kan
phonecard ফোন কার্ড fohn karđ
photo ছবি *ch'o*·bi
police পুলিশ *pu*·lish
postcard পোস্ট কার্ড pohst karđ
post office পোস্ট অফিস pohst *o*·fish
pregnant গর্বভতি *gor*·boh·b'oh·ţi
price n দাম dam

Q

quiet a নিরব *ni*·rob

R

rain n বৃষ্টি *brish*·ti
razor রেজার *re*·zar
receipt n রিসিট ri·*seet*
refund v পয়সা ফেরত *poy*·sha *fe*·rohţ
registered mail রেজিষ্ট্রি মেল *re*·ji·stri mayl
rent v ভাড়া *b'a*·ŗa
repair v মেরামত *me*·ra·moţ
reservation রিজার্ভেশন *ri*·sar·ve·shohn
restaurant রেস্তোরা *res*·ţoh·ra
return v ফেরত *fe*·rohţ
return ticket রিটার্ন টিকেট ri·*tarn ti*·ket
right (direction) ডান đaan
road রাস্তা *raas*·ţa
room n রুম rum

S

safe a নিরাপদ *ni*·ra·pod
sanitary napkin স্যানিটারি প্যাড *sae*·ni·ta·ri paed
seat n সিট seet
send পাঠান *pa*·t'a·noh
sex সেক্স seks
shampoo শ্যাম্পু *shaem*·pu
share (a dorm) সেয়ার *she*·ar

she pol/inf উনি/ও *u*·ni/ oh
sheet (bed) চাদর *cha*·dohr
shirt সার্ট shart
shoes জুতা *ju*·ţa
shop n দোকান *doh*·kan
short খাটো *kha*·toh
shower n সাওয়ার *sha*·war
single room সিঙ্গেল রুম *sin*·gel rum
skin n চামড়া *cham*·ŗa
skirt n স্কার্ট skart
sleep n ঘুম g'um
slowly ধিরে *d'i*·re
small ছোট *ch'oh*·toh
soap সাবান *sha*·ban
some কিছু *ki*·ch'u
soon শিঘ্রি *shig*·ri
south দক্ষিণ *dohk*·k'in
souvenir shop সুভেনিয়ারের দোকান *su*·ve·ni·e·rer *doh*·kan
stamp স্ট্যাম্প staemp
stand-by ticket স্ট্যান্ড বাই টিকেট staend bai *ti*·ket
station (train) স্টেশন *ste*·shohn
stomach পেট pet
stop v থামুন *ţ'a*·mun
stop (bus) n বাস স্টপ bas stop
street রাস্তা *raa*·sţa
student ছাত্র *ch'aţ*·roh
sun সূর্য্য *shur*·joh
sunscreen সানব্লক *san*·blok
swim v সাতার *sha*·ţar

T

tampons ট্যাম্পন *taem*·pohn
teeth দাত daaţ
telephone n টেলিফোন *te*·li·fohn
temperature (weather) টেমপারেচার *tem*·pa·re·char
that (one) ঐ *oh*·i
they pol/inf উনারা/ওরা *u*·na·ra/*oh*·ra
thirst n তেষ্টা *ţesh*·ta
this (one) এই *e*·i
throat গলা *go*·la
ticket টিকেট *ti*·ket
time সময় *sho*·moy
tired টায়ার্ড *tai*·ard
tissues টিস্যু *ti*·shu
today আজ aaj
toilet (city) টয়লেট *toy*·let
toilet (country) পায়খানা *pai*·k'a·na
tomorrow আগামিকাল *aa*·ga·mi·kaal
tonight আজ রাত aaj raaţ
toothbrush টুথব্রাশ *tuţ'*·brash
toothpaste টুথপেস্ট *tuţ'*·pest
torch (flashlight) টর্চ torch
tour v পর্যটন *por*·joh·ton
tourist office পর্যটন কেন্দ্র *pohr*·joh·tohn *ken*·droh
towel তোয়ালে *ţoh*·a·le
train n ট্রেন tren
translate অনুবাদ *oh*·nu·bad
travel agency ট্র্যাভেল এজেন্সি *trae*·vel *e*·jen·si
travellers cheque ট্র্যাভেলার্স চেক *trae*·ve·lars chek
trousers প্যান্ট paent
twin beds টুইন বেড *tu*·in beđ

U

underwear আন্ডারওয়ের *an*·dar·wer
urgent জরুরি *joh*·ru·ri

V

vacant খালি *kh'a*·li
vegetable n সবজি *shohb*·ji
vegetarian a ভেজিটেরিয়ান *ve*·ji·te·ri·an
visa ভিসা *vi*·sa

W

walk v হাটা *ha*·ta
wallet ওয়ালেট *wa*·let
wash (something) ধোয়া *d'oh*·a
watch n ঘড়ি *g'oh*·ŗi
water n পানি *pa*·ni
we আমরা *aam*·ra
weekend উইকএন্ড *wee*·kend
west পশ্চিম *pohsh*·chim
wheelchair হুইলচেয়ার *weel*·che·ar
when কখন *ko*·k'ohn
where কোথায় *koh*·ţ'ay
who কে ke
why কেন *kae*·noh
wife স্ত্রী sţree
window জানালা *ja*·na·la
with সাথে *sha*·ţ'e
without ছাড়া *ch'a*·ŗa
woman মহিলা *moh*·hi·la
write লেখা *le*·k'a

Y

yes হ্যাঁ hang
yesterday গতকাল *go*·toh·kal
you sg আপনি *aap*·ni
you pl আপনারা *aap*·na·ra

Gujarati

alphabet

vowels

અ a	આ aa	ઇ i	ઈ ee	ઉ u	ઊ oo	ઋ ru	એ e	ઐ ai	ઓ o	ઔ ow

consonants

ક ka	ખ k'a	ગ ga	ઘ g'a	ઙ nga
ચ cha	છ ch'a	જ ja	ઝ j'a	ઞ nya
ટ ţa	ઠ ţ'a	ડ đa	ઢ đ'a	ણ ņa
ત ta	થ t'a	દ da	ધ d'a	ન na
પ pa	ફ p'a	બ ba	ભ b'a	મ ma
ય ya	ર ra	લ la	વ va	
સ sa	શ sha	ષ şa		
હ ha	ળ ļa			
ક્ષ ksa	જ્ઞ gna			

numerals

0	1	2	3	4	5	6	7	8	9
૦	૧	૨	૩	૪	૫	૬	૭	૮	૯

introduction

Gujarati (gu·ja·raa·tee ગુજરાતી), spoken by approximately 46 million people in India (primarily in the state of Gujarat), was the mother tongue of Mohandas Karamchand Gandhi. 'Gandhi' means 'grocer' in Gujarati, although the great Mahatma was certainly not restricted by his name! Gandhi, thought of as the father of the modern Indian nation, was also referred to as baa·pu બાપુ (lit: father) throughout India. He was passionate about his native language and wrote a number of works in Gujarati, many of which were later translated into English. Gujarati has a rich literary tradition and is written in the Gujarati script. Like most other languages of northern India, Gujarati is a member of the Indo-Aryan language family, with Sanskrit as its ancestor. The English words 'bungalow' and 'tank' both have their origins in Gujarati, from bang·a·lo બંગલો and tan·kung ટાંકું respectively. Have a crack at the language of the champion of nonviolence – should you make mistakes, there's certainly nothing to fear from its generous speakers!

gujarati

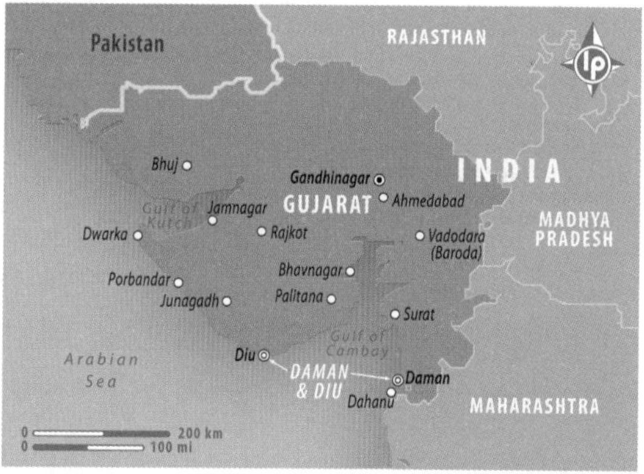

pronunciation

Vowels		Consonants	
Symbol	**English sound**	**Symbol**	**English sound**
a	run	b	bed
aa	father	ch	cheat
ai	aisle	d	dog
e	bet	đ	retroflex d
ee	see	f	fun
i	hit	g	go
o	pot	h	hat
oo	zoo	j	jar
ow	now	k	kit
u	put	l	lot
		ļ	retroflex l
		m	man
		n	not
		ņ	retroflex n
		ng	ring
		p	pet
		r	red
		s	sun
		ş	retroflex s
		sh	shot
		t	top
		ţ	retroflex t
		v	very
		w	win
		y	yes
		z	zoo

In this chapter, the Gujarati pronunciation is given in green after each phrase.

Aspirated consonants (pronounced with a puff of air after the sound) are represented with an apostrophe after the letter – b', ch', d', đ', g', j', k', p', t' and ţ'. Retroflex consonants (pronounced with the tongue bent backwards) are included in this table.

Each syllable is separated by a dot. For example:

નમસ્તે. na·mas·te

essentials		
Yes.	હા.	haa
No.	ના.	naa
Please.	પ્લીઝ.	pleez
Thank you.	આભાર.	aa·b'aar
Excuse me. (to get past)	જરા જવા દેશો.	ja·raa ja·vaa de·sho
Excuse me. (to get attention)	એકસક્યુઝ મી .	eks·kyuz mi
Sorry.	માફ કરજો.	maap' kar·jo

language difficulties

Do you speak English?
તમે ઈન્ગલીશ બોલો છો? — ta·me ing·lish bo·lo ch'o

Do you understand (English)?
તમે (ઈન્ગલીશ) સમજો છો? — ta·me (ing·lish) sam·jo ch'o

I understand.
સમજાયું. — sam·jaa·yung

I don't understand.
સમજાયું નહીં. — sam·jaa·yung na·heeng

Could you please ...?	જરા ...?	ja·raa ...
repeat that	જી	jee
speak more slowly	ધીમે ધીમે બોલો તો	d'ee·me d'ee·me bo·lo to

numbers					
0	શૂન્ય	shoon·ya	20	વીસ	vees
1	એક	ek	30	ત્રીસ	trees
2	બે	be	40	ચાલીસ	chaa·lis
3	ત્રણ	traṇ	50	પચાસ	pa·chaas
4	ચાર	chaar	60	સાઠ	saaţ
5	પાંચ	panch	70	સિત્તેર	sit·ter
6	છ	ch'a	80	એંશી	ehn·si
7	સાત	saat	90	નેવું	ne·vung
8	આઠ	aaţ'	100	એક સો	ek so
9	નવ	nav	1000	એક હજાર	ek ha·jaar
10	દસ	das	100,000	એક લાખ	ek laak'

time & dates

What time is it?	કેટલા વાગ્યા?	keţ·laa vaa·gyaa
It's (two) o'clock.	(બે) વાગ્યા છે.	(be) vaa·gyaa ch'e
Quarter past (two).	(બે)ને પંદર.	(be)·ne pan·dar
Half past (two).	(બે)ને ત્રીસ.	(be)·ne tris
Quarter to (two).	(બે)ને પીસ્તાલીસ.	(be)·ne pis·taa·lis
At what time ...?	... કેટલા વાગ્યે ...?	... keţ·laa vaa·gye ...
At ...	સમયઃ ...	sa·mai ...
It's (15 December).	આજે (પંદર ડિસેમ્બર) છે.	aa·je (pan·dar đi·sem·bar) ch'e

yesterday	ગઈ કાલે	ga·ee kaa·le
today	આજે	aa·je
tomorrow	આવતી કાલે	aav·tee kaa·le

Monday	સોમવાર	som·vaar
Tuesday	મંગળવાર	man·gaļ·vaar
Wednesday	બુધવાર	bud'·vaar
Thursday	ગુરુવાર	gu·ru·vaar
Friday	શુક્રવાર	shuk·ra·vaar
Saturday	શનિવાર	sha·ni·vaar
Sunday	રવિવાર	ra·vi·vaar

border crossing

I'm here ...	હું અહીયાં ... છું.	hung a·hee·yaang ... ch'ung
in transit	ટ્રાન્ઝિટમાં	tran·j'iţ·mang
on business	કામ અંગે આવ્યો/આવી	kaam an·ge aa·vyo/aa·vi m/f
on holiday	ફરવા માટે આવ્યો/આવી	far·vaa maa·ţe aa·vyo/aa·vi m/f

I'm here for ...	હું અહીયાં ... માટે આવ્યો/આવી છું.	hung a·hee·yang ... maa·ţe aa·vyo/aa·vi ch'ung m/f
(10) days	(દસ) દિવસ	(das) di·vas
(three) weeks	(ત્રણ) અઠવાડિયાં	(traņ) aţ'·vaa·đi·yaang
(two) months	(બે) મહિના	(be) ma·hi·naa

I'm going to (Ahmedabad).

હું (અમદાવાદ) જાઉ છું.	hung (am·daa·vaad) jaa·ung ch'ung

I'm staying at the (Deepa hotel).
હું (દીપા હોટલ) પર ઊતર્યો/ઊતરી છું. — hung (dee·paa ho·ţal) par oo·ta·ryo/oo·ta·ri ch'ung **m/f**

I have nothing to declare.
કાંઈ ડિક્લેર કરવાનું નથી. — kaa·in đik·ler kar·vaa·nung na·t'ee

I have this to declare.
મારે આ ડિક્લેર કરવાનું છે. — maa·re aa đik·ler kar·vaa·nung ch'e

That's mine.
એ વસ્તુ મારી છે. — e vas·tu maa·ri ch'e

That's not mine.
એ વસ્તુ મારી નથી. — e vas·tu maa·ri na·t'ee

tickets & luggage

Where can I buy a ticket?
ટિકિટ ક્યાંથી મળશે? — ţi·kiţ kyaang·t'i maļ·she

Do I need to book a seat?
મારે સીટ બુક કરાવવાની જરૂર છે? — maa·re seeţ buk kar·vaa·ni ja·roor ch'e

One … ticket (to Vadodara), please.	(વડોદરા)ની એક … ટિકિટ આપશો પ્લીઝ?	(va·do·da·ra)·ni ek … ţi·kiţ aap·sho pleez
one-way	વન વે	van vey
return	રિટર્ન	ri·ţarn

I'd like to … my ticket, please.	મારે મારી ટિકિટ … છે.	maa·re maa·ri ţi·kiţ … ch'e
cancel	કેન્સલ કરાવવી	ken·sal ka·raav·vi
change	ચેન્જ કરાવવી	chenj ka·raav·vi
collect	કલેક્ટ કરવી	ka·lekţ kar·vee

I'd like a nonsmoking/smoking seat, please.
મને નોનસ્મોકિંગ/સ્મોકિંગ સીટ આપશો, પ્લીઝ? — ma·ne non·smo·king/smo·king seeţ aap·sho pleez

Is there a toilet/air conditioning?
ત્યાં ટોયલેટ/એર કન્ડિશન છે? — tyaan ţoy·leţ/e·yar kan·đi·shan ch'e

How long does the trip take?
આ ટ્રીપ કેટલા સમયની છે? — aa ţrip keţ·laa smai·ni ch'e

Is it a direct route?
એ ડાયરેક્ટ રૂટ છે? — e đaay·rekţ rooţ ch'e

My luggage has been …	મારો લગેજ … છે.	maa·ro la·gej … ch'e
damaged	ડેમેજ થયેલો	đe·mej t'a·ye·lo
lost	ખોવાયો થયેલો	goom t'a·ye·lo
stolen	ચોરાઈ ગયો	cho·raa·ee ga·yo

transport

Where does (flight number 12) arrive/depart?
(ફ્લાઈટ નંબર ૧૨) ક્યારે આવે/ઊપડે છે? — (flait nam·bar baar) kyaa·re aa·ve/oop·đe ch'e

Is this the … to (Mumbai)?	આ … (મુંબઈ) જશે કે?	aa … (mum·ba·ee) ja·she ke
boat	બોટ	boţ
bus	બસ	bas
plane	પ્લેન	pla·in
train	ટ્રેન	ţre·in

What time's the … bus?	… બસ કેટલા વાગ્યાની છે?	… bas keţ·laa vaa·gyaa·ni ch'e
first	સૌથી પહેલી	sow·t'i pa·he·li
last	છેલ્લી	ch'el·li
next	હવે પછીની	ha·ve pa·ch'i·ni

How long will it be delayed?
તે કેટલી લેઈટ છે? — te keţ·li le·iţ ch'e

Please tell me when we get to (Kankaria).
(કાંકરિયા) આવે ત્યારે મને કહેશો? — (kan·ka·ri·a) aa·ve tyaa·re ma·ne ka·he·sho

That's my seat.
આ સીટ મારી છે. — aa seeţ maa·ri ch'e

I'd like a taxi …	મારે … ટેક્સી જોઈએ છે.	maa·re … ţek·see jo·ee·ye ch'e
at (9am)	(સવારે નવ) વાગ્યે	(sa·vaa·re nav) vaa·gye
now	અત્યારે જ	at·yaa·rej

How much is it to (Iskon)?
(ઈસકોન)ના કેટલા થશે? — (is·kon)·na keţ·laa t'a·she

Please put the meter on.
મીટર ઓન કરો. — mee·ţar on ka·ro

Please take me to (this address).
મારે (આ એડ્રેસ ઉપર) જવું છે, ત્યાં લઈ લો. — maa·re (aa eđ·res u·par) ja·vung ch'e tyaang la·ee·lo

Please stop here.
અહીં ગાડી ઊભી રાખો. — a·heeng gaa·đi oo·b'i raa·k'o

Please wait here.
જરા વેઈટ કરજો. — ja·raa ve·iţ kar·jo

I'd like to hire a car/4WD (with a driver).
મારે એક કાર/ફોર વ્હીલર (ડ્રાઈવર સાથે) ભાડે કરવી છે. — maa·re ek kaar/for·wee·lar (đraa·ee·ver saa·t'e) b'a·đe kar·vee ch'e

How much for daily/weekly hire?
રોજનું/અઠવાડિયાનું ભાડું કેટલું થશે? — ro·j·nung/aţ'·vaa·đi·yaa·nung b'aa·đung keţ·lung t'a·she

directions

Where's the ...?	... ક્યાં છે?	... kyaang ch'e
bank	બેન્ક	bengk
foreign currency exchange	ફોરેન કરન્સી એક્સચેન્જ	fo·ren ka·ran·si eks·chenj
post office	પોસ્ટ ઓફિસ	posţ o·fis

Is this the road to (Naranpura)?
આ રોડ (નારણપુરા) જાય છે? — aa rođ (na·raan·pu·ra) jaay ch'e

Can you show me (on the map)?
તે જરા (આ નકશામાં) બતાવશો? — te ja·raa (aa nak·shaa·maang) ba·taav·sho

What's the address?	તેનું એડ્રેસ શું છે?	te·nung eđ·res shung ch'e
How far is it?	તે કેટલે દૂર છે?	te keţ·le door ch'e
How do I get there?	ત્યાં કઈ રીતે જવાય?	tyaang ka·ee ree·te ja·vaay
Turn left/right.	લેફ્ટ/રાઈટ બાજુ જાઓ.	lefţ/ra·yiţ baa·ju jaa·o

It's ...	તે ... છે.	te ... ch'e
behind ...	... ની પાછળ	... ni paa·ch'aļ
in front of ...	... ની આગળ	... ni aa·gaļ
near (to ...)	... ની પાસે	... ni paa·se
on the corner	... ના કોરનર ઉપર	... na kor·nar u·par
opposite ...	... ની સામે	... ni saa·me
straight ahead	એકદમ સીધા	ek·dam see·d'aa
there	ત્યાં	tyaang

accommodation

Where's a guesthouse/hotel nearby?
પાસે કોઈ ગેસ્ટ હાઉસ/હોટેલ છે કે? — paa·se ko·i gest hows/ho·ţal ch'e ke

Can you recommend somewhere cheap/good?
કોઈ સસ્તી/સારી જગ્યા બતાવશો? — ko·i sas·ti/saa·ri jag·yaa ba·taav·sho

I'd like to book a room, please.
એક રૂમ આપશો પ્લીઝ? — ek room aap·sho pleez

I have a reservation.
મારે રિઝરવેશન છે. — maa·re ri·zar·ve·shan ch'e

Do you have a … room?	એક … રૂમ મળશે?	ek … room maļ·she
single	સિન્ગલ	sin·gal
double	ડબલ	đa·bal
twin	ટ્વીન	ţwin

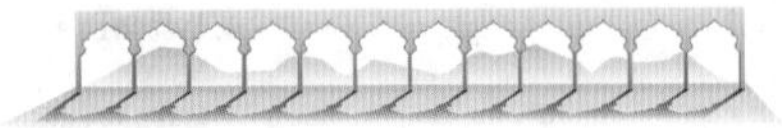

How much is it per night?
એક નાઈટનો ચાર્જ શું છે? — ek na·yit·no chaarj shung ch'e

How much is it per person?
પર પરસનનો ચાર્જ શું છે? — par par·san·no chaarj shung ch'e

I'd like to stay for (two) nights.
હું (બે) નાઈટ રહેવાનો/
રહેવાની છું. — hung (be) na·yit ra·he·vaa·no/
ra·he·vaa·ni ch'ung **m/f**

Can I have my key, please?
મારી કી આપશો, પ્લીઝ? — maa·ri kee aap·sho pleez

Can I get another (blanket)?
એક બીજો (બ્લેન્કેટ) આપશો, પ્લીઝ? — ek bee·jo (bleng·keţ) aap·sho pleez

The (air conditioning) doesn't work.
(એર કન્ડિશન) ચાલતું નથી. — (e·yar kan·đi·shan) chaal·tung na·t'ee

Is there an elevator/a safe?
ત્યાં લિફ્ટ/સેઈફ છે? — tyaang lift/saif ch'e

What time is checkout?
ચેક આઉટનો ટાઈમ શું છે? — chek owt·no ţaa·im shung ch'e

Can I have my ..., please?	મને ... આપશો, પ્લીઝ?	ma·ne ... aap·sho pleez
deposit	મારી ડિપોઝિટ પાછી	maa·ri di·po·zit paa·ch'i
passport	મારો પાસપોર્ટ પાછો	maa·ro pas·porţ paa·ch'o
valuables	મારાં વેલ્યુએબલ્સ પાછાં	maa·rang vel·yu·a·bals paa·ch'ang

banking & communications

Where's an ATM/a public phone?
પાસે કોઈ એટીએમ/પબ્લિક ફોન છે? paa·se ko·i ey·tee·em/pab·lik p'on ch'e

I'd like to ...	મારે ...	ma·re ...
arrange a transfer	એક ટ્રાન્સફર કરાવવું છે	ek trans·far ka·raav·vung ch'e
change a travellers cheque	ટ્રાવેલર્સ ચેક કેશ કરાવવો છે	ţraa·ve·lars chek kesh ka·raav·vo ch'e
change money	ના રૂપિયા કરાવવા છે	na ru·pi·yaa ka·raav·vaa ch'e
withdraw money	પૈસા વિથડ્રો કરવા છે	pai·saa wit'·dro kar·vaa ch'e

What's the ...?	... શું છે?	... shung ch'e
charge for that	તેનો ચાર્જ	te·no chaarj
exchange rate	એક્સચેન્જ રેઈટ	eks·chenj re·yit

Where's the local internet café?
પાસે કોઈ સાયબર કાફે છે? paa·se ko·i sai·bar kaa·fe ch'e

How much is it per hour?
કલાકનો ચાર્જ શું છે? ka·laak·no charj shung ch'e

I'd like to ...	મારે ... છે.	maa·re ... ch'e
get internet access	ઈન્ટરનેટ ઉપર જવું	in·ţar·neţ u·par ja·vung
use a printer/scanner	પ્રિન્ટરનું/સ્કેનરનું કામ	prin·ţar·nug/ske·nar·nug kaam

I'd like a ...	મારે ... છે.	maa·re ... ch'e
mobile/cell phone for hire	મોબાઈલ ફોન રેન્ટ કરવો	mo·baa·il p'on renţ kar·vo
SIM card for your network	તમારા નેટવર્કનું સિમ કાર્ડ જોઈએ	ta·maa·raa neţ·vark·nung sim kaarđ jo·i·ye

What are the rates?
રેઈટ શું છે? | re·yit shung ch'e

What's your phone number?
તમારો ફોન નંબર શું છે? | ta·maa·ro p'on nam·bar shung ch'e

The number is …
નંબર છે … | nam·bar ch'e …

I'd like to buy a phonecard.
મારે એક ફોન કાર્ડ લેવું છે. | maa·re ek p'on kaarđ le·vung ch'e

I want to …	મારે … છે.	maa·re … ch'e
call (Canada)	(કેનેડા) કોલ કરવો	(ke·ne·đaa) kol kar·vo
call collect	કલેક્ટ કોલ કરવો	ka·lekţ kol kar·vo

I want to send a fax.
મારે એક ફેક્સ કરવો છે. | maa·re ek feks kar·vo ch'e

I want to send a parcel.
મારે એક પારસલ મોકલવું છે. | maa·re ek par·sal mo·kal·vung ch'e

I want to buy a stamp.
મારે એક સ્ટેમ્પ લેવી છે. | maa·re ek sţemp le·vi ch'e

I want to buy an envelope.
મારે એક કવર લેવું છે. | maa·re ek ka·var le·vung ch'e

Please send it to (Australia).
પ્લીઝ આને (ઓસ્ટ્રેલિયા) મોકલવાનું છે. | pleez aa·ne (os·ţra·li·yaa) mo·kal·vaa·nung ch'e

sightseeing

What time does it open?
એનો ખૂલવાનો ટાઈમ શું છે? | eh·no k'ool·vaa·no taa·yim shung ch'e

What time does it close?
એનો બંધ થવાનો ટાઈમ શું છે? | eh·no band' t'a·vaa·no taa·yim shung ch'e

What's the admission charge?
તેની ટિકિટ કેટલી છે? | teh·ni ţi·kiţ keţ·li ch'e

Is there a discount for students/children?
સ્ટુડન્ટ/બાળકો માટે કાંઈ કન્સેસન છે? | sţu·đent/baaḷ·ko maa·ţe kaa·yin kan·se·san ch'e

I'd like to hire a guide.
મારે એક ગાઈડ રાખવો છે. | maa·re ek gaa·yiđ raak'·vo ch'e

I'd like a catalogue/map.
મને એક કેટલોગ/નકશો આપશો? — ma·ne ek keţ·log/nak·sho aap·sho

I'd like to see …
જરા તે … બતાવશો? — ja·raa teh … ba·taav·sho

What's that?
તે શું છે? — teh shung ch'e

Can I take a photo?
એક ફોટો પાડું તો વાંધો નથી ને? — ek p'o·ţo paa·đung toh vaan·d'o na·t'i ne

I'd like to go somewhere off the beaten track.
બહુ ઓછા લોકો જતા હોય તેવી જગ્યાએ મારે જવું છે. — ba·hu o·ch'a lo·ko ja·taa hoy te·vi ja·gyaa·e maa·re ja·vung ch'e

When's the next tour?
નેક્સ ટૂર ક્યારે છે? — neksţ ţoor kyaa·re ch'e

How long is the tour?
ટૂર કેટલી લાંબી છે? — ţoor keţ·li lam·bi ch'e

Is … included?	તેમાં … ઈન્ક્લુડેડ છે?	teh·maang … in·klu·đeđ ch'e
accommodation	એકોમોડેશન	e·ko·mo·đe·shan
admission	દાખલ ફી	eđ·mi·shan
food	ભોજન	b'o·jan
transport	વાહન	vaa·han

sightseeing

fort	કિલ્લો	kil·lo
main square	મોટો ચોક	mo·ţo chok
mosque	મસ્જિદ	mas·jid
palace	મહેલ	ma·hel
ruins	રૂઈન્સ	roo·yins
temple	મંદિર	man·dir
tomb	મજાર	ma·jaar
walled city	કોટ વિસ્તાર	kot vis·taar

shopping

Where's a … ?	પાસે કોઈ … છે?	paa·se ko·i … ch'e
camera shop	કેમેરાની દુકાન	ke·me·raa·ni du·kaan
market	બજાર	ba·jaar
souvenir shop	ગિફ્ટ શોપ	gifţ shop

I'm looking for ...
મારે ... જોઈએ છે. — maa·re ... jo·i·ye ch'e

Can I look at it?
જરા બતાવશો? — ja·raa ba·taav·sho

Can I have it sent overseas?
તેને તમે ઓવરસીઝ મોકલી શકો? — teh·ne ta·me o·var·seez mok·li sha·ko

Can I have my (camera) repaired?
અહીં (કેમેરા) રિપેર થશે? — a·heeng (ke·me·raa) ri·pair t'a·she

It's faulty.
આ ... બરાબર ચાલતો/ચાલતી/ ચાલતું નથી. — aa ... ba·raa·bar chaal·to/chaal·ti/ chaal·tung na·t'i **m/f/n**

How much is it?
આની પ્રાઈસ શું છે? — aa·ni praa·yis shung ch'e

Can you write down the price?
પ્રાઈસ જરા લખી આપશો? — praa·yis ja·raa la·k'i aap·sho

That's too expensive.
એ તો બહુ ભાવ કહેવાય. — eh to ba·hu b'aav ka·he·vaay

I'll give you (300 rupees).
(ત્રણસો રૂપિયા) આપું. — (traṇ·so ru·pi·ya) aa·pung

There's a mistake in the bill.
બિલમાં ભૂલ છે. — bil·mang b'ool ch'e

Do you accept ...?	તમે ... સ્વીકારો છો?	ta·me ... svi·kaa·ro ch'o
credit cards	ક્રેડિટ કાર્ડ	kre·điţ kaarđ
debit cards	ડેબિટ કાર્ડ	de·biţ kaarđ
travellers cheques	ટ્રાવેલર્સ ચેક	ţraa·ve·lars chek

I'd like (a) ..., please.	મને ... આપશો, પ્લીઝ?	ma·ne ... aap·sho pleez
bag	એક બેગ	ek beg
my change	મારું ચેન્જ	maa·rung chenj
receipt	રસીદ	ra·seed
refund	મારું રિફન્ડ	maa·rung ri·fanđ

Less.	ઓછું.	o·ch'ung
Enough.	ઈનફ.	i·naf
More.	વધુ.	va·d'u

photography

Can you ...?	તમે મને ... આપશો?	ta·me ma·ne ... aap·sho
burn a CD from my memory card/ stick	મારા મેમરી કાર્ડ/ સ્ટિક ઉપરથી એક સીડી બનાવી	maa·raa me·ma·ri kaarđ/ sţik u·par·t'i ek si·đi ba·naa·vi
develop this film	આ રોલ ડેવલપ કરી	aa rol dev·lap ka·ri

I need a film for this camera.
મારે આ કેમેરા માટે રોલ જોઈએ છે. maa·re aa ke·me·raa maa·ţe rol jo·i·ye ch'e

When will it be ready?
ક્યારે રેડી થઈ જશે? kyaa·re re·đi t'a·yi ja·she

making conversation

Hello.	નમસ્તે.	na·mas·te
Good night.	ગુડ નાઈટ.	guđ naa·yiţ
Goodbye.	આવજો.	aav·jo
Mr/Mrs	ભાઈ/ બહેન	b'aai/ba·hen
Miss/Ms	મિસ/મિઝ	mis/miz
How are you?	કેમ છો?	kem ch'o
Fine, and you?	મજામાં, તમે કેમ છો?	ma·jaa·mang ta·me kem ch'o
What's your name?	તમારું નામ શું છે?	ta·maa·rung naam shung ch'e
My name is ...	મારું નામ ... છે.	maa·rung naam ... ch'e
I'm pleased to meet you.	તમને મળીને ખૂબ આનંદ થયો.	tam·ne ma·ļi·ne k'oob aa·nand t'a·yo
This is ...	આ ... છે.	aa ... ch'e
my brother	મારો ભાઈ	maa·ro b'aai
my daughter	મારી દીકરી	maa·ri dik·ri
my father	મારા બાપા	maa·raa baa·paa
my friend	મારો/મારી ફ્રેન્ડ	maa·ro/maa·ri frenđ m/f
my husband	મારા પતિ	maa·raa pa·tee
my mother	મારાં બા	ma·raang baa
my sister	મારી બહેન	maa·ri ba·hen
my son	મારો દીકરો	maa·ro dik·ro
my wife	મારાં પત્ની	maa·raan pat·nee

Here's my (address).	આ મારું (એડ્રેસ) છે.	aa maa·rung (eđ·res) ch'e
What's your (email)?	તમારો (ઈમેઈલ) શું છે?	ta·maa·ro (ee·me·yil) shung ch'e
Where are you from?	તમે ક્યાંથી આવો છો?	ta·me kyaang·t'i aa·vo ch'o
I'm from …	હું … થી આવું છું.	hung … t'i aa·vung ch'ung
Australia	ઓસ્ટ્રેલિયા	os·tre·li·yaa
Canada	કેનેડા	ke·ne·đaa
New Zealand	ન્યુ ઝીલેન્ડ	nyu zee·lenđ
the UK	બ્રિટન	yoo·ke
the USA	અમેરિકા	yoo·es·e

What's your occupation?
તમે શાનું કામ કરો છો? ta·me shaa·nung kaam ka·ro ch'o

I'm a/an …	હું …	hoong …
businessperson	બિઝનેસ કરું છું	bij'·nes ka·rung ch'ung
office worker	સર્વિસ કરું છું	sar·vis ka·rung ch'ung
Do you like …?	તમને … ગમે છે?	tam·ne … ga·me ch'e
I like …	મને … ગમે છે.	ma·ne … ga·me ch'e
I don't like …	મને … નથી ગમતી/ ગમતું/ગમતાં.	ma·ne … na·t'i gam·ti/ gam·tung/gam·ta **f/n/pl**
art	આર્ટ	aarţ **f**
movies	ફિલ્મ	fi·lam **f**
music	સંગીત	san·geet **n**
reading	પુસ્તકો	pus·ta·ko **pl**
sport	રમત ગમત	ra·mat·ga·mat **f**

eating out

I'd like (a/the) …, please.	પ્લીઝ, જરા … આપશો?	pleez ja·raa … aap·sho
bill	બિલ	bil
local speciality	અહીંની કોઈ ખાસ આઈટમ હોય તે	a·heeng·ni ko·i k'aas aay·ţam hoy teh
menu	મેન્યુ	men·yu
(non)smoking section	(નોન)સ્મોકિંગ સેક્શન	(non·)smo·king sek·shan
table for (four)	(ચાર) જણ માટે એક ટેબલ	(chaar) jaņ maa·ţe ek ţe·bal
that dish	પેલી આઈટમ	pe·li aay·ţam

Can you recommend a ...?	કોઈ ... રેકેમેન્ડ કરશો?	ko·i ... ri·ka·menđ kar·sho
bar	સારો બાર	saa·ro baar
place to eat	સારી રેસ્ટોરાં	saa·ri res·ţo·ranţ
breakfast	બ્રેકફાસ્ટ	brek·fasţ
lunch	લંચ	lanch
dinner	ડિનર	đi·nar
(cup of) coffee/tea ...	(એક કપ) કોફી/ચાય ...	(ek kap) ko·fi/chaay...
with milk	દૂધ સાથે	dood' saa·t'ey
without sugar	સૂગર વિના	soo·gar vi·naa
(orange) juice	(ઓરેન્જ) જૂસ	(o·renj) joos
lassi	લસ્સી	las·si
soft drink	સોફ્ટ ડ્રિન્ક	softţ đrink

I'll have boiled water.
હું ઉકાળેલું પાણી લઈશ. — hoong u·kaa·ļe·lung paa·ņi la·yeesh

I'll have mineral water.
હું મિનરલ વોટર લઈશ. — hoong mi·na·ral vo·ţar la·yeesh

I'll buy you a drink.
તમારા માટે એક ડ્રિન્ક મંગાવું છું. — ta·maa·raa maa·ţe ek đrink man·gaa·vung ch'ung

What would you like?
તમે શું લેશો? — ta·me shung le·sho

a bottle of beer	બીયરની એક બોટલ	bi·yar·ni ek bo·ţal
a glass of beer	બીયરનો એક ગ્લાસ	bi·yar·no ek glaas
a bottle/glass of ... wine	એક બોટલ/ગ્લાસ ... વાઈનનો	ek bo·ţal/glaas ... vaa·yin·no
red	રેડ	ređ
white	વ્હાઈટ	waa·yit

special diets & allergies

Do you have ... food?	તમે ... ફૂડ રાખો છો?	ta·me ... foođ raa·k'o ch'o
halal	હલાલ	ha·laal
kosher	કોશર	ko·shar
vegetarian	શાકાહારી	shaa·kaa·haa·ri

Could you prepare a meal without …?	પ્લીઝ, જરા … વિનાનું ભોજન મળશે?	pleez ja·raa … vi·naa·nung b'o·jan maḷ·she
I'm allergic to …	મને … એલરજી છે.	ma·ne … e·lar·jee ch'e
eggs	ઈંડાંની	een·daang·ni
meat	મટનની	ma·ţan·ni
milk	દૂધની	dood'·ni
nuts	નટ્સની	naţs·ni
seafood	સી ફૂડની	si·foođ·ni

emergencies

Help!	હેલ્પ!	help
Stop!	સ્ટોપ!	sţop
Go away!	જાઓ ભાગો!	jaa·o b'aa·go
Thief!	ચોર! ચોર!	chor chor
Fire!	આગ! આગ!	aag aag
Watch out!	જો જો!	jo jo
Call …!	જલદી … બોલાવો!	jal·di … bo·laa·vo
an ambulance	એમબ્યુલન્સ	em·byu·lans
a doctor	ડોક્ટર	đok·ţar
the police	પોલીસ	po·lis

Could you help me, please?
જરા એક હેલ્પ કરશો? — ja·raa ek help kar·sho

I have to use the phone.
મારે જરા એક ફોન કરવો છે. — maa·re ja·raa ek p'on kar·vo ch'e

I'm lost.
હું ભૂલો પડ્યો/પડી છું. — hoong b'oo·lo pa·đyo/pa·đee ch'ung m/f

Where are the toilets?
ટોયલેટ ક્યાં છે? — ţoy·leţ kyaang ch'e

Where's the police station?
પોલીસ સ્ટેશન ક્યાં છે? — po·lis sţey·shan kyaang ch'e

I have insurance.
મારે ઈન્શ્યોરન્સ છે. — maa·re een·shyo·rans ch'e

I want to contact my embassy.
મારે મારી એમ્બેસીનો કોન્ટાક્ટ કરવો છે. — maa·re maa·ri em·bey·see·no kon·ţakţ kar·vo ch'e

I've been …	મને કોઈએ … છે.	ma·ne ko·yi·e … ch'e
raped	રેઈપ કરેલ	re·yip ka·rel
robbed	લૂંટી લીધેલ	loong·tee li·d'el

I've lost my …	… ખોવાયા છે.	… k'o·vaa·yaa ch'e
bag	મારી બેગ	maa·ri beg
money	મારા પૈસા	maa·raa pai·saa
passport	મારો પાસપોર્ટ	maa·ro pas·porţ

health

Where's the nearest …?	પાસે કોઈ … હશે?	paa·se ko·i … ha·she
dentist	ડેન્ટિસ્ટ	đen·ţisţ
doctor	ડોક્ટર	đok·ţar
hospital	હોસ્પિટાલ	hos·pi·ţaal
pharmacist	દવાની દુકાન	da·vaa·ni du·kan

I need a doctor (who speaks English).
કોઈ (ઈન્ગલીશ બોલતા હોય તેવા) ડોક્ટર મળશે?
ko·i (ing·lish bol·taa hoy te·va) đok·ţar maļ·she

Could I see a female doctor?
કોઈ લેડી ડોક્ટર મળશે?
ko·i le·đi đok·ţar maļ·she

I've run out of my medication.
મારી દવા ખલાસ થઈ ગઈ છે.
maa·ri da·vaa k'a·laas t'a·yee ga·yee ch'e

It hurts here.
મને અહીયાં દુખે છે.
ma·ne a·hee·yang du·k'e ch'e

I have (a) …	મને … છે.	ma·ne … ch'e
asthma	અસ્થમા	as·t'a·maa
constipation	અપચો થયો	a·pa·cho t'a·yo
diarrhoea	ઝાડા થયા	j'aa·đaa t'a·yaa
fever	તાવ	taav
heart condition	હાર્ટ કન્ડિશન	haarţ kan·đee·shan
nausea	ઊબકા આવે	oob·kaa aa·ve

I'm allergic to …	મને … એલરજી છે.	ma·ne … e·lar·jee ch'e
antibiotics	એન્ટિબાયોટિક્સની	en·ţee·baa·yo·ţiks·ni
anti-inflammatories	એન્ટિ ઈન્ફ્લેમેટોરિઝની	en·ţee in·fle·me·ta·rees·ni
aspirin	એસ્પિરીનની	es·pi·reen·ni
bees	મધમાખીની	mad'·maa·k'i·ni
codeine	કોડીનની	ko·đin·ni

responsible travel

I'd like to learn some Gujarati.

મારે થોડું ગુજરાતી શીખવું છે.	maa·re t'o·đung gu·ja·raa·tee shee·k'a·vung ch'e

What's this called in Gujarati?

આને ગુજરાતીમાં શું કહેવાય?	aa·ne gu·ja·raa·tee·mang shung ka·he·vaay

Would you like me to teach you some English?

તમારે થોડું ઈન્ગલીશ શીખવું છે?	ta·maa·re t'o·đung ing·lish shee·k'a·vung ch'e

I didn't mean to do/say anything wrong.

કાંઈ ખોટું કહેવાનો/ કરવાનો મારો આશય નહોતો.	kaa·ying k'o·tung ka·he·vaa·no/ ka·ra·vaa·no maa·ro aa·shai na·ho·to

Is this a local or national custom?

આ અહીંનો કોઈ ખાસ રિવાજ છે કે?	aa a·heeng·no ko·i k'aas ri·vaaj ch'e ke

I'd like to stay at a locally run hotel.

મારે અહીંની કોઈ લોકલ માલિકીની હોટેલમાં રહેવું છે.	maa·re a·heeng·ni ko·i lo·kal maa·li·ki·ni ho·ţal·maang ra·he·vung ch'e

Where can I buy locally produced goods/souvenirs?

મારે અહીંની કોઈ ખાસ વસ્તુ/ યાદગીરી લેવી છે તે ક્યાં મલે?	maa·re a·heeng·ni ko·i k'aas vas·tu/ yaad·gi·ri le·vi ch'e te kyaang ma·le

What's this made from?

આ શામાંથી બને છે?	aa shaa·maang·t'i ba·ne ch'e

Does your company have responsible tourism policies?

તમારી કંપનીએ રિસ્પોન્સિબલ ટૂરિઝમની પોલિસી અપનાવી છે કે?	ta·maa·ri kamp·nee·ye ris·pon·si·bal too·ri·sam po·li·si ap·naa·vi ch'e ke

I'd like to do some volunteer work (for your organisation).

(તમારી સંસ્થામાં) મારે કોઈ વોલન્ટીયર કામ કરવું છે.	(ta·maa·ri sangs·t'aa·maang) maa·re kaa·yingk vo·lan·ti·yar kaam ka·ra·vung ch'e

I'm an (English teacher). Can I volunteer my skills?

હું (ઈન્ગલીશ ટીચર) છું.	hoong (ing·lish tee·char) ch'ung
મારે લાયક કોઈ વોલન્ટીયર કામ છે?	maa·re laa·yak ko·i vo·lan·ti·yar kaam ch'e

english–gujarati dictionary

Words in this dictionary are marked as n (noun), a (adjective) and v (verb) where necessary. Adjectives are given in the masculine form only.

A

accident એક્સીડેન્ટ ek·si·đent
accommodation એકોમોડેશન e·ko·mo·đe·shan
adaptor એડેપ્ટર e·đep·ţar
address n એડ્રેસ eđ·res
after પછી pach·hee
air-conditioned એર કન્ડીશન્ડ e·yar kan·đi·shand
airplane એરોપ્લેન e·ro·pla·in
airport એરપોર્ટ er·porţ
alcohol દારૂ da·roo
all બધો ba·d'o
allergy એલરજી e·lar·jee
ambulance એમ્બ્યુલન્સ em·byu·lans
and અને/ને a·ne/ne
ankle પગની ઘૂંટી pag·ni g'oon·tee
antibiotics એન્ટીબાયોટીક en·ţee·baa·yo·ţik
arm હાથ haat'
ATM એટીએમ ey·tee·em

B

baby બાળક baa·ļak
back (of body) પીઠ peeţ'
backpack બેક પેક bek pek
bad ખરાબ k'a·raab
bag બેગ beg
baggage claim બેગેજ ક્લેમ be·gej klem
bank બેન્ક bengk
bar બાર baar
bathroom બાથરૂમ baat'·room
battery બેટરી bet·ree
beautiful સુંદર sun·dar
bed પથારી pa·t'aa·ree
before ની પહેલાં ni pa·he·laang
behind ની પાછળ ni paa·ch'aļ
bicycle સાયકલ saay·kal
big મોટો mo·ţo
bill બિલ bil
blanket બ્લેન્કેટ bleng·keţ
blood group બ્લડ ગ્રૂપ blađ groop
boat બોટ boţ
book (make a reservation) v રિઝરવેશન કરાવવું ri·zar·ve·shan ka·raav·vung
bottle બોતલ bo·ţal
boy છોકરો ch'ok·ro
brakes (car) (કાર) ની બ્રેક (kaar·ni) brek
breakfast બ્રેકફાસ્ટ brek·fasţ
broken (faulty) ખોટકેલો k'ot·ke·lo
bus બસ bas
business બિઝનેસ bij'·nes
buy v ખરીદવું k'a·reed·vung

C

camera કેમેરા ke·me·raa
cancel કેનસલ ken·sal
car કાર kaar
cash n કેશ kesh
cash (a cheque) v (ચેક) કેશ કરાવવો (chek) kesh ka·raav·vo
cell phone મોબાઈલ ફોન mo·baa·il p'on
centre n સેન્ટર sen·tar
change (money) v (પૈસા) એક્સચેન્જ કરાવવા (pai·saa) eks·chenj ka·raav·vaa
cheap ચીપ cheep
check (bill) બિલ bil
check-in n ચેક ઈન chek in
chest (body) છાતી ch'aa·tee
child બાળક ba·ļak
cigarette સિગારેટ si·gaa·reţ
city શહેર sha·her
clean a સાફ saaf
closed બંધ band'
cold a ઠંડો ţ'an·đo
collect call કલેક્ટ કોલ ka·lekţ kol
come આવવું aav·vung
computer કોમ્પયુટર kom·pu·ţar
condom કોન્ડોમ kon·đom
contact lenses કોન્ટાક્ટ લેન્સીસ kon·ţakţ len·sis
cook v રસોઈ કરવી ra·so·ee kar·vee
cost n કીમત kee·mat
credit card ક્રેડિટ કાર્ડ kre·điţ kaarđ
currency exchange કરન્સી એકસચેન્જ ka·ran·si eks·chenj
customs (immigration) કસ્ટમ્સ kas·ţam

D

dangerous ખતરનાક k'a·tar·naak
date (time) તારીખ taa·rik'
day દિવસ di·vas

delay n વાર vaar
dentist ડેન્ટિસ્ટ đen·ţisţ
depart ડિપાર્ટ đi·parţ
diaper ડાયપર đaa·yaa·par
dinner ડિનર đi·nar
direct a ડાયરેક્ટ đai·rekţ
dirty ડર્ટી đar·ţee
disabled (person) વિકલાંગ vi·ka·laang
discount n કન્સેસન kan·se·san
doctor ડોક્ટર đok·ţar
double bed ડબલ બેડ đa·bal beđ
double room ડબલ રૂમ đa·bal room
drink n ડ્રિન્ક đrink
drive v ડ્રાઈવ કરવું đraa·eev kar·vung
drivers licence ડ્રાઈવર્સ લાઈસન્સ
đraa·ee·vars laa·ee·sans
drug (illicit) (નશીલાં) ડ્રગ (na·shee·lang) đrag

E

ear કાન kaan
east પૂર્વ poor·va
eat જમવું jam·vung
economy class ઈકોનોમી ક્લાસ i·ko·no·mi klaas
electricity ઈલેક્ટ્રિસિટી i·lek·tri·si·ti
elevator લિફ્ટ lift
email ઈમેઈલ ee·me·yil
embassy એમ્બેસી em·bey·see
emergency ઈમરજન્સી i·mer·jen·see
English (language) ઈન્ગલીશ ing·lish
entrance એન્ટ્રેન્સ en·trens
evening સાંજ saanj'
exit n એક્ઝીટ ek·zit
expensive મોંઘો mon·g'o
eye આંખ aank'

F

far દૂર đoor
fast ફાસ્ટ faast
father બાપા baa·paa
film (camera) ફિલ્મ film
finger આંગળી aang·ḷee
first-aid kit ફર્સ્ટ એઈડ કિટ farst aid kit
first class ફર્સ્ટ ક્લાસ farst klaas
fish n માછલી maach'·lee
food ફૂડ foođ
foot પગ pag·foot
free (of charge) મફત ma·fat
friend ફ્રેન્ડ frenđ
fruit ફળ p'aḷ
full ભરેલો b'a·re·lo

G

gift ગિફ્ટ gift
girl છોકરી ch'ok·ri
glass (drinking) ગ્લાસ glaas
glasses ચશમાં chash·maang
go જવું ja·vung
good સરસ sa·ras
guide n ગાઈડ gaa·yiđ

H

half અરધો ar·d'o
hand હાથ haat'
happy સુખી su·k'ee
have પાસે paa·se
he તે tey
head n માથું maa·t'ung
heart હ્દય hru·dey
heavy ભારી b'aa·ree
help v હેલ્પ કરવી help kar·vee
here અહીયાં a·hee·yaang
high ઊંચો oon·cho
highway હાઈવે hai·vey
hike v હાઈક કરવું haik kar·vung
holiday રજા ra·jaa
homosexual n&a હોમોસેક્સુઅલ ho·mo·sek·su·al
hospital હોસ્પિટાલ hos·pi·ţaal
hot ગરમ ga·ram
hotel હોટલ ho·ţal
hungry ભૂખ્યો b'oo·k'yo
husband પતિ pa·tee

I

identification (card) આઈડેન્ટિફિકેશન (કાર્ડ)
i·đen·ţi·fi·ke·shan (kaarđ)
ill બીમાર bee·maar
important ઈમ્પોર્ટન્ટ im·por·ţanţ
injury ઈજા ee·jaa
insurance વીમો een·shyo·rans
internet ઈન્ટરનેટ in·ţar·neţ
interpreter ઈન્ટરપ્રિટર in·ţer·pre·ţar

J

jewellery દાગીના g'a·re·ṇaang
job કામ kaam

K

key ચાવી chaa·vee
kilogram કિલોગ્રામ ki·lo·gram

kitchen કિચન ki·chan
knife ચાકુ chaa·ku

L

laundry (place) લોન્ડ્રી lonđ·ree
lawyer લોયર lo·yar
left (direction) લેફ્ટ lefţ
leg (body) પગ pag
lesbian n&a લેસબીયન les·bi·yan
less ઓછો o·ch'o
letter (mail) લેટર le·ţar
light n લાઈટ laa·yiţ
like v ગમવું gam·vung
lock n તાળું taa·ļung
long લાંબો laam·bo
lost ગુમ gum
love v પ્રેમ કરવો prem kar·vo
luggage લગેજ la·gej
lunch લન્ચ lanch

M

mail n ટપાલ ţa·paal
man માણસ ma·ņas
map નકશો nak·sho
market બજાર ba·jaar
matches માચીસ maa·chis
meat માંસ maans
medicine દવા da·vaa
message સંદેશો san·desh
milk દૂધ dood'
minute મિનિટ mi·niţ
mobile phone મોબાઈલ ફોન mo·baa·il p'on
money પૈસા pai·saa
month મહિનો ma·hi·no
morning સવાર sa·vaar
mother બા baa
motorcycle મોટર સાયકલ mo·ţar saay·kal
mouth મોઢું mo·đ'ung

N

name n નામ naam
near નજીક na·jeek
neck ગરદન gar·dan
new નવો na·vo
newspaper છાપું ch'aa·pung
night રાત raat
no ના naa
noisy નોઈઝી noy·zee
nonsmoking નોનસ્મોકિંગ non·smo·king
north ઉત્તર ut·tar
nose નાક naak
now હવે ha·vey
number નંબર nam·bar

O

old (person) મોટો mo·ţo
old (thing) જૂનો joo·no
one-way ticket વન વે ટિકિટ van vey ţi·kiţ
open a ખુલ્લો k'ul·lo
outside બહાર ba·haar

P

passport પાસપોર્ટ pas·porţ
pay v પગાર pa·gaar
pharmacy દવાની દુકાન da·vaa·ni du·kan
phonecard ફોન કાર્ડ p'on kaarđ
photo ફોટો p'o·ţo
police પોલીસ po·lis
postcard પોસ્ટ કાર્ડ posţ kaarđ
post office પોસ્ટ ઓફિસ posţ o·fis
pregnant પ્રેગનન્ટ preg·nanţ
price n કીમત kee·mat

Q

quiet a શાંત shaant

R

rain n વરસાદ var·saad
razor રેઝર re·zar
receipt n રસીદ ra·seed
refund n રિફન્ડ ri·fanđ
registered mail રજિસ્ટર્ડ મેઈલ ra·jis·terđ meyl
rent v રેન્ટ કરવું renţ kar·vung
repair v રિપેર કરવું ri·per kar·vung
reservation રિઝર્વેશન ri·zar·ve·shan
restaurant રેસ્ટોરન્ટ res·ţo·ranţ
return v રિટર્ન ri·ţarn
return ticket રિટર્ન ટિકિટ ri·ţarn ţi·kiţ
right (direction) રાઈટ ra·yiţ
road રોડ rođ
room રૂમ room

S

safe a સેઈફ se·yif
sanitary napkin સેનિટરી નેપકીન se·ni·ta·ri nep·kin
seat n સીટ seeţ

send મોકલવું mo·kal·vung
sex સેક્સ seks
shampoo શેમ્પુ shem·pu
share (a dorm) v (ડોર્મ) શેર કરવી (đorm) sher kar·vee
she તે tey
sheet (bed) ચાદર chaa·dar
shirt શર્ટ shart̨
shoes શૂઝ shooz
shop n દુકાન du·kaan
short ટૂંકો t̨oong·ko
shower n શાવર shaa·var
single room સિંગલ રૂમ sin·gal room
skin n ચામડી chaam·đee
skirt n સ્કર્ટ skart̨
sleep v સૂવું soo·vung
slowly ધીમે d'ee·mey
small નાનો na·no
soap સાબુ saa·bu
some થોડો t'o·đo
soon તરત ta·rat
south દક્ષિણ dak·shiṇ
souvenir shop ગિફ્ટ શોપ gift̨ shop
stamp સ્ટેમ્પ st̨emp
stand-by ticket સ્ટેન્ડ બાય ટિકિટ st̨enđ bai t̨i·kit̨
station (train) સ્ટેશન st̨ey·shan
stomach પેટ st̨a·mak
stop v અટકવું a·t̨a·ka·vung
stop (bus) n (બસ) સ્ટોપ (bas) st̨op
street સ્ટ્રીટ st̨reet̨
student સ્ટુડન્ટ st̨u·đent
sun સૂરજ soo·raj
sunscreen સન સ્કીન san·skrin
swim v તરવું tar·vung

T

tampons ટેમ્પોન t̨em·pon
teeth દાંત daant
telephone n ટેલિફોન t̨e·li·p'on
temperature (weather) ટેમ્પરેચર t̨em·pa·re·char
that (one) તે tey
they તેઓ te·o
thirsty તરસ્યો tar·syo
this (one) આ aa
throat ગળું ga·ḷung
ticket ટિકિટ t̨i·kit̨
time ટાઈમ t̨aa·im
tired થાકેલો t'aa·ke·lo
tissues પેપર નેપકીન pe·par nep·kin
today આજે aa·je
toilet ટોયલેટ t̨oy·let̨
tomorrow આવતી કાલે aav·tee kaa·le
tonight આજે રાતે aa·je raa·te
toothbrush ટૂથ બ્રશ t̨ut'·brash
toothpaste ટૂથ પેસ્ટ t̨ut'·pest̨
torch (flashlight) ટોર્ચ t̨orch
tour n ટૂર t̨oor
tourist office ટૂરિસ્ટ ઓફિસ t̨u·rist̨ o·fis
towel ટુવાલ t̨u·vaal
train n ટ્રેઈન t̨re·in
translate ટ્રાન્સલેટ t̨raan·slet̨
travel agency ટ્રાવેલ એજેન્સી t̨raa·vel e·jen·si
travellers cheque ટ્રાવેલર્સ ચેક t̨raa·ve·lars chek
trousers પાટલૂન paat̨·loon
twin beds ટવીન બેડઝ t̨vin bedz

U

underwear અન્ડરવેર an·đar·ver
urgent અરજન્ટ ar·jant

V

vacant ખાલી k'aa·lee
vegetable n શાક shaak
vegetarian a શાકાહારી shaa·kaa·haa·ri

W

walk v ચાલવું chaal·vung
wallet પાકિટ paa·kit̨
wash (something) ધોવું d'o·vung
watch n ઘડિયાળ g'a·đi·yaaḷ
water n પાણી paa·ṇi
we (excluding 'you') અમે a·mey
we (including 'you') આપણે aap·ṇey
weekend વીકએન્ડ vi·kenđ
west પશ્ચિમ pash·chim
wheelchair વ્હીલ ચેર vil·cher
when ક્યારે kyaa·rey
where ક્યાં kyaang
who કોણ koṇ
why કેમ kem
wife પત્ની pat·nee
window બારી baa·ree
with સાથે saa·t'ey
without વિના vi·naa
woman સ્ત્રી stree
write વીકએન્ડ lak'·vung

Y

yes હા haa
yesterday ગઈ કાલે ga·ee kaa·le
you તમે ta·me

Hindi

alphabet

vowels

अ a	आ aa	इ i	ई ee	उ u	ऊ oo	ऋ ri	ए e	ऐ ay	ओ o	औ ow

consonants

क ka	ख k'a	ग ga	घ g'a	ङ na		
च cha	छ ch'a	ज ja	झ j'a	ञ na		
ट ṭa	ठ ṭ'a	ड ḍa	ढ ḍ'a	ण na	ड़ ra	ढ़ ra
त ta	थ t'a	द da	ध d'a	न na		
प pa	फ p'a	ब ba	भ b'a	म ma		
य ya	र ṛa	ल la	व va			
श sha	ष sha	स sa				
ह ha						

numerals

0	1	2	3	4	5	6	7	8	9
०	१	२	३	४	५	६	७	८	९

introduction

Hindi (*hin*·dee हिन्दी) belongs to the the Indo-Aryan group of the Indo-European language family. It has about 600 million speakers worldwide, of which 180 million are in India. Hindi developed from Classical Sanskrit, which appeared in the Indus Valley at about the start of the Common Era, and by the European Middle Ages it became known as 'Hindvi'. During the Islamic Mughal Empire, which ruled northern India from the 16th century until the mid-19th century, the Hindu population adopted many new words from Arabic, Persian and Turkish but continued to write in Devanagari script, while the version written in Arabic script became known as Urdu. However, Hindi and Urdu share a common core vocabulary and are generally considered to be one spoken language with two different scripts. After the end of the British rule and Partition in 1947, Hindi was granted official status along with English, with 21 other languages recognised in the Constitution. The contact between the two languages is reflected in the vocabulary – 'jungle', 'khaki', 'pyjama', 'shampoo' and 'veranda' are just some of the common words that entered English from Hindi.

hindi

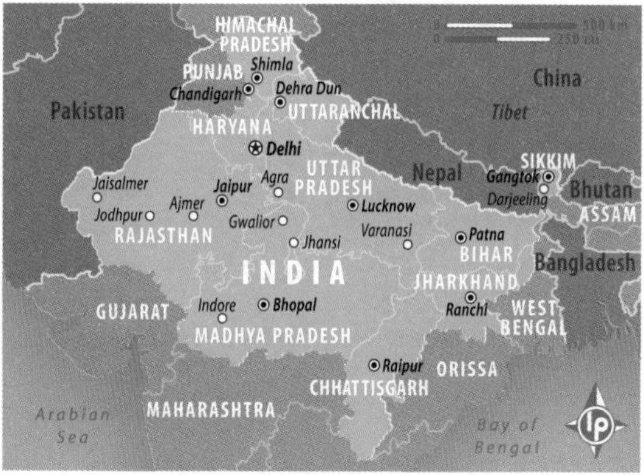

pronunciation

Vowels		Consonants	
Symbol	English sound	Symbol	English sound
a	run	b	bed
aa	father	ch	cheat
ai	aisle	d	dog
ay	day	đ	retroflex d
e	bed	f	fun
ee	see	g	go
i	hit	h	hat
o	pot	j	joke
oh	note	k	kit
oo	zoo	l	lot
u	put	m	man
ow	how	n	not
		ng	ring
		p	pet
		r	run
		ŗ	retroflex r
		s	sun
		sh	shut
		t	top
		ţ	retroflex t
		v	very
		w	win
		y	yes
		z	zero

In this chapter, the Hindi pronunciation is given in green after each phrase.

Aspirated consonants (pronounced with a puff of air after the sound) are represented with an apostrophe after the letter – b′, ch′, d′, đ′, g′, j′, k′, p′, t′ and ţ′. Retroflex consonants (pronounced with the tongue bent backwards) are included in this table.

Each syllable is separated by a dot, and the syllable stressed in each word is italicised. For example:

शुन्या *shoon*·yaa

essentials

Yes.	जी हाँ।	jee haang
No.	जी नहीं।	jee na·*heeng*
Please.	कृपया।	kri·pa·*yaa*
Thank you.	थैंक्यू।	*thayn*·kyoo
Excuse me. (to get past)	रास्ता दे दीजिये।	*raas*·ţaa de *dee*·ji·ye
Excuse me. (to get attention)	सुनिये।	su·ni·*ye*
Sorry.	माफ़ कीजिये।	maaf *kee*·ji·ye

language difficulties

Do you speak English?
क्या आपको अंग्रेज़ी आती है? — kyaa aap ko an·*gre*·zee *aa*·ţee hay

Do you understand?
क्या आप समझे? — kyaa aap *sam*·j'e

I understand.
मैं समझ गया/गयी। — mayng sa·*maj'* ga·*yaa*/ga·*yee* **m/f**

I don't understand.
मैं नहीं समझा/समझी। — mayng na·*heeng* *sam*·j'aa/*sam*·j'ee **m/f**

Could you please ...?	कृपया ...	kri·pa·*yaa* ...
repeat that	फिर से कहिये	p'ir se ka·*hi*·ye
speak more slowly	धीरे बोलिये	*d'ee*·re bo·*li*·ye

numbers

0	शून्या	*shoon*·yaa	**20**	बीस	bees
1	एक	ek	**30**	तीस	ţees
2	दो	do	**40**	चालीस	*chaa*·lees
3	तीन	ţeen	**50**	पचास	pa·*chaas*
4	चार	chaar	**60**	साठ	saat
5	पाँच	paanch	**70**	सत्तर	*saţ*·ţar
6	छह	ch'ay	**80**	अस्सी	*as*·see
7	सात	saaţ	**90**	नब्बे	*nab*·be
8	आठ	aat	**100**	सौ	sow
9	नौ	now	**1,000**	एक हज़ार	ek ha·*zaar*
10	दस	das	**100,000**	एक लाख	ek laak'

time & dates

What time is it?	टाइम क्या है?	*taa*·im kyaa hay
It's (ten) o'clock.	(दस) बजे हैं।	(das) ba·*je* hayng
Quarter past (ten).	सवा (दस)।	sa·*vaa* (das)
Half past (ten).	साढ़े (दस)।	*saa*·ṛe (das)
Quarter to (ten).	पौने (दस)।	*pow*·ne (das)
At what time ...?	कितने बजे ...?	*kiṭ*·ne ba·*je* ...
At 7.57pm.	आठ बजने में तीन मिनट।	aat ba·*je* meng ṭeen mi·*nat*
It's (18 October).	आज (अठारह अक्टूबर) है।	aaj (a·*t'aa*·rah ak·*too*·bar) hay

yesterday	कल	kal
today	आज	aaj
tomorrow	कल	kal

Monday	सोमवार	*som*·vaar
Tuesday	मंगलवार	man·*gal*·vaar
Wednesday	बुधवार	*bud'*·vaar
Thursday	गुरुवार	gu·ru·*vaar*
Friday	शुक्रवार	*shuk*·ra·vaar
Saturday	शनिवार	sha·ni·*vaar*
Sunday	रविवार	ra·vi·*vaar*

border crossing

I'm ...	मैं ... हूँ।	mayng ... hoong
in translit	रास्ते में	*raa*·sṭe meng
on business	व्यापार करने आया/आयी	*vyaa*·paar *kar*·ne *aa*·yaa/*aa*·yee **m/f**
on holiday	छुट्टी मनाने आया/आयी	*ch'ut*·tee ma·*naa*·ne *aa*·yaa/*aa*·yee **m/f**

I'm here for (three) ...	मैं (तीन) ... के लिये आया/आयी हूँ।	mayng (ṭeen) ... ke li·*ye* *aa*·yaa/*aa*·yee hoong **m/f**
days	दिन	din
months	महीने	ma·*hee*·ne
weeks	हफ्ते	*haf*·ṭe

I'm going to (Karachi).

मैं (कराची) जा रहा/रही हूँ।
mayng (ka·*raa*·chee) jaa ra·*haa*/ra·*hee* hoong **m/f**

I'm staying at the (Awadh Hotel).

मैं (अवध होटल) में ठहरा/ठहरी हूँ।
mayng (*a*·wad' ho·*tel*) meng *t'eh*·raa/*t'eh*·ree hoong **m/f**

I have nothing to declare.

कुछ डिक्लेर करने के लिये नहीं है।
kuch' đik·*ler kar*·ne ke li·*ye* na·*heeng* hay

I have this to declare.

मुझे यह डिक्लेर करना/करनी हैं।
mu·j'e yeh đik·*ler kar*·naa/*kar*·nee hayng **m/f**

That's (not) mine.

वह मेरा (नहीं) है।
voh *me*·raa (na·*heeng*) hay

tickets & luggage

Where do I buy a ticket?

टिकट कहाँ मिलता है?
ti·*kat* ka·*haang mil*·ţaa hay

Do I need to book well in advance?

जाने से बहुत पहले बुकिंग होनी चाहिये?
jaa·ne se ba·*huţ peh*·le bu·*king ho*·nee *chaa*·hi·ye

A … ticket to (Kanpur).	(कानपुर) के लिये … टिकट दीजिये।	(*kaan*·pur) ke li·*ye* … ti·*kat dee*·ji·ye
one-way	एक तरफ़ा	ek ţa·ra·*faa*
return	आने जाने का	*aa*·ne *jaa*·ne kaa

I'd like to … my ticket, please.	मुझे टिकट … है।	mu·*j'e* ti·*kat* … hay
cancel	कैंसल कराना	*kayn*·sal ka·*raa*·naa
change	बदलना	ba·*dal*·naa
confirm	कंफर्म कराना	*kan*·farm ka·*raa*·naa

I'd like a (non)smoking seat.

मुझे (नॉन) स्मोकिंग सीट चाहिये।
mu·*j'e* (naan) *smo*·king seet *chaa*·hi·ye

Is there a toilet/air conditioning?

क्या टाइलेट/ए० सी० है?
kyaa *taa*·i·let/e see hay

How long does the trip take?
जाने में कितनी देर लगती है? — *jaa*·ne meng *kiţ*·nee der *lag*·ţee hay

Is it a direct route?
क्या सीधे जाते हैं? — kyaa *see*·d'e *jaa*·ţe hayng

My luggage has been ...	मेरा सामान ... गया है।	*me*·raa *saa*·man ... ga·*yaa* hay
damaged	ख़राब हो	k'a·*raab* ho
lost	खो	k'o
stolen	चोरी हो	*cho*·ree ho

transport

Where does flight number (12) arrive/depart?
फ्लाइट नम्बर (बारह) कहाँ उतरती/उड़ती है? — *flaa*·it *nam*·bar (*baa*·rah) ka·*haang* u·*ţar*·ţee/*uŗ*·ţee hay

Is this the ... to (Agra)?	क्या यह ... (आगरा) जाता है?	kyaa yeh ... (*aag*·raa) *jaa*·ţaa hay
boat	जहाज़	ja·*haaz*
bus	बस	bas
plane	हवाई जहाज़	ha·*vaa*·ee ja·*haaz*
train	ट्रेन	tren

When's the ... (bus)?	... (बस) कब जाती है?	... (bas) kab *jaa*·ţee hay
first	पहली	*peh*·lee
last	आख़िरी	*aa*·k'i·ree
next	अगली	*ag*·lee

How long will it be delayed?
उसे कितनी देर हुई है? — u·*se kiţ*·nee der hu·*ee* hay

Please tell me when we get to (Islamabad).
जब (इसलामाबाद) आता है, मुझे बताइये। — jab (is·laa·*maa*·baad) *aa*·taa hay mu·*j'e* ba·*ţaa*·i·ye

That's my seat.
वह मेरी सीट है। — voh *me*·ree seet hay

I'd like a taxi ...	मुझे ... टैक्सी चाहिये।	mu·*j'e* ... *tayk*·see *chaa*·hi·ye
at (9am)	(सुबह नौ) बजे	(su·*bah* now) ba·*je*
now	अभी	a·*b'ee*

How much is it to (Lahore)?
(लाहौर) तक कितने रुपये लगते हैं? — *(laa*·howr) ţak *kiţ*·ne ru·pa·*ye lag*·ţe hayng

Please put the meter on.
मीटर लगाना। — *mee*·tar la·*gaa*·naa

Please take me to …	… ले जाइये।	… le *jaa*·i·ye
Please stop here.	यहाँ रुकिये।	ya·*haang* ru·ki·*ye*
Please wait here.	यहाँ इंतज़ार कीजिये।	ya·*haang in*·ţa·zaar *kee*·ji·ye

I'd like to hire a car/4WD (with a driver).
मुझे कार/फ़ोर व्हील ड्राइव (ड्राइवर के साथ) किराये पर लेना है। — mu·*je* kaar/for weel *draa*·iv (*draa*·i·var ke saaţ') ki·*raa*·ye par *le*·naa hay

How much for daily hire?
एक रोज़ के लिये किराया कितना है? — ek roz ke li·*ye* ki·*raa*·yaa *kiţ*·naa hay

How much for weekly hire?
हफ़्ते के लिये किराया कितना है? — *haf*·ţe ke li·*ye* ki·*raa*·yaa *kiţ*·naa hay

directions

Where's the …?	… कहाँ है?	… ka·*haang* hay
bank	बैंक	baynk
foreign currency exchange	फ़ॉरेन एक्स्चेंज ऑफ़िस	*faa*·ren *eks*·chenj *aa*·fis
post office	डाक ख़ाना	đaak *k'aa*·naa

Is this the road to (Ajmer)?
क्या यह (अजमीर) का रास्ता है? — kyaa yeh (*aj*·meer) kaa *raas*·ţaa hay

Can you show me (on the map)?
(नक्शे में) दिखा सकते है? — (*nak*·she meng) di·*k'aa sak*·ţe hayng

What's the address?
पता क्या है? — pa·*ţaa* kyaa hay

How far is it?
वह कितनी दूर है? — voh *kiţ*·nee door hay

How do I get there?
मैं चहां कैसे जौंगा/जौंगी? — mayng *va*·hang *kay*·se *ja*·ung·ga/*ja*·ung·gee **m/f**

Turn left/right.	लेफ़्ट/राइट मुड़िये।	left/*raa*·it mu·ṛi·*ye*
It's …	वह … है।	voh … hay
behind …	… के पीछे	… ke *pee*·che
in front of …	… के सामने	… ke *saam*·ne
near …	… के पास	… ke paas
on the corner	कोने पर	*ko*·ne par
opposite …	… के सामने	… ke *saam*·ne
straight ahead	सीधे	*see*·d'e
there	वहाँ	va·*haang*

accommodation

Where's a guesthouse/hotel nearby?
गेस्टहाउस/होटल कहाँ है? — gest·*haa*·us/*ho*·tal ka·*haang* hay

Can you recommend somewhere cheap/good?
सस्ती/अच्छी जगह का पता दे सकते हैं? — *sas*·tee/*ach'*·ch'ee ja·*gah* kaa pa·*ṭaa* de *sak*·ṭe hayng

I'd like to book a room, please.
मुझे कमरा चाहिये। — mu·*j'e kam*·raa *chaa*·hi·ye

I have a reservation.
बुकिंग तो है। — bu·*king* ṭo hay

Do you have a … room?	क्या … कमरा है?	kyaa … *kam*·raa hay
single	सिंगल	*sin*·gal
double	डबल	ḍa·*bal*
twin	टुईन	*tu*·in

How much is it per night?
एक रात के लिय कितने पैसे लगते हैं? — ek raaṭ ke li·*ye kiṭ*·ne *pay*·se *lag*·ṭe hayng

How much is it per person?
हर व्यक्ति के लिय कितने पैसे लगते हैं? — har *vyak*·ti ke li·*ye kiṭ*·ne *pay*·se *lag*·ṭe hayng

For (three) nights.
(तीन) दिन के लिये। — (ṭeen) din ke li·*ye*

Can I have my key, please?
चाबी दीजिये। — *chaa*·bee *dee*·ji·ye

हिन्दी – accommodation

Can I have another (blanket)?

क्या एक और (कम्बल) मिलेगा/मिलेगी?	kyaa ek owr *kam*·bal mi·*le*·gaa/mi·*le*·gee **m/f**

The (air conditioner) doesn't work.

(ए० सी०) ख़राब है।	(e see) k'a·*raab* hay

Is there an elevator/a safe?

क्या यहाँ लिफ़्ट/तिजोरी है?	kyaa ya·*haang* lift/ţi·*jo*·ree hay

What time is checkout?

कितने बजे कमरा ख़ाली करना है?	*kiţ*·ne ba·*je kam*·raa *k'aa*·lee *kar*·naa hay

Can I have my ..., please?	... दे दीजिये।	... de *dee*·ji·ye
deposit	डिपासिट	đi·*paa*·sit
passport	पासपोर्ट	*paas*·port
valuables	बेशक़ीमती चीज़ें	besh·*keem*·ţee *chee*·zeng

banking & communications

Where's an ATM?

ए टी एम कहाँ है?	e tee em ka·*haang* hay

Where's the nearest public phone?

यहाँ पी० सी० ओ० कहाँ है?	ya·*haang* pee see o ka·*haang* hay

I'd like to ...	मैं ... चाहता/चाहती हूँ।	mayng ... *chaah*·ţaa/*chaah*·ţee hoong **m/f**
arrange a transfer	बदली करना	*bad*·li *kar*·naa
change a travellers cheque	ट्रेवलर्स चेक कैश करना	*tre*·va·lars chek kaysh *kar*·naa
change money	पैसे बदलना	*pay*·se ba·*dal*·naa
withdraw money	पैसे निकालना	*pay*·se ni·*kaal*·naa

What's the ...?	... क्या है?	... kyaa hay
charge for that	उस के लिये चार्ज	us ke li·*ye* chaarj
exchange rate	एक्स्चेंज रेट	*eks*·chenj ret

Where's the local internet café?

इंटरनेट कैफ़े कहाँ है?	in·*tar*·net *kay*·fe ka·*haang* hay

How much is it per hour?

प्रति घंटे कितने पैसे लगते हैं?	*pra*·ti *g'an*·te *kiţ*·ne *pay*·se *lag*·ţe hayng

I'd like to …	मुझे … है।	mu·*j'e* … hay
get internet access	इंटरनेट देखना	in·*tar*·net *dek'*·naa
use a printer	कॉपी निकालनी	*kaa*·pee ni·*kaal*·nee
use a scanner	कुछ स्कैन करना	kuch' skayn *kar*·naa

I'd like a …	मुझे … चाहिये।	mu·*j'e* … *chaa*·hi·ye
mobile/cell phone for hire	सेल फ़ोन किराये पर	sel fon ki·*raa*·ye par
SIM card for your network	आप के नेटवर्क के लिये सिम कार्ड	aap ke *net*·vark ke li·*ye* sim kaarđ

What are the rates?
दर क्या है? — đar kyaa hay

What's your phone number?
आप का नम्बर क्या है? — aap kaa *nam*·bar kyaa hay

The number is …
नम्बर … है। — *nam*·bar … hay

I'd like to buy a phonecard.
मैं फ़ोनकार्ड ख़रीदना चाहता/चाहती हूँ। — mayng *fon*·kaarđ k'a·*reed*·naa *chaah*·taa/*chaah*·tee hoong **m/f**

I want to …	मैं … चाहता/चाहती हूँ।	mayng … *chaah*·ţaa/*chaah*·ţee hoong **m/f**
call (Canada)	(कनडा को) फ़ोन करना	(ka·na·*đaa* ko) fon *kar*·naa
call collect	रिवर्स चार्जेज़ करना	ri·*vars chaar*·jez *kar*·naa

I want to send a fax/parcel.
मुझे फ़ैक्स/पार्सल भेजना है। — mu·*j'e* fayks/*paar*·sal *b'ej*·naa hay

I want to buy a stamp/an envelope.
मुझे टिकट/लिफ़ाफ़ा दीजिये। — mu·*j'e* ti·*kat*/li·*faa*·faa *dee*·ji·ye

Please send it to (Australia).
उसे (ऑस्ट्रेलिया) को भेजिये। — i·*se* (aas·*tre*·li·yaa) ko *b'e*·ji·ye

sightseeing

What time does it open?
कितने बजे खुलता है? — *kiţ*·ne ba·*je k'ul*·ţaa hay

What time does it close?
कितने बजे बंद होता है? — *kiţ*·ne ba·*je* banđ *ho*·ţaa hay

What's the admission charge?

अंदर जाने का क्या दाम लगता है?	*an*·dar *jaa*·ne kaa kyaa daam *lag*·ţaa hay

Is there a discount for students/children?

क्या छात्रों/बच्चों के लिय विशेष छूट है?	kyaa *chaa*·trong/*bach*·chong ke li·*ye* vi·*shesh* ch'oot hay

I'd like to hire a guide.

मुझे गाइड चाहिये।	mu·*j'e gaa*·id *chaa*·hi·ye

I'd like a catalogue/map.

मुझे कैटेलॉग/नक्शा चाहिये।	mu·*j'e* kay·*te*·laag/*nak*·shaa *chaa*·hi·ye

I'd like to see ...

मैं ... देखना चाहता/चाहती हूँ।	mayng ... *dek'*·naa *chaah*·ţaa/*chaah*·ţee hoong **m/f**

What's that?

वह क्या है?	voh kyaa hay

Can I take a photo?

क्या मैं फ़ोटो ले सकता/सकती हूँ?	kyaa mayng *fo*·to le *sak*·ţaa/*sak*·ţee hoong **m/f**

I'd like to go somewhere off the beaten track.

मैं अनोखा जगह जाना चाहता/चाहती हू।	mayng *aa*·no·k'a *ja*·ga *jaa*·na *chaah*·ţaa/*chaah*·ţee hung **m/f**

When's the next tour?

अगला टूर कब है?	*ag*·laa toor kab hay

How long is the tour?

टूर कितनी देर की है?	toor *kit*·nee der kee hay

Is ... included?	क्या ... वी शामिल है?	kyaa ... b'ee *shaa*·mil hay
accommodation	रहना	*reh*·naa
admission	पृवेश	*pra*·ves
food	खाना	*k'aa*·naa
transport	आना जाना	*aa*·naa *jaa*·naa

sightseeing

fort	किला	*ki*·la
mosque	मसजिद	*mas*·jid
palace	महल	*ma*·hal
ruins	ध्वंसावशेष	*d'ang*·sa·va·shes
temple	मंदिर	*man*·dir

shopping

Where's a ...?	... कहाँ है?	... ka·*haang* hay
camera shop	कैमरा शॉप	*kaym*·raa shaap
market	बाज़ार	*baa*·zaar
souvenir shop	निशानियों की दुकान	ni·*shaa*·ni·yong kee du·*kaan*

I'd like to buy ...
मुझे ... चाहिये। — mu·*j'e* ... *chaa*·hi·ye

Can I look at it?
दिखाइये। — di·*k'aa*·i·ye

Can I have it sent overseas?
क्या आप बाहर भिजवा देंगे/देंगी? — kyaa aap *baa*·har *b'ij*·vaa *deng*·ge/*deng*·gee **m/f**

Can I have my (camera) repaired?
यहाँ (कैमरा) की मरम्मत होती है? — ya·*haang* (*kaym*·raa) kee ma·*ram*·maṭ *ho*·ṭee hay

It's faulty.
यह ख़राब है। — yeh k'a·*raab* hay

How much is it?
कितने का है? — *kiṭ*·ne kaa hay

Can you write down the price?
दाम काग़ज़ पर लिखिये? — daam *kaa*·gaz par li·k'i·*ye*

That's too expensive.
यह बहुत महंगा/महंगी है। — yeh ba·*huṭ* ma·*han*·gaa/ma·*han*·gee hay **m/f**

I'll give you (30 rupees).
मैं (तीस रुपये) दूँगा/दूँगी। — mayng (ṭees ru·pa·*ye*) *doong*·gaa/*doong*·gee **m/f**

There's a mistake in the bill.
बिल में गलती है। — bil meng *gal*·ṭee hay

Do you accept ...?	क्या आप ... लेते/लेती हैं?	kyaa aap ... *le*·ṭe/*le*·ṭee hayng **m/f**
credit cards	क्रेडिट कार्ड	*kre*·đit kaarđ
debit cards	डेबिट कार्ड	*đe*·bit kaarđ
travellers cheques	ट्रेवलर्स चेक	*tre*·va·lars chek

I'd like (a) …, please.	मुझे … चाहिये।	mu·*j'e* … *chaa*·hi·ye
bag	बैग	bayg
my change	बाक़ी पैसे	*baa*·kee *pay*·se
receipt	रसीद	ra·*seed*
refund	पैसे वापस	*pay*·se *vaa*·pas

Less.	कम।	kam
Enough.	काफ़ी।	*kaa*·fee
A bit more.	थोड़ा और।	*tho*·ṛaa owr

photography

Can you transfer photos from my camera to CD?
क्या आप मेरे कैमरे की फ़ोटो सी० डी० पर लगा सकते हैं? — kyaa aap *me*·re *kaym*·re kee foto see đee par la·*gaa sak*·te hayng

Can you develop this film?
क्या आप यह रील धो सकते/सकती हैं? — kyaa aap yeh reel d'o *sak*·ṭe/*sak*·ṭee hayng **m/f**

I need a film for this camera.
मुझे इस कैमरे के लिये एक रील चाहिये। — mu·*je* is *kaym*·re ke li·*ye* ek reel *chaa*·hi·ye

When will it be ready?
कब तैयार होगा/होगी? — kab *ṭay*·yaar *ho*·gaa/*ho*·gee **m/f**

making conversation

Hello./Goodbye.	नमस्ते।	na·mas·*ṭe*
Good night.	शुभ रात्रि।	shub *raa*·tri

Mr/Mrs	श्रीमन/श्रीमती	*shree*·man/*shree*·ma·ṭee
Miss	कुमारी	ku·*maa*·ree

How are you?	आप कैसे/कैसी हैं?	aap *kay*·se/*kay*·see hayng **m/f**
Fine.	मैं ठीक हूँ।	mayng t'eek hoong
And you?	आप सुनाइये।	aap su·*naa*·i·ye
What's your name?	आप का नाम क्या है?	aap kaa naam kyaa hay
My name is …	मेरा नाम … है।	*me*·raa naam … hay
I'm pleased to meet you.	आपसे मिलकर बहुत ख़ुशी हुई।	aap se *mil*·kar ba·*huṭ* k'u·*shee* hu·*ee*

This is my …	यह मेरा/मेरे … है।	yeh *me*·raa/*me*·ree … hay **m/f**
brother	भाई	*b'aa*·ee
daughter	बेटी	*be*·tee
father	पिता	pi·*ţaa*
friend	दोस्त	dosţ **m&f**
husband	पति	*pa*·ţi
mother	माँ	maang
sister	बहन	be·*han*
son	बेटा	*be*·taa
wife	पत्नी	*paţ*·nee

What's your email address?
आप का ई-मेल का पता क्या है? — aap kaa *ee*·mayl kaa pa·*ţaa* kyaa hay

Here's my phone number.
यह मेरा फ़ोन नम्बर है। — yeh *me*·raa fon *nam*·bar hay

Where are you from?
आप कहाँ के/की हैं? — aap ka·*haang* ke/kee hayng **m/f**

I'm from (New Zealand).
मैं (न्यू ज़ीलैंड) का/की हूँ। — mayng (nyoo *zee*·lanđ) kaa/kee hoong **m/f**

What's your occupation?
आप क्या करते/करती हैं? — aap kyaa *kar*·ţe/*kar*·ţee hayng **m/f**

I'm a …	मैं … हूँ।	mayng … hoong
journalist	पत्रकार	*paţ*·ra·kaar
teacher	टीचर	*tee*·char

Do you like …?	क्या आपको … पसंद है?	kyaa *aap*·ko … pa·*sand* hay
I (don't) like …	मुझे … पसंद (नहीं) है।	mu·*je* … pa·*sand* (na·heeng) hay
meditation	ध्यान लगाना	d'yaan la·*gaa*·naa
puppetry	कठपुतलियाँ	kat·*puţ*·li·yaang
yoga	योगासन	yo·*gaa*·san

eating out

Can you recommend a …?	क्या आप … का नाम बता सकते/सकती हैं?	kyaa aap … kaa naam ba·*ţaa* *sak*·ţe/*sak*·ţee hayng **m/f**
bar	एक बार	ek baar
dish	खाना	*k'aa*·naa
place to eat	ढाबा	*d'aa*·baa

I'd like (a/the) …, please.	मुझे … चाहिये।	mu·*j'e* … *chaa*·hi·ye
bill	बिल	bil
menu	मेन्यू	*men*·yoo
(non)smoking section	(नॉन) स्मोकिंग	(naan) *smo*·king
that dish	वो खाना	vo *k'aa*·na

I'd like to reserve a table for (two) people.
मैं (दो) लोगों के लिये बुकिंग कराना चाहता/चाहती हूँ।
mayng (do) lo·*gong* ke li·*ye* bu·*king* ka·*raa*·naa *chaah*·ṭaa/*chaah*·ṭee hoong **m/f**

What's the local speciality?
ख़ास लोकल चीज़ क्या है?
k'aas *lo*·kal cheez kyaa hay

breakfast	नाश्ता	*naash*·ṭaa **m**
lunch	दिन का खाना	din kaa *k'aa*·naa **m**
dinner	रात का खाना	raaṭ kaa *k'aa*·naa **m**
(cup of) coffee …	(एक कप) काईफ़ी …	(ek kap) *kaa*·fee …
(cup of) tea …	(एक कप) चाय …	(ek kap) chai …
with milk	दूध के साथ	dood' ke saaṭ'
without sugar	चीनी के बिना	*chee*·nee ke bi·*naa*
(orange) juice	(ओरेंज) जूस	(*o*·renj) joos **m**
lassi	लस्सी	*las*·see **m**
boiled water	उबला हुआ पानी	*ub*·laa hu·aa *paa*·nee **m**
mineral water	मिनरल वाटर	*min*·ral *vaa*·tar **m**

I'll buy you a drink.
मैं ही इस ड्रिंक के पैसे दूँगा/दूँगी।
mayng hee is drink ke *pay*·se *doong*·gaa/*doong*·gee **m/f**

What would you like?
आप क्या लेंगे/लेंगी?
aap kyaa *leng*·ge/*leng*·gee **m/f**

I'll have …
मुझे … दीजिये।
mu·*j'e* … *dee*·ji·ye

a bottle of beer	की बोतल बियर	kee *bo*·ṭal bi·*yar*
a glass of beer	का ग्लास बियर	kaa glaas bi·*yar*
a bottle of … wine	… शराब की बोतल	… sha·*raab* kee *bo*·ṭal
a glass of … wine	… शराब का गिलास	… sha·*raab* kaa glaas
red	लाल	laal
white	सफ़ेद	sa·*fed*

special diets & allergies

Do you have … food?	क्या आप का खाना … है?	kyaa aap kaa *k'aa*·naa … hay
halal	हलाल	ha·*laal*
kosher	कोशर	*ko*·shar
vegetarian	शाकाहारी	shaa·kaa·*haa*·ree
I'm allergic to …	मुझे … की एलर्जी है।	mu·*j'e* … kee e·*lar*·jee hay
dairy products	दूध से बनी चीज़ों	dood' se ba·*nee chee*·zong
eggs	अंडे	*an*·ḍe
nuts	मेवे	*me*·ve
seafood	मछली	*mach'*·lee

emergencies

Help!	मदद कीजिये!	ma·*dad kee*·ji·ye
Stop that!	बस करो!	bas ka·*ro*
Stop there!	रुको!	ru·*ko*
Go away!	जाओ!	*jaa*·o
Thief!	चोर!	chor
Fire!	आग!	aag
Watch out!	ख़बरदार!	k'a·*bar*·daar
Call …!	… को बुलाओ।	… ko bu·*laa*·o
a doctor	डॉक्टर	*ḍaak*·tar
an ambulance	एम्बुलेन्स	*em*·bu·lens
the police	पुलिस	pu·*lis*

Could you please help?
मदद कीजिये। — ma·*dad kee*·ji·ye

Can I use your phone?
क्या मैं फ़ोन कर सकता/सकती हूँ? — kyaa mayng fon kar *sak*·ṭaa/*sak*·ṭee hoong **m/f**

I'm lost.
मैं रास्ता भूल गया/गयी हूँ। — mayng *raas*·ṭaa b'ool ga·*yaa*/ga·*yee* hoong **m/f**

Where's the toilet?
टॉइलेट कहाँ है? — *taa*·i·let ka·*haang* hay

Where's the police station?
थाना कहाँ है? — *ṭ'aa*·naa ka·*haang* hay

I have insurance.
मेरे पास बीमा है। — *me*·re paas *bee*·maa hay

I want to contact my embassy.
मैं अपने दूतावास को फ़ोन करना चाहता/चाहती हूँ। — mayng *ap*·ne doo·*taa*·vaas ko fon *kar*·naa *chaah*·ṭaa/*chaah*·ṭee hoong **m/f**

I've been raped.
मेरे साथ बलात्कार हुआ। — *me*·re saaṭ' ba·*laat*·kaar hu·*aa*

I've been robbed.
मेरा सामान चोरी हुआ है। — *me*·raa *saa*·man *cho*·ree hu·*aa* hay

I've lost my …	… खो गया/गयी है।	… k'o ga·*yaa*/ga·*yee* hay **m/f**
bag	बैग	bayg
money	पैसे	*pay*·se
passport	पासपोर्ट	*paas*·port

health

Where's the nearest …?	सब से क़रीब … कहाँ है?	sab se ka·*reeb* … ka·*haang* hay
dentist	डेंटिस्ट	*đen*·tist
doctor	डॉक्टर	*đaak*·tar
hospital	अस्पताल	*as*·pa·ṭaal
pharmacist	दवाख़ाना	da·vaa·*k'aa*·naa

I need a doctor (who speaks English).
मुझे (अंग्रेज़ी बोलनेवाला) डॉक्टर चाहिये। — mu·*j'e* (an·*gre*·zee *bol*·ne·*vaa*·laa) *đaak*·tar *chaa*·hi·ye

Could I see a female doctor?
मुझे लेडी डॉक्टर चाहिये। — mu·*j'e* *le*·đee *đaak*·tar *chaa*·hi·ye

I've run out of my medication.
मेरी दवा ख़त्म हुई है। — *me*·ree da·*vaa* k'atm hu·*ee* hay

It hurts here.	इधर दर्द हो रहा है।	i·*d'ar* dard ho ra·*haa* hay
I'm allergic to …	मुझे … की एलरजी है।	mu·*j'e* … kee e·*lar*·jee hay

antibiotics	एंटीबायोटिकिस	*en*·tee·baa·*yo*·tiks **m**
anti-inflammatories	एंटी-इंफ्लैमिटोरीज़	*en*·tee·in·flay·mi·*to*·rees **m**
aspirin	अस्प्रिन	*as*·prin **m**
bees	मधुमक्खी	*ma*·d'u·*mak*·k'ee **f**
codeine	कोडीन	*ko*·đeen **m**

health – HINDI

I have (a/an) …	मुझे … है।	mu·*j'e* … hay

asthma	दमा	da·*maa* **m**
constipation	कब्ज़	kabz **m**
diarrhoea	दस्त	dasţ **m**
fever	बुख़ार	bu·*k'aar* **m**
heart condition	दिल की बीमारी	dil kee bee·*maa*·ree **f**
nausea	उल्टी का एहसास	*ul*·tee kaa *eh*·saas **m**

responsible travel

I'd like to learn some Hindi.
मैं कुछ हिन्दी सीखना चाहता/चाहती हूँ।
mayng kuch' *hin*·di *sik'*·na *chaah*·ţaa/*chaah*·ţee hoong **m/f**

What's this called in Hindi?
इसे हिन्दी मे क्या बोलदे हैं?
i·se *hin*·di me kya *bohl*·ţe hayng

Would you like me to teach you some English?
क्या मैं आपको कुछ अंग्रेज़ी सिखौं?
kya mayng *aap*·ko kuch' ang·*re*·zee *si*·k'a·ung

I didn't mean to do/say anything wrong.
माफ़ कीजिये, जानबूझकर मैं ने यह नहीं किया/कहा।
maaf *kee*·ji·ye jaan·*booj'*·kar mayng ne yeh na·*heeng* ki·*yaa*/ka·*haa*

Is this a local or national custom?
क्या यह लोकल या राष्ट्रीय प्रथा है?
kyaa yeh *lo*·kal yaa *raash*·tree·yo *pra*·t'aa hay

I'd like to stay at a locally run hotel.
मैं लोकल होटल मे रहना चाहता/चाहती हूँ।
mayng *lo*·kal *ho*·tal me *reh*·na *chaah*·ţaa/*chaah*·ţee hoong **m/f**

Where can I buy locally produced goods?
मैं लोकल निशानियां खरीदना चाहता/चाहती हूँ।
mayng *lo*·kal ni·*shaa*·ni·yang *k'a*·rid·na *chaah*·ţaa/*chaah*·ţee hoong **m/f**

What's this made from?
यह किस चीज शे बानाया हुया हैं?
yeh kis cheez se *ba*·na·ya *hu*·aa hay

I'm (an English teacher). Can I volunteer my skills?
मैं (अंग्रेज़ी टिचार) हु। क्या मैं वलानटारि काम कर सकता/सकती हूँ।
mayng (*ang*·re·zi *ti*·char) hung kya mayng *vo*·lan·ta·ri kam kar *sak*·ţa/*sak*·ţee hoong **m/f**

english–hindi dictionary

Words in this dictionary are marked as n (noun), a (adjective), v (verb), sg (singular), pl (plural), inf (informal) and pol (polite) where necessary. Adjectives are given in the masculine form.

A

accident दुर्घटना *dur·g'at·naa*
accommodation रहने की जगह *reh·ne kee ja·gah*
adaptor अडप्टर *a·đap·tar*
address n पता *pa·ţaa*
after बाद *baad*
air conditioner ए० सी० *e see*
airplane हवाई जहाज़ *ha·vaa·ee ja·haaz*
airport हवाई अड्डा *ha·vaa·ee ađ·đaa*
alcohol शराब *sha·raab*
all सब *sab*
allergy एलरजी *e·lar·jee*
ambulance एंबुलेन्स *em·bu·lens*
and और *owr*
ankle टखना *tak·naa*
antibiotics एंटिबायोटिक्स *en·ti·baa·yo·tiks*
arm बाज़ू *baa·zoo*
ATM ए० टी० एम० *e tee em*

B

baby शिशु *shi·shu*
back (body) पीठ *peet'*
backpack बैकपैक *bayk·payk*
bad बुरा *bu·raa*
bag बैग *bayg*
baggage claim सामान प्राप्ति *saa·maan praap·ţi*
bank बैंक *baynk*
bar बार *baar*
bathroom बाथरूम *baaţ·room*
battery सेल *sel*
beautiful सुन्दर *sun·dar*
bed पलंग *pa·lang*
before पहले *peh·le*
behind पीछे *pee·ch'e*
bicycle साइकिल *saa·i·kil*
big बड़ा *ba·ŗaa*
bill n बिल *bil*
blanket कम्बल *kam·bal*
blood group ब्लडग्रुप *blad·grup*
boat जहाज़ *ja·haaz*
book (make a reservation) v बुकिंग कराना *bu·king ka·raa·naa*
bottle बोतल *bo·ţal*
boy लड़का *laŗ·kaa*
brakes (car) ब्रेक *brek*
breakfast नाश्ता *naash·ţaa*
broken (faulty) टूटा *too·taa*
bus बस *bas*
business व्यापार *vyaa·paar*
buy v ख़रीदना *k'a·reed·naa*

C

camera कैमरा *kaym·raa*
cancel कैंसल करना *kayn·sal kar·naa*
car गाड़ी *gaa·ŗee*
cash n नक़द *na·kad*
cash (a cheque) v कैश करना *kaysh kar·naa*
cell phone सेल फ़ोन *sel fon*
centre n केंद्र *ken·dra*
change (money) v भूनाना *boo·naa·naa*
cheap सस्ता *sas·ţaa*
check (bill) बिल *bil*
check-in n चेक-इन *chek in*
chest (body) सीना *see·naa*
child बच्चा *bach·chaa*
cigarette सिगरेट *sig·ret*
city शहर *sha·har*
clean a साफ़ *saaf*
closed बंद *band*
cold (weather) n सर्दी *sar·dee*
collect call कलेक्ट कॉल *ka·lekt kaal*
come आना *aa·naa*
computer कम्प्यूटर *kam·pyoo·tar*
condom कांडम *kaan·đam*
contact lenses कांटिक्ट लेन्स *kaan·tekt lens*
cook v पकाना *pa·kaa·naa*
cost n दाम *daam*
credit card क्रेडिट कार्ड *kre·đit kaarđ*
currency exchange मुद्रा विनिमय *mu·dra vi·ni·mai*
customs (immigration) सीमाधिकार *see·maa·d'i·kaar*

D

dangerous ख़तरनाक *k'a·ţar·naak*
date (time) तारीख़ *ţaa·reek*

A

english–hindi

day दिन din
delay n देर der
dentist डेंटिस्ट *đen*·tist
depart प्रस्थान करना *pra*·staan *kar*·naa
diaper नैपी *nay*·pee
dinner रात का खाना raaţ kaa *k'aa*·naa
direct a सीधा *see*·d'aa
dirty गंदा *gan*·daa
disabled विकलांग vi·ka·*laang*
discount n छूट ch'oot
doctor डॉक्टर *đaak*·tar
double bed डबल बेड đa·*bal* beđ
double room डबल कमरा đa·*bal kam*·raa
drink n पीने की चीज़ें *pee*·ne kee *chee*·zeng
drive v चलाना cha·*laa*·naa
drivers licence गाड़ी चलाने का लाइसेंस
gaa·ŗee cha·*laa*·ne kaa *laa*·i·sens
drug (illicit) नशीली दवा na·*shee*·lee da·*vaa*

E

ear कान kaan
east पूर्व *poor*·va
eat खाना *k'aa*·naa
economy class इकॉनमी क्लास i·*kaa*·na·mee klaas
electricity बिजली *bij*·lee
elevator लिफ़्ट lift
email ई मेल ee mayl
embassy दूतावास doo·*taa*·vaas
emergency आपत *aa*·pat
English (language) अंग्रेज़ी an·*gre*·zee
entrance प्रवेश *pra*·ves
evening शाम shaam
exit n निकास ni·*kaas*
expensive महंगा ma·*han*·gaa
eye आँख aangk'

F

far दूर door
fast जल्दी *jal*·dee
father पिता pi·*ţaa*
film (camera) रील reel
finger उँगली *ung*·lee
first-aid kit फ़र्स्ट एड किट farst eđ kit
first class प्रथम श्रेणी *pra*·tam *shre*·nee
fish n मछली *mach'*·lee
food खाना *k'aa*·naa
foot पैर payr
free (of charge) मुफ़्त mufţ
friend दोस्त dosţ
fruit फल p'al
full भरा हुआ b'a·*raa* hu·*aa*

G

gift तोहफ़ा *ţoh*·faa
girl लड़की *laŗ*·kee
glass (drinking) गिलास glaas
glasses चश्मा *chash*·maa
go जाना *jaa*·naa
good अच्छा *ach'*·ch'aa
guide n गाइड *gaa*·iđ

H

half n आधा *aa*·d'aa
hand हाथ haaţ
happy ख़ुश k'ush
he वे voh
head n सिर sir
heart दिल dil
heavy भारी *b'aa*·ree
help v मदद करना ma·*dad kar*·naa
here यहाँ ya·*haang*
high ऊँचा *oon*·chaa
hike n हाइक *haa*·ik
holiday छुट्टी *ch'ut*·tee
homosexual a समलैंगिक sam·*layn*·gik
hospital अस्पताल *as*·pa·ţaal
hot गर्म garm
hotel होटल *ho*·tal
hungry भूखा *b'oo*·kaa
husband पति *pa*·ţi

I

I मैं mayng
identification (card) परिचय pa·ri·*chai*
ill बीमार *bee*·maar
important अहम a·*ham*
injury चोट chot
insurance बीमा *bee*·maa
interpreter दुभाषिया du·*baa*·shi·yaa

J

jewellery गहने *geh*·ne
job नौकरी *nowk*·ree

K

key चाबी *chaa*·bee
kilogram किलोग्राम ki·*lo*·graam
kitchen रसोई ra·*so*·ee
knife चाकू *chaa*·koo

L

laundry (clothes) धुलाई d'u·*laa*·ee
lawyer वकील va·*keel*
left (direction) लेफ़्ट left
leg (body) भ५ taangg
lesbian n लेज़्बियन *lez*·bi·yan
less कम kam
letter (mail) पत्र pa·*ţra*
light n रोशनी *rosh*·nee
lock n ताला *ţaa*·laa
long लम्बा *lam*·baa
lost खोया हुआ *k'o*·yaa hu·*aa*
love n प्यार pyaar
luggage सामान *saa*·maan
lunch दिन का खाना din kaa *k'aa*·naa

M

mail n डाक đaak
man आदमी *aad*·mee
map नक्शा *nak*·shaa
market बाज़ार *baa*·zaar
matches माचिस *maa*·chis
meat गोश्त gosht
medicine दवा da·*vaa*
message संदेश *san*·desh
milk दूध dood'
minute मिनट mi·*nat*
mobile phone सेल फ़ोन sel fon
money पैसे *pay*·se
month महीना ma·*hee*·naa
morning सवेरा sa·*ve*·raa
mother माँ maang
motorcycle मोटरसाइकिल *mo*·tar·*saa*·i·kil
motorway मोटरवे mo·*tar*·ve
mouth मुँह mung

N

name नाम naam
near पास paas
neck n गला ga·*la*
new नया na·*yaa*
newspaper अख़बार *ak'*·baar
night रात raaţ
no नहीं na·*heeng*
noise शोर-गुल *shor*·gul
nonsmoking नॉन स्मोकिंग naan *smo*·king
north उत्तर *uţ*·ţar
nose नाक naak
now अब ab
number नम्बर *nam*·bar

O

old पुराना pu·*raa*·naa
one-way ticket एक तरफ़ा टिकट
ek ţa·ra·*faa* ti·*kat*
open a खुला k'u·*laa*
outside बाहर *baa*·har

P

passport पासपोर्ट *paas*·port
pay v पैसे देना *pay*·se *de*·naa
pharmacy दवाख़ाना da·vaa·*k'aa*·naa
phonecard फ़ोन कार्ड fon kaarđ
photo फ़ोटो *fo*·to
police पुलिस pu·*lis*
postcard पोस्टकार्ड *post*·kaarđ
post office डाक ख़ाना đaak *k'aa*·naa
pregnant गर्भवती *garb*·va·tee
price n दाम daam

Q

quiet a शान्त shaant

R

rain n बारिश *baa*·rish
razor उस्तरा *us*·ţa·raa
receipt n रसीद ra·*seed*
refund n रिफ़ंड ri·*fanđ*
registered mail रेजिस्टड मेल re·*jis*·tađ mayl
rent n किराया ki·*raa*·yaa
repair v मरम्मत करना ma·*ram*·maţ *kar*·naa
reservation बुकिंग bu·*king*
restaurant रेस्टोरेंट res·*to*·rent
return v वापस आना *vaa*·pas *aa*·naa
return ticket वापसी टिकट *vaa*·pa·see ti·*kat*
right (direction) दाहिना *daa*·hi·naa
road सड़क sa·*rak*
room n कमरा *kam*·raa

S

safe a तिजोरी ţi·*jo*·ree
sanitary napkin सैनिट्री नैपकिन्स
say·*nit*·ree *nayp*·kin
seat n कुरसी *kur*·see
send भेजना *b'ej*·naa
sex संभोग *sam*·bog
shampoo शम्पू *shqm*·pu
share (a dorm) बाँटना *baangt*·naa

she वे voh
sheet (bed) चादर *chaa*·dar
shirt कुरता *kur*·ṭaa
shoes जूते *joo*·ṭe
shop n दुकान du·*kaan*
short छोटा *ch'o*·taa
shower n शॉवर *shaa*·var
single room सिंगल कमरा *sin*·gal *kam*·raa
skin n चमड़ा *cham*·ṛa
skirt n लहंगा la·*han*·gaa
sleep n नींद neend
slowly धीरे धीरे *d'ee*·re *d'ee*·re
small छोटा *cho*·taa
soap साबुन *saa*·bun
some कुछ kuch'
soon जल्दी *jal*·dee
south दक्षिण *dak*·shin
souvenir shop निशानियों की दुकान
ni·*shaa*·ni·yong kee du·*kaan*
stamp n टिकट ti·*kat*
stand-by ticket स्टैंड-बाई टिकट
staynd *baa*·ee ti·*kat*
station (train) स्टेशन *ste*·shan
stomach पेट pet
stop v ठहरना *ṭ'ehr*·naa
stop (bus) n बस स्टॉप bas *is*·taap
street सड़क sa·*ṛak*
student छात्र *chaa*·tra
sun सूरज *soo*·raj
sunscreen सनब्लॉक *san*·blaak
swim v तैरना *ṭayr*·naa

T

tampons टैम्पाईन *taym*·paan
teeth दाश्वत dangṭ
telephone n टेलीफ़ोन *te*·lee·fohn
temperature (weather) तापमान *ṭaap*·maan
that (one) वह voh
they वे voh
thirst प्यास pyaas
this (one) यह yeh
throat गला ga·*laa*
ticket टिकट ti·*kat*
time समय sa·*mai*
tired थका हुआ ṭ'a·*kaa* hu·*aa*
tissues टिश्यू tish·*yoo*
today आज aaj
toilet टॉइलेट *taa*·i·let
tomorrow कल kal
tonight आज रात aaj raaṭ
toothbrush ब्रुश brush
toothpaste दाँतमंजन daant·*man*·jan
torch (flashlight) टॉर्च taarch
tour n दौरा *dow*·raa
tourist office पर्यटन ऑफ़िस *par*·ya·tan *aa*·fis
towel तौलिया *ṭow*·li·yaa
train n ट्रेन tren
translate अनुवाद करना a·nu·*vaad kar*·naa
travel agency ट्रेवल एजेंट *tre*·val e·jent
travellers cheque ट्रेवलर्स चेक *tre*·va·lars chek
trousers पैंट paynt
twin beds ट्विन बेड्ज़ tvin bedz

U

underwear कच्छा *kach*·ch'aa
urgent ज़रूरी za·*roo*·ree

V

vacant ख़ाली *K'aa*·lee
vegetable n सब्ज़ी *sab*·zee
vegetarian a शाकाहारी shaa·k'aa·*haa*·ree
visa वीसा *vee*·saa

W

walk v पैदल जाना *pay*·dal *jaa*·naa
wallet बटुआ ba·tu·*aa*
wash (something) धोना *d'o*·naa
watch n घड़ी g'a·*ṛee*
water n पानी *paa*·nee
we हम ham
weekend वीक एंड veek end
west पश्चिम *pash*·chim
wheelchair व्हील चैयर vheel *chay*·ar
when कब kab
where कहाँ ka·*haang*
who कौन kown
why क्यों kyong
wife पत्नी *paṭ*·nee
window खिड़की *K'ir*·kee
with के साथ ke saaṭ'
without के बिना ke bi·*naa*
woman स्त्री sṭree
write लिखना *lik'*·naa

Y

yes जी हाँ jee haang
yesterday कल kal
you sg pol&pl आप aap

Kannada

alphabet

vowels				
ಅ a	ಆ aa	ಇ i	ಈ ee	ಉ u
ಊ oo	ಎ e	ಏ ey	ಐ ai	ಒ o
ಓ oh	ಔ ow			

consonants				
ಕ ka	ಖ k'a	ಗ ga	ಘ g'a	ಙ nya
ಚ cha	ಛ ch'a	ಜ ja	ಝ j'a	ಞ nga
ಟ ta	ಠ t'a	ಡ da	ಢ d'a	ಣ ṇa
ತ ţa	ಥ ţ'a	ದ đa	ಧ đ'a	ನ na
ಪ pa	ಫ p'a	ಬ ba	ಭ b'a	ಮ ma
ಯ ya	ರ ra	ಲ la	ವ va	ಶ şa
ಷ sha	ಸ sa	ಹ ha	ಳ ļa	ಕ್ಷ ksha

numerals									
0	1	2	3	4	5	6	7	8	9
೦	೧	೨	೩	೪	೫	೬	೭	೮	೯

KANNADA

ಕನ್ನಡ

introduction

Fancy being able to impress former Miss World and darling of Bollywood, Aishwarya Rai, in her native tongue? Try some Kannada phrases, such as: nee·vu ba·ha·ḷa sun·da·ra·vaa·gi·dee·ra ನೀವು ಬಹಳ ಸುಂದರವಾಗಿದೀರ! (You're very beautiful!). Native speakers of Kannada (kan·na·da ಕನ್ನಡ), like Ms Rai, are called kan·na·di·ga·ru ಕನ್ನಡಿಗರು (Kannadigas) and there are about 38 million of them in India, mostly in Karnataka. A Dravidian language related to Tamil and Malayalam, Kannada is written in its own distinct script. It has a long written tradition – copper-plate inscriptions of the Ganga kings of Talakadu date back at least 1500 years. There are several different dialects of Kannada and, in the past, they were closely linked to caste (determined by the structure of Hindu society), although class (determined by wealth and education) is becoming more important in modern times. The literary and spoken versions of Kannada also differ considerably, with the spoken version provided in this chapter – so you can talk to the people at the local market, as well as Bollywood celebrities!

kannada

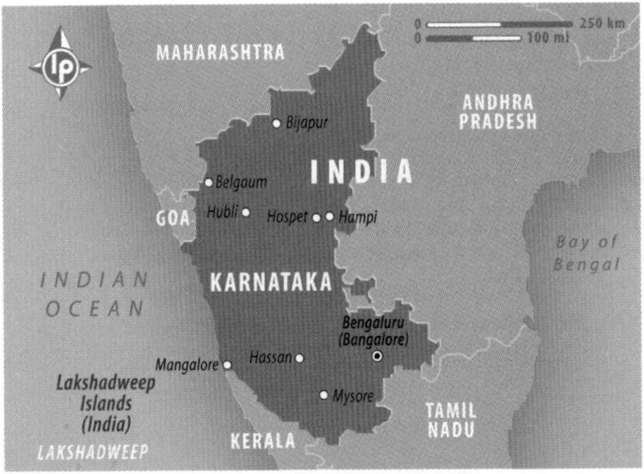

pronunciation

Vowels		Consonants	
Symbol	English sound	Symbol	English sound
a	run	b	bed
aa	father	ch	cheat
ai	aisle	d	dog
e	bet	đ	retroflex d
ee	see	f	fun
ey	as in 'bet', but longer	g	go
i	hit	h	hat
o	pot	j	jar
oh	note	k	kit
oo	zoo	l	lot
ow	now	ļ	retroflex l
u	put	m	man
		n	not
		ņ	retroflex n
		ng	ring
		ny	canyon
		p	pet
		r	red
		s	sun
		ş	retroflex s
		sh	shot
		t	top
		ţ	retroflex t
		v	very
		y	yes

In this chapter, the Kannada pronunciation is given in purple after each phrase.

Aspirated consonants (pronounced with a puff of air after the sound) are represented with an apostrophe after the letter – b', ch', d', đ', g', j', k', p', t' and ţ'. Retroflex consonants (pronounced with the tongue bent backwards) are included in this table.

Each syllable is separated by a dot. For example:

ನಮಸ್ಕಾರ. na·mas·kaa·ra

essentials

Yes.	ಹೌದು.	how·đu
No.	ಇಲ್ಲ.	il·la
Please.	ದಯವಿಟ್ಟು.	đa·ya·vit·tu
Thank you.	ಥ್ಯಾಂಕ್ಯೂ.	t'ank·yoo
Excuse me.	ಸ್ವಲ್ಪ ದಾರಿ ಬಿಡಿ.	sval·pa đaa·ri bi·di
Sorry.	ಕ್ಷಮಿಸಿ.	ksha·mi·si

language difficulties

Do you speak English?
ನೀವು ಇಂಗ್ಲೀಷ್ ಮಾತಾಡುತ್ತೀರ? nee·vu ing·lee·shu maa·taa·duţ·ţee·ra

Do you understand?
ನಿಮಗೆ ಅರ್ಥವಾಗತ್ತ? ni·ma·ge ar·ţ'a·vaa·gaţ·ţa

I understand.
ನನಗೆ ಅರ್ಥವಾಗತ್ತೆ. na·na·ge ar·ţ'a·vaa·gaţ·ţe

I don't understand.
ನನಗೆ ಅರ್ಥವಾಗುವುದಿಲ್ಲ. na·na·ge ar·ţ'a·aa·gu·vu·đil·la

Could you please ...?	ದಯವಿಟ್ಟು ನೀವು ...?	đa·ya·vit·tu nee·vu ...
repeat that	ರಿಪೀಟ್ ಮಾಡಿ	re·peet maa·di
speak more slowly	ಇನ್ನಷ್ಟು ನಿಧಾನ ಮಾತನಾಡಿ	in·nash·tu ni·đ'aa·na maa·ţa·naa·di

numbers

0	ಸೊನ್ನೆ	son·ne	20	ಇಪ್ಪತ್ತು	ip·paţ·ţu
1	ಒಂದು	on·đu	30	ಮೂವತ್ತು	moo·vaţ·ţu
2	ಎರಡು	e·ra·đu	40	ನಲವತ್ತು	na·la·vaţ·ţu
3	ಮೂರು	moo·ru	50	ಐವತ್ತು	ai·vaţ·ţu
4	ನಾಲ್ಕು	naa·ku	60	ಅರವತ್ತು	a·ra·vaţ·ţu
5	ಐದು	ai·đu	70	ಎಪ್ಪತ್ತು	ep·paţ·ţu
6	ಆರು	aa·ru	80	ಎಂಬತ್ತು	em·baţ·ţu
7	ಏಳು	ey·ļu	90	ತೊಂಬತ್ತು	tom·baţ·ţu
8	ಎಂಟು	en·tu	100	ನೂರು	noo·ru
9	ಒಂಬತ್ತು	om·baţ·ţu	1000	ಸಾವಿರ	saa·vi·ra
10	ಹತ್ತು	haţ·ţu	1,000,000	ಹತ್ತು ಲಕ್ಷ	haţ·ţu lak·sha

time & dates

What time is it?	ಗಂಟೆ ಎಷ್ಟು?	gan·te esh·tu
It's (two) o'clock.	ಈಗ (ಎರಡು) ಗಂಟೆ.	ee·ga (e·ra·đu) gan·te
Quarter past (two).	(ಎರಡು) ಹದಿನೈದು.	(e·ra·đu) ha·đi·nai·đu
Half past (two).	(ಎರಡು) ವರೆ.	(e·ra·đu) va·re
Quarter to (three).	(ಮೂರಕ್ಕೆ) ಹದಿನೈದು.	(moo·rak·ke) ha·đi·nai·đu
At what time ...?	ಎಷ್ಟು ಸಮಯಕ್ಕೆ ...?	esh·tu sa·ma·yak·ke ...
At ...	... ಸಮಯಕ್ಕೆ.	... sa·ma·yak·ke
It's (15 December).	ಇವತ್ತು (ಹದಿನೈದು ಡಿಸೆಂಬರ್).	i·vaţ·ţu (ha·đi·nai·đu di·sem·bar)

yesterday	ನಿನ್ನೆ	nin·ne
today	ಇವತ್ತು	i·vaţ·ţu
tomorrow	ನಾಳೆ	naa·ļe
Monday	ಸೋಮವಾರ	soh·ma·vaa·ra
Tuesday	ಮಂಗಳವಾರ	man·ga·ļa·vaa·ra
Wednesday	ಬುಧವಾರ	bu·đ'a·vaa·ra
Thursday	ಗುರುವಾರ	gu·ru·vaa·ra
Friday	ಶುಕ್ರವಾರ	şuk·ra·vaa·ra
Saturday	ಶನಿವಾರ	şa·ni·vaa·ra
Sunday	ಭಾನುವಾರ	b'aa·nu·vaa·ra

border crossing

I'm here ...	ನಾನು ...	naa·nu ...
in transit	ಪ್ರಯಾಣದಲ್ಲಿರುವೆ	pra·yaa·ņa·đal·li·ru·ve
on business	ಬಿಸಿನೆಸ್ ಮೇಲೆ ಬಂದಿರುವೆ	bi·si·nes mey·le ban·đi·ru·ve
on holiday	ರಜೆ ಮೇಲೆ ಬಂದಿರುವೆ	ra·je mey·le ban·đi·ru·ve
I'm here for ...	ನಾನಿಲ್ಲಿ ಬಂದಿರುವುದು ...	naa·nil·li ban·đi·ru·vu·đu ...
(10) days	(ಹತ್ತು) ದಿನಗಳು	(haţ·ţu) đi·na·ga·ļu
(three) weeks	(ಮೂರು) ವಾರಗಳು	(moo·ru) vaa·ra·ga·ļu
(two) months	(ಎರಡು) ತಿಂಗಳು	(e·ra·du) ţin·ga·ļu

I'm going to (Hampi).

ನಾನು (ಹಂಪಿ)ಗೆ ಹೋಗುತ್ತಿರುವೆ.	naa·nu (ham·pi)·ge hoh·guţ·ţi·ru·ve

I'm staying at the (Ashoka hotel).
ನಾನು (ಅಶೋಕ ಹೋಟೆಲ್)ನಲ್ಲಿ ಇರುವೆ. — naa·nu (a·shoh·ka hoh·tel)·nal·li i·ru·ve

I have nothing to declare.
ಡಿಕ್ಲೇರ್ ಮಾಡುವಂತದ್ದು ನನ್ನ ಬಳಿ ಏನೂ ಇಲ್ಲ. — dik·leyr maa·du·van·ţađ·đu nan·na ba·ļi ey·noo il·la

I have this to declare.
ಡಿಕ್ಲೇರ್ ಮಾಡಬಹುದಾದ್ದು ಇದು. — dik·leyr maa·đa·ba·hu·đaađ·đu i·du

That's mine.
ಅದು ನನ್ನದು. — a·đu nan·na·đu

That's not mine.
ಅದು ನನ್ನದಲ್ಲ. — a·đu nan·ṇa·đal·la

tickets & luggage

Where can I buy a ticket?
ಟಿಕೀಟು ಎಲ್ಲಿ ಕೊಳ್ಳಬಹುದು? — ti·kee·tu el·li koļ·ļa·ba·hu·đu

Do I need to book a seat?
ಸೀಟು ಬುಕ್ ಮಾಡಬೇಕ? — see·tu buk maa·da·bey·ke

One … ticket (to Mysore), please.	ದಯವಿಟ್ಟು ಒಂದು … ಟಿಕೀಟು (ಮೈಸೂರಿ)ಗೆ.	đa·ya·vit·tu on·đu … ti·kee·tu (mai·soo·ri)·ge
one-way	ಒನ್-ವೇ	on·vey
return	ರಿಟರ್ನ್	ri·tarn

I'd like to … my ticket, please.	ನನ್ನ ಟಿಕೀಟು … ಮಾಡಬೇಕು, ದಯವಿಟ್ಟು.	nan·na ti·kee·tu … maa·da·bey·ku đa·ya·vit·tu
cancel	ಕ್ಯಾನ್ಸಲ್	kyaan·sel
change	ಬದಲಾವಣೆ	ba·đa·laa·va·ṇe

I'd like a nonsmoking/smoking seat, please.
ನನಗೆ ನಾನ್-ಸ್ಮೋಕಿಂಗ್/ಸ್ಮೋಕಿಂಗ್ ಸೀಟು ಬೇಕು, ದಯವಿಟ್ಟು. — na·na·ge naan·smoh·king/smoh·king see·tu bey·ku đa·ya·vit·tu

Is there a toilet/air conditioning?
ಟಾಯ್ಲೆಟ್/ಏರ್ ಕಂಡೀಶನಿಂಗ್ ಇದೆಯಾ? — taay·let/eyr kan·dee·sha·ning i·de·yaa

How long does the trip take?
ಈ ಪ್ರವಾಸ ಎಷ್ಟು ಹೊತ್ತು ಹಿಡಿಯತ್ತೆ? — ee pra·vaa·sa esh·tu hoţ·ţu hi·di·yaţ·ţe

Is it a direct route?
ಇದು ಡೈರೆಕ್ಟ್ ರೂಟಾ? — i·đu dai·rekt roo·taa

My luggage has been …	ನನ್ನ ಲಗೇಜು …	nan·na la·gey·ju …
damaged	ಹಾಳಾಗಿದೆ	haa·ḷaa·gi·đe
lost	ಕಳೆದುಹೋಗಿದೆ	ka·ḷe·du·hoh·gi·đe
stolen	ಕಳ್ಳತನವಾಗಿದೆ	kaḷ·ḷa·ţa·na·vaa·gi·đe

transport

Where does flight (IA-564) arrive/depart?
ಫ್ಲೈಟು (IA-564) ಎಲ್ಲಿ ಆಗಮನ/ನಿರ್ಗಮನ? — flai·tu (ai ey ai·đu aa·ru naa·ku) el·li aa·ga·ma·na/nir·ga·ma·na

Is this the … to (Mangalore)?	(ಮಂಗಳೂರ್)ಗೆ … ಇದೇನಾ?	(mang·ḷoor)·ge … i·đey·naa
boat	ದೋಣಿ	đoh·ṇi
bus	ಬಸ್ಸು	bas·su
plane	ವಿಮಾನ	vi·maa·na
train	ರೈಲು	rai·lu

What time's the … bus?	… ಬಸ್ಸು ಎಷ್ಟು ಹೊತ್ತಿಗೆ?	… bas·su esh·tu hoţ·ţi·ge
first	ಮೊದಲ	mo·đa·la
last	ಕೊನೆಯ	ko·ne·ya
next	ಮುಂದಿನ	mun·đi·na

How long will it be delayed?
ಎಷ್ಟು ಹೊತ್ತು ಲೇಟಾಗುತ್ತೆ? — esh·tu hoţ·ţu ley·taa·guţ·ţe

Please tell me when we get to (the palace).
(ಅರಮನೆ)ಗೆ ತಲುಪಿದ ಕೂಡ್ಲೆ ದಯವಿಟ್ಟು ನನಗೆ ತಿಳಿಸಿ. — (a·ra·ma·ne)·ge ţa·lu·pi·da koo·da·le đa·ya·vit·tu na·na·ge ţi·ḷi·si

That's my seat.
ಅದು ನನ್ನ ಸೀಟು. — a·đu nan·na see·tu

I'd like a taxi …	ನನಗೆ … ಟ್ಯಾಕ್ಸಿ ಬೇಕು.	na·na·ge … tyaak·si bey·ku
at (9am)	(ಬೆಳಿಗ್ಗೆ ಒಂಬತ್ತಕ್ಕೆ)	(be·ḷig·ge oṃ·bat·tak·ke)
now	ಈಗ	ee·ga

How much is it to (Mysore)?
(ಮೈಸೂರ್)ಗೆ ಎಷ್ಟು? — (mai·soor)·ge esh·tu

Please put the meter on.
ಮೀಟರ್ ಆನ್ ಮಾಡಿ. — mee·tar aan maa·di

Please take me to (this address).

(ಈ ವಿಳಾಸ)ಕ್ಕೆ ದಯವಿಟ್ಟು ನನ್ನನ್ನು ಕರೆದುಕೊಂಡು ಹೋಗಿ. — (ee vi·ḷaa·sak)·ke đa·ya·vit·tu nan·na·nu ka·re·đu·kon·du hoh·gi

Please stop/wait here.

ದಯವಿಟ್ಟು ಇಲ್ಲಿ/ನಿಲ್ಲಿ. — đa·ya·vit·tu il·li/nil·li

I'd like to hire a car/4WD (with a driver).

ನನಗೊಂದು ಕಾರು/4WD ಬಾಡಿಗೆಗೆ ಬೇಕು (ಡ್ರೈವರ್ ಜೊತೆಗೆ). — na·na·gon·đu kaa·ru/fohr·dab·lu·di baa·di·ge·ge bey·ku (drai·var jo·ţe·ge)

How much for daily/weekly hire?

ದಿನಕ್ಕೆ/ವಾರಕ್ಕೆ ಬಾಡಿಗೆ ಎಷ್ಟು? — đi·nak·ke/vaa·rak·ke baa·di·ge esh·tu

directions

Where's the ...?	... ಎಲ್ಲಿದೆ?	... el·li·đe
bank	ಬ್ಯಾಂಕು	byaan·ku
foreign currency exchange	ಫಾರಿನ್ ನೋಟು ವಿನಿಮಯ	faa·rin noh·tu vi·ni·ma·ya
post office	ಅಂಚೆ ಕಛೇರಿ	an·che ka·ch'ey·ri

Is this the road to (Hampi)?

(ಹಂಪಿ)ಗೆ ಇದೇನ ರಸ್ತೆ? — (ham·pi)·ge i·đey·na ras·ţe

Can you show me (on the map)?

(ಮ್ಯಾಪ್ ಮೇಲೆ) ತೋರಿಸುತ್ತೀರ? — (myaap mey·le) ţoh·ri·suţ·ţee·ra

What's the address?

ವಿಳಾಸ ಏನು? — vi·ḷaa·sa ey·nu

How far is it?

ಎಷ್ಟು ದೂರ ಇದೆ? — esh·tu đoo·ra i·de

How do I get there?

ಅಲ್ಲಿಗೆ ಹೋಗುವುದು ಹೇಗೆ? — al·li·ge hoh·gu·vu·đu hey·ge

Turn left/right.

ಎಡಕ್ಕೆ/ಬಲಕ್ಕೆ ತಿರುಗಿ. — e·dak·ke/ba·lak·ke ţi·ru·gi

It's ...	ಅದು ...	a·đu ...
behind ...	... ಹಿಂದೆ	... hin·đe
in front of ...	... ಮುಂದೆ	... mun·đe
near (to ...)	(... ಅದರ) ಹತ್ತಿರ	(... a·đa·ra) haţ·ţi·ra
on the corner	ಕೊನೆಯಲ್ಲಿ	ko·ne·yal·li
opposite ...	... ಎದುರು	... e·đu·ru
there	ಅಲ್ಲಿ	al·li

accommodation

Where's a guesthouse/hotel nearby?

ಹತ್ತಿರದಲ್ಲಿ ಗೈಸ್ಟ್‌ಹೌಸ್/ಹೋಟ್ಲು ಎಲ್ಲಿದೆ? — haţ·ţi·ra·đal·li gest·hows/hoht·lu el·li·đe

Can you recommend somewhere cheap?

ಕಡಿಮೆ ಬೆಲೆಯ ಯಾವುದಾದರೂ ತಿಳಿಸುವಿರಾ? — ka·di·me be·le·ya yaa·vu·đaa·đa·roo ţi·ļi·su·vi·raa

I'd like to book a room, please.

ದಯವಿಟ್ಟು ನನಗೊಂದು ರೂಮು ಬುಕ್ ಮಾಡಿ. — đa·ya·vit·tu na·na·gon·đu roo·mu buk maa·di

I have a reservation.

ನನ್ನದೊಂದು ರಿಸರ್ವೇಶನ್ನು ಇದೆ. — nan·na·đon·đu ri·sar·vey·shan·nu i·đe

Do you have a … room?	… ರೂಮು ಇದೆಯೇ?	… roo·mu i·đe·yey
single	ಸಿಂಗಲ್	sin·gal
double	ಡಬ್ಬಲ್	dab·baļ
twin	ಅಕ್ಕಪಕ್ಕ	ak·ka pak·ka

How much is it per night?

ಪ್ರತಿ ರಾತ್ರಿ ಎಷ್ಟು? — pra·ţi raaţ·ri esh·tu

How much is it per person?

ಪ್ರತಿಯೊಬ್ಬರಿಗೆ ಎಷ್ಟು? — pra·ţi·yob·ba·ri·goo esh·tu

I'd like to stay for (two) nights.

(ಎರಡು) ರಾತ್ರಿಗಳು ಇರ್ತೀನಿ. — (e·ra·đu) raaţ·ri·ga·ļu ir·ţee·ni

Can I have my key, please?

ದಯವಿಟ್ಟು ನನ್ನ ಕೀಲಿ ಕೊಡುತ್ತೀರ? — đa·ya·vit·tu nan·na kee·li ko·duţ·ţee·ra

Can I get another (blanket)?

ಮತ್ತೊಂದು (ಹೊದಿಕೆ) ಸಿಗುವುದಾ? — maţ·ţon·du (ho·đi·ke) si·gu·vu·đaa

The (air conditioning) doesn't work.

(ಏರ್ ಕಂಡೀಶನಿಂಗ್) ಕೆಲಸ ಮಾಡುತ್ತಿಲ್ಲ. — (eyr kan·dee·şa·ning) ke·la·sa maa·duţ·ţil·la

Is there an elevator/a safe?

ಲಿಫ್ಟು/ತಿಜೋರಿ ಇದೆಯಾ? — lif·tu/ţi·joh·ri i·đe·yaa

What time is checkout?

ಚೆಕೌಟ್ ಸಮಯ ಎಷ್ಟು? — chek·owt sa·ma·ya esh·tu

Can I have my ..., please?	ನನ್ನ ... ಕೊಡುತ್ತೀರ, ದಯವಿಟ್ಟು?	nan·na ... ko·duţ·ţee·ra đa·ya·vit·tu
deposit	ಡಿಪಾಸಿಟ್	di·paa·sit
passport	ಪಾಸ್ಪೋರ್ಟ್	paas·pohr·tu

banking & communications

Where's an ATM/a public phone?
ಎ ಟಿ ಎಂ/ಪಬ್ಲಿಕ್ ಫೋನು ಎಲ್ಲಿದೆ? — e ti em/pab·lik foh·nu el·li·đe

I'd like to ...	... ಮಾಡ್ಬೇಕು.	... maad·bey·ku
arrange a transfer	ಹಣ ಹಸ್ತಾಂತರ	ha·ņa has·ţaan·ţa·ra
change a travellers cheque	ಟ್ರಾವೆಲ್ಲರ್ಸ್ ಬದಲಾವಣೆ	traa·ve·lars chek·ku ba·đa·laa·va·ņe
change money	ಹಣ ಬದಲಾವಣೆ	ha·ņa ba·đa·laa·va·ņe
withdraw money	ಹಣ ವಿತ್–ಡ್ರಾ	ha·ņa viţ·draa

What's the ...?	... ಎಷ್ಟು?	... esh·tu
charge for that	ಇದರ ವೆಚ್ಚ	i·da·ra vech·cha
exchange rate	ವಿನಿಮಯ ರೇಟು	vi·ni·ma·ya rey·tu

Where's the local internet café?
ಇಂಟರ್ನೆಟ್ ಸೆಂಟರ್ ಹತ್ತಿರದಲ್ಲಿ ಎಲ್ಲಿದೆ? — in·tar·net sen·tar haţ·ţi·ra·đal·li el·li·đe

How much is it per hour?
ಗಂಟೆಗೆ ಎಷ್ಟು? — gan·te·ge esh·tu

I'd like to ...	ನನಗೆ ... ಬೇಕು.	na·na·ge ... bey·ku
get internet access	ಇಂಟರ್ನೆಟ್	in·tar·net
use a printer/ scanner	ಪ್ರಿಂಟರು/ಸ್ಕ್ಯಾನರು ಬಳಸಲು	prin·tar·ru/skyaa·nar·ru ba·ļa·sa·lu

I'd like a ...	ನನಗೆ ... ಬೇಕು.	na·na·ge ... bey·ku
mobile/cell phone for hire	ಮೊಬೈಲು ಬಾಡಿಗೆಗೆ	mo·bai·lu baa·di·ge·ge
SIM card for your network	ನಿಮ್ಮ ನೆಟ್ವರ್ಕಿನ ಸಿಮ್ ಕಾರ್ಡು	nim·ma net·var·ki·na sim kaar·du

What are the rates?
ರೇಟು ಎಷ್ಟು? — rey·tu esh·tu

What's your phone number?
ನಿಮ್ಮ ಫೋನ್ ನಂಬರ್ ಏನು? — nim·ma foh·nu nam·bar ey·nu

The number is ...
ನಂಬರ್ರು ... — nam·bar·ru ...

I'd like to buy a phonecard.
ನನಗೊಂದು ಕಾಲ್ಲಿಂಗ್ ಕಾರ್ಡು ಬೇಕು. — na·na·gon·du kaa·ling kaar·du bey·ku

I want to ...	ನಾನು ... ಮಾಡಬೇಕಿದೆ.	naa·nu ... maa·da·bey·ki·đe
call (Canada)	ಕಾಲ್ (ಕೆನಡ)	kaal (ke·na·da)
call collect	ಕಾಲ್ ಕಲೆಕ್ಟ್	kaal ka·lekt

I want to send a fax/parcel.
ನಾನು ಒಂದು ಫ್ಯಾಕ್ಸ್/ಪಾರ್ಸಲ್ ಕಳಿಸಬೇಕಿದೆ. — naa·nu on·du fyaaks/paar·sel ka·ḷi·sa·bey·ki·đe

I want to buy a stamp.
ನನಗೊಂದು ಅಂಚೆ ಚೀಟಿ ಕೊಳ್ಳಬೇಕಿದೆ. — na·na·gon·đu an·che chee·ti koḷ·ḷa·bey·ki·đe

I want to buy an envelope.
ನನಗೊಂದು ಎನ್ವಲಪ್ ಕೊಳ್ಳಬೇಕಿದೆ. — na·na·gon·đu en·va·lap koḷ·ḷa·bey·ki·đe

Please send it to (Australia).
ದಯವಿಟ್ಟು ಇದನ್ನು (ಆಸ್ಟ್ರೇಲಿಯ)ಕ್ಕೆ ಕಳುಹಿಸಿ. — đa·ya·vit·tu i·dan·nu (aas·trey·li·ya)·ke ka·ḷu·hi·si

sightseeing

What time does it open/close?
ಎಷ್ಟು ಸಮಯಕ್ಕೆ ಇದು ತೆರೆಯತ್ತೆ/ಮುಚ್ಚುತ್ತೆ? — esh·tu sa·ma·yak·ke i·đu ţe·re·yaţ·ţe/much·chaţ·ţe

What's the admission charge?
ಪ್ರವೇಶ ಶುಲ್ಕ ಎಷ್ಟು? — pra·vey·şa şul·ka esh·tu

Is there a discount for students/children?
ವಿದ್ಯಾರ್ಥಿಗಳಿಗೆ/ಮಕ್ಕಳಿಗೆ ರಿಯಾಯಿತಿ ಇದೆಯೇ? — viđ·yaar·ţ'i·ga·ḷi·ge/mak·ka·ḷi·ge ri·yaa·yi·ţi i·đey·yey

I'd like to hire a guide.
ನನಗೊಬ್ಬ ಗೈಡ್ ಬೇಕು. — na·na·gob·ba gai·du bey·ku

I'd like a catalogue/map.
ನನಗೊಂದು ಕೆಟೆಲಾಗ್/ ಮ್ಯಾಪು ಬೇಕು. — na·na·gon·du ke·te·laag/ myaa·pu bey·ku

I'd like to see …
ನನಗೊಂದು ... ತೋರಿಸಿ. — na·na·gon·du … ţoh·ri·si

What's that?
ಏನದು? — ey·na·đu

Can I take a photo?
ಫೋಟೊ ತೆಗೆದುಕೊಳ್ಳಬಹುದಾ? — foh·to ţe·ge·đu·koḷ·ḷa·ba·hu·đaa

I'd like to go somewhere off the beaten track.
ಕೆಟ್ಟಿರುವ ರೋಡು ತಪ್ಪಿಸಲಾಗುವುದೆ? — ket·ti·ru·va roh·du tap·pi·sa·laa·gu·vu·đe

When's the next tour?
ಮುಂದಿನ ಪ್ರವಾಸ ಯಾವಾಗ? — mun·đi·na pra·vaa·sa yaa·vaa·ga

How long is the tour?
ಎಷ್ಟು ಹೊತ್ತು ಪ್ರವಾಸ? — esh·tu hoţ·ţu pra·vaa·sa

Is … included?	... ಇದರಲ್ಲಿ ಸೇರಿದೆಯಾ?	… i·đa·ral·li sey·ri·đe·yaa
accommodation	ವಸತಿ	va·sa·ţi
admission	ಪ್ರವೇಶ	pra·vey·sa
food	ಊಟ	oo·ta
transport	ಸಾರಿಗೆ	saa·ri·ge

sightseeing		
fort	ಕೋಟೆ	koh·te
main square	ಪ್ರಮುಖ ಚೌಕಟ್ಟು	pra·mu·k'a chow·kat·tu
mosque	ಮಸೀದಿ	ma·see·đi
museum	ಸಂಗ್ರಹಾಲಯ	san·gra·haa·la·ya
old city	ಹಳೆ ಊರು	ha·ḷe oo·ru
palace	ಅರಮನೆ	a·ra·ma·ne
ruins	ಪಾಳು	paa·ḷu
temple	ದೇವಾಲಯ	đey·vaa·la·ya

shopping

Where's a … ?	... ಎಲ್ಲಿದೆ?	… el·li·đe
camera shop	ಕ್ಯಾಮೆರ ಅಂಗಡಿ	kyaa·me·ra an·ga·di
market	ಮಾರ್ಕೆಟ್ಟು	maar·ket·tu
souvenir shop	ಸೂವನಿಯರ್ ಅಂಗಡಿ	soo·va·neer an·ga·di

I'm looking for ...
... ಹುಡುಕುತ್ತಿದ್ದೇನೆ. — ... hu·du·ku·ţiđ·đey·ne

Can I look at it?
ನಾನು ಇದನ್ನು ನೋಡಬಹುದೆ? — naa·nu i·đan·nu noh·đa·ba·hu·đey

Can I have it sent overseas?
ಇದನ್ನು ಹೊರದೇಶಕ್ಕೆ ಕಳಿಸಿಕೊಡಬಹುದೆ? — i·đan·nu ho·ra·đey·shak·ke ka·li·si·ko·da·ba·hu·đe

Can I have my (camera) repaired?
(ಕ್ಯಾಮೆರಾ) ರಿಪೇರಿ ಮಾಡಿಸಬಹುದೆ? — (kyaa·me·ra) ri·pey·ri maa·di·sa·ba·hu·đe

It's faulty.
ಇದರಲ್ಲಿ ತೊಂದರೆಯಿದೆ. — i·đa·ral·li ţon·đa·re·yi·đe

How much is it?
ಎಷ್ಟು ಇದು? — esh·tu i·đu

Can you write down the price?
ಬೆಲೆ ಬರೆದು ತಿಳಿಸುತ್ತೀರಾ? — be·le ba·re·đu ţi·ļi·suţ·ţee·raa

That's too expensive.
ಇದು ಬಹಳ ದುಬಾರಿ. — i·đu ba·ha·ļa đu·baa·ri

I'll give you (300 rupees).
ನಾನು ನಿಮಗೆ (ಮುನ್ನೂರು ರುಪಾಯಿ) ಕೊಡುವೆ. — naa·nu ni·ma·ge (mun·noo·ru ru·paa·yi) ko·du·ve

There's a mistake in the bill.
ಬಿಲ್ಲು ತಪ್ಪಾಗಿದೆ. — bil·lu ţap·paa·gi·đe

Do you accept ...?	ನೀವು ... ತಗೋತೀರಾ?	nee·vu ... ţa·goh·ţee·raa
credit cards	ಕ್ರೆಡಿಟ್ ಕಾರ್ಡುಗಳು	kre·dit kaar·du·ga·ļu
debit cards	ಡೆಬಿಟ್ ಕಾರ್ಡುಗಳು	de·bit kaar·du·ga·ļu
travellers cheques	ಟ್ರಾವೆಲ್ಲರ್ಸ್ ಚೆಕ್ಕು	traa·ve·lars chek·ku

I'd like (a) ..., please.	ದಯವಿಟ್ಟು ನನಗೆ ... ಕೊಡಿ.	đa·ya·vit·tu na·na·ge ... ko·di
bag	ಒಂದು ಚೀಲ	on·đu chee·la
my change	ನನ್ನ ಚಿಲ್ಲರೆ	na·na chil·la·re
receipt	ಒಂದು ರಸೀದಿ	on·đu ra·see·đi
refund	ರೀಫಂಡ್	ree·fund

Less./More./Enough.	ಕಡಿಮೆ./ಜಾಸ್ತಿ./ಸಾಕು.	ka·di·me/jaas·ţi/saa·ku

photography

Can you ...?	... ಮಾಡಿಕೊಡ್ತೀರಾ?	... maa·di·kod·tee·raa
burn a CD from my memory card/ stick	ನನ್ನ ಮೆಮೋರಿ ಕಾರ್ಡಿನಿಂದ/ ಸ್ಟಿಕ್‌ನಿಂದ ಸಿಡಿ	nan·na me·moh·ri kaar·di·nin·đa/ stik·nin·đa see·di
develop this film	ಈ ಫಿಲ್ಮು ಡೆವಲಪ್	ee fil·mu de·va·lap

I need a film for this camera.

ಈ ಕ್ಯಾಮೆರಕ್ಕೆ ಫಿಲ್ಮು ಬೇಕು.	ee kyaa·me·rak·ke fil·mu bey·ku

When will it be ready?

ಯಾವಾಗ ರೆಡಿಯಾಗಬಹುದು?	yaa·vaa·ga re·di·yaa·ga·ba·hu·du

making conversation

Hello.	ನಮಸ್ಕಾರ.	na·mas·kaa·ra
Good night.	ಶುಭರಾತ್ರಿ.	şu·b'a·raa·ţri
Goodbye.	ಸಿಗೋಣ.	si·goh·ṇa
How are you?	ಹೇಗಿದ್ದೀರಿ?	hey·gi·đee·ri
Fine, thanks. And you?	ಚೆನ್ನಾಗಿದೀನಿ, ವಂದನೆಗಳು. ನೀವು?	chen·naa·gi·đee·ni van·đa·ne·ga·ḷu nee·vu
What's your name?	ನಿಮ್ಮ ಹೆಸರೇನು?	nim·ma he·sa·rey·nu
My name is ...	ನನ್ನ ಹೆಸರು ...	nan·na he·sa·ru ...
I'm pleased to meet you.	ನಿಮ್ಮನ್ನು ಭೇಟಿ ಮಾಡಿ ಖುಷಿ ಆಯ್ತು.	nim·man·nu b'ey·ti maa·di k'u·shi aay·ţu
This is my ...	ಇವರು ನನ್ನ ...	i·va·ru nan·na ...
brother (older)	ಅಣ್ಣ	aṇ·ṇa
brother (younger)	ತಮ್ಮ	tam·ma
daughter	ಮಗಳು	ma·ga·ḷu
father	ಅಪ್ಪ	ap·pa
friend	ಸ್ನೇಹಿತ ಸ್ನೇಹಿತೆ	sney·hi·ţa m sney·hiţ·ţey f
husband	ಗಂಡ	gan·da
mother	ಅಮ್ಮ	am·ma
sister (older)	ಅಕ್ಕ	ak·ka
sister (younger)	ತಂಗಿ	ţan·gi
son	ಮಗ	ma·ga
wife	ಹೆಂಡತಿ	hen·da·ţi

Here's my (address).	ನನ್ನ (ವಿಳಾಸ) ಇಲ್ಲಿದೆ.	nan·na (vi·ḷaa·sa) il·li·de
What's your (email)?	ನಿಮ್ಮ (ಇಮೇಯ್ಲು) ಏನು?	nim·ma (ee·mey·lu) ey·nu
Where are you from?	ಎಲ್ಲಿಯವರು ನೀವು?	el·li·ya·va·ru nee·vu
I'm from …	ನಾನು ...ನು/ಳು	naa·nu … ·nu/·ḷu **m/f**
Australia	ಆಸ್ಟ್ರೇಲಿಯದವ	aas·trey·li·ya·đa·va
Canada	ಕೆನಡಾದವ	ke·na·daa·đa·va
New Zealand	ನ್ಯೂ ಝಿಲಿಂಡ್	nyoo j'i·lend·na·va
the UK	ಯೂ ಕೆಯವ	yoo·key ya·va
the USA	ಯೂಎಸ್ ಎಯವ	yoo·es·ey ya·va
What's your occupation?	ನಿಮ್ಮ ಉದ್ಯೋಗ ಏನು?	nim·ma uđ·yoh·ga ey·nu
I'm a/an …	ನಾನು ಒಬ್ಬ ...	naa·nu ob·ba …
businessperson	ವ್ಯಾಪಾರಿ	vyaa·paa·ri
office worker	ಸಂಬಳದ ಕೆಲಸಗಾರ	sam·ba·ḷa·đa ke·la·sa·gaa·ra
tradesperson	ದಲ್ಲಾಳಿ	đal·laa·ḷi
Do you like …?	... ನಿಮಗಿಷ್ಟವೇ?	… ni·ma·gish·ta·vey
I (don't) like …	ನನಗೆ ... ಇಷ್ಟ (ಆಗುವುದಿಲ್ಲ).	na·na·ge … ish·ta (aa·gu·vu·đil·la)
art	ಕಲೆ	ka·le
movies	ಚಲನಚಿತ್ರಗಳು	cha·la·na·chiţ·ra·ga·ḷu
music	ಸಂಗೀತ	san·gee·ţa
reading	ಓದು	oh·đu
sport	ಕ್ರೀಡೆ	kree·de

eating out

I'd like (a/the) …, please.	ದಯವಿಟ್ಟು ನನಗೆ ... ಕೊಡಿ.	đa·ya·vit·tu na·na·ge … ko·di
bill	ಬಿಲ್ಲು	bil·lu
drink list	ಪಾನೀಯಗಳ ಪಟ್ಟಿ	paa·nee·ya·ga·ḷa pat·ti
local speciality	ಇಲ್ಲಿನ ವಿಶೇಷ	il·li·na vi·şey·sha
menu	ಮೆನು	me·nu
(non)smoking section	(ನಾನ್)ಸ್ಮೋಕಿಂಗ್ ಜಾಗ	(naan·)smoh·king jaa·ga
table for (four)	(ನಾಲ್ಕು) ಜನರಿಗೆ ಟೇಬಲ್ಲು	(naa·ku) ja·na·ri·ge tey·bal·lu
that dish	ಆ ತಿಂಡಿ	aa ţin·di

Can you recommend a ...?	ಒಂದು ... ಸೂಚಿಸುತ್ತೀರಾ?	on·đu ... soo·chi·suţ·ţee·raa
bar	ಬಾರನ್ನು	baa·ran·nu
dish	ತಿಂಡಿಯನ್ನು	ţin·di·yan·nu
place to eat	ಊಟಕ್ಕೆ ಒಂದು ಜಾಗವನ್ನು	oo·tak·ke on·đu jaa·ga·van·nu

breakfast	ತಿಂಡಿ	ţin·di
lunch	ಊಟ	oo·ta
dinner	ಊಟ	oo·ta

(cup of) coffee ...	(ಒಂದು ಕಪ್) ಕಾಫಿ ...	(on·đu kap) kaa·fi ...
(cup of) tea ...	(ಒಂದು ಕಪ್) ಚಹ ...	(on·đu kap) ch'a ...
with milk	ಹಾಲಿನೊಂದಿಗೆ	haa·li·non·đi·ge
without sugar	ಸಕ್ಕರೆ ಇಲ್ಲದೆ	sak·ka·re il·la·đe

(orange) juice	(ಕಿತ್ತಳೆ) ರಸ	(kiţ·ţa·ļe) ra·sa
lassi	ಲಸ್ಸಿ	las·si
soft drink	ತಂಪು ಪಾನೀಯ	tam·pu paa·nee·ya

I'll have boiled/mineral water.
ನನಗೆ ಕುದಿಸಿದ ನೀರು/ಮಿನರಲ್ ವಾಟರ್ ಕೊಡಿ. — na·na·ge ku·đi·si·đa nee·ru/mi·na·ral vaa·tar ko·di

I'll buy you a drink.
ನಾನು ನಿನಗೊಂದು ಪಾನೀಯ ಕೊಡಿಸುವೆ. — naa·nu ni·na·gon·đu paa·nee·ya ko·di·su·ve

What would you like?
ನೀನೇನು ತಗೊಳ್ತೀಯ? — nee·ney·nu ţa·goļ·ţee·ya

a bottle/glass of beer	ಒಂದು ಬಾಟಲು/ಗ್ಲಾಸು ಬೀರು	on·du baa·ta·lu/glaa·su bee·ru
a bottle/glass of wine	ಒಂದು ಬಾಟಲು/ಗ್ಲಾಸು ವೈನ್	on·du baa·ta·lu/glaa·su vai·nu

special diets & allergies

Do you have ... food?	ನಿಮ್ಮಲ್ಲಿ ... ಊಟ ಇದೆಯೇ?	nim·mal·li ... oo·ta i·de·ye
halal	ಹಲಾಲ್	ha·laal
kosher	ಕೋಶರ್	koh·şar
vegetarian	ಸಸ್ಯಾಹಾರಿ	sas·yaa·haa·ri

I'm allergic to …	… ನಾನು ಅಲರ್ಜಿಕ್.	… naa·nu a·lar·jik
dairy products	ಡೈರಿ ಉತ್ಪಾದನೆಗಳಿಗೆ	dai·ri uţ·paa·đa·ne·ga·ļi·ge
eggs	ಮೊಟ್ಟೆಗಳಿಗೆ	mot·te·ga·ļi·ge
meat stock	ಶೇಖರಿಸಿದ ಮಾಂಸಕ್ಕೆ	shey·k'a·ri·si·da maam·sak·ke
nuts	ನಟ್ಟುಗಳಿಗೆ	nat·tu·ga·ļi·ge
seafood	ಸೀ ಫುಡ್‌ಗೆ	see·fud·ge

emergencies

Help!	ಸಹಾಯ ಮಾಡಿ!	sa·haa·ya maa·di
Stop!	ನಿಲ್ಲಿ!	nil·li
Go away!	ದೂರ ಹೋಗಿ!	đoo·ra hoh·gi
Thief!	ಕಳ್ಳ!	kaļ·ļa
Fire!	ಬೆಂಕಿ!	ben·ki
Watch out!	ಹುಷಾರು!	hu·shaa·ru

Call …!	… ಕಾಲ್ ಮಾಡಿ!	… kaal maa·di
an ambulance	ಆಂಬುಲೆನ್ಸಿಗೆ	aam·bu·len·si·ge
a doctor	ಡಾಕ್ಟರಿಗೆ	daak·ta·ri·ge
the police	ಪೋಲೀಸಿಗೆ	poh·lee·si·ge

Could you help me, please?
ದಯವಿಟ್ಟು ನನಗೆ ಸಹಾಯ ಮಾಡುತ್ತೀರ? — đa·ya·vit·tu na·na·ge sa·haa·ya maa·duţ·ţee·raa

I have to use the phone.
ನಾನು ಫೋನ್ ಬಳಸಬೇಕು. — naa·nu foh·nu ba·ļa·sa·bey·ku

I'm lost.
ನಾನು ಕಳೆದುಹೋಗಿರುವೆ. — naa·nu ka·ļe·đu·hoh·gi·ru·ve

Where are the toilets?
ಟಾಯ್ಲೆಟ್ಟುಗಳು ಎಲ್ಲಿ? — taay·let·tu·ga·ļu el·li

Where's the police station?
ಪೋಲೀಸ್ ಸ್ಟೇಶನ್ ಎಲ್ಲಿ? — poh·lees stey·shan el·li

I have insurance.
ನನ್ನ ಹತ್ತಿರ ವಿಮೆ ಇದೆ. — nan·na haţ·ţi·ra vi·me i·de

I want to contact my embassy.
ನಾನು ನನ್ನ ಎಂಬೆಸಿಯನ್ನ ಸಂಪರ್ಕಿಸಬೇಕು. — naa·nu nan·na em·be·si·yan·na sam·par·ki·sa·bey·ku

I've been …	ನನಗೆ … ಆಗಿದೆ.	na·na·ge … aa·gi·de
raped	ಅತ್ಯಾಚಾರ	aţ·yaa·chaa·ra
robbed	ಕಳ್ಳತನ	kaḷ·ḷa·ţa·na
I've lost my …	ನಾನು ನನ್ನ … ಕಳೆದುಕೊಂಡಿರುವೆ.	naa·nu nan·na … ka·ḷe·đu·kon·di·ru·ve
bag	ಬ್ಯಾಗು	byaa·gu
money	ಹಣ	ha·ṇa

health

Where's the nearest …?	ಹತ್ತಿರದ … ಎಲ್ಲಿ?	haţ·ţi·ra·đa … el·li
dentist	ದಂತ ವೈದ್ಯ	đan·ţa vaiđ·ya
doctor	ಡಾಕ್ಟರು	daak·ta·ru
hospital	ಆಸ್ಪತ್ರೆ	aas·paţ·re
pharmacist	ಮೆಡಿಕಲ್ ಸ್ಟೋರು	me·di·kal stoh·ru

I need a doctor (who speaks English).
ನನಗೊಬ್ಬ (ಇಂಗ್ಲೀಷ್ ಬರುವ) ಡಾಕ್ಟರು ಬೇಕು. — na·na·gob·ba (ing·lee·shu ba·ru·va) daak·ta·ru bey·ku

Could I see a female doctor?
ನಾನು ಒಬ್ಬ ಲೇಡಿ ಡಾಕ್ಟರನ್ನು ಕಾಣಬಹುದೆ? — naa·nu ob·ba ley·di daak·ta·ran·nu kaa·ṇa·ba·hu·đe

I've run out of my medication.
ನನ್ನ ಔಷಧಿ ಮುಗಿದುಹೋಗಿದೆ. — nan·na ow·sha·đ'i mu·gi·đu·hoh·gi·đe

It hurts here.
ಇಲ್ಲಿ ನೋವುತ್ತೆ. — il·li noh·vuţ·ţe

I have (a) …	ನನಗೆ … ಇದೆ.	na·na·ge … i·đe
asthma	ಅಸ್ತಮಾ	as·ţ'a·maa
constipation	ಭೇದಿ	b'ey·đi
diarrhoea	ಡಯೇರಿಯಾ	da·yey·ri·yaa
fever	ಜ್ವರ	jva·ra
heart condition	ಹೃದಯದ ತೊಂದರೆ	hru·đa·ya·đa ţon·đa·re
nausea	ಹೊಟ್ಟೆ ತೊಳಸು	hot·te ţo·ḷa·su
I'm allergic to …	ನಾನು … ಅಲರ್ಜಿಕ್.	naa·nu … a·lar·jik
antibiotics	ಆಂಟಿ ಬಯಾಟಿಕ್ಸ್	aan·ti·ba·yaa·tik
aspirin	ಆಸ್ಪಿರಿನ್	aas·pi·rin
bees	ಜೇನು ನೊಣಗಳಿಗೆ	jey·nu no·ṇa·ga·ḷi·ge

responsible travel

I'd like to learn some Kannada.

ನಾನು ಸ್ವಲ್ಪ ಕನ್ನಡ ಕಲಿಯಬೇಕು.
naa·nu sval·pa kan·na·da ka·li·ya·bey·ku

What's this called in Kannada?

ಕನ್ನಡ ದಲ್ಲಿ ಇದಕ್ಕೆ ಏನಂತಾರೆ?
kan·na·da đal·li i·dak·ke ey·nan·ţaa·re

Would you like me to teach you some English?

ನಿಮಗೆ ಇಂಗ್ಲೀಷ್ ಕಲಿಸಿಕೊಡಲೆ?
ni·ma·ge ing·lee·shu ka·li·si·ko·da·le

I didn't mean to do/say anything wrong.

ನಾನು ತಪ್ಪಾದದ್ದು ಏನೂ
ಮಾಡಲು/ಹೇಳಲು ಹೊರಟಿರಲಿಲ್ಲ.
naa·nu ţap·paa·đađ·đu ey·noo
maa·da·lu/hey·ḷa·lu ho·ra·ti·ra·lil·la

Is this a local or national custom?

ಇದು ಇಲ್ಲಿಯದೋ ಅಥವ
ರಾಷ್ಟ್ರೀಯ ಪದ್ಧತಿಯೋ?
i·du il·li·ya·đoh a·t'a·va
raash·tree·ya pađ·đa·ţi·yoh

I'd like to stay at a locally run hotel.

ಇಲ್ಲಿಂದಲೇ ನಡೆಸಲ್ಪಡುವ
ಹೋಟ್ಲು ಬೇಕು.
il·lin·đa·ley na·de·sal·pa·du·va
hoht·lu bey·ku

Where can I buy locally produced goods/souvenirs?

ಇಲ್ಲೇ ಉತ್ಪಾದಿಸಿರುವ ವಸ್ತುಗಳು/
ಸೂವನಿಯರ್‌ಗಳು ಎಲ್ಲಿ
ಕೊಳ್ಳಬಹುದು?
il·ley uţ·paa·đi·si·ru·va vas·ţu·ga·ḷu/
soo·va·neer·ga·ḷu el·li
koḷ·ḷa·ba·hu·đu

What's this made from?

ಇದನ್ನು ಯಾವ ವಸ್ತು ಬಳಸಿ
ಮಾಡಿದ್ದಾರೆ?
i·đan·nu yaa·va vas·ţu ba·ḷa·si
maa·di·đaa·re

Does your company have responsible tourism policies?

ನಿಮ್ಮ ಕಂಪೆನಿ ಜವಾಬ್ದಾರಿ ಇರುವ
ಟೂರಿಸಂ ಪಾಲಿಸಿಗಳನ್ನು
ಇಟ್ಟುಕೊಂಡಿದೆಯೇ?
nim·ma kam·pe·ni ja·vaab·đaa·ri i·ru·va
too·rism paa·li·si·ga·ḷan·na
it·tu·kon·di·đe·yey

I'd like to do some volunteer work (for your organisation).

(ನಿಮ್ಮ ಸಂಸ್ಥೆಗೆ) ನಾನು ಸ್ವಯಂ
ಸೇವಕನಾಗಬೇಕು.
(nim·ma sam·sţ'e·ge) naa·nu sva·yam
sey·va·ka·naa·ga·bey·ku

I'm an (English teacher). Can I volunteer my skills?

ನಾನು (ಇಂಗ್ಲೀಷ್ ಟೀಚರ್).
ನನ್ನ ಸ್ಕಿಲ್ಸ್ ಸ್ವಯಂ ಸೇವೆಗೆ
ಸೇರಿಸಿಕೊಳ್ಳಬಹುದೆ?
naa·nu (ing·lee·shu tee·char)
nan·na skils sva·yam sey·ve·ge
ba·ḷa·si·koḷ·ḷa·ba·hu·đey

english–kannada dictionary

Words in this dictionary are marked as n (noun), a (adjective), v (verb), m (masculine), f (feminine), sg (singular), pl (plural), inf (informal) and pol (polite) where necessary.

A

accident ಅಪಘಾತ a·pa·gaa·ţa
accommodation ವಸತಿ va·sa·ţi
adaptor ಅಡಾಪ್ಟರ್ a·daap·tar
address n ವಿಳಾಸ vi·ḷaa·sa
after ನಂತರ nang·ţa·ra
air-conditioned ಏ ಸಿ ey si
airplane ವಿಮಾನ vi·maa·na
airport ವಿಮಾನ ನಿಲ್ದಾಣ vi·maa·na nil·daa·ṇa
alcohol ಸಾರಾಯಿ saa·raa·yi
all ಎಲ್ಲ el·la
allergy ಅಲರ್ಜಿ a·lar·ji
ambulance ಆಂಬುಲೆನ್ಸ್ aam·bu·lens
and ಮತ್ತು maţ·ţu
ankle ಹಿಮ್ಮಡಿ him·ma·di
antibiotics ಆಂಟಿ ಬಯಾಟಿಕ್ಸ್ aan·ti ba·yaa·tik
arm ಕೈ kai
ATM ಎ ಟಿ ಎಂ e ti em

B

baby ಮಗು ma·gu
back (of body) ಬೆನ್ನು ben·nu
backpack ಬ್ಯಾಗು byaa·gu
bad ಕೆಟ್ಟ ket·ta
bag ಚೀಲ chee·la
baggage claim ಬ್ಯಾಗೇಜ್ ಕ್ಲೇಯ್ಮು byaa·gey·ju kley·mu
bank ಬ್ಯಾಂಕು byaan·ku
bar ಬಾರು baa·ru
bathroom ಬಚ್ಚಲು bach·cha·lu
battery ಬ್ಯಾಟರಿ byaa·ta·ri
beautiful ಸುಂದರ sun·đa·ra
bed ಹಾಸಿಗೆ haa·si·ge
before ಮುಂಚೆ mun·che
behind ಹಿಂದೆ hin·đe
bicycle ಸೈಕಲ್ಲು sai·kal·lu
big ದೊಡ್ಡ đod·da
bill ಬಿಲ್ಲು bil·lu
blanket ಹೊದಿಕೆ ho·đi·ke
blood group ರಕ್ತ ಗುಂಪು rak·ţa gum·pu
boat ದೋಣಿ đoh·ni
book (make a reservation) v ಪುಸ್ತಕ pus·ţa·ka
bottle ಬಾಟಲು baa·ta·lu
boy ಹುಡುಗ hu·du·ga
brakes (car) ಬ್ರೇಕುಗಳು brey·ku·ga·lu
breakfast ತಿಂಡಿ ţin·di
broken (faulty) ಮುರಿದ mu·ri·đa
bus ಬಸ್ಸು bas·su
business ವ್ಯಾಪಾರ vyaa·paa·ra
buy v ಕೊಳ್ಳು koḷ·ḷu

C

camera ಕ್ಯಾಮೆರ kyaa·me·ra
cancel ಕ್ಯಾನ್ಸಲ್ kyaan·sel
car ಕಾರು kaa·ru
cash n ದುಡ್ಡು đud·du
cash (a cheque) v ಕ್ಯಾಶ್ kyaaş
cell phone ಮೊಬೈಲು mo·bai·lu
centre n ಮಧ್ಯೆ mađ'·ye
change (money) v ಬದಲಿಸಿ ba·đa·li·si
cheap ಕಡಿಮೆ ಬೆಲೆ ka·di·me be·le
check (bill) ಬಿಲ್ಲು bil·lu
check-in n ಚೆಕ್–ಇನ್ chek·in
chest (body) ಎದೆ e·đe
child ಮಗು ma·gu
cigarette ಸಿಗರೇಟು si·ga·rey·tu
city ನಗರ na·ga·ra
clean a ಸ್ವಚ್ಛ svach·cha
closed ಮುಚ್ಚಿದ much·chi·đa
cold a ತಣ್ಣಗಿರುವ ţan·na·gi·ru·va
collect call ಕಾಲ್ ತಗೊಳಿ kaal ţa·go·ḷi
come ಬನ್ನಿ ban·ni
computer ಕಂಪ್ಯೂಟರು kam·pyu·tar
condom ಕಾಂಡಮ್ kaan·dam
contact lenses ಕಾಂಟ್ಯಾಕ್ಟ್ ಲೆನ್ಸು kaant·yaakt len·su
cook v ಅಡುಗೆ a·du·ge
cost n ಬೆಲೆ be·le
credit card ಕ್ರೆಡಿಟ್ ಕಾರ್ಡು kre·dit kaar·du
currency exchange ನೋಟುಗಳ ವಿನಿಮಯ noh·tu·ga·la vi·ni·ma·ya
customs (immigration) ಕಸ್ಟಮ್ಸ್ kas·tam

D

dangerous ಅಪಾಯಕರ a·paa·ya·ka·ra
date (time) ದಿನಾಂಕ đi·naang·ka
day ದಿನ đi·na
delay n ವಿಳಂಬ vi·ḷam·ba
dentist ದಂತ ವೈದ್ಯ đan·ta vaiđ·ya
depart ಹೊರಡು ho·ra·du
diaper ಡೈಪರ್ dai·par

dinner ಊಟ oo·ta
direct a ನೇರ ney·ra
dirty ಗಲೀಜು ga·lee·ju
disabled ಅಂಗವಿಕಲ an·ga·vi·ka·la
discount n ರಿಯಾಯಿತಿ ri·yaa·yi·ţi
doctor ಡಾಕ್ಟರು daak·ta·ru
double bed ಡಬ್ಬಲ್ ಬೆಡ್ಡು dab·bal bed·du
double room ಡಬಲ್ ರೂಮು dab·bal roo·mu
drink n ಪಾನೀಯ paa·nee·ya
drive v ಡ್ರೈವು drai·vu
drivers licence ಲೈಸೆನ್ಸು lai·san·su
drug (illicit) ಡ್ರಗ್ಸು drag·su

E

ear ಕಿವಿ ki·vi
east ಪೂರ್ವ poor·va
eat ತಿನ್ನಿ ţin·ni
economy class ಎಕಾನಮಿ ಕ್ಲಾಸು e·kaa·na·mi klaa·su
electricity ಲೈಟು lai·tu
elevator ಲಿಫ್ಟು lif·tu
email ಇಮೇಯ್ಲು ee·mey·lu
embassy ಎಂಬೆಸಿ em·be·si
emergency ಎಮರ್ಜೆನ್ಸಿ e·mar·jen·si
English (language) ಇಂಗ್ಲೀಷು ing·lee·shu
entrance ಪ್ರವೇಶ pra·vey·şa
evening ಸಂಜೆ san·je
exit n ನಿರ್ಗಮನ nir·ga·ma·na
expensive ದುಬಾರಿ đu·baa·ri
eye ಕಣ್ಣು kaņ·ņu

F

far ದೂರ đoo·ra
fast ಬೇಗ bey·ga
father ಅಪ್ಪ ap·pa
film (camera) ಕ್ಯಾಮೆರ ಫಿಲ್ಮು kyaa·me·ra fil·mu
finger ಬೆರಳು be·ra·ļu
first-aid kit ಫಸ್ಟ್ ಏಡ್ ಕಿಟ್ಟು fast ey·du kit·tu
first class ಮೊದಲ ದರ್ಜೆ mo·đa·la dar·je
fish n ಮೀನು mee·nu
food ಊಟ oo·ta
foot ಪಾದ paa·đa
free (of charge) ಉಚಿತ u·chi·ţa
friend ಸ್ನೇಹಿತ/ಸ್ನೇಹಿತೆ sney·hi·ţa/sney·hit·tey m/f
fruit ಹಣ್ಣು haņ·ņu
full ಪೂರ್ಣ poor·ņa

G

gift ಉಡುಗೊರೆ u·du·go·re
girl ಹುಡುಗಿ hu·du·gi
glass (drinking) ಗ್ಲಾಸು glaa·su
glasses ಗ್ಲಾಸುಗಳು glaa·su·ga·ļu
go ಹೋಗು hoh·gu
good ಒಳ್ಳೇದು oļ·ļey·đu
guide n ಗೈಡು gai·du

H

half n ಅರ್ಧ ar·đ'a
hand ಕೈ kai
happy ಸಂತೋಷ san·ţoh·sha
have ಇದೆ i·đe
he ಅವನು a·va·nu
head n ಮುಖ್ಯಸ್ಥ muk'·yas·ţ'a
heart ಹೃದಯ hru·đa·ya
heavy ಭಾರ b'aa·ra
help v ಸಹಾಯ sa·haa·ya
here ಇಲ್ಲಿ il·li
high ಎತ್ತರ eţ·ţa·ra
highway ಹೈವೇ hai·vey
hike v ಪಾದಯಾತ್ರೆ paa·đa·yaaţ·re
holiday ರಜೆ ra·je
homosexual n&a ಸಲಿಂಗಕಾಮಿ sa·ling·ga·kaa·mi
hospital ಆಸ್ಪತ್ರೆ aas·paţ·re
hot ಬಿಸಿ bi·si
hotel ಹೋಟ್ಲು hoht·lu
hungry ಹಸಿವು ha·si·vu
husband ಗಂಡ gan·da

I

I ನಾನು naa·nu
identification (card) ಗುರುತು ಚೀಟಿ gu·ru·ţu chee·ti
ill ಹುಷಾರಿಲ್ಲ hu·shaa·ril·la
important ಮುಖ್ಯ muk'·ya
injury ಗಾಯ gaa·ya
insurance ವಿಮೆ vi·me
internet ಇಂಟರ್ನೆಟ್ in·tar·net
interpreter ಅನುವಾದ ಮಾಡುವವ a·nu·vaa·đa maa·du·va·va

J

jewellery ಆಭರಣ aa·b'a·ra·na
job ಕೆಲಸ ke·la·sa

K

key ಕೀಲಿ kee·li
kilogram ಕೆಜಿ ke·ji
kitchen ಅಡುಗೆಮನೆ a·du·ge·ma·ne
knife ಚಾಕು chaa·ku

L

laundry (place) ಧೋಬಿ đ'oh·bi
lawyer ಲಾಯರು laa·ya·ru
left (direction) ಎಡ e·da
leg (body) ಕಾಲು kaa·lu
lesbian n&a ಸಲಿಂಗಕಾಮಿ sa·ling·ga·kaa·mi
less ಕಡಿಮೆ ka·di·me
letter (mail) ಪತ್ರ paţ·ra
light n ಲೈಟು lai·tu
like v ಇಷ್ಟ ish·ta
lock n ಬೀಗ bee·ga
long ಉದ್ದ uđ·đa
lost ಕಳೆದುಹೋದ ka·ļe·đu·hoh·đa
love v ಪ್ರೀತಿ pree·ţi
luggage ಲಗೇಜು la·gey·ju
lunch ಊಟ oo·ta

M

mail n ಅಂಚೆ an·che
man ಮನುಷ್ಯ ma·nush·ya
map ಮ್ಯಾಪು myaa·pu
market ಮಾರ್ಕೆಟ್ಟು maar·ket·tu
matches ಬೆಂಕಿಕಡ್ಡಿ ben·ki·kad·di
meat ಮಾಂಸ maam·sa
medicine ಔಷಧ ow·sha·đ'a
message ಸಂದೇಶ san·đey·sha
milk ಹಾಲು haa·lu
minute ನಿಮಿಷ ni·mi·sha
mobile phone ಮೊಬೈಲು mo·bai·lu
money ಹಣ/ಕಾಸು/ದುಡ್ಡು ha·ņa/kaa·su/đud·du
month ತಿಂಗಳು ţin·ga·ļu
morning ಬೆಳಿಗ್ಗೆ be·ļig·ge
mother ಅಮ್ಮ am·ma
motorcycle ಬೈಕು bai·ku
mouth ಬಾಯಿ baa·yi

N

name ಹೆಸರು he·sa·ru
near ಹತ್ತಿರ haţ·ţi·ra
neck n ಕತ್ತು kaţ·ţu
new ಹೊಸ ho·sa
newspaper ಸುದ್ದಿಪತ್ರಿಕೆ suđ·đi·paţ·ri·ke
night ರಾತ್ರಿ raaţ·ri
no ಇಲ್ಲ il·la
noisy ಸದ್ದು sađ·đu
nonsmoking ನಾನ್–ಸ್ಮೋಕಿಂಗ್ naan·smoh·king
north ಉತ್ತರ uţ·ţa·ra
nose ಮೂಗು moo·gu
now ಈಗ ee·ga
number ನಂಬರ್ nam·bar

O

old ಹಳೆಯ ha·ļe·ya
one-way ticket ಒನ್–ವೇ ಟಿಕೀಟ್ಟು on·vey ti·kee·tu
open a ತೆರೆ ţe·re
outside ಹೊರಗೆ ho·ra·ge

P

passport ಪಾಸ್ಪೋರ್ಟು paas·pohr·tu
pay v ಪಾವತಿ paa·va·ţi
pharmacy ಮೆಡಿಕಲ್ ಸ್ಟೋರು me·di·kal stoh·ru
phonecard ಕಾಲ್ಲಿಂಗ್ ಕಾರ್ಡು kaa·ling kaar·du
photo ಫೋಟೊ foh·to
police ಪೋಲಿಸ್ poh·lees
postcard ಅಂಚೆ ಕಾರ್ಡು an·che kaar·du
post office ಅಂಚೆ ಕಛೇರಿ an·che ka·ch'ey·ri
pregnant ಬಸುರಿ ba·su·ri
price n ಬೆಲೆ be·le

Q

quiet a ಸದ್ದು ಮಾಡದೆ sađ·đu maa·da·đe

R

rain n ಮಳೆ ma·ļe
razor ರೇಝರ್ rey·jar
receipt n ರಸೀದಿ ra·see·đi
refund n ರೀಫಂಡ್ ree·fund
registered mail ರಿಜಿಸ್ಟರ್ ಅಂಚೆ re·jis·tar an·che
rent v ಬಾಡಿಗೆ baa·di·ge
repair v ರಿಪೇರಿ ri·pey·ri
reservation ರಿಸರ್ವೇಶನ್ನು ri·sar·vey·shan·nu
restaurant ಹೋಟ್ಲು hoht·lu
return v ವಾಪಸ್ vaa·pas
return ticket ರಿಟರ್ನ್ ಟಿಕೀಟ್ಟು ri·tarn ti·kee·tu
right (direction) ಬಲ ba·la
road ರಸ್ತೆ ras·ţe
room n ರೂಮು roo·mu

S

safe a ಸುರಕ್ಷಿತ su·rak·shi·ţa
sanitary napkin ಟಿಶ್ಯೂ tis·yoo
seat n ಸೀಟು see·tu
send ಕಳುಹಿಸಿ ka·ļu·hi·si
sex ಸೆಕ್ಸು sek·su
shampoo ಶಾಂಪೂ shaam·poo
share (a dorm) ಶೇರ್ ಮಾಡು sheyr maa·du

she ಅವಳು a·va·ḷu
sheet (bed) ಮಗಲಾಸಿಗೆ ma·ga·laa·si·ge
shirt ಅಂಗಿ an·gi
shoes ಶೂ shoo
shop n ಅಂಗಡಿ an·ga·di
short ಕಿರಿದಾದ ki·ri·đaa·đa
shower n ಶವರ್ sha·var
single room ಸಿಂಗಲ್ ರೂಮು sin·gal roo·mu
skin n ಚರ್ಮ char·ma
skirt n ಸ್ಕರ್ಟು skar·tu
sleep v ನಿದ್ರೆ niđ·re
slowly ನಿಧಾನವಾಗಿ ni·đ'aa·na·vaa·gi
small ಚಿಕ್ಕ chik·ka
soap ಸೋಪು soh·pu
some ಕೆಲವು ke·la·vu
soon ಸದ್ಯದಲ್ಲೇ sađ·ya·đal·le
south ದಕ್ಷಿಣ đak·shi·na
souvenir shop ಸೂವನೀರ್ ಅಂಗಡಿ
soo·va·neer an·ga·di
stamp ಅಂಚೆ ಚೀಟಿ an·che chee·ti
stand-by ticket ಸ್ಟಾಂಡ್ ಬೈ ಟಿಕೀಟು
staand bai ti·kee·tu
station (train) ಸ್ಟೇಶನ್ನು stey·shan·nu
stomach ಹೊಟ್ಟೆ hot·te
stop v ನಿಲ್ಲಿಸಿ nil·li·si
stop (bus) n ನಿಲ್ದಾಣ nil·đaa·na
street ಬೀದಿ bee·đi
student ವಿದ್ಯಾರ್ಥಿ viđ·yaar·ti
sun ಸೂರ್ಯ soor·ya
sunscreen ಸನ್ ಸ್ಕ್ರೀನ್ san skreen
swim v ಈಜು ee·ju

T

tampons ಹತ್ತಿ haţ·ţi
teeth ಹಲ್ಲು hal·lu
telephone n ಟೆಲಿಫೋನು te·li·foh·nu
temperature (weather) ತಾಪಮಾನ ţaa·pa·maa·na
that (one) ಅದು a·đu
they ಅವರು a·va·ru
thirsty ಬಾಯಾರಿಕೆ baa·yaa·ri·ke
this (one) ಇದು i·đu
throat ಗಂಟಲು gan·ta·lu
ticket ಟಿಕೆಟ್ಟು ti·kee·tu
time ಸಮಯ sa·ma·ya
tired ಸುಸ್ತಾಗಿದೆ su·saa·gi·đe
tissues ಟಿಶ್ಯೂಗಳು tis·yoo·ga·lu
today ಇವತ್ತು i·vaţ·ţu
toilet ಟಾಯ್ಲೆಟ್ taay·let
tomorrow ನಾಳೆ naa·ḷe
tonight ಇಂದು ರಾತ್ರಿ in·đu raaţ·ri
toothbrush ಹಲ್ಲು ತಿಕ್ಕುವ ಬ್ರಶ್ಶು
hal·lu tik·ku·va brash·shu
toothpaste ಟೂತ್ ಪೇಸ್ಟ್ tooţ peysh·tu
torch (flashlight) ಟಾರ್ಚು taar·chu
tour n ಪ್ರವಾಸ pra·vaa·sa
tourist office ಪ್ರವಾಸಿ ಕಛೇರಿ pra·vaa·si ka·chey·ri
towel ಟವಲ್ಲು ta·val·lu
train n ರೈಲು rai·lu
translate ಅನುವಾದ a·nu·vaa·đa
travel agency ಟ್ರಾವೆಲ್ ಏಜೆನ್ಸಿ traa·vel ey·jen·si
travellers cheque ಟ್ರಾವೆಲ್ಲರ್ಸ್ ಚೆಕ್ಕು
traa·ve·lars chek·ku
trousers ಷರಾಯಿ sha·raa·yi
twin beds ಜೋಡಿ ಹಾಸಿಗೆ joh·di haa·si·ge

U

underwear ಅಂಡರ್‌ವೇರ್ an·dar·veyr
urgent ತುರ್ತು ţur·ţu

V

vacant ಖಾಲಿ k'aa·li
vegetable n ತರಕಾರಿ ţar·kaa·ri
vegetarian a ಸಸ್ಯಾಹಾರಿ sas·yaa·haa·ri
visa ವೀಸ vee·sa

W

walk v ನಡೆದಾಡು na·de·đaa·du
wallet ವ್ಯಾಲೆಟ್ vyaa·let
wash (something) ತೊಳೆ ţo·ḷi
watch n ನೋಡು noh·du
water n ನೀರು nee·ru
we ನಾವು naa·vu
weekend ವಾರಾಂತ್ಯ vaa·raanţ·ya
west ಪಶ್ಚಿಮ pas·chi·ma
wheelchair ಗಾಲಿಕುರ್ಚಿ gaa·li·kur·chi
when ಯಾವಾಗ yaa·vaa·ga
where ಎಲ್ಲಿ el·li
who ಯಾರು yaa·ru
why ಯಾಕೆ yaa·ke
wife ಹೆಂಡತಿ hen·da·ţi
window ಕಿಟಕಿ ki·ta·ki
with ಜೊತೆಗೆ jo·ţe·ge
without ಇಲ್ಲದೆ il·la·đe
woman ಮಹಿಳೆ ma·hi·ḷe
write ಬರಿ ba·ri

Y

yes ಹೌದು how·đu
yesterday ನಿನ್ನೆ nin·ne
you sg inf ನೀನು nee·nu
you sg pol&pl ನೀವು nee·vu

DICTIONARY

T

Kashmiri

alphabet

vowels

अ a	आ aa	इ i	ई ee	अ’ iu	आ’ iū	ॲ eu	ऑ eū
ऍ e	ए ey	उ u	ऊ oo	ओ’ o	ओ oh	अ्व wa	ऐ ai

consonants

क ka	ख k’a	ग ga	गं nga			
च cha	छ ch’a	च़ tsa	छ़ ts’a	ज ja	ज़ za	
ट ţa	ठ ţ’a	ड đa				
त ta	थ t’a	द da	न na			
प pa	फ p’a	ब ba	म ma			
य ya	र ra	ल la	व va			
श sha	ष sha	स sa	ह ha	क्ष ksha	त्र tra	ज्ञ gya

KASHMIRI

कश्मीरी

introduction

We can thank the Kashmiri, experts in cheating the Himalayan chill, for the word 'cashmere' in English. Kashmiri (kash·mee·ree कश्मीरी) is spoken in the valley of Kashmir at the foothills of the Himalayas: a beautiful area, situated mostly in the Jammu and Kashmir state of India. There are about 5.5 million speakers of Kashmiri, a member of the Dardic subgroup of the Indo-Aryan language family. It's written using a variation of the Perso-Arabic script or, as in this chapter, in the Devanagari script. You might try impressing the locals with your knowledge of some of their colourful proverbs, such as euky sund keu·syaa·niu bey·i sund giu·zaa ॲक्य सुंद कॅसियान' बेयि सुंद ग'ज़ा (literally 'One person's vomit is another's food'), meaning 'One person's trash is another's treasure'; or eu·kis da·zaan deūr byaak' vush·naa·vaan at' ॲकिस दज़ान दॉर ब्याख वुशनावान अथ' (literally 'When one man's beard is on fire, another man warms his hands on it'), meaning 'People often take advantage of someone else's misery'.

kashmiri

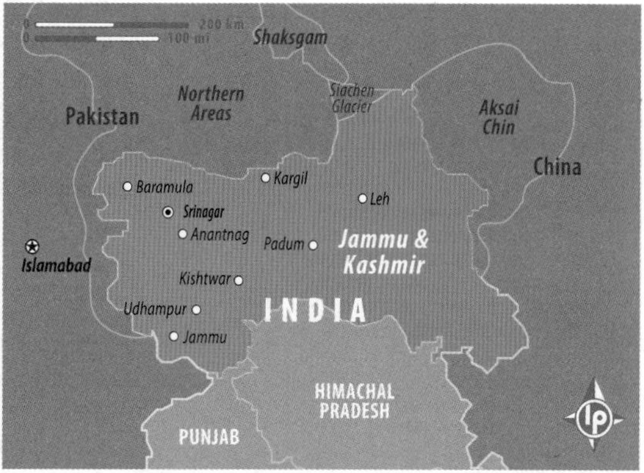

Vowels		Consonants	
Symbol	English sound	Symbol	English sound
a	run	b	bed
aa	father	ch	cheat
ai	aisle	d	dog
e	bet	đ	retroflex d
ee	see	g	go
eu	nurse	h	hat
eū	as eu, but longer	j	joke
ey	as e, but longer	k	kit
i	hit	l	lot
iu	similar to the 'e' in 'open'	m	man
iū	as iu, but longer	n	not
o	pot	ng	ring
oh	note	p	pet
oo	zoo	r	rose
u	put	s	sun
		sh	shot
		t	top
		ţ	retroflex t
		ts	hats
		v	very
		w	win
		y	yes
		z	zero

In this chapter, the Kashmiri pronunciation is given in pink after each phrase.

Aspirated consonants (pronounced with a puff of air after the sound) are represented with an apostrophe after the letter – ch', k', p', t', ţ' and ts'. Retroflex consonants (pronounced with the tongue bent backwards) are included in this table.

Each syllable is separated by a dot. For example:

आदाब । aa·daab

essentials		
Yes.	आ।	aa
No.	न।	na
Please.	मेहरबॉनी।	me·har·beū·nee
Thank you.	शुकिया।	shuk·ri·yaa
Excuse me. (to get past)	वथ त्रॉविव।	vat' treū·viv
Excuse me. (to get attention)	यपॉरय।	ya·peūry
Sorry.	माफ कॅरिव।	maap' keu·riv

language difficulties

Do you speak English?
तोहय छिवा अंगरीज़ी बोलान? — tohy ch'i·vaa ang·ree·zee bo·laan

Do you understand?
त्वहि छा फिकिरि तरान? — twa·hi ch'aa p'i·kri ta·raan

I understand.
व' छुस/छस ज़ानान। — biu ch'us/ch'as zaa·naan **m/f**

I don't understand.
व' छुस/छस न' ज़ानान। — biu ch'us/ch'as niu zaa·naan **m/f**

Could you please ...?	तोहय हेकिवा ...?	tohy he·ki·vaa ...
repeat that	दुवार' वॅनिथ	du·baa·riu veu·nit'
speak more slowly	वार' वार' वॅनिव	vaa·riu vaa·riu veu·niv

numbers					
0	ज़ीरो	zee·ro	20	वुह	vuh
1	अख	ak'	30	त्र'ह	triuh
2	ज़'	ziu	40	चतजी	tsat·jee
3	त्रे	tre	50	पंचाह	pan·tsah
4	चोर	tsohr	60	शेठ	sheyṭ'
5	पांछ	paants'	70	सतथ	sa·tat'
6	शे	she	80	शीथ	sheet'
7	सथ	sat'	90	नमथ	na·mat'
8	ऑठ	eūṭ'	100	हथ	hat'
9	नव	nav	1000	सास	saas
10	दॅह	deuh	1,000,000	मिलियन	mi·li·yan

time & dates

What time is it?	कॅ़च बजेयि?	keuts ba·je·yi
It's (two) o'clock.	(ज़') बजेयि।	(ziu) ba·je·yi
Quarter past (two).	स्वाद' (ज़')।	swaa·diu (ziu)
Half past (three).	साड' (त्रे)।	saa·điu (tre)
Quarter to (three).	दून' (त्रे)।	doo·ni·e (tre)
At what time ...?	कॅ़चि बजि ...?	keu·tsi ba·ji ...
It's (15 December).	अज़ छु (पंदाह दिसंम्बर)।	az ch'u (pan·dah di·sam·bar)
yesterday	राथ	raat'
today	अज़	az
tomorrow	पगाह	pa·gaah
Monday	चॅंद'रवार	tseun·diur·vaar
Tuesday	बोमवार	bom·vaar
Wednesday	ब्यदवार	bwad·vaar
Thursday	ब्रसवार	bras·vaar
Friday	जुमाह	ju·maah
Saturday	बट'वार	baţ·vaar
Sunday	आथ'वार	aa·t'iu·vaar

border crossing

I'm here ...	ब' छुस/छस येति ...	biu ch'us/ch'as ye·ti ... **m/f**
in transit	पडावस	pa·đaa·vas
on business	कारबर'किस	kaa·riu·baar·kis
	सिलसिलस मंज़	sil·si·las manz
on holiday	छुटी पेठ	ch'u·ţee pet'
I'm here for ...	ब' छुस/छस येति ...	biu ch'us/ch'as ye·ti ... **m/f**
(10) days	(दॅहन) दोहन	(deu·han) dwa·han
(three) weeks	(त्रे) हफ़्त'	(tre) hap'·tiu
(two) months	(ज़') रेथ	(ziu) ret'

I'm going to (Pahalgam).
ब' गछ़' (पहलगाम)। biu ga·ts'iu (pa·hal·gaam)

I'm staying at the (Breadway).
ब' रोज़' (ब्राडवे)। biu ro·ziu (braađ·ve)

I have nothing to declare.
मे छुन' कें‍ह डिकलियर करुन्। — me ch'u·niu kenh đik·li·yar ka·run

I have this to declare.
मे छु यि डिकलियर करुन। — me ch'u yi đik·li·yar ka·run

That's (not) mine.
हु छु (न') म्योन। — hu ch'u (niu) myon

tickets & luggage

Where can I buy a ticket?
ब' कति हेक' टिकट हेथ? — biu ka·ti he·kiu ţi·kaţ' het'

Do I need to book a seat?
मे छे सीट बुक कर'न्य। — me cha seeţ buk ka·riuny

One … ticket (to Gulmarg), please.	अख टिकठ … (गुलमरग) खॉतर'।	ak' ţi·kaţ' … (gul·ma·rag) k'eū·triu
one-way	अकि तरफ'च	a·ki tar·p'iuch
return	वापसी	vaap·see

I'd like to … my ticket, please.	ब' छुस/छस पन'न्य टिकट यछान …	biu ch'us/ch'as pa·niuny ţi·kaţ' ye·ts'aan … **m/f**
cancel	रद कर'न्य	rad ka·riuny
change	बदल'न्य	bad·liuny
collect	हॉसिल कर'न्य	heū·sil ka·riuny

I'd like a (non)smoking seat, please.
मे गछ़ि (नान) स्मोकिंग सीट। — me ga·ts'i (naan) smo·king seeţ

Is there a toilet/air conditioning?
अति छा टायलेट/ए सी? — ati ch'aa ţaay·leţ/e see

How long does the trip take?
सफर का'ति कालुक छु? — sa·p'ar keū·ti kaa·luk ch'u

Is it a direct route?
यि छा सेदि स्योद वथ? — yi ch'aa se·di syod vat'

My luggage has been …	म्योन सामान छु …	myon saa·maan chu …
damaged	खराब गोमुत	k'a·raab go·mut
lost	रोवमुत	rohv·mut
stolen	चूरि निन' आमुत	tsoo·ri ni·niu aa·mut

transport

Where does flight (IA 404) arrive/depart?
फलायट नम्बर (चोर ज़ीरो चोर) कतेन छे यिवान/नेरान? — p'a·laiţ nam·bar (tsohr zee·ro tsohr) ka·ten ch'a yi·vaan/ne·raan

Is this the … to (Srinagar)?	यि … गछ्या (सिरीनगर)?	yi … gats'·yaa (si·ree·na·gar)
boat	नाव	naav
bus	बस	bas
plane	जहाज़'	ja·haaz
train	ट्रेन	tren

What time's the … bus?	… कॅचि बजि छे?	… keu·tsi ba·ji ch'a
first	ग्वडनिच	gwađ·nich
last	ऑखरी	eūk'·ree
next	दोयिम	do·yim

How long will it be delayed?
यथ कोताह चेर लगि? — yat' ko·taah tseyr la·gi

Please tell me when we get to (Pahalgam).
अॅस्य कॅचि बजि वातव (पहलगाम)। — eusy keu·tsi ba·ji vaa·tav (pa·hal·gaam)

That's my seat.
ह्व छे मेन्य सीट। — hwa ch'a meyny seet

I'd like a taxi …	मे गछ़ि टेक्सी …	me ga·ts'i ţek·see …
at (9am)	सुबहन (नव बजे)	sub·han (nav ba·je)
now	वुन्य	vuny

How much is it to (Verinag)?
(वेरनाग) ताम कोताह छु? — (veer·naag) taam koh·taa ch'u

Please put the meter on.
मीटर चलॉविव। — mee·tar cha·leū·viv

Please take me to (this address).
मे नियिव (यथ पताहस पेठ)। — me ni·yiv (yat' pa·taa·has pet')

Please stop/wait here.
येत्यन ठॅहरिव/प्रॉरिव। — ye·tyen ţ'iuh·riv/preū·riv

I'd like to hire a car (with a driver).
ब' छुस/छस यछ़ान (ड्रायवर हेथ) कार किरायस प्यठ हेन्य। — biu ch'us/ch'as ye·ts'aan (đrai·var het') kaar ki·raay·as pet' heny **m/f**

कशमीरी – transport

I'd like to hire a 4WD (with a driver).

ब' छुस/छस यछ़ान (ड्रायवर हेथ) चोर डबल्यो डी किरायस प्यठ हेन्य ।	biu ch'us/ch'as ye·ts'aan (đrai·var het') tsohr blyod ee ki·raay·as pet' heny m/f

How much for daily/weekly hire?

दवहस/हफ्तस कॉचा किराय छे?	dwa·has/hap'·tas keū·tsaa ki·raay ch'a

directions

Where's the ...?	... कति छु?	... ka·ti ch'u
bank	बैंक	bank
foreign currency exchange	फारीन करंसी अक्सचेंज	p'aa·reen ka·ran·see aks·cheynj
post office	डाक खान'	đaak k'aa·niu

Is this the road to (Nishat Bagh)?

यि वथ छा (निशात बाग) गछ़ान?	yi vat' ch'aa (ni·shaat baag) ga·ts'aan

Can you show me (on the map)?

तोहय हेकिवा (नक्शस पेठ) हॉविथ?	tohy he·ki·vaa (nak·shas peţ') heū·vit'

What's the address?

पताह क्याह छु?	pa·taah kyaa ch'u

How far is it?

यि कोताह दूर छु?	yi ko·taah door ch'u

How do I get there?

ब' किथ'क'न्य वात' ओर?	biu ki·t'iu·kiuny vaa·tiu oor

Turn left/right.

खोवुर/दॅछुन कुन फीरिव ।	k'oh·vur/deu·ch'un kun p'ee·riv

It's ...	यि छु ...	yi ch'u ...
behind ...	... पत' कनि	... pa·tiu ka·ni
in front of ...	... ब्रोंह कनि	... bronh ka·ni
near (to ...)	... निश	... nish
on the corner	कूनस पेठ	koo·nas peţ'
opposite ...	... बुथि	... bu·t'i
straight ahead	स्येदि स्योद	sye·di syod
there	होति	ho·ti

Where's a guesthouse/hotel nearby?
नज़दीख'य कति छु गेस्टहाऊस/होटल? — naz·dee·k'iuy ka·ti ch'u gesţ·ha·us/ho·ţal

Can you recommend somewhere cheap/good?
तोह्य हेकिवा कुनि सस्त'/जान जायि ह'ज़ सिफॉरिश कॅरिथ? — tohy he·ki·vaa ku·ni sas·tiu/jaan jaa·yi hiunz si·p'eū·rish keu·rit'

I'd like to book a room, please.
ब' छुस/छस यछ़ान अख कमर' बुक करुन। — biu ch'us/ch'as ya·ts'aan ak' kam·riu buk ka·run **m/f**

I have a reservation.
मे छे रिज़रवशन। — me ch'a ri·zar·ve·shan

Do you have a … room?	तोहि छा कांह … कमर'?	toh·i ch'aa kaanh … kam·riu
single	सिन्गल	sin·gal
double	डवल	đa·bal
twin	टुविन	ţu·vin

How much is it per night?
रातस कॉचाह किराय छे? — raa·tas keū·tsaa ki·raay ch'a

How much is it per person?
फी नफरस कॉचाह किराय छे? — p'ee nap'·ras keū·tsaa ki·raay ch'a

I'd like to stay for (two) nights.
ब' छुस/छस यछ़ान (दवन) रॉचन रोज़ुन। — biu ch'us/ch'as ye·ts'aan (dwan) reū·tsan ro·zun **m/f**

Can I have my key, please?
मे मेल्या कुन्ज़? — me mey·lyaa kunz

Can I get another (blanket)?
दोयिम (कम्बल) हेक्या मीलिथ? — do·yim (kam·bal) he·kyaa mee·lit'

The (air conditioning) doesn't work.
(ए सी) छुन' चलान। — (e see) ch'u·niu cha·laan

Is there an elevator/a safe?
येति छा लिफ्ट/सेफ? — ye·ti ch'aa lip'ţ/sef

What time is checkout?
कमर' कमि सात' छु खॉली करुन? — kam·riu ka·mi saa·tiu ch'u k'eū·lee ka·run

Can I have my ..., please?	मे मेल्या पनुन ... वापस?	me mee·lyaa pa·nun ... vaa·pas
deposit	डिपाज़िट	đi·paa·ziţ
passport	पासपोर्ट	paas·porţ
valuables	का'मती सामान	keŭm·tee saa·maan

banking & communications

Where's an ATM/a public phone?
ए टी एम/पवलिक फोन कति छु?
ey ţee em/pab·lik p'ohn ka·ti ch'u

I'd like to ...	ब' छुस यछ़ान ...	biu ch'us/ch'as ye·ts'aan ... **m/f**
arrange a transfer	ट्रान्सफर कर'नावुन	ţraans·p'ar ka·riu·naa·vun
change a travellers cheque	ट्रवलरस चेक' बदलाव'न्य	ţrav·lars chek bad·laa·viuny
change money	पॉन्स' बदलाव'न्य	peŭn·siu bad·laa·viuny
withdraw money	पॉन्स' कडुन	peŭn·siu ka·đun

What's the ...?	... कोताह छु?	... koo·taah ch'u
charge for that	अम्युक चारज	a·myuk chaa·riuj
exchange rate	मवादल' दर	mu·baa·dal dar

Where's the local internet café?
लोकल इन्टरनेट केफे कत्यन छु?
lo·kal in·ţar·neţ ke·p'e ka·ten ch'u

How much is it per hour?
गन्टस कॉत्या पॉन्स' छि लगान?
gan·ţas keu·tyaa peŭn·siu ch'i la·gaan

I'd like to ...	ब' छुस/छस यछ़ान ...	biu ch'us/ch'as ye·ts'aan ... **m/f**
get internet access	इन्टरनेट अक्सेस	in·ţar·neţ ak·ses
use a printer/ scanner	प्रिन्टर/स्केनर इसतिमाल करुन	priun·ţar/ske·nar is·ti·maal ka·run

I'd like a ...	ब' छुस/छस यछ़ान ...	biu ch'us/ch'as ye·ts'aan ... **m/f**
mobile/cell phone for hire	'किरायस प्यठ मोबाइल फोन ह्योन	ki·raa·yas peţ' mo·bail p'ohn hyon
SIM card for your network	तुहन्दि नेटवरकुक सिम काड	tu·hun·di net·veur·kuk sim kaađ

What are the rates?
रेट क्या छे? — reyt' kyaa ch'a

What's your phone number?
त्वहि क्या छु टेलीफोन नम्बर? — twa·hi kyaa ch'u te·li·p'ohn nam·bar

The number is ...
नम्बर छु ... — nam·bar ch'u ...

I'd like to buy a phonecard.
ब' छुस/छस यछ़ान फोन काड मॅल्य ह्योन। — biu ch'us/ch'as ye·ts'aan p'ohn kaađ meuly hyon **m/f**

I want to ...	ब' छुस/छस यछ़ान ...	biu ch'us/ch'as ye·ts'aan ... **m/f**
call (Canada)	(केनाडा) टेलिफोन करुन	(ka·na·đaa) p'ohn ka·run
call collect	कल्यकट काल करुन	ka·lekţ kaal ka·run

I want to send a (fax/parcel).
ब' छुस/छस यछ़ान (फेक्स/पार्सल) सोज़ुन। — biu ch'us/ch'as ye·ts'aan (p'eks/paar·sal) so·zun **m/f**

I want to buy (a stamp/an envelope).
ब' छुस/छस यछ़ान (टिकट/ लिफाफ') मॅल्य ह्योन। — biu ch'us/ch'as ye·ts'aan (ţi·kaţ'/ li·p'aa·p'iu) meuly hyon **m/f**

Please send it to (Australia).
यि सूज़िव (अस्ट्रेलिया)। — yi soo·ziv (as·ţre·li·yaa)

sightseeing

What time does it open?
यि कॅचि बजि छु खुलान? — yi keu·tsi ba·ji ch'u k'u·laan

What time does it close?
यि कॅचि बजि छु बन्द गछ़ान? — yi keu·tsi ba·ji ch'u band ga·ts'aan

What's the admission charge?
दॉखल' फीस क्या छु? — deūk'·liu p'ees kyaa ch'u

Is there a discount for students?
तॉलिब' ॲलिमन छा रियायथ? — teū·li·bi eu·li·man ch'aa ri·yaa·yat'

Is there a discount for children?
शुऱ्यन छा रियायथ? — shu·ren ch'aa ri·yaa·yat'

I'd like to hire a guide.
ब' छुस/छस यछ़ान गाईड न्युन। — biu ch'us/ch'as ye·ts'aan gaiđ nyun **m/f**

I'd like a catalogue/map.
मे गोछ़ केटलाग/नक्श' ।	me ga·ts'i kaiţ·laag/nak·shiu

I'd like to see ...
ब' छुस/छस यछ़ान यि ... वुछुन ।	biu ch'us/ch'as ye·ts'aan yi ... vu·ch'un **m/f**

What's that?
हु क्या छु?	hu kyaa ch'u

Can I take a photo?
ब' ह्यका फोटू तुलिथ?	biu he·kaa p'o·too tu·lit'

I'd like to go somewhere off the beaten track.
ब' छुस/छस यछ़ान येमि आम ट्रेकि अलग कुनि वति गछुन ।	biu ch'us/ch'as ye·ts'aan ye·mi aam ţre·ki a·lag ku·ni va·ti ga·ts'un **m/f**

When's the next tour?
दोयिम टुयूर कर छु?	do·yim ţyoor kar ch'u

How long is the tour?
टयूर का'ति कालुक छु?	ţyoor keū·ti kaa·luk ch'u

Is ... included?	यथ मन्ज़ छा ... शॉमिल?	yat' manz ch'aa ... sheū·mil
accommodation	रोज़न जाय	roh·zan jaay
admission	दॉखल'	deūk'·liu
food	ख्यन चेन	k'en chen
transport	ट्रान्सपोर्ट	ţraan·spot

sightseeing		
fort	क'ल'	kiu·liu
mosque	मसजिद	mas·jid
old city	प्रोन शहर	pron sha·har
palace	मॅहल	meu·hal
ruins	खन्डहर	k'anđ·har

shopping

Where's a ... ?	... कति छु?	... ka·ti ch'u
camera shop	केमरा दुकान	kem·raa du·kaan
market	बाज़र	baa·zar
souvenir shop	सोविनियर दुकान	so·vi·ni·yar du·kaan

I'm looking for …
व' छुस/छस छांडान … — biu ch'us/ch'as ts'aan·d'aan … **m/f**

Can I look at it?
व' हेका वुछिथ? — biu he·kaa vu·ch'it'

Can I have it sent overseas?
व' हेका यि मुल्क' नेबर सोज़'नॉविथ? — biu he·kaa yi mul·kiu ne·bar soz·ne·vit'

Can I have my (camera) repaired?
व' छुस/छस यछ़ान पनुन (केमरा) शेर'नावुन। — biu ch'us/ch'as ye·ts'aan pa·nun (kem·raa) sher·naa·vun **m/f**

It's faulty.
यथ छु नोकुस। — yat' ch'u no·kus

How much is it?
यि का'तिस छु? — yi keū·tis ch'u

Can you write down the price?
तोह्य हेकिवा का'मथ लीखिथ? — tohy he·ki·vaa kiu·iu·mat' lee·k'it'

That's too expensive.
यि गव स्यठाह द्रोग। — yi gav se·ţ'aa drog

I'll give you (300 rupees).
व' दिमोव' (त्रे हथ रवपयि)। — biu di·mo·viu (tre hat' rwa·pyi)

There's a mistake in the bill.
यथ बिलि मन्ज़ छे गलती। — yat' bi·li manz ch'a gal·tee

Do you accept …?	तोह्य छिवा रटान …?	tohy ch'i·vaa ra·ţaan …
credit cards	केडिट काड	kre·điţ kaađ
debit cards	डेबिट काड	đe·biţ kaađ
travellers cheques	ट्रवलरस चेक'	ţrav·lars chek
I'd like (a) …, please.	मे गछ़ि …	me ga·ts'i …
bag	अख बैग	ak' beūg
my change	फुट'वोट	p'uţ·voţ
receipt	रसीद	reu·seed
refund	रिफन्ड	ri·p'anđ
Less.	कम।	kam
Enough.	कॉफी।	keū·p'ee
More.	ज़्याद'।	zyaa·diu

photography

Can you …?	तोहृय हेकिवा …?	tohy he·ki·vaa …
burn a CD from my memory card/stick	येमि यादाश्त कार्डुं/ सिटिक पेठ' सी डी बनॉविथ	ye·mi yaa·daash kaa·điu/ sti·ki peţ' see đee ba·neū·vit'
develop this film	यि फिल्म डिवेल्प कॅरिथ	yi p'i·lim đi·velp keu·rit'

I need a film for this camera.
मे गछि येमि केमरा खॉतर' फिल्म। — me ga·ts'i ye·mi kem·raa k'eū·triu p'i·lim

When will it be ready?
यि कर आसि तयार? — yi kar aa·si ta·yaar

making conversation

Hello.	आदाब।	aa·daab
Good night.	शबे खैर।	sha·bey k'eūr
Goodbye.	अल्विदा।	al·vi·daa
Mr	जिनाब	ji·naab
Mrs	मोहतरमा	moh·tar·maa
Miss/Ms	मिस	mis
How are you?	तोहृय छिवा वारय?	tohy ch'i·vaa vaa·rai
Fine, thanks. And you?	वारय, शुक्रिया। त' तोहृय?	vaa·rai shuk·ri·yaa tiu tohy
What's your name?	त्वहि क्या छु नाव?	twa·hi kyaa ch'u naav
My name is …	मे छु नाव …	me ch'u naav …
I'm pleased to meet you.	मे सप'ज़ खोशी त्वहि मीलिथ।	me sa·piuz k'o·shee twa·hi mee·lit'
This is my father.	यिम छि मेन्य वॉलिद।	yim ch'i meyny veū·lid
This is my …	यि छु म्योन …	yi ch'u myon …
brother	बॉय	bohy
friend	दोस	dohs
husband	रून	roon
son	नेचुव	ne·chuv
This is my …	यि छे मेन्य …	yi ch'a meyny …
mother	मॉज	meūj
sister	बेनि	be·ni
wife	ज़नान	za·naan

photography – KASHMIRI

Here's my (address).	यि छु म्यान (पताह)।	yi ch'u myon (pa·taah)
What's your (email)?	तुहुन्द (ई मेल) क्या छु?	tu·hund (ee meyl) kyaa ch'u
Where are you from?	तोह्य कतिक छिव?	tohy ka·tik ch'iv
I'm from ...	ब' छुस/छस रोज़ान ...	biu ch'us/ch'as ro·zaan ... **m/f**
Australia	अस्ट्रेलिया	as·ţre·li·yaa
Canada	केनाडा	ka·naa·đaa
New Zealand	न्यूज़ीलैंड	nyoo·zi·leynđ
the UK	यू के	yoo ke
the USA	यू एस ए	yoo es e
What's your occupation?	तोह्य क्या छिव करान?	tohy kyaa ch'iv ka·raan
I'm a/an ...	ब' छुस/छस ...	biu ch'us/ch'as ... **m/f**
businessperson	कारबार करान	kaar·baar ka·raan
office worker	दफ्तरस मंज़ कॉम करान	dap'·ta·ras manz keũm ka·raan
tradesperson	कारबार करन वोल	kaar·baar ka·ran vohl
Do you like ...?	त्वहि छा पसंन्द ...?	twa·hi ch'aa pa·sand ...
I (don't) like ...	मे छु (न') पसंन्द ...	me ch'u (niu) pa·sand ...
art	आर्ट	aarţ
movies	फिल्म'	p'il·miu
music	म्यूज़िक	myoo·zik
reading	परुन	pa·run
sport	गिन्दुन	gin·dun

eating out

I'd like (a/the) ..., please.	मे गछ़ि ...	me ga·ts'i ...
bill	बिल	bil
drink list	ड्रिंक लिस्ट	đrink lisţ
local speciality	येतिच खास ज़ियाफ्त	ye·tich k'aas zi·yaa·p'at
menu	मेनू	me·noo
(non)smoking section	(नान) स्मोकिंग जाय	(naan) smo·king jaay
table for (four)	(च्वन) ह'न्दि खॉतर' मेज़	(tswan) hiun·di k'eũt·riu meyz
that dish	हु ख्यन	hu k'en

Can you recommend a ...?	तोह्य कॅरिवा सिफॉरिश कुनि ...?	tohy keury·vaa si·p'eū·rish ku·ni ...
bar	बार'च	baa·riuch
dish	ख्यन'च	k'e·niuch
place to eat	ख्यन चनचि जायि ह'न्ज़	k'en chan·chi jaa·yi hiunz
breakfast	ब्रेकफस्ट	brek·p'aasţ
lunch	लंच	lanch
dinner	डिनर	đi·nar
(cup of) coffee/tea ...	(अख कप) काफी/चाय ...	(ak' kap) kaa·p'ee/chaay ...
with milk	दवद' सान	dwa·diu saan
without sugar	मॅदरेर वरॉय	meud·reyr va·reūy
(orange) juice	(संतर') जूस	(san·tar) joos
lassi	लॅस्य	leusy
soft drink	साफ्ट ड्रिंक	saap'ţ đrink

I'll have boiled water.
मे गछ़ि ग्रक'नॉवम'च त्रेश।
me ga·ts'i gra·kiu·neūv·miuts treysh

I'll have mineral water.
मे गछ़ि मिनरल वाटर।
me ga·ts'i min·ral vaa·ţar

I'll buy you a drink.
ब' चावथ केंह।
biu chaa·vat' kenh

What would you like?
त्वहि क्या छु पसन्द?
twa·hi kyaa ch'u pa·sand

special diets & allergies

Do you have ... food?	त्वहि छा ...?	twa·hi ch'aa ...
halal	हलहाल माज़	hal·haal maaz
kosher	कोशर माज़	ko·shar maaz
vegetarian	शाकाहॉरी ख्यन	shaa·kaa·haa·ree k'en
Could you prepare a meal without ...?	तोह्य हेकिवा ... वरॉय ख्यन बनॉविथ?	tohy he·ki·vaa ... va·reūy k'yen ba·neū·vit'
dairy products	दव्द' चीज़न ह'न्ज़	dwa·diu chey·zan hiunz
eggs	ठूलन ह'ज़	ţ'oo·lan hiunz
meat stock	माज़ वगॉर'च	maaz va·geū·riuch
nuts	नटन ह'ज़	na·ţan hiunz
seafood	सी फूड'च	see·p'oo·điuch

emergencies

Help!	मदथ!	ma·dat'
Stop!	ठहर!	ţ'eu·har
Go away!	चल!	tsal
Thief!	चूर!	tsoor
Fire!	नार!	naar
Watch out!	खबरदार!	k'a·bar·daar

Call ...!	बुलॉविव ...!	bu·leū·viv ...
an ambulance	अम्बुलंस	am·bu·lans
a doctor	डाक्टर	đaak·ţar
the police	पुलीस	pu·lees

Could you help me, please?
मेहरबॉनी कॅरिथ कॅरिवा मे मदथ। — me·har·beū·nee keu·rit' keu·riv me ma·dat'

I have to use the phone.
मे छु फोन करुन। — me ch'u p'ohn ka·run

I'm lost.
ब' रोवुस। — biu ro·vus

Where are the toilets?
टायलेट कति छि? — ţaay·leţ ka·ti ch'u

Where's the police station?
पुलीस स्टेशन कति छु? — pu·lees sţey·shan ka·ti chu

I have insurance.
मे छु बीम'। — me ch'u bee·miu

I want to contact my embassy.
ब' छुस/छस यछ़ान पननि अम्बेसी सा'त्य रॅबत' कॉयिम करुन। — biu ch'us/ch'as ye·ts'aan pa·niu·ni em·bey·see siūty reūb·tiu keū·yim ka·run **m/f**

I've been ...	मे कोरुख ...	me ko·ruk' ...
assaulted	हमल'	ham·liu
raped	मे सा'त्य कोरुख बदकार	me siūty ko·ruk' bad·kaar
robbed	लूठ	looţ'

I've lost my ...	मे रोव ...	me rov ...
bag	बैग	beūg
money	पॉन्स'	peūn·siu
passport	पासपोट	paas·porţ

health

Where's the nearest …?	सारिव'य ख्वत' … कति छु?	saa·ri·viuy k'wa·tiu … ka·ti ch'u
dentist	दन्द' डाक्टर	dan·diu đaak·ţar
doctor	डाक्टर	đaak·ţar
hospital	हस्पताल	has·pa·taal
pharmacist	दवा दुकान	da·vaa du·kaan

I need a doctor (who speaks English).
मे छु डाक्टर ज़रूरत (युस अंग्रीज़ी आसि ज़ानान)। — me ch'u đaak·ţar zo·roo·rat (yus ang·ree·zee aa·si zaa·naan)

Could I see a female doctor?
मे छु ज़नान डाक्टरस समखुन। — me ch'u za·naan đaak·ţars sam·k'un

I've run out of my medication.
मे म्वकल्योव दवा। — me mwak·lyov da·vaa

It hurts here.
येत्यन छुम लगान। — ye·ten ch'um la·gaan

I have (a) …	मे छु …	me ch'u …
constipation	कब'ज़	ka·biuz
fever	तफ	tap'
heart condition	दिलस दोद	di·las dod
nausea	मन गॅहलान	man geuh·laan

I have (a) …	मे छि …	me ch'a …
asthma	शांश	shaansh
diarrhoea	दस्त'	das·tiu
cough	ॖचास	tsaas

I'm allergic to …	मे छे अलरजी … 'च।	me ch'a a·lar·jee … iuch
antibiotics	अंटीबयोटिक्स	an·ţee·bai·ţiks
anti-inflammatories	अंटी इंफ्लेमेटरीज	an·ţee in·p'aa·neţ·reez
aspirin	असप्रिन	as·preen
bees	त'लरि	tiul·ri

responsible travel

I'd like to learn some Kashmiri.

ब' छुस/छस कॉशुर यछ़ान हेछुन। — biu ch'us/ch'as keū·shur ye·ts'aan he·ch'un **m/f**

What's this called in Kashmiri?

यथ क्या छि वनान कॉशिरिस मंज़? — yat' kyaa ch'i va·naan keūsh·ris manz

Would you like me to teach you some English?

ब' हेछनावोवा केंह अंगरीज़ी? — biu he·ch'iu·naa·viu·vo·aa kenh ang·ree·zee

I didn't mean to (do/say) anything wrong.

ब' ओसुस/ऑस'स न' केंह गलथ (करुन/वनुन) यछ़ान। — biu os·sus/eū·sius niu kenh ga·lat' (ka·run/va·nun) ye·ts'aan **m/f**

Is this a local or national custom?

यि छा मुकॉमी रस'म या कौमी? — yi ch'aa mu·keū·mee ra·sium yaa kau·mee

I'd like to stay at a locally run hotel.

ब' छुस/छस कुनि मुकॉमी होटलस मंज़ रोज़ुन यछान। — biu ch'us/ch'as ku·ni mu·keū·mee ho·ta·las manz ro·zun ye·ts'aan **m/f**

Where can I buy locally produced goods/souvenirs?

ब' कति हेक' येतिक्य बनेमित्य चीज़ मॅल्य हेथ? — biu ka·ti he·kiu ye·tiky ba·ne·miuty cheez meuly het'

What's this made from?

यि कति छु बन्योमुत? — yi ka·ti ch'u ban·yo·mut

Does your company have responsible tourism policies?

तुहंज़ि कम्पनी छा ज़िम'दारान' ट्यूरिजम पाल्सी? — tu·hiun·zi kam·pa·nee ch'aa zi·miu·daa·raa·niu ţyoo·rizm paal·si

I'd like to do some volunteer work (for your organisation).

ब' छुस/छस यछ़ान (तुहंदिस अदारस मंज़) रज़ाकारान' कॉम कॅर'न्य। — biu ch'us/ch'as ye·ts'aan (tu·hiun·dis a·daa·ras manz) ra·zaa·kaa·raa·niu keūm ka·riuny **m/f**

I'm (an English teacher). Can I volunteer my skills?

ब' छुस/छस (अंग्रीज़ी टीचर)। ब' हेका रज़ाकारान' कॉम कॅरिथ? — biu ch'us/ch'as (ang·ree·zee tee·char) biu he·kaa ra·zaa·kaa·raan keūm keu·rit' **m/f**

english–kashmiri dictionary

Words in this dictionary are marked as n (noun), a (adjective), v (verb), sg (singular), pl (plural), inf (informal) and pol (polite) where necessary.

A

accident हॉदिस' heŭd·siu
accommodation रोज़न जाय roh·zan jaay
adaptor अडापटर a·daap·ţar
address n पताह pa·taah
after पत' pa·tiu
air-conditioned एयर कंडीशंड e·yar kan·đi·shanđ
airplane हवॉई जहाज़' ha·veŭ·ee ja·haaz
airport हवॉई अड' ha·veŭ·ee a·điu
alcohol शराब sha·raab
all सोरूय soh·ruy
allergy अलर्जी a·lar·jee
ambulance अम्बुलंस am·bu·lans
and त' tiu
ankle ग्वड gwađ
antibiotics अंटीबयटिक्स an·ţee·bai·ţiks
arm नॅर neur
ATM ए टी एम ey ţee em

B

baby शुर shur
back (of body) थर t'ar
backpack बैकपैक beŭk·peŭk
bad खराब k'a·raab
bag बैग beŭg
baggage claim बैगेज क्लेम beu·geyj kleym
bank बैंक bank
bar बार baar
bathroom बाथरूम baat'·room
battery बैटरी baiţ·ree
beautiful खूबसूरत k'oob·soo·rat'
bed बिस्तर' bis·tar
before ब्रोंह bronh
behind पत'कनि pa·tiu
bicycle सयकल sai·kal
big बोड bođ
bill बिल bil
blanket कम्बल kam·bal
blood group ब्लड ग्रुप blađ grup
boat नाव naav
book (make a reservation) v बुक करुन buk ka·run
bottle बोतल bo·tal
boy लॅडक' leuđ·kiu

brakes (car) ब्रेक breyk
breakfast ब्रेकफस्ट brek·p'aasţ
broken (faulty) फुटमुत p'uţ·mut
bus बस bas
business कार'बार kaa·riu·baar
buy v मॅल्य ह्योन meuly hyon

C

camera केमरा kem·raa
cancel रद rad
car कार kaar
cash n नक'द na·kiud
cash (a cheque) v बुनाव'न्य ba·naa·viuny
cell phone मोबाइल फोन mo·bail p'ohn
centre n मरकज़ mar·kaz
change (money) v बदलावुन bad·laa·vun
cheap सस्त' sas·tiu
check (bill) बिल bil
check-in n चेक इन chek in
chest (body) सीन' see·niu
child शुर shur
cigarette सिगरेठ sig·reţ'
city शहर sha·har
clean a साफ saap'
closed बंद band
cold a सर'द sa·riud
collect call क्लेक्ट काल ka·lekţ kaal
come यि yi
computer कम्प्यूटर kam·pyoo·ţar
condom कंडोम kan·đom
contact lenses कंटेक्ट लेंसिस kan·teykţ len·sis
cook v रनुन ra·nun
cost n का'मथ keŭ·mat'
credit card केडिट कार्ड kre·điţ kaađ
currency exchange ज़र' मुबादल' zar mu·baa·da·liu
customs कस्टमज़ kas·ţamz

D

dangerous खतरनाख k'a·tar·naak'
date (time) तॉरीख teŭ·reek'
day द्वह dwah
delay n चेर tser
dentist दन्द' डाक्टर dan·diu đaak·ţar
depart नेरुन ne·run

diaper डाइपर dai·par
dinner डिनर đi·nar
direct a सेदि स्योद se·di syod
dirty गन्द' gan·diu
disabled नाकार' naa·kaa·riu
discount n डिस्कऊंट đis·ka·unţ
doctor डाक्टर đaak·ţar
double bed डबल बेड đa·bal beđ
double room डबल कमर' đa·bal kam·riu
drink n ड्रिंक đrink
drive v चलावुन cha·laa·vun
drivers licence ड्राइवर्स लाइसंस đrai·veürs lai·sans
drug (illicit) ड्रग drag

E

ear कन kan
east मशरिक mash·rik
eat ख्योन k'en
economy class इकानमी क्लास i·kaan·mee klaas
electricity बिजली bij·lee
elevator लिफ्ट lip'ţ
email ई मेल ee meyl
embassy अम्बेसी em·bey·see
emergency अमरजेंसी a·mar·jan·see
English (language) अंग्रीज़ी ang·ree·zee
entrance दॉखल' deü·k'liu
evening शाम shaam
exit n नेबर नेरनुक दरवाज़' ne·bar ner·nuk dar·vaa·ziu
expensive द्रोग drog
eye ॲछ euch'

F

far दूर door
fast तेज़ tez
father वॉलिद veü·lid
film (camera) फिल्म p'i·lim
finger ओंग'ज ong·iuj
first-aid kit फर्स्ट एड किट p'eusţ eyđ kiţ
first class फर्स्ट क्लास p'eusţ klaas
fish n गाड gaa·điu
food ख्यन k'en
foot ख्वर k'war
free (of charge) मूफ्त mu·p'ut
friend दोस dohs
fruit फल p'al
full वॅरिथ beu·rit'

G

gift तोफ' toh·p'iu
girl कूर koor
glass (drinking) गिलास gi·laas
glasses ऑनख eü·nak'
go गछ़ gats'
good जान jaan
guide n गाइड gaiđ

H

half n ओड ođ
hand अथ' a·t'iu
happy ख्वश k'wash
have आसुन aa·sun
he हु hu
head n कल' ka·liu
heart दिल dil
heavy गोब gob
help v मदथ दयुन ma·dat' dyun
here येति ye·ti
high थोद t'od
highway हयवे hai·ve
hike v खसुन k'a·sun
holiday छुटी ch'u·ţee
homosexual n&a हमजिंस परस्त ham·jins pa·rast
hospital हस्पताल has·pa·taal
hot गर'म ga·rium
hotel होटम ho·ţal
hungry बोछ boch'
husband रून roon

I

I ब' biu
identification (card) शिनाख्त कार्ड shi·naak't kaađ
ill ब्यमार be·maar
important ज़रूरी za·roo·ree
injury ज़ख'म za·k'ium
insurance बीम' bee·miu
internet इनटरनेट in·ţar·neţ
interpreter तरजमान tar·ju·maan

J

jewellery ज़ेवर zey·var
job नोकरी nohk·ree

K

key कुंज़ kunz
kilogram किलोग्राम ki·lo·graam
kitchen चोक' choh·kiu
knife श्रापुच shraa·puch

L

laundry (place) पलव छलन जाय pa·lav ch'a·lan jaay
lawyer वॅकील va·keel
left (direction) खोवुर k'oh·vur
leg (body) ज़ंग zang
lesbian n&a लेसबियन les·bi·yan
less कम kam
letter (mail) चिठ्ठय chiṭ'y
light n गाश gaash
like v पसन्द करुन pa·sand ka·run
lock n कूलुफ ku·lup'
long ज़्यूठ zyooṭh
lost रोवमुत roov·mut
love v मोहबथ करुन moh·bat' ka·run
luggage सामान saa·maan
lunch लंच lanch

M

mail n डाख đaak'
man मर'द ma·riud
map नक्श' nak·shiu
market बाज़र baa·zar
matches गंदक डॅब्य gan·dak đeuby
meat माज़ maaz
medicine दवा da·vaa
message शेछ shech'
milk द्वद dwad
minute मिनठ mi·nat'
mobile phone मोबाइल फोन mo·bail p'ohn
money पॉन्स' peũn·siu
month र्‍यथ ret'
morning सुबुह su·buh
mother मॉज meũj
motorcycle मोटर साइकल mo·ṭar sai·kal
mouth ऑस eũs

N

name नाव naav
near नज़दीख neuz·deek'
neck n गर्दन gar·dan
new नोव nov
newspaper अखबार ak'·baar
night राथ raat'
no न na
noise शोर shohr
nonsmoking नान स्मोकिंग naan smo·king
north शुमाल shu·maal
nose नस nas

now व्वन्य vwany
number नम्बर nam·bar

O

old प्रोन prohn
one-way ticket अकि तरफ'च टिकठ a·ki tar·p'iuch ṭi·kaṭ'
open a खुल' k'u·liu
outside नेबर ne·bar

P

passport पासपोर्ट paas·porṭ
pay v अदा करुन a·daa ka·run
pharmacy दवा दुकान da·vaa du·kaan
phonecard फान कार्ड p'ohn kaađ
photo फाटू p'o·too
police पुलीस pu·lees
postcard पोस्ट कार्ड pohsṭ kaađ
post office डाक खान' đaak k'aa·niu
pregnant बॅर'च beu·riuts
price n का'मथ keũ·mat'

Q

quiet a शांत shaant

R

rain n रूद rood
razor रेज़र rey·zar
receipt n रॅसीद reu·seed
refund n रिफंड ri·p'ađ
registered mail रजस्टर्ड मेल ra·jes·teũrd meyl
rent v किरायस पेठ ह्योन ki·raa·yas peṭ' hyon
repair v मरमथ कर'न्य mar·mat' ka·riuny
reservation रिज़रवेशन ri·zar·ve·shan
restaurant रेस्तरान res·ta·raan
return v वापस करुन vaa·pas ka·run
return ticket वापसी टिकठ vaap·see ṭi·kaṭ'
right (direction) दॅछुन deu·ch'un
road वथ vat'
room n कमर' kam·riu

S

safe a सेफ seyp'
sanitary napkin सानिट्री नेपकिन sai·ni·ṭree neyp·kin
seat n सीट seeṭ
send सोज़ुन soh·zun
sex जिनस ji·nas

shampoo शम्पू sham·poo
share (a dorm) यिकवट' रोज़ुन yi·kiu·va·ţiu roh·zun
she हव hwa
sheet (bed) कपर चादर ka·par tsaa·dar
shirt कॅमीज़ keu·meez
shoes बूठ booţ'
shop n दुकान du·kaan
short छोट ts'oţ
shower n शावर shaa·var
single room सिंगल कमर' sin·gal kam·riu
skin n म'सल' mius·liu
skirt n स्कर्ट skeürţ
sleep v श्वंगुन shwan·gun
slowly वार' वार' vaa·riu vaa·riu
small ल्वकुट lwa·kuţ
soap सावन saa·ban
some केंह kenh
soon जल'द ja·liud
south जनूब ja·noob
souvenir shop सोविनियर दुकान so·vi·ni·yar du·kaan
stamp टिकठ ţi·kaţ
stand-by ticket स्टैंड बय टिकठ steynđ bai ţi·kaţ'
station (train) स्टेशन sţey·shan
stomach म्याद' myaa·diu
stop v ठहर ţ'eu·har
stop (bus) n बस स्टाप bas sţaap
street सडख sa·đak'
student तॉलिवि ॲलिम teü·li·bi eu·lim
sun अफताब ap'·taab
sunscreen सन स्कीन san skreen
swim v छांठ वायिन्य ts'aanţ vaa·yiny

T

tampons फाहा p'aa·haa
teeth दन्द dand
telephone n टेलिफोन ţe·li·p'ohn
temperature (weather) दरजे हरारथ dar·je ha·raa·rat'
that (within sight) हु hu
that (out of sight) सु su
they (within sight) हुम hum
they (out of sight) तिम tim
thirsty त्रेशिहोत trey·shi·hot
this (one) यि yi
throat होट hoţ
ticket टिकठ ţi·kaţ'
time वख'त va·k'iut
tired थोकमुत t'ok·mut
tissues टिशूज़ ţi·shooz
today अज़ az
toilet टोयलेट ţaay·leţ
tomorrow पगाह pa·gaah
tonight अज़ राथ az raat'
toothbrush दन्द' ब्रश dan·diu brash
toothpaste टुथपेस्ट ţut'·peysţ
torch (flashlight) टार'च ţaa·riuch
tour n ट्यूर ţyoor
tourist office ट्यूरिस्ट दफतर ţyoo·rist dap'·tar
towel तवलिया tav·li·yaa
train n ट्रेन tren
translate तरजम' tar·ja·miu
travel agency ट्रवल अजंसी tra·val a·jen·see
travellers cheque ट्रवलरस चेक' ţrav·lars chek
trousers पतलून pat·loon
twin beds टुविन बेड्ज़ा ţu·vin beđz

U

underwear कछ' ka·ch'iu
urgent फोरी poh·ree

V

vacant खॉली k'eü·lee
vegetable n सब्ज़ी sab·zee
vegetarian a शाकाहॉरी shaa·kaa·haa·ree
visa वीज़ा vee·zaa

W

walk v पकुन pa·kun
wallet बॅटव' beuţ·viu
wash (something) छलुन ch'a·lun
watch n गॅर geur
water n आव aab
we ॲस्य eusy
weekend वीकएंड vee·kend
west मगरिब mag·rib
wheelchair व्हीलचियर veel·chi·yar
when येलि ye·li
where कति ka·ti
who कुस kus
why क्याज़ि kyaa·zi
wife ज़नान za·naan
window दॉर deür
with सान/सॉत्य saan/seüty
without वरॉय va·reüy
woman ज़नान za·naan
write लेखुन ley·k'un

Y

yes आ aa
yesterday राथ raat'
you sg inf च' tsiu
you sg pol&pl तोहय tohy

DICTIONARY

Konkani

alphabet

vowels					
ಅ a	ಆ aa	ಇ i	ಈ ee	ಉ u	ಊ oo
ಎ e	ಏ ay	ಒ o	ಓ oh	ಔ ow	

consonants				
ಕ ka	ಖ k'a	ಗ ga	ಘ g'a	
ಚ cha	ಚ ts'a			
ಜ ja	ಜ za			
ಟ ta	ಡ da	ಣ ṇa	ತ ṭa	ದ đa
ನ na	ಪ pa	ಫ fa	ಬ ba	ಭ b'a
ಮ ma	ಮ್ಹ m'a			
ಯ ya	ರ ra	ಲ la	ವ wa	
ಶ sha	ಸ sa	ಹ ha	ಳ ḷa	

introduction

The 2.5 million Konkani speakers living in India are a diverse lot: they live on the west coast of India in the states of Goa, Karnataka, Maharashtra, Gujarat and Kerala, they practise Hinduism, Christianity and Islam, and they write in the Devanagari, Roman, Arabic, Kannada and Malayalam scripts. In 1987, after years of political debate, Konkani (*konk*·ṇee ಕೊಂಕ್ಣಿ) finally became the official language of Goa, the home of trance music and Goan prawn curry. The name Goa is reportedly derived from the Konkani word *go*·yan ಗೊಂಯಾಂ (meaning 'a patch of tall grass'), though Goa is probably better known for its beautiful beaches. An Indo-Aryan language related to Gujarati and Marathi, Konkani has also been influenced by Sanskrit, Portuguese, Perso-Arabic and Kannada. The Devanagari script (used to write Hindi and Marathi) is now the official writing system for Konkani in Goa. However, a large number of Konkani speakers in Karnataka use the Kannada script, as given in this chapter. So don't get stuck in a Goan trance – get out there and have a go at speaking Konkani.

konkani

pronunciation

Vowels	
Symbol	**English sound**
a	run
aa	father
ae	act
ai	aisle
ay	say
e	bet
ee	see
eu	nurse (short sound)
eū	as eu, but longer
i	hit
o	pot
oh	note
oo	zoo
ow	how
ōw	as ow, but longer
u	put

In this chapter, the Konkani pronunciation is given in red after each phrase. Aspirated consonants (pronounced with a puff of air after the sound) are represented with an apostrophe after the letter – b′, đ′, g′, k′, m′, t′ and ţ′. Retroflex consonants (pronounced with the tongue bent backwards) are included in this table. Each syllable is separated by a dot, and the syllable stressed in each word is italicised. For example:

ಮೆಳ್ಯಾಂ. *meḷ*·yaang

Consonants	
Symbol	**English sound**
b	bed
ch	cheat
d	dog
đ	retroflex d
f	fat
g	go
h	hat
j	jar
k	kit
l	lot
ḷ	retroflex l
m	man
n	not
ņ	retroflex n
ng	sing (indicates nasalisation of preceding vowel)
p	pet
r	rose
s	sun
sh	shot
t	top
ţ	retroflex t
ts′	as in hats, aspirated
w	win
y	yes
z	zero

essentials		
Yes.	ವ್ಹಯ್.	*weu*-i
No.	ನಾಂ.	naang
Please.	ಉಪ್ಕಾರ್ ಕರ್ನ್.	*up*-kaar keürn
Thank you.	ದೇವ್ ಬರೆಂ ಕರುಂ.	*đay*-u *bo*-reng *ko*-roong
Excuse me. (to get past)	ಮ್ಹಾಕಾ ವಚೊಂಕ್ ಸೊಡ್.	*m'aa*-kaa *wo*-ts'onk ts'od
Excuse me. (to get attention)	ಉಪ್ಕಾರ್ ಕರ್ನ್.	*up*-kaar keürn
Sorry.	ಚೂಕ್ ಜ಼ಾಲಿ, ಮಾಫ್ ಕರ್.	ts'ook *zaa*-li maaf keür

language difficulties

Do you speak English?
ಇಂಗ್ಲಿಶ್ ಉಲೈತಾಯ್ಗೀ? — *ing*-leesh *u*-leuy-ţaay-gee

Do you understand?
ಸಮ್ಜಾಲೆಂಗೀ? — *som*-zaa-leng-gee

I understand.
ಸಮ್ಜಾಲೆಂ. — *som*-zaa-leng

I don't understand.
ನಾಂ, ಸಮ್ಜೊಂಕ್–ನಾಂ. — naang *som*-zonk-naang

Could you please ...?	ಉಪ್ಕಾರ್ ಕರ್ನ್ . . .?	*up*-kaar keürn ...
repeat that	ಪರ್ತ್ಯಾಕ್ ಸಾಂಗ್	*porţ*-yaak ts'aang
speak more slowly	ಸವ್ಕಾಸ್ ಉಲಯ್	*seu*-u-kaas *u*-leuy

numbers					
0	ಸೊನ್ನೊ	*son*-no	20	ವೀಸ್	wees
1	ಏಕ್	ayk	30	ತೀಸ್	ţees
2	ದೋನ್	đohn	40	ಚಾಳೀಸ್	*ts'aa*-ļees
3	ತೀನ್	ţeen	50	ಪನ್ನಾಸ್	*pon*-naas
4	ಚಾರ್	chaar	60	ಸಾಟ್	saat'
5	ಪಾಂಚ್	paants'	70	ಸತ್ತರ್	*seuţ*-ţeür
6	ಸೊ	so	80	ಐಂಶಿಂ	*eüyng*-shing
7	ಸಾತ್	saaţ	90	ನೊವ್ವೋದ್	*no*-wođ
8	ಆಟ್	aat'	100	ಶೆಂಭರ್	*shem*-bor
9	ನೋವ್	nohw	1000	ಹಜ಼ಾರ್	*ha*-zaar
10	ಧಾ	đ'aa	1,000,000	ಧಾ ಲಾಖ್	đ'aa laak

time & dates

What time is it?	ವೇಳ್ ಕಿತ್ಲೊ ಜ಼ಾಲೊ?	wayļ *kiţ*·lo *zaa*·lo
It's (three) o'clock.	ಆತಾಂ (ತೀನ್) ವರಾಂ ಜ಼ಾಲಿಂ.	*aa*·ţaang (ţeen) *weū*·raang *zaa*·ling
Quarter past (three).	ಸವಾಯ್ (ತೀನ್).	*seu*·waay (ţeen)
Half past (three).	ಸಾಡೇ (ತೀನ್).	*saa*·de (ţeen)
Quarter to (three).	ಪಾವ್ಣೆಂ (ತೀನ್).	*pow*·ņeng (ţeen)
At what time ...?	ಕಿತ್ಲ್ಯಾ ವೆಳಾರ್ . . .?	*kiţ*·lyaa *we*·ļaar ...
At ...	. . . ವೆಳಾರ್.	... *we*·ļaar
It's (15 December).	ಆಜ಼್ (ಪಂದ್ರಾ ದಿಸೆಂಬ್ರ್).	aaz (*peūnđ*·raa *đi*·sembr)

yesterday	ಕಾಲ್	kaal
today	ಆಜ಼್	aaz
tomorrow	ಫ಼ಾಲ್ಯಾಂ	*faal*·yaang

Monday	ಸೊಮಾರ್	*so*·maar
Tuesday	ಮಂಗ್ಳಾರ್	*mong*·ļaar
Wednesday	ಬುಧ್ವಾರ್	*buđ*·waar
Thursday	ಬ್ರೇಸ್ತಾರ್	*bray*·sţaar
Friday	ಸುಕ್ರಾರ್	*suk*·raar
Saturday	ಸನ್ವಾರ್	*seun*·waar
Sunday	ಆಯ್ತಾರ್	*aay*·ţaar

border crossing

I'm here ...	ಹಾಂವ್ಂ . . .	*haang*·ung ...
in transit	ಟ್ರಾಂಸಿಟಾಂತ್ ಆಸಾಂ	*traan*·si·taanţ *aa*·saang
on business	ಬಿಜ಼್ನೆಸಾರ್ ಆಯ್ಲಾಂ	*biz*·ne·saar *aay*·laang
on holiday	ಸುಟ್ಯೆರ್ ಆಯ್ಲಾಂ	*su*·ti·yer *aay*·laang

I'm here for ...	ಹಾಂವ್ಂ ಹಾಂಗಾ . . . ಆಸಾಂ.	*haang*·ung *haang'*·aa ... *aa*·saang
(10) days	(ಧಾ) ದೀಸಾಂಕ್	(đ'aa) *đee*·saank
(three) weeks	(ತೀನ್) ಹಫ಼್ತ್ಯಾಂಕ್	(ţeen) *haf*·ţi·aank
(two) months	(ದೋನ್) ಮ್ಹಯ್ನ್ಯಾಂಕ್	(đohn) *m'ai*·nyaank

I'm going to (Kundapur).
ಹಾಂವ್ಂ (ಕುಂದಾಪುರ್) ವೆತಾಂ. *haang*·ung (*kun*·đ'aa·pur) *we*·ţaang

I'm staying at the (Kodiyal hotel).
ಹಾಂವ್ಂ (ಕೊಡಿಯಾಳ್ ಹೊಟೆಲಾಂತ್) ರಾವ್ತಾಂ. — *haang*·ung (*ko*·di·yaaļ *ho*·te·lanţ) *rōw*·ţaang

I have nothing to declare.
ಮ್ಹಾಕಾ ಡಿಕ್ಲೇರ್ ಕರುಂಕ್ ಕಾಂಯ್ ನಾಂ. — *m'aa*·kaa *dik*·laer *keū*·roonk *kaang*·ee naang

I have this to declare.
ಮ್ಹಾಕಾ ಹೆಂ ಡಿಕ್ಲೇರ್ ಕರುಂಕ್ ಆಸಾ. — *m'aa*·kaa heng *dik*·laer *keū*·roonk *aa*·saa

That's (not) mine.
ತೆಂ ಮ್ಹಜೆಂ (ನ್ಹಂಯ್). — ţeng *m'eū*·jeng (*neu*·ing)

tickets & luggage

Where can I buy a ticket?
ಟಿಕೇಟ್ ಖೈಂಯ್ ಮೆಳ್ತಾ? — *ti*·kayt *k'eu*·ing *meļ*·ţaa

Do I need to book a seat?
ಬುಕ್ ಕರ್ಚಿ ಘ಼ರ್ಜ಼್ ಆಸಾಗೀ? — buk *keur*·chi g'eürz *aa*·saa·gee

One … ticket to (Permude), please.	(ಪೆರ್ಮುದೆ) . . . ಮ್ಹಾಕಾ ಏಕ್ ಟಿಕೇಟ್ ಜ಼ಾಯ್.	(*per*·mu·đe) … *m'aa*·kaa ayk *ti*·kayt zaay
one-way	ವಚೊಂಕ್ ಮಾತ್ರ್	*wo*·ts'onk maaţr
return	ವಚೊಂಕ್ ಆನಿಂ ಪಾಟೀಂ ಯೇಂವ್ಕ್	*wo*·ts'onk *aan*·ing *paa*·ting *ayng*·wuk

I'd like to … my ticket, please.	ಮ್ಹಜೀ ಟಿಕೇಟ್ . . . ಜ಼ಾಯ್ ಆಸ್-ಲ್ಲಿ.	*m'eu*·jee *ti*·kayt … zaay *aa*·sul·li
cancel	ಕೇನ್ಸಲ್ ಕರುಂಕ್	*kayn*·sal *keū*·roonk
change	ಬದ್ಲುಂಕ್	*beuđ*·loonk
collect	ಕಲೆಕ್ಟ್ ಕರುಂಕ್	*ka*·lekt *keū*·roonk

Is there a toilet/air conditioning?
ಟೊಯ್ಲೆಟ್/ಏರ್ ಕಂಡಿಶನ್ ಆಸಾಗೀ? — *toy*·let/ayr *kan*·di·shan *aa*·saa·gee

How long does the trip take?
ಪಾವಂವ್ಕ್ ಕಿತ್ಲೊ ವೇಳ್ ಜ಼ಾಯ್? — *paa*·weünk *kiţ*·lo wayļ zaay

Is it a direct route?
ಹಿ ಸೀಧಾ ವಾಟ್ಗೀ? — hi *see*·đ'a *waat*·gee

My luggage has been …	ಮ್ಹಜೀ ಲಗೇಜ್ . . .	*m'eu*·jee *la*·gayj …
lost	ಮೆಳೊಂಕ್ನಾಂ	*me*·ļonk·naang
stolen	ಸೊರ್ಲ್ಯಾ	*sor*·lyaa

transport

Where does flight (IC-7559) arrive?

(ಐಸೀ–7559) ನಂಬ್ರಾಚೆಂ ವಿಮಾನ್ ಕೆದಾಳಾ ಪಾವ್ತಾ?	(aay see saaţ paants' paants' nohw) *neũm*·braa·cheng *wi*·maan *ke*·đaa·ļaa *paaw*·ţaa

Where does flight (IC-7559) depart?

(ಐಸೀ–7559) ನಂಬ್ರಾಚೆಂ ವಿಮಾನ್ ಕೆದಾಳಾ ಪಾಟಿಂ ವೆತಾ?	(aay see saaţ paants' paants' nohw) *neũm*·braa·cheng *wi*·maan *ke*·đaa·ļaa *paa*·ting *we*·ţaa

Is this the boat to (Goa)?

(ಗೊಯಾಂ) ವಚೊಂಕ್ ಹಿಚ್ಚ್ ಗೀ ಬೋಟ್?	(*go*·yaang) *wo*·ts'onk *hits'*·gee boht

Is this the bus to (Karkal)?

(ಕಾರ್ಕೊಳ್) ವಚೊಂಕ್ ಹೆಂಚ್ಚ್ ಗೀ ಬಸ್?	(*kaar*·koļ) *wo*·ts'onk *hents'*·gee bas

Is this the plane to (Mangalore)?

(ಮಂಗ್ಳುರ್) ವಚೊಂಕ್ ಹೆಂಚ್ಚ್ ಗೀ ವಿಮಾನ್?	(*mong*·ļoor) *wo*·ts'onk *hents'*·gee *wi*·maan

Is this the train to (Kundapur)?

(ಕುಂದಾಪುರ್) ವಚೊಂಕ್ ಹೆಂಚ್ಚ್ ಗೀ ರೈಲ್?	(*kun*·đ'aa·pur) *wo*·ts'onk *hents'*·gee reuyl

What time's the ... bus?	... ಬಸ್ ಕಿತ್ಲ್ಯಾ ವೆಳಾರ್ ಯೆತಾ?	... bas *kiţ*·lyaa *we*·ļaar *ye*·ţaa
first	ಪಯ್ಲೆಂ	*peuy*·leng
last	ಆಖ್ರೇಚೆಂ	ak'·*ray*·cheng
next	ದುಸ್ರೆಂ	*đus*·reng

How long will it be delayed?

ಕಿತ್ಲೊ ತಡವ್ ಜ಼ಾಯ್ತ್?	*kiţ*·lo *ţeu*·deũw zaayţ

Please tell me when we get to (Moodbidri).

(ಬಿದ್ರ್ಯಾಂ) ಪಾವ್ತಾನಾ ಮ್ಹಾಕಾ ಸಾಂಗ್.	(*biđ*·ryaang) *pōw*·ţaa·naa *m'aa*·kaa saang'

I'd like a taxi ...	... ಮ್ಹಾಕಾ ಟೆಕ್ಸೀ ಜ಼ಾಯ್ ಆಸ್–ಲ್ಲಿ.	... *m'aa*·kaa *tek*·si zaay *aa*·sul·li
at (9am)	(ಸಕಾಳಿಂ ನೋವ್ ವರಾಂ) ಚೆರ್	(*sa*·kaa·ļing nohw *weũ*·raang) cher
now	ಆತಾಂ	*aa*·ţaang

How much is it to (Sultan Battery)?

(ಸುಲ್ತಾನ್ ಬತ್ತೆರಿ) ವಚೊಂಕ್ ಕಿತ್ಲೆ ಪೈಶೆ? — *(sul*·ţaan *baţ*·ţe·ri) *wo*·ts'onk *kiţ*·le *peu*·i·she

Please put the meter on.

ಮೀಟರ್ ಘಾಲ್. — *mee*·tar g'aal

Please take me to (this address).

(ಹ್ಯಾ ಜ಼ಾಗ್ಯಾಕ್) ವ್ಹರ್. — (hyaa *zaag*·yaak) weur

Please stop/wait here.

ಹಾಂಗಾ ರಾವಯ್/ರಾವ್. — *haang'*·aa *rōw*·euy/*rōw*

I'd like to hire a car/4WD (with a driver).

ಮ್ಹಾಕಾ (ಡ್ರಾಯ್ವಾರಾ ಸಾಂಗಾತಾ) ಕಾರ್/ಜೀಪ್ ಭಾಡ್ಯಾಕ್ ಜ಼ಾಯ್ ಆಸ್-ಲ್ಲೆಂ. — *m'aa*·kaa (*draay*·wa·raa *sang*·a·ţaa) kaar/jeep *b'aa*·dyaak *zaa*·i *aa*·sul·leng

How much for daily/weekly hire?

ದೀಸಾಕ್/ಹಫ್ತ್ಯಾಕ್ ಭಾಡೆಂ ಕಿತ್ಲೆಂ? — *đee*·saak/*heuf*·ţyaak *b'a*·deng *kiţ*·leng

directions

Where's the ...?	... ಖೈಂ ಆಸಾ?	... k'euyng *aa*·saa
bank	ಬೇಂಕ್	baynk
foreign currency exchange	ಭಾಯ್ಲೆ ಪೈಶೆ ಬದ್ಲುಂಚೊ ಜ಼ಾಗೊ	*b'aay*·le *peuy*·she *beuđ*·lun·ts'o *zaa*·go
post office	ಪೊಸ್ಟ್ ಒಫಿಸ್	post *o*·fis

Is this the road to (Udipi)?

(ಉಡ್ಪಿ) ವಚೊಂಕ್ ರಸ್ತೊ ಹೊಚ್ಗೀ? — (*ud*·pi) *wo*·ts'onk *reu*·sţo *hots'*·gee

Can you show me (on the map)?

(ಮೇಪಾಚೆರ್) ದಾಕೈಶಿಗೀ? — (*mae*·paa·cher) đaa·*keuy*·shi·gee

What's the address?

ವಿಳಾಸ್ ಕಸ್ಲೊ? — *wi*·ļaas *keus*·lo

How far is it?

ಕಿತ್ಲೆಂ ಪೈಸ್ ಆಸಾ? — *kiţ*·leng peūys *aa*·saa

How do I get there?

ಹಾಂವೆಂ ಥೈಂ ಕಶೆಂ ಪಾವೈತ್? — *haang*·weng *ţ'eū*·ing *keū*·sheng *pow*·yeţ

Turn left/right.

ದಾವ್ಯಾಕ್/ಉಜ್ವ್ಯಾಕ್ ಘುಂವ್. — *đaa*·wyaak/*uz*·wyaak *g'ung*·u

It's …	ತೆಂ . . .	ţ'eng …
behind …	. . . ಪಾಟ್ಲ್ಯಾನ್	… *paat*·lyaan
in front of …	. . . ಮುಕ್ಲ್ಯಾನ್	… *muk*·lyaan
near (to …)	(. . . ಚ್ಯಾ) ಲಾಗಿಂ	(… chya) *laa*·ging
on the corner	ಕೊನ್ಶ್ಯಾರ್	*kon*·shyaar
opposite …	. . . ಸಾಮ್ಕಾರ್	… *saam*·kaar
there	ಥೈಂ	*ţ'eū*·ing

accommodation

Where's a guesthouse/hotel nearby?
ಹಾಂಗಾ ಲಾಗ್ಶಿಲೆಂ ಗ್ಯಸ್ಟ್–ಹೌಸ್/ ಹೊಟೆಲ್ ಖೈಂ ಆಸಾ?
haang'·aa *lag*·shi·leng *gyast*·hows/ *ho*·tel *k'eu*·ing *aa*·saa

Can you recommend somewhere cheap/good?
ಸವಾಯೆಚೆಂ/ಬರೆಂ ಖೈಂ ಮ್ಹಣೀ ಮೆಳಾತ್ಗೀ?
seu·waa·ye·cheng/*beu*·reng *k'eu*·ing *m'eū*·ṇee *me*·ḷaaţ·gee

I'd like to book a room, please.
ಮ್ಹಾಕಾ ಏಕ್ ರೂಮ್ ಬುಕ್ ಕರುಂಕ್ ಜ಼ಾಯ್.
m'aa·kaa ayk room buk *keū*·roonk zaay

I have a reservation.
ಮ್ಹಜೆಂ ರಿಸರ್ವೇಶನ್ ಆಸಾ.
m'eū·jeng ri·ser·*way*·shan *aa*·saa

Do you have a … room?	. . . ರೂಮ್ ಮೆಳಾತ್ಗೀ?	… room *me*·ḷaaţ·gee
single	ಸಿಂಗಲ್	*sin*·gal
double	ಡಬಲ್	*da*·bal
twin	ಟ್ವಿನ್	twin

How much is it per night?
ಏಕಾ ರಾತೀಚೆಂ ಭಾಡೆಂ ಕಿತ್ಲೆಂ?
e·kaa *raa*·ţi·cheng *b'aa*·deng *kiţ*·leng

How much is it per person?
ಏಕ್ಲ್ಯಾಕ್ ಭಾಡೆಂ ಕಿತ್ಲೆಂ?
ek·lyaak *b'aa*·deng *kiţ*·leng

I'd like to stay for (two) nights.
ಮ್ಹಾಕಾ (ದೋನ್) ರಾತೀ ರಾವೊಂಕ್ ಜ಼ಾಯ್.
m'aa·kaa (đohn) *raa*·ţi *ra*·wonk zaay

Can I have my key, please?
ಮ್ಹಜೀ ಚಾವೀ ದಿವ್ಶಿಗೀ?
m'eu·ji *ts'aa*·wi *điw*·shi·gee

Can I get another (blanket)?
ಆನ್ಯೇಕ್ (ವೋಲ್) ದಿವ್ಶಿಗೀ?
aan·yayk (wohl) *điw*·shi·gee

The (air conditioning) doesn't work.
(ಏರ್ ಕಂಡಿಶನ್) ಚಲಾನಾಂ. — (ayr *kan*·di·shan) *ts'eu*·laa·naang

Is there an elevator/a safe?
ಲಿಫ್ಟ್/ಆಲ್ಮಾರ್ ಆಸಾಗೀ? — lift/*al*·maar *aa*·saa·gee

What time is checkout?
ಚೆಕ್–ಆವ್ಟಾಚೊ ವೇಳ್ ಕಿತ್ಲೊ? — *chek*·ōwt·aa·ts'o wayḷ *kiţ*·lo

Can I have my ..., please?	... ಪಾಟಿಂ ದಿವ್ಶಿಗೀ?	... *paa*·ting *đîw*·shi·gee
deposit	ಮ್ಹುಜೆಂ ಡಿಪೊಜ಼ಿಟ್	*m'eu*·jeng *di*·po·zit
passport	ಮ್ಹುಜ಼ೊ ಪಾಸ್ಪೋರ್ಟ್	*m'eu*·zo *paas*·port

banking & communications

Where's an ATM/a public phone?
ಲಾಗ್ಶಿಲೆಂ ಏ–ಟೀ–ಎಮ್/
ಪಬ್ಲಿಕ್ ಫೊನ್ ಖ್ಯೆಂ ಆಸಾ? — *lag*·shi·leng *ay*·tee·em/ *pab*·lik fon *k'eu*·ing *aa*·saa

I'd like to ...	... ಜ಼ಾಯ್ ಆಸ್–ಲ್ಲೆ.	... zaay *aa*·sul·le
arrange a transfer	ಪೈಶೆ ಟ್ರಾನ್ಸ್ಫರ್ ಕರುಂಕ್	*peuy*·she *traans*·far *keū*·roonk
change money	ಭಾಯ್ಲೆ ಪೈಶೆ ಬದ್ಲುಂಕ್	*b'aay*·le *peuy*·she *bađ*·loonk
withdraw money	ಬೇಂಕಾಂತ್ ಥಾವ್ನ್ ಪೈಶೆ ಕಾಡುಂಕ್	*bayn*·kaanţ ţ'aawn *peuy*·she *kaa*·doonk

What's the ...?		
charge for that	ತಾಚೊ ಖರ್ಚ್ ಕಿತ್ಲೊ?	*ţaa*·ts'o k'eurts' *kiţ*·lo
exchange rate	ಎಕ್ಸ್ಚೆಂಜ್ ರೇಟ್ ಕಿತ್ಲಿ?	*eks*·chaynj rayt *kiţ*·li

Where's the local internet café?
ಲಾಗ್ಶಿಲೆಂ ಇನ್ಟರ್ನೆಟ್ ಕಫ಼ೇ
ಖ್ಯೆಂ ಆಸಾ? — *lag*·shi·leng *in*·tar·net *ka*·fay *k'eu*·ing *aa*·saa

How much is it per hour?
ಏಕಾ ವರಾಕ್ ಕಿತ್ಲೆ? — *ay*·kaa *weū*·raak *kiţ*·le

I'd like to ...	ಮ್ಹಾಕಾ ... ಆಸಾ.	*m'aa*·kaa ... *aa*·saa
get internet access	ಇನ್ಟರ್ನೆಟಾಚಿ ಘರ್ಜ್	*in*·tar·ne·ta·chi geūrz
use a printer/ scanner	ಪ್ರಿಂಟರಾಚಿ/ ಸ್ಕೇನ್ನಾರಾಚಿ ಘರ್ಜ್	*prin*·ta·raa·chi/ *skay*·na·raa·chi geūrz

I'd like a …	. . . ಜ಼ಾಯ್ ಆಸ್–ಲ್ಲೆಂ.	… zaay *aa*·sul·leng
mobile/cell phone for hire	ಭಾಡ್ಯಾಕ್ ಮೊಬಾಇಲ್ ಫೊನ್	*b'aa*·dyaak *mo*·bail fon
SIM card for your network	ಫೊನಾಕ್ ತುಮ್ಚ್ಯಾ ಫೊನ್–ಕಂಪೆನಿಚೆಂ ಏಕ್ ಸಿಮ್ ಕಾರ್ಡ್	*fo*·naak *ţum*·chyaa *fon*·kam·pe·ni·cheng ayk sim kaard

What are the rates?
ಕಿತ್ಲೆ ಪೈಶೆ? — *kiţ*·le *peuy*·she

What's your phone number?
ತುಜೆಂ ಫೊನ್ ನಂಬರ್ ಕಿತೆಂ? — *ţu*·jeng fon *nam*·bar *ki*·ţeng

The number is …
ನಂಬರ್ . . . — *nam*·bar …

I'd like to buy a phonecard.
ಮ್ಹಾಕಾ ಏಕ್ ಫೊನ್ ಕಾರ್ಡ್ ಜ಼ಾಯ್ ಆಸ್–ಲ್ಲೆಂ. — *m'aa*·kaa ayk fon kaard zaay *aa*·sul·leng

I want to call (Canada).
(ಕೆನಾಡಾಕ್) ಫೊನ್ ಕರುಂಕ್ ಆಸಾ. — (*ke*·naa·dak) fon *keū*·roonk *aa*·saa

I want to send a fax/parcel.
ಏಕ್ ಫ್ಯೇಕ್ಸ್/ಪಾರ್ಸೆಲ್ ಧಾಡುಂಕ್ ಆಸ್–ಲ್ಲೆಂ. — ayk faks/*paar*·sel *đ'aa*·dunk *aa*·sul·leng

I want to buy a stamp.
ಏಕ್ ಸ್ಟೇಂಪ್ ಜ಼ಾಯ್ ಆಸ್–ಲ್ಲೆಂ. — ayk staemp zaay *aa*·sul·leng

I want to buy an envelope.
ಏಕ್ ಪೊಸ್ಟಾಚೆಂ ಕವರ್ ಜ಼ಾಯ್ ಆಸ್–ಲ್ಲೆಂ. — ayk *pos*·ta·cheng *ka*·war zaay *aa*·sul·leng

Please send it to (Australia).
(ಆಸ್ಟ್ರೇಲಿಯಾ) ಆಕ್ ಧಾಡ್. — (*aas*·tray·li·ya) ak đ'aad

sightseeing

What time does it open/close?
ಕಿತ್ಲ್ಯಾ ವೆಳಾರ್ ಉಗ್ತೆಂ/ಬಂಧ್ ಜ಼ಾತಾ? — *kiţ*·lya *we*·ļaar *ug*·teng/banđ' *zaa*·ţaa

Is there a discount for students?
ಇಸ್ಕಾಲಾಚ್ಯಾ ಭುರ್ಗ್ಯಾಂಕ್ ಕನ್ಸೆಶನ್ ಆಸಾಗೀ? — *is*·kaa·la·chyaa *b'ur*·gyaank *kan*·se·shan *aa*·saa·gee

Is there a discount for children?
ಭುರ್ಗ್ಯಾಂಕ್ ಕನ್ಸೆಶನ್ ಆಸಾಗೀ? — *b'ur*·gyaank *kan*·se·shan *aa*·saa·gee

I'd like to hire a guide.
ಭಾಡ್ಯಾಕ್ ಏಕ್ ಗಾಯ್ಡ್ ಝ಼ಾಯ್ ಆಸ್-ಲ್ಲೊ. — *b'aa*·dyaak ayk gaayd zaay *aa*·sul·lo

I'd like a catalogue.
ಏಕ್ ವಸ್ತುಂಚಿ ಪಟ್ಟಿ ಝ಼ಾಯ್ ಆಸ್-ಲ್ಲೆಂ. — ayk *was*·ţun·chi *pat*·ti zaay *aa*·sul·leng

I'd like a map.
ಏಕ್ ಮೇಪ್ ಝ಼ಾಯ್ ಆಸ್-ಲ್ಲೆಂ. — ayk maep zaay *aa*·sul·leng

I'd like to see …
. . . ಪಳೊಂವ್ಕ್ ಝ಼ಾಯ್ ಆಸ್-ಲ್ಲಿ. — … *peū*·ļong·uk zaay *aa*·sul·li

What's that?
ತೆಂ ಕಿತೆಂ? — ţeng *ki*·ţeng

Can I take a photo?
ಏಕ್ ಫೊಟೊ ಕಾಡುಂವ್-ಯೇ? — ayk *fo*·to *kaa*·dung·yay

When's the next tour?
ಆನ್ಯೇಕ್ ಟೂರ್ ಕೆದಾಳಾ? — *aa*·ni·ayk toor *ke*·đaa·ļaa

How long is the tour?
ಟೂರ್ ಕಿತ್ಲೆಂ ಲಾಂಬಾಯೆಚೆಂ? — toor *kiţ*·leng *laam*·baa·ye·cheng

Is … included?	. . . ಸಾಂಗಾತಾಗೀ?	… *saang'*·aa·ţaa·gee
accommodation	ರಾಂವ್ಚ್ಯಾ ಝ಼ಾಗ್ಯಾ	*raang*·u·chaa *zaa*·gyaa
admission	ಎದ್ಮಿಶನಾ	*ed*·mi·shaa·naa
food	ಜೆವ್ಣಾ	*jew*·ņaa
transport	ಪಯ್ಣಾ	*peuy*·ņaa

sightseeing		
fort	ಕೊಟೆಂ	*ko*·teng
Jain temple	ಬಸ್ದಿ	*beūs*·đee
mosque	ಮಶೀದ್	*meū*·sheeđ
palace	ರಾವ್ಳೆರ್	*raa*·u·ļer
ruins	ಕೊಸಾಳ್ಳಿಂ ಬಾಂದ್ಪಾಂ	*ko*·saaļ·ļing *baanđ*·paang
temple	ದೆವಾಳ್	*đe*·waaļ

shopping

Where's a . . . ?	. . . ಖೈಂ ಆಸಾ?	. . . k'euyng *aa*·saa
camera shop	ಕೆಮಾರಾ ಶೊಪ್	*ke*·maa·raa shop
market	ಸಾಂತ್	saanţ
souvenir shop	ಸುವ್ನೀರ್ ಶೊಪ್	*suw*·neer shop

I'm looking for . . .
ಮ್ಹಾಕಾ . . . ಜ಼ಾಯ್ ಆಸ್–ಲ್ಲೆಂ. — *m'aa*·kaa . . . aay *aa*·sul·leng

Can I look at it?
ಪಳಯೆತ್ಗೀ? — *peū*·ļeū·yeţ·gee

Can I have it sent overseas?
ಭಾಯ್ಲ್ಯಾ ಗಾಂವಾಕ್ ಧಾಡುನ್ ದಿವ್ಯೆತ್ಗೀ? — *b'aay*·lyaa *gaang*·waak *đ'aa*·dun *điw*·yeţ·gee

Can I have my (camera) repaired?
ಮ್ಹುಜ಼ೊ (ಕೆಮರಾ) ರಿಪೆರ್ ಕರ್ಯೆತ್ಗೀ? — *m'eu*·zo (*ke*·maa·raa) *ri*·payr *keur*·yeţ·gee

It's faulty.
ಪಾಡ್ ಜ಼ಾಲಾ. — paad *zaa*·laa

How much is it?
ತಾಕಾ ಕಿತ್ಲೆ ಪೈಶೆ? — *ţaa*·kaa *kiţ*·le *peuy*·she

Can you write down the price?
ಕಿತ್ಲೆ ಪೈಶೆ ತೆ ಬರವ್ನ್ ದಿವ್ಶಿಗೀ? — *kiţ*·le *peuy*·she ţe *beu*·reū·wun *điw*·shi·gee

That's too expensive.
ತೆಂ ಏಕ್ಧಮ್ ಮ್ಹಾರಗ್. — ţeng *ayk*·đ'am *m'aa*·reūg

I'll give you (300 rupees).
(ತಿಣ್ಶಿಂ ರುಪೈ) ದೀತಾಂ. — (*ţiṇ*·shing *ru*·pai) *đi*·ţang

There's a mistake in the bill.
ಬಿಲ್ಲಾಂತ್ ಏಕ್ ಚೂಕ್ ಜ಼ಾಲ್ಯಾ. — *bil*·laanţ ayk ts'ook *zaa*·lyaa

I'd like my change, please.
ಉರುಲ್ಲೆ ಚಿಲ್ಲರ್ ಪೈಶೆ ಜ಼ಾಯ್ ಆಸ್–ಲ್ಲೆ. — *u*·rul·le *chil*·lar *peuy*·she zaay *aa*·sul·le

Do you accept . . . ?	. . . ಘೆತಾಯ್ಗೀ?	. . . *g'e*·ţaay·gee
credit cards	ಕ್ರೆಡಿಟ್ ಕಾರ್ಡಾಂ	*kre*·dit *kaar*·daang
debit cards	ಡೆಬಿಟ್ ಕಾರ್ಡಾಂ	*de*·bit *kaar*·daang
travellers cheques	ಟ್ರಾವೆಲರ್ಸ್ ಚೆಕ್ಸ್	*traa*·we·lars cheks

I'd like a ..., please.	... ಝ಼ಾಯ್ ಆಸ್-ಲ್ಲೆಂ.	... zaay *aa*·sul·leng
bag	ಏಕ್ ಬೇಗ್	ayk bayg
receipt	ಬಿಲ್ಲ್	bil
refund	ಮ್ಹುಜೆಂ ರಿಫ಼ಂಡ್	*m'eu*·jeng *ri*·fand

Less.	ಉಣೆಂ.	*u*·ṇeng
Enough.	ಪುರೊ.	*pu*·ro
More.	ಚಡ್.	ts'eūd

photography

Can you ...?	... ಕರ್ಶಿವೇ?	... *keur*·shi·way
burn a CD from my memory card/stick	ಹ್ಯಾ ಮೆಮರಿ ಕಾರ್ಡಾ/ ಸ್ಟಿಕಾ ಚೆಂ ಏಕ್ ಸೀ-ಡೀ ತಯಾರ್	hyaa *me*·ma·ri *kaar*·daa/ *sti*·kaa cheng ayk *see*·dee *ţeūy*·aar
develop this film	ಹೆಂ ಫ಼ಿಲ್ಮ್ ಡೆವೆಲಪ್	heng film *de*·we·lap

I need a film for this camera.

ಹ್ಯಾ ಕೆಮಾರಾಕ್ ಫ಼ಿಲ್ಮ್ ಝ಼ಾಯ್ ಆಸ್-ಲ್ಲೆಂ. — hyaa *ke*·maa·raak film zaay *aa*·sul·leng

When will it be ready?

ಕೆದಾಳಾ ತಯಾರ್ ಝ಼ಾಯ್ತ್? — *ke*·đaa·ḷaa *ţeū*·yaar zaayţ

making conversation

Hello.	ಹಲ್ಲೋ.	*hal*·lo
Good night.	ದೇವ್ ಬರಿ ರಾತ್ ದೀಂವ್.	đayw *beū*·ri raaţ *đeeng*·wu
Goodbye.	ಮೆಳ್ಯಾಂ.	*meḷ*·yaang

Mr/Mrs	ಶ್ರೀ/ಶ್ರೀಮತಿ	shree/*shree*·ma·ţi
Miss/Ms	ಕುಮಾರಿ	*ku*·maa·ri

How are you?	ಕಸೊ/ಕಶಿ ಆಸಾಯ್?	*keū*·so/*keū*·shi *aa*·saay **m/f**
Fine, thanks. And you?	ಹಾಂವ್ಂ ಬರೊಂ ಆಸಾಂ. ತುಂ ಕಸೊ/ಕಶಿ ಆಸಾಯ್?	*haang*·ung *beū*·rong *aa*·saang ţung *keū*·so/*keū*·shi *aa*·saay **m/f**
What's your name?	ತುಜೆಂ ನಾಂವ್ಂ ಕಿತೆಂ?	*ţu*·jeng *naang*·ung *ki*·ţeng
My name is ...	ಮ್ಹುಜೆಂ ನಾಂವ್ಂ ...	*m'eu*·jeng *naang*·ung ...
I'm pleased to meet you.	ತುಕಾ ಮೆಳೊಂಕ್ ಮ್ಹಾಕಾ ಖುಶಿ ಝ಼ಾಲಿ.	*ţu*·kaa *me*·ḷonk *m'aa*·kaa *k'u*·shi *zaa*·li
This is my mother.	ಹಿ ಮ್ಹುಜಿ ಆವೈ.	hi *m'eu*·jee *aa*·wai

This is my …	ಹೊ ಮ್ಹುಜ಼ೊ . . .	ho *m'eu*·zo …
brother	ಭಾವ್	b'aaw
father	ಬಾಪ್ಪೈ	*baa*·pai
friend (male)	ಈಶ್ಟ್	eesht
husband	ಘೊವ್	g'ow
son	ಪೂತ್	pooţ
This is my …	ಹೆಂ ಮ್ಹುಜೆಂ . . .	heng *m'eu*·jeng …
daughter	ಧುವ್	đ'uw
friend (female)	ಈಶ್ಟ್	eesht
sister	ಭೈಣ್	b'aiņ
wife	ಬಾಯ್ಲ್	baayl
Here's my (address).	ಹೊ ಮ್ಹುಜ಼ೊ (ವಿಳಾಸ್).	ho *m'eu*·zo (*wi*·ļaas)
What's your (email)?	ತುಜೆಂ (ಈಮೇಲ್) ಕಿತೆಂ?	*ţu*·jeng (*ee*·mayl) *ki*·ţeng
Where are you from?	ತುಜ಼ೊ ಗಾಂವ್ಂ ಖೈಂಚೊ?	*ţu*·zo *gaang*·ung *k'eu*·ing·ts'o
I'm from …	ಹಾಂವ್ಂ . . . ಚೊ/ಚೆಂ.	*haang*·ung … ts'o/cheng **m/f**
Australia	ಆಸ್ಟ್ರೇಲಿಯಾ	*aas*·tray·li·yaa
Canada	ಕೆನಾಡಾ	*ke*·naa·daa
New Zealand	ನ್ಯೂ ಜ಼ೆಲೇಂಡ್	nyoo *zi*·laynd
the UK	ಬ್ರಿಟಾನ್	*bri*·tan
the USA	ಆಮೇರಿಕಾ	*aa*·me·ri·kaa

What's your occupation?

ತುಂ ಖೈಂಚೆಂ ಕಾಮ್ ಕರ್ತಾಯ್? — ţung *k'eu*·ing·cheng kaam *keūr*·ţaay

I'm a/an …	ಹಾಂವ್ಂ . . .	*haang*·ung …
businessperson	ಬಿಸ್ನೆಸ್ ಮನಿಸ್	*biz*·nes *meū*·nis
office worker	ಒಫ಼ಿಸ್ ಕಾಮೆಲಿ	*o*·fis *kaa*·me·li
tradesperson	ಕಾಮೆಲಿ	*kaa*·me·li
Do you like …?	. . . ಪಸಂದ್ ಆಸಾ–ಗೀ?	… *pa*·sanđ *aa*·saa·gee
I like …	. . . ಪಸಂದ್ ಆಸಾ.	… *pa*·sanđ *aa*·saa
I don't like …	. . . ಪಸಂದ್ ನಾಂ.	… *pa*·sanđ naang
art	ಕಲಾ	*keū*·laa
movies	ಫ಼ಿಲ್ಮಾಂ	*fil*·mang
music	ಸಂಗೀತ್	*seūng*·eeţ
reading	ಬೂಕ್	book
sport	ಖೆಳ್	kheļ

eating out

Can you recommend a bar?

ಹಾಂಗಾ ಲಾಗ್ಶಿಲ್ಯಾನ್ ಬರೆಂ ಏಕ್ ಬಾರ್ ಆಸಾಗೀ? — *haang'*·aa *laag*·shi·lyaan *beū*·reng ayk baar *aa*·saa·gee

Can you recommend a dish?

ಬರೆಂ ಏಕ್ ನಿಸ್ತೆಂ ಜ಼ಾಲ್ಯಾರ್ ಖ್ಯೆಂಚೆಂ? — *beū*·reng ayk *nis*·ţeng *zaa*·lyaar *k'eu*·ing·cheng

Can you recommend a place to eat?

ಬರೊ ಏಕ್ ಜೆವ್ಣಾಚೊ ಜ಼ಾಗೊ ಜ಼ಾಲ್ಯಾರ್ ಖ್ಯೆಂಚೊ? — *beū*·ro ayk *jew*·ņa·ts'o *zaa*·go *zaa*·lyaar *k'eu*·ing·ts'o

I'd like the menu.

ಮೆನೂ ಜ಼ಾಯ್ ಆಸ್-ಲ್ಲೊ. — *me*·noo zaay *aa*·sul·lo

I'd like (a/the) ..., please.	... ಜ಼ಾಯ್ ಆಸ್-ಲ್ಲೆಂ.	... zaay *aa*·sul·leng
bill	ಬಿಲ್ಲ್	bil
local speciality	ಗಾಂವ್ಚೆಂ ಖಾಣ್-ಜೆವಾಣ್	*gaa*·ung·cheng *k'aņ*·je·waaņ
table for (five)	(ಪಾಂಚ್) ಜ಼ಣಾಂಕ್ ಏಕ್ ಮೇಜ಼್	(paants') *zeu*·ņaank ayk mayz
that dish	ತೆಂ ಖಾಣ್	ţeng k'aņ

breakfast	ಸಕಾಳಿಂಚೊ ನಾಸ್ಟೊ	sa·*kaa*·ļing·ts'o *naas*·to
lunch	ದೊನ್ಪಾಂರಾಂಚೆಂ ಜೆವಾಣ್	*đon*·paa·raang·cheng *je*·waaņ
dinner	ಸಾಂಜೆಚೆಂ ಜೆವಾಣ್	*saan*·je·cheng *je*·waaņ

(cup of) coffee/tea ...	... ಕಾಫಿ಼/ಚಾಯ್	... *kaa*·fee/ chaay
with milk	ದುದಾ-ಸಾಂಗಾತಾ	*đu*·đaa·saang'·aa·ţaa
without sugar	ಸಾಕ್ರಿ-ವಿಣೆಂ	*saak*·ri·wi·ņeng

(orange) juice	(ಸಂತ್ರಾಂ) ರೋಸ್	(*san*·ţraang) rohs
lassi	ತಾಕ್	ţaak
soft drink	ಸೊಡಾ ಪೀವನ್	*so*·da *pee*·wan

I'll have boiled/mineral water.

ಉಕ್ಡೈಲ್ಲೆಂ/ಬೊತ್ಲಿಚೆಂ ಉದಾಕ್ ಜ಼ಾಯ್ ಆಸ್-ಲ್ಲೆಂ. — *uk*·dai·leng/*boţ*·li·cheng *u*·đaak zaay *aa*·sul·leng

I'll buy you a drink.

ತುಜ್ಯಾ ಪೀವನಾಚೆ ಪೈಶೆ ಹಾಂವ್ಂ ದೀತಾಂ. — *ţuj*·yaa *pee*·wa·naa·che *peuy*·she *haang*·ung *đi*·ţang

What would you like?	ಕಿತೆಂ ಝ಼ಾಯ್ ಸಾಂಗ್?	*ki*·ţeng zaay saang'
a bottle/glass of beer	ಏಕ್ ಬೊತ್ಲ್/ಗ್ಲಾಸ್ ಬೀರ್	ayk bohţl/glaas beer
a bottle/glass of wine	ಏಕ್ ಬೊತ್ಲ್/ಗ್ಲಾಸ್ ವೈನ್	ayk bohţl/glaas waayn

special diets & allergies

Do you have ... food?	. . . ಜೆವಾಣ್ ಮೆಳಾತ್ಗೀ?	... *je*·waaṇ *me*·ḷaaţ·gee
halal	ಹಲಾಲ್	*ha*·laal
kosher	ಕೊಶೆರ್	*ko*·sher
vegetarian	ಸಸ್ಯಾಹಾರಿ	*sa*·syaa·haa·ri
I'm allergic to ...	. . . ಮ್ಹಾಕಾ ಪಿಡಾ ದಿತಾ.	... *m'aa*·kaa *pi*·daa *đi*·ţaa
dairy products	ದುದಾಳ್ ಖಾಣ್	*đu*·đaaḷ k'aaṇ
eggs	ತಾಂತಿಂ	*ţaan*·ţing
meat stock	ಮಾಸಾಳ್ ಖಾಣ್	*maa*·saaḷ k'aaṇ
nuts	ಬಿಯೊ	*bi*·yo
seafood	ಮಾಸ್ಳಿ	*maas*·ḷi

emergencies

Help!	ಮ್ಹಾಕಾ ಕುಮಕ್ ಕರ್!	*m'aa*·kaa *ku*·meŭk keŭr
Stop!	ರಾವ್!	raaw
Go away!	ವಸ್!	weŭts'
Thief!	ಚೋರ್!	ts'ohr
Fire!	ಉಜ಼ೊ ಪೆಟ್ಲಾ!	*u*·zo *pet*·laa
Watch out!	ಝ಼ಾಗ್ರುತ್!	*zaag*·ruţ
Call ...!	. . . ಆಪೈ!	... *aa*·pai
an ambulance	ಎಂಬ್ಯುಲೆಂಸಾಕ್	*em*·byu·len·saak
a doctor	ದಾಕ್ತೆರಾಕ್	*đaak*·ţe·raak
the police	ಪೊಲಿಸಾಂಕ್	*po*·li·saank

Could you help me, please?
ಮ್ಹಾಕಾ ಇಲ್ಲೊಚೊ ಉಪ್ಕಾರ್ ಕರ್ಶಿಗೀ? — *m'aa*·kaa *il*·lo·ts'o *up*·kaar *keur*·shi·gee

I have to use the phone.
ಮ್ಹಾಕಾ ಫೊನಾಚಿ ಘರ್ಜ್ ಆಸಾ. — *m'aa*·kaa *fo*·na·chi g'eŭrz *aa*·saa

I'm lost.
ಮ್ಹುಜೀ ವಾಟ್ ಚುಕ್ಲ್ಯಾ. — *m'eu*·ji waat *ts'uk*·lyaa

Where are the toilets?
ಟೊಯ್ಲೆಟ್ ಖ್ಯೆಂಚರ್ ಆಸಾತ್? — *toy*·let *k'eu*·ing·ts'eūr *aa*·saaţ

Where's the police station?
ಪೊಲಿಸ್ ಸ್ಟೇಶನ್ ಖ್ಯೆಂಚರ್ ಆಸಾ? — *po*·lis *stay*·shan *k'eu*·ing·ts'eūr *aa*·saa

I have insurance.
ಮ್ಹುಜೆಂ ಇನ್ಶುರೆನ್ಸ್ ಆಸಾ. — *m'eu*·jeng *in*·shu·rens *aa*·saa

I want to contact my embassy.
ಮ್ಹುಜ್ಯಾ ಎಂಬೆಸೀಕ್ ಸಂಪರ್ಕ್ ಕರುಂಕ್ ಆಪೇಕ್ಶಿತಾಂ. — *m'eu*·jyaa *em*·be·seek *sam*·park *keū*·roonk *aa*·pek·shi·ţaang

I've been assaulted/raped.
ಮ್ಹಾಕಾ ಘಾಯಾಳ್/ಝುಲೂಮ್ ಕೆಲಾಂ. — *m'aa*·kaa *gaa*·yaaḷ/*zu*·loom *ke*·laang

I've lost my passport.
ಹಾಂವೆಂ ಮ್ಹುಝೊ ಪಾಸ್ಪೋರ್ಟ್ ಹೊಗ್ಡಾಯ್ಲಾ. — *haang*·weng *m'eu*·zo *paas*·port *hog*·daay·laa

I've lost my money.
ಹಾಂವೆಂ ಮ್ಹುಜೆ ಪೈಶೆ ಹೊಗ್ಡಾಯ್ಲ್ಯಾತ್. — *haang*·weng *m'eu*·je *peuy*·she *hog*·daay·lyaaţ

health

Where's the nearest ...?	... ಖ್ಯೆಂ ಆಸಾ?	... *k'eu*·ing *aa*·saa
dentist	ಲಾಗ್ಶಿಲೊ ದಾಂತಾಂಚೊ ದಾಕ್ತೆರ್	*laag*·shi·lo *đaan*·ţaang·ts'o *đaak*·ţer
doctor	ಲಾಗ್ಶಿಲೊ ದಾಕ್ತೆರ್	*laag*·shi·lo *đaak*·ţer
hospital	ಲಾಗ್ಶಿಲಿ ಆಸ್ಪತ್ರ್	*laag*·shi·li *aas*·peūţr
pharmacist	ಲಾಗ್ಶಿಲೆಂ ವಕ್ತಾಚೆಂ ಶೊಪ್	*laag*·shi·leng *wak*·ţaang·cheng shop

I need a doctor (who speaks English).
ಮ್ಹಾಕಾ (ಇಂಗ್ಲಿಶ್ ಉಲಪ್ಪಿ) ದಾಕ್ತೆರ್ ಜ಼ಾಯ್. — *m'aa*·kaa (*ing*·leesh *u*·leū·u·pi) *đaak*·ţer zaay

Could I see a female doctor?
ಮ್ಹಾಕಾ ಬಾಯ್ಲ್ ದಾಕ್ತೆರ್ ಮೆಳಾತ್ಗೀ? — *m'aa*·kaa baayl *đaak*·ţer *me*·ḷaaţ·gee

I've run out of my medication.
ಮ್ಹುಜೆಂ ವಕಾತ್ ಮುಗ್ಧಾಲಾಂ. — *m'eu*·jeng *wo*·kaaţ *mug*·đ'aa·laang

It hurts here.
ಹಾಂಗಾ ಧೂಕ್ ಆಸಾ. — *haang'*·aa đ'ook *aa*·saa

I have (a) … | ಮ್ಹಾಕಾ . . . | *m'aa*·kaa …
asthma | ಉಸ್ಮಡ್ ಆಸಾ | *us*·meūd *aa*·saa
diarrhoea | ಹಾಗೊಣ್ ಝ಼ಾಲ್ಯಾ | *haa*·goṇ *zaa*·lyaa
fever | ತಾಪ್ ಝ಼ಾಲಾ | ţaap *zaa*·laa
heart condition | ಕಾಳ್ಜ಼ಾಚಿ ಪಿಡಾ ಆಸಾ | *kaaḷ*·zaa·chi *pi*·daa *aa*·saa
nausea | ವೊಂಕಾರೊ ಝ಼ಾಲಾ | *won*·kaa·ro *aa*·saa

responsible travel

I'd like to learn some Konkani.
ಮ್ಹಾಕಾ ಇಲ್ಲಿಶಿ ಕೊಂಕ್ಣಿ ಶಿಕೊಂಕ್ ಉರ್ಭಾ ಆಸಾ.
m'aa·kaa *il*·le·sheng *konk*·ṇee *shi*·konk ur·b'aa *aa*·saa

What's this called in Konkani?
ಕೊಂಕ್ಣೆಂತ್ ಹಾಕಾ ಕಿತೆಂ ಮ್ಹಣ್ತಾತ್?
konk·ṇenţ *haa*·kaa *ki*·ţeng *m'euṇ*·ţaaţ

Would you like me to teach you some English?
ತುಕಾ ಇಲ್ಲೆಶೆಂ ಇಂಗ್ಲಿಶ್ ಶಿಕೊಂವ್-ಯೇ?
ţu·kaa *il*·le·sheng *ing*·leesh *shi*·kong·way

I didn't mean to do/say anything wrong.
ಚೂಕ್ ಕರುಂಕ್/ಸಾಂಗೊಂಕ್ ಮ್ಹುಜ್ಯಾ ಮತಿಂತ್ ನಾತ್-ಲ್ಲೆಂ.
ts'ook *keū*·roonk/*saang'*·onk *m'eu*·jyaa *meū*·ţeenţ *naa*·ţul·leng

Is this a local or national custom?
ಹಿ ಹ್ಯಾ ಗಾಂವ್ಚಿ ಚಾಲ್-ಗೀ ಯ್ಹಾ ದೇಶಾಚಿ ಚಾಲ್?
hi hyaa *gaang*·u·chi *ts'aal*·gee yaa *đe*·sha·chi ts'aal

I'd like to stay at a locally run hotel.
ಹಾಂವ್ಂ ಗಾಂವ್ಚ್ಯಾ ಲೋಕಾನ್ ಚಲಂವ್ಚ್ಯಾ ಹೊಟೆಲಾಂತ್ ರಾವೊಂಕ್ ಆಪೆಕ್ಷಿತಾಂ.
haang·ung *gaang*·u·chaa *lo*·kaan *ts'eū*·long·u·cha *ho*·te·laanţ *raa*·wonk *aa*·pek·shi·ţaang

Where can I buy locally produced goods/souvenirs?
ಗಾಂವ್ಚ್ಯಾ ಲೋಕಾನ್ ತಯಾರ್ ಕೆಲ್ಲ್ಯೊ ವಸ್ತು/ಸುವ್ನೀರ್ ಖ್ಯೆಂ ಘೆಂವ್ಕ್ ಮೆಳ್ತಾತ್?
gaang·ung·chaa *lo*·kaan *ţa*·yaar *kel*·lyo *wos*·ţu/*suw*·neer *k'eu*·ing *g'e*·unk *meḷ*·ţaaţ

What's this made from?
ಹೆಂ ಖ್ಯೆಂಚಾ ವಸ್ತುನಿಂ ತಯಾರ್ ಕೆಲಾಂ?
heng *k'eu*·ing·cha *wos*·ţu·ning *ţa*·yaar *ke*·lang

I'd like to do some volunteer work (for your organisation).
ಹಾಂವ್ಂ (ತುಮ್ಚ್ಯಾ ಸಂಘಾಕ್) ಫುಂಕ್ಯಾಕ್ ವಾವ್ರ್ ಕರುಂಕ್ ಆಪೆಕ್ಷಿತಾಂ.
haang·ung (*ţum*·cha *sang'*·aak) *fun*·ki·aak *waa*·ur *keū*·roonk *aa*·pek·shi·ţaang

english–konkani dictionary

Words in this dictionary are marked as n (noun), a (adjective), v (verb), sg (singular) and pl (plural) where necessary.

A

accident ಅಪ್ಘಾತ್ *ap*·g'aaţ
accommodation ರಾವೊಂಕ್ ಸುವಾತ್ *raa*·wonk *su*·waaţ
adaptor ಎಡಾಪ್ಟರ್ e·*daap*·tar
address n ವಿಳಾಸ್ *wi*·ļaas
after ಉಪ್ರಾಂತ್ *up*·raanţ
air-conditioned ಏರ್ ಕಂಡಿಶನ್ ಆಸ್‌–ಲ್ಲೆಂ ayr *kan*·di·shan *aa*·sul·leng
airplane ವಿಮಾನ್ *wi*·maan
airport ವಿಮಾನ್ ಥಳ್ *wi*·maan ţaļ
alcohol ಸೊರೊ *so*·ro
all ಸಕ್ಕಡ್ *sak*·kad
allergy ಎಲರ್ಜೀ *e*·lar·jee
ambulance ಎಂಬ್ಯುಲೆಂಸ್ *em*·byu·lens
and ಆನಿಂ *aa*·ning
ankle ಖುಬೊ *k'u*·bo
antibiotics ಎಂಟಿಬಯೋಟಿಕ್ಸ್ en·ti·ba·*yo*·tiks
arm ಬಾವ್ಳೊ *baa*·u·ļo
ATM ಏ–ಟೀ–ಎಮ್ *ay*·tee·em

B

baby ಬಾಳ್ಶೆಂ *baaļ*·sheng
back (of body) ಪಾಟ್ paat
backpack ಪಾಟಿಚೆಂ ಬೇಗ್ *paa*·ti·cheng bayg
bad ಪಾಡ್ paad
bag ಬೇಗ್ bayg
baggage claim ಬೇಗೆಜ್ ಕ್ಲೇಇಮ್ *bay*·gej klaym
bank ಬೇಂಕ್ baynk
bar ಬಾರ್ baar
bathroom ನಾಣಿಂ *naa*·ņing
battery ಬೆಟ್ರಿ *be*·tri
beautiful ಸೊಭಿತ್ *so*·b'iţ
bed ಖಾಟ್ಲೆಂ *k'aat*·leng
before ಪೈಲೆಂ *peüy*·leng
behind ಪಾಟ್ಲ್ಯಾನ್ *paat*·lyaan
bicycle ಸಾಯ್ಕಲ್ *saay*·kal
big ವ್ಹಡ್ಲೆಂ *weud*·leng
bill ಬಿಲ್ಲ್ bil
blanket ವೋಲ್ wohl
blood group ರಗ್ತಾಚೊ ನಮುನೊ *reüg*·ţaa·ts'o *neü*·mu·no
boat ಬೋಟ್ boht
book (make a reservation) v ಬುಕ್ ಕರ್ buk keür
bottle ಬೊತ್ಲ್ bohţl
boy ಚೆಡೊ *che*·do
brakes (car) ಬ್ರೇಕ್ brayk
breakfast ಸಕಾಳಿಂಚೊ ನಾಸ್ಟೊ sa·*kaa*·ļing·ts'o *naas*·to
broken (faulty) ಸಮಾ ನಾಂ *seü*·maa naang
bus ಬಸ್ bas
business ಬಿಜ್ನೆಸ್ *biz*·nes
buy v ಮೊಲಾಕ್ ಘೆ *moh*·laak g'e

C

camera ಕೆಮಾರಾ *ke*·maa·raa
cancel ಕೇನ್ಸಲ್ *kayn*·sal
car ಕಾರ್ kaar
cash n ಪೈಶೆ *peuy*·she
cash (a cheque) v ಚೆಕ್ ಕೇಶ್ ಕರ್ chek kaysh keür
cell phone ಮೊಬಾಯ್ಲ್ ಫೊನ್ *mo*·bail fon
centre n ಮಧೆಂ *meü*·đeng
change (money) v ಪೈಶೆ ಬದ್ಲ್ಲೆ *peuy*·she *bađ*·leüy
cheap ಸವಾಯ್ *seu*·waa·i
check (bill) ಬಿಲ್ಲ್ bil
check-in n ಚೆಕ್ ಇನ್ chek in
chest (body) ಹರ್ಧೆಂ *heur*·đeng
child ಭುರ್ಗೆಂ *b'ur*·geng
cigarette ಸಿಗ್ರೆಟ್ *sig*·ret
city ಶೆಹರ್ *she*·har
clean a ನಿರ್ಮಳ್ *nir*·maļ
closed ಬಂಧ್ banđ'
cold a ಥಂಡ್ ţeund
collect call ಕೊಲ್ ಕಲೆಕ್ಟ್ ಕರ್ kol *ka*·lekt keür
come ಯೇ yay
computer ಕಂಪ್ಯೂಟರ್ kamp·*yoo*·tar
condom ಕೊಂಡಮ್ *kon*·dam
contact lenses ಕೊನ್ಟೇಕ್ಟ್ ಲೆನ್ಸ್ *kon*·tekt lens
cook v ರಾಂದಾಪ್ ಕರ್ *raan*·đaap keür
cost n ಖರ್ಚ್ k'eurs
credit card ಕ್ರೆಡಿಟ್ ಕಾರ್ಡ್ *kre*·dit kaard
currency exchange ಭಾಯ್ಲೆ ಪೈಶೆ ಬದ್ಲುಂಚೊ ಜ಼ಾಗೊ *b'aay*·le *peuy*·she *beuđ*·lun·ts'o *zaa*·go
customs (immigration) ಕಸ್ಟಮ್ಸ್ *kas*·tams

D

dangerous ಭಿರಾಂಕುಳ್ *b'i*·raan·kuļ
date (time) ತಾರೀಖ್ *ţaa*·reek'
day ದೀಸ್ đees
delay n ತಡವ್ *ţeu*·deüw

dentist ದಾಂತಾಂಚೊ ದಾಕ್ತೆರ್ *đaan*·ţaang·ts'o *đaak*·ţer
depart ಪಾಟಿಂ ವಚ್ *paa*·ting weūs
diaper ಡಯಾಪರ್ da·*yaa*·par
dinner ಸಾಂಜೆಚೆಂ ಜೆವಾಣ್ *saan*·je·cheng *je*·waaņ
direct a ಸೀಧಾ *see*·đ'a
dirty ಮೆಳೆಂ *me*·ļeng
discount n ಕನ್ಸೆಶನ್ *kan*·se·shan
doctor ದಾಕ್ತೆರ್ *đaak*·ţer
double bed ದೊಗಾಂಚೆಂ ಖಾಟ್ಲೆಂ
đ'o·gang·cheng *k'aat*·leng
double room ಡಬಲ್ ರೂಮ್ *da*·bal room
drink n ಪೀವನ್ *pee*·wan
drive v ಚಲಯ್ *seū*·leūy
drivers licence ಡ್ರಾಯ್ವಾರ್ ಲೈಸನ್ಸ್
draay·waar *laay*·sans
drug (illicit) ಚರಸ್ ಗಾಂಜಾ *cha*·ras *gaan*·jaa

E

ear ಕಾನ್ kaan
east ಉದೆಂತ್ *u*·đenţ
eat ಖಾ k'aa
economy class ಇಕೊನೊಮಿ ಕ್ಲಾಸ್ i·*ko*·no·mi klaas
electricity ಎಲೆಕ್ಟ್ರಿಕ್ ಪವರ್ e·*lek*·trik *pa*·war
elevator ಲಿಫ್ಟ್ lift
email ಈಮೇಲ್ *ee*·mayl
embassy ಎಂಬೆಸಿ *em*·be·see
emergency ಎಮರ್ಜೆನ್ಸಿ e·*mar*·jen·si
English (language) ಇಂಗ್ಲಿಶ್ *ing*·leesh
entrance ಪ್ರವೇಶನ್ *pra*·way·shan
evening ಸಾಂಝ್ saanz
exit n ಭಾಯ್ರ್ ವೆಚೆಂ ದಾರ್ b'aayr *we*·cheng đaar
expensive ಮ್ಹಾರಗ್ *m'aa*·reūg
eye ದೊಳೊ *đo*·ļo

F

far ಪೈಸ್ *peū*·is
fast ವೆಗಿಂಚ್ *we*·gins
father ಬಾಪೈ *baa*·pai
film (camera) ಫಿಲ್ಮ್ film
finger ಬೊಟ್ bot
first-aid kit ಫಸ್ಟ್ ಏಡ್ ಕಿಟ್ farst ayd kit
first class ಪಯ್ಲಿ ಕ್ಲಾಸ್ *peūy*·li klaas
fish n ಮಾಸ್ಳಿ *mas*·ļi
food ಜೆವಾಣ್ *je*·waaņ
foot ಪಾಯ್ paay
free (of charge) ಫುಂಕ್ಯಾಕ್ *fun*·ki·aak
friend ಈಶ್ಟ್ eesht
fruit ಫಳ್ faļ
full ಭರ್ನ್ b'eūrn

G

gift ಇನಾಮ್ *i*·naam
girl ಚೆಡುಂ *che*·dung
glass (drinking) ಗ್ಲಾಸ್ glaas
glasses ವಕ್ಲ್ weūkl
go ವಸ್ weūts'
good ಬರೆಂ *beū*·reng
guide n ಗಾಯ್ಡ್ gaayd

H

half n ಅರ್ಧೆಂ *eūr*·đeng
hand ಹಾತ್ haaţ
happy ಖುಶಿ *k'u*·shi
have ಆಸಾ *aa*·saa
he ತೊ ţo
head n ತಕ್ಲಿ *ţeūk*·li
heart ಉಂಡ್ oond
heavy ಝಡ್ zeūd
help v ಕುಮಕ್ *ku*·meūk
here ಹಾಂಗಾ *haang'*·aa
high ವೈರ್ *weū*·ir
highway ಹೈವೇ *haay*·way
hike v ಹಾಯ್ಕ್ haayk
holiday ಸುಟಿ *su*·ti
hospital ಆಸ್ಪತ್ರ್ *aas*·peūţr
hot ಹುನ್ hun
hotel ಹೊಟೆಲ್ *ho*·tel
hungry ಭುಕ್ ಲಾಗ್ಲ್ಯಾ b'uk *laag*·lyaa
husband ಘೊವ್ g'ow

I

I ಹಾಂವ್ಂ *haang*·ung
identification (card) ಆಯ್ ಡೀ ಕಾರ್ಡ್ aay dee kaard
ill ಪಿಡಾ *pee*·daa
important ಘರ್ಜೆಚೆಂ *g'eūr*·je·cheng
injury ಮಾರ್ ಝಾಲಾ maar *zaa*·laa
insurance ಇನ್ಶುರೆನ್ಸ್ in·*shu*·rens
internet ಇನ್ಟರ್ನೆಟ್ *in*·tar·net
interpreter ಭಾಶಾಂತರ್ ಕರ್ಪಿ *b'aa*·shaan·ţar *keūr*·pi

J

job ಕಾಮ್ kaam

K

key ಚಾವಿ *ts'aa*·wi
kilogram ಕಿಲೊ *ki*·lo

kitchen ರಾಂದ್ಚೆಂ ಕೂಡ್ *raand*·cheng kood
knife ಸುರಿ *su*·ri

L

lawyer ವಕೀಲ್ *wa*·keel
left (direction) ದಾವ್ಯಾಕ್ *đaa*·wyaak
leg (body) ಪಾಯ್ paay
less ಉಣೆಂ *u*·ṇeng
letter (mail) ಪತ್ರ್ peüţr
light n ದಿವೊ *đi*·wo
like v ತಶೆಂ *ţeü*·sheng
lock n ಬೀಗ್ beeg
long ಲಾಂಬ್ laamb
lost ಹೊಗ್ಡಾಯ್ಲಾಂ *hog*·daay·laang
love v ಮೋಗ್ ಕರ್ mohg keür
luggage ಲಗೇಜ್ *la*·gayj
lunch ದೊನ್ಪಾಂರಾಂಚೆಂ ಜೆವಾಣ್ *saan*·je·cheng *je*·waaṇ

M

mail n ಟಪ್ಪಾಲ್ *tap*·paal
man ಮನಿಸ್ *meü*·nees
map ಮೇಪ್ maep
market ಸಾಂತ್ saanţ
meat ಮಾಸ್ maas
medicine ವಕಾತ್ *wo*·kaaţ
message ಖಬಾರ್ *k'eu*·baar
milk ದೂಧ್ đoođ
minute ಮಿನಿಟ್ *mi*·nit
mobile phone ಮೊಬಾಯ್ಲ್ ಫೊನ್ *mo*·bail fon
money ಪೈಶೆ *peuy*·she
month ಮಹಿನೊ *meuy*·no
morning ಸಕಾಳಿಂ sa·*kaa*·ḷing
mother ಆವೈ *aa*·wai
motorcycle ಮೊಟರ್ ಸಾಯ್ಕಲ್ *mo*·tar *saay*·kal
mouth ತೊಂಡ್ ţond

N

name ನಾಂವ್ಂ *naang*·ung
near ಲಾಗಿಂ *laa*·ging
neck n ಗೊಮ್ಟಿ *gom*·ti
new ನವೆಂ *neü*·weng
newspaper ದಿಸಾಳೆಂ *đi*·saa·ḷeng
night ರಾತ್ raaţ
no ನಾಂ naang
noisy ಗೌಜಿ ಆಸೊನ್ *gow*·ji *aa*·son
nonsmoking ಧೂಮ್ರಪಾನ್ ನಾ ಆಸುಲ್ಲೊ
đ'oom·ra·paan naa *aa*·sul·lo
north ಬಡ್ಗಾ *beüd*·gaa
nose ನಾಕ್ naak
now ಆತಾಂ *aa*·ţaang
number ನಂಬರ್ *nam*·bar

O

old ಪರ್ನೆಂ *peür*·neng
one-way ticket ವಚೊಂಕ್ ಮಾತ್ರ್ ಟಿಕೇಟ್
wo·ts'onk maaţr *ti*·kayt
open a ಉಗ್ತೆಂ *ug*·ţeng
outside ಭಾಯ್ರ್ b'aayr

P

passport ಪಾಸ್ಪೋರ್ಟ್ *paas*·port
pay v ಪೈಶೆ ದೀ *peuy*·she đee
pharmacy ವಕ್ತಾಚೆಂ ಶೊಪ್ *wak*·ţaang·cheng shop
phonecard ಫೊನ್ ಕಾರ್ಡ್ fon kaard
photo ಫೊಟೊ *fo*·to
police ಪೊಲಿಸ್ *po*·lis
postcard ಪೊಸ್ಟ್–ಕಾರ್ಡ್ *post*·kaard
post office ಪೊಸ್ಟ್ ಒಫೀಸ್ post *o*·fis
pregnant ಗುರ್ವಾರ್ *gur*·waar
price n ಖರ್ಚ್ k'eurs

Q

quiet a ವೊಗೆತ್ *wo*·geţ

R

rain n ಪಾವ್ಸ್ *paa*·us
razor ವಾಕೊರ್ *waa*·kor
receipt n ಬಿಲ್ಲ್ bil
refund n ರಿಫಂಡ್ *ri*·fand
registered mail ರಜಿಸ್ತ್ರ್ ಟಪ್ಪಾಲ್ *reü*·jeesţr *tap*·paal
rent v ಭಾಡೆಂ *b'aa*·deng
repair v ರಿಪೆರ್ *ri*·payr
reservation ರಿಸರ್ವೇಶನ್ ri·ser·*way*·shan
restaurant ರೆಸ್ಟೊರೆಂಟ್ *res*·to·rent
return v ಪಾಟಿಂ ಧೀ *paa*·ting đee
return ticket ವಚೊಂಕ್ ಆನಿಂ ಪಾಟೀಂ ಯೇಂವ್ಕ್
wo·ts'onk aa·ning paa·ting ayng·wuk *ti*·kayt
right (direction) ಉಜ್ವ್ಯಾಕ್ *uz*·wyaak
road ರಸ್ತೊ *reü*·sţo
room n ರೂಮ್ room

S

safe a ಭದ್ರತಿ *b'eu*·dra·ţee
sanitary napkin ಸೆನಿಟರಿ ನೆಪ್ಕಿನ್ *se*·ni·ta·ri *nep*·kin
seat n ಸೀಟ್ seet
send ಧಾಡ್ đaad
sex ಸಂಭೋಗ್ *sam*·b'og
shampoo ಶಾಂಪೂ *shaang*·poo
she ತೆಂ ţeng

sheet (bed) ವ್ಹೋಲ್ wohl
shirt ಕೊಮಿಸ್ *ko*·mis
shoes ಮೊಚೆ *mo*·che
shop n ಶೊಪ್ shop
short ಮಟ್ವೆಂ *meūt*·weng
shower n ನಾಣಿ *naa*·ṇi
single room ಸಿಂಗಲ್ ರೂಮ್ *sin*·gal room
skin n ಕಾತ್ kaaţ
skirt n ಗಾಗ್ರೊ *gaa*·gro
sleep v ನಿದೆ *ni*·đe
slowly ಸವ್ಕಾಸ್ *seu*·u·kaas
small ಲ್ಹಾನ್ laan
soap ಸಾಬು *saa*·bu
some ಥೊಡೆ *ţo*·de
soon ವೆಗಿಂ *we*·ging
south ತೆಣ್ಕಾ *ţeṇ*·kaa
souvenir shop ಸುವ್ನೆರ್ ಶೊಪ್ *suw*·neer shop
stamp ಸ್ಟೇಂಪ್ staemp
station (train) ಸ್ಟೇಶನ್ *stay*·shan
stomach ಪೊಟ್ pot
stop v ರಾವ್ rōw
stop (bus) n ರಾಂವ್ಸೊ ಜ಼ಾಗೊ *raang*·u·so *zaa*·go
street ರಸ್ತೊ *reū*·sţo
student ವಿದ್ಯಾರ್ಥಿ *wiđ*·yaar·ţi
sun ಸುರ್ಯೊ *sur*·yo
sunscreen ಸನ್–ಸ್ಕ್ರೀನ್ san skreen
swim v ಉಪ್ಯೇ *up*·yay

T

tampons ಟೇಂಪೊನ್ *taym*·pon
teeth ದಾಂತ್ đaanţ
telephone n ಫೊನ್ fon
temperature (weather) ಹವೊ *ha*·wo
that (one) ತೆಂ ţeng
they ತಿಂ ţing
thirsty ತಾನ್ ಲಾಗ್ಲ್ಯಾ ţaan *laag*·lyaa
this (one) ಹೆಂ heng
throat ಗಳೊ *geū*·ḷo
ticket ಟಿಕೇಟ್ *ti*·kayt
time ವೇಳ್ wayḷ
tired ಪುರಾಸಾಣ್ ಜ಼ಾಲ್ಯಾ *pu*·raa·saṇ *zaa*·lyaa
tissues ಪೇಪರಾಚೆ ತುವಾಲೆ *pay*·pa·ra·che *ţu*·wa·le
today ಆಜ಼್ aaz
toilet ಟೊಯ್ಲೆಟ್ *toy*·let
tomorrow ಫಾಲ್ಯಾಂ *faal*·yaang
tonight ಆಜ಼್ ರಾತಿಂ aaz *raa*·ţing
toothbrush ದಾಂತಾಂಚೆಂ ಬ್ರಶ್
đaan·ţaang·cheng brash
toothpaste ದಾಂತಾಂಚೊ ಪೇಸ್ಟ್
đaan·ţaang·ts'o payst
torch (flashlight) ಟೊರ್ಚ್ torch
tour n ಟೂರ್ toor
tourist office ಟೂರಿಸ್ಟ್ ಒಫ್ಫೀಸ್ *too*·rist *o*·fis
towel ತುವಾಲೊ *ţu*·waa·lo
train n ರೈಲ್ reuyl
translate ಭಾಶಾಂತರ್ ಕರ್ *b'aa*·shaan·ţar keūr
travel agency ಟ್ರಾವೆಲ್ ಏಜನ್ಸೀ *traa*·wel *ay*·jen·si
travellers cheque ಟ್ರಾವೆಲರ್ಸ್ ಚೆಕ್
traa·we·lars chek
trousers ಪೇಂಟ್ paent

U

underwear ಭಿತರ್ಲಿಂ ವಸ್ತುರಾಂ
b'i·ţar·ling *wos*·ţu·raang
urgent ತುರ್ತಾನ್ *ţur*·ţaan

V

vacant ಖಾಲಿ ಆಸಾ *k'aa*·li *aa*·saa
vegetable n ತರ್ಕಾರಿ *ţar*·kaa·ri
vegetarian a ಸಸ್ಯಾಹಾರಿ *sa*·syaa·haa·ri
visa ವೀಜ಼ಾ *wee*·zaa

W

walk v ಚಲ್ seūl
wash (something) ಧು đoo
watch n ಘಡಿಯಾಳ್ *g'a*·di·yaaḷ
water n ಉದಾಕ್ *u*·đaak
we ಆಮಿಂ *aa*·ming
weekend ಸನ್ವಾರಾ ಆಯ್ತಾರಾ
seun·waa·raa *aay*·ţaa·raa
west ಅಸ್ತಮ್ತಿಂ *as*·ţam·ţing
wheelchair ವೀಲ್ ಚೇರ್ weel chayr
when ಕೆದಾಳಾ *ke*·đaa·ḷaa
where ಖೈಂ *k'eu*·ing
who ಕೋಣ್ kohṇ
why ಕಿತ್ಯಾಕ್ *kiţ*·yaak
wife ಬಾಯ್ಲ್ baayl
window ಜ಼ನೆಲ್ *zeū*·nel
with ಸಾಂಗಾತಾ *saang'*·aa·ţaa
without ನಾಸ್ತಾನಾ *naas*·ţaa·naa
woman ಬಾಯ್ಲ್ ಮನಿಸ್ baayl *meū*·nees
write ಬರೈ *beū*·reūy

Y

yes ವ್ಹಯ್ *w'eu*·i
yesterday ಕಾಲ್ kaal
you sg/pl ತುಂ/ತುಮಿಂ ţung/*ţu*·ming

Malayalam

alphabet

vowels				
അ a	ആ aa	ഇ i	ഈ ee	ഉ u
ഊ oo	എ e	ഏ ey	ഐ ai	ഒ o
ഔ ow	അം um	അഃ ah	ഓ aw	

consonants				
ക ka	ഖ k'a	ഗ ga	ഘ g'a	ങ nga
ച cha	ഛ ch'a	ജ ja	ത്ധ j'a	ഞ nya
ട ta	ഠ t'a	ഡ da	ഢ d'a	ണ ṇa
ത ţa	ഥ ţ'a	ദ đa	ധ đ'a	ന na
പ pa	ഫ fa	ബ ba	ഭ b'a	മ ma
യ ya	ര ra	ല la	വ va	ശ sh'a
ഷ sha	സ şa	ഹ ha	ള ḷa	ഴ zha
റ ṛa	റ്റ ta	ഷ്പ p'a	സ് sa	

MALAYALAM

മലയാളം

introduction

Malayalam (ma·la·ya·*lam* മലയാളം) is a Dravidian language related to Tamil, in which its name is purported to mean 'language of the mountain region'. It has around 33 million speakers, primarily in the Indian state of Kerala. Malayalam is written in the curly Malayalam script, used in this chapter, and occasionally in the Arabic script. This language is the source of the English words 'copra' (dried coconut), from the Malayalam kop·*pa*·ra കൊപ്പറ, and 'teak' (brown colour), from the Malayalam tek·*ka* തേക്ക്. Other culturally significant Malayalam terms include mun·*tu* മുണ്ട്, the local white- or cream-coloured version of the ubiquitous Indian *dhoti* (loincloth), and ka·la·*rip*·pa·jat·*t'i* കളരിപ്പയറ്റ്, a local form of martial arts. A huge 40% of Malayalam vocabulary can be traced back to borrowings from Sanskrit. The language is rapidly moving into modern times, with influence from English and the coining of new terms, such as a·*di*·po·*li* അടിപൊളി, equivalent to 'awesome' or 'wow' in English. So give the following words and phrases a try – they're totally, like, *adipoli*!

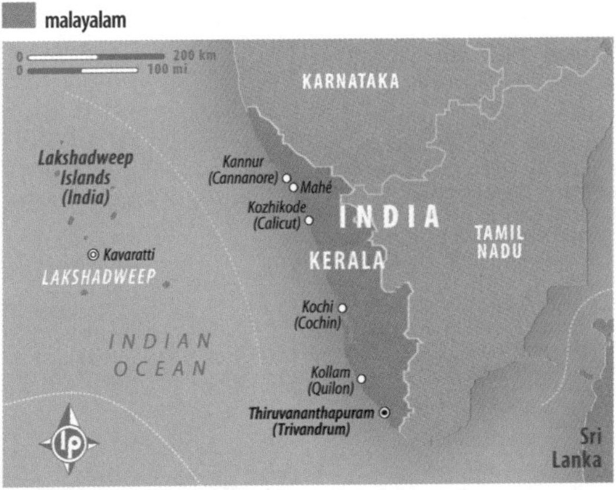

pronunciation

Vowels	
Symbol	**English sound**
a	run
aa	father
ai	aisle
aw	law
e	bet
ee	see
ey	as in 'bet', but longer
i	hit
o	pot
oo	zoo
ow	now
u	put

In this chapter, the Malayalam pronunciation is given in orange after each phrase.

Aspirated consonants (pronounced with a puff of air after the sound) are represented with an apostrophe after the letter – b', ch', d', đ', g', j', k', p', t' and ţ'. Retroflex consonants (pronounced with the tongue bent backwards) are included in this table.

Each syllable is separated by a dot, and the syllable stressed in each word is italicised. For example:

ദയവായി. đa·ya·va·*yi*

Consonants	
Symbol	**English sound**
b	bed
ch	cheat
d	dog
đ	retroflex d
f	fun
g	go
h	hat
j	jar
k	kit
l	lot
ļ	retroflex l
m	man
n	not
ņ	retroflex n
ng	ring
ny	canyon
p	pet
r	rose
ŗ	retroflex r
s	sun
ş	retroflex s
sh	shot
t	top
ţ	retroflex t
v	very
w	win
y	yes
zh	measure

essentials

Yes./No.	അതെ./അല്ല.	a·t'e/al·la
Please.	ദയവായി.	đa·ya·va·yi
Thank you.	നന്ദി.	nan·n'i
Excuse me. (to get past)	ക്ഷമിക്കണം.	ksha·mi·ka·nam
Excuse me. (to get attention)	ക്ഷമിക്കണം.	ksha·mi·ka·nam
Sorry.	ക്ഷമിക്കുക.	ksha·mi·ku·ka

language difficulties

Do you speak English?
നിങ്ങൾ ഇംഗ്ലീഷ് സംസാരിക്കുമോ? ning·al in·glish şam·saa·ri·ku·mo

Do you understand?
നിങ്ങൾക്ക് മനസ്സിലാകുന്നുണ്ടോ? ning·al·ku ma·na·şi·la·ku·nun·do

I understand.
എനിക്ക് മനസ്സിലാകും. e·ni·ku ma·na·şi·la·kum

I don't understand.
എനിക്ക് മനസ്സിലാകില്ല. e·ni·ku ma·na·şi·la·ki·la

Could you please ...?	നിങ്ങൾ ദയവായി ...?	ning·al đ'a·ya·va·yi ...
repeat that	അത് ആവർത്തിക്കൂ	a·t'u aa·var·t'i·koo
speak more slowly	കുറച്ചു കൂടി വേഗത കുറച്ച് സംസാരിക്കൂ	ku·ra·chu koo·di ve·ga·t'a ku·ra·chu şam·saa·ri·koo

numbers

0	പൂജ്യം	poo·jyam	20	ഇരുപത്	i·ru·pa·t'a
1	ഒന്ന്	on·na	30	മുപ്പത്	mu·p'a·t'a
2	രണ്ട്	ran·d'a	40	നാൽപത്	naal·pa·t'a
3	മൂന്ന്	moo·na	50	അമ്പത്	an·ba·t'a
4	നാല്	naa·la	60	അറുപത്	a·ru·pa·t'a
5	അഞ്ച്	an·ja	70	എഴുപത്	e·zhu·pa·t'a
6	ആറ്	aa·ra	80	എൺപത്	en·pa·t'a
7	ഏഴ്	e·zha	90	തൊണ്ണൂറ്	t'on·noo·ra
8	എട്ട്	e·t'a	100	നൂറ്	n'oo·ra
9	ഒമ്പത്	on·pa·t'a	1000	ആയിരം	aa·ye·ram
10	പത്ത്	pa·t'a	1,000,000	പത്തു ലക്ഷം	pa·t'u lak·sham

time & dates

What time is it?	സമയം എന്തായി?	ṣa·ma·*yam* en·*t'a*·yi
It's (two) o'clock.	(രണ്ടു) മണിയായി.	(*ran*·d'u) ma·ni·ya·*yi*
Quarter past (two).	(രണ്ടേ) കാലായി.	(ran·*d'e*) *kaa*·la·yi
Half past (two).	(രണ്ടര) ആയി.	(ran·d'a·*ra*) aa·*yi*
Quarter to (three).	(രണ്ടേ) മുക്കാലായി. (lit: (two) and-three-quarters)	(ran·*d'e*) mu·*k'aa*·la·yi
At what time ...?	എത്ര മണിക്ക് ...?	et'·*ra* ma·*ni*·ka ...
At ...	... മണിക്ക്.	... ma·*ni*·ka
It's (15 December).	അത് (ഡിസംബർ പതിനഞ്ച്) ആണ്.	a·*t'u* (de·*sem*·bar pa·ţi·nan·*ja*) aa·*na*

yesterday	ഇന്നലെ	in·na·*le*
today	ഇന്ന്	in·*na*
tomorrow	നാളെ	*naa*·l'ey

Monday	തിങ്കൾ	*t'in*·kal
Tuesday	ചൊവ്വ	cho·*wa*
Wednesday	ബുധൻ	b'u·*d'an*
Thursday	വ്യാഴം	vya·*zham*
Friday	വെള്ളി	ve·*l'i*
Saturday	ശനി	sha·*ni*
Sunday	ഞായർ	*nyaa*·yar

border crossing

I'm here ...	ഞാൻ ഇവിടെ ...	nyan i·*vi*·te ...
in transit	യാത്രയിലാണ്	yaa·t'ra·*yi*·laa·na
on business	ബിസിനസിലാണ്	be·*se*·na·si·laa·na
on holiday	അവധിക്കാലം ചെലവഴിക്കുന്നു	a·va·*d'i*·kaa·lam che·la·va·*zhe*·k'u·nu

I'm here for ...	ഞാൻ ഇവിടെ വന്നത് ...	nyan i·*vi*·te van·*na*·t'a ...
(10) days	(പത്ത്) ദിവസം	(*pa*·t'a) đi·va·*sam*
(three) weeks	(മൂന്ന്) ആഴ്ച	(moo·*na*) aazh·*cha*
(two) months	(രണ്ട്) മാസം	(ran·*d'u*) ma·*sam*

I'm going to (Kochi).

ഞാൻ (ഒകാചചിക്ക്) പോകുന്നു. nyan (ko·chi·*k'ye*) *po*·ku·na

I'm staying at the (Taj Malabar).
ഞാൻ (താജ് മലബാറിൽ) തങ്ങുന്നു. nyan (taj ma·la·*baa*·ril) t'ang·un·*nu*

I have nothing to declare.
എനിക്കൊന്നും പ്രഖ്യാപിക്കുവാനില്ല. e·ni·ko·*num* pra·*g'ya*·pi·ku·*va*·ni·la

I have this to declare.
എനിക്കിത് പ്രഖ്യാപിക്കുവാനുണ്ട്. e·ni·ki·*t'a* pra·*g'ya*·pi·ku·*va*·nun·da

That's mine.
അത് എൻേറതാണ്. a·*t'u* en·tey·*t'a*·na

That's not mine.
അത് എന്റേതല്ല. a·*t'u* en·tey·t'a·*la*

tickets & luggage

Where can I buy a ticket?
എനിക്ക് എവിടെ നിന്നാണ് ഒരു ടിക്കറ്റ് വാങ്ങുവാൻ സാധിക്കുക? e·ni·*ku* e·vi·*tey* nin·*na*·nu o·*ru* ti·*ka*·tu *vang*·u·van *şaa*·d'i·ku·ka

Do I need to book a seat?
ഞാൻ ഒരു ഇരിപ്പിടം ബുക്ക് ചെയ്യേണ്ടതുണ്ടോ? nyan o·*ru* i·ri·pi·*tam* *bu*·ka chey·yen·*ta*·t'un·to

One … ticket (to Kochi), please.	(കൊച്ചിക്ക്) … ഒരു ടിക്കറ്റ്, ദയവായി തരൂ.	(ko·chi·*k'ye*) … o·*ru* ti·*ka*·tu đ'a·ya·va·*yi* t'a·*roo*
one-way	ഒരു വശത്തേക്കുള്ള	o·*ru* va·sha·*t'e*·ku·la
return	മടങ്ങാനുള്ള	ma·*tang*·a·nu·*la*

I'd like to … my ticket, please.	ദയവായി എൻെറ ടിക്കറ്റ് ഒന്ന് …	đ'a·ya·va·*yi* en·*te* ti·*ka*·tu on·*nu* …
cancel	റദ്ദ് ചെയ്യണം	ra·*d'u* che·*ya*·nam
change	മാറ്റണം	maa·*ta*·nam
collect	വാങ്ങിക്കൊണ്ടുവരണം	van·*gi*·kon·*tu*·va·ra·nam

Is there a toilet/air conditioning?
അവിടെ കക്കൂസ്/ എയർകണ്ടീഷൻ ഉണ്ടോ? a·vi·*de* ka·*koos*/ e·yar·kan·di·*shan* un·*to*

How long does the trip take?
എത്ര നേരം ഉണ്ടാകും ഈ യാത്ര? et'·*ra* ney·*ram* un·ta·*kum* ee ya·*tra*

Is it a direct route?
നേരിട്ടുള്ള വഴിയിലൂടെയാണോ ഇത്? ney·ri·*tul*·la va·zhi·yi·*loo*·te·yaa·no i·*t'u*

My luggage has been …	എന്റെ ലഗേജ് …	en·*te* la·*geyj* …
damaged	കേടായി	ke·ta·*yi*
lost	നഷ്ടപ്പെട്ടു	nash·*ta*·pe·tu
stolen	കളവുപോയി	ka·la·*vu*·po·*yi*

transport

Where does flight (AI 137) arrive/depart?
എപ്പോഴാണ് ഐസി (ഏഐ ഒന്ന് മൂന്ന് ഏഴ്) വിമാനം എത്തുന്നത്/പുറപ്പെടുന്നത്?
e·*po*·zha·*nu* (ey ai *on*·na *moo*·na e·zha) *vi*·ma·nam e·*tu*·na·*tu*/pu·*ra*·pe·*du*·na·t'u

Is this the … to (Kochi)?	ഈ … (കൊച്ചിക്ക്) പോകുന്ന താണോ?	ee … (ko·chi·*k'ye*) po·ku·*na*·t'aa·no
boat	ബോട്ട്	bot
bus	ബസ്	ba·*sa*
plane	വിമാനം	vi·maa·*nam*
train	ട്രെയിൻ	tre·*yin*

What time's the … bus?	എത്ര മണിക്കാണ് … ബസ് പുറപ്പെടുന്നത്?	et'·*ra* ma·ni·*ka*·nu … ba·*sa* pu·ra·*pe*·du·na·*t'u*
first	ആദ്യം	aa·*đ'yam*
last	അവസാനം	a·va·*saa*·nam
next	അടുത്ത	a·du·*t'a*

How long will it be delayed?
എത്ര നേരം ഇത് താമസിക്കും?
et'·*ra ne*·ram i·*tu ta*·ma·si·kum

Please tell me when we get to (the zoo).
നമ്മൾ എപ്പോഴാണ് (മൃഗശാലയിൽ) എത്തുന്നതെന്ന് ദയവായി പറയുമോ?
nam·*mal* e·po·*zha*·nu (me·ru·ga·*shaa*·la·*yil*) e·tu·*na*·te·nu đ'a·ya·va·*yi* pa·ra·ya·*mo*

That's my seat.
അതെന്റെ ഇരിപ്പിടം ആണ്.
a·ten·*te* i·ri·pi·*tam* aa·*na*

I'd like a taxi …	… ഒരു ടാക്സി കിട്ടിയാൽ കൊള്ളാം.	… o·*ru* tak'·*si* ki·*ti*·yaal ko·*lam*
at (9am)	(രാവിലെ ഒമ്പത്) മണിക്ക്	(raa·vi·*ley on*·pa·t'a) ma·ni·*ku*
now	ഇപ്പോൾ	i·*pol*

How much is it to (the zoo)?

(മൃഗശാലയിലേക്ക്) എത്രയാവും? | (me·ru·ga·*shaa*·la·yi·le·*ku*) et'·ra·ya·*vum*

Please put the meter on.

ദയവായി മീറ്റർ ഇടൂ. | đ'a·ya·vaa·*yi mee*·ter i·*doo*

Please take me to (this address).

എന്നെ (ഈ വിലാസത്തിൽ) ദയവായി കൊണ്ടുപോകൂ. | e·*ne* (ee vi·laa·sat·*t'il*) đ'a·ya·va·*yi* kon·*du*·po·*ku*

Please stop/wait here.

ദയവായി ഇവിടെ നിർത്തൂ/കാത്തു. | đ'a·ya·va·*yi* i·vi·*de* kaa·*t'u*/nil·*ku*

I'd like to hire a car/4WD (with a driver).

ഒരു കാർ/4ഡബ്ല്യുഡി വാടകയ്ക്കെടുക്കണമെന്നുണ്ട് (ഡ്രൈവർ സഹിതം). | o·*ru* kaar/for·weel·*draiv* vaa·da·ka·*ke*·tu·*ka*·na·me·*nun*·tu (*drai*·ver şa·*hi*·t'am)

How much for daily/weekly hire?

എത്രയാണ് ദിവസ/ആഴ്ച വാടക? | et'·ra·ya·*nu* đ'i·va·*sa*/aazh·*cha* va·ta·*ka*

directions

Where's the ...?	എവിടെയാണ് ...?	e·vi·*te*·ya·*nu* ...
bank	ബാങ്ക്	baank
foreign currency exchange	വിദേശ നാണയ എക്സ്ചേഞ്ച്	vi·đe·*sha* naa·*n'a*·ya eks·cheyn·*ju*
post office	തപാൽ ഓഫീസ്	t'a·*paal* o·*fees*

Is this the road to (Kochi)?

ഈ റോഡ് (കൊച്ചിക്ക്)? | ee raw·*du* (ko·*chik*) *aa*·no

Can you show me (on the map)?

എനിക്കത് (ഭൂപടത്തിൽ) കാട്ടിത്തരുമോ? | e·ni·ka·*t'u* (b'oo·pa·ta·*t'il*) kaa·*t'i*·t'a·ru·*mo*

What's the address?

വിലാസം എന്താണ്? | vi·laa·*sam* en·t'a·*na*

How far is it?

എത്ര ദൂരമുണ്ട് അവിടേക്ക്? | et'·*ra* đ'oo·*ra*·mun·*ta* a·vi·te·*ku*

How do I get there?

എനിക്കെങ്ങനെ അവിടെ എത്താൻ കഴിയും? | e·ni·keng·a·*ney* a·vi·*te* e·*t'an* ka·zhi·*yum*

Turn left/right.

ഇടത്തേക്ക്/വലത്തേക്ക് തിരിയുക. | i·ta·*t'ey*·ku/va·la·*t'ey*·ku t'i·ri·yu·*ka*

It's …	അത് …	a·*t'u* …
behind …	… ന്റെ പിന്നിലാണ്	… nte pi·*ni*·laa·nu
in front of …	… ന്റെ മുന്നിലാണ്	… nte mu·*ni*·laa·nu
near (to …)	… (ന്റെ) അടുത്താണ്	… (nte) a·tu·t'aa·*nu*
on the corner	മൂലയിലാണ്	moo·*la*·yi·laa·*nu*
opposite …	… ന്റെ എതിർ വശത്താണ്	… nte e·*t'ir*·va·sha·t'a·*nu*
straight ahead	നേരെ മുന്നിൽ	ney·*re* mu·*nil*
there	അവിടെ	a·vi·*de*

accommodation

Where's a guesthouse/hotel nearby?
അടുത്ത് എവിടെയാണ് അതിഥിമന്ദിരം/ഹോട്ടൽ ഉള്ളത്?
a·tu·*t'u* e·vi·*te*·yaa·*nu* a·t'i·*d'i*·man·d'i·*ram*/ho·*tal* u·la·*t'u*

Can you recommend somewhere cheap/good?
ചെലവു കുറഞ്ഞ/നല്ല ഇടം താങ്കൾക്ക് അറിയാമോ?
chi·la·*vu* ku·ran·*ja*/nal·*la* i·*dam* t'ang·al·*ku* a·ri·yaa·*mo*

I'd like to book a room, please.
എനിക്ക് ഒരു മുറി ബുക്ക് ചെയ്യണം.
e·ni·*ku* o·*ru* mu·*ṛi* bu·*ku* che·*ya*·nam

I have a reservation.
എനിക്ക് റിസർവേഷൻ ഉണ്ട്.
e·ni·*ku* re·ser·va·*shan* un·*tu*

Do you have a … room?	ഇവിടെ … റൂം ഒഴിവുണ്ടോ?	i·vi·*te* … room o·zhi·vun·*to*
single	സിംഗിൾ	şing·*il*
double	ഡബിൾ	da·*bil*
twin	ട്വിൻ	t'vin

How much is it per night/person?
ഒരു രാത്രിക്ക്/വ്യക്തിക്ക് എത്രയാണ്?
o·*ru* raa·*t'ri*·ku/vyak·t'i·*ku* et'·ra·yaa·*nu*

I'd like to stay for (two) nights.
എനിക്ക് (രണ്ട്) രാത്രികൾ തങ്ങണം.
e·ni·*ku* (ran·*d'u*) raa·t'ri·*kal* t'an·g'a·*nam*

Can I have my key, please?
ദയവായി എന്റെ താക്കോൽ തരുമോ?
d'a·ya·vaa·*yi* en·*te* t'a·*kol* t'a·ru·*mo*

Can I get another (blanket)?
എനിക്ക് മറ്റൊരു (കരിമ്പടം) കൂടി തരുമോ?
e·ni·*ku* ma·to·*ru* (ka·rim·pa·*dam*) koo·*de* t'a·ru·*mo*

The (air conditioning) doesn't work.
(എയർകണ്ടീഷനിങ്) പ്രവർത്തിക്കുന്നില്ല. — (e·yar·kan·di·sha·*ning*) pra·var·*t'i*·ku·ni·*la*

Is there an elevator/a safe?
അവിടെ എലിവേറ്റർ/ സെയ്ഫ് ഉണ്ടോ? — a·vi·*te* e·li·vai·*t'ar*/ şeyf un·*to*

What time is checkout?
ചെക്ക്ഔട്ട് ചെയ്യേണ്ട സമയം ഏതാണ്? — che·kow·*tu* che·yen·*ta* şa·ma·*yam* ey·t'a·*nu*

Can I have my …, please?	ദയവായി എനിക്കെന്റെ …, തരുമോ?	đ'a·ya·va·*yi* eni·ken·*te* … t'a·ru·*mo*
deposit	ഡിപ്പോസിറ്റ്	de·po·*sit*
passport	പാസ്പോർട്ട്	pas·*port*

banking & communications

Where's an ATM/a public phone?
എവിടെയാണ് എടിഎം/ പബ്ലിക് ഫോൺ? — e·vi·de·yaa·*nu* ey·tee·*yam*/ pub·*lik* fon

I'd like to …	എനിക്ക് …	e·ni·*ku* …
arrange a transfer	പണം ട്രാൻസ്ഫർ ചെയ്യണമായിരുന്നു	pa·*nam* trans·*far* che·*ya*·na·maa·*yi*·ru·*nu*
change a travellers cheque	ഒരു ട്രാവലേഴ്സ് ചെക്ക് മാറ്റണമായിരുന്നു	o·*ru* tra·ve·ler·*su* chek maa·ta·*na*·maa·yi·ru·*nu*
change money	കറൻസി മാറ്റണമായിരുന്നു	ka·ran·*si* maa·ta·*na*·maa·yi·ru·*nu*
withdraw money	പണം പിൻവലിക്കണ-മായിരുന്നു	pa·*nam* pin·va·li·*ka*·na·maa·yi·ru·*nu*

What's the …?	എത്രയാണ് …?	et'·*ra*·yaa·*nu* …
charge for that	അതിനുള്ള നിരക്ക്	a·t'i·nu·*la* ni·ra·*ku*
exchange rate	എക്സ്ചേഞ്ച് നിരക്ക്	eks·chan·*ju* ni·ra·*ku*

Where's the local internet café?
എവിടെയാണ് ലോക്കൽ ഇന്റർനെറ്റ് കഫേ? — e·vi·te·yaa·*nu* lo·*kal* in·ter·*net* ka·*fey*

How much is it per hour?
മണിക്കൂറിന് എത്രയാണ് ചാർജ്? — ma·ni·koo·ri·*nu* et'·ra·yaa·*nu* char·*ja*

I'd like to …	എനിക്കൊരു …	e·ni·ko·*ru* …
get internet access	ഇന്റർനെറ്റ് ആക്സെസ് കിട്ടിയാൽ നന്നായിരുന്നു	in·ter·*net* ak·*ses* ki·ti·*yaal* na·naa·*yi*·ru·*nu*
use a printer/scanner	പ്രിന്റർ/സ്കാനർ ഉപയോഗിച്ചാൽ കൊള്ളാമായിരുന്നു	prin·*tar*/ska·*nar* u·pa·yo·gi·*chal* ko·*laa*·maa·yi·ru·*nu*

I'd like a …	എനിക്കൊരു … കിട്ടിയാൽ കൊള്ളാമായിരുന്നു.	e·ni·ko·*ru* … ki·*ti*·yaal ko·*la*·ma·yi·ru·*nu*
mobile/cell phone for hire	മൊബൈൽ ഫോൺ വാടകയ്ക്ക്	mo·*bail* fon vaa·ta·ka·*ku*
SIM card for your network	നിങ്ങളുടെ നെറ്റ്‌വർക്കിലേക്ക് ഒരു സിം കാർഡ്	ning·a·lu·*te* neyt·var·*ki*·ley·*ku* o·*ru* şim kard

What are the rates?
എത്രയാണ് നിരക്കുകൾ? — et'·*ra*·yaa·*nu* ni·ra·*ku*·kal

What's your phone number?
താങ്കളുടെ ഫോൺ നമ്പർ എത്രയാണ്? — t'ang·a·lu·*te* fon num·*bar* et'·*ra*·yaa·*nu*

The number is …
നമ്പർ … ആണ്. — num·*bar* … aa·*nu*

I'd like to buy a phonecard.
എനിക്ക് ഒരു ഫോൺ കാർഡ് വാങ്ങിയാൽ കൊള്ളാമായിരുന്നു. — e·ni·*ku* o·*ru* fon kard vaa·ngi·*yaal* ko·laa·ma·*yi*·ru·*nu*

I want to …	എനിക്ക് … വിളിക്കണം.	e·ni·*ku* … vi·li·ka·*nam*
call (Canada)	(കാനഡയിലേക്ക്)	(ka·na·da·yi·le·*ku*)
call collect	കളക്ടിലേക്ക്	ka·lak·ti·ley·*ku*

I want to send a fax/parcel.
എനിക്ക് ഒരു ഫാക്സ്/ പാഴ്സൽ അയക്കണം. — e·ni·*ku* o·*ru* faks/ par·*sel* a·ya·ka·*nam*

I want to buy a stamp/an envelope.
എനിക്ക് ഒരു സ്റ്റാമ്പ്/ കവർ വാങ്ങണം. — e·ni·*ku* o·*ru* stamp/ ka·*var* vaa·nga·*nam*

Please send it (to Australia).
ഇത് ദയവായി (ഓസ്ട്രേലിയയിലേക്ക്) അയക്കൂ. — i·*t'u* d'a·ya·va·*yi* (os·tra·li·*ya*·yi·le·*ku*) a·ya·*koo*

sightseeing

What time does it open/close?
എത്ര മണിക്ക് ഇത് തുറക്കും/അടയ്ക്കും? — e·*t'ra* ma·ni·*ku* i·t'u t'u·ra·*kum*/a·ta·*kum*

What's the admission charge?
പ്രവേശനത്തിന് എത്രയാണ് നിരക്ക്? — pra·ve·zha·na·*t'i*·nu et'·*ra*·yaa·*nu* ni·ra·*ku*

Is there a discount for students/children?
വിദ്യാർത്ഥികൾക്ക്/കുട്ടികൾക്ക് ഇളവുണ്ടോ? — vi·đ'yaar·t'i·kal·*ku*/ku·*ti*·kal·*ku* i·la·vun·*do*

I'd like to hire a guide.
എനിക്ക് വാടകയ്ക്ക് ഒരു വഴികാട്ടി വേണമായിരുന്നു. — e·ni·*ku* vaa·ta·ka·*ku* o·*ru* va·*zhi*·kaa·*ti* ve·na·*maa*·yi·ru·*nu*

I'd like a catalogue/map.
എനിക്ക് ഒരു കാറ്റലോഗ്/ ഭൂപടം വേണമായിരുന്നു. — e·ni·*ku* o·*ru* ka·ta·*log*/ b'oo·pa·*tam* ve·na·maa·yi·ru·*nu*

I'd like to see ...
എനിക്ക് ... കാണണമായിരുന്നു. — e·ni·*ku* ... kaa·na·*na*·maa·yi·ru·*nu*

What's that?
അതെന്താണ്? — a·t'en·t'aa·*nu*

Can I take a photo?
ഫോട്ടോ എടുക്കാമോ? — fo·*to* e·du·ka·*mo*

I'd like to go somewhere off the beaten track.
മറ്റ് പുതിയ എവിടേക്കെങ്കിലും പോകണമെന്നുണ്ട്. — ma·*tu* pu·t'i·*ya* e·vi·de·ke·ngi·*lum* po·ka·*na*·me·nun·*tu*

How long is the tour?
എത്ര ദൈർഘ്യമുണ്ട് ഈ പര്യടനത്തിന്? — et'·*ra* đ'air·*g'ya*·mun·*tu* ee pa·rya·ta·*na*·t'i·na

When's the next tour?
അടുത്ത പര്യടനം എപ്പോഴാണ്? — a·tu·*t'a* pa·rya·ta·*nam* e·po·zha·*nu*

Is ... included?	... ഇതിൽപെടുമോ?	... i·*t'il* pe·tu·*mo*
accommodation	താമസം	*t'aa*·ma·sam
admission	പ്രവേശനം	pra·ve·sha·*nam*
food	ഭക്ഷണം	b'ak·sha·*nam*
transport	യാത്ര	yaa·*t'ra*

sightseeing		
fort	കോട്ട	ko·*ta*
mosque	പള്ളി	pal·*li*
palace	കൊട്ടാരം	ko·taa·*ram*
ruins	ജീർണാവശിഷ്ടങ്ങൾ	jeer·*naa*·va·shis·stang·*al*
temple	ക്ഷേത്രം	kshe·*t'ram*

shopping

Where's a … ?	എവിടെയാണ് …?	e·vi·de·yaa·*nu* …
camera shop	ക്യാമറാ ഷോപ്പ്	ka·me·*ra* shop
market	ചന്ത	chan·*d'a*
souvenir shop	സുവനീർ ഷോപ്പ്	ş̧u·va·*neer* shop

I'm looking for …
ഞാൻ തേടുന്നത് … — nyaan t'e·du·na·*t'u* …

Can I look at it?
ഞാൻ അത് നോക്കട്ടെ? — nyaan a·*t'u* no·ka·*te*

Can I have it sent overseas?
എനിക്ക് അത് വിദേശത്തേക്ക് അയക്കാമോ? — e·ni·*ku* a·*t'u* vi·đe·*sha*·t'e·*ku* a·ya·ka·*mo*

Can I have my (camera) repaired?
എന്റെ (ക്യാമറ) റിപ്പയർ ചെയ്തു തരുമോ? — en·*te* (ka·me·*ra)* ri·*per* chey·*t'u* t'a·ru·*mo*

It's faulty.
അത് കേടാണ്. — a·*t'u* ke·daa·*nu*

How much is it?
എത്രയാണ് ഇതിന്? — et'·ra·yaa·*nu* i·t'i·*nu*

Can you write down the price?
താങ്കൾക്ക് വിലയെഴുതി വയ്ക്കാമോ? — t'ang·al·*ku* vi·la·ye·zhu·*t'i* vey·*ka*·mo

That's too expensive.
ഇത് വളരെ വിലക്കൂടുതലാണ്. — i·*t'u* va·la·*re* vi·la·koo·du·*t'a*·laa·*nu*

I'll give you (300 rupees).
ഞാൻ നിങ്ങൾക്ക് (മൂന്ന് നൂറ് രൂപ) തരും. — nyaan ning·al·*ku* (*moo*·na *n'oo*·ra roo·*pa*) t'a·*rum*

There's a mistake in the bill.
ബില്ലിൽ തെറ്റുണ്ടല്ലോ. — bi·*lil* t'e·tun·da·*lo*

Do you accept ...?	താങ്കൾ ... സ്വീകരിക്കുമോ?	t'ang·*al* ... şwee·ka·ri·*ku*·mo
credit cards	ക്രെഡിറ്റ് കാർഡ്	kre·*dit* kard
debit cards	ഡെബിറ്റ് കാർഡ്	de·*bit* kard
travellers cheques	ട്രാവലേഴ്സ് ചെക്ക്	tra·ve·ler·*su* chek
I'd like (a) ..., please.	എനിക്ക് ..., വേണമായിരുന്നു.	e·ni·*ku* ... ve·na·*maa*·yi·ru·*nu*
bag	ഒരു ബാഗ്	o·*ru* bag
my change	എന്റെ ബാക്കി	en·*te* baa·*ki*
receipt	ഒരു രസീത്	o·*ru* ra·see·*t'u*
refund	പണം തിരികെ	pa·*nam* t'i·ri·*ke*
Less.	കുറച്ച്.	ku·ra·*chu*
Enough.	വേണ്ടത്ര.	ven·dat'·*ra*
More.	ധാരാളം.	d'a·raa·*lam*

photography

Can you develop this film?
താങ്കൾക്ക് ഈ ഫിലിം ഡെവലപ് ചെയ്യാനാകുമോ — t'ang·al·*ku* ee fi·*lim* de·va·*lap* che·*yaa*·na·ku·*mo*

I need a film for this camera.
ഈ ക്യാമറയ്ക്ക് എനിക്ക് ഫിലിം വേണം. — ee ka·me·rai·*ku* e·ni·*ka* fi·*lim* ve·*nam*

When will it be ready?
എപ്പോൾ ഇത് തയാറാകും? — e·pol i·*t'u* t'a·ya·raa·*kum*

making conversation

Hello./Goodbye.	ഹലോ./ഗുഡ് ബൈ.	ha·*lo*/good bai
Good night.	ഗുഡ് നൈറ്റ്.	good nait
Mr/Mrs	ശ്രീ/ശ്രീമതി	shree/shree·ma·*t'i*
Miss/Ms	കുമാരി	ku·*ma*·ri
How are you?	താങ്കൾക്ക് സുഖമാണോ?	t'ang·al·*ku* şu·*k'a*·maa·no
Fine, thanks.	അതെ, നന്ദി.	a·*t'e* nan·*d'i*
And you?	താങ്കൾക്കോ?	t'ang·al·*ko*

What's your name?	താങ്കളുടെ പേര് എന്താണ്?	t'ang·a·lu·*te* pey·*ru* en·t'aa·*nu*
My name is ...	എന്റെ പേര് ...	en·*te* pey·*ru* ...
I'm pleased to meet you.	താങ്കളെ കണ്ടതിൽ വളരെ സന്തോഷമുണ്ട്.	t'ang·a·*le* kan·ta·*t'il* va·la·*re* şan·t'o·*sha*·mun·*tu*

This is my ...	ഇതെന്റെ ...	i·t'en·*te* ...
brother	സഹോദരനാണ്	şa·ho·da·*ra*·naa·*nu*
daughter	മകളാണ്	ma·ka·laa·*nu*
father	അച്ഛനാണ്	a·*ch'a*·naa·nu
friend	സുഹൃത്താണ്	şuh·ru·t'aa·*nu*
husband	ഭർത്താവാണ്	b'ar·*t'aa*·vaa·*nu*
mother	അമ്മയാണ്	am·ma·yaa·*nu*
sister	സഹോദരിയാണ്	şa·ho·đa·*ri*·yaa·*nu*
son	മകനാണ്	ma·ka·*naa*·nu
wife	ഭാര്യയാണ്	b'a·rya·*yaa*·nu

Here's my (address).
ഇതാണെന്റെ (മേൽവിലാസം). — i·t'a·nen·*te* (meyl·vi·laa·*sam*)

What's your (email)?
എന്താണ് താങ്കളുടെ (ഇമെയിൽ)? — ent'a·*nu* t'ang·alu·*de* (i·me·*yil*)

Where are you from?
താങ്കൾ എവിടെ നിന്നു വരുന്നു? — t'ang·*al* e·vi·*de* ni·*nu* va·ru·*nu*

I'm from (New Zealand).
ഞാൻ (ന്യുസിലാൻഡിൽ) നിന്ന്. — nyaan (nyu·si·lan·*dil*) ni·*nu*

What's your occupation?
എന്താണ് താങ്കളുടെ ജോലി? — en·t'a·*nu* t'an·ka·lu·*de* jo·*li*

I'm a ...	ഞാൻ ഒരു ...	nyaan o·*ru* ...
businessperson	ബിസിനസുകാരനാണ്	bi·si·*nas*·kaa·ra·naa·*nu*
tradesperson	വ്യാപാരിയാണ്	vyaa·paa·*ri*·yaa·*nu*

Do you like ...?	താങ്കൾക്ക് ... ഇഷ്ടമാണോ?	t'ang·al·*ku* ... ish·ta·*maa*·nu
I like ...	എനിക്ക് ... ഇഷ്ടമാണ്.	e·ni·*ku*... ish·ta·*maa*·nu
I don't like ...	എനിക്ക് ... ഇഷ്ടമല്ല.	e·ni·*ku*... ish·ta·mal·*la*
art	കല	ka·*la*
movies	സിനിമ	şi·ni·*ma*
music	സംഗീതം	şan·gee·*t'am*
reading	വായന	vaa·ya·*na*
sport	സ്പോർട്	şpot

eating out

Can you recommend a …?	താങ്കൾക്ക് ഒരു … നിർദ്ദേശിക്കാമോ?	t'ang·al·*ku* o·*ru* … nir·*d'e*·shi·ka·*mo*
bar	ബാർ	baar
place to eat	ഭക്ഷണം കഴിക്കാനിടം	b'ak·sha·*nam* ka·zhi·ka·ni·*dam*
I'd like a/the …, please.	എനിക്ക് ദയവായി … വേണമായിരുന്നു.	e·ni·*ku* đa·*ya*·va·*yi* … *vey*·na·maa·yi·ru·*nu*
bill	ബിൽ	bil
local speciality	നാടൻ വിഭവങ്ങൾ	naa·*tan* vi·b'a·vang·*al*
menu	മെനു	me·*noo*
table for (four)	ഒരു ടേബിൾ (നാലു പേർക്ക്)	o·*ru ta*·bil (naa·*lu* per·*ku*)

breakfast	പ്രഭാതഭക്ഷണം	pra·b'a·*t'a*·b'ak·sha·*nam*
lunch	ഉച്ചഭക്ഷണം	u·cha·b'ak·sha·*nam*
dinner	അത്താഴം	a·t'aa·*zham*
(cup of) coffee …	(ഒരു കപ്പ്) കോഫി …	(o·*ru* kap) ko·*fee* …
(cup of) tea …	(ഒരു കപ്പ്) ചായ …	(o·*ru* kap) chaa·*ya* …
with milk	പാലൊഴിച്ച്	paa·lo·zhi·*chu*
without sugar	പഞ്ചസാരയില്ലാതെ	pan·cha·saa·*ra*·yil·la·*t'e*
(orange) juice	(ഓറഞ്ച്) ജ്യൂസ്	(o·ran·*ju*) joos
lassi	ലസി	la·*si*
soft drink	ലഘുപാനീയം	la·*g'u*·paa·nee·*yam*

I'll have boiled/mineral water.
എന്റെ കൈയിൽ തിളപ്പിച്ച/ മിനറൽ വെള്ളമുണ്ടാകും. — en·*te* ka·*yil* t'i·la·pi·*cha*/ mi·na·*ral* ve·*la*·mun·daa·*kum*

What would you like?
താങ്കൾക്ക് എന്താണ് വേണ്ടത്? — t'ang·al·*ku* en·t'a·*nu* veyn·ta·*t'u*

a bottle/glass of beer	ഒരു കുപ്പി/ഗ്ലാസ് ബിയർ	o·*ru* ku·*pi*/glas bi·*yar*
a bottle/glass of wine	ഒരു കുപ്പി/ഗ്ലാസ് വീഞ്ഞ്	o·*ru* ku·*pi*/glas vee·*nya*

special diets & allergies

Do you have vegetarian food?

താങ്കളുടെ പക്കൽ സസ്യാഹാരി ഭക്ഷണം ഉണ്ടോ?	t'an·ka·lu·*de* pak·*kal* sa·sya·ha·*ri* b'ak·sha·*nam* un·*to*

I'm allergic to ...	എനിക്ക് ... അലർജിയാണ്.	e·ni·*ku* ... a·lar·*ji*·yaa·*nu*
dairy products	പാലുൽപന്നങ്ങൾ	*paa*·lul·pa·*nang*·al
eggs	മുട്ടകൾ	mut·ta·*kal*
meat stock	മാംസ ചാറ്	maam·*sam* cha·*ru*
nuts	കായ്കൾ	kai·*kal*
seafood	കടൽവിഭവങ്ങൾ	ka·*tal*·vi·*b'a*·vang·*al*

emergencies

Help!	സഹായിക്കൂ!	şa·ha·yi·*koo*
Stop!	നിർത്തൂ!	nir·*t'oo*
Go away!	ഇവിടുന്ന് പോകൂ!	i·vi·du·*nu* po·*koo*
Thief!	കള്ളൻ!	kal·*lan*
Fire!	തീ!	tee
Watch out!	ശ്രദ്ധിക്കുക!	shra·d'i·ku·*ka*

Call ...!	... വിളിക്കൂ!	... vi·li·*koo*
an ambulance	ഒരു ആംബുലൻസിനെ	o·*ru* aam·bu·lan·si·*ne*
a doctor	ഒരു ഡോക്ടറെ	o·*ru* dok·ta·*re*
the police	പൊലീസിനെ	po·li·si·*ne*

Could you help me, please?

ദയവായി താങ്കൾക്ക് എന്നെ സഹായിക്കാമോ?	đa·ya·va·*yi* t'ang·al·*ku* e·*ne* şa·haa·*yi*·ka·*mo*

I have to use the phone.

എനിക്ക് ഈ ഫോൺ ഒന്നു വേണമായിരുന്നു.	e·ni·*ku* ee fon o·*nu* *vey*·na·maa·yi·ru·*nu*

I'm lost.

എനിക്ക് വഴി അറിഞ്ഞുകൂട.	e·ni·*ku* va·*zhi* a·ri·*nyu*·koo·*da*

Where are the toilets?

എവിടെയാണ് കക്കൂസ്?	e·vi·de·yaa·*nu* ka·koo·*su*

Where's the police station?

എവിടെയാണ് പൊലീസ് സ്റ്റേഷൻ?	e·vi·de·yaa·*nu* po·*lis* *ştey*·shan

I have insurance.
എനിക്ക് ഇൻഷുറൻസ് ഉണ്ട്. e·ni·*ku* in·shu·*rans* un·*du*

I want to contact my embassy.
എനിക്ക് എന്റെ എംബസിയുമായി ബന്ധപ്പെടണം. e·ni·*ku* en·*te* em·ba·*si*·yu·ma·*yi* ban·*d'a*·pe·da·*nam*

I've been ...	എന്നെ ...	e·*ne* ...
raped	ബലാത്സംഗം ചെയ്തു	ba·laal·sang·*am* chey·*t'u*
robbed	കൊള്ളയടിച്ചു	kol·*la*·ya·ti·*chu*

I've lost my ...	എനിക്ക് എന്റെ ... നഷ്ടപ്പെട്ടു.	e·ni·*ku* en·*te* ... nash·*ta*·pe·*tu*
money	പണം	pa·*nam*
passport	പാസ്പോർട്ട്	pas·*port*

health

Where's the nearest ...?	... തൊട്ടടുത്ത് എവിടെയാണ്?	... t'o·ta·du·*t'u* e·vi·de·yaa·*nu*
dentist	ദന്തിസ്റ്റ്	đan·*t'ist*
doctor	ഡോക്ടർ	dok·*tar*
hospital	ആശുപത്രി	aa·shu·pa·*t'ri*
pharmacist	ഫാർമസിസ്റ്റ്	far·ma·*sist*

I need a doctor (who speaks English).
എനിക്ക് ഒരു ഡോക്ടറെ വേണം (ഇംഗ്ലീഷ് പറയാൻ അറിയുന്ന). e·ni·*ku* o·*ru* dok·ta·*re* vey·*nam* (in·*glish* pa·ra·*yaan* a·ri·yu·*na*)

Could I see a female doctor?
എനിക്കൊരു വനിതാ ഡോക്ടറെ കാണാൻ കഴിയുമോ? e·ni·ko·*ru* va·ni·*t'a* dok·ta·*re* ka·*naan* ka·zhi·yu·*mo*

I've run out of my medication.
എന്റെ മരുന്ന് തീർന്നു. en·*te* ma·ru·*nu* t'eer·*nu*

I have (a) ...	എനിക്ക് ... ഉണ്ട്.	e·ni·*ku* ... un·*du*
asthma	ആസ്തമ	*aast'*·ma
constipation	മലബന്ധം	ma·la·ban·*d'am*
diarrhoea	വയറിളക്കം	va·ya·ri·la·*kam*
fever	പനി	pa·*ni*
heart condition	ഹൃദ്രോഗം	hruđ·ro·*gam*
nausea	ഓക്കാനം	aw·*kaa*·nam

I'm allergic to ...	എനിക്ക് ... അലർജിയാണ്.	e·ni·*ku* ... a·lar·*ji*·yaa·*nu*
antibiotics	ആന്റിബയോട്ടിക്കുകൾ	an·ti·ba·yo·*ti*·ku·kal
anti-inflammatories	ആന്റി-ഇൻഫ്ലമേറ്ററികൾ	an·ti·in·*fley*·mey·ta·ri·*kal*
aspirin	ആസ്പിരിൻ	as·pi·*rin*
bees	തേനീച്ചകൾ	t'ey·nee·cha·*kal*
painkillers	വേദനസംഹാരികൾ	vey·đa·*naa*·ṣam·haa·ri·*kal*

responsible travel

I'd like to learn some Malayalam.

എനിക്ക് കുറച്ച് മലയാളം പഠിച്ചാൽ കൊള്ളാം.
e·ni·*ku* ku·ra·*chu* ma·la·ya·*lam* pa·di·*chaal* ko·*lam*

Would you like me to teach you some English?

ഞാൻ നിങ്ങൾക്ക് കുറച്ച് ഇംഗ്ലീഷ് പഠിപ്പിച്ച് തരണമെന്ന് നിങ്ങൾ ആഗ്രഹിക്കുന്നുണ്ടോ?
nyaan ning·al·*ku* ku·ra·*chu* in·*glish* pa·*di*·pi·*chu* t'a·ra·na·me·*nu* ning·*al* aa·gra·hi·*ku*·nun·to

I didn't mean to do/say anything wrong.

ഞാൻ അങ്ങനെ തെറ്റായൊന്നും ചെയ്യാൻ/പറയാൻ ഉദ്ദേശിച്ചില്ല.
nyaan an·ga·*ne* t'e·ta·yo·*num* che·*yaan*/pa·ra·*yaan* u·*d'e*·shi·chi·*la*

Is this a local or national custom?

ഈ ആചാരം പ്രാദേശികമാണോ ദേശീയമാണോ?
ee aa·chaa·*ram* pra·*đe*·shi·ka·maa·*no* d'e·*see*·ya·maa·*no*

I'd like to stay at a locally run hotel.

ഏതെങ്കിലും നാടൻ ഹോട്ടലിൽ തങ്ങാൻ എനിക്ക് ആഗ്രഹമുണ്ട്.
ey·d'en·ki·*lum* naa·*tan* ho·ta·*lil* t'ang·*an* e·ni·*ku* aa·gra·ha·mun·*tu*

Where can I buy locally produced goods/souvenirs?

തദ്ദേശീയമായി ഉണ്ടാക്കിയ വസ്തുക്കൾ/സുവനീറുകൾ എനിക്ക് എവിടെ വാങ്ങുവാൻ കിട്ടും?
t'a·*d'e*·shee·ya·maa·*yi* un·*ta*·ki·*ya* va·st'u·*kal*/sow·ve·*nee*·ru·*kal* e·ni·*ku* evi·*de* vaan·gu·*vaan* ki·*tum*

What's this made from?

ഇത് എന്തു കൊണ്ടാണ് നിർമ്മിച്ചിരിക്കുന്നത്?
i·*t'u* en·*t'u* kon·taa·*nu* nir·*mi*·chi·ri·ku·na·*t'u*

I'm (an English teacher). Can I volunteer my skills?

ഞാൻ (ഒരു ഇംഗ്ലീഷ് ടീച്ചർ ആണ്). ഞാൻ വളണ്ടിയറായി പഠിപ്പിച്ചോട്ടെ?
nyaan (o·*ru* in·*glish* tee·*char* aa·*nu*) nyaan va·lan·ti·ya·raa·*yi* pa·*t'i*·pi·cho·*te*

english–malayalam dictionary

Words in this dictionary are marked as n (noun), a (adjective), v (verb), sg (singular) and pl (plural) where necessary.

A

accident അപകടം a·pa·ka·*tam*
accommodation താമസം *t'aa*·ma·sam
adaptor അഡാപ്റ്റർ a·dap·*tar*
address n മേൽവിലാസം meyl·vi·laa·*sam*
after ശേഷം she·*sham*
air-conditioned എയർ-കണ്ടീഷൻഡ് e·yar·kan·di·*shand*
airplane വിമാനം vi·maa·*nam*
airport വിമാനത്താവളം vi·maa·*na*·t'aa·va·*lam*
alcohol ആൽക്കഹോൾ aal·ka·*hol*
all എല്ലാം el·*lam*
allergy അലർജി a·lar·*ji*
ambulance ആംബുലൻസ് aam·bu·*lans*
and കൂടെ koo·*te*
ankle കണങ്കാൽ ka·nan·*kaal*
antibiotics ആന്റിബയോട്ടിക്കുകൾ an·ti·ba·yo·*ti*·ku·kal
arm കൈ kai
ATM എടിഎം ey·tee·*yam*

B

baby കുഞ്ഞ് kun·*nyu*
back (of body) പുറം ശരീരത്തിന്റെ pu·*ṛam* sha·*ree*·ra·t'in·*te*
backpack പുറത്തു തൂക്കുന്ന ബാഗ് pu·ra·*tu* too·ku·*na* bag
bad മോശം mo·*sham*
bag ബാഗ് bag
baggage claim ബാഗേജ് ക്ലെയിം ba·ga·*je* kley·*yim*
bank ബാങ്ക് baank
bar ബാർ baar
bathroom കുളിമുറി ku·li·mu·*ṛi*
battery ബാറ്ററി baa·ta·*ri*
beautiful സൗന്ദര്യമുള്ള ṣown·dar·*ya*·mu·*la*
bed കിടക്ക ki·da·*ka*
before മുമ്പിൽ mun·*pil*
behind പിന്നിൽ pi·*nil*
bicycle സൈക്കിൾ ṣai·*kil*
big വലിപ്പമുള്ള va·li·*pa*·mu·*la*
bill ബിൽ bil
blanket കരിമ്പടം ka·rim·pa·*dam*
blood group രക്ത ഗ്രൂപ്പ് rak·*t'a* groop
boat ബോട്ട് bot
book (make a reservation) v ബുക്ക് ചെയ്യൽ റിസർവേഷൻ buk che·*yal* re·ser·va·*shan*
bottle കുപ്പി ku·*pi*
boy ആൺകുട്ടി aan·ku·*ti*
brakes (car) ബ്രേക്ക് brey·*ku*
breakfast പ്രഭാതഭക്ഷണം pra·b'a·*t'a*·b'ak·sha·*nam*
broken (faulty) പൊട്ടിയ po·ti·*ya*
bus ബസ് bas
business ബിസിനസ് bi·si·*nas*
buy v വാങ്ങൽ vaan·*gal*

C

camera ക്യാമറ ka·me·*ra*
cancel റദ്ദു ചെയ്യുക ṛa·*du* che·yu·*ka*
car കാർ kaar
cash n പണം pa·*nam*
cash (a cheque) v പണമാക്കൽ (ഒരു ചെക്ക്) pa·*na*·maa·kal (o·*ru* chek)
cell phone മൊബൈൽ ഫോൺ mo·*bail* fon
centre n കേന്ദ്രസ്ഥാനം keyn·*dra*·ṣt'aa·*nam*
change (money) v വിനിമയം ചെയ്യൽ (പണം) vi·ni·ma·*yam* che·*yal* (pa·*nam*)
cheap വിലകുറഞ്ഞ vi·*la* ku·ṛa·*nya*
check (bill) ബിൽ bil
chest (body) നെഞ്ച് nen·*ju*
child കുട്ടി ku·*t'i*
cigarette സിഗററ്റ് ṣi·ga·*rat*
city നഗരം na·ga·*ram*
clean a വൃത്തിയുള്ള vru·t'i·yu·*la*
closed വളരെ അടുത്ത va·la·*re* a·du·*t'a*
cold a തണുത്ത t'a·nu·*t'a*
collect call കളക്ട് കോൾ ka·*lak*·tu kol
come വരിക va·ri·*ka*
computer കമ്പ്യൂട്ടർ kan·pyoo·*tar*
condom ഉറ u·*ṛa*
contact lenses കോൺടാക്ട് ലെൻസുകൾ kon·*takt* len·su·*kal*
cook v പാചകം ചെയ്യൽ paa·cha·*kam* che·*yal*
cost n വില vi·*la*
credit card ക്രെഡിറ്റ് കാർഡ് kre·*dit* kard
currency exchange നാണയ വിനിമയം naa·*n'a*·ya vi·ni·ma·*yam*

A

english–malayalam

D

dangerous ആപൽക്കരം aa·pal·ka·*ram*
date (time) തീയതി t'ee·ya·*t'i*
day ദിവസം đi·va·*sam*
delay n വിലംബം vi·lam·*bam*
dentist ദന്തിസ്റ്റ് đan·*t'ist*
depart വേർപിരിയുക *veyr*·pi·ri·yu·*ka*
diaper ഡയെപർ da·ya·*par*
dinner അത്താഴം a·t'aa·*zham*
direct a നേരെ ney·*re*
dirty അശുദ്ധമായ a·shu·*đa*·maa·*ya*
disabled അശക്തനായ a·shak·*t'a*·naa·*ya*
discount n കിഴിവ് ki·zhi·*vu*
doctor ഡോക്ടർ dok·*tar*
double bed ഡബിൾ ബെഡ് da·*bil* bed
double room ഡബിൾ റൂം da·*bil* room
drink n പാനീയം paa·nee·*yam*
drive v ഓടിക്കുക aw·di·ku·*ka*
drivers licence ഡ്രൈവർമാരുടെ ലൈസൻസ്
drai·var·maa·ru·*de* lai·*sans*

E

ear കാത് kaa·*t'u*
east കിഴക്ക് ki·zha·*ku*
eat കഴിക്കുക ka·zhi·ku·*ka*
electricity വൈദ്യുതി vai·đyu·*t'i*
elevator എലിവേറ്റർ e·li·vai·*t'ar*
email ഇമെയിൽ i·me·*yil*
embassy എംബസി em·ba·*si*
emergency അടിയന്തരം a·ti·yan·t'a·*ram*
English (language) ഇംഗ്ലീഷ് in·*glish*
entrance പ്രവേശദ്വാരം pra·*vey*·shad·*wa*·ram
evening വൈകുന്നേരം vai·ku·ne·*ram*
exit n നിർഗമനം nir·ga·ma·*nam*
expensive അമിതവിലയുള്ളത് a·mi·*t'a*·vi·la·yu·la·*t'u*
eye കണ്ണ് kan·*nu*

F

far അകലെ a·ka·*ley*
fast ദ്രുതം đru·*t'am*
father അച്ഛൻ a·*ch'an*
film (camera) ഫിലം fi·*lam*
finger കൈ വിരൽ kai vi·*ral*
first-aid kit പ്രഥമ ശുശ്രൂഷാ കിറ്റ്
pra·t'a·*ma* shush·roo·*sha* kit
first class ഫസ്റ്റ് ക്ലാസ് fast klas
fish n മത്സ്യം mat'·*syam*
food ഭക്ഷണം b'ak·sha·*nam*
foot പാദം paa·*đam*
free (of charge) സൗജന്യം sow·ja·*nyam*
friend സുഹൃത്ത് suh·*rut*
fruit പഴം pa·*zham*
full സമ്പൂർണമായ sam·poor·*na*·maa·*ya*

G

gift സമ്മാനം sam·ma·*nam*
girl പെൺകുട്ടി pen·ku·*t'i*
glass (drinking) ഗ്ലാസ് glas
glasses ഗ്ലാസുകൾ gla·su·*kal*
go പോകുക po·ku·*ka*
good ഗുണകരമായ gu·*na*·ka·ra·ma·*ya*
guide n വഴികാട്ടി va·*zhi*·kaa·*t'i*

H

half n പകുതി pa·ku·*t'i*
hand കൈ kai
happy സന്തോഷം san·t'o·*sham*
have കൈവശമുണ്ടായിരിക്കുക
kai·va·*sha*·mun·daa·yi·*ri*·ku·ka
he അവൻ a·*van*
head n ശിരസ്സ് shi·*ras*
heart ഹൃദയം hru·đa·*yam*
heavy കനത്ത ka·na·*t'a*
help v ഉപകരിക്കുക u·pa·ka·*ri*·ku·*ka*
here ഇവിടെ i·vi·*dey*
high ഉയർന്നത് u·yar·na·*t'u*
highway ഹൈവേ hai·*wey*
hike v വർധന var·*đ'a*·*na*
holiday അവധിദിനം a·va·*đ'i*·đi·*nam*
homosexual n സ്വവർഗസംഭോഗി,
swa·var·*ga*·sam·b'o·*gi*
hospital ആശുപത്രി aa·shu·pat'·*ri*
hot ചൂടുള്ള choo·du·*la*
hotel ഹോട്ടൽ ho·*tal*
hungry വിശപ്പ് vi·*sha*·pu
husband ഭർത്താവ് b'ar·t'aa·*vu*

I

I ഞാൻ nyaan
identification (card) തിരിച്ചറിയൽ കാർഡ്
t'i·*ri*·ch'a·ri·*yal* kard
ill അസുഖമായ a·su·k'a·maa·*ya*
important സുപ്രധാനമായ sup·ra·*đ'aa*·na·maa·*ya*
injury പരിക്ക് pa·ri·*ku*
interpreter ദ്വിഭാഷി đwi·b'a·*shi*

J

jewellery ആഭരണം aa·b'a·ra·*nam*
job ജോലി jo·*li*

K

key താക്കോൽ taa·*k'ol*
kitchen അടുക്കള a·tu·ka·*la*
knife കത്തി ka·*t'i*

L

laundry (place) അലക്കു കമ്പനി a·la·*ku* kam·pa·*ni*
lawyer അഭിഭാഷകൻ a·*b'i*·b'a·sha·*kan*
left (direction) ഇടത് i·da·*tu*
leg (body) കാൽ kaal
less കുറഞ്ഞ ku·ra·*nya*
letter (mail) കത്ത് ka·*t'u*
light n പ്രകാശം pra·kaa·*sham*
like v ഇഷ്ടപ്പെടുക ish·ta·pe·tu·*ka*
lock n പൂട്ട് poo·*tu*
long നീളമുള്ള nee·la·mu·*la*
lost നഷ്ടപ്പെട്ട nash·ta·pe·*ta*
love v സ്നേഹിക്കുക sney·*hi*·ku·*ka*
luggage ലഗേജ് la·*geyj*
lunch ഉച്ചഭക്ഷണം u·*ch'a*·b'ak·sha·*nam*

M

mail n തപാൽ t'a·*paal*
man മനുഷ്യൻ ma·nu·*shyan*
map ഭൂപടം b'oo·pa·*tam*
market ചന്ത chan·*d'a*
matches തീപ്പെട്ടി t'ee·pe·*ti*
meat മാംസം maam·*sam*
medicine ഔഷധം ow·sha·*d'am*
message സന്ദേശം san·d'ey·*sham*
milk പാൽ paal
minute മിനിട്ട് mi·*nit*
mobile phone മൊബൈൽ ഫോൺ mo·*bail* fon
money പണം pa·*nam*
month മാസം maa·*sam*
morning പ്രഭാതം pra·b'a·*t'am*
mother അമ്മ am·*ma*
motorcycle മോട്ടോർസൈക്കിൾ mo·*tor*·sai·*kel*
mouth വായ് vaa·*yu*

N

name പേര് pey·*ru*
near അരികത്തുള്ള a·ri·ka·t'u·*la*
neck n കഴുത്ത് ka·zhu·*t'u*
new പുതിയത് pu·t'i·ya·*t'u*
newspaper വാർത്താ പത്രിക vaar·*t'a* pat'·ri·*ka*
night രാത്രി raa·*tri*
no അല്ല. al·*la*
noisy ശബ്ദായമാനമായ shab·*d'a*·maa·*na*·maa·*ya*
nonsmoking പുകവലിക്കാത്ത pu·*ka*·va·li·kaa·*t'a*
north വടക്ക് va·ta·*ku*
nose മൂക്ക് moo·*ku*
now ഇപ്പോൾ i·*pol*
number സംഖ്യ sam·*k'ya*

O

old പഴയ pa·zha·*ya*
one-way ticket ഒരു വശത്തേക്കുള്ള ടിക്കറ്റ്
o·*ru* va·sha·*t'e*·k'u·la ti·*ka*·tu
open a തുറന്ന t'u·ra·*na*
outside പുറംഭാഗം pu·*ram*·b'a·*gam*

P

passport പാസ്പോർട്ട് pas·*port*
pay v വേതനം നൽകുക ve·ta·*nam* nal·ku·*ka*
pharmacy ഔഷധാലയം ow·sha·*d'a*·la·*yam*
postcard പോസ്റ്റ്കാർഡ് post·*kard*
post office തപാൽ ഓഫീസ് t'a·*paal* o·*fees*
pregnant ഗർഭമുള്ള gar·*b'a*·mu·*la*
price n വില vi·*la*

Q

quiet a പ്രശാന്തമായ pra·shan·*t'a*·maa·*ya*

R

rain n മഴ ma·*zha*
razor ക്ഷൗരക്കത്തി kshow·ra·ka·*t'i*
receipt n രസീത് ra·see·*t'u*
refund n പണം തിരികെ pa·*nam* t'i·ri·*ke*
registered mail രജിസ്ട്രേഡ് തപാൽ
re·gi·stra·*tu* t'a·*paal*
rent v വാടക vaa·ta·*ka*
repair v കേടുപാട് തീർക്കുക
key·*tu*·paa·*tu* teer·ku·*ka*
reservation റിസർവേഷൻ re·ser·va·*shan*
restaurant ഭക്ഷണശാല b'ak·sha·*na*·sha·*la*
return v തിരിച്ചെത്തുക t'i·ri·*che*·t'u·*ka*
return ticket മടങ്ങാനുള്ള ടിക്കറ്റ്
ma·*tang*·a·nu·*la* ti·*ka*·tu
right (direction) വലത് va·la·*tu*
road നിരത്ത് raw·*du*
room n മുറി mu·*ri*

S

safe a സുരക്ഷിതമായ su·rak·shi·*t'a*·maa·*ya*
seat n ഇരിപ്പിടം i·ri·pi·*tam*

send അയക്കുക a·ya·ku·*ka*
sex സംഭോഗം sam·b'o·*gam*
share (a dorm) പങ്കുവയ്ക്കൽ (ഒരേ മുറി) pan·ku·ve·*kal* (o·*rey* mu·*ri*)
she അവൾ a·*val*
sheet (bed) വിരിപ്പ് vi·*rip'*
shirt ഷർട്ട് shart
shoes പാദരക്ഷകൾ paa·*đa*·rak·sha·*kal*
shop n കട ka·*ta*
short ഹ്രസ്വമായ hru·*swa*·maa·*ya*
shower n ഷവർ sha·*var*
single room സിംഗിൾ റൂം şing·*il* room
skin n ചർമ്മം char·*mam*
skirt n പാവാട paa·vaa·*ta*
sleep v ഉറങ്ങുക u·ran·gu·*ka*
slowly മന്ദമായി man·*d'a*·maa·*yi*
small ചെറിയ che·ri·*ya*
soap സോപ്പ് sop
some അൽപം al·*pam*
soon ഉടനെ u·ta·*ne*
south തെക്ക് t'ek
stamp സ്റ്റാമ്പ് stamp
station (train) സ്റ്റേഷൻ *stey*·shan
stomach ഉദരം u·đa·*ram*
stop v തടയുക t'a·ta·yu·*ka*
stop (bus) n സ്റ്റോപ്പ് stop
street തെരുവ് t'e·ru·*vu*
student വിദ്യാർത്ഥി vi·đ'yaar·*t'i*
sun സൂര്യൻ soor·*yan*
swim v നീന്തുക neen·*t'u*·ka

T

teeth പല്ലുകൾ pa·lu·*kal*
telephone n ടെലിഫോൺ te·li·*fon*
temperature (weather) താപനില t'aa·pa·ni·*la*
that (one) ഏതൊന്ന് ey·t'o·*nu*
they അവർ a·*var*
thirsty തൃഷാർത്തമായ t'ru·shaar·*t'a*·maa·*ya*
this (one) ഇത് i·*t'u*
throat കണ്ഠം ka'n·*dam*
ticket ടിക്കറ്റ് ti·*kat*
time സമയം şa·ma·*yam*
tired ക്ഷീണിച്ച kshee·ni·*cha*
tissues ടിഷ്യുകൾ ti·shu·*kal*
today ഇന്ന് in·*na*
toilet കക്കൂസ് ka·*koos*
tomorrow നാളെ *naa*·l'ey
tonight ഇന്നു രാത്രി in·*nu* raat'·*ri*
toothbrush പല്ല് തേയ്ക്കാനുള്ള ബ്രഷ് pa·*lu* t'e·ka·nu·*la* brash
toothpaste പല്ല് തേയ്ക്കാനുള്ള പേസ്റ്റ് pa·*lu* t'e·ka·nu·*la* peyst

tour n പര്യടനം pa·rya·ta·*nam*
tourist office വിനോദ സഞ്ചാര ഓഫീസ് vi·no·*đa* san·cha·*ra* o·*fees*
towel തോർത്ത് t'ort
train n ട്രെയിൻ tre·*yin*
translate പരിഭാഷപ്പെടുത്തുക pa·ri·b'a·*sha*·pe·tu·t'u·*ka*
travellers cheque ട്രാവലേഴ്സ് ചെക്ക് tra·ve·ler·*su* chek
trousers ട്രൗസർ trow·*ser*
twin beds ഇരട്ടക്കിടക്ക i·ra·*ta*·ki·ta·*ka*

U

underwear അടിവസ്ത്രം a·ti·vas·*t'ram*
urgent തിടുക്കമുള്ള t'i·tu·*ka*·mu·*la*

V

vacant ഒഴിഞ്ഞ o·zhin·*ja*
vegetable n ഭക്ഷ്യയോഗ്യമായ സസ്യം b'a·*shya*·yo·*gya*·maa·*ya* sa·*syam*
vegetarian a സസ്യാഹാരി sa·sya·ha·*ri*
visa വിസ *vi*·sa

W

walk v നടക്കുക na·ta·ku·*ka*
wallet പണസഞ്ചി pa·na·san·*ji*
wash (something) കഴുകൽ ka·zhu·*kal*
watch n കാവൽ kaa·*val*
water n വെള്ളം ve·*lam*
we നമ്മൾ nam·*mal*
weekend വാരാന്ത്യം vaa·raan·*t'yam*
west പടിഞ്ഞാറ് pa·tin·ja·*ru*
wheelchair വീൽചെയർ veel·che·*yar*
when എപ്പോൾ e·*pol*
where എവിടെ e·vi·*tey*
who ആര് aa·*ru*
why എന്തിന് en·t'i·*nu*
wife ഭാര്യ b'a·*rya*
window ജാലകം jaa·la·*kam*
with കൂടെ koo·*te*
without ഇല്ലാതെ il·la·*t'e*
woman സ്ത്രീ st'ree
write എഴുതുക e·zhu·t'u·*ka*

Y

yes അതെ a·*t'e*
yesterday ഇന്നലെ in·na·*le*
you sg/pl നീ/നിങ്ങൾ nee/ning·*al*

T

DICTIONARY

Marathi

alphabet

vowels					
अ a	आ aa	इ i	ई ee	उ u	ऊ oo
ए e	ऐं ai	ओ o	औ ow		

consonants					
क ka	ख k'a	ग ga	घ g'a	फ fa	
च cha	छ ch'a	ज ja	झ j'a	ग nga	
ट ta	ठ t'a	ड da	ढ d'a	ण ṇa	य nya
त ţa	थ ţ'a	द đa	ध đ'a	न na	
प pa	फ p'a	ब ba	भ b'a	म ma	
य ya	र ra	ल la	व va		
श sha	ष şa	स sa			
ह ha	ळ ḷa				
क्ष ksa	ज्ञ gya	त्स tsa			

numerals									
0	1	2	3	4	5	6	7	8	9
०	१	२	३	४	५	६	७	८	९

introduction

Bollywood fans may already recognise some of the more colourful Marathi expressions. Mumbai slang (mum·bai·*cha* मुंबईचा), a rough-and-ready mix of Hindi, Marathi, Gujarati, Konkani and English, often features in the popular Hindi films. Spoken by an estimated 71 million people, Marathi (ma·raa·*t'i* मराठी) is the official language in Maharashtra and is spoken in bordering areas. It's also the language of cricketing icon and Mumbai native Sachin Tendulkar. Marathi belongs to the southern branch of the Indo-Aryan language family, with influences from Telugu and Kannada. Turkish, Arabic, Portuguese and Persian have also left their mark. Present-day written Marathi is a slightly modified version of the Devanagari script (used for Hindi) and is encouragingly called bal·*bod* बाळबोध, meaning 'can be understood by a child'. While you don't need to master the writing to communicate with the mum·bai·*kar* मुंबईकर (people of Mumbai), the phrases in this chapter will certainly help you on your way.

marathi

pronunciation

Vowels	
Symbol	**English sound**
a	run
aa	father
ai	aisle
e	bet
ee	see
i	hit
o	pot
oh	note
oo	zoo
ow	now
u	put

In this chapter, the Marathi pronunciation is given in brown after each phrase.

Aspirated consonants (pronounced with a puff of air after the sound) are represented with an apostrophe after the letter – b', ch', d', đ', g', j', k', p', t' and ţ'. Retroflex consonants (pronounced with the tongue bent backwards) are included in this table.

Each syllable is separated by a dot, and the syllable stressed in each word is italicised. For example:

कृपया. kri·pa·*yaa*

Consonants	
Symbol	**English sound**
b	bed
ch	cheat
d	dog
đ	retroflex d
f	fun
g	go
h	hat
j	jar
k	kit
l	lot
ļ	retroflex l
ly	million
m	man
n	not
ņ	retroflex n
ng	ring
ny	canyon
p	pet
r	rose
s	sun
ş	retroflex s
sh	shot
t	top
ţ	retroflex t
ts	hats
v	very
y	yes

essentials		
Yes.	होय.	hoy
No.	नाही.	naa-*hee*
Please.	कृपया.	kri-pa-*yaa*
Thank you.	धन्यवाद.	đ'an-ya-*vaađ*
Excuse me. (to get past)	जरा जाऊ देता.	ja-*raa* jaa-*oo* *đe*-ţaa
Excuse me. (to get attention)	क्षमस्व	ksha-mas-*va*
Sorry.	खेद आहे.	k'eđ aa-*he*

language difficulties

Do you speak English?
आपण इंग्रजी बोलता का ? — aa-*paṇ* ing-re-*jee* bol-*ţaa* kaa

Do you understand?
आपणाला समजते का ? — aa-pa-ṇaa-*laa* sa-ma-ja-*ţe* kaa

I understand.
मला समजते. — ma-*laa* sam-*jaţ*

I don't understand.
मला समजत नाही. — ma-*laa* sam-*jaţ* naa-*hee*

Could you please ...?	कृपया आपण ... ?	kri-pa-*yaa* aa-*paṇ* ...
repeat that	ते पुन्हा सांगाल	ţe pun-*haa* saan-*gaal*
speak more slowly	जास्त सावकाश बोला	jaasţ saa-va-*kaash* *bo*-laa

numbers					
0	शून्य	shoo-*nya*	20	वीस	vees
1	एक	ek	30	तीस	ţees
2	दोन	đon	40	चाळीस	chaa-*lees*
3	तीन	ţeen	50	पन्नास	pan-*naas*
4	चार	chaar	60	साठ	saat'
5	पाच	paach	70	सत्तर	sat-*ţar*
6	सहा	sa-*haa*	80	ऐंशी	ain-*shee*
7	सात	saaţ	90	नव्वद	nav-*vađ*
8	आठ	aat'	100	शंभर	sham-*b'ar*
9	नऊ	na-*oo*	1000	एक हजार	ek ha-*jaar*
10	दहा	đa-*haa*	1,000,000	दहा लाख	đa-*haa* laak'

time & dates

What time is it?	किती वाजले आहेत ?	ki·ţee vaa·ja·*le* aa·*heţ*
It's (two) o'clock.	(दोन) वाजले आहेत.	(đon) vaa·ja·*le* aa·*heţ*
Quarter past (two).	सव्वा (दोन).	sa·*vaa* (đon)
Half past (three).	साडे(तीन).	sa·re·(*ţeen*)
Quarter to (three).	पावणे(तीन).	paa·va·ṇe·(*ţeen*)
At what time ...?	किती वाजता ... ?	ki·ţee vaa·ja·*ţaa* ...
At ...	... वाजता.	... vaa·ja·*ţaa*
It's (15 December).	(पंधरा डिसेंबर) आहे.	(pan·d'a·*ra* di·*sem*·bar) aa·*he*
yesterday	काल	kaal
today	आज	aaj
tomorrow	उद्या	ud·*ya*
Monday	सोमवार	som·*vaar*
Tuesday	मंगळवार	man·gal·*vaar*
Wednesday	बुधवार	bu·đ'a·*vaar*
Thursday	गुरूवार	gu·roo·*vaar*
Friday	शुक्रवार	shu·kra·*vaar*
Saturday	शनिवार	sha·ni·*vaar*
Sunday	रविवार	ra·vi·*vaar*

border crossing

I'm here ...	मी इथे आहे ...	mee i·*ţ'e* aa·*he* ...
in transit	प्रवासात	pra·vaa·*saaţ*
on business	व्यवसायाच्या कामासाठी	vya·va·saa·yaa·*chyaa* kaa·maa·saa·*t'ee*
on holiday	सुटीवर	su·*tee*·var
I'm here for ...	मी ... साठी इथे आहे.	mee ... saa·*t'ee* i·*ţ'e* aa·*he*
(10) days	(दहा) दिवस	(đa·*haa*) đi·*vas*
(three) weeks	(तीन)आठवडे	(ţeen) aa·t'a·va·*de*
(two) months	(दोन) महिने	(đon) ma·hi·*ne*

I'm going to (Pune).
मी (पुणे) जात आहे. — mee (pu·*ne*) jaaţ aa·*he*

I'm staying at the (Surya Hotel).
मी (द सूर्य हॉटिल) येथे रहात आहे. — mee (su·*rya* ho·*tel*) ye·*ţ'e* ra·*haaţ* aa·*he*

I have nothing to declare.
सांगण्यासारखे काहीच नाही. saan·ga·*nyaa*·saa·ra·*k'e* kaa·*heech* naa·*hee*

I have this to declare.
हे सांगण्यासारखे आहे. he saan·ga·*ṇyaa*·saa·ra·*k'e* aa·*he*

That's mine.
ते माझे. ţe maa·*j'e*

That's not mine.
ते माझे नाही. ţe maa·*j'e* naa·*hee*

tickets & luggage

Where can I buy a ticket?
मी तिकीट कोठे खरेदी करु शकतो ? mee ţi·*keet* ko·*t'e* k'a·re·*đee* ka·*ru* sha·ka·*ţo*

Do I need to book a seat?
मला सीट आरक्षित करण्याची गरज आहे का ? ma·*laa* seet aa·rak·*shiţ* ka·ra·*nyaa*·chee ga·*raj* aa·*he* kaa

One … ticket (to Pune), please.	कृपया एक (पुण्याचे) … तिकीट.	kri·pa·*yaa* ek (pu·*ne*) … ţi·*keet*
one-way	एकेरी	e·ke·*ree*
return	जाण्यायेण्याचे	jaa·*nyaa*·yeṇ·yaa·*che*

I'd like to … my ticket, please.	मला कृपया माझे तिकीट. … आहे.	ma·*laa* kri·pa·*yaa* maa·*j'e* ţi·*keet* … aa·*he*
cancel	रद्द करायचे	rađ ka·*raa*·ya·che
change	बदलावयाचे	ba·đa·*laa*·va·yaa·*che*
collect	घ्यायचे	đ'yaa·ya·*che*

I'd like a nonsmoking/smoking seat, please.
मला धूम्रपानरहित/ धूम्रपानाच्या जागेची सीट हवी आहे. ma·*laa* đ'oo·ma·paa·na·ra·*hiţ*/ đ'oo·ma·paa·na·ra·*cha* jaa·ge·*chee* seet ha·*vee* aa·*he*

Is there a toilet/air conditioning?
तिथे शौचालय/वातानुकुल यंत्रणा आहे का ? ţi·*ţ'e* shoh·chaa·*lai*/vaa·ţaa·nu·*kool* yan·ţra·*ṇaa* aa·*he* kaa

How long does the trip take?
प्रवासाला किती वेळ लागतो ? pra·vaa·saa·*laa* ki·*ţee* vel laa·ga·*ţo*

Is it a direct route?
थेट प्रवास आहे का ? ţ'et pra·*vaas* aa·*he* kaa

tickets & luggage – MARATHI

My luggage has been …	माझे सामान …	maa·*j'e* saa·*maan* …
damaged	त्याचे नुकसान झाले	ţyaa·*che* nu·ka·*saan* j'aa·*le*
lost	हरवले	ha·ra·va·*le*
stolen	चोरीला गेले	cho·ree·*laa* ge·*le*

transport

Where does flight (Air India 567) arrive/depart?
फ्लाईट (एअर इंडिया ५६७) कुठून येते/सुटते ?
flaa·eet (er in·di·*a* paach sa·*haa* saaţ) ku·*t'oon* ye·*ţe*/su·ta·*ţe*

Is this the … to (Pune)?	हा (पुणे) … ज चा मार्ग आहे ?	haa (pu·*ne*) … chaa maarg aa·*he*
boat	बोट	noh·*kaa*
bus	बसचा	ba·sa·*chaa*
plane	विमानाचा	vi·maa·naa·*chaa*
train	रेल्वेचा	rel·ve·*chaa*

What time's the … bus?	… बस कधी आहे ?	… bas ka·*đ'ee* aa·*he*
first	पहिली	pa·hi·*lee*
last	शेवटची	she·va·ta·*chee*
next	पुढची	pu·d'a·*chee*

How long will it be delayed?
तिला किती उशीर होईल ?
ţi·*laa* ki·*ţee* u·*sheer* ho·*eel*

Please tell me when we get to (Khandala).
कृपया मला सांगा आपण कधी पोहोचू (खंडाळा).
kri·pa·*yaa* ma·*laa* saa·*ngaa* aa·*paņ* ka·*đ'ee* po·hu·*choo* (k'an·da·*la*)

That's my seat.
ती माझी सीट आहे.
ţee maa·*j'ee* seet aa·*he*

I'd like a taxi …	मला टैक्सी … पाहिजे	ma·*laa* taik·*see* … paa·hi·*je*
at (9am)	सकाळी (नऊ वाजता)	sa·kaa·*lee* (na·*oo* vaa·ja·*ţaa*)
now	आत्ता	aa·*ţaa*

How much is it to (Khandala)?
(खंडाळा) पर्यंत किती घेणार ?
(k'an·da·*la*) pa·*ryanţ* ki·*ţee* g'e·*ņaar*

Please put the meter on.
कृपया मीटर चालू करा. — kri·pa·*yaa* mee·*tar* chaa·*loo* ka·*raa*

Please take me to (this address).
कृपया मला (या पत्त्यावर) घेऊन चला. — kri·pa·*yaa* ma·*laa* (yaa pa·ţaa·*var*) g'e·*oon* cha·*laa*

Please stop/wait here.
कृपया येथे थांबा/प्रतिक्षा करा. — kri·pa·*yaa* ye·ţ'e ţ'aan·*baa*/pra·ţik·*shaa* ka·*raa*

I'd like to hire a car/4WD (with a driver).
मला कार/4WD भाड्याने घ्यायची आहे (ड्रायव्हरसहित). — ma·*laa* kaar/for veel draiv b'aa·daa·*ne* đ'yaa·ya·*chee* aa·*he* (draa·yav·ha·ra·sa·*hiţ*)

How much for daily/weekly hire?
रोजचे/आठवड्याचे भाडे किती ? — ro·ja·*che*/aa·t'a·va·da·yaa·*che* b'aa·*de* ki·*ţee*

directions

Where's the ...?	... कुठे आहे ?	... u·*t'e* aa·*he*
bank	बँक	baank
foreign currency exchange	परकीय चलन बदली	pa·ra·*keey* cha·*lan* ba·đa·*lee*
post office	पोस्ट ऑफीस	post o·*fees*

Is this the road to (Pune)?
हा रस्ता (पुणे) चा आहे का ? — haa ras·*ţaa* (pu·*ne*) cha aa·*he* kaa

Can you show me (on the map)?
मला (नकाशात) दाखवू शकता ? — ma·*laa* (na·kaa·*shaaţ*) đaa·k'a·*voo* sha·ka·*ţaa*

What's the address?
पत्ता काय ? — pa·*ţaa* kaay

How far is it?
किती दूर आहे ? — ki·*ţee* đoor aa·*he*

How do I get there?
मी तिथे कसा जाऊ ? — mee ţi·*ţ'e* ka·*saa* jaa·*oo*

Turn left/right.
डावीकडे/उजवीकडे वळा. — *daa*·vee·ka·de/u·*ja*·vee·ka·de va·*laa*

It's …	ते …	ţe …
behind …	… मागे आहे	… maa·*ge* aa·*he*
in front of …	… पुढे आहे	… pu·*d'e* aa·*he*
near (to …)	… च्या जवळ आहे	… chyaa ja·*val* aa·*he*
on the corner	कोपऱ्यावर आहे	ko·pa·*ryaa*·var aa·*he*
opposite …	समोर आहे …	sa·*mor* aa·*he* …
straight ahead	सरळ पुढे आहे	sa·*ral* pu·*d'e* aa·*he*
there	तेथे आहे	ţe·*ţ'e* aa·*he*

accommodation

Where's a guesthouse/hotel nearby?
जवळ गेस्टहाऊस/हॉटेल कोठे आहे ? — ja·*val* gest haa·*oos*/ho·*tel* ko·*t'e* aa·*he*

Can you recommend somewhere cheap/good?
आपण स्वस्त/चांगले काही सुचवाल का ? — aa·*paņ* svasţ/chaa·nga·*le* kaa·*hee* su·cha·*vaal* kaa

I'd like to book a room, please.
मला खोली बुक करायची आहे. — ma·*laa* k'o·*lee* buk ka·raa·ya·*chee* aa·*he*

I have a reservation.
मी आरक्षण केले आहे. — mee aa·rak·*shaņ* ke·*le* aa·*he*

Do you have a … room?	तुमच्या कडे … खोली आहे ?	ţu·ma·*chyaa* ka·*de* … k'o·*lee* aa·*he*
single	सिंगल	sin·*gal*
double	डबल	da·*bal*
twin	जुळी	ju·*lee*

How much is it per night/person?
दर रात्रीसाठी/माणशी किती भाडे आहे ? — đar raa·ţree·saa·*t'ee*/maa·ņa·*shee* ki·*ţee* b'aa·*de* aa·*he*

I'd like to stay for (two) nights.
मला (दोन) रात्री रहावयाचे आहे. — ma·*laa* (đon) raa·*ţree* ra·haa·va·yaa·*che* aa·*he*

Can I have my key, please?
मला माझी चावी कृपया द्याल का ? — ma·*laa* maa·*j'ee* chaa·*vee* kri·pa·*yaa* dyal kaa

Can I get another (blanket)?
मला आणखी एक (ब्लँकेट) मिळेल का ? — ma·*laa* aa·ņa·*k'ee* ek (blan·*ket*) mi·*la* kaa

The (air conditioning) doesn't work.
(वातानुकूल यंत्रणा) चालत नाही. — (vaa·ţaa·nu·*kool* yan·ţra·*ņaa*) chaa·*laţ* naa·*hee*

Is there an elevator/a safe?
इथे सरकता जिना/कपाट आहे का ? — i·ţ'e sa·ra·ka·*ţaa* ji·*naa*/ka·*paat* aa·*he* kaa

What time is checkout?
खोली सोडण्याची वेळ काय आहे ? — k'o·*lee* so·daṇ·yaa·*chee* vel kaay aa·*he*

Can I have my ..., please?	मी माझे ... घेऊ का ?	mee maa·*j'e* ... g'e·*oo* kaa
deposit	डिपॉझिट	di·po·*j'it*
passport	पासपोर्ट	paa·sa·*port*
valuables	मूल्यवान वस्तू	mool·ya·*vaan* vas·*ţoo*

banking & communications

Where's an ATM?
ATM कुठे आहे ? — e·tee·*em* ku·*t'e* aa·*he*

Where'sa public phone?
सार्वजनिक फोन कुठे आहे ? — saar·va·ja·*nik* p'on ku·*t'e* aa·*he*

I'd like to ...	मला ...	ma·*laa* ...
arrange a transfer	ट्रान्सफरची व्यवस्था करायची आहे	traan·sa·fa·ra·*chee* vya·vas·*ţ'a* a·ka·raa·ya·*chee* aa·*he*
change a travellers cheque	ट्रॅव्हर्स चेज़ बदलायचा आहे	tra·va·*lars* chek ba·đa·laa·ya·*che* aa·*he*
change money	पैसे बदलून हवे आहेत	pai·*se* ba·đa·*loon* ha·*ve* aa·*heţ*
withdraw money	पैसे काढायचे आहेत	pai·*se* kaa·d'aa·ya·*che* aa·*heţ*

What's the ...?	त्यासाठी ... ?	ţyaa·saa·*t'ee* ...
charge for that	शुल्क किती	shulk ki·*ţee*
exchange rate	विनिमय दर किती	vi·ni·*mai* đar ki·*ţee*

Where's the local internet café?
स्थानिक इंटरनेट कॅफे कुठे आहे ? — sţ'aa·*nik* in·ta·ra·*net* ka·*fe* ku·*t'e* aa·*he*

How much is it per hour?
दर तासाला त्याचे भाडे ज़्ति ? — đar ţaa·saa·*laa* ţyaa·*che* b'aa·*de* ki·*ţee*

I'd like to ...	मला ... आहे.	ma·*laa* ... aa·*he*
get internet access	इंटरनेट ॲक्सेस पाहिजे	in·ta·ra·*net* ak·*ses* paa·hi·*je*
use a printer/ scanner	प्रिंटर/स्कॅनर वापरायचा	prin·*tar*/ska·*nar* vaa·pa·raa·ya·*chaa*

I'd like a …	मला … पाहिजे आहे.	**ma-*laa* … paa-hi-*je* aa-*he***
mobile/cell phone for hire	सेल फोन भाड्याने	**sel fon b'aa-daa-ya-*ne***
SIM card for your network	तुमच्या नेटवर्कसाठी सिम कार्ड	**ţu-ma-*chyaa* ne-ta-*vark* saa-*t'ee* sim-*kaard***

What are the rates?
दर काय आहेत ? — **đar kaay aa-*heţ***

What's your phone number?
आपला फोन नंबर काय आहे ? — **aa-pa-*laa* fon nam-*bar* kaay aa-*he***

The number is …
नंबर आहे … — **nam-*bar* aa-*he* …**

I'd like to buy a phonecard.
मला फोनकार्ड खरेदी करायचे आहे. — **ma-*laa* fo-na-*kaard* k'a-re-*đee* ka-raa-ya-*che* aa-*he***

I want to …	मला …	**ma-*laa* …**
call (Canada)	(कॅनडाला) कॉल करायचा आहे	**(ka-naa-daa-*laa*) kaal ka-raa-ya-*chaa* aa-*he***
call collect	कलेक्ट कॉल	**ka-*lekt* kaal**

I want to send a fax/parcel.
मला फॅक्स/पार्सल पाठवायचे आहे. — **ma-*laa* faks/paar-*sal* paa-t'a-vaa-ya-*che* aa-*he***

I want to buy a stamp/an envelope.
मला तिज़ीट./लिफाफा खरेदी करायचा आहे. — **ma-*laa* shik-*kaa*/li-faa-*faa* k'a-re-*đee* ka-raa-ya-*chaa* aa-*he***

Please send it (to Australia).
कृपया हे (ऑस्ट्रेलियाला) पाठवा. — **kri-pa-*yaa* he (ohs-tre-li-ya-*laa*) paa-t'a-*vaa***

sightseeing

What time does it open/close?
ते कधी उघडते/बंद होते ? — **ţe ka-*đ'ee* u-g'a-da-*ţe*/banđ ho-*ţe***

What's the admission charge?
प्रवेश शुल्क किती आहे ? — **pra-*vesh* shulk ki-*ţee* aa-*he***

Is there a discount for students/children?
विद्यार्थी/मुले साठी काही सवलत आहे का ? — **vi-dyaar-*ţ'ee*/mu-*le* saa-*t'ee* kaa-*hee* sa-va-*laţ* aa-*he* kaa**

I'd like to hire a guide.
मला वाटाड्या भाड्याने पाहिजे आहे. ma·*laa* vaa·taa·*dyaa* b'aa·daa·*ne* paa·hi·*je* aa·*he*

I'd like a catalogue/map.
मला कॅटलॉग/नकाशा पाहिजे आहे. ma·*laa* ka·ta·*log*/na·kaa·*shaa* paa·hi·*je* aa·*he*

I'd like to see ...
मला ... पहायच्या आहेत. ma·*laa* ... pa·haa·ya·*chyaa* aa·*heţ*

What's that?
ते काय आहे ? ţe kaay aa·*he*

Can I take a photo?
मी फोटो काढू शकतो का ? mee fo·*to* kaa·*d'oo* sha·ka·*ţo* kaa

I'd like to go somewhere off the beaten track.
मला एखाद्या वेगळ्या ठिकाणी जायचे आहे. ma·*laa* e·k'aa·*dyaa* ve·ga·*lyaa* t'i·kaa·*ņee* jaa·ya·*che* aa·*he*

When's the next tour?
पुढची सहल कधी आहे ? pu·d'a·*chee* sa·*hal* ka·*đ'ee* aa·*he*

How long is the tour?
सहल किती वेळाची आहे ? sa·*hal* ki·*ţee* ve·laa·*chee* aa·*he*

Is ... included?	यात ... समाविष्ट आहे ?	yaaţ ... sa·maa·*visht* aa·*he*
accommodation	निवास	ni·*vaas*
admission	प्रवेश	pra·*vesh*
food	खाणेपिणे	k'aa·ņe·pi·*ņe*
transport	वाहतुक खर्च	vaa·ha·*ţuk* k'arch

sightseeing		
fort	किल्ला	kil·*laa*
mosque	मशीद	ma·*sheeđ*
old city	जुने शहर	ju·*ne* sha·*har*
palace	राजवाडा	raa·ja·vaa·*daa*
ruins	अवशेष	a·va·*shesh*
temple	मंदीर	man·*đeer*

shopping

Where's a ...?	... कुठे आहे ?	... ku·*t'e* aa·*he*
camera shop	कॅमेऱ्याचे दुकान	ka·me·yaa·*che* đu·*kaan*
market	बाजारपेठ	baa·jaa·ra·*pet'*
souvenir shop	स्मरण वस्तुंचे दुकान	sma·*raņ* vas·ţun·*che* đu·*kaan*

I'm looking for ...
मी ... पाहातो आहे. — mee ... paa·haa·*to* aa·*he*

Can I look at it?
मी ते पाहू शकतो का? — mee ţe paa·*hoo* sha·ka·*ţo* kaa

Can I have it sent overseas?
ते परदेशी पाठवून मिळेल का? — ţe pa·ra·đe·*shee* paa·t'a·*voon* mi·*lel* kaa

Can I have my (camera) repaired?
मला माझा (कॅमेरा) दुरुस्त करून मिळेल का? — ma·*laa* maa·*j'aa* (kai·me·*raa*) đu·*rusţ* ka·*roon* mi·*lel* kaa

It's faulty.
त्यात बिघाड आहे. — ţyaaţ bi·*g'aad* aa·*he*

How much is it?
याची काय किंमत आहे? — yaa·*chee* kaay ki·*maţ* aa·*he*

Can you write down the price?
किंमत लिहून दाखवाल का? — ki·*maţ* li·*hoon* đaa·k'a·*vaal* kaa

That's too expensive.
हे खूप महाग आहे. — he k'oop ma·*haag* aa·*he*

I'll give you (300 rupees).
मी (तीनशे रुपये) देईन. — mee (*ţeen*·she ru·pa·*ye*) đe·*een*

There's a mistake in the bill.
बिलात चूक झाली आहे. — bi·*laaţ* chook j'aa·*lee* aa·*he*

Do you accept ...?	आपण ... स्वीकारता का?	aa·*paņ* ... svee·kaa·ra·*ţaa* kaa
credit cards	क्रेडिट कार्ड	kre·*dit* kaard
debit cards	डेबिट कार्ड	de·*bit* kaard
travellers cheques	ट्रॅव्हलर्स चेक	tra·va·*lars* chek

I'd like (a) ..., please.	कृपया मला ... पाहिजे आहे.	kri·pa·*yaa* ma·*laa* ... paa·hi·*je* aa·*he*
bag	पिशवी	pi·sha·*vee*
my change	वरचे सुटे पैसे	va·ra·*che* su·*te* pai·*se*
receipt	पावती	paa·va·*ţee*
refund	पैसे परत	pai·*se* pa·*raţ*

Less./More./Enough. कमी./जास्त./पुरेसे. — ka·*mee*/jaasţ/pu·re·*se*

photography

Can you develop this film?
आपण ही फिल्म डेव्हलप ज़रुन द्या ज़ा ? — aa·*paṇ* hee film dev·ha·*lap* ka·*run* dyaal kaa

I need a film for this camera.
मला या कॅमेऱ्यासाठी फिल्म हवी आहे. — ma·*laa* yaa ka·me·raa·saa·*t'ee* film ha·*vee* aa·*he*

When will it be ready?
ते कधी तयार होतील ? — ţe ka·*đ'ee* ţa·*yaar* ho·*ţeel*

making conversation

Hello./Goodbye.	नमस्कार./बाय.	na·mas·*kaar*/bai
Good night.	शुभरात्री.	shu·b'a·raa·*ţree*
Mr/Mrs	श्रीयुत/श्रीमती	shree·*yuţ*/shree·ma·*ţee*
Miss/Ms	कुमारी	ku·maa·*ree*
How are you?	आपण कसे आहात ?	aa·*paṇ* ka·*se* aa·*haaţ*
Fine, thanks.	छान आहे, आभार.	ch'aan aa·*he* aa·*b'aar*
And you?	आणि आपण ?	aa·*ṇi* aa·*paṇ*
What's your name?	आपले नांव ?	aa·pa·*le* naa·*nav*
My name is …	माझे नांव …	maa·*j'e* naa·*nav* …
I'm pleased to meet you.	आपल्याला भेटून मला आनंद झाला.	aa·pa·lyaa·*laa* b'e·*toon* ma·*laa* aa·*nanđ* j'aa·*laa*
This is my father.	हे माझे वडी आहेत.	haa maa·*j'e* va·*deel* aa·*he*
This is my …	हा माझा … आहे.	haa maa·*j'aa* … aa·*he*
brother	भाऊ	b'aa·*oo*
friend (male)	मित्र	miţr
husband	पती	pa·*ţee*
son	मुलगा	mu·la·*gaa*
This is my …	हा माझी … आहे.	haa maa·*j'ee* … aa·*he*
daughter	मुलगी	mu·la·*gee*
friend (female)	मैत्रीण	miţr
mother	आई	aa·*ee*
sister	बहीण	ba·*heeṇ*
wife	पत्नी	paţ·*nee*

Here's my (address).	हा माझा (पत्ता).	haa maa·*j'aa* (pa·*ţaa*)
What's your (email)?	आपला (ई-मेल) काय आहे ?	aa·pa·*laa* (ee·*mel*) kaay aa·*he*
Where are you from?	आपण कुठले ?	aa·*paņ* ku·t'a·*le*

I'm from ...	मी ...	mee ...
Australia	ऑस्ट्रेलियाचा	ohs·tre·li·yaa·*chaa*
Canada	कॅनडाचा	ka·naa·daa·*chaa*
New Zealand	न्यूझीलंडचा	nyoo·j'ee·lan·da·*chaa*
the UK	इंग्लंडचा	in·glan·da·*chaa*
the USA	अमेरिकेचा	a·me·ri·ke·*chaa*

What's your occupation?
आपला व्यवसाय काय आहे ? — aa·pa·*laa* vya·va·*saay* kaay aa·*he*

I'm a/an ...	मी ... आहे.	mee ... aa·*he*
businessperson	व्यावसायिक	vyaa·va·saa·*yik*
office worker	नोकरदार	no·ka·ra·*đaar*
tradesperson	व्यापारी	vyaa·paa·*ree*

Do you like ...?	आपल्याला ... आवडते ?	aa·pa·lyaa·*laa* ... aa·va·da·*ţe*
I like ...	मला ... आवडते.	ma·*laa* ... aa·va·da·*ţe*
I don't like ...	मला ... आवडत नाही.	ma·*laa* ... aa·va·*daţ* naa·*hee*
art	कला	ka·*laa*
movies	चित्रपट	chi·ţra·*pat*
music	संगीत	san·*geeţ*
reading	वाचन	vaa·*chan*
sport	खेळ	k'el

eating out

I'd like (a/the) ..., please.	मला ... पाहिजे आहे.	ma·*laa* ... paa·hi·*je* aa·*he*
bill	बिल	bil
drink list	पेयांची सूची	pe·yaan·*chee* soo·*chee*
local speciality	इथला स्थानिक खास पदार्थ	i·ţ'a·*laa* sţ'aa·*nik* k'aas pa·*đaarţ'*
menu	पदार्थांची सूची	pa·đaar·ţ'aan·*chee* soo·*chee*
nonsmoking/ smoking section	धूम्रपानसहित/ धूम्रपानाच्या विभाग	đ'oo·ma·paa·na·ra·*hiţ*/ đ'oo·ma·paa·na·ra·*cha* vi·*b'aag*
table for (four)	(चार) लोकांसाठी टेबल	(chaar) lo·kaan·saa·*t'ee* te·*bal*
that dish	तो पदार्थ	ţo pa·*đaarţ'*

Can you recommend a ...?	आपण एखादे ... सुचवाल का ?	aa·*paṇ* e·k'aa·*đe* ... su·cha·*vaal* kaa
bar	बार	baar
dish	पदार्थ	pa·*đaarţ'*
place to eat	खाण्यासाठी जागा	k'aa·nyaa·saa·*t'ee* jaa·*gaa*

breakfast	नाश्ता	naash·*ţaa*
lunch	दुपारचे भोजन	đu·paa·ra·*che* b'o·*jan*
dinner	रात्रीचे भोजन	raa·ţree·*che* b'o·*jan*

(cup of) coffee ...	(कपभर) कॉफी ...	(ka·pa·*b'ar*) ko·*fee* ...
(cup of) tea ...	(कपभर) चहा ...	(ka·pa·*b'ar*) cha·*haa* ...
with milk	दूध घातलेला	đoođ' g'aa·ţa·le·*laa*
without sugar	साखरेशिवाय	saa·k'a·re·shi·*vaiţ*

(orange) juice	(संत्र्याचा) ज्यूस	(sanţ·ryaa·*chaa*) jyoos
lassi	लस्सी	ţaak
soft drink	शीतपेय	shee·ţa·*pey*

I'll have boiled/mineral water.
मला उकळलेले/मिनरल पाणी हवे आहे. — ma·*laa* u·ka·la·le·*le*/mi·na·*ral* paa·*ṇee* ha·*ve* aa·*he*

I'll buy you a drink.
मी तुझ्यासाठी पेय विकत घेतो. — mee ţuj'·yaa·saa·*t'ee* pey vi·*kaţ* g'e·*ţo*

What would you like?
आपल्याला काय आवडेल ? — aa·pa·lyaa·*laa* kaay aa·va·*del*

a bottle/glass of beer	एक बाटली/ग्लास बिअर	ek baa·tal·*ee*/glaas bi·*ar*

a bottle/glass of ... wine	एक बाटली/ग्लास ... वाईन	ek baa·ta·*lee*/glaas ... vaa·*een*
red	लाल	laal
white	पांढरी	paan·d'a·*ree*

special diets & allergies

Do you have ... food?	आपल्याकडे ... पदार्थ आहेत ?	aa·pa·lyaa·ka·*de* ... pa·đaar·*ţ'a* aa·*heţ*
halal	हलाल	ha·*laal*
kosher	कोशर	ko·*shar*
vegetarian	शाकाहारी	shaa·kaa·haa·*ree*

I'm allergic to ...	मला ... ची ॲलर्जी आहे.	ma·*laa* ... chee a·lar·*jee* aa·*he*
dairy products	दुग्धजन्य पदार्थ	đug·đ'a·*jany* pa·*đaarţ'*
eggs	अंडी	an·*dee*
meat stock	मांसाचा स्टॉक	maan·saa·*chaa* stok
nuts	दाणे	đaa·*ṇe*
seafood	सागरी अन्न	saa·ga·*ree* an

emergencies

Help!	मदत !	ma·*đaţ*
Stop!	थांबा !	ţ'aam·*baa*
Go away!	दूर जा !	đoor jaa
Thief!	चोर !	chor
Fire!	आग !	aag
Watch out!	लक्ष ठेवा !	laksh t'e·*vaa*

Call ...!	कॉल करा ... !	kaal ka·*raa* ...
an ambulance	रुग्णवाहिनीला	rug·ṇa·vaa·hi·nee·*laa*
a doctor	डॉक्टरांना	dok·ta·raan·*naa*
the police	पोलिसांना	po·li·saa·*naa*

Could you help me, please?
आपण मला कृपया मदत कराल का ? — aa·*paṇ* ma·*laa* kri·pa·*yaa* ma·*đaţ* ka·*raal* kaa

I have to use the phone.
मला फोन वापरायचा आहे. — ma·*laa* fon vaa·pa·raa·ya·*chaa* aa·*he*

I'm lost.
मी हरवले आहे. — mee ha·ra·va·*le* aa·*he*

Where are the toilets?
शौचालय कुठे आहे ? — shoh·chaa·*lai* ku·*t'e* aa·*he*

Where's the police station?
पोलिस स्थानक कुठे आहे ? — po·*lis* sţ'aa·*nak* ku·*t'e* aa·*he*

I have insurance.
माझा विमा आहे. — maa·*j'aa* vi·*maa* aa·*he*

I want to contact my embassy.
मला माझ्या दूतावासाशी संपर्क करायचा आहे. — ma·*laa* maa·*j'yaa* đoo·ţaa·vaa·saa·*shee* sam·par·*ka* ka·raa·ya·*chaa* aa·*he*

I've been …	माझ्यावर … झाला आहे.	maa·j'yaa·*var* … j'aa·*laa* aa·*he*
raped	बलात्कार	ba·laaţ·*kaar*
robbed	माझी चोरी झाली आहे	maa·*j'ee* cho·*ree* j'aa·*lee* aa·*he*

I've lost my …	मी माझे … हरवले.	mee maa·*j'e* … ha·ra·va·*le*
bag	पिशवी	pi·sha·*vee*
money	पैसे	pai·*se*

health

Where's the nearest …?	इथे जवळ … कुठे आहे ?	i·*ţ'e* ja·*val* … ku·*t'e* aa·*he*
dentist	दंतवैद्य	đan·ţa·va·*iđ'*
doctor	डॉक्टर	dok·*tar*
hospital	इस्पितळ	is·pi·*ţal*
pharmacist	औषधांचे दुकान	oh·sha·đ'aan·*che* đu·*kaan*

I need a doctor (who speaks English).
मला डॉक्टर पाहिजेत (जे इंग्रजी बोलतात). — ma·*laa* dok·*tar* paa·hi·*jeţ* (je ing·re·*jee* bo·la·*ţaaţ*)

Could I see a female doctor?
कोणी महिला डॉक्टर आहेत का ? — ko·*ņee* ma·hi·*laa* dok·*tar* aa·*heţ* kaa

I've run out of my medication.
माझी औषधे संपली आहेत. — maa·*j'ee* oh·sha·*đ'e* sam·pa·*lee* aa·*heţ*

I have (a) …	मला … चा त्रास आहे.	ma·*laa* … chaa ţraas aa·*he*
asthma	दमा	đa·*maa*
constipation	बद्धकोष्ठता	bađ·đ'a·kosh·t'a·*ţaa*
diarrhoea	अतिसार	a·ţi·*saar*
fever	ताप	ţaap
heart condition	हृदयाचा त्रास	hri·đa·yaa·*chaa* ţraas
nausea	मळमळ	ma·la·*mal*

I'm allergic to …	मला … ची ॲलर्जी आहे.	ma·*laa* … chee a·lar·*jee* aa·*he*
antibiotics	प्रतिजैविकांची	pra·ţi·jai·vi·kaan·*chee*
anti-inflammatories	सूजविरोधी औषधांची	soo·ja·vi·ro·*đ'ee* oh·sha·đ'aan·*chee*
aspirin	ॲस्पिरिनची	as·pi·ri·na·*chee*
bees	बीजची	bee·ja·*chee*
codeine	कोडीनची	ko·dee·na·*chee*

responsible travel

I'd like to learn some Marathi.

मला एखादी मराठी शिकायची आहे.	ma·*laa* e·k'aa·*đee* ma·*raa*·t'i sha·ki·a·ya·*chee* aa·*he*

What's this called in Marathi?

याला मराठी त ज़ायम्हणतात ?	yaa·*laa* ma·*raa*·t'i kaay ma·ṇa·*ţaaţ*

Would you like me to teach you some English?

मी तुहाला थोडेफार इंग्रजी शिकवू का ?	mee ţu·haa·*laa* ţ'o·de·*faar* ing·re·*jee* shi·ka·*oo* kaa

I didn't mean to do/say anything wrong.

काहीही चुकीचे करण्याचा/ सांगण्याचा माझा हेतू नव्हता.	kaa·hee·*hee* chu·kee·*che* ka·ra·nyaa·*chaa*/ saa·nga·nyaa·*chaa* maa·*j'aa* he·*ţoo* na·va·*ţaa*

Is this a local or national custom?

ही स्थानिक की राष्ट्रीय रुढी आहे ?	hee sţ'aa·*nik* kee raash·tree·*ya* ru·*d'ee* aa·*he*

I'd like to stay at a locally run hotel.

मला स्थानिक हॉटेलात रहाण्यास आवडेल.	ma·*laa* sţ'aa·*nik* ho·te·*laaţ* ra·haa·*nyaas* aa·va·*del*

Where can I buy locally produced goods/souvenirs?

मला स्थानिक उत्पादित वस्तू/ स्मरणवस्तू कुठे मिळतील ?	ma·*laa* sţ'aa·*nik* uţ·paa·*điţ* vas·*ţoo*/ sma·ra·ṇa·vas·*ţoo* ku·*t'e* mi·la·*ţeel*

What's this made from?

हे कशाचे बनवलेले आहे ?	he ka·shaa·*che* ba·na·va·le·*le* aa·*he*

Does your company have responsible tourism policies?

आपल्या कंपनीत जबाबदार पर्यटन धोरणे आहेत ?	aa·pa·*lyaa* kam·pa·*neeţ* ja·baa·ba·*đaar* pa·rya·*tan* đ'o·ra·*ṇe* aa·*heţ*

I'd like to do some volunteer work (for your organisation).

मला काहीतरी स्वयंसेवी काम करायचे आहे (आपल्या संघटनेसाठी).	ma·*laa* kaa·hee·ţa·*ree* sva·yam·se·*vee* kaam ka·raa·ya·*che* aa·*he* (aa·pa·*lyaa* san·g'a·ta·ne·saa·*t'ee*)

I'm (an English teacher). Can I volunteer my skills?

मी (इंग्रजीचा शिक्षक) आहे. मी स्वेच्छेने माझे कौशल्य देऊ का ?	mee (ing·re·jee·*chaa* shik·*shak*) aa·*he* mee sve·che·ch'e·*ne* maa·*j'e* koh·sha·*lya* đe·*oo* kaa

english–marathi dictionary

Words in this dictionary are marked as n (noun), a (adjective), v (verb), sg (singular), pl (plural), inf (informal) and pol (polite) where necessary.

A

accident अपघात a-pa-*g'aaṭ*
accommodation निवास ni-*vaas*
adaptor जुळवून घेणारा ju-la-*voon* g'e-ṇaa-*raa*
address n पत्ता pa-*ṭaa*
after नंतर nan-*ṭar*
air-conditioned वातानुकूलित vaa-ṭaa-*nu*-koo-*liṭ*
airplane विमान vi-*maan*
airport विमानतळ vi-maa-na-*ṭal*
alcohol अल्कोहोल al-ko-*hol*
all सर्व sarv
allergy ॲलर्जी a-lar-*jee*
ambulance रुग्णवाहिका rug-ṇa-vaa-hi-*kaa*
and आणि aa-*ṇi*
ankle घोटा g'o-*taa*
antibiotics प्रतिजैविके pra-ṭi-*jai*-vi-*ke*
arm बाहू baa-*hoo*
ATM ATM e-tee-*em*

B

baby बाळ baal
back (of body) पाठ paat'
backpack पाठीवरची पिशवी paa-t'ee-va-ra-*chee* pi-sha-*vee*
bad वाईट vaa-*eet*
bag पिशवी pi-sha-*vee*
baggage claim सामानाचा दावा saa-maa-naa-*chaa* đaa-*vaa*
bank बँक baank
bar बार baar
bathroom बाथरुम baa-ṭ'a-*rum*
battery बॅटरी bai-ta-*ree*
beautiful सुंदर *sun*-đar
bed बिछाना bi-ch'aa-*naa*
before पूर्वी poor-*vee*
behind मागे maa-*ge*
bicycle सायकल saa-ya-*kal*
big मोठा mo-*t'aa*
bill बिल bil
blanket ब्लँकेट blan-*ket*
blood group रक्तगट rak-ṭa-*gat*
boat बोट noh-*kaa*
book (make a reservation) v बुक buk
bottle बाटली baa-ta-*lee*
boy मुलगा mu-la-*gaa*
brakes (car) ब्रेक brek
breakfast नाश्ता naash-*ṭaa*
broken (faulty) तुटलेला ṭu-ta-le-*la*
bus बस bas
business व्यवसाय vya-va-*saay*
buy v विकत घेणे vi-*kaṭ* g'e-*ṇe*

C

camera कॅमेरा kai-me-*raa*
cancel रद्द करणे rađ ka-ra-*ṇe*
car कार kaar
cash n रोख रक्कम rok' ra-*kam*
cash (a cheque) v धनादेश वटविणे đ'a-naa-*đesh* va-ta-vi-*ne*
cell phone सेल फोन sel fon
centre n केंद्र ken-*đra*
change (money) v मोड mod (pai-*se*)
cheap स्वस्त svasṭ
check (bill) बिल bil
check-in n चेक-इन che-ka-*in*
chest (body) छाती ch'aa-*ṭee*
child मूल mool
cigarette सिगरेट si-ga-*ret*
city शहर sha-*har*
clean a स्वच्छ sva-*chech'*
closed बंद bанđ
cold a थंड ṭ'and
collect call कलेक्ट कॉल ka-*lekt* kaal
come या yaa
computer संगणक sa-nga-*ṇak*
condom कॉन्डोम kan-*dom*
contact lenses कॉन्टॅक्ट लेन्सेस *kon*-takt *len*-ses
cook v शिजवणे shi-ja-va-*ṇe*
cost n किंमत ki-*maṭ*
credit card क्रेडिट कार्ड kre-*dit* kaard
currency exchange चलन विनिमय cha-*lan* vi-ni-*mai*
customs (immigration) कस्टम्स *kas*-tams

D

dangerous धोकादायक đ'o-kaa-đaa-*yak*
date (time) तारीख ṭaa-*reek'*
day दिवस đi-*vas*
delay n विलंब vi-*lamb*
dentist दंतवैद्य đan-ṭa-va-*iđ'*
depart निघणे ni-g'a-*ṇe*
diaper लंगोट lan-*got*

A

english–marathi

dinner रात्रीचे भोजन raa·ţree·*che* b'o·*jan*
direct a थेट ţ'et
dirty खराब k'a·*raab*
disabled अपंग a·pan·*ga*
discount n सवलत sa·va·*laţ*
doctor डॉक्टर dok·*tar*
double bed डबल बेड da·*bal* bed
double room डबल खोली da·*bal* k'o·*lee*
drink n पेय pey
drive v चालवणे chaa·la·va·*ņe*
drivers licence चालक परवाना chaa·*lak* pa·ra·vaa·*naa*
drug (illicit) ड्रग drag

E

ear कान kaan
east पूर्व poorv
eat खाणे k'aa·*ņe*
economy class इकॉनॉमी वर्ग i·ko·no·*mee* varg
electricity विद्युत पुरवठा vi·*dyuţ* pu·ra·va·*t'aa*
elevator जिना ji·*naa*
email ई-मेल ee·*mel*
embassy दूतावास đoo·ţaa·*vaas*
emergency आणीबाणी aa·*ņee* baa·*ņee*
English (language) इंग्रजी ing·re·*jee*
entrance प्रवेश pra·*vesh*
evening संध्याकाळ sanđ'·*yaa*·kaal
exit n बाहेर baa·*her*
expensive महाग ma·*haag*
eye डोळा do·*laa*

F

far दूर đor
fast जलद ja·*lađ*
father वडील va·*deel*
film (camera) फिल्म film
finger बोट bot
first-aid kit प्रथमोपचार साहित्य pra·ţ'a·mo·pa·*chaar* saa·hiţ·*ya*
first class प्रथम वर्ग pra·*ţ'am* varg
fish n मासा maa·*saa*
food अन्न an·*na*
foot पाय paay
free (of charge) मोफत mo·*faţ*
friend मित्र miţr
fruit फळ fal
full पूर्ण poorņ

G

gift भेटवस्तू b'e·ta·vas·*ţoo*
girl मुलगी mu·la·*gee*
glass (drinking) ग्लास glaas
glasses चष्मा chash·*maa*
go जा jaa
good चांगले chaan·ga·*le*
guide n वाटाड्या vaa·taa·*dyaa*

H

half n अर्धा ar·*đ'aa*
hand हात haaţ
happy आनंदी aa·nan·*đee*
have असणे a·sa·*ņe*
he तो ţo
head n डोके do·*ke*
heart हृदय hri·*đai*
heavy जड jad
help v मदत ma·*đaţ*
here येथे ye·*ţ'e*
high उंच unch
highway महामार्ग ma·haa·*maarg*
hike v वर जाणे var jaa·*ņe*
holiday सुटी su·*tee*
homosexual n&a समलिंगी sa·ma·lin·*gee*
hospital इस्पितळ is·pi·*ţal*
hot गरम ga·*ram*
hotel हॉटेल ho·*tel*
hungry भुकेला b'u·ke·*laa*
husband पती pa·*ţee*

I

I मी mee
identification (card) ओळख पत्र o·*lak'* pa·*ţra*
ill आजारी aa·jaa·*ree*
important महत्वाचे ma·haţ·vaa·*che*
injury दुखापत đu·k'aa·*paţ*
insurance विमा vi·*maa*
internet इंटरनेट in·ta·ra·*net*
interpreter दुभाषा đu·b'aa·*shaa*

J

jewellery जडजवाहिर ja·da·ja·vaa·*hir*
job नोकरी no·ka·*ree*

K

key किल्ली *kil*·lee
kilogram किलोग्रॅम ki·lo·*graam*
kitchen स्वयंपाकघर sva·yan·paa·ka·*g'ar*
knife सुरी su·*ree*

L

laundry (place) लाँड्री laan·*dree*
lawyer वकील va·*keel*
left (direction) डावी daa·*vee*
leg (body) पाय paay
lesbian a समलिंगी संबंध ठेवणारी स्त्री sa·ma·lin·*gee* san·*band'* t'e·va·ṇaa·*ree* sṭree
less कमी ka·*mee*
letter (mail) पत्र paṭr
light n प्रकाश pra·*kaash*
like v आवडणे aa·va·da·*ṇe*
lock n कुलूप ku·*loop*
long लांब laanb
lost हरवलेले ha·ra·va·le·*le*
love v प्रेम prem
luggage सामान saa·*maan*
lunch दुपारचे भोजन đu·paa·ra·*che* b'o·*jan*

M

mail n टपाल ta·*paal*
man पुरुष pu·*rush*
map नकाशा na·kaa·*shaa*
market बाजारपेठ baa·jaa·ra·*pet'*
matches सामने saa·ma·*ne*
meat मांस maans
medicine औषध oh·*shađ'*
message संदेश san·*đesh*
milk दूध đoođ'
minute मिनिट *mi*·nit
mobile phone सेल फोन sel fon
money पैसे pai·*se*
month महिना ma·hi·*naa*
morning सकाळ sa·*kaal*
mother आई aa·*ee*
motorcycle मोटारसायकल mo·taa·ra·saa·ya·*kal*
mouth तोंड ṭond

N

name नांव naa·*nav*
near जवळ ja·*val*
neck n मान maan
new नवीन na·*veen*
newspaper वर्तमानपत्र var·ṭa·maa·na·pa·*ṭra*
night रात्र raaṭr
no नाही naa·*hee*
noisy आवाज होणारा aa·*vaaj* ho·ṇaa·*raa*
nonsmoking धूम्रपानरहित đ'oo·ma·paa·na·ra·*hiṭ*
north उत्तर uṭ·*ṭar*
nose नाक naak
now आता aa·*ṭaa*
number नंबर nam·*bar*

O

old जुना ju·*naa*
one-way ticket एकेरी तिकीट e·ke·*ree* ṭi·*keet*
open a उघडा u·g'a·*daa*
outside बाहेरच्या बाजूला baa·he·ra·*chyaa* baa·joo·*laa*

P

passport पासपोर्ट paa·sa·*port*
pay v पैसे देणे pai·*se* đe·*ṇe*
pharmacy औषधांचे दुकान oh·sha·đ'aan·*che* đu·*kaan*
phonecard फोनकार्ड fo·na·*kaard*
photo फोटो fo·*to*
police पोलीस po·*lis*
postcard पोस्टकार्ड pos·*ta*·kaard
post office पोस्ट ऑफीस post o·*fees*
pregnant गरोदर ga·ro·*đar*
price n किंमत ki·*maṭ*

Q

quiet a शांत shaanṭ

R

rain n पाऊस paa·*oos*
razor वस्तरा vas·ṭa·*raa*
receipt n पावती paa·va·*ṭee*
refund n परतावा pa·ra·ṭaa·*vaa*
registered mail पोच पावतीचे टपाल poch paa·va·ṭee·*che* ta·*paal*
rent v भाडे b'aa·*de*
repair v दुरुस्ती करणे đu·rus·*ṭee* ka·ra·*ṇe*
reservation आरक्षण aa·rak·*shaṇ*
restaurant उपाहारगृह u·paa·haa·ra·*gruh*
return v परत येणे pa·*raṭ* ye·*ṇe*
return ticket जाण्यायेण्याचे तिकीट jaa·*nyaa*·yeṇ·yaa·*che* ṭi·*keet*
right (direction) उजवा u·ja·*vaa*
road रस्ता ras·*ṭaa*
room n खोली k'o·*lee*

S

safe a सुरक्षित su·rak·*shiṭ*
sanitary napkin सॅनिटरी नॅपकिन sai·ni·ta·*ree* *nai*·pa·kin
seat n सीट seet
send पाठवा paa·t'a·*vaa*
sex समागम sa·ma·gam

L

english–marathi

shampoo शांपू shaam·*poo*
share (a dorm) विभागणे (खोली) vi·b'aa·ga·*ṇe* (k'o·*lee*)
she ती ţee
sheet (bed) चादर chaa·*đar*
shirt शर्ट shart
shoes जोडे jo·*de*
shop n दुकान đu·*kaan*
short आखूड aa·*k'ood*
shower n शॉवर sho·*var*
single room सिंगल खोली sin·*gal* k'o·*lee*
skin n त्वचा ţva·*chaa*
skirt n स्कर्ट skart
sleep v झोपणे j'o·pa·*ṇe*
slowly हळूहळू ha·*loo*·ha·*loo*
small लहान la·*haan*
soap साबण saa·*baṇ*
some काही kaa·*hee*
soon लवकर la·va·*kar*
south दक्षिण đak·*shiṇ*
souvenir shop स्मरण वस्तुंचे दुकान
sma·*raṇ* vas·ţun·*che* đu·*kaan*
stamp शिक्का shik·*kaa*
stand-by ticket पर्यायी तिकीट par·yaa·*yee* ţi·*keet*
station (train) स्थानक sţ'aa·*nak*
stomach पोट pot
stop v थांबणे ţ'aam·ba·*ṇe*
stop (bus) n थांबा ţ'aam·*baa*
street गल्ली ga·*lee*
student विद्यार्थी vi·dyaar·*ţ'ee*
sun सूर्य soo·*ri*
sunscreen सनस्क्रीन sa·na·*skrin*
swim v पोहणे po·i·ha·*ṇe*

T

tampons टॅम्पन्स tam·*pans*
teeth दात đaaţ
telephone n दूरध्वनी đoo·rađ'·va·*nee*
temperature (weather) तापमान ţaa·pa·*maan*
that (one) तो ţo
they ते ţe
thirsty तहानलेला ţa·haa·na·le·*laa*
this (one) हा haa
throat गळा ga·*laa*
ticket तिकीट ţi·*keet*
time वेळ vel
tired दमलेला đa·ma·le·*laa*
tissues टिश्यू ti·*shoo*
today आज aaj
toilet शौचालय shoh·chaa·*lai*
tomorrow उद्या u·*dya*
tonight आज रात्री aaj raa·*ţree*
toothbrush टूथब्रश too·ţ'a·*brash*
toothpaste टूथपेस्ट too·ţ'a·*pest*
torch (flashlight) टॉर्च torch
tour n सहल sa·*hal*
tourist office पर्यटन कार्यालय pa·rya·*tan* kaa·ryaa·*lai*
towel टॉवेल to·*vel*
train n रेल्वेगाडी rel·ve·gaa·*dee*
translate भाषांतर करा b'aa·shaan·*ţar* ka·*raa*
travel agency पर्यटन एजन्सी pa·rya·*tan* e·jan·*see*
travellers cheque ट्रॅव्हलर्स चेक tra·va·*lars* chek
trousers विजार vi·*jaar*
twin beds दुहेरी बिछाना đu·he·*ree* bi·ch'aa·*naa*

U

underwear अंतर्वस्त्र an·ţar·*vasţr*
urgent तातडीचा ţaa·ţa·dee·*chaa*

V

vacant रिक्त rikţ
vegetable n भाजी b'aa·*jee*
vegetarian a शाकाहारी shaa·kaa·haa·*ree*
visa व्हिसा vi·*saa*

W

walk v चालणे chaa·la·*ṇe*
wallet पैशांचे पाकिट pai·shaan·*che* paa·*kit*
wash (something) धुणे đ'u·*ṇe*
watch n घडयाळ g'a·da·*yaal*
water n पाणी paa·*ṇee*
we आम्ही aam·*hee*
weekend सप्ताहान्त saap·ţa·*haanţ*
west पश्चिम pash·*chim*
wheelchair चाकांची खुर्ची chaa·kaan·*chee* k'ur·*chee*
when केव्हा kev·*haa*
where कोठे ko·*t'e*
who कोण koṇ
why का kaa
wife पत्नी paţ·*nee*
window खिडकी vi·*đ'a*·*vaa*
with च्या सहित chyaa sa·*hiţ*
without च्या शिवाय chyaa shi·*vai*
woman स्त्री sţree
write लिहा li·*haa*

Y

yes होय hoy
yesterday काल kaal
you sg inf तुम्ही *ţu*·mee
you sg pol&pl आपण *aa*·paṇ

Marwari (Rajasthani)

alphabet

vowels				
अ a	आ aa	इ i	ई ee	उ u
ऊ oo	ए e	ऐ ai	ओ o	औ ow

consonants				
क ka	ख k'a	ग ga	घ g'a	ड. ng
च cha	छ ch'a	ज ja	झ j'a	
ट ta	ठ t'a	ड da	ढ d'a	ण ṇa
त ţa	थ ţ'a	द đa	ध đ'a	न na
प pa	फ p'a	ब ba	भ b'a	म ma
य ya	र ra	ल la	व va	श s'a
स sa	ह ha	ळ ḷa	ड. ṛa	

MARWARI (RAJASTHANI)

मारवाडी (राजस्थानी)

introduction

To be recognised or not to be recognised – that has been the controversial question for Rajasthani (raa·jas·t̯'aa·nee राजस्थानी). This Indo-Aryan language of the state of Rajasthan, spoken by around 25 million people, is said to be the sum of its dialects rather than a language in itself. As such, it's not recognised by the Indian Constitution. Interestingly, those who lobbied for its recognition have met with impassioned opposition from fellow Rajasthanis. In 2005, some concerned citizens of this region protested that recognition would in effect give official status to the dominant dialect, Marwari (maa·ra·vaa·ṛee मारवाडी), leaving speakers of other dialects out in the linguistic cold. Marwari, used in this chapter, is spoken by about 13 million people in Rajasthan's west, with Jaipuri, Malvi and Mewari predominant in the east, southeast and northeast respectively. Despite the number of dialects, they're all closely related and their speakers generally understand each other. Language politics aside, the Rajasthani on the street will be impressed with any effort to communicate in their language, whatever you choose to call it.

marwari (rajasthani)

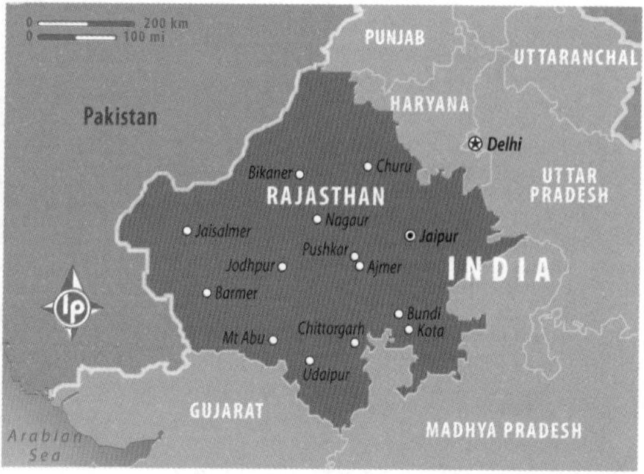

pronunciation

Vowels		Consonants	
Symbol	English sound	Symbol	English sound
a	run	b	bed
aa	father	ch	cheat
ai	aisle	d	dog
aw	law	đ	retroflex d
e	bet	f	fat
ee	see	g	go
ey	as in 'bet', but longer	h	hat
i	hit	j	jar
o	pot	k	kit
oo	zoo	l	lot
ow	how	ļ	retroflex l
u	put	m	man
		n	not
		ņ	retroflex n
		ny	canyon
		p	pet
		r	red
		ŗ	retroflex r
		s	sun
		t	top
		ţ	retroflex t
		v	very
		w	win
		y	yes

In this chapter, the Marwari (Rajasthani) pronunciation is given in brown after each phrase.

Aspirated consonants (pronounced with a puff of air after the sound) are represented with an apostrophe after the letter – b', ch', d', đ', g', j', k', m', p', s', t' and ţ'. Retroflex consonants (pronounced with the tongue bent backwards) are included in this table.

Each syllable is separated by a dot. For example:

धन्न-बाद । đ'an·baađ

essentials

Yes./No.	हाँ।/नइ सा।	haany/nai saa
Please.	किरपा-करनै।	kir·paa·kar·nai
Thank you.	धन्न-बाद।	đ'an·baađ
Excuse me. (to get past)	म्हाने जाण दौ सा।	m'aa·nai jaaṇ đow saa
Excuse me. (to get attention)	सुणियो जी।	su·ṇi·yo ji
Sorry.	माफ कर ज्यो।	maaf kar jyo

language difficulties

Do you speak English?
आप ईंग्रेजी जाणो कोंई? — aap ing·re·jee jaa·ṇo kaa·nyee

Do you understand?
आप सम-झिया कोंई? — aap sam·j'i·yaa kaa·nyee

I understand.
मैं आप-री बात समझ-ग्यो। — mai aap·ree baaţ sa·maj'·gyo

I don't understand.
मैं आप-री बात नी समझयौ। — mai aap·ree baaţ nee sam·j'yo

Could you please ...?	आप ...	aap ...
repeat that	पाछो बतावो	paa·ch'o ba·ţaa·vo
speak more slowly	थोडो होले बोलो	ţ'o·ŗo ho·lai bo·lo

numbers

0	शून्य	s'un·ya	20	बीस	bees
1	एक	ek	30	तीस	ţees
2	दो	đo	40	चाळीस	chaa·ļees
3	तीन	ţeen	50	पचास	pa·chaas
4	चार	chaar	60	साठ	saat'
5	पाँच	paanch	70	सित्तर	siţ·ţar
6	छः	ch'ah	80	अस्सी	as·see
7	सात	saaţ	90	नब्बे	nab·bai
8	आठ	aat'	100	सौ	sow
9	नो	no	1000	एक हजार	ek ha·jaar
10	दस	đas	1,000,000	दस लाख	đas laak'

time & dates

What time is it?	अबार कित्ता बज्या है?	a·baar kiţ·ţaa baj·yaa hai
It's (two) o'clock.	(दो) बज्या है।	(đo) baj·yaa hai
Quarter past (two).	(दो) बजकै पन्द्रा मिनट।	(đo) ba·ja·ke pan·đra mi·nut
Half past (two).	(दो) बजकै तीस मिनट।	(đo) ba·ja·ke ţees mi·nut
Quarter to (two).	(दो) बजवा मैं पन्द्रा मिनट।	(đo) ba·ja·wa meyn pan·đra mi·nut
At what time ...?	कित्ते बज्यॉं ...?	kiţ·ţee ba·jyaany ...
At ...	... बज्यॉं।	... ba·jyaany
It's (15 December).	आज (पन्द्रा दिसम्बर) है।	aaj (pan·đraa đi·sam·bar) hai

yesterday	गुजरे काल	gu·ja·re kaal
today	आज	aaj
tomorrow	काल	kaal

Monday	सोमबार	som·baar
Tuesday	मंगळबार	man·gaļ·baar
Wednesday	बुद्धबार	buđ·đ'baar
Thursday	बिस्पत-बार	bis·paţ·baar
Friday	ुक्रबार	s'u·kar·baar
Saturday	सनीबार	sa·nee·baar
Sunday	दीत-बार	đeeţ·baar

border crossing

I'm here ...	मै अठै ... हुं।	mai a·t'ai ... hoony
in transit	रास्ते मै	ras·ţai mai
on business	ब्योपार रै काम सूं आयो	bo·paar rai kaam soony aa·yoo
on holiday	छुट्टियॉं मनाण रै वास्ते आयो	ch'ut·ti·yaan ma·naaņ rai vaas·ţai aa·yoo

I'm here for ...	मै अठै ... रे वास्तै आयो हुं।	mai a·t'ai ... rai vaas·ţai aa·yo hoony
(10) days	(दस) दिन	(đas) đin
(three) weeks	(तीन) हफ्ता	(ţeen) haf·ţaa
(two) months	(दो) मिन्हा	(đo) min·ha

I'm going to (Delhi).	मै (दिल्ली) जाउँ।	mai (đil·lee) jaa·oony

I'm staying at the (Taaj Palace).

मै (ताज पैलेस) में ठहर्यो हूं।	mai (ţaaj pai·les) me t'a·ha·ryo hoony

I have nothing to declare.

म्हारे कनै कस्टम ड्यूटी रो कोई समान कोनी।	m'aa·rai kan·nai kas·tam dyu·tee ro koo·ee sa·maan koo·nee

I have this to declare.

मनै यो डिक्लेयर करणो है।	man·ne yo dik·le·ar kar·ņo hai

That's (not) mine.

ओ म्हारो (कोनी) है।	o m'aa·ro (ko·nee) hai

tickets & luggage

Where can I buy a ticket?

टि–गट कठै मिलै?	ti·gat ka·t'ai mi·lai

Do I need to book a seat?

सीट बुक कराणी जरूरी है कॉई?	seet buk ka·raa·ņe ja·roo·ree hai kaa·nyee

One … ticket (to Jaipur), please.	(जयपुर) रो एक … टिगट सा।	(jai·pur) ro ek … ti·gat saa
one-way	एक तरफ रो	ek ţa·raf ro
return	आणजाण रो	aaņ·jaaņ ro

I'd like to … my ticket, please.	मै म्हारो टिगट … चावूं।	m'ai m'aa·ro ti·gat … chaa·voony
cancel	केन्सल कराणो	ken·sal ka·raa·ņo
change	बदलाणो	ba·đa·laa·ņo
collect	लेवणो	le·va·ņo

I'd like a nonsmoking/smoking seat, please.

मनै धुम्रपान वरजित/ हाळी सीट चाइजै।	m'aa·nai đ'um·ra·paan var·jiţ/ haa·ļee seet chaa·e·je

Is there a toilet/air conditioning?

अठै टोयलेट/ऐसी है कॉई?	a·t'ai toy·let/ey·see hai kaa·nyee

How long does the trip take?

सफर मे कित्तौ बखत लागै?	sa·p'ar mai kiţ·ţo ba·k'aţ laa·gai

Is it a direct route?

यो सीधो रास्तो है कॉई?	o see·đ'o raas·ţo hai kaa·nyee

My luggage has been …	म्हारो सामान … व्है ग्यो।	m'aa·ro sa·maan … hwai gyo
damaged	खराब	k'a·raab
lost	गुम	gum
stolen	चोरी	cho·ree

transport

Where does flight (211) arrive/depart?
फलाइट (211) कठै उतरै/कठै सूँ जावै? — flaa·eet (đo ek ek) ka·t'ai u·ţa·rai/ka·t'aa soony jaa·wai

Is this the … to (Mumbai)?	कॉई ओ/आ … (मुम्बई) जावै?	kaa·nyee o/aa … (mum·bai) jaa·wai m/f
boat	नाव	naav f
bus	बस	bas f
plane	हवाई जहाज	ha·vaa·ee ja·haaj m
train	रेलगाडी	rel·gaa·ŗee f

What time's the … bus?	… बस कित्ती बज्याँ चालै?	… bas kiţ·ţee ba·jyaa chaa·lai
first	पैल्ली	pail·lee
last	आखरी	aak'·ree
next	आगली	aa·ga·lee

How long will it be delayed?
कित्ती लेट व्हेला? — kiţ·ţi let hwe·laa

Please tell me when we get to (Ajmer).
जद (अजमेर) आजावै म्हाने बताज्यो। — jađ (aj·mer) aa·jaa·vai m'a·nai ba·ţaa·jyow

That's my seat.
आ म्हारी सीट है। — aa m'aa·ree seet hai

I'd like a taxi …	म्हानै … एक टैक्सी चाइजे।	m'a·nai … ek tek·si chaa·e·je
at (9am)	सुबै (नो बज्याँ)	su·bai (no ba·jyaan)
now	अबार	a·baar

How much is it to (Hawaa Mahal)?
(हवा महल) जाण रो कित्तो किरायो? — (ha·waa ma·hal) jaaņ ro kiţ·ţo ki·raa·yoo

Please put the meter on.
मीटर चालू करो सा। — mee·tar chaa·loo ka·ro sa

Please take me to (this address).
मनै (ई पता) पै ले चालो। — ma·nai (ee pa·ţaa) pai le chaa·lo

Please stop/wait here.
अठै रूको/इंतजार करो। — a·t'ai ru·ko/in·ţa·jaar ka·ro

I'd like to hire a car/4WD (with a driver).
मै एक कार/फोर व्हील ड्राइव (ड्राइवर कै सागै) किराया पर लेबो चांउ। — m'ai ek kaar/for weel draiv (di·rai·var ke sag·ge) ki·ra·ya par le·bo chaa·voony

How much for daily/weekly hire?
एक दिन/हफ्ता रो कित्तो किरायो? — ek đin/haf·ţaa ro kiţ·ţo ki·raa·yoo

directions

Where's the ...?	... कठै है?	... ka·t'ai hai
bank	बैंक	baink
foreign currency exchange	विदेशी मुद्रा बदलवाणै री ाखा	vi·đe·s'ee mu·đraa ba·đal·vaa·ṇai ree s'aa·k'aa
post office	डाक खाणों	daak k'aa·ṇo

Is this the road to (Sikar)?
आ सडक (सीकर) जावै कॉई? — aa sa·ṛak (si·kar) jaa·vai kaa·nyee

Can you show me (on the map)?
कॉई थे म्हाने (नक्शो माय–न) दिखा सको? — kaa·nyee ţ'e m'aa·nai (nak·s'o maay·ne) đi·k'aa sa·ko

What's the address?
पतो कॉई है? — pa·ţo kaa·nyee hai

How far is it?
ओ/आ कित्ती दूर है? — o/aa kiţ·ţee đoor hai m/f

How do I get there?
मै उठै कियां पूगूँ? — mai u·t'ai ki·yan poo·goony

Turn left/right.
उल्ट/सीधे हाथ मुडो। — ul·te/see·đ'e haaţ' mu·ṛo

It's ...	ओ/आ ... है।	o/aa ... hai m/f
behind ...	... रै लारै	... rai laa·rai
in front of ...	... रै सामै	... rai saa·mai
near (to ...)	... रै कन्नै	... rai kan·nai
on the corner	खूणा माथै	k'oo·ṇaa maa·ţ'ai
opposite ...	... रै सामै	... rai saa·mai
there	बठै	ba·t'e

Where's a guesthouse/hotel nearby?
अठै पास मैं कोई गेस्टहाउस/होटल है कॉई?
a·t'ai paas me ko·ee gest·hows/ho·tal hai kaa·nyee

Can you recommend somewhere cheap/good?
कॉई थे एक सस्ती/चोखी जग्यॉं रो पतो दे सको?
kaa·nyee ţ'e ek sas·ţee/cho·k'ee ja·gyan ro pa·ţo đe sa·ko

I'd like to book a room, please.
मैं एक कमरो लेणों चावूँ सा।
mai ek ka·ma·ro le·ṇo chaa·voony saa

I have a reservation.
म्हारी बुकिंग है।
m'aa·ree bu·king hai

Do you have a ... room?	एक ... कमरो खाली है कॉई?	ek ... ka·ma·ro k'aa·lee hai kaa·nyee
single	सिंगल	sin·gal
double	डबल	da·bal
twin	दो बिस्तरॉं हाळो	đo bis·ţa·ran haa·ḷo

How much is it per night/person?
एक रात/जणा रो कित्तो किराया है?
ek raaţ/ja·ṇai ro kiţ·ţo ki·raa·yo hai

I'd like to stay for (two) nights.
मै (दो) रात रूकणो चावूँ।
mai (đo) raaţ ru·ka·ṇo chaa·voony

Can I have my key, please?
म्हारी चाबी सा?
m'aa·ree chaa·bee saa

Can I get another (blanket)?
कॉई म्हाने एक और (कम्बल) मिल सकै?
kaa·nyee m'a·nai ek awr (kaam·bal) mil sa·kai

The (air conditioning) doesn't work.
(ऐसी) काम कोन्नी करै।
(ey·see) kaam ko·nee ka·rai

Is there an elevator/a safe?
कॉई अठै लिफ्ट/तिजौरी है?
kaa·nyee a·t'ai lift/ţi·jow·ree hai

What time is checkout?
कमरो कित्ती बज्यॉं खाली करनो है?
kam·ro kiţ·ţee ba·jyaan k'aa·lee kar·no hai

Can I have my ..., please?	म्हारो/म्हारी ... वापस करदो सा?	m'a·ro/m'aa·ree ... vaa·pas ka·ra·do sa m/f
deposit	जमा रकम	ja·maa ra·kam f
passport	पासपोर्ट	paas·port m

banking & communications

Where's an ATM/a public phone?		
एटीएम/पीसीओ कठै है?		e·tee·em/pee·see·o ka·t'ai hai
I'd like to ...	मैं ... चावूँ।	m'ai ... chaa·voony
arrange a transfer	पइसा भेजणा री व्यवस्था	pai·saa b'ej·naa ri vya·vas·ṱ'a
change a travellers cheque	ट्रेवलर चैक कैश कराणो	tre·va·lar chai·ka kais' ka·raa·ṇo
change money	पईसा बदलणा	pa·ee·saa ba·đal·ṇaa
withdraw money	पईसा निकालणा	pa·ee·saa ni·kaal·ṇa
What's the ...?	... कॉई है?	... kaa·nyee hai
charge for that	फीस	fees
exchange rate	इक्सचेन्ज रेट	iks·chenj ret
Where's the local internet café?		
ई जग्यॉं इन्टरनैट कैफे कठै है?		ee ja·gyan in·tar·net kai·fe ka·t'ai hai
How much is it per hour?		
एक घन्टा रा कित्ता रिपिया?		ek g'an·tai raa kiṱ·ṱaa ri·pi·yaa
I'd like to ...	मैं ... चावूँ।	m'ai ... chaa·voony
get internet access	इन्टरनेट इस्तेमाल करणो	in·tar·net is·ṱe·maal kar·ṇo
use a printer/scanner	प्रिंटर/स्कैनर इस्तेमाल करणो	prin·tar/skai·nar is·ṱe·maal kar·ṇo
I'd like a ...	मैं ... लेणो चावूँ।	m'ai ... le·no chaa·voony
mobile/cell phone for hire	मोबाईल फोन किराया पै लेणों	mo·baa·eel fon ki·raa·yaa pai le·ṇo
SIM card for your network	आपरै नेटवर्क रै वास्तै सिमकारड	aap·rai net·wark rai vaas·ṱai sim·kaard
What are the rates?		
कॉई रेट है?		kaa·nyee ret hai
What's your phone number?		
आपरो फोन नम्बर कॉई है?		aap·ro fon nam·bar kaa·nyee hai
The number is ...		
नम्बर है ...		nam·bar hai ...
I'd like to buy a phonecard.		
मैं एक फोन कार्ड खरीदनो चावूँ।		m'ai ek fon kaard k'a·reeđ·no chaa·voony

I want to ...	मैं ... चावूं।	mai ... chaa·voony
call (Canada)	(कनाडा) फोन करणो	(ka·naa·daa) fon kar·ṇo
call collect	काल कलेक्ट करणी	kol ko·lekt kar·ṇee

I want to send a parcel/fax.
मै एक पारसल/फैक्स भेजणी चावूं। — m'ai ek paar·sal/p'ek·sa b'e·ja·ṇo chaa·voony

I want to buy a stamp/an envelope.
मै एक डाक टिगट/लिफाफो खरीदणो चावूं। — m'ai ek daak ti·gat/li·faa·fo k'a·reeđ·ṇo chaa·voony

Please send it to (Australia).
इन्ने (आस्ट्रेलिया) भेज दयो सा। — in·nai (aas·tre·li·yaa) b'ej đyo saa

sightseeing

What time does it open/close?
ईणरे खुलण/बन्द व्हेणा रो कॉई टेम है? — iṇ·rai k'u·la·ṇa/banđ hwai·ṇaa ro kaa·nyee tem hai

What's the admission charge?
प्रवेश ृल्क कित्तो है? — pra·ves' s'ulk kiţ·ţo hai

Is there a discount for students/children?
कांई विद्यार्थियां/टाबरों रै वास्ते छूट है? — kaa·nyee vi·đyaar·ţ'i·yaa/taa·ba·raany rey vaas·ţai ch'oot hai

I'd like to hire a guide.
मैं एक गाइड करणो चावूं। — m'ai ek gaa·eed kar·ṇo chaa·voony

I'd like a catalogue/map.
मनै एक कैटेलोग/नक्शो चाइजे। — m'a·nai ek kai·te·log/nak·s'o chaa·e·je

I'd like to see ...
मै कोई ... देखणो चावूं। — m'ai ko·ee ... đe·k'a·ṇo chaa·voony

What's that?
बो कॉई है? — bo kaa·nyee hai

Can I take a photo?
कॉई मै फोटू खींच सकूं? — kaa·nyee m'ai fo·too k'eench sa·koony

I'd like to go somewhere off the beaten track.
मै कोई अलग जग्यॉं जाणौ चावूं। — m'ai ko·ee a·lag ja·gi·yaan jaa·ṇo chaa·voony

When's the next tour?
अगलो टूर कठे है? — ag·lo toor ka·đe hai

How long is the tour?
यो टूर कित्तो लम्बो है? — yo toor kiţ·ţo lam·bo hai

Is … included?	इण मै … ़ामिल है?	iṇ mai … s'aa·mil hai
accommodation	रहबा की जग्यॉं	ra·ha·ba ri ja·gi·yaan
food	खाणो	k'aa·ṇo
transport	सवारी रो इन्तजाम	sa·waa·ree ro inţ·jaam

sightseeing

fort	किलो	ki·lo
mosque	मस्जिद	mas·zid
palace	म्हल	ma·hal
ruins	खंडहर	k'an·da·har
temple	मिन्दर	min·đar

shopping

Where's a … ?	… कठै है?	… ka·t'ai hai
camera shop	कैमरो री दुकान	kai·ma·ro ree đu·kaan
market	बजार	ba·jaar
souvenir shop	सेविनियर री दुकान	soo·vee·ni·ar ree đu·kaan

I'm looking for …
मै ढूंढ रियो हूं … — m'ai d'ood' ri·yo hoon …

Can I look at it?
कॉंई मै ओ देख सकुं? — kaa·nyee mai o đek' sa·koony

Can I have it sent overseas?
कॉंई आप इनै बिदेस भिजवा सको? — kaa·nyee aap ee·nai bi·đe·sa b'ij·waa sa·ko

Can I have my (camera) repaired?
कॉंई मै (कैमरा) ठीक करा सकुं? — kaa·nyee m'ai (kai·ma·ro) t'eek ka·raa sa·koony

It's faulty.
ओ खराब है। — o k'a·raab hai

How much is it?
यो कित्ता रो है? — o kiţ·ţaa ro hai

Can you write down the price?
कॉंई थै दाम लिख सको? — kaa·nyee ţ'ai đaam lik' sa·ko

That's too expensive.
यो भोत मैंगो है। — o b'oţ main·g'o hai

I'll give you (300 rupees).
म्है थानै (तीन सौ रिपिया) दूँला। — m'ai ţ'aa·nai (ţeen sow ri·pi·yaa) đoo·laa

There's a mistake in the bill.
ई बिल माय कुछ गलती है। — ee bil mai kuch' ga·la·ţee hai

Do you accept ...?	कॉई थे लेवो ...?	kaa·nyee ţ'e le·vo ...
credit cards	क्रेडिट कारड	kre·dit kaa·rad
debit cards	डेबिट कारड	de·bit kaa·rad
travellers cheques	ट्रेवलर चैक	tre·va·lar chai·ka

I'd like (a) ..., please.	मैने ... चाइजे सा।	m'a·nai ... chaa·e·je saa
bag	एक थैलो	ek ţ'ai·lo
my change	म्हारा खुला पईसा	m'aa·raa k'u·laa pa·ee·saa
receipt	एक रसीद	ek ra·seeđ
refund	पईसा वापस	pa·ee·saa vaa·pas

Less.	कम।	kam
Enough.	भोत।	b'oţ
More.	जादा।	jaa·đaa

photography

Can you ...?	कॉई थे ...?	kaa·nyee ţ'ai ...
burn a CD from my memory card/stick	म्हारा मेमोरी कारड/स्टिक सूं सीडी बणा सको	m'aa·raa mai·mo·ree kaa·rad/stik soony see·dee ba·ṇaa sa·ko
develop this film	आ रील धो सको	aa reel đ'o sa·ko

I need a film for this camera.
म्हानै ई कैमरो रै वास्ते फिलम चाहिजै। — m'a·nai ee kai·ma·ro rai vaas·ţai fi·lam chaa·e·je

When will it be ready?
ओ कद तैयार होसी? — o kađ ţyaar ho·see

making conversation

Hello./Good night.	राम-राम सा।	raam·raam saa
Goodbye.	मै अब चालूँ सा।	mai ab chaa·loony saa
Mr/Mrs	श्रीमान/श्रीमती	sree·maan/sree·ma·ţee
Miss	कुमारी	ku·maa·ree

How are you?
थे कयान हो? — ţ'ai ka·yaan ho

Fine, thanks. And you?
ठीक, धनबाद। और थै? — t'eek đ'an·baađ owr ţ'ai

What's your name?
थारो नाम कॉई है? — ţ'aan·ro naam kaa·nyee hai

My name is ...
म्हारो नाम है ... — m'aa·ro naam hai ...

I'm pleased to meet you.
आप सूं मिलर भोत चोखो लाग्यो। — aap soony mi·lar b'oţ cho·k'o la·gyo

This is my ...	ओ म्हारो ... है।	o m'aa·ro ... hai m
	आ म्हारी ... है।	aa m'aa·ree ... hai f
brother	भाई	b'aa·ee
daughter	बेटी	be·tee
father	बापू	baa·poo
friend	दोस्त	đosţ
husband	धणी	đ'a·ņee
mother	माँ	maany
sister	भैण	b'eņ
son	बेटो	be·to
wife	घरवाळी	g'ar·waa·ļee

Here's my (address).	यो म्हारो (पत्तो) है।	o m'aa·ro (pa·ţo) hai
What's your (email)?	थारो (ई-मेल) कॉई है?	ţ'aa·ro (ee·mel) kaa·nyee hai
Where are you from?	थे कठै रहो?	ţ'ai ka·t'ai raa·ho

I'm from ...	मै ... रो हूं।	m'ai ... ro hoony
Australia	आस्ट्रेलिया	aas·tre·li·yaa
Canada	कनाडा	ka·naa·daa
New Zealand	न्यूजीलैंड	nyu zee·land
the UK	इंग्लैंड	eng·land
the USA	अमरिका	am·ree·kaa

What's your occupation?
थांरो धंधो कॉई है? — ţ'aa·ro đ'an·đ'o kaa·nyee hai

I'm a/an ...	मै ... एक।	m'ai ... ek
businessperson	ब्योपारी	byo·paa·ree
office worker	करमचारी	kar·ma·chaa·ree
tradesperson	ब्योपारी	byo·paa·ree
Do you like ...?	थांनै ... पसंद है?	ţ'aa·nai ... pa·sanđ hai
I (don't) like ...	म्हानै ... पसंद (कोनी) है।	m'a·nai ... pa·sanđ (ko·nee) hai
art	कला	ka·laa
movies	फिलम	fi·lam
music	गाणो-बजाणो	ga·ṇo·ba·ja·ṇo
reading	पढणो	pa·d'a·ṇo
sport	खेलणो	k'e·la·ṇo

eating out

Can you recommend a ...?	कॉई थे बता सको ...?	kaa·nyee ţ'ai ba·ţaa sa·ko ...
bar	बार	baar
dish	पकवान	pa·ka·vaa·na
place to eat	ढाबो	d'aa·bo
I'd like (a/the) ..., please.	म्हाने ... चाहिजे सा।	m'a·nai ... chaa·hi·jai sa
bill	बिल	bil
drink list	ड्रिंक्स रो मीनू	drinks ro me·noo
local speciality	अठा री खास चीज	a·t'aa ree k'aas cheej
menu	मीनू	mee·noo
(non)smoking section	धुम्रपान (निखेध) जग्यॉ	đ'um·ra·paan (ni·k'eđ') ja·gyany
table for (four)	(चार) जणां रै वास्ते टेबुल	(chaar) ja·ṇaa rai vaas·ţai te·bu·la
that dish	बो पकवान	bo pa·ka·vaa·na
breakfast	नाश्तो	naas·ţo
lunch	दोपहर रो खाणो	đo·pair ro k'aa·ṇo
dinner	रात रो खाणो	raaţ ro k'aa·ṇo

(cup of) coffee …	(एक कप) कोफी …	(ek kap) ko·fee …
(cup of) tea …	(एक कप) चाय …	(ek kap) chaay …
with milk	दूध रै साग्गै	đoođ' rai saag·gai
without sugar	बिना चीणी रै	bi·naa chee·ṇee rai
(orange) juice	(संतरा रो) रस	(san·ţa·raa ro) ras
lassi	लस्सी	las·see
soft drink	ठण्डो	t'an·do

I'll have boiled/mineral water.
म्हाने उबलेडो/मिनरल वाटर चाहिजे। m'a·nai ub·le·ŗo/mi·na·ral vaa·tar chaa·e·je

I'll buy you a drink.
आप रै ड्रिंक रा पइसा मैं देवूँला। aap rai drink raa pa·ee·saa m'ai đe·voony·laa

What would you like?
थाने कॉई पसन्द है? ţ'aa·nai kaa·nyee pa·sanđ hai

a bottle/glass of beer	एक बोतल/गिलास बियर	ek bo·ţal/gi·laas bi·yar
a bottle/glass of wine	एक बोतल/गिलास अंगूर री शराब	ek bo·ţal/gi·laas an·goor ree s'a·raab

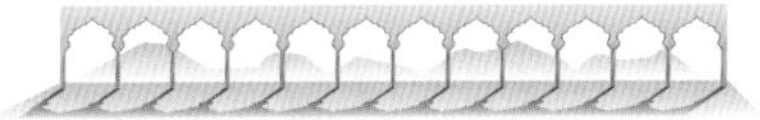

special diets & allergies

Do you have … food?	कॉई थारै कन्नै … खाणो है?	kaa·nyee ţ'aa·rai kan·nai … k'aa·ṇo hai
halal	हलाल	ha·laal
kosher	झटको	j'a·ta·ko
vegetarian	शाकाहारी	s'aa·kaa·haa·ree
I'm allergic to …	मन्नै … सूं एलर्जी है।	m'a·nai … soony e·lar·jee hai
dairy products	दूध सूँ बणेडो सामान	đoo·đ'a soony ba·ṇe·ŗo sa·maan
eggs	अण्डा	aṇ·da
meat stock	गोश्त	gos'ţ
nuts	मेवो	me·vo
seafood	मछली	ma·ch'a·lee

emergencies

Help!	मदद!	ma·đađ
Stop!	रूको!	ru·ko
Go away!	चल्यो जा!	cha·lyo jaa
Thief!	चोर!	chor
Fire!	आग!	aag
Watch out!	खबरदार!	k'a·bar·đaar

Call ...!	बुलावो ...!	bu·laa·vo ...
an ambulance	एम्बूलेंस	em·boo·lens
a doctor	डाक्टर	daak·tar
the police	पुलिस	pu·lis

Could you help me, please?
कॉई थै म्हारी मदद करस्यो? — kaa·nyee ţ'ai m'aa·ree ma·đađ ka·ra·syo

I have to use the phone.
मन्नै फोन रो इस्तेमाल करणो है। — man·nai fon ro is·ţe·maal ka·ra·ṇo hai

I'm lost.
मै खो ग्यो हूं। — m'ai k'o gyo hoony

Where are the toilets?
टोयलेट कठै है? — toy·let ka·t'ai hai

Where's the police station?
पुलिस थाणो कठै है? — pu·lis ţ'aa·ṇo ka·t'ai hai

I have insurance.
म्हारो बीमो है। — m'aa·ro bee·mo hai

I want to contact my embassy.
म्है म्हारा दूतावास सूं सम्पर्क करणो चाहूं। — m'ai m'aa·raa đoo·ţaa·vaas soony sam·park ka·ra·ṇo chaa·voony

I've been ...	म्हारे साग्गै ...	m'aa·re saag·gai ...
assaulted	दुर्व्यवहार	đur·vya·va·haar
raped	बलात्कार	ba·laaţ·kaar
robbed	लूटमार	loot·maar

I've lost my ...	म्हारो ... खो ग्यो।	m'aa·ro ... k'o gyo
bag	थैलो	ţ'ai·lo
credit card	क्रेडिट कार्ड	kre·dit kaa·rad
money	पईसा	pa·ee·saa
passport	पासपोर्ट	paas·port
travellers cheques	ट्रेवलर चैक	tre·va·lar chai·ka

health

Where's the nearest ...?	अठै पास मै कोइ ... है?	a·t'ai paas me ko·ee ... hai
dentist	दाँतां रो डाक्टर	đaa·ţaany ro daak·tar
doctor	डाक्टर	daak·tar
hospital	हस्पताल	has·pa·ţaal
pharmacist	फारमेसी	p'aa·ra·me·see

I need a doctor (who speaks English).
मन्नै (इंग्रेजी बोलण वाळो) डाक्टर चाहिजे। — m'an·nai (ing·re·jee bo·laṇ waa·ḷo) daak·tar chaa·e·je

Could I see a female doctor?
मन्नै महिला डाक्टर चाहिजे? — m'an·nai ma·hi·laa daak·tar chaa·e·je

I've run out of my medication.
म्हारी दवायाँ खतम व्हैगी। — m'aa·ree đa·vaa·yaany k'a·ţam hwai·gee

It hurts here.
अठै दर्द हुवै। — a·t'ai đarđ hu·wai

I have (a) ...	मन्नै ... है।	m'a·nai ... hai
asthma	दमो	đa·mo
constipation	कब्ज	kabj
diarrhoea	हैजो	hai·jo
fever	बुखार	bu·k'aar
heart condition	दिल री बिमारी	đil ree bee·maa·ree
nausea	उबकाई रो एहसास	ub·kaa·ee ro eh·saas

I'm allergic to ...	मन्नै ... सूं एलर्जी है।	m'an·nai ... soony e·lar·jee hai
antibiotics	एन्टी बॉयटिक	en·tee bo·ya·tik
anti-inflammatories	एन्टी इंफ्लेमेट्रीज	en·tee in·fle·me·ta·reej
aspirin	एस्प्रिन	es·pi·rin
bees	मोम री माखी	mom ree maak·k'ee
codeine	कोडीन	ko·deen

responsible travel

I'd like to learn some Marwari/Rajasthani.
मै कोई मारवाडी/राजस्थानी सीखणी चावूं।
mai ko·ee maa·ra·vaa·ṛee/raa·jas·ţ'aa·nee see·k'a·ṇee chaa·voony

What's this called in Marwari/Rajasthani?
इ नै मारवाडी/राजस्थानी मै कॉई कैवै?
ee nai maa·ra·vaa·ṛee/raa·jas·ţ'aa·nee me kaa·nyee kai·vai

Would you like me to teach you some English?
मैं आपनै थोडी इंग्रेजी सिखाणी चावूं?
mai aap·nai ţ'o·ree ing·re·jee si·k'aa·ṇee chaa·voony

I didn't mean to do/say anything wrong.
म्हारो इरादो आपने बुरो बताण/करणा रो बिल्कुल नी हो।
m'aa·ro i·ra·đo aap·nai bu·ro ba·ţaṇ/ka·ra·ṇa ro bil·kul nee ho

Is this a local or national custom?
कॉई यो स्थानीय या रा-ट्रीय रिवाज है?
kaa·nyee o sţ'aa·neey ya raas'·treey ri·vaaj hai

I'd like to stay at a locally run hotel.
मै स्थानीय होटल मै ठहरणो चावूंला।
mai sţ'aa·neey ho·tal me t'a·har·ṇo chaa·voony·laa

Where can I buy locally produced goods/souvenirs?
अठैरी बण्योडी चीजां/सोविनियर मैं कठै सूँ खरीद सकूँ?
a·t'ai·ree ba·ṇyo·ṛee chee·jaa/soo·vee·ni·ar mai ka·t'ai soony k'a·ree·đa sa·koony

What's this made from?
यो कॉई सूं बण्यो है?
yo kaa·nyee soony ba·ṇyo hai

Does your company have responsible tourism policies?
कॉई आपरी कम्पनी री कोई जिम्मेदार पर्यटन नीति है?
kaa·nyee aap·ree kam·pa·nee ree ko·ee jim·me·đar pa·rya·tan nee·ţi hai

I'd like to do some volunteer work (for your organisation).
मै (आपरी संस्था रे वास्तै) कुछ योगदान देणो चावूं।
m'ai (aap·ree sans·ţ'aa rai vaas·ţai) kuch' yog·đaan đe·ṇo chaa·voony

I'm (an English teacher). Can I volunteer my skills?
मैं (अँग्रेजी रो अध्यापक हूँ)। मै म्हारी योग्यता रो योगदान देणो सकूँ?
m'ai (ing·re·jee ro ađ'·yaa·pak hoony) mai m'aa·ree yo·gya·ţaa ro yog·đaan đe sa·koony

english–marwari dictionary

Words in this dictionary are marked as n (noun), a (adjective), v (verb), sg (singular) and pl (plural) where necessary.

A

accident हादसो haad·so
accommodation रहणा रो ठिकाणो ra·ha·nai ro t'i·kaa·no
adaptor एडोप्टर e·dop·tar
address n पतो pa·ţo
after पाछै paa·ch'ai
air-conditioned एयरकंडिशन e·ya·ra·kan·di·s'an
airplane हवाई जहाज ha·vaa·ee ja·haaj
airport हवाई अड्डो ha·vaa·ee ad·do
alcohol दारू đaa·roo
all सगळा sa·ga·ļaa
allergy एलर्जी e·lar·jee
ambulance एम्बुलैंस em·boo·lens
and और owr
ankle टखणो ta·k'a·ņo
antibiotics एन्टी बॉयटिक en·tee bo·ya·tik
arm बाजू baa·joo
ATM एटीएम e·tee·em

B

baby छोटो टाबर ch'o·to taa·bar
back (of body) पीठ peet'
backpack थैलो ţ'ai·lo
bad बुरो bu·ro
bag थैलो ţ'ai·lo
baggage claim सामान वापसी saa·maan vaa·pa·see
bank बैंक baink
bar बार baar
bathroom गुसलखाणों gu·sa·la·k'aa·ņo
battery बैटरी bai·ta·ree
beautiful फूटरो p'oo·ta·ro
bed बिस्तरो vis·ţa·ro
before पेल्लो pel·lo
behind लारै laa·rai
bicycle सायकल saa·ya·kal
big बडो ba·ŗo
bill बिल bil
blanket कम्बल kaam·bal
blood group ब्लड ग्रुप blad grup
boat नाव naav
book (make a reservation) v बुक करणो buk kar·no
bottle बोतल bo·ţal
boy छोरो ch'o·ro
brakes (car) ब्रेक brek
breakfast नास्तो naas·ţo
broken (faulty) टूट्योडो tu·tyo·ŗo
bus बस bas
business ब्योपार byo·paar
buy v खरीदणो k'a·ree·đa·ņo

C

camera कैमरो kai·ma·ro
cancel रद्द rađ·đa
car कार kaar
cash n पईसो pa·ee·so
cash (a cheque) v चैक कैश कराणो chaik kais' ka·raa·no
cell phone मोबाईल फोन mo·baa·eel fon
centre n केन्द्र ken·đra
change (money) v छुट्टा पईसा ch'ut·taa pa·ee·saa
cheap सस्तो sas·to
check (bill) बिल bil
check-in n चैक-इन chaik·in
chest (body) छाती ch'aa·ţee
child छोटो टाबर ch'o·to taa·bar
cigarette सिगरेट si·ga·ret
city शहर sair
clean a साफ saap'
closed बन्द banđ
cold a ठंडो t'an·do
collect call कलैक्ट कॉल ka·lek·ta kaa·la
come आणों aa·ņo
computer कम्प्युटर kam·pu·tar
condom कन्डोम kan·do·ma
contact lenses कान्टेक्ट लैंस kaan·tek·ta lens
cook v रसोइयो ra·soy·yo
cost n कीमत kee·ma·ţa
credit card क्रेडिट कारड kre·dit kaa·rad
customs (immigration) कस्टम kas·ta·ma

D

dangerous खतरनाक k'a·ţa·ra·naa·ka
date (time) तारीख ţaa·ree·k'a
day दिन đi·na
delay n देरी đe·ree

dentist दांता रो डाक्टर đaa·ţaany ro daak·ta·ra
depart रवानगी ra·vaa·na·gee
diaper पोतडो po·ţa·ŗo
dinner रात रो खाणो raaţ ro k'aa·ņo
direct a सीधो see·d'o
dirty गन्दो gan·đo
disabled अपाहिज a·paa·hi·ja
discount n छूट ch'oo·ta
doctor डाक्टर daak·ta·ra
double bed डबल बैड da·ba·la bai·da
double room डबल कमरो da·ba·la ka·ma·ro
drink n ड्रिंक drin·ka
drive v गाडी चलाणो gaa·dee cha·ļaa·ņo

E

ear कान kaan
east पूरब poo·rab
eat खाणों k'aa·ņo
economy class रिआयती दर्जो ri·aay·tee dar·jo
electricity बिजली bi·ja·lee
elevator लिफ्ट lif·ta
email ई-मेल ee·me·la
embassy दूतावास đoo·ţaa·vaa·sa
emergency आपातकाल aa·paa·ţa·kaa·la
English (language) इंग्रेजी ing·re·jee
evening ्ााम s'aa·ma
exit n निकास ni·kaa·sa
expensive मंहगों ma·han·go
eye आँख aany·k'a

F

far दूर đoo·ra
fast तेज ţe·ja
father बापु baa·poo
film (camera) रील ree·la
finger उंगळी ung·ļee
first class पैलो दर्जो pai·lo dar·jo
fish n मछली ma·ch'a·lee
food खाणो k'aa·ņo
foot पग pa·ga
free (of charge) मुफत mu·fa·ţa
friend दोस्त đos·ţa
fruit फल p'a·la
full भरयोडो b'a·ryo·ŗo

G

gift तोफो to·p'o
girl छोरी ch'o·ree
glass (drinking) गिलास gi·laa·sa
glasses काँच kaanych
go जावो jaa·vo
good अच्छो aa·ch'o
guide n गाइड gaa·ee·da

H

half n आधो aa·đ'o
hand हाथ haa·ţ'a
happy राजी raa·jee
have कन्नै kan·nai
he बो bo
head n माथो maa·ţ'o
heart दिल đi·la
heavy भारी b'aa·ree
help v मदद ma·đa·đa
here अठै a·ţ'ai
high उँचो oony·cho
highway हाईवै haa·ee·vai
hike v पगाँ घूमणो pa·g'aany g'oo·ma·ņo
holiday छुट्टी रो दिन ch'ut·tee ro đi·na
homosexual n&a समलैंगी sa·ma·lain·gee
hospital अस्पताल has·pa·ţaa·la
hot तातो ţaa·ţo
hotel होटल ho·ta·la
hungry भूखो b'oo·k'o
husband धणीं đ'a·ņee

I

identification (card) पहचान पत्र pa·ha·chaa·na paţ·ra
ill बिमार bi·maa·ra
important जरूरी ja·roo·ree
injury जखम ja·k'a·ma
insurance बीमो bee·mo
internet इंटरनेट in·tar·ne·ta
interpreter दुभा-ियो du·b'aa·s'i·yo

J

jewellery गहणो gai·ņo
job नौकरी now·ka·ree

K

key कूँची koony·chee
kilogram किलोग्राम ki·lo·graa·ma
kitchen रसोई ra·so·ee
knife चाकू chaa·koo

L

laundry (place) गाबा धोणा री जग्यॉं
ga·ba đ'o·ṇa ri ja·gyaṇ
lawyer वकील va·kee·la
left (direction) बांयो baany·yo
leg (body) टांग taaṇg
lesbian n&a लेसबियन les·bi·an
less कम ka·ma
letter (mail) चिट्ठी chi·t'ee
light n चानणो chaa·na·ṇo
like v पसन्द pa·san·đa
lock n ताळो ṭaa·ḷo
long लम्बो lam·bo
lost गुमग्यो gu·ma·gyo
love v प्यार pyaa·ra
luggage सामान sa·maa·na
lunch दुपैर रो खाणों đo·pai·ra ro k'aa·ṇo

M

mail n डाक daa·ka
man आदमी aa·đa·mee
map नक्शो nak·s'o
market बजार ba·jaa·ra
matches माचिसपेटी maa·chi·sa·pe·tee
meat गोश्त gos'·ṭa
medicine दवाई đa·vaa·ee
message संदेस san·đe·sa
milk दूध đoo·đ'a
minute मिनट mi·na·ta
mobile phone मोबाईल फोन mo·baa·eel fon
money पईसा pa·ee·saa
month मिन्हो min·ho
morning सुबह su·ba·ha
mother माँ maany
motorcycle मोटरसाइकल mo·ta·ra·saa·i·ka·la
mouth मुंडो mun·do

N

name नाम naa·ma
near कन्नैं kan·ney
neck n गरदन gar·đa·na
new नवो na·vo
newspaper इखबार i·k'a·baa·ra
night रात raa·ṭa
no ना/नी naa/nee
noisy ॄोरगुल वाळी जग्यॉं s'or·gul waa·ḷee ji·gyany
nonsmoking धूम्रपान वर्जित đ'um·ra·paa·na var·ji·ṭa
north उत्तर uṭ·ṭa·ra
nose नाक naa·ka
now अबार a·baa·ra
number नम्बर nam·ba·ra

O

old पूराणों pu·raa·ṇo
one-way ticket एक तरफ रो टिगट
e·ka ṭa·ra·fa ro ti·ga·ta
open a खुल्लो k'ul·lo
outside बारे baa·rai

P

passport पासपोर्ट paas·por·ta
pay v तनखा ṭa·na·k'aa
pharmacy फारमेसी p'aa·ra·me·see
phonecard फोन कारड fon kaa·ra·da
photo फोटू fo·too
police पुलिस pu·li·sa
postcard पोस्टकार्ड pos·ta·kaar·da
post office डाकखाणों daa·ka·k'aa·ṇo
pregnant गरभवती ga·ra·b'a·va·ṭee
price n दाम daa·ma

Q

quiet a ांत s'aan·ta

R

rain n बरसात ba·ra·saa·ṭa
razor उस्तरो us·ṭa·ro
receipt n रसीद ra·see·đa
refund n पइसा वापस pa·ee·saa vaa·pa·sa
registered mail रजिस्टर्ड डाक ra·jis·tar·da daa·ka
rent v किरायो ki·raa·yo
repair v मरम्मत करणों ma·ra·ma·ṭa ka·ra·ṇo
reservation रिजर्वेशन ri·jar·ve·s'a·na
restaurant रैसटोरेन्ट rai·sa·to·ren·ta
return v वापस vaa·pa·sa
return ticket वापसी टिगट vaa·pa·see ti·ga·ta
right (direction) जीमणो jee·ma·ṇo
road सडक sa·ṛa·ka
room n कमरो ka·ma·ro

S

safe a सुरक्षित su·rak·s'i·ṭa
seat n सीट see·ta
send भेजणो b'e·ja·ṇo

L

english–marwari

sex संभोग sam·b'o·ga
share (a dorm) साझे में (कमरो) लेणो saa·j'e me (kam·ro) le·ṇo
she बा baa
sheet (bed) चादर chaa·đa·ra
shirt कमीज ka·mee·ja
shoes जुत्ता ju·ţaa
shop n दुकान đu·kaa·na
short छोटो ch'o·to
shower n फवारो p'a·vaa·ro
single room सिंगल कमरो sin·ga·la ka·ma·ro
skin n चमडी cha·ma·ṛee
skirt n स्कर्ट skar·ta
sleep v सोणो so·ṇo
slowly होले-होले ho·lai·ho·lai
small छोटो ch'o·to
soap साबण saa·ba·ṇa
some कुछ ku·ch'a
soon बेग्गो beg·go
south दक्षिण đak·s'i·ṇa
souvenir shop सेविनियर री दुकान soo·vee·ni·ar ree đu·kaa·na
stamp टिगट ti·ga·ta
station (train) स्टेशन ste·s'a·na
stomach पेट pet
stop v रूकाणो roo·kaa·ṇo
stop (bus) n बस स्टाप bas staa·pa
street गली ga·lee
student विद्यार्थी vi·đyaar·ţ'ee
sun सूरज soo·ra·ja
sunscreen सनस्कीन sa·na·skree·na
swim v तैरणों ţai·ra·ṇo

T

tampons टैम्पून taim·poo·na
teeth दांत đaaṇ·ţa
telephone n टेलीफोन te·lee·p'o·na
temperature (weather) तापमान ţaa·pa·maa·na
that (one) बो bo
they बै bai
thirsty प्यासो pyaa·so
this (one) ओ o
throat गळो ga·ḷo
ticket टिगट ti·ga·ta
time बखत ba·k'a·ţa
tired थक्योडो ţ'ak·yo·ṛo
tissues उत्तक uţ·ţa·ka
today आज aa·ja
toilet टोलेट toy·le·ta
tomorrow काल kaa·la
tonight आज aa·ja
toothbrush टूथब्रश too·ţ'a·bra·s'a
toothpaste टूथपेस्ट too·ţ'a·pes·ta
torch (flashlight) बैटरी bai·ta·ree
tour n टूर too·ra
tourist office टूरिस्ट ओफिस too·ri·sa o·fi·sa
towel तौलियो ţow·li·yo
train n रेलगाडी re·la·gaa·ṛee
translate अनुवाद a·nu·vaa·đa
travellers cheque ट्रेवलर चैक tre·va·lar chai·ka
trousers पतलून pat·loo·na
twin beds डबल बैड da·ba·la bai·da

U

underwear जांघियो jaaṇ·g'i·yo
urgent जरूरी ja·roo·ree

V

vacant खाली k'aa·lee
vegetable n सबजी sa·ba·jee
vegetarian a शाकाहारी s'aa·kaa·haa·ree
visa बीजो bee·jo

W

walk v घूमणो g'oo·ma·ṇo
wallet बटुवो ba·tu·vo
wash (something) धोणो đ'o·ṇo
watch n घडी g'a·ṛee
water n पाणी paa·ṇee
we म्हें m'eny
weekend वीकेन्ड wee·kain·da
west पश्चिम pas'·chi·ma
wheelchair पहिया वाळी कुर्सी pa·hi·yaa vaa·ḷee kur·see
when कद ka·da
where कठै ka·t'ai
who कुण ku·ṇa
why क्यूं kyoony
wife घरवाळी g'ar·waa·ḷee
window खिडकी k'i·ṛa·kee
with सागै saag·gai
without बिना bi·naa
woman लुगाई lu·gaa·ee
write लिखणों li·k'a·ṇo

Y

yes हाँ haany
yesterday गुजरे काल gu·ja·re kaa·la
you sg/pl थे/आप ţ'e/aa·pa

DICTIONARY

Oriya

alphabet

vowels									
ଅ a	ଆ aa	ଇ i	ଈ ee	ଉ u	ଊ oo	ଏ e	ଐ ai	ଓ o	ଔ *o*·woo

consonants				
କ ka	ଖ k'a	ଗ ga	ଘ g'a	ଙ woon
ଚ cha	ଛ chaa	ଜ ja	ଝ j'a	ଞ *ga*·yan
ଟ ta	ଠ t'a	ଡ da	ଢ d'a	ଣ na
ତ ta	ଥ t'a	ଦ da	ଧ d'a	ନ na
ପ pa	ଫ p'a	ବ ba	ଭ b'a	ମ ma
ଯ jya	ୟ ya	ର ra	ଲ la	ଳ ḷa
ଵ b'a	ୱ wo	ଶ sha	ଷ şa	ସ sa
ହ ha	କ୍ଷ k'ya			

numerals									
0	1	2	3	4	5	6	7	8	9
୦	୧	୨	୩	୪	୫	୬	୭	୮	୯

introduction

The Jagannatha temple at Puri in Orissa houses some of the earliest Oriya writing, contained in the 12th-century *Madala Panji* (Palm-leaf Chronicles). Now spoken by around 31 million people, Oriya (o·di·aa ଓଡ଼ିଆ) is the state language of Orissa, with speakers in West Bengal and Gujarat. Historically very similar to Bengali, Oriya is believed to have come into its own in the 10th and 11th centuries, when a common language evolved from the western and coastal dialects of the Orissa region. It developed a rich literary tradition, with many writers mastering the art of poetry in particular. The modern state of Orissa wasn't declared until after Indian independence in 1947, when the Oriya-speaking peoples were united. Oriya belongs to the Indo-Aryan language family and, in addition to Bengali, it has a close relative in Assamese. Despite these connections, the Oriya speakers preferred a different writing system to that of other Indo-Aryan languages, and adopted a script with fewer straight lines.

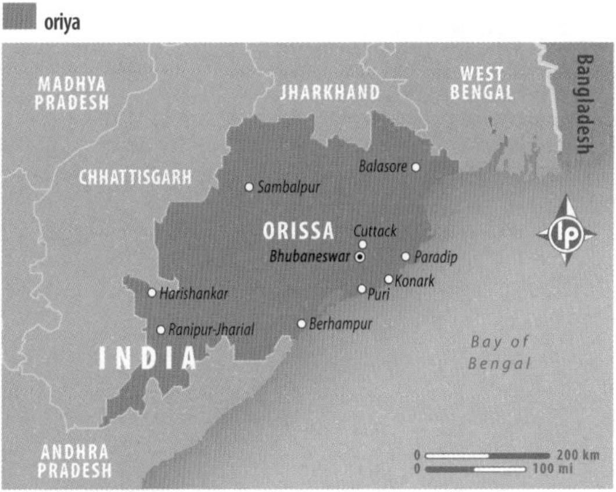

pronunciation

Vowels		Consonants	
Symbol	**English sound**	**Symbol**	**English sound**
a	run	b	bed
aa	father	ch	cheat
ai	aisle	d	dog
e	bet	g	go
ee	see	h	hat
i	hit	j	jar
o	pot	k	kit
oo	zoo	l	lot
u	put	ḷ	retroflex l
		m	man
		n	not
		ng	ring
		p	pet
		r	red
		s	sun
		ş	retroflex s
		sh	shut
		t	top
		w	win
		y	yes

In this chapter, the Oriya pronunciation is given in blue after each phrase.

Aspirated consonants (pronounced with a puff of air after the sound) are represented with an apostrophe after the letter – b', d', g', j', k', n', p' and t'. Retroflex consonants (pronounced with the tongue bent backwards) are included in this table.

Each syllable is separated by a dot. For example:

ଦୁଃଖିତ. du·k'i·ta

essentials		
Yes.	ହଁ.	han
No.	ନା.	naa
Please.	ଦୟାକରୀ.	da·yaa·ka·ri
Thank you.	ଧନ୍ୟବାଦ.	d'an·ya·baa·da
Excuse me. (to get past)	କ୍ଷମା କରିବେ.	k'ya·maa ka·ri·be
Excuse me. (to get attention)	କ୍ଷମା କରନ୍ତୁ.	k'ya·maa ka·ran·tu
Sorry.	ଦୁଃଖିତ.	du·k'i·ta

language difficulties

Do you speak English?
ଆପଣ ଇଁରାଜୀ କୁହନ୍ତି କୀ? — aa·pa·na eng·li·sha ku·han·ti ki

Do you understand?
ଆପଣ ବୁଝନ୍ତି କୀ? — aa·pa·na bu·jhan·ti ki

I understand.
ମୁଁ ବୁଝେ. — mu bu·j'e

I don't understand.
ମୁଁ ବୁଝେ ନାହିଁ. — mu bu·j'e naa·hi

Could you please ...?	ଆପଣ ଦୟାକରୀ ...?	aa·pa·na da·yaa·ka·ri ...
repeat that	ପୁନର୍ବାର କର	pu·nar·baa·ra ka·ra
speak more slowly	ଆହୁରି ଧୀରେ କଥାକୁହନ୍ତୁ	aa·hu·ri d'ee·re ka·t'a·ku·han·tu

numbers					
0	ଶୁନ୍ୟ	sun·ya	20	କୋଡୀଏ	ko·dee·e·a
1	ଏକ	e·ka	30	ତିରିଶ	ti·ri·şi
2	ଦୁଇ	do·e	40	ଚାଳିଶି	cha·li·şi
3	ତିନ	ti·ni	50	ପଚାଶ	pa·cha·şa
4	ଚାରି	cha·ri	60	ଷାଠିଏ	sha·t'i·e
5	ପାନ୍ଚ	pan·cha	70	ସତୁରି	sa·tu·ri
6	ଛଅ	cha·a	80	ଅଶୀଏ	a·şee·e
7	ସାତ	saa·t'a	90	ନବେ	na·be
8	ଆଠ	aa·t'a	100	ଶହେ	sa·he
9	ନଅ	na·aa	1000	ଏକ ହଜାର	e·ka ha·ja·ra
10	ଦଶ	da·sa	1,000,000	ଦଶ ଲକ୍ଷ	da·şa lak'·ya

time & dates

What time is it?	ଏବେ କେତେଟା ସମୟ ହେଲା?	e·be ke·te·ta sa·ma·ya he·laa
It's (two) o'clock.	ଏବେ (ଦୁଇ) ଘଣ୍ଟା ବାଜିଛି.	e·be (do·e) g'an·ta ba·ji·chi
Quarter past (two).	(ଦୁଇ) ଘଣ୍ଟା ବାଜି ପନ୍ଦର ମିନିଟ ହେଇଛି.	(do·e) g'an·ta ba·ji pan·da·ra mi·ni·ta ho·e·chi
Half past (two).	(ଦୁଇ) ଘଣ୍ଟା ବାଜି ଅଧଘଣ୍ଟା ହେଇଛି.	(do·e) g'an·taa baa·ji aa·d'a·g'an·taa ho·e·chi
Quarter to (three).	(ତିନି) ଘଣ୍ଟା ହେବାକୁ ପନ୍ଦର ମିନିଟ ଅଛି.	(ti·ni) g'an·taa he·baa·ku pan·da·ra mi·ni·ta aa·chi
At what time ...?	କେଉଁ ସମୟରେ ...?	ke·un sa·ma·ya·re ...
At ...	ସ୍ଥାନ ...	st'a·na ...
It's (15 December).	ଏହା (ପନ୍ଦର ଡିସେମ୍ବର).	e·haa (pan·da·ra de·sem·ber)

yesterday	ଗତକାଲି	ga·ta·kaa·li
today	ଆଜି	aa·ji
tomorrow	ଆସନ୍ତା କାଲି	aa·san·t'a kaa·li

Monday	ସୋମବାର	so·ma·baa·ra
Tuesday	ମଗଂଳବାର	man·ga·la·baa·ra
Wednesday	ବୁଧୁବାର	bu·d'u·baa·ra
Thursday	ଗୁରୁବାର	gu·ru·baa·ra
Friday	ଶୁକ୍ରୁବାର	suk·ru·baa·ra
Saturday	ଶନିବାର	sa·ni·baa·ra
Sunday	ରବିବାର	ra·bi·baa·ra

border crossing

I'm here ...	ମୁଁ ଏଠାରେ ...	mu a·t'a·re ...
in transit	ଯାତ୍ରା କରୁଛି	jaat·ra ka·ru·chi
on business	ବ୍ୟବସାୟ କରୁଛ	bya·ba·saa·ya ka·ru·chi
on holiday	ଛୁଟିରେ ଅଛି	chu·ti·re aa·chi

I'm here for ...	ମୁଁ ଏଠାରେ ଅଛି ... ପାଇଁ.	mu a·t'a·re aa·chi ... pai
(10) days	(ଦଶ) ଦିନ	(da·sa) di·na
(three) weeks	(ତିନି) ସପ୍ତାହ	(ti·ni) sap·t'a
(two) months	(ଦୁଇ) ମାସ	(do·e) maa·sa

I'm going to (Puri).
ମୁଁ (ପୁରୀ) ଯାଉଛି. mu (pu·ri) ja·u·chi

I'm staying at the (Taj hotel).

ମୁଁ (ତାଜ୍ ହୋଟେଲ୍) ରେ ରହୁଛି.	mu (taj ho·te·la) re ra·hu·chi

I have nothing to declare.

ମୋର କିଛି ପ୍ରକାଶ କରିବାର ନାହିଁ.	mo·ra ki·chi pra·kaa·ṣa ka·ri·baa·ra naa·hi

tickets & luggage

Where can I buy a ticket?

ମୁଁ କେଉଁଠାରୁ ଗୋଟେ ଟିକଟ କିଣି ପାରିବି?	mu ke·u·t'a·ru go·te ti·ka·ta ki·n'i pa·ri·bi

Do I need to book a seat?

ମୋର ଗୋଟିଏ ସ୍ଥାନ ସଂରକ୍ଷଣ କରିବା ଦରକାର କି?	mo·ra go·ti·e·a st'a·na san·ra·kya·n'a ka·ri·baa da·ra·kaa·ra ki

One … ticket (to Bhunaneswar), please.	ଦୟାକରୀ, ଗୋଟେ … (ଭୁବନେଶ୍ୱର) କୁ ଟିକଟ ଦିୟନ୍ତୁ.	da·yaa·ka·ri go·te … (b'u·ba·nes·wa·ra) ku ti·ka·ta di·yan·tu
one-way	ଗୋଟିଏ ପଟ	go·ti·e·a pa·ta
return	ଫେରନ୍ତା	p'e·ran·ta

I'd like to … my ticket, please.	ମ ଚାହୁଁଛି, ଦୟାକରି ଟିକଟିକୁ …	mu cha·hu·chi da·yaa·ka·ri ti·ka·ta·ti·ku …
cancel	ରଦ୍ଦ	rad·d'a
change	ପରିବର୍ତ୍ତନ	pa·ri·bar·ta·na
collect	ସଂଗ୍ରହ	san·gra·ha

I'd like a (non)smoking seat, please.

ମୁଁ ଚାହୁଁଛି ଗୋଟେ ଧୂମପାନ (ବିହିନ) ସ୍ଥାନ, ଦୟାକରି.	mu cha·hu·chi go·te d'u·ma·paa·na (bi·hi·na) st'a·na da·yaa·ka·ri

Is there a toilet?

ସେଠାରେ ଗୋଟେ ଶୌଚାଗାର ଯନ୍ତ୍ର ଅଛି କି?	se·t'a·re go·te so·u·cha·gaa·ra jaan·tra aa·chi ki

Is there air conditioning?

ସେଠାରେ ଗୋଟେ ଶୀତତାପ ନିୟନ୍ତ୍ରଣ ଯନ୍ତ୍ର ଅଛି କି?	se·t'a·re go·ti·e si·ta·taa·pa ni·yaan·tra·n'a jaan·tra aa·chi ki

How long does the trip take?

ଏଇ ଯାତ୍ରା କେତେ ସମୟ ନେବ?	aa·e jaa·traa ke·te sa·ma·ya ne·ba

Is it a direct route?

ଏହା ଗୋଟେ ସିଧା ରାସ୍ତା କି?	a·ha go·te si·d'a ras·taa ki

My luggage has been …	ମୋର ଜିନିଷ ...	mo·ra ji·ni·sha …
lost	ହଜିଯାଇଛି	ha·ji·jaa·e·chi
stolen	ଚୋରି ହୋଇଯାଇଛି	cho·ri ho·e·jaa·e·chi

transport

Where does flight (268) arrive/depart?
କେଉଁଠାରେ ଉଡାଜାହାଜ ସଂଖ୍ୟା (ଦୁଇଶହ ଅଠଷଠୀ) ଆସିବ/ଛାଡିବ? — ke·u·t'a·re u·da·ja·ha·ja sam·kya (do·e·sa·ha a·t'a·sha·t'i) aa·si·ba/cha·di·ba

Is this the … to (Puri)?	ଏହା (ପୁରୀ) ଯିବା ପାଇଁ ... କି?	e·ha (pu·ri) ji·baa paa·e … ki
bus	ବସ୍	bus
train	ରେଳଗାଡି	re·ḷa·gaa·di

What time's the … bus?	କୋଉ ସମୟରେ ... ବସ୍ ଅଛି?	ko·oo sa·ma·ya·re … bus ki
first	ପ୍ରଥମ	pra·t'a·ma
last	ଶେଷ	ṣe·sha
next	ପରବର୍ତ୍ତି	pa·ra·bar·t'i

How long will it be delayed?
ଏହା କେତେ ସମୟ ଡେରି ହେବ? — e·ha ke·te sa·ma·ya de·ri he·ba

Please tell me when we get to …
ଦୟାକରି ମତେ କହିବ, ଯେତେବେଳେ ଆମେ ... ରେ ପହଁଚିବା. — da·yaa·ka·ri ma·te ka·hi·ba ke·te·be·ḷe aa·me … re pa·han·chi·baa

That's my seat.
ତାହା ମୋର ସ୍ଥାନ. — ta·ha mo·ra st'a·na

I'd like a taxi …	ମୁଁ ଗୋଟେ ଭଡାଗାଡି ଚାହୁଁଛି ...	mu go·te b'a·daa·gaa·di cha·hu·chi …
at (9am)	(ସକାଳ ନଅ ଘଣ୍ଟା) ରେ	(sa·kaa·ḷa na·aa g'an·taa) re
now	ଏବେ	e·be

How much is it to (Konark)?
(କୋଣାର୍କ) ଯିବା ପାଇଁ କେତେ ପଇସା ଲାଗିବ? — (ko·nar·ka) ji·baa paa·e ke·te pa·e·saa laa·gi·ba

Please put the meter on.
ଦୟାକରି ମିଟର ଟିକୁ ଚାଲୁ କରନ୍ତୁ. — da·yaa·ka·ri mi·ta·ra ti·ku cha·lu ka·ran·tu

Please take me to …	ଦୟାକରି ମତେ … କୁ ନେଇଯାଆନ୍ତୁ.	da·yaa·ka·ri ma·te … ku ne·e·jaa·aan·tu
Please stop/wait here.	ଦୟାକରି ଏଠାରେ ରୁହନ୍ତୁ/ ଅପେକ୍ଷା କରନ୍ତୁ.	da·yaa·ka·ri e·t'a·re ru·han·tu/ a·pek·k'yaa ka·ran·tu
I'd like to hire a car (with a driver).	ମୁଁ ଗୋଟିଏ ମଟର ଗାଡି (ଚାଳକ ସହିତ) ଭଡାରେ ନେବାକୁ ଚାହୁଁଛି.	mu go·ti·e·a ma·ta·ra gaa·di (cha·ḷa·ka sa·hi·ta) b'a·daa·re ne·ba·ku cha·hun·chi
How much for daily/weekly hire?	ଦିନ/ସପ୍ତାହ ପାଇଁ କେତେ ଭଡା ଲାଗିବ?	di·na/sap·ta·ha paa·e ke·te b'a·daa laa·ji·ba

directions

Where's the …?	କେଉଁଠାରେ ଅଛି …?	ke·un·t'aa·re aa·chi …
bank	ବ୍ୟାଙ୍କ	bank
foreign currency exchange	ବୈଦେଶିକ ମୁଦ୍ରା ବିନିମୟ କେନ୍ଦ୍ର	bai·de·şi·ka mud·ra bi·ni·ma·ya ken·dra
post office	ଡାକ ଘର	daa·ka g'a·ra

Is this the road to …?	ଏହା … ଯିବାକୁ ରାସ୍ତା କି?	e·ha … ji·baa·ku ras·ta ki
Can you show me (on the map)?	ଆପଣ ମତେ (ନକ୍ସାରେ) ଦର୍ଶାଇ ପାରିବେ କି?	aa·pa·na ma·te (nak·shaa·re) dar·sa·e paa·ri·be ki
What's the address?	ଠିକଣାଟି କ'ଣ?	t'i·ka·n'aa ti ka·n'a
How far is it?	ଏହା କେତେ ଦୂର?	e·ha ke·te doo·ra
How do I get there?	ମୁଁ ସେଠାରେ କେମିତି ପହଁଚିବି?	mu se·t'aa·re ke·mi·ti pa·han·chi·bi
Turn left/right.	ବାମ/ଡାହାଣ ପଟକୁ ବୁଲନ୍ତୁ.	baa·ma/daa·ha·na pa·ta·ku bu·lan·tu

It's …	ଏହା …	e·ha …
behind …	ପଛରେ …	pa·cha·re …
in front of …	ଆଗରେ …	aa·ga·re …
near (to …)	ପାଖରେ …	paa·k'a·re …
on the corner	କୋଣରେ	ko·n'a·re

accommodation

Where's a guesthouse/hotel nearby?
ଆଖପାଖରେ ଯାତ୍ରିନିବାସ/ ହୋଟେଲ କେଉଁଠାରେ ଅଛି ?
aa·k'a·paa·k'a·re jaa·tri·ni·baa·sha/ ho·te·la ke·un·t'aa·re aa·chi

Can you recommend somewhere cheap/good?
କେଉଁଠାରେ ଶସ୍ତା/ଭଲ ଅଛି, ଶୁପାରିଶ କରିପାରିବେ କି ?
ke·un·t'aa·re şas·t'a/b'a·la aa·chi su·paa·ri·şa ka·ri·paa·ri·be ki

I'd like to book a room, please.
ମୁଁ ଗୋଟିଏ ବଖରା ସଂରକ୍ଷଣ କରିବାକୁ ଚହୁଁଛି, ଦୟାକରି.
mu go·ti·ea ba·k'a·raa san·ra·kya·na ka·ri·baa·ku cha·hun·chi da·yaa·ka·ri

I have a reservation.
ମୋର ଗୋଟିଏ ସଂରକ୍ଷଣ ସ୍ଥାନ ଅଛି.
mo·ra go·ti·e·a san·ra·kya·na st'aa·na aa·chi

Do you have a … room?	ଆପଣଙ୍କର ଗୋଟେ … ବଖରା ଅଛି ?	aa·pa·nan·ka·ra go·te … ba·k'a·raa aa·chi
single	ଗୋଟିଏ	go·ti·e·a
double	ଯୋଡା	jo·daa
twin	ଏକାପରି	e·ka·pa·ri

How much is it per night/person?
ଗୋଟେ ରାତି/ବ୍ୟକ୍ତିକୁ କେତେ ?
go·te raa·ti/bak·ti·ku ke·te

I'd like to stay for (two) nights.
ମୁଁ (ଦୁଇ) ରାତି ରହିବା ପାଇଁ ଚାହୁଁଛି.
mu (do·e) raa·ti ra·hi·baa paa·e cha·hun·chi

Can I have my key, please?
ଦୟାକରି, ମୁଁ ମୋର ଚାବି ନେଇପାରିବି କି ?
da·yaa·ka·ri mu mo·ra cha·bi ne·e·pa·ri·bi ki

Can I get another (blanket)?
ମୁଁ ଆଉ ଗୋଟିଏ (କମ୍ବଳ) ପାଇପାରିବି କି ?
mu aa·u go·ti·e (kam·ba·ḷa) paa·e·paa·ri·bi ki

The (air conditioning) doesn't work.
(ଶୀତତାପ ନିୟନ୍ତ୍ରଣ ଯନ୍ତ୍ର) କାମ କରୁନାହିଁ.
(si·ta·taa·pa ni·yan·tra·na jan·tra) kaa·ma ka·ru·naa·hi

Is there an elevator?
ଏଠାରେ ଉତ୍ତୋଳକ ଯନ୍ତ୍ର ଅଛି କି ?
e·t'aa·re u·t'o·ḷa·ka jaan·tra aa·chi ki

Is there a safe?
ଏଠାରେ ଆଲମାରୀ ଅଛି କି ?
e·t'aa·re aa·la·ma·ree aa·chi ki

What time is checkout?
ଛାଡିବାର ସମୟ କ'ଣ ?
chaa·di·baa·ra sa·ma·ya ka·na

Can I have my …, please?	ଦୟାକରି, ମୁଁ ମୋର ... ନେଇପାରିବି କି?	da·yaa·ka·ri mu mo·ra … ne·e·pa·ri·bi ki
deposit	ଜମା	ja·maa
passport	ପାଶପୋର୍ଟ	paa·şa·port
valuables	ମୂଲ୍ୟବାନ୍ ସାମଗ୍ରୀ	mul·yaa·baa·na sa·mag·ree

banking & communications

Where's an ATM?

କେଉଁଠାରେ ଗୋଟେ ଏ.ଟି.ମ ଅଛି? — ke·un·t'aa·re go·te ey·ti·em aa·chi

Where's a public phone?

 କେଉଁଠାରେ ଗୋଟେ ଜନତା ଦୂରଭାଷ ଅଛି? — ke·un·t'aa·re go·te ja·na·taa du·ra·b'aa·sha aa·chi

I'd like to …	ମୁଁ ଚାହୁଁଛି ...	mu cha·hun·chi …
arrange a transfer	ଏକ ବଦଳ ବ୍ୟବସ୍ଥା	e·ka ba·da·ḷa bya·bas·t'aa
change a travellers cheque	ପର୍ଯ୍ୟଟକ ଚେକ୍ ପରିବର୍ତ୍ତନ କରିବାକୁ	par·jya·ta·ka chek pa·ri·bar·ta·na ka·ri·baa·ku
change money	ଅର୍ଥ ପରିବର୍ତ୍ତନ କରିବାକୁ	ar·t'a pa·ri·bar·ta·na ka·ri·baa·ku
withdraw money	ଅର୍ଥ କାଢିବାକୁ	ar·t'a ka·d'i·baa·ku

What's the …?	କେତେ ଲାଗିବ ...?	ke·te laa·gi·ba …
charge for that	ତାହାପାଇଁ ମୂଲ୍ୟ	ta·ha·pa·e mul·ya
exchange rate	ବିନିମୟ ଦର	bi·ni·ma·ya da·ra

Where's the local internet café?

ସ୍ଥାନୀୟ ଇଣ୍ଟରନେଟ କ୍ୟାଫେ କେଉଁଠି ଅଛି? — st'aa·ni·ya in·ta·ra·net kya·p'e ke·un·t'i aa·chi

How much is it per hour?

ଏଠାରେ ଘଣ୍ଟାକୁ କେତେ ଲାଗେ? — e·t'aa·re g'an·ta·ku ke·te laa·ge

I'd like to …	ମୁଁ ... ଚାହୁଁଛି.	mu … cha·hun·chi
get internet access	ଇଣ୍ଟରନେଟ ପ୍ରବେଶ ପାଇବା ପାଇଁ	in·ta·ra·net pra·be·şa paa·e·baa paa·e
use a printer/ scanner	ମୁଦ୍ରଣ/ କ୍ରମବିକ୍ଷକ ଯନ୍ତ୍ର ବ୍ୟବହାର କରିବା ପାଇଁ	mud·ra·na/ kra·ma·bi·kya·ka jan·tra bya·ba·haa·ra ka·ri·baa paa·e

I'd like a ...	ମୁଁ ଗୋଟେ ... ଚାହୁଁଛି.	mu go·te ... cha·hu·chi
mobile/cell phone for hire	ଚଳନଶୀଳ ଦୂରଭାଷ ଭଡାରେ	cha·ḷa·na·ṣe·ḷa du·ra·b'a·sha b'a·daa·re
	ନବା ପାଇଁ	na·baa paa·e
SIM card for your network	ସିମ୍ ପତ୍ର ଅପଣଙ୍କର ସଂଯୁକ୍ତ କେନ୍ଦ୍ର ପାଇଁ	ṣi·ma pat·ra aa·paa·nan·ka·ra san·juk·ta ken·dra paa·e

What are the rates?
ମୂଲ୍ୟ ଗୁଡିକ କ'ଣ? — mul·ya gu·di·ka ka·na

What's your phone number?
ଆପଣଙ୍କର ଦୂରଭାଷ ସଂଖ୍ୟା କ'ଣ? — aa·paa·nan·ka·ra du·ra·b'aa·sha san·kyaa ka·na

The number is ...
ସଂଖ୍ୟାଟି ହେଲା ... — san·kyaa·ti he·laa ...

I'd like to buy a phonecard.
ମୁଁ ଗୋଟିଏ ଦୂରଭାଷ ପତ୍ର କିଣିବାକୁ ଚାହୁଁଛି. — mu go·ti·e du·ra·b'aa·sha pat·ra ki·ni·baa·ku cha·hun·chi

I want to ...	ମୁଁ ... କରିବାକୁ ଚାହୁଁଛି.	mu ... ka·ri·baa·ku cha·hun·chi
call (Canada)	କଥାବର୍ତ୍ତା (କାନାଡା)	ka·t'a·bar·t'a (kaa·naa·daa)
call collect	କଥାବର୍ତ୍ତା ସଂଗ୍ରହ	ka·t'a·bar·t'a san·gra·ha

I want to send a fax.
ମୁଁ ଗୋଟିଏ ପ୍ରତିଲିପି ପ୍ରେରଣ କରିବାକୁ ଚାହୁଁଛି. — mu go·ti·e pra·ti·li·pi pre·ra·na ka·ri·baa·ku cha·hun·chi

I want to send a parcel.
ମୁଁ ଗୋଟିଏ ପୁଟୁଳୀ ଡାକରେ ପଠାଇବା ପାଇଁ ଚାହୁଁଛି. — mu go·ti·e·a pu·tu·lee daa·ka·re pa·t'aa·e·ba paa·e cha·hun·chi

I want to buy a stamp.
ମୁଁ ଗୋଟିଏ ଡାକ ଟିକଟ କିଣିବାକୁ ଚାହୁଁଛି. — mu go·ti·e·a daa·ka ti·ka·ta ki·ni·baa·ku cha·hun·chi

I want to buy an envelope.
ମୁଁ ଗୋଟିଏ ଲଫାଫା କିଣିବାକୁ ଚାହୁଁଛି. — mu go·ti·e la·p'aa·paa ki·ni·baa·ku cha·hun·chi

Please send it to (Australia).
ଦୟାକରି, ଏହାକୁ ପଠାନ୍ତୁ (ଅଷ୍ଟ୍ରେଲିଆ) କୁ. — da·yaa·ka·ri e·ha·ku pa·t'an·tu (a·u·straa·li·aa) ku

sightseeing

What time does it open/close?
କେଉଁ ସମୟରେ ଏହା ଖୋଲା/ ବନ୍ଦ ହୁଏ? — ke·un sa·ma·ya·re e·ha k'o·laa/ ban·da hu·e

What's the admission charge?
ଏହାର ପ୍ରବେଶ ଶୁଳ୍କ କେତେ? — e·ha·ra pra·be·sha suk·la ke·te

Is there a discount for students/children?
ଛାତ୍ରମାନଙ୍କ/ପିଲାମାନଙ୍କ ପାଇଁ କିଛି ରିହାତି ଅଛି କି? — cha·tra·maa·nan·ka/pi·laa·maa·nan·ka paa·e ki·chi ri·ha·ti aa·chi ki

I'd like to hire a guide.
ମୁଁ ଜଣେ ପଥପ୍ରଦର୍ଶକଙ୍କୁ ଭଡାରେ ନେବାକୁ ଚାହୁଁଛି. — mu ja·ne pa·t'a·pra·dar·sha·ka·nan·ku b'a·daa·re ne·baa·ku cha·hu·chi

I'd like a catalogue/map.
ମୁଁ ଗୋଟେ ତାଲିକା/ନକ୍ସା ଚାହୁଁଛି. — mu go·te taa·li·kaa·baa/nak·shaa cha·hun·chi

I'd like to see …
ମୁଁ … ଦେଖିବାକୁ ଚାହୁଁଛି. — mu … de·k'i·baa·ku cha·hun·chi

What's that?
ତାହା କ'ଣ? — taa·haa ka·na

Can I take a photo?
ମୁଁ ଗୋଟିଏ ଚିତ୍ର ଉତ୍ତୋଳନ କରିପାରିବିକି? — mu go·ti·e·a chit·ra u·t'o·ḷa·na ka·ri·paa·ri·bi·ki

I'd like to go somewhere off the beaten track.
ମୁଁ ନଷ୍ଟ ହୋଇଥିବା ରାସ୍ତାରୁ ଅନ୍ୟ କୁଆଡେ ଯିବାକୁ ଚାହୁଁଛି. — mu nas·t'a ho·e·t'i·baa ras·ta·ru an·ya ku·aa·de ji·baa·ku cha·hun·chi

When's the next tour?
ପରବର୍ତ୍ତି ଭ୍ରମଣ କେତେବେଳେ? — pa·ra·bar·t'i b'ra·ma·na ke·te·be·ḷe

How long is the tour?
ଭ୍ରମଣଟି କେତେ ସମୟର? — b'ra·ma·na·ti ke·te sa·ma·ya·ra

Is … included?	… ଅନ୍ତର୍ଭୁକ୍ତ କି?	… an·tar·b'uk·ta ki
accommodation	ଆବାସ	aa·baa·sa
food	ଖାଦ୍ୟ	k'ad·ya
transport	ପରିବହନ	pa·ri·ba·ha·na

sightseeing		
fort	ଦୁର୍ଗ	dur·ga
mosque	ମସଜିଦ୍	mas·jit
palace	ରାଜଭବନ	ra·ja·b'a·ba·na
ruins	ଧ୍ୱଂସାବଶେଷ	d'on·saa·ba·se·sa
temple	ମନ୍ଦିର	man·di·ra

shopping

Where's a ...?	... କେଉଁଠାରେ ଅଛି ?	... ke·un·t'aa·re aa·chi
camera shop	ଚିତ୍ର ଉତ୍ତୋଳକ ଯନ୍ତ୍ର ଦୋକାନ	chit·ra u·t'o·ḷa·na jant·ra do·kaa·na
market	ବଜାର	ba·jaa·ra
souvenir shop	ସ୍ମରଣୀକା ଦୋକାନ	sma·ra·n'ee·kaa do·kaa·na

I'm looking for ...
ମୁଁ ଖୋଜୁଛି ... — mu ko·ju·chi ...

Can I look at it?
ମୁଁ ଏହାକୁ ଦେଖିପାରିବି କି ? — mu e·ha·ku de·k'i·paa·ri·bi ki

Can I have it sent overseas?
ମୁଁ ଏହାକୁ ବିଦେଶ କୁ ପଠାଇପାରିବି କି ? — mu e·ha·ku bi·de·sha ku pa·t'aa·e·paa·ri·bi ki

Can I have my (camera) repaired?
ମୁଁ ମୋର (ଚିତ୍ର ଉତ୍ତୋଳକ ଯନ୍ତ୍ର) କୁ ତିଆରି କରାଇପାରିବି କି ? — mu mo·ra (chit·ra u·t'o·ḷa·na jant·ra) ku ti·aa·ri ka·raa·e·paa·ri·bi ki

It's faulty.
ଏହା ଦୋଷଯୁକ୍ତ ଅଟେ. — e·ha do·sha·juk·ta a·te

How much is it?
ଏହା କେତେ ? — e·ha ke·te

Can you write down the price?
ଆପଣ ଏହାର ମୂଲ୍ୟ ଲେଖିଦେଇ ପାରିବେ କି ? — aa·pa·na e·ha·ra mul·ya le·k'i·de·e paa·ri·be ki

That's too expensive.
ତାହା ଅନେକ ଦାମୀକା. — taa·haa a·ne·ka da·mee·kaa

I'll give you (300 rupees).
ମୁଁ ଆପଣଙ୍କୁ (ତିନିଶହ ଟଙ୍କା) ଦେବି. — mu aa·pa·nan·ku (ti·ni·sa·ha tan·ka) de·bi

There's a mistake in the bill.
ଏହି ରସିଦରେ ଗୋଟିଏ ଭୁଲ ଅଛି. — e·hi ra·si·da·re go·ti·e·a b'u·la aa·chi

Do you accept ...?	ଆପଣ ... ଗ୍ରହଣ କରନ୍ତି କି?	aa·pa·na ... gra·ha·na ka·ran·ti ki
credit cards	ଉଧାର ପତ୍ର	u·d'aa·ra pat·ra
debit cards	ଲିପିବଦ୍ଧ ପତ୍ର	li·pi·bad·ha pat·ra
travellers cheques	ପର୍ଯ୍ୟଟକ ଚେକ୍	par·jya·ta·ka chek
I'd like (a) ..., please.	ଦୟାକରି ମୁଁ ଚାହୁଁଛି ...	da·yaa·ka·ri mu cha·hun·chi ...
bag	ଗୋଟେ ଥଳି	go·te t'a·ḷee
my change	ମୋର ଖୁଚୁରା	mo·ra k'u·chu·raa
receipt	ଗୋଟେ ରସିଦ	go·te ra·si·da
refund	ଫେରସ୍ତ	p'e·ras·ta
Less./Enough./More.	କମ୍./ଯଥେଷ୍ଟ./ଅଧିକ.	ka·ma/ja·t'es·t'a/a·d'i·ka

photography

Can you develop this film?	
ଆପଣ ଏହି ଆଲୋକ ଚିତ୍ର କୁ ଦୃଶ୍ୟମାନ କରିପାରିବେ କି?	aa·pa·na e·hi aa·lo·ka chit·ra ku drus·ya·maa·na ka·ri·pa·ri·be ki
I need a film for this camera.	
ମତେ ଏହି ଚିତ୍ର ଉତ୍ତୋଳକ ଯନ୍ତ୍ର ପାଇ ଆଲୋକ ଚିତ୍ର ଦରକାର.	ma·te e·hi chit·ra u·t'o·ḷa·ka jant·ra paa·e aa·lo·ka chit·ra da·ra·kaa·ra
When will it be ready?	
ଏହା କେତେବେଳେ ତିଆରି ହୋଇଯିବ?	e·haa ke·te·be·ḷe ti·aa·ri ho·e·ji·ba

making conversation

Hello./Goodbye.	ଆହେ./ବିଦାୟ.	aa·he/bi·daa·ya
Good night.	ଶୁଭ ରାତ୍ରି.	su·b'a raat·ri
Mr/Mrs/Miss	ଶ୍ରୀମାନ/ଶ୍ରୀମତୀ/କୁମାରୀ	sri·maan/sri·ma·ti/ku·maa·ree
How are you?	ଆପଣ କେମିତି ଅଛନ୍ତି?	aa·pa·na ke·mi·ti a·chan·ti
Fine, thanks. And you?	ଉତ୍ତମ, ଧନ୍ୟବାଦ. ଏବଂ ଆପଣ?	u·t'a·ma d'an·ya·bad e·bam aa·pa·na
What's your name?	ଆପଣଙ୍କ ନାମ କ'ଣ?	aa·pa·na·ka naa·ma ka·na
My name is ...	ମୋ ନାମ ହେଲା ...	mo naa·ma he·laa ...
I'm pleased to meet you.	ଆପଣଙ୍କ ସହିତ ଦେଖାକରି ମୁଁ ଆନନ୍ଦୀତ.	aa·pa·na·ka sa·hi·ta de·k'aa·ka·ri mu aa·nan·di·ta

This is my …	ଇୟେ ହେଲେ ମୋର …	e·ye he·le mo·ra …
brother	ଭାଇ	b'ai
daughter	ଝିଅ	j'i·a
father	ବାପା	baa·paa
friend	ସାଙ୍ଗ	san·ga
husband	ସ୍ୱାମୀ	swa·mi
mother	ମା	maa
sister	ଭଉଣୀ	b'a·u·nee
son	ପୁତ୍ର	put·ra
wife	ସ୍ତ୍ରୀ	stri

Here's my (address).
ଏହା ହେଲା ମୋର (ଠିକଣା). — e·ha he·laa mo·ra (t'i·ka·naa)

What's your (email)?
ଆପଣଙ୍କର (ବୈଦୁତିକ ଠିକଣା) କ'ଣ? — aa·pa·nan·ka·ra (bai·du·ti·ka t'i·ka·naa) ka·na

Where are you from?
ଆପଣ କେଉଁଠାରୁ ଆସିଛନ୍ତି? — aa·pa·na ke·un·t'aa·ru aa·si·chan·ti

I'm from (New Zealand).
ମୁଁ ଆସିଛି (ନିୟୁଜିଲ୍ୟାଣ୍ଡ). — mu aa·si·chi (nyu·ji·laan·da)

What's your occupation?
ଆପଣଙ୍କ ବୃତ୍ତି କ'ଣ? — aa·pa·na·ka bru·ti ka·na

I'm (an office worker).
ମୁଁ ହେଲି (କାର୍ଯ୍ୟାଳୟ କର୍ମଚାରୀ). — mu he·li (kar·jyaa·ḷa·ya kar·ma·cha·ree)

Do you like …?	ଆପଣ … ପସନ୍ଦ କରନ୍ତି କି?	aa·pa·na·ka … pa·san·da ka·ran·ti ki
I (don't) like …	ମୁଁ … ପସନ୍ଦ କରେ (ନାହିଁ).	mu … pa·san·da ka·re (naa·hi)
movies	ଚଳଚ୍ଚିତ୍ର	cha·ḷa·chit·ra
music	ସଂଗୀତ	san·gi·ta
reading	ପଠନ	pa·t'a·na
sport	କ୍ରୀଡା	kri·daa

eating out

Can you recommend a …?	ଆପଣ ଗୋଟେ … ପରାମର୍ଶ ଦେଇପାରିବେ କି?	aa·pa·na go·te … pa·raa·mar·şa de·e·paa·ri·be ki
bar	ମଦ୍ୟଶାଳା	mad·ya·şaa·ḷaa
place to eat	ଖାଦ୍ୟ ଖାଇବା ପାଇଁ ସ୍ଥାନ	k'aad·ya k'aa·e·baa paa·e staa·na

I'd like (a/the) ..., please.	ମୁଁ ଚାହୁଁଛି ... ଦୟାକରି.	mu cha·hun·chi ... da·yaa·ka·ri
bill	ରସିଦ	ra·si·da
local speciality	ସ୍ଥାନୀୟ ବିଶେଷ ପଦାର୍ଥ	st'a·nee·ya bi·se·sha pa·daar·t'a
menu	ଭୋଜନ ତାଲିକା	b'o·ja·na ta·li·kaa
(non)smoking section	ଧୂମପାନ (ବିହିନ) ବିଭାଗ	d'u·ma·paa·na (bi·hi·na) bi·b'a·ga
table for (four)	ଗୋଟିଏ ଟେବୁଲ (ଚାରି) ଜଣଙ୍କ ପାଇଁ	go·ti·e·a te·bu·la (cha·ri) ja·nan·ka paa·e
that dish	ସେହି ଥାଳି	se·hi t'aa·ḷee

breakfast	ଜଳଖିଆ	ja·ḷa·k'i·aa
lunch	ମଧ୍ୟାନ୍ନ ଭୋଜନ	maad·hyan·na b'o·ja·na
dinner	ରାତ୍ରି ଭୋଜନ	rat·ri b'o·ja·na

(cup of) coffee ...	ଗୋଟେ (କପ୍) କଫି ...	go·te (kap) ka·p'i ...
(cup of) tea ...	ଗୋଟେ (କପ୍) ଚାହା ...	go·te (kap) cha·haa ...
with milk	ଦୁଗ୍ଧ ସହିତ	dug·d'a sa·hi·ta
without sugar	ବିନା ଚିନି	bi·naa chi·ni

(orange) juice	(କମଳା) ରସ	(ka·ma·ḷaa) ra·sa
lassi	ଲସୀ	la·see
soft drink	ମୃଦୁ ପାନୀୟ	mru·du paa·nee·ya

I'll have boiled/mineral water.
ମୁଁ ସିଝା/ଖଣିଜ ପାନିୟ ନେବି. — mu si·j'a/k'a·ni·ja paa·nee·ya ne·bi

I'll buy you a drink.
ମୁଁ ତୁମ ପାଇଁ ଏକ ପାନୀୟ କିଣୁଛି. — mu tu·ma paa·e e·ka paa·nee·ya ki·nu·chi

What would you like?
ତୁମେ କ'ଣ ପସନ୍ଦ କର? — tu·me ka·na pa·san·da ka·ra

a bottle/glass of beer	ବିୟର୍ ର ଗୋଟିଏ ବୋଟଲ/ଗ୍ଲାସ	bi·ya·ra ra go·ti·e·a bo·ta·la/gla·sa
a bottle/glass of wine	ଗୋଟିଏ ବୋଟଲ/ଗ୍ଲାସ ୱାଇନ୍ ର	go·ti·e·a bo·ta·la/gla·sa wa·e·na ra

special diets & allergies

Do you have vegetarian food?		
	ଆପଣଙ୍କ ପାଖରେ ନିରାମୀଷ ଖାଦ୍ୟ ଅଛି କି?	aa·pa·nan·ka paa·k'a·re ni·raa·mee·sha k'ad·ya aa·chi ki
I'm allergic to ...	ମୋର ... କୁ ଅସହିଷ୍ଣୁତା ଅଛି.	mo·ra ... ku a·sa·his·sta·taa aa·chi
dairy products	ଦୁଗ୍ଧ ଜାତୀୟ ଦ୍ରବ୍ୟ	dug·d'a jaa·ti·ya drab·ya
eggs	ଅଣ୍ଡା	an·daa
nuts	ବାଦାମ	baa·daa·ma
seafood	ସାମୁଦ୍ରିକ ଖାଦ୍ୟ	saa·mu·dri·ka k'ad·ya

emergencies

Help!	ରକ୍ଷା କର!	rak·hya ka·ra
Stop!	ରୁହ!	ru·ha
Go away!	ଏଠାରୁ ଚାଲିଯାଅ!	e·t'aa·ru cha·li·jaa·a
Thief!	ଚୋର!	cho·ra
Fire!	ନିଆଁ!	ni·aa
Watch out!	ଦେଖିକରି!	de·k'i·ka·ri
Call ...!	ଡାକ ... କୁ!	daa·ka ... ku
an ambulance	ରୋଗୀଯାନ	ro·gi·jaa·na
a doctor	ଡାକ୍ତର	daak·ta·ra
the police	ପୋଲିସ୍	po·li·sa
Could you help me, please?		
	ଆପଣ ଦୟାକରି ମତେ ସାହାର୍ଯ କରିପାରିବେ କି?	aa·pa·na da·yaa·ka·ri ma·te saa·har·jya ka·ri·paa·ri·be ki
I have to use the phone.		
	ମୋର ଦୂରଭାଷ ବ୍ୟବହାର କରିବାର ଅଛି.	mo·ra du·ra·b'aa·sha bya·ba·haa·ra ka·ri·baa·ra aa·chi
I'm lost.		
	ମୁଁ ହଜିଯାଇଛି.	mu ha·ji·jaa·e·chi
Where are the toilets?		
	ଶୌଚାଗାର କେଉଁଠାରେ ଅଛି?	so·u·cha·gaa·ra ke·un·t'aa·re aa·chi
Where's the police station?		
	ଥାନା କେଉଁଠାରେ ଅଛି?	t'a·naa ke·un·t'aa·re aa·chi

I have insurance.
ମୋର ବିମା ଅଛି. mo·ra bi·maa aa·chi

I want to contact my embassy.
ମୁଁ ମୋର ଦୂତାବାସକୁ ସମ୍ପର୍କ କରିବାକୁ ଚାହୁଁଛି. mu mo·ra du·taa·baa·sa·ku sam·par·ka ka·ri·baa·ku cha·hun·chi

I've been raped/robbed.
ମୋତେ ଧର୍ଷଣ/ଲୁଣ୍ଠନ କରାଯାଇଛି. mo·te dar·sha·na/lun·t'a·na ka·raa·jaa·e·chi

I've lost my ...	ମୁଁ ମୋର ... ହଜାଇ ଦେଇଛି.	mu mo·ra ... ha·jaa·e de·e·chi
bag	ଥଳି	t'a·ḷee
money	ଟଙ୍କା ପଇସା	tan·ka pa·e·saa

health

Where's the nearest ...?	ନିକଟସ୍ଥ ... କେଉଁଠାରେ ଅଛି?	ni·ka·tas·t'a ... ke·un·t'aa·re aa·chi
dentist	ଦାନ୍ତ ଡାକ୍ତର	daan·ta daak·ta·ra
doctor	ଡାକ୍ତର	daak·ta·ra
hospital	ଡାକ୍ତରଖାନା	daak·ta·ra·k'aa·naa
pharmacist	ଭେଷଜଜ୍ଞ	b'e·sha·jag·ya

I need a doctor (who speaks English).
ମୋର ଜଣେ ଡାକ୍ତର ଦରକାର (ଯିଏ ଇଂଲିଶ କହିପାରୁଥିବେ). mo·ra ja·ne daak·ta·ra da·ra·kaa·ra (ji·e eng·li·sha ka·hi·paa·ru·t'i·be)

Could I see a female doctor?
ମୁଁ ଜଣେ ମହିଳା ଡାକ୍ତରଙ୍କୁ ଦେଖା ହେଇପାରିବି କି? mu ja·ne ma·hi·laa daak·ta·ran·ku de·k'aa ho·e·paa·ri·baa ki

I've run out of my medication.
ମୋର ଔଷଧ ସରିଯାଇଛି. mo·ra o·sa·d'a sa·ri·jaa·e·chi

It hurts here.
ଏହା ଏହିଠାରେ କାଟୁଛି. e·haa e·hi·t'aa·re kaa·tu·chi

I have (a) ...	ମୋର ... ଅଛି.	mo·ra ... aa·chi
asthma	ଶ୍ୱାସ ରୋଗ	swa·sa ro·ga
constipation	କୋଷ୍ଠ କାଠିନ୍ୟ ରୋଗ	kos·t'a kaa·t'in·ya ro·ga
diarrhoea	ଅତିସାର ରୋଗ	a·di·saa·ra ro·ga
fever	ଜର	ja·ra
heart condition	ହୃଦୟ ରୋଗ	hru·da·ya ro·ga
nausea	ବାନ୍ତି ରୋଗ	ban·ti ro·ga

I'm allergic to ...	ମୋର ... ପ୍ରତି ଅସହିଷ୍ଣୁତା ରୋଗ ଅଛି.	mo·ra ... pra·ti a·sa·his·sta·taa ro·ga aa·chi
antibiotics	ଜୀବାଣୁ ପ୍ରତିରୋଧକ ଔଷଧ	jee·baa·nu pra·ti·ro·dha·ka o·sa·dha
anti-inflammatories	ଉଦ୍ଦୀପକ ବିରୋଧୀ ଔଷଧ	ud·bee·pa·ka bi·ro·dhee ow·sa·dha
aspirin	ଯନ୍ତ୍ରଣା ହ୍ରାସ ଔଷଧ	jan·tra·naa hra·sa ow·sa·dha
bees	ମଧୁମକ୍ଷିକା	ma·dhu·ma·khi·kaa
codeine	ନିଦ ଔଷଧ	ni·da ow·sa·dha

responsible travel

I'd like to learn some Oriya.
ମୁଁ କିଛି ଓଡିଆ ଭାଷା ଶିଖିବାକୁ ଚାହୁଁଛି. — mu ki·chi o·di·aa bhaa·shaa si·khi·baa·ku cha·hu·chi

What's this called in Oriya?
ଏହାକୁ ଓଡିଆରେ କ'ଣ କୁହାଯାଏ? — e·ha·ku o·di·aa·re ka·na ku·haa·jaa·e

Would you like me to teach you some English?
ଆପଣ ଚାହାନ୍ତି କି, ମୁଁ ଆପଣଙ୍କୁ କିଛି ଇଂଲିଶ ଶିଖେଇବି ବୋଲି? — aa·pa·na cha·han·ti ki mu aa·pa·nan·ku ki·chi eng·li·sha si·khe·e·bi bo·li

I didn't mean to do/say anything wrong.
ମୁଁ କିଛି ଭୁଲ କରିବାକ/ କହିବାକୁ ଚାହୁଁନଥିଲି. — mu ki·chi bhu·la ka·ri·baa·ku/ ka·hi·baa·ku cha·hu·na·thi·li

Is this a local or national custom?
ଏହା ଗୋଟିଏ ସ୍ଥାନୀୟ ନୀତି ନା ରାଜ୍ୟ ନୀତି? — e·haa go·ti·e·a stha·nee·ya nee·ti naa raj·ya nee·ti

I'd like to stay at a locally run hotel.
ମୁଁ ସ୍ଥାନୀୟ ହୋଟେଲରେ ରହିବାକୁ ଚାହୁଁଛି. — mu sthaa·nee·ya ho·te·la·re ra·hi·baa·ku cha·hu·chi

Where can I buy locally produced goods/souvenirs?
ମୁଁ କେଉଁଠାରୁ ସ୍ଥାନୀୟ ବସ୍ତୁ/ ସ୍ମରଣୀକା କିଣିପାରିବି? — mu ke·un·tha·ru stha·nee·ya bas·tu/ sma·ra·nee·kaa ki·ni·paa·ri·bi

What's this made from?
ଏହା କେଉଁଥିରୁ ପ୍ରସ୍ତୁତ? — e·haa ke·un·thi·ru pras·tu·ta

I'm (an English teacher). Can I volunteer my skills?
ମୁଁ ଜଣେ (ଇଂଲିଶ ଶିକ୍ଷକ). ମୁଁ ମୋର ଦକ୍ଷତା ଉପଯୋଗ କରିପାରିବି କି? — mu ja·ne (eng·li·sha şi·khya·ka) mu mo·ra da·khya·taa u·pa·jo·ga ka·ri·paa·ri·bi ki

english–oriya dictionary

Words in this dictionary are marked as n (noun), a (adjective), v (verb), sg (singular) and pl (plural) where necessary.

A

accident ଦୁର୍ଘଟଣା dur·g'a·ta·naa
accommodation ଆବାସ ସ୍ଥାନ aa·baa·sa st'a·na
adaptor ବୈଦୁତିକ ପ୍ଲଗ bai·dyu·ti·ka plak
address n ଠିକଣା t'i·ka·n'aa
after ପରେ pa·re
air-conditioned ଶିତତାପ ନିୟନ୍ତ୍ରିତ
si·ta·taa·pa ni·yan·tri·ta
airplane ଉଡାଜାହାଜ u·daa·jaa·haa·ja
airport ବିମାନ ବନ୍ଦର bi·maa·na ban·da·ra
alcohol ମାଦକ ଦ୍ରବ୍ୟ maa·da·ka dra·bya
all ସମସ୍ତେ sa·mas·te
allergy ପ୍ରତିକୂଳ ପ୍ରତିକ୍ରିୟା pra·ti·ku·la pra·ti·kri·ya
ambulance ରୋଗୀଯାନ ro·gi·jaa·na
and ଓ o
ankle ପାଦର ଗଣ୍ଠି paa·ra·da gan·t'i
antibiotics ଜୀବାଣୁ ପ୍ରତିରୋଧକ ଔଷଧ
jee·baa·nu pra·ti·ro·d'a·ka ow·sa·d'a
arm ହାତ haa·ta
ATM ଏ.ଟି.ଏମ୍ ey·ti·em

B

baby ଛୋଟ ଶିଶୁ cho·ta shi·shu
back (of body) ପିଠି pi·t'i
backpack ପିଠିରେ ବନ୍ଧା ବ୍ୟାଗ pi·t'i·re ban·d'aa bag
bad ଖରାପ k'a·raa·pa
bag ଥଳି t'a·ļee
baggage claim ଜିନିଷ ପତ୍ର ଦାବି
ji·ni·sha pa·tra daa·bee
bank ବ୍ୟାଙ୍କ bank
bar ମଦ୍ୟଶାଳା mad·ya·şaa·ļaa
bathroom ଶୌଚାଗାର so·u·chaa·gaa·ra
battery ବିଦ୍ୟୁତ ଧାରକ ଓ ବିତରକ ଉପକରଣ
bid·yut d'aa·ra·ka o bi·ta·ra·ka u·pa·ka·ra·na
beautiful ସୁନ୍ଦର sun·da·ra
bed ଖଟ k'a·ta
before ପୂର୍ବରୁ pur·ba·ru
behind ପଛରେ pa·cha·re
bicycle ଦୁଇଚକିଆ ଯାନ duy·chak·yi·yaa jaa·na
big ବଡ ba·da
bill ରସିଦ ra·si·da
blanket କମ୍ବଳ kam·ba·ļa
blood group ରକ୍ତ ବର୍ଗ rak·ta bar·ga
boat ନୌକା no·u·kaa
book (make a reservation) v ସଂରକ୍ଷଣ କରିବା
sam·ra·kya·na ka·ri·baa
bottle ବୋତଲ bo·ta·la
boy ପୁଅ pu·a
brakes (car) ବ୍ରେକ bre·a·ka
breakfast ଜଳଖିଆ ja·ļa·k'i·aa
broken (faulty) ଭାଂଗିଯାଇଥିବା b'an·gi·ja·e·t'i·baa
bus ବସ୍ bus
business ବ୍ୟବସାୟ bya·ba·saa·ya
buy v କିଣିବା ki·ni·baa

C

camera ଚିତ୍ର ଉତ୍ତୋଳନ ଯନ୍ତ୍ର chit·ra u·t'o·ļa·na jan·tra
cancel ରଦ୍ଦ rad·d'a
car କାର kar
cash n ଟଙ୍କା tan·ka
cash (a cheque) v ମୁଦ୍ରା ବିନିମୟ କରିବା
mud·raa bi·ni·ma·ya ka·ri·baa
cell phone ଚଳମାନ ଦୂରଭାଷ
cha·ļa·maa·na du·ra·b'a·sha
centre n କେନ୍ଦ୍ର ken·dra
change (money) v ଖୁଚୁରା କରିବା
k'u·chu·raa ka·ri·baa
cheap ଶସ୍ତା şas·t'aa
check (bill) ରସିଦ ra·si·da
check-in n ତାଲିକଭୁକ୍ତ ହେବା taa·li·ka·b'uk·ta he·baa
chest (body) ଛାତି chaa·ti
child ପିଲା pi·laa
cigarette ସିଗାରେଟ୍ si·gaa·ret
city ସହର sa·ha·ra
clean a ସଫା sa·p'aa
closed ବନ୍ଦ ban·da
cold a ଥଣ୍ଡା t'an·da
collect call ଡାକରା ସଂଗ୍ରହ daa·ka·raa san·gra·ha
come ଆସ aa·sa
computer ଆଭିକଳକ aa·b'i·ka·ļa·ka
condom କୋନଡମ kon·dam
contact lenses କୃତ୍ରିମ ଚକ୍ଷୁ ପୁତୁଳି
ku·tri·ma cha·kyu pu·tu·ļe
cook v ରୋଷେଇ କରିବା ro·she·e ka·ri·baa
cost n ମୂଲ୍ୟ mul·ya
credit card ଉଧାର ପତ u·d'aa·ra pat·ra
currency exchange ବୈଦେଶିକ ମୁଦ୍ରା ବିନିମୟ
bai·de·şi·ka mud·raa bi·ni·ma·ya
customs (immigration) କଷ୍ଟମ୍ସ kas·tam·sa

D

dangerous ବିପଦପୂର୍ଣ୍ଣ bi·pa·da·pur·na
date (time) ଆରିଖ ta·ri·k'a
day ଦିନ di·na
delay n ଡେରି de·ri
dentist ଦାନ୍ତ ଡାକ୍ତର daan·ta daak·ta·ra
depart ପ୍ରସ୍ଥାନ pras·t'aa·na
diaper ଶିଶୁର ଅନ୍ତଃବସ୍ତ୍ର si·su·ra an·ta·ha·bas·tra
dinner ରାତ୍ରି ଭୋଜନ rat·ri b'o·ja·na
direct a ସିଧା si·d'aa
dirty ମଇଳା ma·e·laa
disabled ଅସମର୍ଥ a·sa·mar·t'a
discount n ରିହାତ ri·haa·ti
doctor ଡାକ୍ତର daak·ta·ra
double bed ଦୁଇଟି ଶଯ୍ୟା do·e·ti sar·jyaa
double room ଯୋଡା ବଖରା jo·daa ba·k'a·raa
drink n ପାନୀୟ paa·nee·ya
drive v ଚଳାଇବା cha·ḷaa·e·baa
drivers licence ଚାଳକ ଅନୁମତି ପତ୍ର chaa·ḷa·ka a·nu·ma·ti pat·ra
drug (illicit) ନିଶା ଦ୍ରବ୍ୟ ବେଆଇନ ni·ṣa dra·bya be·aa·e·na

E

ear କାନ kaa·na
east ପୂର୍ବ pur·ba
eat ଖାଇବା k'aa·e·baa
economy class ମିତବ୍ୟୟ ଶ୍ରେଣୀ mi·ta·bya·ya ṣre·ni
electricity ବିଦ୍ୟୁତ୍ bi·dyu·t'a
elevator ଉତ୍ତୋଳକ ଯନ୍ତ୍ର u·t'o·ḷa·ka jaan·tra
email ବୈଦୁତିକ ଚିଠି bai·du·ti·ka chi·t'i
embassy ଦୂତାବାସ du·ta·baa·sa
English (language) ଇଂଲିଶ eng·li·sha
entrance ପ୍ରବେଶ pra·be·ṣa
evening ସଂନ୍ଧ୍ୟା san·d'ya
exit n ପ୍ରସ୍ଥାନ pras·t'aa·na
expensive ଦାମୀକା daa·mee·kaa
eye ଆକ୍ଷୀ aa·k'e

F

far ଦୂରରେ du·ra·re
fast ଜୋରରେ jo·ra·re
father ବାପା baa·paa
film (camera) ଆଲୋକଚିତ୍ର aa·lo·ka chi·tra
finger ଆଙ୍ଗୁଳି aan·gu·li
first-aid kit ଆଶୁଚିକିତ୍ସା ଉପକରଣ aa·su·chi·kis·cha u·pa·ka·ra·na
first class ପ୍ରଥମ ଶ୍ରେଣୀ pra·t'a·ma sre·ni
fish n ମାଛ maa·cha
food ଖାଦ୍ୟ k'aad·ya
foot ପାଦ paa·da
free (of charge) ମାଗଣା maa·ga·naa
friend ସାଙ୍ଗ san·ga
fruit ଫଳ p'a·la
full ପୂରା pu·raa

G

gift ଉପହାର u·pa·haa·ra
girl ଝିଅ j'i·a
glass (drinking) ଗ୍ଲାସ gla·sa
glasses ଚଷମା cha·sha·maa
go ଯାଅ jaa·a
good ଭଲ b'a·la
guide n ପଥପ୍ରଦର୍ଶକ pa·t'a·pra·dar·sha·ka

H

half n ଅଧା a·d'aa
hand ହାତ haa·ta
happy ଖୁସି k'u·si
have ଅଛି a·chi
he ପୁରୁଷ pu·ru·sha
head n ମୁଣ୍ଡ mun·da
heart ହୃଦୟ hru·da·ya
heavy ଭାରି b'aa·ri
help v ସାହାର୍ଯ saa·haar·jya
here ଏଠାରେ e·t'a·re
high ଉଚ୍ଚ u·cha
highway ରାଜପଥ raa·ja·pa·t'a
hike v ଚାଲିବା chaa·li·baa
holiday ଛୁଟିଦିନ chu·ti·di·na
hospital ଡାକ୍ତରଖାନା daak·ta·ra·k'aa·naa
hot ଗରମ ga·ra·ma
hotel ହୋଟେଲ ho·te·la
hungry ଭୋକିଲା b'o·ki·laa
husband ସ୍ୱାମୀ swa·mi

I

I ଇ e
identification (card) ଚିହ୍ନଟପତ୍ର chin·ha·ta·pat·ra
ill ରୁଗ୍ଣ ru·gu·na
important ଗୁରୁତ୍ୱପୂର୍ଣ୍ଣ gu·rut·wa·pur·na
injury କ୍ଷତ k'ya·ta
insurance ବିମା bi·maa
interpreter ଅନୁବାଦକ a·nu·baa·da·ka

J

jewellery ଅଳଙ୍କାର aa·lan·kaa·ra
job ବୃତି bru·ti

DICTIONARY

D

K

key ଚାବି cha·bi
kitchen ରୋଷେଇଘର ro·se·e·g'a·ra
knife ଛୁରୀ chu·ree

L

lawyer ଓକିଲ o·ki·la
left (direction) ବାମ ପଟ baa·ma pa·ta
leg (body) ଗୋଡ go·da
less ଅଳ୍ପ al·pa
letter (mail) ଚିଠି chi·t'i
light n ଆଲୋକ aa·lo·ka
like v ପସନ୍ଦ କରିବା pa·san·da ka·ri·baa
lock n ତାଲା taa·laa
long ଲମ୍ବା lam·baa
lost ହଜିଯାଇଛି ha·ji·jaa·e·chi
love v ପ୍ରେମ କରିବା pre·ma ka·ri·baa
luggage ଜିନିଷ ji·ni·sha
lunch ମଧ୍ୟାହ୍ନ ଭୋଜନ maad·hyan·na b'o·ja·na

M

mail n ଚିଠି chi·t'i
man ପୁରୁଷ pu·ru·sha
map ନକ୍ସା nak·shaa
market ବଜାର ba·jaa·ra
matches ଦିଆସିଲି di·aa·si·li
meat ମାଂସ man·sa
medicine ଔଷଧ ow·sa·d'a
message ବାର୍ତ୍ତା bar·taa
milk ଦୁଗ୍ଧ dug·d'a
minute ମିନିଟ mi·ni·ta
mobile phone ଚଳମାନ ଦୂରଭାଷ cha·ḷa·maa·na du·ra·b'aa·sha
money ଟଙ୍କା ପଇସା tan·ka pa·e·saa
month ମାସ maa·sa
morning ସକାଳ sa·kaa·ḷa
mother ମା maa
motorcycle ଦୁଇଚକିଆ ଯାନ do·e·cha·ki·yaa jaa·na
mouth ପାଟି paa·ti

N

name ନାମ naa·ma
near ପାଖରେ paa·k'a·re
neck n ବେକ be·ka
new ନୂତନ nu·ta·na
newspaper ଖବର କାଗଜ k'aa·ba·ra ka·ga·ja
night ରାତି raa·ti
no ନା naa
noisy କୋଳାହଳ ପୂର୍ଣ୍ଣ ko·ḷaa·ha·ḷa pur·na
nonsmoking ଧୂମପାନ ବିହିନ d'u·ma·paa·na bi·hi·na
north ଉତ୍ତର ଦିଗ u·ta·ra di·ga
nose ନାକ naa·ka
now ଏବେ e·be
number ସଂଖ୍ୟା san·kya

O

old ପୁରୁଣା pu·ru·naa
one-way ticket ଗୋଟିଏ ଦିଗ ଟିକଟ go·ti·e·a pa·ta ti·ka·ta
open a ଖୋଲା k'o·la
outside ବାହାରେ baa·haa·re

P

pay v ଅର୍ଥ aar·t'a
pharmacy ଔଷଧ ଦୋକାନ ow·sa·d'a do·kaa·na
phonecard ଦୂରଭାଷ ପତ୍ର du·ra·b'aa·sha pat·ra
photo ଚିତ୍ର ଉତ୍ତୋଳନ chit·ra u·t'o·ḷa·na
postcard ଡାକ ପତ୍ର daa·ka pat·ra
post office ଡାକ ଘର daa·ka g'a·ra
pregnant ଗର୍ଭବତୀ gar·b'a·ba·tee
price n ମୂଲ୍ୟ mul·ya

Q

quiet a ନିରବ ni·ra·ba

R

rain n ବର୍ଷା bar·saa
razor ଖୁର k'u·ra
receipt n ରସିଦ ra·si·da
refund n ଫେରସ୍ତ p'e·ras·ta
registered mail ନିରାପତ୍ତା ଚିଠି ni·raa·pa·taa chi·t'i
rent v ଭଡା b'a·daa
repair v ତିଆରି ti·aa·ri
reservation ସଂରକ୍ଷଣ san·ra·kya·na
restaurant ଭୋଜନାଳୟ b'o·ja·naa·ḷa·ya
return v ଫେରସ୍ତ ଦେବା p'e·ras·ta de·baa
return ticket ଫେରନ୍ତା ଟିକଟ p'e·ran·taa ti·ka·ta
right (direction) ଡାହାଣ ପଟ daa·haa·na pa·ta
road ରାସ୍ତା raas·taa
room n ବଖରା ba·k'a·raa

S

safe a ନିରାପଦ ni·raa·pa·da
sanitary napkin ଅବଶୋଷକ ପଦାର୍ଥ a·ba·ṣo·sha·ka pa·dar·t'a
seat n ଚୌକି cho·u·ki

send ପଠାଇବା pa·t'aa·e·baa
sex ଯୌନ କ୍ରିୟା jo·u·na kri·yaa
share (a dorm) ଭାଗି ହେବା b'aa·gi he·baa
she ସ୍ତ୍ରୀ ଲୋକ stri lo·ka
sheet (bed) ଚାଦର ଖଟ chaa·da·ra k'a·ta
shirt କମିଜ ka·mi·ja
shoes ଯୋତା jo·taa
shop n ଦୋକାନ do·kaa·na
short ଅଳ୍ପ al·pa
shower n ଗାଧୋଇବା gaa·d'o·e·baa
single room ଗୋଟିଏ ବଖରା go·ti·e·a ba·k'a·raa
skin n ଚର୍ମ char·ma
skirt n ସ୍କର୍ଟ skar·ta
sleep v ଶୋଇବା so·e·baa
slowly ଧିରେ d'ee·re
small ଛୋଟ cho·ta
soap ସାବୁନ saa·bu·na
some କିଛି ki·chi
soon ଶୀଘ୍ର si·g'ra
south ଦକ୍ଷିଣ da·k'i·na
souvenir shop ସ୍ମରଣୀକା ଦୋକାନ
sma·ra·nee·kaa do·kaa·na
stamp ଡାକ ଟିକଟ daa·ka ti·ka·ta
stand-by ticket ଅପେକ୍ଷାରତ ଟିକଟ
a·pe·k'yaa·ra·ta ti·ka·ta
station (train) ରେଳ ଷ୍ଟେସ୍‌ନ re·ḷa stey·sa·na
stomach ପେଟ pe·ta
stop v ରହିବା ra·hi·baa
stop (bus) n ବସ୍ ରହିବା ସ୍ଥାନ bus ra·hi·baa st'aa·na
street ଗଳି ga·ḷee
student ଛାତ୍ର chat·ra
sun ସୂର୍ଯ୍ୟ sur·jya
swim v ପହଁରିବା pa·han·ri·baa

T

tampons ଅବାଶୋଷକ ପଦାର୍ଥ a·ba·ṣo·sha·ka pa·dar·t'a
teeth ଦାନ୍ତ daan·ta
telephone n ଦୂରଭାଷ du·ra·b'aa·sha
temperature (weather) ଉତ୍ତାପ u·t'aa·pa
that (one) ତାହା taa·haa
they ସେମାନେ se·maa·ne
thirsty ଶୋଷିଲା so·shi·laa
this (one) ଏହା e·haa
throat ତଣ୍ଟି tan·ti
ticket ଟିକଟ ti·ka·ta
time ସମୟ sa·ma·ya
tired ହାଲିଆ haa·lee·aa
tissues ଅବଶୋଷକ କାଗଜ a·ba·ṣo·sha·ka kaa·ga·ja
today ଆଜି aa·ji
toilet ଶୌଚାଗାର so·u·chaa·gaa·ra
tomorrow ଆସନ୍ତା କାଲି aa·san·taa kaa·li
tonight ଆଜିରାତି aa·ji·raa·ti
toothbrush ଦାନ୍ତ ଘସା ବ୍ରସ୍ dan·ta g'a·saa bra·sa
toothpaste ଦାନ୍ତ ଘସା ପ୍ରଲେପ dan·ta g'a·saa pra·le·pa
torch (flashlight) ଆଲୋକ ଉତ୍ସ aa·lo·ka us·t'a
tour n ଭ୍ରମଣ b'ra·ma·na
tourist office ପର୍ଯ୍ୟଟନ କାର୍ଯ୍ୟାଳୟ
par·jya·ta·na kaar·jyaa·ḷa·ya
towel ଗାମୁଛା gaa·mu·chaa
train n ରେଳଗାଡି re·ḷa·gaa·di
translate ଆନୁବାଦ anu·baa·da
travellers cheque ପର୍ଯ୍ୟଟକ ଚେକ୍ par·jya·ta·ka chek
trousers ପୁରାପ୍ୟାଣ୍ଟ pu·raa·pant
twin beds ଶଯ୍ୟା ଜୋଡା sar·jyaa jo·daa

U

underwear ଅନ୍ତଃବସ୍ତ୍ର aan·t'a·ha·bas·tra
urgent ଜରୁରୀ ja·ru·ree

V

vacant ଖାଲି k'aa·li
vegetable n ପରିବା pa·ri·baa
vegetarian a ନିରାମୀଷ ni·raa·mee·sha

W

walk v ଚାଲିବା chaa·li·baa
wallet ବଟୁଆ ba·tu·aa
wash (something) ସଫାକରିବା sa·p'aa·ka·ri·baa
watch n ହାତ ଘଣ୍ଟା haa·ta g'an·taa
water n ପାଣି paa·ni
we ଆମେ aa·me
weekend ସପ୍ତାହର ଶେଷଦିନ
sap·taa·haa·raa ṣe·sa·di·naa
west ପଶ୍ଚିମ ଦିଗ pas·chi·ma di·ga
wheelchair ଚକଲଗା ଚୌକି cha·ka·la·gaa cho·u·ki
when କେତେବେଳେ ke·te·be·ḷe
where କେଉଁଠାରେ ke·un·t'aa·re
who କିଏ ki·e·a
why କାହିଁକି kaan·hi·ki
wife ସ୍ତ୍ରୀ stri
window ଝରକା j'a·ra·kaa
with ସହିତ sa·hi·ta
without ନଥିବା na·t'i·baa
woman ସ୍ତ୍ରୀ ଲୋକ stri lo·ka
write ଲେଖିବା le·k'i·baa

Y

yes ହଁ han
yesterday ଗତକାଲି ga·ta·kaa·li
you sg inf/pol ତୁମେ/ଆପଣ tu·me/aa·pa·na
you pl ତୁମେ ମାନେ tu·me maa·ne

Punjabi

alphabet

vowels				
ੳ oo·raa	ਅ *ae*·raa	ੲ *ee*·ree		

consonants				
ਸ *sa*·sa	ਹ *haa*·haa			
ਕ *ka*·ka	ਖ *k'a*·k'a	ਗ *ga*·ga	ਘ *g'a*·g'aa	ਙ *nga*·ngaa
ਚ *cha*·chaa	ਛ *ch'a*·ch'aa	ਜ *ja*·ja	ਝ *j'a*·jaa	ਞ *nya*·ee·nyaa
ਟ *ţaeng*·kaa	ਠ *ţ'a*·ţ'aa	ਡ *đa*·đaa	ਢ *đ'a*·đ'aa	ਣ *ņaa*·ņaa
ਤ *ta*·taa	ਥ *t'a*·t'aa	ਦ *da*·daa	ਧ *d'a*·d'aa	ਨ *na*·naa
ਪ *pa*·paa	ਫ *p'a*·p'aa	ਬ *ba*·baa	ਫ *b'a*·baa	ਮ *ma*·maa
ਯ *ya*·ee·ya	ਰ *ra*·raa	ਲ *la*·laa	ਵ *wa*·waa	ੜ *ŗaa*·ŗaa
ਸ਼ *sha*·shaa	ਜ਼ *za*·zaa	ਫ਼ *fa*·faa		

numerals									
0	1	2	3	4	5	6	7	8	9
੦	੧	੨	੩	੪	੫	੬	੭	੮	੯

introduction

You may not speak it yet, but with an estimated 60 million Punjabi speakers worldwide chances are you've heard it. If you've seen the film *Bend it like Beckham*, or enjoyed the rhythms of *bhangra* music, then you've already had a taste of this lively language. Part of the Indo-Aryan language family and related to Hindi and Urdu, Punjabi (*pan*·jaa·bee ਪੰਜਾਬੀ) is spoken by more than 27 million people in India. While it's the official language of the state of Punjab, it's also spoken in Pakistan and Bangladesh. Large communities of Punjabi speakers are also found in far-flung places such as Kenya, Singapore, Fiji, the UK, Canada and the US. The Gurmukhi script – meaning 'from the mouth of the guru' – is Punjabi's chief written medium in India (Shahmukhi is used in Pakistan) and was standardised by the Sikh Guru Angad in the 16th century. The alphabet is phonetic, which means that every letter generally corresponds to one sound. But be prepared: like most Indian languages, Punjabi is not for the lazy-tongued – so get your mouth warmed up and start mixing with the locals.

punjabi

pronunciation

Vowels	
Symbol	**English sound**
a	run
aa	father
ae	act
aw	law
e	bet
ee	see
ey	as in 'bet', but longer
i	hit
o	note
oo	zoo
u	put

In this chapter, the Punjabi pronunciation is given in green after each phrase.

Aspirated consonants (pronounced with a puff of air after the sound) are represented with an apostrophe after the letter – b', ch', d', đ', g', j', k', p', t' and ţ'. Retroflex consonants (pronounced with the tongue bent backwards) are included in this table.

The symbol ng is also used after the symbols for vowels to indicate the nasalisation of vowels.

Each syllable is separated by a dot, and the syllable stressed in each word is italicised. For example:

ਧੰਨਵਾਦ। *d'an*-waad

Consonants	
Symbol	**English sound**
b	bed
ch	cheat
d	dog
đ	retroflex d
f	fat
g	go
h	hat
j	jar
k	kit
l	lot
m	man
n	not
ņ	retroflex n
ng	ring
ny	canyon
p	pet
r	red (flapped)
ŗ	retroflex r
s	sun
sh	shot
t	top (softer)
ţ	retroflex t
w	win (between 'v' and 'w')
y	yes
z	zoo

essentials		
Yes./No.	ਹਾਂ।/ਨਹੀ।	haang/neyng
Please.	ਕਿਰਪਾ ਕਰਕੇ।	*kir*·pa kar·*key*
Thank you.	ਧੰਨਵਾਦ।	*d'an*·waad
Excuse me. (to get past)	ਧਿਆਨ ਦੇਣਾ।	d'i·*aan* dey·*naa*
Excuse me. (to get attention)	ਧਿਆਨ ਦੇਣਾ।	d'i·*aan* dey·*naa*
Sorry.	ਮਾਫ ਕਰਨਾ।	maaf *kar*·naa

language difficulties

Do you speak English?
ਕੀ ਤੁਸੀਂ ਅੰਗਰੇਜੀ ਬੋਲਦੇ ਹੋ? — kee tu·*seeng* an·*grey*·jee bol·*dey* ho

Do you understand?
ਕੀ ਤੁਹਾਨੂੰ ਸਮੱਝ ਲੱਗਿਆ? — kee *twaa*·noo *sa*·mij' lag·*gya*

I understand.
ਮੈਂ ਸਮਝਿਆ। — maeng *sa*·mij'·ya

I don't understand.
ਮੈਂ ਨਹੀਂ ਸਮਝਿਆ। — maeng neyng *sa*·mij'·ya

Could you please ...?	ਕੀ ਤੁਸੀਂ ਕਿਰਪਾ ਕਰਕੇ ...?	kee tu·*seeng kir*·pa kar·*key* ...
repeat that	ਇਹ ਦੁਬਾਰਾ ਬੋਲ ਸਕਦੇ ਹੋ	ey du·*baa*·raa bol *sak*·dey ho
speak more slowly	ਹੋਰ ਹੌਲੀ ਬੋਲੋ	hor *ho*·lee *bo*·lo

numbers					
0	ਸਿਫਰ	*si*·far	20	ਵੀਹ	wee
1	ਇਕ	ik	30	ਤੀਹ	tee
2	ਦੋ	do	40	ਚਾਲੀ	*chaa*·lee
3	ਤਿੰਨ	tin	50	ਪੰਜਾਹ	pa·*jaa*
4	ਚਾਰ	chaar	60	ਸੱਠ	saţ'
5	ਪੰਜ	panj	70	ਸੱਤਰ	*sa*·tar
6	ਛੇ	ch'ey	80	ਅੱਸੀ	*a*·see
7	ਸੱਤ	sat	90	ਨੱਬੇ	*na*·bey
8	ਅੱਠ	aţ'	100	ਸੌ	saw
9	ਨੌਂ	nawng	1000	ਹਜਾਰ	ha·*jaar*
10	ਦੱਸ	das	1,000,000	ਦੱਸ ਲੱਖ	das lak'

time & dates

What time is it?	ਕੀ ਸਮਾਂ ਹੋਇਆ ਹੈ?	kee sa·*maang ho*·yaa hae
It's (two) o'clock.	(ਦੋ) ਵੱਜੇ ਹਨ।	(do) *wa*·jey han
Quarter past (ten).	ਸਵਾ (ਦੱਸ) ਹੋਏ ਹਨ।	*sa*·wa (das) *ho*·ey han
Half past (ten).	ਸਾਡੇ (ਦੱਸ) ਵੱਜੇ ਹਨ।	*sa*·dey (das) *wa*·jey han
Quarter to (three).	ਪੌਣੇ (ਤਿੰਨ) ਹੋਏ ਹਨ।	*po*·ṇey (tin) *ho*·ey han
At what time ...?	ਕਿੰਨੇ ਵਜੇ ...?	*ki*·ney *wa*·jey ...
It's (15 December).	(ਪੰਦਰਾ ਦਿਸੰਬਰ) ਹੈ।	(*pand*·raang di·*sam*·bar) hae

yesterday/tomorrow	ਕੱਲ	kal
today	ਅੱਜ	aj
Monday	ਸੋਮਵਾਰ	*som*·waar
Tuesday	ਮੰਗਲਵਾਰ	*man*·gal·waar
Wednesday	ਬੁੱਧਵਾਰ	*bud'*·waar
Thursday	ਵੀਰਵਾਰ	*weer*·waar
Friday	ਸ਼ੁਕਰਵਾਰ	*shu*·kar·waar
Saturday	ਸ਼ਨੀਚਰਵਾਰ	*shnee*·char·waar
Sunday	ਐਤਵਾਰ	*aet*·waar

border crossing

I'm here ...	ਮੈਂ ਇੱਥੇ ਹਾਂ ...	maeng *i*·t'ey haang ...
in transit	ਥੋੜੇ ਸਮੇ ਲਈ	*t'o*·ṛey *sa*·mey *ley*·ee
on business	ਵਪਾਰ ਲਈ	va·*paar ley*·ee
on holiday	ਛੁੱਟੀਆਂ ਲਈ	*ch'u*·ṭee·aang *ley*·ee

I'm here for ...	ਮੈਂ ਇਥੇ ਹਾਂ ... ਲਈ।	maeng *i*·t'ey haang ... *ley*·ee
(10) days	(ਦੱਸ) ਦਿਨਾਂ	(das) *di*·naang
(three) weeks	(ਤਿੰਨ) ਹਫਤਿਆਂ	(tin) *haf*·ti·aang
(two) months	(ਦੋ) ਮਹੀਨਿਆਂ	(do) ma·*hee*·ni·aang

I'm going to (Hoshiarpur).
ਮੈਂ (ਹੋਸ਼ਿਆਰਪੁਰ) ਜਾ ਰਿਹਾ ਹਾਂ। — maeng (ha·shi·*aar*·pur) jaa re·*aa* haang

I'm staying at the (Taj Hotel).
ਮੈਂ (ਤਾਜ ਹੋਟਲ) ਵਿੱਚ ਠਹਿਰ ਰਿਹਾ ਹਾਂ। — maeng (taaj *ho*·ṭal) wich taer re·*aa* haang

I have nothing to declare.
ਮੇਰੇ ਕੋਲ ਦੱਸਣ ਯੋਗ ਕੁੱਛ ਨਹੀਂ ਹੈ। *mey*·rey kol da·*sin* yog kuch' *ne*·heeng hae

I have this to declare.
ਮੇਰੇ ਕੋਲ ਦੱਸਣ ਲਈ ਇਹ ਹੈ। *mey*·rey kol da·*sin* *ley*·ee ey hae

That's (not) mine.
ਇਹ ਮੇਰਾ (ਨਹੀਂ) ਹੈ। ey *mey*·raa (neyng) hae

tickets & luggage

Where can I buy a ticket?
ਮੈਂ ਟਿਕਟ ਕਿੱਥੋਂ ਖਰੀਦ ਸਕਦਾ ਹਾਂ? maeng *ţi*·kiţ *ki*·t'ong ka·*reed* *sak*·da haang

Do I need to book a seat?
ਕੀ ਮੈਨੂੰ ਆਪਣੀ ਸੀਟ ਬੁੱਕ ਕਰਵਾ ਲੈਣੀ ਚਾਹਦੀ ਹੈ? kee *me*·noo *ap*·ņee seeţ buk kar·*vaa* *lae*·ņee *chaa*·ee·dee hae

One … ticket (to Dharamsala), please.	ਕਿਰਪਾ ਕਰਕੇ ਮੈਨੂੰ (ਧਰਮਸ਼ਾਲਾ ਦੀ) ਇਕ … ਟਿਕਟ ਦੇ ਦਿਉ।	*kir*·pa kar·*key* *me*·noo (d'a·ram·*shaa*·laa dee) ik … *ţi*·kiţ dey *de*·o
one-way	ਜਾਣ ਦੀ	jaaņ dee
return	ਵਾਪਸੀ ਦੀ	*waa*·pa·see dee

I'd like to … my ticket, please.	ਮੈਂ ਆਪਣੀ ਟਿਕਟ … ਚਾਹੁੰਦਾ ਹਾਂ।	maeng *ap*·ņee *ţi*·kiţ … *chaa*·ee·daa haang
cancel	ਰੱਦ ਕਰਵਾਉਣਾ	rad kar·*wo*·ņaa
change	ਬਦਲੀ ਕਰਵਾਉਣਾ	*bad*·lee kar·*wo*·naa
collect	ਲੈਣਾ	*lae*·ņaa

I'd like a smoking seat, please.
ਕਿਰਪਾ ਕਰਕੇ ਮੈਨੂੰ ਇਕ ਸਿਗਰੇਟ ਪੀਣ ਵਾਲੀ ਸੀਟ ਚਾਹੀਦੀ ਹੈ। *kir*·pa kar·*key* *me*·noo ik *si*·ga·reyţ peeņ *waa*·lee seeţ *chaa*·ee·dee hae

I'd like a nonsmoking seat, please.
ਕਿਰਪਾ ਕਰਕੇ ਮੈਨੂੰ ਇਕ ਸਿਗਰੇਟ ਰਹਿਤ ਸੀਟ ਚਾਹੀਦੀ ਹੈ। *kir*·pa kar·*key* *me*·noo ik *si*·ga·reyţ *ra*·hit seeţ *chaa*·ee·dee hae

Is there a toilet?
ਕੀ ਇੱਥੇ ਕੋਈ ਪਾਖ਼ਾਨਾਂ ਹੈ? kee *i*·t'ey ko·*ee* *paa*·k'aa·ņaang hae

Is there air conditioning?
ਕੀ ਇੱਥੇ ਕੋਈ ਏਅਰ ਕੰਡੀਸ਼ਨਰ ਹੈ? kee *i*·t'ey ko·*ee* eyr kan·*đee*·sha·nar hae

How long does the trip take?
ਸਫਰ ਨੂੰ ਕਿੰਨਾ ਸਮਾਂ ਲੱਗੇਗਾ? — *sa*·far noo *ki*·naa sa·*maang* la·gey·*gaa*

Is it a direct route?
ਕੀ ਇਹ ਸਿੱਧਾ ਰਾਹ ਹੈ? — kee ey *si*·d'aa raa hae

My luggage has been …	ਮੇਰਾ ਸਮਾਨ … ਹੋ ਗਿਆ ਹੈ।	*mey*·raa sa·*maan* … ho *gey*·aa hae
lost	ਗੁੰਮ	gum
stolen	ਚੋਰੀ	*cho*·ree

transport

Where does flight (AI 80) arrive/depart?
(ਏ ਆਈ ੮੦) ਜਹਾਜ ਕਿੱਥੋਂ ਪਹੁੰਚਣਾ/ਜਾਨਾ ਹੈ? — (ey·*aa*·ee *a*·see) ja·*haaj* ki·*t'ong* *ponch*·ṇa/*jaa*·naa hae

Is this the … to (Ludhiana)?	ਕੀ ਇਹ (ਲੁਧਿਆਣਾ) ਦੀ … ਹੈ?	kee ey (lad'·*yaa*·ṇaa) dee … hae
bus	ਬੱਸ	bas
plane	ਜਹਾਜ	ja·*haaj*
train	ਰੇਲਗੱਡੀ	*reyl*·ga·ḍee

What time's the … bus?	… ਬੱਸ ਕਿੰਨੇ ਵਜੇ ਹੈ?	… bas *ki*·ney *wa*·jey hae
first	ਪਹਿਲੀ	*pe*·lee
last	ਅਖਿਰਲੀ	a·*k'eer*·lee
next	ਅਗਲੀ	*ag*·lee

How long will it be delayed?
ਹੋਰ ਕਿੰਨੀ ਦੇਰ ਲੱਗੇਗੀ? — hor *ki*·nee deyr la·gey·*gee*

Please tell me when we get to (Chandigarh).
ਕਿਰਪਾ ਕਰਕੇ ਮੈਂਨੂ (ਚੰਡੀਗੜ) ਪਹੁੰਚਣ ਤੇ ਦੱਸ ਦਿਉ। — *kir*·pa kar·*key* *me*·noo (*chan*·ḍee·gaaṛ) pon·*chey* dey das de·*o*

That's my seat.
ਇਹ ਮੇਰੀ ਜਗਾਹ ਹੈ। — ey *mey*·ree *ja*·gaa hae

I'd like a taxi …	ਮੈਂਨੂ … ਇਕ ਟੈਕਸੀ ਚਾਹੀਦੀ ਹੈ।	*me*·noo … ik *taek*·see chaa·ee·*dee* hae
at (9am)	(ਸਵੇਰੇ ਦੇ ਨੌਂ ਵਜੇ)	(*sa*·wey·rey dey nawng *wa*·jey)
now	ਹੁਣ	huṇ

ਪੰਜਾਬੀ – transport

How much is it to (Chandigarh)?
(ਚੰਡੀਗੜ) ਤੱਕ ਕਿੰਨੇ ਪੈਸੇ ਲੱਗਣਗੇ? — (*chan*·đee·gaaŗ) tak *ki*·ney *pae*·sey la·gaņ·*gey*

Please put the meter on.
ਕਿਰਪਾ ਕਰਕੇ ਮੀਟਰ ਚਲਾ ਦੇ ਦਿਉ। — *kir*·pa kar·*key mee*·tar cha·*laa* dey de·*o*

Please take me to ...
ਕਿਰਪਾ ਕਰਕੇ ਮੈਨੂੰ ... ਲੈ ਚੱਲੋ। — *kir*·pa kar·*key me*·noo ... lae cha·*lo*

Please stop here.
ਕਿਰਪਾ ਕਰਕੇ ਇਥੇ ਰੁਕੋ। — *kir*·pa kar·*key i*·ťey ru·*ko*

Please wait here.
ਕਿਰਪਾ ਕਰਕੇ ਇਥੇ ਇੰਤਜਾਰ ਕਰੋ। — *kir*·pa kar·*key i*·ťey engt·*jaar* ka·*ro*

I'd like to hire a car (with a driver).
ਮੈਨੂੰ ਗੱਡੀ (ਡਰਾਇਵਰ ਨਾਲ) ਕਿਰਾਏ ਤੇ ਚਾਹੀਦੀ ਹੈ। — *me*·noo *ga*·đee (*đra*·ee·var nal) *ki*·raa·ee·ey tey cha·ee·*dee* hae

I'd like to hire a 4WD (with a driver).
ਮੈਨੂੰ 4×4 ਗੱਡੀ (ਡਰਾਇਵਰ ਨਾਲ) ਕਿਰਾਏ ਤੇ ਚਾਹੀਦੀ ਹੈ। — *me*·noo chaar baa·*ee* chaar *ga*·dee (*đra*·ee·var nal) *ki*·raa·ee·ey tey cha·ee·*dee* hae

How much for daily/weekly hire?
ਰੋਜਾਨਾ/ਹਫਤੇ ਦੇ ਕਿੰਨੇ ਪੈਸੇ ਲਗੱਣਗੇ? — *ro*·jaa·naa/*haf*·taa dey *ki*·ney *pae*·sey la·gan·*gey*

directions

Where's the bank/post office?
ਬੈਂਕ/ਡਾਕਖਾਨਾ ਕਿੱਥੇ ਹੈ? — baenk/*đaak*·k'aa·naa *ki*·tey hae

Where can I exchange foreign currency?
ਵਿਦੇਸ਼ੀ ਮੁੱਦਰਾ ਕਿੱਥੇ ਬਦਲੀ ਕੀਤੀ ਜਾਂਦੀ ਹੈ? — wi·*dey*·shee *mud*·raa *ki*·tey *bad*·lee *kee*·tee *jaan*·dee hae

Is this the road to (Ropar)?
ਕੀ ਇਹ (ਰੋਪੜ) ਦੀ ਸੜਕ ਹੈ? — kee ey (*ro*·paŗ) dee saŗk hae

Can you show me (on the map)?
ਕੀ ਤੁਸੀਂ ਮੈਨੂੰ (ਨਕਸ਼ੇ ਤੇ) ਦਿਖਾ ਸਕਦੇ ਹੋ? — kee tu·*seeng me*·noo (*nak*·shey tey) di·*k'aa sak*·dey ho

What's the address?
ਪਤਾ ਕੀ ਹੈ? — *pa*·taa kee hae

How far is it?
ਕਿੰਨੀ ਦੂਰ ਹੈ? — *ki*·nee door hae

How do I get there?
ਮੈਂ ਉਥੇ ਕਿਵੇ ਪਹੁੰਚਾਂਗਾ/ਪਹੁੰਚਾਂਗੀ?
maeng *u*·t'ey *kee*·wey *pon*·chaang·gaa/*pon*·chaang·gaa **m/f**

Turn left/right.
ਖੱਬੇ/ਸੱਜੇ ਮੁੜੋ।
k'a·bey/*sa*·jey mu·*ṛo*

It's …	ਇਹ ਹੈ …	ey hae …
behind …	… ਦੇ ਪਿੱਛੇ	… dey *pi*·ch'ey
in front of …	… ਦੇ ਸਾਹਮਣੇ	… dey *saam*·ṇey
near (to …)	(… ਦੇ) ਨੇੜੇ	(… dey) *ney*·ṛey
on the corner	ਕੋਨੇ ਤੇ	*ko*·ney tey
opposite …	… ਉਲਟਾ	… *ul*·ṭaa
there	ਉਥੇ	*u*·t'ey

accommodation

Where's a guesthouse/hotel nearby?
ਇੱਥੇ ਨੇੜੇ ਧਰਮਸ਼ਾਲਾ/ਹੋਟਲ ਕਿੱਥੇ ਹੈ?
i·t'ey *ney*·ṛey d'a·ram·*shaa*·laa/*ho*·ṭel *ki*·t'ey hae

Can you recommend somewhere cheap/good?
ਕੀ ਤੁਸੀਂ ਕੋਈ ਸਸਤਾ/ਵਧੀਆ ਦੱਸ ਸਕਦੇ ਹੋ?
kee tu·*seeng* ko·*ee sas*·taa/*wa*·d'ee·aa das *sak*·dey ho

I'd like to book a room, please.
ਕਿਰਪਾ ਕਰਕੇ ਮੇਰੇ ਲਈ ਇੱਕ ਕਮਰਾ ਰਾਖਵਾਂ ਕਰ ਦਿਉ।
kir·pa kar·*key mey*·rey *ley*·ee ik *kam*·raa raak'·*waa* kar de·*o*

I have a reservation.
ਮੇਰਾ ਰਾਖਵਾਂਕਰਨ ਹੈ।
mey·raa raak'·*waang*·karn hae

Do you have a … room?	ਕੀ ਤੁਹਾਡੇ ਕੋਲ … ਕਮਰਾ ਹੈ?	kee *tu*·aa·đey kol … *kam*·raa hae
single	ਇਕ ਬਿਸਤਰ ਦਾ	ik *bis*·tar daa
double	ਡਬਲ ਬਿਸਤਰ ਦਾ	*đa*·bal *bis*·tar daa
twin	ਦੋ ਬਿਸਤਰ ਦਾ	do *bis*·tar daa

How much is it per night/person?
ਇੱਕ ਰਾਤ/ਬੰਦੇ ਦੇ ਕਿੰਨੇ ਪੈਸੇ ਲੱਗਣਗੇ?
ik raat/*ban*·dey dey *ki*·ney *pae*·sey la·gaṇ·*gey*

I'd like to stay for (two) nights.
ਮੈਂ (ਦੋ) ਰਾਤਾਂ ਲਈ ਰੁਕਣਾ ਚਾਹੁੰਦਾ/ਚਾਹੁੰਦੀ ਹਾਂ।
maeng (do) *raa*·taang *ley*·ee ruk·*ṇaa chon*·daa/*chon*·dee haang **m/f**

Can I have my key, please?
ਕਿਰਪਾ ਕਰਕੇ ਕੀ ਮੈਂ ਆਪਣੀ ਚਾਬੀ ਲੈ ਸਕਦਾ/ਸਕਦੀ ਹਾਂ? — *kir*·pa kar·*key* kee maeng *ap*·ṇee *chaa*·bee lae *sak*·daa/*sak*·dee haang **m/f**

Can I get another (blanket)?
ਕੀ ਮੈਨੂੰ ਇਕ ਹੋਰ (ਕੰਬਲ) ਮਿਲ ਸਕਦਾ ਹੈ? — kee *me*·noo ik hor (*kam*·bal) mil *sak*·daa hae

The (air conditioning) doesn't work.
(ਏਅਰ ਕੰਡੀਸ਼ਨਰ) ਕੰਮ ਨਹੀਂ ਕਰਦਾ। — (eyr kan·*đee*·sha·nar) kam neyng *kar*·daa

Is there an elevator/a safe?
ਕੀ ਇਥੇ ਕੋਈ ਲਿਫਟ/ਤਿਜੋਰੀ ਹੈ? — kee *i*·t'ey ko·*ee* lifţ/ti·*jaw*·ree hae

What time is checkout?
ਕਿਹੜੇ ਸਮੇਂ ਕਮਰਾ ਖਾਲੀ ਕਰਨਾ ਹੈ? — *key*·ŗey sa·*meyng* *kam*·raa *k'aa*·lee *kar*·naa hae

Can I have my ..., please?	ਕਿਰਪਾ ਕਰਕੇ ਕੀ ਮੈਂ ਆਪਣਾ ... ਲੈ ਸਕਦਾ/ਸਕਦੀ ਹਾਂ?	*kir*·pa kar·*key* kee maeng *ap*·ṇaa ... lae *sak*·daa/*sak*·dee haang **m/f**
deposit	ਜਮਾਂ	*ja*·maang
passport	ਪਾਸਪੋਰਟ	*paas*·porţ
valuables	ਕੀਮਤੀ ਸਮਾਨ	*keem*·tee sa·*maan*

banking & communications

Where's an ATM/a public phone?
ਏਟੀਐਮ/ਪੱਬਲਿਕ ਫੋਨ ਕਿੱਥੇ ਹੈ? — *ey*·ţee·em/*pab*·lik fon *ki*·t'ey hae

I'd like to ...	ਮੈਂ ... ਚਾਹੁੰਦਾ/ ਚਾਹੁੰਦੀ ਹਾਂ।	maeng ... *chon*·daa/ *chon*·dee haang **m/f**
arrange a transfer	ਪੈਸੇ ਭੇਜਣ ਦਾ ਬੰਦੋਬਸਤ ਕਰਨਾ	*pae*·sey b'ey·*jin* daa *ban*·da·bast *kar*·naa
change money	ਪੈਸੇ ਬਦਲਵਾਉਣਾ	*pae*·sey ba·dal·*wo*·ṇaa
withdraw money	ਪੈਸੇ ਕਢਵਾਉਣਾ	*pae*·sey kađ'·*wo*·ṇaa

What's the charge for that?
ਇਸ ਦੇ ਕਿੰਨੇ ਪੈਸੇ ਲੱਗਣਗੇ? — eys dey *ki*·ney *pae*·sey la·gaṇ·*gey*

What's the exchange rate?
ਪੈਸੇ ਬਦਲਵਾਉਣ ਦੇ ਕਿੰਨੇ ਪੈਸੇ ਲੱਗਣਗੇ? — *pae*·sey ba·dal·*woṇ* dey *ki*·ney *pae*·sey la·gaṇ·*gey*

Where's the local internet café?
ਇੱਥੇ ਨੇੜੇ ਇੰਟਰਨੇਟ ਕੈਫੇ ਕਿੱਥੇ ਹੈ?
i·t'ey *ney*·ŗey *in*·ţar·neţ *kae*·fey *ki*·t'ey hae

How much is it per hour?
ਘੰਟੇ ਦੇ ਕਿੰਨੇ ਪੈਸੇ ਲੱਗਣਗੇ?
ken·ţey dey *ki*·ney *pae*·sey la·gaṇ·*gey*

I'd like to …	ਮੈਂ … ਚਾਹੁੰਦਾ/ ਚਾਹੁੰਦੀ ਹਾਂ।	maeng … *chon*·daa/ *chon*·dee haang **m/f**
get internet access	ਇੰਟਰਨੇਟ ਵਰਤਨਾ	*in*·ţar·neţ wart·*naa*
use a printer/scanner	ਪ੍ਰਿੰਟਰ/ਸਕੈਨਰ ਵਰਤਨਾ	*prin*·ţar/*skae*·nar wart·*naa*

I'd like a …	ਮੈਂ … ਚਾਹੁੰਦਾ/ ਚਾਹੁੰਦੀ ਹਾਂ।	maeng … *chon*·daa/ *chon*·dee haang **m/f**
mobile/cell phone for hire	ਮੋਬਾਇਲ ਫੋਨ ਕਿਰਾਏ ਲਈ	*mo*·baa·eel fon *ki*·raa·ey *ley*·ee
SIM card for your network	ਤੁਹਾਡੇ ਨੈਟਵਰਕ ਲਈ ਸਿਮ ਕਾਰਡ	*tu*·aa·đey *neţ*·wark *ley*·ee sim kaarđ

What are the rates?
ਕੀ ਭਾਅ ਹੈ?
kee b'aa hae

What's your phone number?
ਤੁਹਾਡਾ ਫੋਨ ਨੰਬਰ ਕੀ ਹੈ?
tu·aa·đaa fon *nam*·bar kee hae

The number is …
ਇਹ ਨੰਬਰ ਹੈ …
ey *nam*·bar hae …

I'd like to buy a phonecard.
ਮੈਂ ਇੱਕ ਫੋਨ ਕਾਰਡ ਖਰੀਦਣਾ ਚਾਹੁੰਦਾ/ਚਾਹੁੰਦੀ ਹਾਂ।
maeng ik fon kaarđ k'a·*reed*·ṇaa *chon*·daa/*chon*·dee haang **m/f**

I want to call (Canada).
ਮੈਂ (ਕਨੇਡਾ) ਫੋਨ ਕਰਨਾ ਚਾਹੁੰਦਾ/ਚਾਹੁੰਦੀ ਹੈ।
maeng (ka·*ney*·đaa) fon *kar*·naa *chon*·daa/*chon*·dee hae **m/f**

I want to send a fax/parcel.
ਮੈਂ ਇੱਕ ਫੈਕਸ/ਪਾਰਸਲ ਭੇਜਣਾ ਚਾਹੁੰਦਾ/ਚਾਹੁੰਦੀ ਹਾਂ।
maeng ik faeks/*paar*·sal *b'eyj*·ṇaa *chon*·daa/*chon*·dee haang **m/f**

I want to buy a stamp/an envelope.
ਮੈਂ ਇੱਕ ਸਟੈਂਪ/ਲਿਫਾਫਾ ਖਰੀਦਣਾ ਚਾਹੁੰਦਾ/ਚਾਹੁੰਦੀ ਹਾਂ।
maeng ik sţaemp/li·*faa*·faa k'a·*reed*·ṇaa *chon*·daa/*chon*·dee haang **m/f**

Please send it to (Australia).
ਕਿਰਪਾ ਕਰਕੇ ਇਹ (ਆਸਟ੍ਰੇਲਿਆ) ਭੇਜ ਦਿਉ।
kir·pa kar·*key* ey (aa·*sţrey*·lee·aa) b'eyj de·*o*

sightseeing

What time does it open?
ਇਹ ਕਿੰਨੇ ਵਜੇ ਖੁੱਲਦਾ ਹੈ?
ey *ki*·ney *wa*·jey *k'ul*·daa hae

What time does it close?
ਇਹ ਕਿੰਨੇ ਵਜੇ ਬੰਦ ਹੁੰਦਾ ਹੈ?
ey *ki*·ney *wa*·jey band *hun*·daa hae

What's the admission charge?
ਦਾਖਲੇ ਦੇ ਕਿੰਨੇ ਪੈਸੇ ਲੱਗਣਗੇ?
daak'·ley dey *ki*·ney *pae*·sey la·gaṇ·*gey*

Is there a discount for students/children?
ਕੀ ਇੱਥੇ ਕੋਈ ਵਿਦਿਆਰਥਿਆਂ/
ਬੱਚਿਆਂ ਲਈ ਛੂਟ ਹੈ?
kee *i*·t'ey ko·*ee* wi·di·*aar*·k'i·aang/
ba·chi·aang *ley*·ee ch'ooṭ hae

I'd like to hire a guide.
ਮੈਂ ਇੱਕ ਸਹਾਇਕ ਲੈਣਾ
ਚਾਹੁੰਦਾ/ਚਾਹੁੰਦੀ ਹਾਂ।
maeng ik sa·*haa*·ik *lae*·ṇaa
chon·daa/*chon*·dee haang **m/f**

I'd like a catalogue.
ਮੈਂ ਇੱਕ ਸੂਚਨਾ ਕਿਤਾਬ
ਚਾਹੁੰਦਾ/ਚਾਹੁੰਦੀ ਹਾਂ।
maeng ik *soch*·naa ki·*taab*
chon·daa/*chon*·dee haang **m/f**

I'd like a map.
ਮੈਂ ਇੱਕ ਨਕਸ਼ਾ
ਚਾਹੁੰਦਾ/ਚਾਹੁੰਦੀ ਹਾਂ।
maeng ik *nak*·shaa
chon·daa/*chon*·dee haang **m/f**

I'd like to see ...
ਮੈਂ ... ਦੇਖਣਾ ਚਾਹੁੰਦਾ/
ਚਾਹੁੰਦੀ ਹਾਂ।
maeng ... *dek'*·ṇaa *chon*·daa/
chon·dee haang **m/f**

What's that?
ਇਹ ਕੀ ਹੈ?
ey kee hae

Can I take a photo?
ਕੀ ਮੈਂ ਇੱਕ ਫੋਟੋਂ ਖਿਚ ਸਕਦਾ/
ਸਕਦੀ ਹਾਂ?
kee maeng ik *fo*·ṭo k'ich *sak*·daa/
sak·dee haang **m/f**

I'd like to go somewhere off the beaten track.
ਮੈਂ ਉਸ ਜਗਾਹ ਤੇ ਜਾਣਾ ਚਾਹੁੰਦਾ/
ਚਾਹੁੰਦੀ ਹਾਂ ਜਿੱਥੇ ਆਮ ਲੋਕ
ਨਹੀ ਜਾਂਦੇ।
maeng os *ja*·gaa tey *jaa*·ṇaa *chon*·daa/
chon·dee haang *ji*·t'ey aam lok
neyng *jaan*·dey **m/f**

When's the next tour?
ਅਗਲਾ ਦੌਰਾ ਕਦੋਂ ਹੈ? — *ag*·laa *do*·raa *ka*·dong hae

How long is the tour?
ਦੌਰਾ ਕਿੰਨੀ ਦੇਰ ਦਾ ਹੈ? — *do*·raa *ki*·nee deyr daa hae

Is … included?	ਕੀ … ਨਾਲ ਹੈ?	kee … naal hae
accommodation	ਰਿਹਾਇਸ਼	ri·*haa*·ish
admission	ਦਾਖਲਾ	*daak'*·laa
food	ਖਾਣਾ	*k'aa*·ṇaa
transport	ਟਰਾਂਸਪੋਰਟ	*ṭraan*·sporṭ

sightseeing		
fort	ਕਿਲ੍ਹਾ	*ki*·laa
Hindu temple	ਮੰਦਿਰ	*man*·dar
mosque	ਮਸਜਿਦ	*mas*·jid
palace	ਮਹਿਲ	*ma*·hil
ruins	ਕਾਫੀ ਪੁਰਾਣਾ	*kaa*·fee *praa*·ṇaa
Sikh temple	ਗੁਰੂਦੁਆਰਾ	*gurd*·waa·raa

shopping

Where's a … ?	… ਕਿੱਥੇ ਹੈ?	… *ki*·t'ey hae
camera shop	ਕੈਮਰੇ ਦੀ ਦੁਕਾਨ	*kaem*·rey dee da·*kaan*
market	ਬਜ਼ਾਰ	ba·*zaar*
souvenir shop	ਯਾਦਗਾਰੀ ਚੀਜਾਂ ਵਾਲੀ ਦੁਕਾਨ	*yaad*·gaa·ree *chee*·jaang *waa*·lee da·*kaan*

I'm looking for …
ਮੈਂ … ਦੇਖ ਰਿਹਾ/ਰਹੀ ਹਾਂ। — maeng … deyk' *rey*·aa/*rey*·ee haang **m/f**

Can I look at it?
ਕੀ ਮੈਂ ਦੇਖ ਸਕਦਾ/ਸਕਦੀ ਹਾਂ? — kee maeng deyk' *sak*·daa/*sak*·dee haang **m/f**

Can I have it sent overseas?
ਕੀ ਮੈਂ ਇਹ ਵਿਦੇਸ਼ ਭੇਜ ਸਕਦਾ/ਸਕਦੀ ਹਾਂ? — kee maeng ey wi·*deysh* b'eyj *sak*·daa/*sak*·dee haang **m/f**

Can I have my (camera) repaired?
ਕੀ ਮੈਂ ਆਪਣਾ (ਕੈਮਰਾ) ਠੀਕ ਕਰਵਾ ਸਕਦਾ/ਸਕਦੀ ਹਾਂ? — kee maeng *ap*·ṇaa (*kaem*·raa) ṭ'eek ka·*raa* *sak*·daa/*sak*·dee haang **m/f**

It's faulty.
ਇਹ ਖਰਾਬ ਹੈ। — ey kraab hae

How much is it?
ਇਸ ਦੇ ਕਿੰਨੇ ਪੈਸੇ ਹੈ? — is dey *ki*·ney *pae*·sey hae

Can you write down the price?
ਕੀ ਤੁਸੀਂ ਇਹ ਦਾ ਭਾਅ ਲਿੱਖ ਸਕਦੇ ਹੋ? — kee tu·*seeng* ey daa b'aa lik' *sak*·dey ho

That's too expensive.
ਇਹ ਜਿਆਦਾ ਮਹਿੰਗਾ ਹੈ। — ey *jaa*·daa *men*·gaa hae

I'll give you (300 rupees).
ਮੈਂ ਤੁਹਾਨੂੰ (ਤਿੰਨ ਸੌ ਰੁਪਏ) ਦੇ ਸਕਦਾ/ਸਕਦੀ ਹਾਂ। — maeng *tu*·aa·noo (tin saw roo·*pey*) dey *sak*·daa/*sak*·dee haang **m/f**

There's a mistake in the bill.
ਬਿੱਲ ਦੇ ਵਿੱਚ ਗਲਤੀ ਹੈ। — bil dey wich *gal*·tee hae

Do you accept ...?	ਕੀ ਤੁਸੀਂ ... ਸਵੀਕਾਰਦੇ ਹੋ?	kee tu·*seeng* ... sa·wee·*kaar*·dey ho
credit cards	ਕਰੈਡਿਟ ਕਾਰਡ	*krey*·điţ kaarđ
debit cards	ਡੈਬਿਟ ਕਾਰਡ	*đey*·biţ kaarđ
travellers cheques	ਟਰੈਵਲਰ ਚੈੱਕ	*ţrae*·wa·lar chaek

I'd like (a) ..., please.	ਕਿਰਪਾ ਕਰਕੇ ਮੈਂ ... ਲੈ ਸਕਦਾ/ਸਕਦੀ ਹਾਂ।	*kir*·pa kar·*key* maeng ... lae *sak*·daa/*sak*·dee haang **m/f**
bag	ਇੱਕ ਬਸਤਾ	ik *bas*·taa
my change	ਮੇਰੀ ਭਾਨ	*mey*·ree b'aan
receipt	ਇੱਕ ਰਸੀਦ	ik ra·*seed*
refund	ਵਾਪਸ ਕਰ	*waa*·pas kar

Less./Enough./More.	ਘੱਟ।/ਕਾਫੀ।/ਜਿਆਦਾ।	g'aţ/*kaa*·fee/*jaa*·daa

photography

Can you ...?	ਕੀ ਤੁਸੀਂ ... ਸਕਦੇ ਹੋ?	kee tu·*seeng* ... *sak*·dey ho
burn a CD from my memory card	ਮੇਰੇ ਮੈਮਰੀ ਕਾਰਡ ਤੋਂ ਸੀ ਡੀ ਬਣਾ	*mey*·rey *mae*·ma·ree kaarđ tong see đee ba·*ṇaa*
develop this film	ਇਹ ਰੀਲ ਬਣਾ	ey reel ba·*ṇaa*

I need a film for this camera.
ਮੈਂਨੂ ਇਸ ਕੈਮਰੇ ਦੇ ਲਈ ਰੀਲ ਚਾਹੀਦੀ। — *me*·noo es *kaem*·rey dey *ley*·ee reel chaa·*ee*·dee

When will it be ready?
ਇਹ ਕਦੋਂ ਤਿਆਰ ਹੋਵੇਗੀ? — ey *ka*·dong ti·*aar* ho·*vey*·gee

making conversation

Hello.	ਸਤਿ ਸ੍ਰੀ ਅਕਾਲ।	sat sree a·*kaal*
Good night.	ਸ਼ੁੱਭ ਰਾਤਰੀ।	shub' *raat*·ree
Goodbye.	ਸਤਿ ਸ੍ਰੀ ਅਕਾਲ।	sat sree a·*kaal*
Mr/Mrs	ਸ਼੍ਰੀਮਾਨ/ਸ਼੍ਰੀਮਤੀ	*shree*·maan/*shree*·ma·tee
Miss/Ms	ਕੁਮਾਰੀ	ku·*maa*·ree
How are you?	ਤੁਹਾਡਾ ਕੀ ਹਾਲ ਹੈ?	*tu*·aa·đaa kee haal hae
Fine, thanks.	ਠੀਕ ਹਾਂ।	ţ'eek haang
And you?	ਤੁਸੀਂ ਕਿੱਦਾਂ?	tu·*seeng ki*·daang
What's your name?	ਤੁਹਾਡਾ ਕੀ ਨਾਮ ਹੈ?	*tu*·aa·đaa kee naam hae
My name is …	ਮੇਰਾ ਨਾਂ … ਹੈ।	*mey*·raa naang … hae
I'm pleased to meet you.	ਤੁਹਾਨੂੰ ਮਿਲ ਕੇ ਬਹੁਤ ਖੁਸ਼ੀ ਹੋਈ।	*tu*·aa·noo mil key bot *k'u*·shee ho·*ee*
This is my …	ਇਹ ਮੇਰਾ … ਹੈ।	ey *mey*·raa … hae
brother	ਭਰਾ	b'raa
daughter	ਕੁੜੀ	*ku*·ŗee
friend	ਮਿੱਤਰ/ਸਹੇਲੀ	*mi*·tar/sa·*hey*·lee **m/f**
sister	ਭੈਣ	b'aeņ
son	ਪੁੱਤਰ	*pu*·tar
Here's my (address).	ਇਹ ਮੇਰਾ (ਪਤਾ) ਹੈ।	ey *mey*·raa (*pa*·taa) hae
What's your (email)?	ਤੁਹਾਡਾ (ਈਮੇਲ) ਕੀ ਹੈ?	*tu*·aa·đaa (*ee*·meyl) kee hae
Where are you from?	ਤੁਸੀਂ ਕਿੱਥੋਂ ਹੋ?	tu·*seeng ki*·t'ong ho
I'm from (New Zealand).	ਮੈਂ (ਨਿਊਜ਼ੀਲੈਂਡ) ਤੋਂ ਹਾਂ।	maeng (ni·oo·*jee*·laenđ) tong haang
What's your occupation?	ਤੁਹਾਡਾ ਕਿੱਤਾ ਕੀ ਹੈ?	*tu*·aa·đaa *ki*·taa kee hae
I'm (a student).	ਮੈਂ ਇੱਕ (ਵਿਦਿਆਰਥੀ) ਹਾਂ।	maeng ik (wi·di·*aar*·t'ee) haang
Do you like …?	ਕੀ ਤੁਸੀਂ … ਪਸੰਦ ਕਰਦੇ ਹੋ?	kee tu·*seeng* … pa·*sand kar*·dey ho
I (don't) like …	ਮੈਂ … ਪਸੰਦ (ਨਹੀਂ) ਕਰਦਾ/ਕਰਦੀ।	maeng … pa·*sand* (neyng) *kar*·daa/*kar*·dee **m/f**
art	ਕਲਾ	ka·*laa*
movies	ਫਿਲਮ	film
music	ਸੰਗੀਤ	san·*geet*
reading	ਪੜਾਈ	pa·ŗa·*ee*
sport	ਖੇਲ	k'eyl

eating out

Can you recommend a …?	ਕੀ ਤੁਸੀਂ … ਦੱਸ ਸਕਦੇ ਹੋ?	kee tu·*seeng* … das *sak*·dey ho
bar	ਬਾਰ	baar
dish	ਖਾਣ ਵਾਲੀ ਚੀਜ	k'aaṇ *waa*·lee cheej
place to eat	ਖਾਣ ਵਾਲੀ ਜਗਾਹ	k'aaṇ *waa*·lee *ja*·gaa

I'd like a/the …, please.	ਕਿਰਪਾ ਕਰਕੇ ਮੈਨੂੰ … ਚਾਹੀਦਾ ਹੈ।	*kir*·pa kar·*key me*·noo … cha·*ee*·da hae
bill	ਬਿੱਲ	bil
drink list	ਸ਼ਰਬਤ ਸੂਚੀ	*shar*·bat *soo*·chee
local speciality	ਸਥਾਨਕ ਵਿਸ਼ੇਸ਼ਤਾ	sa·*t'aa*·nak wi·*shey*·shtaa
menu	ਭੋਜਨ ਦੀ ਸੂਚੀ	*b'o*·jan dee *soo*·chee
(non)smoking section	ਧੂਆਂ (ਰਹਿਤ) ਖੰਡ	*d'oo*·aang (raet) k'ađ
table for (four)	(ਚਾਰਾਂ) ਵਾਸਤੇ ਇੱਕ ਮੇਜ	(*chaa*·raang) *waas*·tey ik meyj

breakfast	ਸਵੇਰ ਦਾ ਖਾਣਾ	sa·*weyr* daa *k'aa*·ṇaa
lunch	ਦੁਪਹਿਰ ਦਾ ਖਾਣਾ	da·*paer* daa *k'aa*·ṇaa
dinner	ਰਾਤ ਦਾ ਖਾਣਾ	raat daa *k'aa*·ṇaa

coffee/tea …	ਕਾਹਵਾ/ਚਾਹ …	*kaa*·waa/chaa …
with milk	ਦੁੱਧ ਦੇ ਨਾਲ	dud' dey naal
without sugar	ਖੰਡ ਤੋਂ ਬਗੈਰ	k'anđ tong ba·*gaer*

(orange) juice	(ਸੰਗਤਰੇ ਦਾ) ਜੂਸ	(*sang*·trey daa) joos
lassi	ਲੱਸੀ	*la*·see
soft drink	ਸ਼ਰਬਤ	*shar*·bat

I'll have (boiled/mineral) water.
ਮੈਂ (ਉਬਾਲਿਆ/ਸ਼ੁਧ) ਪਾਣੀ ਲਵਾਂਗਾ/ਲਵਾਂਗੀ। — maeng (a·*waa*·lee·aa/shud') *paa*·ṇee la·*waang*·gaa/la·*waang*·gee **m/f**

I'll buy you a drink.
ਮੈਂ ਤੁਹਾਡੇ ਲਈ ਸ਼ਰਬਤ ਖਰੀਦਾਗਾਂ/ਖਰੀਦਾਗੀਂ। — maeng *tu*·aa·đey *ley*·ee *shar*·bat k'a·*ree*·da·gaang/k'a·*ree*·da·geeng **m/f**

What would you like?
ਤੁਸੀਂ ਕੀ ਲੈਣਾ ਚਾਹੁੰਦੇ ਹੋ? — tu·*seeng* kee *lae*·ṇaa *chon*·dey ho

a bottle/glass of beer	ਬੀਅਰ ਦੀ ਬੋਤਲ/ਗਿਲਾਸ	beer dee *bo*·tal/glaas
a bottle/glass of wine	ਇੱਕ ਬੋਤਲ/ਗਿਲਾਸ ਸ਼ਰਾਬ ਦੀ	ik *bo*·tal/glaas sha·*raab* dee

special diets & allergies

Do you have vegetarian food?		
ਕੀ ਤੁਹਾਡੇ ਕੋਲ ਸ਼ਾਕਾਹਾਰੀ ਭੋਜਨ ਹੈ?		kee *tu*·aa·đey kol shaa·kaa·*haa*·ree *b'o*·jan hae
I'm allergic to ...	... ਮੇਰੇ ਲਈ ਹਾਨੀਕਾਰਕ ਹੈ।	... *mey*·rey *ley*·ee *haa*·nee·kaa·rak hae
dairy products	ਦੁੱਧ ਨਾਲ ਬਣੀਆਂ ਚੀਜ਼ਾਂ	dud' naal ba·ņee·*aang* *chee*·jang
eggs	ਆਂਡੇ	*an*·đey
meat stock	ਮੀਟ ਸਟੋਕ	meeţ sţok
peanuts	ਮੂੰਗਫ਼ਲੀ	*mung*·flee
seafood	ਸਮੁੰਦਰੀ ਭੋਜਨ	sa·*mun*·dree *b'o*·jan

emergencies

Help!	ਮੱਦਦ!	*ma*·dad
Stop!	ਰੁਕੋ!	ru·*ko*
Go away!	ਦੂਰ ਜਾਉ!	door *jaa*·o
Thief!	ਚੋਰ!	chor
Fire!	ਅੱਗ!	ag
Watch out!	ਧਿਆਨ ਨਾਲ!	d'i·*aan* naal
Call ...!	... ਬੁਲਾਓ!	... bu·*laa*
an ambulance	ਐਂਬੁਲੈਂਸ	aem·*boo*·laens
a doctor	ਡਾਕਟਰ	*đaak*·ţar
the police	ਪੁਲਿਸ	plees

Could you help me, please?
ਕੀ ਤੁਸੀਂ ਮੇਰੀ ਮਦਦ ਕਰ ਸਕਦੇ ਹੋ? — kee tu·*seeng* *mey*·ree *ma*·dad kar *sak*·dey ho

I have to use the phone.
ਮੈਂ ਫੋਨ ਕਰਨਾ ਹੈ। — maeng fon *kar*·naa hae

I'm lost.
ਮੈਂ ਗੁਆਚ ਗਿਆ/ਗਈ ਹਾਂ। — maeng gu·*aach* gey·*aa*/gey·*ee* haang **m/f**

Where are the toilets?
ਪਾਖਾਨਾਂ ਕਿੱਥੇ ਹੈ? — *paa*·k'aa·ņaang *ki*·t'ey hae

Where's the police station?
ਪੁਲਿਸ ਥਾਣਾ ਕਿੱਥੇ ਹੈ? — plees *t'aa*·ņaa *ki*·t'ey hae

I have insurance.
ਮੇਰੇ ਕੋਲ ਬੀਮਾਂ ਹੈ। — *mey*·rey kol *bee*·maang hae

I want to contact my embassy.
ਮੈਂ ਆਪਣੇ ਦੂਤਾਵਾਸ ਨਾਲ ਸੰਪਰਕ ਕਰਨਾ ਚਾਹੁੰਦਾ/ਚਾਹੁੰਦੀ ਹਾਂ। — maeng *ap*·ṇey du·*taa*·vaas naal san·*pa*·rak *kar*·naa *chon*·daa/*chon*·dee haang **m/f**

I've been raped.
ਮੇਰਾ ਕਿਸੇ ਨੇ ਬਲਾਤਕਾਰ ਕੀਤਾ। — *mey*·raa *ki*·sey ney ba·*laat*·kaar kee·*taa*

I've been robbed.	ਮੈਂ ਠੱਗਿਆ ਗਿਆ।	maeng *ţ'a*·gi·aa gey·*aa* **m**
	ਮੈਂ ਠੱਗੀ ਗਈ।	maeng *ţ'a*·gee gey·*ee* **f**

I've lost ...	... ਗੁੰਮ ਗਿਆ ਹੈ।	... gum gey·*aa* hae
my bag	ਮੇਰਾ ਬਸਤਾ	*mey*·raa *bas*·taa
my money	ਮੇਰੇ ਪੈਸੇ	*mey*·rey *pae*·sey

health

Where's the nearest ...?	ਇੱਥੇ ਲਾਗੇ ... ਕਿੱਥੇ ਹੈ?	*i*·t'ey laa·*gey* ... *ki*·t'ey hae
dentist	ਦੰਦਾਂ ਵਾਲਾ ਡਾਕਟਰ	*dan*·daang *waa*·laa *đaak*·ţar
doctor	ਡਾਕਟਰ	*đaak*·ţar
hospital	ਹਸਪਤਾਲ	*hasp*·taal
pharmacist	ਫ਼ਾਰਮੈਸਿਸਟ	*faar*·mey·sisţ

I need a doctor (who speaks English).
ਮੈਨੂੰ ਇੱਕ ਡਾਕਟਰ ਚਾਹੀਦਾ ਹੈ (ਜੋ ਅੰਗਰੇਜੀ ਬੋਲਦਾ ਹੋਵੇ)। — *me*·noo ik *đaak*·ţar chaa·*ee*·daa hae (jo an·*grey*·jee bol·*daa ho*·wey)

Could I see a female doctor?
ਕੀ ਮੈਂ ਇੱਕ ਜਨਾਨਾ ਡਾਕਟਰ ਨੂੰ ਮਿਲ ਸਕਦੀ ਹਾਂ? — kee maeng ik ja·*naa*·naa *đaak*·ţar noong mil *sak*·dee haang

I've run out of my medication.
ਮੇਰੀ ਦਵਾਈ ਮੁੱਕ ਗਈ ਹੈ। — *mey*·ree *da*·wa·ee muk gey·*ee* hae

It hurts here.
ਇੱਥੇ ਦੁੱਖਦਾ ਹੈ। — *i*·t'ey *duk'*·daa hae

I have (a) ...	ਮੈਨੂੰ ... ਹੈ।	*me*·noo ... hae
asthma	ਦਮਾ	*da*·maa
constipation	ਕਬਜ	*ka*·bij
diarrhoea	ਟੱਟੀਆਂ	*ţa*·ţee·aang
fever	ਬੁਖਾਰ	ba·*k'aar*
heart condition	ਦਿਲ ਦੀ ਬੀਮਾਰੀ	dil dee bi·*maa*·ree

I'm allergic to …	ਮੈਨੂੰ … ਤੋ ਐਲਰਜੀ ਹੈ।	*me*·noo … to ae·*lar*·jee hae
antibiotics	ਐਂਟੀਬਾਔਟਿਕ	*aen*·ţee·baa·ee·aa·ţik
anti-inflammatories	ਐਂਟੀ–ਇਨਫਲੈਮੈਟੋਰੀਸ	*aen*·ţee in·*flae*·mey·ţo·rees
aspirin	ਦਰਦ ਵਾਹਕ	dard waak
bees	ਮੱਖੀਆਂ	*ma*·k'ee·aang
codeine	ਕੋਡੀਨ	ko·*đeen*

responsible travel

I'd like to learn some Punjabi.
ਮੈਂ ਪੰਜਾਬੀ ਸਿੱਖਣਾ ਚਾਹੁੰਦਾ/ਚਾਹੁੰਦੀ ਹਾਂ। — maeng *pan*·jaa·bee *sik'*·ņaa *chon*·daa/*chon*·dee haang **m/f**

What's this called in Punjabi?
ਇਸ ਨੂੰ ਪੰਜਾਬੀ ਵਿੱਚ ਕੀ ਕਹਿੰਦੇ ਹੈ? — is noo *pan*·jaa·bee wich kee *ken*·dey hae

Would you like me to teach you some English?
ਕੀ ਤੁਸੀਂ ਚਾਹੁੰਦੇ ਹੋ ਕੀ ਮੈਂ ਤੁਹਾਨੂੰ ਅੰਗਰੇਜੀ ਸਿਖਾਵਾਂ? — kee tu·*seeng chon*·dey hae kee maeng *tu*·aa·noo an·*grey*·jee si·*k'aa*·waang

I didn't mean to do anything wrong.
ਮੈਂ ਇਹ ਜਾਣਕੇ ਨਹੀ ਕੀਤਾ। — maeng ey *jaaņ*·key neyng *kee*·taa

I didn't mean to say anything wrong.
ਮੇਰੇ ਕਹਿਣ ਦਾ ਇਹ ਮਤਲਬ ਨਹੀ ਸੀ। — *mey*·rey kaeņ daa ey *ma*·ta·lab neyng see

Is this a local or national custom?
ਕੀ ਇਹ ਸ਼ਹਿਰੀ ਚੂੰਗੀ ਜਾਂ ਗਸ਼ਟਰੀ ਚੂੰਗੀ ਹੈ? — kee ey *shae*·ree *choon*·gee jaang *gash*·ţree *choon*·gee hae

I'd like to stay at a locally run hotel.
ਮੈਂ ਇਲਾਕਾ ਨਿਵਾਸੀਆਂ ਵੱਲੋ ਚਲਾਏ ਜਾਂਦੇ ਹੋਟਲ ਵਿੱਚ ਠਹਿਰਣਾ ਚਾਹੁੰਦਾ/ਚਾਹੁੰਦੀ ਹਾਂ। — maeng ey·*laa*·kaa ni·*waa*·see·aang *wa*·long cha·*laa*·ey *jaang*·dey *ho*·ţel wich *taer*·ņaa *chon*·daa/*chon*·dee haang **m/f**

Where can I buy locally produced goods/souvenirs?
ਮੈਂ ਇੱਥੋਂ ਦੀਆਂ ਬਣੀਆਂ ਹੋਈਆਂ ਚੀਜਾਂ ਕਿੱਥੋ ਖਰੀਦ ਸਕਦਾ/ਸਕਦੀ ਹਾਂ? — maeng *i*·t'ey di·*aang* ba·ņee·*aang* ho·ee·*aang chee*·jaang *ki*·t'ong k'a·*reed sak*·daa/*sak*·dee haang **m/f**

I'm (an English teacher). Can I volunteer my skills?
ਮੈਂ (ਅੰਗਰੇਜੀ ਦਾ ਅਧਿਆਪਕ) ਹਾਂ। ਮੈਂ ਆਪਣੇ ਹੁਨਰ ਨਾਲ ਕੀ ਸੇਵਾ ਕਰ ਸਕਦਾ/ਸਕਦੀ ਹਾਂ? — maeng (an·*grey*·jee daa a·d'i·*aa*·pak) haang maeng *ap*·ņey hu·*nar* naal kee *sey*·vaa kar *sak*·daa/*sak*·dee haang **m/f**

english–punjabi dictionary

Words in this dictionary are marked as n (noun), a (adjective), v (verb), m (masculine), f (feminine), sg (singular), pl (plural), inf (informal) and pol (polite) where necessary.

A

accident ਦੁਰਘਟਨਾ dur·*g'at*·naa
accommodation ਰਿਹਾਇਸ਼ ri·*haa*·ish
adaptor ਅਡਾਪਟਰ a·*ḍaap*·ṭar
address n ਪਤਾ *pa*·taa
after ਬਾਦ baad
air-conditioned ਏਅਰਕਨਦੀਸ਼ਨਡ eyr·kan·*dee*·shanḍ
airplane ਜਹਾਜ ja·*haaj*
airport ਏਅਰਪੋਰਟ *eyr*·porṭ
alcohol ਦਾਰੂ *daa*·roo
all ਸਾਰਾ *saa*·raa
allergy ਐਲਰਜੀ ae·*lar*·jee
ambulance ਐਮਬੁਲੈਂਸ *aem*·boo·laens
and ਅਤੇ *a*·tey
ankle ਗਿੱਟਾ *git*·taa
antibiotics ਐਂਟੀਬਾਔਟਿਕ *aen*·ṭee·baa·ee·aa·ṭik
arm ਬਾਂਹ bang
ATM ਏਟੀਐਮ *ey*·ṭee·em

B

baby ਕਾਕਾ/ਕਾਕੀ *kaa*·kaa/*kaa*·kee m/f
back (of body) ਪਿੱਠ piṭ'
backpack ਪਿੱਠੂ *pi*·ṭ'oo
bad ਬੁਰਾ *bu*·raa
bag ਬਸਤਾ *bas*·taa
bank ਬੈਂਕ baenk
bar ਬਾਰ baar
bathroom ਬਾਥਰੂਮ *baat'*·room
battery ਬੈਟਰੀ *bae*·ṭree
beautiful ਸੁੰਦਰ *sun*·dar
bed ਬਿਸਤਰ *bis*·tar
before ਪਹਿਲਾ *pe*·laa
behind ਪਿੱਛੇ *pi*·ch'ey
bicycle ਸਾਇਕਲ *saa*·ee·kal
big ਬੜਾ *ba*·ṛaa
bill ਬਿੱਲ bil
blanket ਕੰਬਲ *kam*·bal
blood group ਬਲੱਡ ਗਰੁੱਪ blad groop
boat ਕਿਸ਼ਤੀ *kish*·tee
book (make a reservation) v ਬੁੱਕ ਕਰਨਾ buk *kar*·naa
bottle ਬੋਤਲ *bo*·tal
boy ਮੁੰਡਾ *mun*·ḍaa
brakes (car) ਬਰੇਕ breyk
breakfast ਸਵੇਰ ਦਾ ਖਾਣਾ sa·*weyr* daa *k'aa*·ṇaa
broken (faulty) ਟੁੱਟਿਆ ਹੋਇਆ *ṭu*·ṭee·aa *ho*·ee·aa
bus ਬੱਸ bas
business ਵਪਾਰ wa·*paar*
buy v ਖਰੀਦਣਾ k'a·*reed*·ṇaa

C

camera ਕੈਮਰਾ *kaem*·raa
cancel ਰੱਦ ਕਰਨਾ rad *kar*·naa
car ਗੱਡੀ *ga*·ḍee
cash n ਰੋਕੜ *ro*·kaṛ
cash (a cheque) v ਬਦਲਵਾਉਣਾ ba·dal·*wo*·ṇaa
cell phone ਮੋਬਾਇਲ ਫੋਨ *mo*·baa·eel fon
centre n ਵਿਚਕਾਰ wich·*kaar*
change (money) v ਬਦਲਵਾਉਣਾ ba·dal·*wo*·ṇaa
cheap ਸੱਸਤਾ *sas*·taa
check (bill) ਬਿੱਲ bil
check-in n ਚੈੱਕ ਇਨ chek in
chest (body) ਛਾਤੀ *ch'aa*·tee
child ਬੱਚਾ *ba*·chaa
cigarette ਸਿਗਰੇਟ *si*·ga·reyṭ
city ਸ਼ਹਿਰ shaer
clean a ਸਾਫ਼ saaf
closed ਬੰਦ band
cold a ਠੰਡਾ *ṭ'an*·ḍaa
come ਆਉਣਾ *aw*·ṇaa
computer ਕੰਪਿਊਟਰ kam·*poo*·ṭar
condom ਨਿਰੋਧ ni·*rod'*
contact lenses ਅੱਖਾਂ ਦੇ ਲੈਂਸ *a*·k'aang dey laenz
cook v ਪਕਾਉਣਾ pa·*kaw*·ṇaa
cost n ਖ਼ਰਚਾ *kar*·chaa
credit card ਕਰੈਡਿਟ ਕਾਰਡ *krey*·ḍiṭ kaarḍ
currency exchange ਪੈਸੇ ਬਦਲਵਾਉਣਾ *pae*·sey ba·dal·*wo*·ṇaa
customs (immigration) ਕਸਟੱਮ *kas*·ṭam

D

dangerous ਖਤਰਨਾਕ k'a·*tar*·naak
date (time) ਤਾਰੀਖ treek'
day ਦਿਨ din
delay n ਦੇਰ ਕਰਨਾ deyr *kar*·naa
dentist ਦੰਦਾ ਵਾਲਾ ਡਾਕਟਰ *dan*·daa *waa*·laa *ḍaak*·ṭar
depart ਤੁਰ ਜਾਣਾ tur *jaa*·ṇaa
diaper ਡਾਈਪਰ ḍaa·*ee*·par

dinner ਰਾਤ ਦਾ ਖਾਣਾ raat daa *k'aa*·ṇaa
direct a ਸਿੱਧਾ *si*·d'aa
dirty ਗੰਦਾ *gan*·daa
disabled ਅਪਾਹਜ a·*paa*·haj
discount n ਛੂਟ ch'ooṭ
doctor ਡਾਕਟਰ *ḍaak*·ṭar
double bed ਡਬਲ ਬਿਸਤਰ *ḍa*·bal *bis*·tar
double room ਡਬਲ ਬਿਸਤਰ ਦਾ ਕਮਰਾ
ḍa·bal *bis*·tar daa *kam*·raa
drink n ਸ਼ਰਬਤ *shar*·bat
drive v ਗੱਡੀ ਚਲਾਉਣਾ *ga*·ḍee cha·*law*·ṇaa
drivers licence ਡਰਾਇਵਿੰਗ ਲਾਇਸੈਂਸ
ḍraa·ee·wing laa·ee·*saens*
drug (illicit) ਡਰੱਗ ḍrag

E

ear ਕੰਨ kan
east ਪੂਰਬ *poo*·rab
eat ਖਾਣਾ *k'aa*·ṇaa
economy class ਆਮ ਦਰਜੇ ਵਾਲੀ aas *dar*·jey *waa*·lee
electricity ਬਿਜਲੀ *bij*·lee
elevator ਲਿਫ਼ਟ lifṭ
email ਈਮੇਲ *ee*·meyl
embassy ਦੂਤਾਵਾਸ du·*taa*·vaas
emergency ਤੱਤਕਾਲ tat·*kaal*
English (language) ਅੰਗਰੇਜ਼ੀ an·*grey*·jee
entrance ਪ੍ਰਵੇਸ਼ *par*·weysh
evening ਸ਼ਾਮ shaam
exit n ਬਾਹਰ ਦਾ ਰਾਸਤਾ baar daa *raas*·taa
expensive ਮਹਿੰਗਾ *men*·gaa
eye ਅੱਖ ak'

F

far ਦੂਰ door
fast ਤੇਜ਼ teyj
father ਪਿਤਾ/ਪਿਓ *pi*·taa/*pi*·o pol/inf
film (camera) ਰੀਲ reel
finger ਉਂਗਲੀ *ung*·lee
first-aid kit ਫ਼ਸਟ ਏਡ ਕਿੱਟ fasṭ eyḍ kiṭ
first class ਪਹਿਲੇ ਦਰਜੇ ਵਾਲੀ *pe*·ley *dar*·jey *waa*·lee
fish n ਮੱਛੀ *ma*·ch'ee
food ਭੋਜਨ *b'o*·jan
foot ਪੈਰ paer
free (of charge) ਮੁਫ਼ਤ muft
friend ਮਿੱਤਰ/ਸਹੇਲੀ *mi*·tar/sa·*hey*·lee m/f
fruit ਫੱਲ p'al
full ਭਰਿਆ *b'a*·ree·aa

G

gift ਤੋਹਫ਼ਾ *to*·faa
girl ਕੁੜੀ *ku*·ṛee
glass (drinking) ਗਿਲਾਸ glaas
glasses ਐਨਕ aenk
go ਜਾਣਾ *jaa*·ṇaa
good ਚੰਗਾ *chan*·gaa
guide n ਸਹਾਇਕ sa·*haa*·ik

H

half n ਅੱਧਾ *a*·d'aa
hand ਹੱਥ hat'
happy ਖ਼ੁਸ਼ k'ush
have ਲੈਣਾ *lae*·ṇaa
he ਉਹ o
head n ਸਿਰ sir
heart ਦਿੱਲ dil
heavy ਭਾਰਾ *b'aa*·raa
help v ਮੱਦਦ *ma*·dad
here ਇੱਥੇ *i*·t'ey
high ਉਚਾ *u*·chaa
highway ਵੱਡੀ ਸੜਕ *wa*·ḍee saṛk
hike v ਪਹਾੜਾਂ ਦੀ ਸੈਰ pa·*haa*·ṛaang dee saer
holiday ਛੁੱਟੀ *ch'u*·ṭee
homosexual n&a ਸਮਲਿੰਗ-ਭੋਗੀ
sa·ma·ling·*b'o*·gee
hospital ਹਸਪਤਾਲ *hasp*·taal
hot ਗਰਮ garm
hotel ਹੋਟਲ *ho*·ṭel
hungry ਭੁੱਖਾ *b'u*·k'aa
husband ਪਤੀ *pa*·tee

I

I ਮੈਂ maeng
identification (card) ਪਹਿਚਾਣ pey·*chaaṇ*
ill ਬੀਮਾਰ bi·*maar*
important ਜ਼ਰੂਰੀ ja·*roo*·ree
injury ਸੱਟ saṭ
insurance ਬੀਮਾਂ *bee*·maang
internet ਇਨਟਰਨੈਟ *in*·ṭar·neṭ
interpreter ਦੁਭਾਸ਼ੀ du·*b'aa*·shee

J

jewellery ਗਹਿਣੇ *gae*·ṇey
job ਨੌਕਰੀ *nok*·ree

K

key ਚਾਬੀ *chaa*·bee
kilogram ਕੇਜੀ *key*·jee
kitchen ਰਸੋਈ ru·*so*·ee
knife ਚਾਕੂ *chaa*·koo

L

laundry (place) ਧੋਬੀਘਾਟ *d'o*·bee·g'aaţ
lawyer ਵਕੀਲ wa·*keel*
left (direction) ਖੱਬਾ *k'a*·baa
leg (body) ਲੱਤ lat
less ਘੱਟ g'aţ
letter (mail) ਚਿੱਠੀ *chi*·ţ'ee
light n ਰੋਸ਼ਨੀ *hosh*·nee
like v ਪਸੰਦ pa·*sand*
lock n ਤਾਲਾ *taa*·laa
long ਲੰਬਾ *lam*·baa
lost ਗੁਆਚਿਆ gu·*waa*·chi·aa
love v ਪਿਆਰ ਕਰਨਾ pi·*aar kar*·naa
luggage ਸਮਾਨ sa·*maan*
lunch ਦੁਪਹਿਰ ਦਾ ਖਾਣਾ da·*paer* daa *k'aa*·ņaa

M

mail n ਡਾਕ đaak
man ਆਦਮੀ *aad*·mee
map ਨੱਕਸ਼ਾ *nak*·shaa
market ਬਜ਼ਾਰ ba·*zaar*
matches ਤੀਲੀਆਂ *tee*·lee·aang
meat ਮੀਟ meeţ
medicine ਦਵਾਈ *da*·waa·ee
message ਸੁਨੇਹਾ sa·*ney*·haa
milk ਦੁੱਧ dud'
minute ਮਿੰਟ minţ
mobile phone ਮੋਬਾਇਲ ਫੋਨ *mo*·baa·eel fon
money ਪੈਸੇ *pae*·sey
month ਮਹੀਨਾ ma·*hee*·naa
morning ਸਵੇਰ sa·*weyr*
mother ਮਾਤਾ/ਮਾਂ *maa*·taa/maang pol/inf
motorcycle ਮੋਟਰ ਸਾਇਕਲ *mo*·ţar *saa*·ee·kal
mouth ਮੂੰਹ moong

N

name ਨਾਮ naam
near ਨੇੜੇ *ney*·ŗey
neck n ਗਰਦੱਨ *gar*·dan
new ਨਵਾਂ *na*·waang
newspaper ਅਖ਼ਬਾਰ ak'·*baar*
night ਰਾਤ raat
no ਨਹੀ neyng
noisy ਰੌਲਾ *ro*·laa
nonsmoking ਧੂਆਂ ਰਹਿਤ *d'oo*·aang raet
north ਉੱਤਰੀ *ut*·ree
nose ਨੱਕ nak
now ਹੁੱਣ huņ
number ਨੰਬਰ *nam*·bar

O

old ਪੁਰਾਣਾ pa·*raa*·ņaa
one-way ticket ਜਾਣ ਦੀ ਟਿਕਟ jaaņ dee *ţi*·kiţ
open a ਖੁੱਲਾ *k'u*·laa
outside ਬਾਹਰ baar

P

passport ਪਾਸਪੋਰਟ *paas*·porţ
pay v ਤਨਖਾਹ tan·*k'aa*
pharmacy ਫ਼ਾਰਮੈਸੀ *faar*·mae·see
phonecard ਫ਼ੋਨ ਕਾਰਡ fon kaarđ
photo ਫ਼ੋਟੋ *fo*·ţo
police ਪੁਲੀਸ plees
postcard ਪੋਸਟ ਕਾਰਡ posţ kaarđ
post office ਡਾਕਖਾਣਾ *đaak*·k'aa·ņaa
pregnant ਗਰਭਵਤੀ *gar*·b'aw·tee
price n ਭਾਅ b'aa

Q

quiet a ਚੁੱਪ chup

R

rain n ਮੀਂਹ meeng
razor ਬਲੇਡ bleyđ
receipt n ਰਸੀਦ ra·*seed*
refund n ਪੈਸੇ ਵਾਪਸ *pae*·sey *waa*·pas
registered mail ਦਰਜ ਪੱਤਰ darj *pa*·tar
rent v ਕਿਰਾਇਆ ki·*raa*·ee·aa
repair v ਮੁਰੰਮਤ ਕਰਨਾ *moo*·ran·mat *kar*·naa
reservation ਰਾਖਵਾਂਕਰਨ raak'·*waang*·karn
restaurant ਰੈਸਟਰਾਂਟ *res*·ţraanţ
return v ਵਾਪਸ *waa*·pas
return ticket ਵਾਪਸੀ ਟਿਕਟ *waa*·pa·see *ţi*·kiţ
right (direction) ਸੱਜਾ *sa*·jaa
road ਸੜਕ saŗk
room n ਕਮਰਾ *kam*·raa

S

safe a ਸੁਰੱਖਿਅਤ *su*·ra·ki·at
sanitary napkin ਸਟੇ ਫ਼੍ਰੀ sţey free
seat n ਜਗਾਹ *ja*·gaa
send ਭੇਜਣਾ *b'eyj*·ņaa
sex ਸੰਭੋਗ san·*b'og*
shampoo ਸ਼ੈਂਪੂ *shaem*·poo
share (a dorm) ਹਿੱਸਾ ਕਰਨਾ *hi*·saa *kar*·naa
she ਉਹ o
sheet (bed) ਚਾਦਰ *chaa*·dar
shirt ਕਮੀਜ ka·*meej*

shoes ਜੁੱਤੀ *ju*·tee
shop n ਦੁਕਾਨ da·*kaan*
short ਛੋਟਾ *ch'o*·ţaa
shower n ਇਸ਼ਨਾਨ ish·*naan*
single room ਇੱਕ ਬਿਸਤਰ ਦਾ ਕਮਰਾ ik *bis*·tar daa *kam*·raa
skin n ਚੱਮੜੀ *cham*·ŗee
skirt n ਸਕਰਟ skarţ
sleep v ਸੌਣਾ *saw*·ņaa
slowly ਹੌਲੀ *ho*·lee
small ਛੋਟਾ *ch'o*·ţaa
soap ਸਾਬਣ *saa*·baņ
some ਕੋਈ ko·*ee*
soon ਛੇਤੀ *ch'ey*·tee
south ਦੱਖਣ *da*·k'aņ
souvenir shop ਯਾਦਗਾਰੀ ਚੀਜਾਂ ਵਾਲੀ ਦੁਕਾਨ *yaad*·gaa·ree *chee*·jaang *waa*·lee da·*kaan*
stamp ਸਟੈਂਪ sţaemp
stand-by ticket ਬਿਨਾਂ ਆਰਖਣ ਦਾ ਟਿਕਟ bi·*naang aar*·k'aņ daa *ţi*·kiţ
station (train) ਅੱਡਾ *a*·đaa
stomach ਢਿੱਡ đ'iđ
stop v ਰੋਕਣਾ *rok*·ņaa
stop (bus) n ਅੱਡਾ *a*·đaa
street ਗਲੀ *ga*·lee
student ਵਿਦਿਆਰਥੀ wi·di·*aar*·t'ee
sun ਸੂਰਜ surj
swim v ਤਰਨਾ *tar*·naa

T

tampons ਸਟੇ ਫ੍ਰੀ sţey free
teeth ਦੰਦ dand
telephone n ਟੈਲੀਫ਼ੂਨ *te*·lee·foon
temperature (weather) ਤਾਪਮਾਨ taap·*maan*
that (one) ਉਹ o
they ਉਹ o
thirsty ਪਿਆਸ pi·*aas*
this (one) ਇਹ ey
throat ਗਲਾ *ga*·laa
ticket ਟਿਕਟ *ţi*·kiţ
time ਸਮਾਂ sa·*maang*
tired ਥੱਕਿਆ *t'a*·kee·aa
tissues ਟੀਸ਼ੂ *ţee*·shoo
today ਅੱਜ aj
toilet ਪਾਖਾਨਾ *paa*·k'aa·ņaa
tomorrow ਕੱਲ kal
tonight ਅੱਜ ਰਾਤ aj raat
toothbrush ਦੰਦਾਂ ਦਾ ਬਰੱਸ਼ *dan*·daang daa brash
toothpaste ਦੰਦ ਮੰਜਨ dand *man*·jan
torch (flashlight) ਟਾਰਚ ţaarch
tour n ਦੌਰਾ *do*·raa
tourist office ਯਾਤਰੀ ਦਫ਼ਤਰ *yaa*·tree *daf*·tar
towel ਤੌਲੀਆ *to*·lee·aa
train n ਰੇਲਗੱਡੀ *reyl*·ga·đee
translate ਅਨੁਵਾਦ ਕਰਨਾ a·nu·*waad kar*·naa
travel agency ਟਰੈਵਲ ਏਜੰਸੀ *ţrae*·wal ey·*jan*·see
travellers cheque ਟਰੈਵਲਰ ਚੈਕ *ţrae*·wa·lar chaek
trousers ਪਜਾਮਾ pa·*jaa*·maa
twin beds ਦੋ ਬਿਸਤਰ do *bis*·tar

U

underwear ਕੱਛਾ *ka*·ch'ee
urgent ਜ਼ਰੂਰੀ ja·*roo*·ree

V

vacant ਖਾਲੀ *k'aa*·lee
vegetable n ਸਬਜੀ *sab*·jee
vegetarian a ਸ਼ਾਕਾਹਾਰੀ shaa·kaa·*haa*·ree
visa ਵੀਜ਼ਾ *vee*·jaa

W

walk v ਤੁਰਣਾ *tur*·ņaa
wallet ਬਟੂਆ *ba*·ţoo·aa
wash (something) ਧੋਣਾ *d'aw*·ņaa
watch n ਘੜੀ *g'a*·ŗee
water n ਪਾਣੀ *paa*·ņee
we ਅਸੀਂ *a*·seeng
weekend ਹਫ਼ਤੇ ਦਾ ਆਖਿਰੀ ਦਿਨ *haf*·tey daa aa·*k'i*·ree din
west ਪੱਛਮ *pa*·ch'am
wheelchair ਪਹੀਆ ਕੁਰਸੀ *pey*·ee·aa *kur*·see
when ਕਦੋਂ ka·*do*
where ਕਿੱਥੇ *ki*·t'ey
who ਕੌਣ/ਕਿਨ੍ਹਾਂ koņ/*ki*·naang
why ਕਿਉਂ *ki*·ong
wife ਪਤਨੀ *pat*·nee
window ਤਾਕੀ *taa*·kee
with ਨਾਲ naal
without ਬਗੈਰ ba·*gaer*
woman ਤੀਵੀਂ *tee*·meeng
write ਲਿਖਣਾ *lik'*·ņaa

Y

yes ਹਾਂ haang inf
yes ਹਾਂ ਜੀ haang jee pol
yesterday ਕੱਲ kal
you sg inf/pol ਤੂੰ/ਤੁਸੀਂ toong/*tu*·seeng
you pl inf&pol ਤੁਸੀਂ *tu*·seeng

Tamil

alphabet

vowels					
அ a	ஆ aa	இ i	ஈ ee	உ u	ஊ oo
எ e	ஏ ey	ஐ ai	ஒ o	ஓ ow	ஔ aw

consonants					
க ka	ங nga	ச cha	ஞ nya	ட ṭa	ண ṇa
த ta	ந na	ப pa	ம ma	ய ya	ர ra
ல la	வ va	ழ źa	ள ḷa	ற ra	ன na
ஜ ja	ஷ sha	ஹ ha	ஸ sa	பா ba	து da
ஷ şa	சை zai				

introduction

Ever wondered who made the first curry? While experts may dispute the origins of the dish, it's almost certain that the Tamil word *ka*·ri கறி gave us its English name. With records of the language's existence going back more than 2000 years, it's not surprising that many Tamil words have been shared around. English also owes Tamil thanks for mi·la·*ku* tan·*ni* மிளகு தண்ணி (lit: pepper water), known to many as 'mulligatawny', and for kat·*tu* ma·*ram* கட்டு மரம் (lit: tied logs), from which 'catamaran' is derived. Spoken by about 62 million people in India, Tamil (*ta*·mil தமிழ்) is the official language of the Indian state Tamil Nadu, as well as a national language in Sri Lanka, Malaysia and Singapore. Tamil belongs to the Tamil-Kannada group from the southern branch of the Dravidian language family. It was confirmed a 'classical language' of India in 2004 – one of only two languages with this status (Sanskrit is the other). The Tamil script is aptly named vat·*te*·lut·tu வட்டெழுத்து (meaning 'rounded writing') – so styled because curved lines were gentler on palm leaves, the traditional material for writing.

tamil

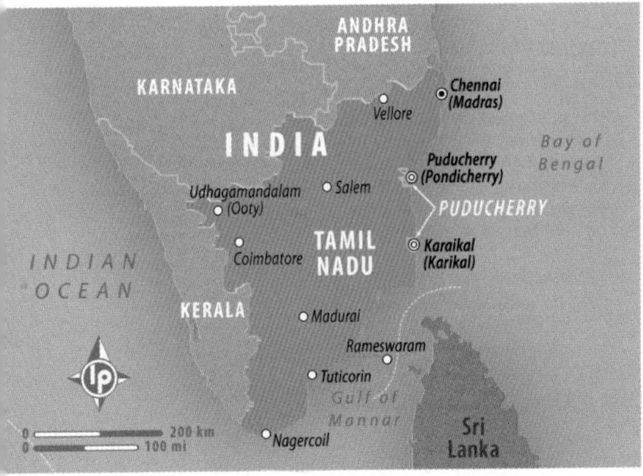

pronunciation

Vowels	
Symbol	**English sound**
a	run
aa	father
ai	aisle
aw	law
e	bet
ee	see
ey	as in 'bet', but longer
i	hit
o	pot
oo	zoo
ow	now
u	put

In this chapter, the Tamil pronunciation is given in pink after each phrase.

Unlike most other Indian languages, Tamil has no 'aspirated' sounds (pronounced with a puff of air). Some consonants can be 'retroflex' (pronounced with the tip of the tongue bent backwards).

Each syllable is separated by a dot, and the syllable stressed in each word is italicised. For example:

மன்னிக்கவும். *man*·nik·ka·vum

Consonants	
Symbol	**English sound**
b	bed
ch	cheat
d	dog
h	hat
j	jar
k	kit
l	lot
ļ	retroflex l
m	man
n	not
ņ	retroflex n
ng	sing
ny	canyon
p	pet
r	red
s	sun
ş	retroflex s
sh	shoot
t	top
ţ	retroflex t
v	very
y	yes
z	zero
ź	retroflex z

essentials

Yes./No.	ஆமாம்./இல்லை.	*aa*·maam/*il*·lai
Please./Thank you.	தயவு செய்து./நன்றி.	ta·ya·*vu* chey·*tu*/*nan*·dri
Excuse me.	தயவு செய்து.	ta·ya·*vu* sei·*du*
Sorry.	மன்னிக்கவும.	*man*·nik·ka·vum

language difficulties

Do you speak English?
நீங்கள் ஆங்கிலம் பேசுவீர்களா? *neeng*·kaḷ *aang*·ki·lam *pey*·chu·*veer*·ka·ḷa

Do you understand?
உங்களுக்கு விளங்குகிறதா? ung·ka·ḷuk·*ku* vi·*ḷang*·ku·ki·ra·*taa*

I understand.
எனக்கு விளங்குகிறது. e·*nak*·ku vi·*ḷang*·ku·ki·ra·*tu*

I don't understand.
எனக்கு விளங்கவில்லை. e·*nak*·ku vi·*ḷang*·ka·vil·*lai*

Could you please ...?	நிங்கள் தயவு செய்து ...?	*neeng*·kaḷ ta·ya·*vu* chey·*tu* ...
repeat that	அதை மீண்டும் கூறுகீர்களா	a·*tai meeṇ*·ṭum *koo*·ru·ki·reer·ka·*ḷa*
speak more slowly	இன்னும் மெதுவாகப் பேசுகிறீர்களா	*in*·num me·tu·va·*ha* *pey*·chu·ki·reer·ka·*ḷaa*

numbers

0	சுழியம்	su·źi·*yam*	20	இருபது	i·ru·pa·*tu*
1	ஒன்று	on·*dru*	30	முப்பது	mup·pa·*tu*
2	இரண்டு	i·*raṇ*·ṭu	40	நாற்பது	naar·pa·*tu*
3	மூன்று	*moon*·dru	50	ஐம்பது	aim·pa·*tu*
4	நான்கு	naan·*ku*	60	அறுபது	a·ru·pa·*tu*
5	ஐந்து	ain·*tu*	70	எழுபது	e·źu·pa·*tu*
6	ஆறு	*aa*·ru	80	எண்பது	eṇ·pa·*tu*
7	ஏழு	*ey*·źu	90	தொன்னூறு	ton·noo·*ru*
8	எட்டு	eṭ·*ṭu*	100	நூறு	noo·*ru*
9	ஒன்பது	on·pa·*tu*	1000	ஓராயிரம்	*aw*·raa·yi·ram
10	பத்து	pat·*tu*	1,000,000	பத்து லட்சம்	*pat*·tu lat·*cham*

time & dates

What time is it?	மணி என்ன?	ma·*ṇi en*·na
It's (two) o'clock.	மணி (இரண்டு).	ma·*ṇi* (i·*raṇ*·ţu)
Quarter past (two).	(இரண்டே) கால்.	(i·*raṇ*·ţey) kaal
Half past (two).	(இரண்டு) முப்பது.	(i·*raṇ*·ţu) mup·pa·*tu*
Quarter to (three).	(மூன்றுக்கு) முக்கால் மணி.	(*moon*·druk·ku) muk·*kaal* ma·*ṇi*
At what time ...?	எத்தனை மணிக்கு ...?	*et*·ta·nai ma·*ṇik*·ku ...
At ...	... மணிக்கு.	... ma·*ṇik*·ku
It's (15 December).	தேதி (பதிண் ஐந்து டிசம்பர்).	*tey*·ti (pat·*tin* ain·*tu* ţi·*cham*·par)

yesterday	நேற்று	*neyt*·tru
today	இன்று	in·*dru*
tomorrow	நாளை	*naa*·ḷai

Monday	திங்கள்	*ting*·kaḷ
Tuesday	செவ்வாய்	chev·*vai*
Wednesday	புதன்	pu·*tan*
Thursday	வியாழன்	vi·*yaa*·źan
Friday	வெள்ளி	veḷ·*ḷi*
Saturday	சனி	cha·*ni*
Sunday	ஞாயிறு	*nyaa*·yi·ru

border crossing

I'm here ...	நான் இங்கே இருக்கிறேன் ...	naan *ing*·key i·*ruk*·ki·reyn ...
in transit	பயணத்தில்	*pa*·ya·ṇat·til
on business	வேலையாக	*vey*·lai·yaa·ka
on holiday	வீடுமுறையில்	*vi*·ţu·mu·rai·*yil*

I'm here for ...	நான் இங்கே இருப்பது ...	naan *ing*·key i·*rup*·pa·tu ...
(10) days	(பத்து) நாட்களுக்கு	(pat·*tu*) *naaţ*·ka·ḷuk·ku
(three) weeks	(மூன்று) வாரங்களுக்கு	(*moon*·dru) *vaa*·rang·ka·ḷuk·ku
(two) months	(இரண்டு) மாதங்களுக்கு	(i·*raṇ*·ţu) *maa*·tang·ka·ḷuk·ku

I'm going to (Chennai).
நான் (சென்னைக்குப்) போகிறேன். — naan (*chen*·naik·kup) *paw*·ki·reyn

I'm staying at the (Taj Hotel).
நான் (தாஜ் ஹோட்டலில்) தங்கியிருக்கிறேன். — naan (taaj *hoţ*·ţa·lil) tang·ki·yi·*ruk*·ki·reyn

I have nothing to declare.
அறிவிப்பதற்கு என்னிடம் எதுவும் இல்லை. — a·*ri*·vip·pa·tar·ku *en*·ni·ţam e·tu·*vum* il·*lai*

tickets & luggage

Where can I buy a ticket?
எங்கே நான் ஒரு டிக்கட் வாங்கலாம்? — *eng*·key naan o·*ru* ţik·*kaţ* *vaang*·ka·laam

Do I need to book a seat?
ஓர் இருக்கையை நான் முன்னேற்பாடு செய்ய வேண்டுமா? — awr i·*ruk*·kai·yai naan mun·neyr·*paa*·ţu chey·*ya* *veyṇ*·ţu·maa

One … ticket (to Madurai), please.	(மதுரைக்கு) தயவு செய்து … டிக்கட் கொடுங்கள்.	(ma·tu·raik·*ku*) ta·ya·*vu* chey·*tu* … ţik·*kaţ* ko·ţung·*kaļ*
one-way	ஒரு வழிப்பயண	o·*ru* va·*źip*·pa·ya·ṇa
return	இரு வழிப்பயண	i·*ru* va·*źip*·pa·ya·ṇa

I'd like to … my ticket, please.	எனது டிக்கட்டை நான் தயவு செய்து … விரும்புகிறேன்.	e·na·*tu* ţik·*kaţ*·ţai naan ta·ya·*vu* chey·*tu* … *vi*·rum·pu·ki·*reyn*
cancel	ரத்து செய்ய	*rat*·tu chey·*ya*
change	மாற்ற	*maat*·tra

Is there a toilet?
கழிவறை இருக்கிறதா? — ka·*źi*·va·rai i·*ruk*·ki·ra·taa

How long does the trip take?
பயணம் எவ்வளவு நேரம் எடுக்கும்? — pa·ya·*ṇam* ev·*va*·ļa·vu ney·*ram* e·*ţuk*·kum

Is it a direct route?
இது நேரடியான பாதையா? — i·*tu* ney·ra·ţi·*yaa*·na *paa*·tai·yaa

My luggage has been ...	எனது பெட்டி ... விட்டது.	e·na·*tu peţ*·ţi ... *viţ*·ţa·tu
lost	காணாமல போய்	*kaa*·ṇaa·mal *pow*·i
stolen	திருடுப்போய்	ti·*ru*·ţup·*pow*·i

transport

Where does flight (IC 975) arrive/depart?
(IC 975) விமானம் எங்கே வந்தடையும்/புறப்படும்?
(ai see on·pa·*tu ey*·źu ain·*tu*) vi·*maa*·nam *eng*·key *van*·ta·ţai·yum/pu·*rap*·pa·ţum

Is this the ... to (New Delhi)?	இது தானா (புதுடில்லிக்குப்) புறப்படும் ...?	i·*tu* taa·*naa* (pu·*tu* ţil·lik·*kup*) pu·*rap*·pa·ţum ...
bus	பஸ்	pas
plane	விமானம்	vi·*maa*·nam
train	இரயில்	i·ra·*yil*

What time's the first/last bus?
எத்தனை மணிக்கு முதல்/இறுதி பஸ் வரும்?
et·ta·nai ma·*ṇik*·ku mu·*tal*/i·ru·*ti* pas va·*rum*

How long will it be delayed?
எவ்வளவு நேரம் அது தாமதப்படும்?
ev·*va*·ļa·vu *ney*·ram a·*tu* taa·ma·*tap*·pa·ţum

Please tell me when we get to (Ooti).
(ஊட்டிக்குப்) போனவுடன் தயவு செய்து எனக்குக் கூறுங்கள்.
(ooţ·ţik·*kup*) paw·na·vu·*ţan* ta·ya·*vu* chey·*tu* e·*nak*·kuk *koo*·rung·kaļ

That's my seat.
அது எனது இருக்கை.
a·*tu* e·na·*tu* i·*ruk*·kai

I'd like a taxi ...	எனக்கு ஒரு டாக்சி ... வேண்டும்.	e·*nak*·ku o·*ru ţaak*·si ... *veyṇ*·ţum
at (9am)	(காலை ஒன்பது) மணிக்கு	(*kaa*·lai on·pa·*tu*) ma·*ṇik*·ku
now	இப்பொழுது	*ip*·po·źu·tu

How much is it to (Maamallapuram)?
(மாமல்லபுரத்துக்கு) என்ன விலை?
(maa·mal·*la*·pu·rat·*tuk*·ku) en·*na* vi·*lai*

Please put the meter on.

தயவு செய்து மீட்டரைப் போடுங்கள்.

ta·ya·*vu* chey·*tu meeţ*·ţa·raip *pow*·ţung·kaļ

Please take me to (this address).

தயவு செய்து என்னை இந்த (விலாசத்துக்குக்) கொண்டு செல்லுங்கள்.

ta·ya·*vu* chey·*tu en*·nai *in*·ta (vi·*laa*·chat·tuk·kuk) *koņ*·ţu *chel*·lung·kaļ

Please stop/wait here.

தயவு செய்து இங்கே நிறுத்துங்கள்/காத்திருங்கள்.

ta·ya·*vu* chey·*tu ing*·key ni·*rut*·tung·kaļ/*kaat*·ti·rung·kaļ

I'd like to hire a car (with a driver).

நான் ஒரு மோட்டார் வண்டி (ஓர் ஓட்டுநருடன்) வாடகைக்கு எடுக்க விரும்புகிறேன்.

naan o·*ru mowţ*·ţaar *vaņ*·ţi (awr aw·*ţu*·na·ru·ţan) vaa·ţa·*haik*·ku e·*ţuk*·ka vi·*rum*·pu·ki·reyn

I'd like to hire a 4WD (with a driver).

நான் ஒரு 4WD (ஓர் ஓட்டுநருடன்) வாடகைக்கு எடுக்க விரும்புகிறேன்.

naan o·*ru* for weel draiv (awr aw·*ţu*·na·ru·ţan) vaa·ţa·*haik*·ku e·*ţuk*·ka vi·*rum*·pu·ki·reyn

How much for daily/weekly hire?

அன்றாட/வார வாடகைக்கு என்ன விலை?

an·ţraa·ţa/*vaa*·ra vaa·ţa·*haik*·ku en·*na* vi·*lai*

directions

Where's the ...?	... எங்கே இருக்கிறது?	... *eng*·key i·*ruk*·ki·ra·tu
bank	வங்கி	*vang*·ki
foreign currency exchange	நாணய மாற்றுச் சந்தை	*naa*·ņa·ya *maat*·truch *chan*·tai
post office	தபால் நிலையம்	ta·*paal* ni·*lai*·yam

Is this the road to (Maamallapuram)?

இது தான் (மாமல்லபுரத்துக்கு) செல்லும் சாலையா?

i·*tu* taan (maa·mal·*la*·pu·rat·*tuk*·ku) *chel*·lum chaa·lai·*yaa*

Can you show me (on the map)?

எனக்கு (வரைபடத்தில்) காட்ட முடியுமா?

e·*nak*·ku (va·*rai*·pa·*ţat*·til) *kaaţ*·ţa mu·ţi·yu·*maa*

What's the address?

விலாசம் என்ன?

vi·*laa*·cham *en*·na

How far is it?

எவ்வளவு தூரத்தில் இருக்கிறது? *ev*·va·ḷa·vu too·*rat*·til i·*ruk*·ki·ra·tu

How do I get there?

நான் அங்கே எவ்வாறு செல்வது? naan *ang*·key *ev*·vaa·ru *chel*·va·tu

Turn left/right.

இடது/வலது புறத்தில் திரும்புக. i·ţa·*tu*/va·la·*tu* pu·*rat*·til *ti*·rum·pu·ka

It's ...	அது இருப்பது ...	a·*tu* i·*rup*·pa·tu ...
behind ...	...க்குப் பின்னால்	... kup *pin*·naal
in front of ...	...க்கு முன்னால்	... ku *mun*·naal
near (to ...)	(...க்கு) அருகே	(... ku) a·ru·*key*
on the corner	ஓரத்தில்	aw·*rat*·til
there	அங்கே	*ang*·key

accommodation

Where's a guesthouse nearby?

அருகே ஒரு விருந்தினர் இல்லம் எங்கே உள்ளது? a·ru·*ke* o·*ru* vi·*run*·ti·nar *il*·lam *eng*·ke *uḷ*·ḷa·tu

Where's a hotel nearby?

அருகே ஒரு ஹோட்டல் எங்கே உள்ளது? a·ru·*ke* o·*ru* *hoţ*·ţal *eng*·ke *uḷ*·ḷa·tu

Can you recommend somewhere cheap/good?

எங்கேனும் மலிவாக/நல்லதாக இருப்பதை பரிந்துரைக்க முடியுமா? *eng*·key·num *ma*·li·vaa·ka/*nal*·la·taa·ka i·*rup*·pa·tai pa·rin·tu·*raik*·ka mu·*ţi*·yu·maa

I'd like to book a room, please.

நான் ஓர் அறையை தயவு செய்து முன்னேற்பாடு செய்ய விரும்புகிறேன. naan awr a·*rai*·yai ta·ya·*vu* chey·*tu* *mun*·neyr·paa·ţu *chey*·ya vi·*rum*·pu·ki·ren

I have a reservation.

எனக்கு ஓர் அறை முன்னேற்பாடு செய்யப்பட்டுள்ளது. e·*nak*·ku awr a·*rai* *mun*·neyr·paa·ţu chey·*yap*·paţ·*ţuḷ*·ḷa·tu

Do you have a ... room?	உங்களிடம் ஓர் ... அறை உள்ளதா?	*ung*·ka·li·ţam awr ... a·*rai* *uḷ*·ḷa·taa
single	தனி	ta·*ni*
double	இரட்டை	i·raţ·*ţai*
twin	இரு பகுதிகளுடைய	i·*ru* pa·*ku*·ti·ka·ḷu·ţai·*ya*

How much is it per night/person?
ஓர் இரவுக்கு/ஒருவருக்கு என்னவிலை? — awr i·ra·*vuk*·ku/o·ru·va·*ruk*·ku *en*·na·vi·lai

I'd like to stay for (two) nights.
நான் (இரண்டு) இரவுகள் தங்க விரும்புகிறேன். — naan (i·*raṇ*·ţu) i·*ra*·vu·kaļ *tang*·ka vi·*rum*·pu·ki·reyn

Can I have my key, please?
எனது சாவியை தயவு செய்து கொடுக்க முடியுமா? — e·*na*·tu *chaa*·vi·yai ta·ya·*vu* chey·*tu* ko·*ţuk*·ka mu·*ţi*·yu·maa

Can I get another (blanket)?
எனக்கு மேலும் ஒரு (போர்வை) கிடைக்குமா? — e·*nak*·ku *mey*·lum o·*ru* (*pawr*·vai) ki·*ţaik*·ku·maa

The (air conditioning) doesn't work.
(குளிர்சாதனம்) வேலை செய்யவில்லை. — (ku·*ļir*·chaa·ta·*nam*) vey·*lai* *chey*·ya·*vil*·lai

Is there an elevator?
லிப்ட் உள்ளதா? — lipt *uļ*·ļa·taa

Is there a safe?
பாதுகாப்புப் பெட்டி உள்ளதா? — paa·tu·kaap·*pup* peţ·*ţi* *uļ*·ļa·taa

What time is checkout?
எத்தனை மணிக்கு வெளியேற வேண்டும? — *et*·ta·nai ma·*ṇik*·ku ve·*ļi*·yey·ra *veyṇ*·ţum

Can I have my (passport), please?
தயவு செய்து நான் எனது (பாஸ்போர்ட்) பெற முடியுமா? — ta·ya·*vu* chey·*tu* naan e·na·*tu* (*paas*·powrţ) pe·*ra* mu·*ţi*·yu·maa

banking & communications

Where's an ATM?
எங்கே ஒரு ATM இருக்கிறது? — *eng*·key o·*ru* ey ti em i·*ruk*·ki·ra·tu

Where's a public phone?
எங்கே ஒரு பொது தொலைபேசி இருக்கிறது? — *eng*·key o·*ru* po·*tu* *to*·lai·pey·*chi* i·*ruk*·ki·ra·tu

I'd like to …	நான் … விரும்புகிறேன்.	naan … vi·*rum*·pu·ki·*reyn*
arrange a transfer	பணம் அனுப்ப	pa·*ṇam* a·*nup*·pa
change money	பணத்தை மாற்ற	pa·*ṇat*·tai *maat*·tra
withdraw money	பணத்தை எடுக்க	pa·*ṇat*·tai e·*ţuk*·ka

What's the ...?	... கட்டணம் என்ன?	... *kaţ*·ţa·*ṇam en*·na
charge for that	அதற்குரிய	a·*tar*·ku·ri·ya
exchange rate	பங்கு மாற்று	*pang*·ku *maat*·tru

Where's the local internet café?
அருகே இணைய க.:.பே எங்கே உள்ளது? — a·*ru*·key i·ṇai·*ya* ka·*pey* *eng*·key *uḷ*·ḷa·tu

How much is it per hour?
ஒரு மணிக்கு என்ன விலை? — o·*ru* ma·*ṇik*·ku *en*·na vi·*lai*

I'd like to ...	நான் ... பெற விரும்புகிறேன்.	naan ... pe·*ra* vi·*rum*·pu·ki·reyn
get internet access	இணையத் தொடர்பு	i·ṇai·*yat* to·*ţar*·pu
use a printer/ scanner	அச்சுப்பொறி/ ஒளியியல் சாட்டணம்	ach·*chup*·po·ri/ o·*ḷi*·yi·yal *chaa*·ta·nam

I'd like a ...	நான் ... பெற விரும்புகிறேன்.	naan ... pe·*ra* vi·*rum*·pu·ki·reyn
mobile/cell phone for hire	வாடகைக்கு கைத்தொலைபேசி	vaa·ţa·*kaik*·ku *kait*·to·lai·pey·*chi*
SIM card for your network	உங்கள் தொடர்புக்கு அட்டை	*ung*·kal to·ţar·*puk*·ku sim·*aţ*·ţai

What are the rates?
கட்டணங்கள் என்ன? — kaţ·ţa·*ṇang*·kaḷ *en*·na

The number is ...
இவை தான் எண்கள் ... — i·*vai* taan *eṇ*·kaḷ ...

I'd like to buy a phonecard.
நான் ஒரு தொலைபேசி அட்டை வாங்க விரும்புகிறேன். — naan o·*ru to*·lai·pey·*chi aţ*·ţai *vaang*·ka vi·rum·*pu*·ki·reyn

I want to ...	நான் ... விரும்புகிறேன்.	naan ... vi·rum·*pu*·ki·reyn
call (Canada)	(கனடா) வுக்கு அழைக்க	(ka·na·*ţaa*) vuk·*ku* a·źaik·*ka*
call collect	கலெக்ட் அழைப்பு செய்ய	ka·*lekt* a·źaip·*pu* chey·*ya*

I want to send a fax/parcel.
நான் ஒரு தொலைநகல்/ பொட்டலம் அனுப்ப விரும்புகிறேன். — naan o·*ru* to·*lai*·na·kal/ *poţ*·ţa·lam a·nup·*pa* vi·rum·*pu*·ki·reyn

I want to buy a stamp.

நான் ஓர் அஞ்சல் தலை
வாங்க விரும்புகிறேன்.

naan owr *an*·nyal ta·*lai*
vaang·ka vi·rum·*pu*·ki·reyn

I want to buy an envelope.

நான் ஓர் கவர்கூடு
வாங்க விரும்புகிறேன்.

naan owr ka·var·*koo*·ţu
vaang·ka vi·rum·*pu*·ki·reyn

Please send it (to Australia).

தயவு செய்து இதை
(ஆஸ்திரேலியாவுக்கு) அனுப்பவும்.

ta·ya·*vu* chey·*tu* i·*tai*
(*aas*·ti·*rey*·li·yaa·vuk·ku) a·*nup*·pa·vum

sightseeing

What time does it open/close?

அது எத்தனை மணிக்கு
திறக்கும்/மூடும்?

a·*tu* *et*·ta·nai ma·ṇik·*ku*
ti·rak·*kum*/*moo*·ţum

What's the admission charge?

நுழைவு கட்டணம் என்ன?

nu·*źai*·vu *kaţ*·ţa·nam *en*·na

Is there a discount for students/children?

மாணவர்களுக்கு/
சிறுவர்களுக்கு கழிவு
இருக்கிறதா?

maa·ṇa·*var*·ka·*ļuk*·ku/
chi·ru·*var*·ka·*ļuk*·ku ka·*źi*·vu
i·*ruk*·ki·ra·taa

I'd like to hire a guide.

நான் ஒரு வழிகாட்டியை
வாடகைக்கு பெற விரும்புகிறேன்.

naan o·*ru* va·*źi*·kaaţ·*ţi*·yai
vaa·ţa·*kaik*·ku pe·*ra* vi·rum·*pu*·ki·reyn

I'd like a catalogue/map.

எனக்கு ஒரு பொருள்பட்டியல்/
வரைபடம் வேண்டும்.

e·*nak*·ku o·*ru* po·*ruļ*·paţ·*ţi*·yal/
va·*rai*·pa·ţam veeṇ·*ţum*

I'd like to see …

நான் ஒரு … பார்க்க
விரும்புகிறேன்.

naan o·*ru* … *paark*·ka
vi·rum·*pu*·ki·reyn

Can I take a photo?

நான் ஒரு புகைப்படம்
எடுக்கலாமா?

naan o·*ru* pu·*kaip*·pa·ţam
e·*ţuk*·ka·*laa*·maa

I'd like to go somewhere off the beaten track.

வழக்கமாக இல்லாத பகுதிக்கு
நான் செல்ல விரும்புகிறேன்.

va·*źak*·ka·maa·ha *il*·laa·ta pa·ku·*tik*·ku
naan *chel*·la vi·*rum*·pu·ki·reyn

When's the next tour?

அடுத்த சுற்றுப்பயணம் எப்போது? — a·*ţut*·ta *chut*·trup·pa·ya·ņam *ep*·pow·tu

How long is the tour?

அந்த சுற்றுப்பயணம் எவ்வளவு தூரம்? — *an*·ta *chut*·trup·pa·ya·ņam *ev*·va·ļa·vu *too*·ram

Is ... included?	... சேர்க்கப்பட்டுள்ளதா?	... cheyr·*kap*·paţ·*ţuļ*·ļa·taa
accommodation	தங்குமிடம்	*tang*·ku·mi·ţam
food	உணவு	u·*ņa*·vu
transport	போக்குவரத்து	*powk*·ku·va·*rat*·tu

sightseeing

fort	கோட்டை	*kowţ*·ţai
mosque	பள்ளி வாசல்	*paļ*·ļi vaa·*chal*
palace	அரண்மனை	a·*raņ*·ma·nai
ruins	பாழடைந்த இடம்	paa·*źa*·*ţain*·ta i·*ţam*
temple	கோவில்	*kow*·vil

shopping

Where's a ... ?	எங்கே ... இருக்கிறது?	*eng*·key ... i·*ruk*·ki·ra·tu
camera shop	காமிரா கடை	kaa·mi·*raa* ka·*ţai*
market	சந்தை	*chan*·tai
souvenir shop	நினைவுச் சின்ன கடை	ni·nai·*vu chin*·na ka·*ţai*

I'm looking for ...

நான் தேடிக்கொண்டிருப்பது ... — naan tey·ţik·koņ·ţi·*rup*·pa·tu ...

Can I look at it?

நான் இதைப் பார்க்கலாமா? — naan i·*taip paark*·ka·laa·maa

Can I have it sent overseas?

நான் இதை வெளியூருக்கு அனுப்பலாமா? — naan i·*tai* ve·ļi·yoo·*ruk*·ku a·*nup*·pa·laa·maa

Can I have my (camera) repaired?

நான் எனது (காமிராவை) பழுது பார்க்க முடியுமா? — naan e·na·*tu* (kaa·mi·raa·*vai*) pa·*źu*·tu *paark*·ka mu·*ţi*·yu·*maa*

It's faulty.

இது பாழடைந்துள்ளது. — i·*tu* paa·*źa*·*ţain*·tuļ·ļa·*tu*

How much is it?
இது என்ன விலை? — i·*tu* *en*·na vi·*lai*

That's too expensive.
அது அதிக விலையாக இருக்கிறது. — a·*tu* a·*ti*·ka vi·*lai*·yaa·ka i·*ruk*·ki·ra·tu

I'll give you (300 rupees).
நான் உங்களுக்கு (300 ரூபா) தருகிறேன். — naan *ung*·ka·*luk*·ku (*moon*·noo·ru roo·*paai*) ta·ru·*ki*·reyn

There's a mistake in the bill.
இந்த விலைச்சீட்டில் ஒரு தவறு இருக்கிறது. — *in*·ta vi·*laich*·cheeṭ·ṭil o·*ru* *ta*·va·ru i·*ruk*·ki·ra·tu

Do you accept ...?	நீங்கள் ... ஏற்றுக் கொள்கிறீர்களா?	*neeng*·kaḷ ... eyt·*truk* *koḷ*·ki·*reer*·ka·ḷaa
credit cards	கிரேடிட் அட்டைகள்	ki·rey·*ṭit* *aṭ*·ṭai·kaḷ
travellers cheques	பயணிகள் காசோலைகள்	pa·ya·ṇi·*kal* kaa·*chow*·lai·kaḷ

I'd like (a) ..., please.	தயவு செய்து எனக்கு ... வேண்டும்.	ta·ya·*vu* chey·*tu* e·*nak*·ku ... *veyṇ*·ṭum
receipt	ஒரு ரசீது	o·*ru* ra·*chee*·tu
refund	என் பணம் திரும்ப	en pa·*ṇam* ti·*rum*·pa

Less./More.	குறைவு./அதிகம்.	ku·rai·*vu*/a·*ti*·kam
Enough.	போதும்.	*pow*·tum

photography

Can you ...?	நீங்கள் ... முடியுமா?	*neeng*·kaḷ ... mu·*ṭi*·yu·maa
burn a CD from my memory card/stick	எனது சேமிப்பு ஊடகத்திலிருந்து CD உருவாக்க	e·*na*·tu chey·*mip*·pu *oo*·ṭa·*kat*·ti·li·*run*·tu see dee u·ru·*vaak*·ka
develop this film	இந்தப் படச்சுருளை உருவாக்க	in·*tap* pa·*ṭach*·chu·ru·ḷai u·ru·*vaak*·ka

I need a film for this camera.
இந்த காமிராவுக்கு படச்சுருள் தேவை. — *in*·ta kaa·mi·raa·*vuk*·ku pa·*ṭach*·chu·ruḷ tey·*vai*

When will it be ready?
இது எப்பொழுது தயாராகும்? — i·*tu* ep·po·*źu*·*tu* ta·*yaa*·raa·*kum*

making conversation

Hello.	வணக்கம்.	va·*ṇak*·kam
Good night.	இரவு வணக்கம்.	i·ra·*vu* va·*ṇak*·kam
Goodbye.	போய் வருகிறேன்.	*po*·i va·*ru*·ki·reyn
Mr/Mrs	திருவாளர்/திருமதி	ti·ru·*vaa*·ḷar/ti·ru·ma·*ti*
Miss/Ms	குமாரி/திருவாட்டி	ku·*maa*·ri/ti·ru·*vaṭ*·ṭi
How are you?	நீங்கள் நலமா?	*neeng*·kaḷ na·*la*·maa
Fine, thanks. And you?	நலம், நன்றி. நீங்கள்?	na·*lam nan*·dri *neeng*·kaḷ
What's your name?	உங்கள் பெயர் என்ன?	*ung*·kal pe·*yar en*·na
My name is ...	என் பெயர் ...	en pe·*yar* ...
I'm pleased to meet you.	உங்களைச் சந்தித்ததில் நான் மகிழ்ச்சி அடைகிறேன்.	*ung*·ka·ḷaich chan·*tit*·ta·til naan ma·*kiźch*·chi a·*ṭai*·ki·reyn
This is my ...	இவர் என் ...	i·*var* en ...
brother	தம்பி	*tam*·pi
daughter	மகள்	ma·*kaḷ*
friend	நண்பன்	*naṇ*·pan
sister	தங்கை	*tang*·kai
son	மகன்	ma·*kan*

Here's my (address).
இதோ என் (விலாசம்). — i·*tow* en (vi·*laa*·cham)

What's your (email)?
உங்கள் (மின்னஞ்சல் முகவரி) என்ன? — *ung*·kaḷ (min·nan·*chal* mu·ka·va·*ri*) *en*·na

Where are you from?
நீங்கள் எங்கிருந்து வருகிறீர்கள்? — *neeng*·kaḷ *eng*·ki·run·tu va·ru·*ki*·reer·kaḷ

I'm from (New Zealand).
நான் இங்கிருந்து வருகிறேன் (நியுசிலாந்து). — naan *ing*·ki·run·tu va·ru·*ki*·reyn (ni·yoo·chi·*laan*·tu)

What's your occupation?
உங்கள் வேலை என்ன? — *ung*·kaḷ vey·*lai en*·na

I'm a/an ...	நான் ஒரு ...	naan o·*ru* ...
businessperson	வியாபாரி	vi·yaa·paa·*ri*
office worker	அலுவலக ஊழியர்	a·*lu*·va·la·ka *oo*·źi·yar
tradesperson	தொழிற்துறையாளர்	to·*źir*·tu·rai·yaa·ḷar

Do you like ...?	உங்களுக்கு ... பிடிக்குமா?	*ung*·ka·*ļuk*·ku ... pi·*ţik*·ku·maa
I like ...	எனக்கு ... பிடிக்கும்.	e·*nak*·ku ... pi·*ţik*·kum
I don't like ...	எனக்கு ... பிடிக்காது.	e·*nak*·ku ... pi·*ţik*·kaa·tu
art	கலை	*ka*·lai
sport	விளையாட்டு	vi·ļai·*yaaţ*·ţu

eating out

Can you recommend a ...?	நீங்கள் ஒரு ... பரிந்துரைக்க முடியுமா?	*neeng*·kaļ o·*ru* ... pa·rin·tu·*raik*·ka mu·ţi·*yu*·maa
bar	பார்	paar
place to eat	உணவகம்	u·ņa·va·*ham*
I'd like (a/the) ..., please.	எனக்கு தயவு செய்து ... கொடுங்கள்.	e·*nak*·ku ta·ya·*vu* chey·*tu* ... ko·*ţung*·kaļ
bill	விலைச்சீட்டு	vi·*laich*·cheeţ·ţu
menu	உணவுப்பட்டியல்	u·ņa·*vup*·paţ·ţi·yal
table for (four)	(நான்கு) பேருக்குரிய ஒரு மேசை	(naan·*ku*) pey·*ruk*·ku·ri·ya o·*ru* mey·*chai*
that dish	அந்த உணவு வகை	*an*·ta u·ņa·*vu* va·*hai*
breakfast	காலை உணவு	kaa·*lai* u·ņa·*vu*
lunch	மதிய உணவு	ma·*ti*·ya u·ņa·*vu*
dinner	இரவு உணவு	i·ra·*vu* u·ņa·*vu*

I'll have boiled/mineral water.

எனக்கு கொதிக்க வைக்கப்பட்ட/மினரல் தண்ணீர் வேண்டும். — e·*nak*·ku ko·*tik*·ka vaik·*kap*·paţ·ţa/mi·na·*ral taņ*·ņeyr *veyņ*·ţum

What would you like?

உங்களுக்கு எது வேணடும்? — *ung*·ka·ļuk·ku e·*tu veyn*·ţum

(cup of) coffee/tea ...	(கப்) காப்பி/தேனீர் ...	(kap) *kaap*·pi/*tey*·neer ...
with milk	பாலுடன்	paa·lu·*ţan*
without sugar	சர்க்கரைஇல்லாமல	*chark*·ka·rai·*il*·laa·mal
(orange) juice	(ஆரஞ்சு) சாறு	(aa·ra·*nyu*) chaa·*ru*
lassi	லாசி	laa·*chi*
soft drink	குளிர் பானம்	ku·*ļir* paa·*nam*
a bottle/glass of beer	ஒரு பாட்டில்/கிளாஸ் பீர்	o·*ru paaţ*·ţil/ki·*ļaas* peer

a bottle/glass of ... wine	ஒரு பாட்டில்/ கிளாஸ ... வைன்	o·*ru paaţ*·ţil/ ki·*ļaas* ... vain
red	சிவப்பு	chi·*vap*·pu
white	வெள்ளை	*veļ*·ļai

special diets & allergies

Do you have vegetarian food?

உங்களிடம சைவ உணவு உள்ளதா? — *ung*·ka·ļi·ţam *chai*·va u·ņa·*vu uļ*·ļa·taa

I'm allergic to ...	எனக்கு ... உணவு சேராது.	e·*nak*·ku ... u·ņa·*vu* *chey*·raa·tu
dairy products	பால் சார்ந்த	paal *chaarn*·ta
eggs	முட்டை	*muţ*·ţai
meat stock	இறைச்சி வகை	i·*raich*·chi va·*kai*
nuts	பருப்பு வகை	pa·*rup*·pu va·*kai*
seafood	கடல் சார்ந்த	ka·*ţal chaarn*·ta

emergencies

Help!	உதவ!	u·ta·*vi*
Stop!	நிறுத்து!	ni·*rut*·tu
Go away!	போய் விடு!	*pow*·i *vi*·ţu
Thief!	திருடன்!	*ti*·ru·ţan
Fire!	நெருப்பு!	ne·*rup*·pu
Watch out!	கவனிக்கவும!	ka·va·*nik*·ka·vum

Call ...!	ஐ அழைக்கவும் ...!	i a·*źai*·ka·vum ...
an ambulance	ஒரு ஆம்புலன்ஸ்	o·*ru aam*·pu·lans
a doctor	ஒரு மருத்துவர்	o·*ru* ma·*rut*·tu·var
the police	போலிஸ்	pow·*lees*

Could you help me, please?

நீங்கள் எனக்கு தயவு செய்து உதவி செய்ய முடியுமா? — *neeng*·kaļ e·*nak*·ku ta·ya·*vu* chey·*tu* u·ta·*vi chey*·ya mu·ţi·yu·maa

I have to use the phone.

நான் தொலைபேசியை பயன்படுத்த வேண்டும. — naan *to*·lai·pey·*chi*·yai pa·*yan*·pa·*ţut*·ta veyņ·*ţum*

I'm lost.

நான் வழி தவறி போய்விட்டேன். naan va·*źi* ta·va·*ri* pow·i·*viţ*·ţeyn

Where are the toilets?

கழிவறைகள் எங்கே? ka·*źi*·va·rai·kaļ *eng*·key

Where's the police station?

காவல் நிலையம் எங்கே உள்ளது? kaa·*val* ni·*lai*·yam *eng*·key *uļ*·ļa·tu

I have insurance.

என்னிடம் காப்பீடு உள்ளது. *en*·ni·ţam *kaap*·pee·ţu *uļ*·ļa·tu

I want to contact my embassy.

நான் எனது தூதரகத்துடன் தொடர்பு கொள்ள விரும்புகிறேன். naan e·na·*tu* too·ta·ra·*kat*·tu·ţan to·*ţar*·pu *koļ*·ļa vi·*rum*·pu·ki·ren

I've been raped.

நான் கற்பழிக்கப்பட்டுள்ளேன். naan kar·pa·*źik*·kap·paţ·*ţuļ*·ļeyn

I've been robbed.

நான் கொள்ளையிடப்பட்டுள்ளேன். naan koļ·ļai·yi·*ţap*·paţ·*ţuļ*·ļeyn

I've lost my bag/money.

நான் எனது பை/பணம் தொலைத்து விட்டேன். naan e·na·*tu* pai/pa·*ņam* to·*lait*·tu viţ·*ţeyn*

health

Where's the nearest ...?	அருகிலுள்ள ... எங்கே?	a·ru·ki·*luļ*·ļa ... *eng*·key
dentist	பல் மருத்துவர்	pal ma·*rut*·tu·var
doctor	மருத்துவர்	ma·*rut*·tu·var
hospital	மருத்துவமனை	ma·*rut*·tu·va·ma·nai
pharmacist	மருந்தகம்	ma·*run*·ta·kam

I need a doctor (who speaks English).

(ஆங்கிலம் பேசக்கூடிய) ஒரு மருத்துவர் எனக்கு தேவை. (*aang*·ki·lam pey·chak·*koo*·ţi·ya) o·*ru* ma·*rut*·tu·var e·*nak*·ku *tey*·vai

Could I see a female doctor?

நான் ஒரு பெண் மருத்துவரை பார்க்க முடியுமா? naan o·*ru* peņ ma·*rut*·tu·va·rai paark·*ka* mu·ţi·*yu*·maa

I've run out of my medication.

எனது மருந்துகள் முடிந்து விட்டன. e·na·*tu* ma·*run*·tu·kaļ mu·*ţin*·tu *viţ*·ţa·na

I have (a) ...	எனக்கு ... உள்ளது.	e·*nak*·ku ... *uḷ*·ḷa·tu
constipation	மலச்சிக்கல்	ma·*lach*·chik·kal
diarrhoea	வயிற்றுப்போக்கு	va·yit·*trup*·powk·ku
fever	காய்ச்சல்	*kaich*·chal
heart condition	இருதய நோய்	i·*ru*·ta·ya *now*·i
nausea	குமட்டல்	ku·*maṭ*·ṭal

I'm allergic to ...	எனக்கு ... சேராது.	e·*nak*·ku ... *chey*·raa·tu
anti-inflammatories	அழற்சிக்கான மருந்து	a·źar·*chik*·kaa·na ma·*run*·tu
bees	தேனிக்கள்	*tey*·ni·kaḷ
codeine	கொடெய்ன் மருந்து வகை	ko·*ṭeyn* ma·*run*·tu va·*kai*

responsible travel

I'd like to learn some Tamil.
நான் தமிழ் கற்க விரும்புகிறேன். — naan *ta*·mil *kar*·ka vi·*rum*·pu·ki·reyn

Would you like me to teach you some English?
உங்களுக்கு நான் சிறிது ஆங்கிலம் கற்றுத் தரட்டுமா? — *ung*·ka·*ḷuk*·ku naan *chi*·ri·tu *aang*·ki·lam *kat*·trut ta·*raṭ*·ṭu·maa

I didn't mean to do anything wrong.
நான் தவறாக எதையும் செய்யவோ நினைக்கவில்லை. — naan ta·va·raa·*ka* e·*tai*·yum chey·ya·*vow* ni·*naik*·ka·*vil*·lai

Is this a local or national custom?
இது ஓர் உள்ளூர் வழக்கமா அல்லது நாட்டு வழக்கமா? — i·*tu* owr *uḷ*·ḷoor va·*źak*·ka·maa *al*·la·tu *naaṭ*·ṭu va·*źak*·ka·maa

I'd like to stay at a locally run hotel.
நான் உள்ளூரில் நடத்தப்படும் ஒரு ஹோட்டலில் தங்க விரும்புகிறேன். — naan *uḷ*·ḷoo·ril na·*ṭat*·tap·pa·ṭum o·*ru hoṭ*·ṭa·lil *tang*·ka vi·*rum*·pu·ki·reyn

Where can I buy locally produced goods?
உள்ளூரில் தயாரிக்கப்பட்ட பொருட்கள் நான் எங்கே வாங்க முடியும்? — *uḷ*·ḷoo·ril ta·yaa·*rik*·kap·paṭ·ṭa po·*ruṭ*·kaḷ naan *eng*·key *vang*·ka mu·ṭi·*yum*

I'd like to do some volunteer work.
நான் சில பொதுநலத் தொண்டுகள் செய்ய விரும்புகிறேன். — naan *chi*·la po·*tu*·na·*lat* *toṇ*·ṭu·kaḷ *chey*·ya vi·*rum*·pu·ki·reyn

english–tamil dictionary

Words in this dictionary are marked as n (noun), a (adjective), v (verb), m (masculine), f (feminine), sg (singular), pl (plural), inf (informal) and pol (polite) where necessary.

A

accident விபத்து vi·*pat*·tu
accommodation தங்குமிடம் *tang*·ku·mi·ţam
adaptor பொருத்துங்கருவி po·*rut*·tung·ka·ru·vi
address n விலாசம் vi·*laa*·cham
after பிறகு pi·ra·*ku*
air-conditioned குளிர்சாதன வசதியுடையது ku·*ḷir*·chaa·ta·na va·*cha*·ti·yu·*ţai*·ya·tu
airplane விமானம் vi·*maa*·nam
airport விமான நிலையம் *vi*·maa·na *ni*·lai·yam
alcohol சாராயம் *chaa*·raa·yam
all அனைத்தும் a·*nait*·tum
allergy ஒவ்வாமை *ov*·vaa·mai
ambulance ஆம்புலன்ஸ் *aam*·pu·lans
and மற்றும் *mat*·trum
ankle கணுக்கால் ka·*ṇuk*·kaal
antibiotics எந்திபயோட்டிக் en·ti·pa·*yowţ*·ţik
arm மேற்கை *meyr*·kai
ATM ATM ey ti em

B

baby குழந்தை ku·*źan*·tai
back (of body) முதுகு mu·*tu*·ku
backpack முதுகுப்பை mu·tu·*kup*·pai
bad கெட்ட *keţ*·ţa
bag பை pai
baggage claim பயணப்பெட்டி பெறுமிடம் pa·ya·ṇap·*peţ*·ţi pe·*ru*·mi·ţam
bank வங்கி *vang*·ki
bar பார் paar
bathroom குளியலறை ku·ḷi·*ya*·la·rai
battery பாட்டரி *paaţ*·ţa·ri
beautiful அழகு a·*źa*·ku
bed படுக்கை pa·*ţuk*·kai
before முன் mun
behind பின்புறம் *pin*·pu·ram
bicycle சைக்கிள் *chaik*·kiḷ
big பெரிய pe·*ri*·ya
bill விலைச்சீட்டு vi·*laich*·cheeţ·ţu
blanket போர்வை *pawr*·vai
blood group இரத்தப் பிரிவு i·*rat*·tap pi·*ri*·vu
boat படகு pa·ţa·*ku*
book (make a reservation) v புத்தகம் *put*·ta·kam
bottle பாட்டில் *paaţ*·ţil
boy பையன் *pai*·yan
brakes (car) வேகத்தடைகள் vey·*kat*·ta·ţai·kaḷ
breakfast காலை உணவு kaa·*lai* u·ṇa·*vu*
broken (faulty) உடைந்தது u·*ţain*·ta·tu
bus பஸ் pas
business வியாபாரம் *vi*·yaa·paa·ram
buy v வாங்குதல் *vaang*·ku·tal

C

camera காமிரா kaa·mi·*raa*
cancel தடைசெய்தல் *ta*·ţai·*chey*·tal
car மோட்டார் வண்டி *mowţ*·ţaar *vaṇ*·ţi
cash n ரொக்கம் *rok*·kam
cash (a cheque) v பணம் பெறுதல் pa·*ṇam* pe·*ru*·tal
cell phone கைத்தொலைபேசி *kait*·to·lai·pey·*chi*
centre n மையம் *mai*·yam
change (money) v மாற்றுதல் *maat*·tru·tal
cheap மலிவு ma·*li*·vu
check (bill) விலைச்சீட்டு vi·*laich*·cheeţ·ţu
check-in n பதிவிடம் pa·ti·*vi*·ţam
chest (body) நெஞ்சு *nen*·ju
child சிறுவன்/சிறுமி chi·*ru*·van/chi·*ru*·mi m/f
cigarette சிகரெட் *chi*·ka·ret
city நகரம் na·ka·*ram*
clean a சுத்தம் *chut*·tam
closed மூடப்பட்டுள்ளது moo·ţap·*paţ*·ţuḷ·ḷa·*tu*
cold a குளிர் ku·*ḷir*
collect call கலெக்ட் அழைப்பு ka·*lekt* a·*źaip*·pu
come வா vaa
computer கணினி ka·*ṇi*·ni
condom ஆணுறை *aa*·ṇu·rai
contact lenses உள் கண்ணாடி வில்லை uḷ *kaṇ*·ṇaa·ţi *vil*·lai
cook v சமையல்காரர் *cha*·mai·*yal*·kaa·rar
cost n விலை vi·*lai*
credit card கிரேடிட் அட்டை ki·rey·*ţiţ aţ*·ţai
currency exchange நாணய மாற்றம் *naa*·ṇa·ya *maat*·tram
customs (immigration) சுங்கத்துறை *chung*·kat·tu·rai

D

dangerous அபாயம் a·*paa*·yam
date (time) தேதி *tey*·ti

day நாள் naaḷ
delay n தாமதம் *taa*·ma·tam
dentist பல் மருத்துவர் pal ma·*rut*·tu·var
depart புறப்பாடு pu·*rap*·paa·ṭu
diaper குழந்தை அணையாடைத் துணி ku·*źan*·tai a·ṇai·yaa·*ṭait* tu·*ṇi*
dinner இரவு உணவு i·ra·*vu* u·ṇa·*vu*
direct a நேரடி ney·ra·*ṭi*
dirty அழுக்கு a·*źuk*·ku
disabled முடக்கிவிடுதல் mu·*ṭak*·ki·vi·ṭu·tal
discount n கழிவு ka·*źi*·vu
doctor மருத்துவர் ma·*rut*·tu·var
double bed இரட்டைப்படுக்கை i·*raṭ*·ṭaip·pa·*ṭuk*·kai
double room இரட்டையறை i·*raṭ*·ṭai·ya·rai
drink n பானம் paa·*nam*
drive v ஓட்டுதல் *owṭ*·ṭu·tal
drivers licence வாகனமோட்டும் லைசன்ஸ் vaa·ka·na·*mowṭ*·ṭum lai·*chans*
drug (illicit) போதைப்பொருள் pow·*taip*·po·ruḷ

E

ear காது kaa·*tu*
east கிழக்கு ki·*źak*·ku
eat சாப்பிடு *chaap*·pi·ṭu
economy class சிக்கன வகுப்பு *chik*·ka·na va·*kup*·pu
electricity மின்சாரம் min·*chaa*·ram
elevator லிப்ட் lipt
email மின்னஞ்சல் min·nan·*chal*
embassy தூதரகம் *too*·ta·ra·kam
emergency நெருக்கடி ne·ruk·ka·*ṭi*
English (language) ஆங்கிலம் *aang*·ki·lam
entrance நுழைவாயில் nu·zai·vaa·*yil*
evening மாலை maa·*lai*
exit n வெளியேறுமிடம் ve·ḷi·yey·*ru*·mi·ṭam
expensive விலையுயர்ந்தது vi·*lai*·yu·yarn·ta·tu
eye கண் kaṇ

F

far தூரம் *too*·ram
fast வேகம் *vey*·kam
father அப்பா *ap*·paa
film (camera) படச்சுருள் pa·*ṭach*·chu·ruḷ
finger விரல் *vi*·ral
first-aid kit முதலுதவிப்பெட்டி mu·ta·lu·ta·*vip peṭ*·ṭi
first class முதல் வகுப்பு mu·*tal* va·*kup*·pu
fish n மீன் meen
food உணவு u·ṇa·*vu*
foot கால் kaal
free (of charge) இலவசம் i·la·va·*cham*
friend நண்பன் *naṇ*·pan
fruit பழம் pa·*źam*
full நிறைய ni·*rai*·ya

G

gift பரிசு pa·ri·*chu*
girl சிறுமி *chi*·ru·mi
glass (drinking) கிளாஸ் ki·*ḷaas*
glasses மூக்குக் கண்ணாடி mook·*kuk kaṇ*·ṇaa·ṭi
go போவது *pow*·va·tu
good நல்லது *nal*·la·tu
guide n வழிகாட்டி va·*źi*·kaaṭ·ṭi

H

half n பாதி paa·*ti*
hand கை kai
happy மகிழ்ச்சி ma·*kiźch*·chi
have இருத்தல் i·*rut*·tal
he அவன் a·*van*
head n தலை ta·*lai*
heart இருதயம் i·*ru*·ta·yam
heavy பாரம் paa·*ram*
help v உதவி u·ta·*vi*
here இங்கே *ing*·key
high உயரம் u·ya·*ram*
highway நெடுஞ்சாலை ne·*ṭuny*·chaa·lai
hike v நடைப்பயணம் na·*ṭaip*·pa·ya·ṇam
holiday விடுமுறை vi·ṭu·*mu*·rai
hospital மருத்துவமனை ma·*rut*·tu·va·ma·nai
hot சூடு *choo*·ṭu
hotel ஹோட்டல் *hoṭ*·ṭal
hungry பசி pa·*chi*
husband கணவன் ka·ṇa·*van*

I

I நான் naan
identification (card) அடையாள அட்டை a·*ṭai*·yaa·ḷa *aṭ*·ṭai
ill உடல்நலக்குறைவு u·ṭal·na·*lak*·ku·rai·vu
important முக்கியம் *muk*·ki·yam
injury காயம் kaa·*yam*
insurance காப்பீடு *kaap*·pee·ṭu
internet இணையம் i·ṇai·*yam*
interpreter துபாஷி *tu*·paa·shi

J

jewellery நகை na·*kai*
job வேலை *vey*·lai

K

key சாவி *chaa*·vi
kilogram கிலோகிராம் ki·*low*·ki·raam
kitchen சமையலறை cha·mai·ya·*la*·rai
knife கத்தி *kat*·ti

L

laundry (place) துணி துவைக்குமிடம் *tu*·ṇi tu·*vaik*·ku·mi·ṭam
lawyer வழக்கறிஞர் va·*źak*·ka·ri·nyar
left (direction) இடது i·ṭa·*tu*
leg (body) கால் kaal
less குறைவு ku·rai·*vu*
letter (mail) கடிதம் ka·ṭi·*tam*
light n ஒளி o·*ḷi*
like v பிடித்தல் pi·*ṭit*·tal
lock n பூட்டு *pooṭ*·ṭu
long நீண்டது *neeṇ*·ṭa·tu
lost தொலைதல் to·*lai*·tal
love v அன்பு *an*·pu
luggage பெட்டி *peṭ*·ṭi
lunch மதிய உணவு ma·*ti*·ya u·ṇa·*vu*

M

mail n கடிதம் ka·ṭi·*tam*
man ஆண் aaṇ
map வரைபடம் va·*rai*·pa·ṭam
market சந்தை *chan*·tai
matches தீக்குச்சி *teek*·kuch·chi
meat இறைச்சி i·*raich*·chi
medicine மருந்து ma·*run*·tu
message தகவல் ta·ka·*val*
milk பால் paal
minute நிமிடம் ni·*mi*·ṭam
money பணம் pa·*ṇam*
month மாதம் *maa*·tam
morning காலை kaa·*lai*
mother அம்மா *am*·maa
motorcycle மோட்டார் சைக்கிள் *mowṭ*·ṭaar *chaik*·kiḷ
mouth வாய் vai

N

name பெயர் pe·*yar*
near அருகே a·ru·*key*
neck n கழுத்து ka·*źut*·tu
new புதிது pu·ti·*tu*
newspaper பத்திரிகை *pat*·ti·ri·kai
night இரவு i·ra·*vu*
no இல்லை *il*·lai
noisy இரைச்சல் i·*raich*·chal
nonsmoking புகை பிடிக்காத pu·*hai* pi·*ṭik*·kaa·ta
north வடக்கு va·*ṭak*·ku
nose மூக்கு *mook*·ku
now இப்பொழுது ip·*po*·zu·tu
number எண் eṇ

O

old பழையது pa·*źai*·ya·tu
open a திறந்த ti·*ran*·ta
outside வெளியே ve·ḷi·*yey*

P

passport பாஸ்போர்ட் *paas*·powrt
pay v பணம் கொடுத்தல் pa·*ṇam* ko·*ṭut*·tal
pharmacy மருந்தகம் ma·*run*·ta·kam
photo புகைப்படம் pu·*kaip*·pa·ṭam
police போலீஸ் pow·*lees*
postcard அஞ்சல் அட்டை *any*·chal *aṭ*·ṭai
post office தபால் நிலையம் ta·*paal* ni·*lai*·yam
pregnant கர்ப்பம் *karp*·pam
price n விலை vi·*lai*

Q

quiet a அமைதி a·mai·*ti*

R

rain n மழை ma·*źai*
razor சவரக்கத்தி cha·va·*rak*·kat·ti
receipt n ரசீது ra·*chee*·tu
registered mail பதியப்பட்ட அஞ்சல் pa·ti·yap·*paṭ*·ṭa *any*·chal
rent v வாடகை vaa·*ṭa*·kai
repair v பழுது பார்த்தல் pa·*źu*·tu *paart*·tal
reservation முன்பதிவு *mun*·pa·ti·vu
restaurant உணவகம் u·ṇa·va·*kam*
return v திரும்புதல் ti·*rum*·pu·tal
right (direction) வலது va·la·*tu*
road சாலை *chaa*·lai
room n அறை a·*rai*

S

safe a பாதுகாப்பு paa·tu·*kaap*·pu
sanitary napkin சுகாதார நாப்கின் chu·kaa·*taa*·ra *naap*·kin
seat n இருக்கை i·*ruk*·kai

send அனுப்புதல் a·*nup*·pu·tal
sex பாலியல் உறவு paa·*li*·yal u·ra·*vu*
shampoo ஷாம்பு *shaam*·pu
she அவள் a·*vaḷ*
sheet (bed) விரிப்பு vi·*rip*·pu
shirt சட்டை *chaṭ*·ṭai
shoes காலணி kaa·la·*ṇi*
shop n கடை ka·*ṭai*
short கட்டை *kaṭ*·ṭai
shower n மழை பொழிதல் ma·*żai* po·*żi*·tal
single room தனியறை ta·*ni*·ya·rai
skin n தோள் towḷ
skirt n பாவாடை paa·vaa·*ṭai*
sleep v தூக்கம் *took*·kam
slowly மெதுவாக me·*tu*·vaa·ka
small சிறியது *chi*·ri·ya·tu
soap சவர்க்காரம் cha·*vark*·kaa·ram
some சில *chi*·la
soon உடனே u·ṭa·*ney*
south தெற்கு *ter*·ku
stamp அஞ்சல் தலை *an*·nyal ta·*lai*
station (train) நிலையம் ni·*lai*·yam
stomach வயிறு va·*yi*·ru
stop v நிறுத்தும் ni·*rut*·tum
stop (bus) n பஸ் நிறுத்தும் pas ni·*rut*·tum
street சாலை *chaa*·lai
student மாணவன் maa·ṇa·*van*
sun சூரியன் *choo*·ri·yan
swim v நீந்துதல் *neen*·tu·tal

T

tampons பெண்களுக்குரிய தாம்போன் *peṇ*·ka·*ḷuk*·ku·ri·ya *tam*·pon
teeth பற்கள் *pat*·kaḷ
telephone n தொலைபேசி *to*·lai·pey·*chi*
temperature (weather) வெப்ப நிலை *vep*·pa ni·*lai*
that (one) அது a·*tu*
they அவர்கள் a·*var*·kaḷ
thirsty தாகம் taa·*kam*
this (one) இது i·*tu*
throat தொண்டை *toṇ*·ṭai
ticket டிக்கட் ṭik·*kaṭ*
time நேரம் *ney*·ram
tired களைப்பு ka·*ḷaip*·pu
tissues உறிஞ்சு தாள் u·*riny*·ju·taaḷ
today இன்று in·*dru*
toilet கழிவறை ka·*żi*·va·rai
tomorrow நாளை *naa*·ḷai
tonight இன்றிரவு in·*dri*·ra·vu
toothbrush பல் தூரிகை pal *too*·ri·kai
toothpaste பற்பசை *par*·pa·chai
torch (flashlight) கைவிளக்கு kai·vi·ḷa·*ku*
tour n சுற்றுலா *chut*·tru·laa
towel துண்டு *tuṇ*·ṭu
train n இரயில் i·ra·*yil*
translate மொழிபெயர்த்தல் mo·*żi*·pe·*yart*·tal
travel agency பிரயாண அலுவலகம் *pi*·ra·yaa·ṇa a·*lu*·va·la·kam
travellers cheque பயணிகள் காசோலை pa·ya·ṇi·*kal* kaa·*chow*·lai
trousers காற்சட்டை kaar·*chaṭ*·ṭai
twin beds இரட்டைப் படுக்கைகள் i·raṭ·*ṭaip* pa·*ṭuk*·kai·kaḷ

U

underwear உள்ளாடை *uḷ*·ḷaa·ṭai
urgent அவசரம் a·va·*cha*·ram

V

vacant காலி kaa·*li*
vegetable n காய்கறி *kai*·ka·ri
vegetarian a சைவம் *chai*·vam
visa விசா vi·*chaa*

W

walk v நடத்தல் na·*ṭat*·tal
wallet பணப்பை pa·*ṇap*·pai
wash (something) கழுவுதல் ka·*żu*·vu·tal
watch n கடிகாரம் ka·*ṭi*·kaa·ram
water n தண்ணீர் *taṇ*·ṇeyr
we நாம் naam
weekend வார இறுதி *vaa*·ra i·ru·*ti*
west மேற்கு *meyr*·ku
wheelchair சக்கர நாற்காலி *chak*·ka·ra *naar*·kaa·li
when எப்பொழுது ep·po·*żu*·*tu*
where எங்கே *eng*·key
who யார் yaar
why ஏன் eyn
wife மனைவி ma·*nai*·vi
window சன்னல் *chan*·nal
with உடன் u·*ṭan*
without இல்லாமல் *il*·laa·mal
woman பெண் peṇ
write எழுது e·*żu*·tu

Y

yes ஆமாம் *aa*·maam
yesterday நேற்று *neyt*·tru
you sg inf நீ nee
you sg pol & pl நீங்கள் *neeng*·kaḷ

Telugu

alphabet

vowels				
అ a	ఆ aa	ఇ i	ఈ ee	ఉ u
ఊ oo	ఎ e	ఏ ay	ఐ ai	ఒ oh
ఓ ōh	ఔ ow			

consonants				
క ka	ఖ k'a	గ ga	ఘ g'a	
చ cha	ఛ ch'a	జ ja	ఝ j'a	
ట ţa	ఠ ţ'a	డ đa	ఢ đ'a	ణ ņa
త ta	థ t'a	ద da	ధ d'a	న na
ప pa	ఫ p'a	బ ba	భ b'a	మ ma
య ya	ర ra	ల la	వ va	శ şa
ష sha	స sa	హ ha	ళ ļa	క్ష ksha

introduction

There are many theories about the origins of the name 'Telugu' (also known as Tenugu), but perhaps the most endearing one is that it's derived from the word te·ne తేనె (honey), thus making Telugu (te·lu·gu తెలుగు) 'the language of honey'. The official home of this south-central Dravidian language is Andhra Pradesh, where it achieved official status in 1966. It's spoken by around 70 million people there, as well as in parts of Tamil Nadu. As with many Indian languages, migration has taken Telugu offshore and it's spoken in Malaysia, Singapore, Fiji, Mauritius and parts of the Middle East. The geography of its home state, which spreads into the heart of India, has allowed Telugu to be enriched over time by both Indo-Aryan and Dravidian languages. Local poets first mused in the language in the 11th century and it has long been associated with the classical Carnatic music. Telugu has four regional dialects – northern, southern, eastern and central – with central considered the standard. A few honeyed Telugu phrases will go a long way whichever region you're in!

■ telugu

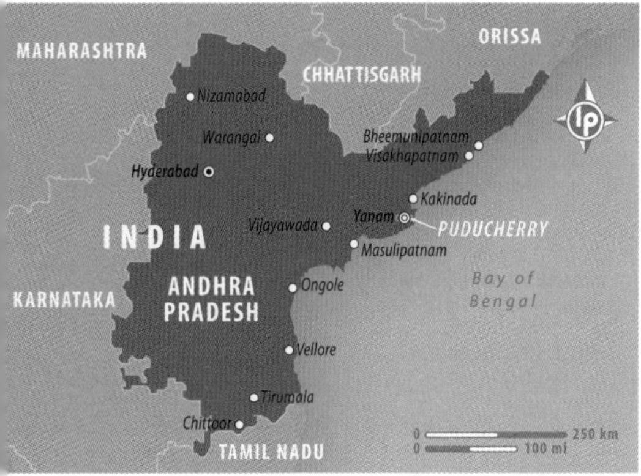

pronunciation

Vowels		Consonants	
Symbol	English sound	Symbol	English sound
a	run	b	bed
aa	father	ch	cheat
ai	aisle	d	dog (pronounced with tongue more forward)
ay	day	đ	retroflex d
e	bet	g	go
ee	need	h	hat
i	hit	j	jar
oh	note	k	kit
ōh	as oh, but longer	l	lot
oo	zoo	ļ	retroflex l
ow	how	m	man
u	put	n	not
		ņ	retroflex n
		p	pet
		r	red
		s	sun
		ş	retroflex s
		sh	shot
		t	top (pronounced with tongue more forward)
		ţ	retroflex t
		v	very (close to the English 'w')
		y	yes

In this chapter, the Telugu pronunciation is given in purple after each phrase.

Aspirated consonants (pronounced with a puff of air after the sound) are represented with an apostrophe after the letter – b', ch', d', đ', g', j', k', p', t' and ţ'. Retroflex consonants (pronounced with the tongue bent backwards) are included in this table.

Each syllable is separated by a dot. For example:

దయచేసి. da·ya·chay·si

essentials

Yes./No.	అవును./కాదు.	a·vu·nu/kaa·du
Please.	దయచేసి.	da·ya·chay·si
Thank you.	ధన్యవాదాలు.	d'an·ya·vaa·daa·lu
Excuse me. (to get past)	కొంచెం పక్కకు జరగండి.	kohn·chem pak·ka·ku ja·ra·gan·đi
Excuse me. (to get attention)	ఏమండి.	ay·an·đi
Sorry.	క్షమించండి.	ksha·min·chan·đi

language difficulties

Do you speak English?
మీరు ఇంగ్లీషు మాట్లాడుతారా? — mee·ru ing·lee·shu maaţ·laa·đu·taa·raa

Do you understand?
మీకు అర్థం అవుతుందా? — mee·ku ar·t'am ow·tun·daa

I understand.
అర్థం అవుతుంది. — ar·t'am ow·tun·di

I don't understand.
అర్థం కాదు. — ar·t'am kaa·du

Could you please ...?	కొంచెం ...?	kohn·chem ...
repeat that	మళ్ళీ చెప్తారా	maḷ·ḷee che·pu·taa·raa
speak more slowly	మెల్లిగా మాట్లాడుతారా	mel·li·gaa maaţ·laa·đu·taa·raa

numbers

0	సున్నా	sun·naa	20	ఇరవై	i·ra·vai
1	ఒకటి	oh·ka·ţi	30	ముప్పై	mup·p'ai
2	రెండు	ren·đu	40	నలభై	na·la·b'ai
3	మూడు	moo·đu	50	యాభై	yaa·b'ai
4	నాలుగు	naa·lu·gu	60	అరవై	a·ra·vai
5	ఐదు	ai·du	70	డెబ్బై	đeb·b'ai
6	ఆరు	aa·ru	80	ఎనభై	e·na·b'ai
7	ఏడు	ay·đu	90	తొంభై	tohm·b'ai
8	ఎనిమిది	e·ni·mi·di	100	వంద	van·da
9	తొమ్మిది	tohm·mi·di	1000	వెయ్యి	vey·yi
10	పది	pa·di	1,000,000	లక్ష	lak·sha

time & dates

What time is it?	టైం ఎంత?	taim en·ta
It's (two) o'clock.	(రెండు) గంటలు.	(ren·đu) gan·ţa·lu
Quarter past (two).	(రెండుం)బావు.	(ren·đum)·baa·vu
Half past (two).	(రెండు)న్నర.	(ren·đun)·na·ra
Quarter to (three).	పావు తక్కువ (మూడు).	paa·vu tak·ku·va (moo·đu)
At what time ...?	ఎన్ని గంటలకి ...?	en·ni gan·ţa·la·ki ...
At (nine) o'clock.	(తొమ్మిది) గంటలకి.	(tohm·mi·di) gan·ţa·la·ki
It's (15 December).	ఈ రోజు (డిసెంబరు పదిహేను).	ee rōh·ju (đi·sem·ba·ru pa·di·hay·mu)
yesterday	నిన్న	ni·na
today	ఇవాళ	i·vaa·ļa
tomorrow	రేపు	ray·pu
Monday	సోమ వారం	sōh·ma vaa·ram
Tuesday	మంగళ వారం	man·ga·ļa vaa·ram
Wednesday	బుధ వారం	bu·d'a vaa·ram
Thursday	గురు వారం	gu·ru vaa·ram
Friday	శుక్ర వారం	şuk·ra vaa·ram
Saturday	శని వారం	şa·ni vaa·ram
Sunday	ఆది వారం	aa·di vaa·ram

border crossing

I'm here ...	నేను ఇక్కడ ... ఉన్నాను.	nay·nu ik·ka·đa ... un·naa·nu
in transit	ప్రయాణంలో	pra·yaa·ņam·lōh
on business	పని మీద	pa·ni mee·da
on holiday	సెలవలకి	se·la·va·la·ki
I'm here for ...	నేను ఇక్కడ ... ఉంటాను.	nay·nu ik·ka·đa ... un·ţaa·nu
(10) days	(పది) రోజులు	(pa·di) rōh·ju·lu
(three) weeks	(మూడు) వారాలు	(moo·đu) vaa·raa·lu
(two) months	(రెండు) నెలలు	(ren·đu) ne·la·lu

I'm going to (Charminar).
నేను (చార్మినారుకు) వెళ్తున్నాను. nay·nu (chaar·mee·naar·ku) veļ·tun·naa

I'm staying at the (Hotel Golconda).

నేను (హోటల్ గోల్కొండలో) ఉంటున్నాను. — nay·nu (hōh·ţal gōhl·kohn·đa·lōh) un·ţun·naa·nu

I have nothing to declare.

నా దగ్గిర డిక్లేరు చేయడానికేమీ లేవు. — naa dag·gi·ra đik·lay·ru chay·a·đaa·ni·kay·mee lay·vu

I have this to declare.

నా దగ్గిర డిక్లేరు చేయడానికిది ఉంది. — naa dag·gi·ra đik·lay·ru chay·a·đaa·ni·ki·di un·di

tickets & luggage

Where can I buy a ticket?

టిక్కెట్టు ఎక్కడ దొరుకుతుంది? — ţik·keţ·ţu ek·ka·đa doh·ru·ku·tun·di

Do I need to book a seat?

నేను టిక్కెట్టు బుక్ చేసుకోవాలా? — nay·nu ţik·keţ·ţu buk chay·su·kōh·vaa·laa

One one-way ticket to (Vizag), please.

(వైజాగుకు) వెళ్ళేందుకు మాత్రమే ఒక టిక్కెట్టు ఇవ్వండి. — (vai·jaa·gu·ku) veḷ·ḷayn·du·ku maat·ra·may oh·ka ţik·keţ·ţu iv·van·đi

One return ticket to (Vizag), please.

(వైజాగుకు) రాను-పోను ఒక టిక్కెట్టు ఇవ్వండి. — (vai·jaa·gu·ku) raa·nu·pōh·nu oh·ka ţik·keţ·ţu iv·van·đi

I'd like to … my ticket, please.	నా టిక్కెట్టు ...	naa ţik·keţ·ţu …
cancel	క్యాన్సిలు చేసుకోవాలి	kyaan·si·lu chay·su·kōh·vaa·li
change	మార్చుకోవాలి	maar·chu·kōh·vaa·li
collect	తీసుకోవాలి	tee·su·kōh·vaa·li

I'd like a nonsmoking seat, please.

నాకు పొగ తాగని సీటు కావాలి. — naa·ku pōh·ga taa·ga·ni see·ţu kaa·vaa·li

I'd like a smoking seat, please.

నాకు పొగ తాగే సీటు కావాలి. — naa·ku pōh·ga taa·gay see·ţu kaa·vaa·li

Is there a toilet?

టాయిలెట్ ఉందా? — ţaa·yi·leţ un·daa

Is there air conditioning?

ఎయిరు కండిషనింగు ఉందా? — e·yi·ru kan·đi·sha·nin·gu un·daa

How long does the trip take?
ప్రయాణం ఎంత సేపు పడుతుంది? **pra·yaa·ṇam en·ta say·pu pa·đu·tun·di**

Is it a direct route?
ఇది నేరుగా పోతుందా? **i·di nay·ru·gaa pōh·tun·daa**

My luggage has been ...	నా సామాను ...	**naa saa·maa·nu ...**
lost	పోయింది	**pōh·yin·di**
stolen	దొంగిలించారు	**dohn·gi·lin·chaa·ru**

transport

Where does flight (353) arrive?
ఫ్లైట్ నంబరు (353) ఎక్కడికి వస్తుంది? **p'laiţ nam·ba·ru (moo·đu ai·du moo·đu) ek·ka·đi·ki vas·tun·di**

Where does flight (353) depart?
ఫ్లైట్ నంబరు (353) ఎక్కడి నించి పోతుంది? **p'laiţ nam·ba·ru (moo·đu ai·du moo·đu) ek·ka·đi nin·chi pōh·tun·di**

Is this the ... to (Eluru)?	ఇది (ఏలూరు) ...?	**i·di (ay·loo·ru) ...**
bus	బస్సా	**bas·saa**
plane	విమానమా	**vi·maa·na·maa**
train	రైలా	**rai·laa**

What time's the ... bus?	... బస్సు ఎన్ని గంటలకి?	**... bas·su en·ni gan·ţa·la·ki**
first	మొదటి	**moh·da·ţi**
last	చివరి	**chi·va·ri**
next	తర్వాతి	**tar·vaa·ti**

How long will it be delayed?
అది ఎంతసేపు ఆలస్యం? **a·di en·ta·say·pu aa·las·yam**

Please tell me when we get to (Golconda).
(గోల్కొండ) వచ్చినప్పుడు చెప్పండి. **(gōhl·kohn·đa) vach·chi·nap·pu·đu chep·pan·đi**

That's my seat.
అది నా సీటు. **a·di naa see·ţu**

I'd like a taxi ...	నాకు టాక్సీ ... కావాలి.	**naa·ku ţaak·see ... kaa·vaa·li**
at (9am)	(పొద్దున తొమ్మిది) గంటలకి	**(pohd·du·na tohm·mi·di) gan·ţa·la·ki**
now	ఇప్పుడే కావాలి	**ip·pu·đay**

How much is it to (Golconda)?

(గోల్కొండకి) ఎంత అవుతుంది? — (gōhl·kohn·đa·ki) en·ta a·vu·tun·di

Please put the meter on.

మీటరు వెయ్యి. — mee·ţa·ru vey·yi

Please take me to (this address).

(ఈ అడ్రస్సుకి) తీసుకెళ్ళు. — (ee ađ·đras·su·ki) tee·su·keḷ·ḷu

Please stop here.

ఇక్కడ ఆపు. — ik·ka·đa aa·pu

Please wait here.

ఇక్కడ వెయిట్ చెయ్యి. — ik·ka·đa ve·yiţ chey·yi

I'd like to hire a car/4WD (with a driver).

నాకు ఒక కారు/జీపు (డ్రైవరుతో) అద్దెకు కావాలి. — naa·ku oh·ka kaa·ru/jee·pu (đrai·va·ru tōh) ad·de·ku kaa·vaa·li

How much for daily/weekly hire?

రోజుకి/వారానికి అద్దె ఎంత? — rōh·ju·ki/vaa·raa·ni·ki ad·de en·ta

directions

Where's the ...?	... ఎక్కడ ఉంది?	... ek·ka·đa un·di
bank	బ్యాంకు	byaan·ku
foreign currency exchange	ఫారిన్ కరెన్సీ ఎక్చేంజి	p'aa·rin ka·ren·see eks·chayn·ji
post office	పోస్టాఫీసు	pōhs·ţaa·p'ee·su

Is this the road to (Tank Bund)?

ఇది (ట్యాంక్ బండుకు) పోయే రోడ్డా? — i·di (ţyank ban·đu·ku) pōh·yay rōhđ·đaa

Can you show me (on the map)?

(మ్యాపులో) చూపిస్తారా? — (myaap·lōh) choo·pis·taa·raa

What's the address?

అడ్రస్సు ఏంటి? — ađ·đras·su ayn·ţi

How far is it?

ఎంత దూరం? — en·ta doo·ram

How do I get there?

అక్కడికెట్లా వెళ్ళాలి? — ak·ka·đi·keţ·laa veḷ·ḷaa·li

Turn left/right.

ఎడమ/కుడి పక్కకి తిరగండి. — e·đa·ma/ku·đi pak·ka·ki ti·ra·gan·đi

It's …	అది … ఉంది.	a·di … un·di
behind …	… వెనక	… ve·na·ka
in front of …	… ముందు	… mun·du
near …	… దగ్గర్లో	… dag·gar·lōh
on the corner …	… మూలలో	… moo·la·lōh
opposite …	… ఎదురుగా	… e·du·ru·gaa
straight ahead	నేరుగా	nay·ru·gaa
there	అక్కడ	ak·ka·đa

accommodation

Where's a guesthouse/hotel nearby?
దగ్గర్లో గెస్టుహౌసు/హోటలు ఎక్కడ ఉంది?
dag·gar·lōh ges·ţu·how·su/hōh·ţa·lu ek·ka·đa un·di

Can you recommend somewhere cheap/good?
మీరు ఏదన్నా చౌక/మంచి హోటలు చెప్తారా?
mee·ru ay·dan·naa chow·ka/man·chi hōh·ţa·lu chep·taa·raa

I'd like to book a room, please.
నేను ఒక రూము బుక్ చేసుకోవాలి.
nay·nu oh·ka roo·mu buk chay·su·kōh·vaa·li

I have a reservation.
నాకు రిజర్వేషన్ ఉంది.
naa·ku ri·jar·vay·shan un·di

Do you have a … room?	మీ దగ్గర … రూము ఉందా?	mee dag·ga·ra … roo·mu un·daa
single	సింగల్	sin·gil
double	డబల్	đa·bal
twin	జంట	jan·ţa

How much is it per night/person?
ఒక రాత్రికి/మనిషికి ఎంత అవుతుంది?
oh·ka raat·ri·ki/ma·ni·shi·ki en·ta a·vu·tun·di

I'd like to stay for (two) nights.
నేను (రెండు) రాత్రులు ఉంటాను.
nay·nu (ren·đu) raat·ru·lu un·ţaa·nu

Can I have my key, please?
నా తాళంచెవి ఇస్తారా?
naa taa·ļam·che·vi is·taa·raa

Can I get another (blanket)?
నాకు ఇంకొక (దుప్పటి) ఇస్తారా?
naa·ku in·koh·ka (dup·pa·ţi) is·taa·raa

The (air conditioning) doesn't work.
(ఎయిరు కండిషనింగు) పని చేయటం లేదు. — (e·yi·ru kan·đi·sha·nin·gu) pa·ni chay·ya·ţam lay·du

Is there an elevator/a safe?
ఇక్కడ లిఫ్ట్/లాకరు ఉందా? — ik·ka·đa lip'·ţu/laa·ka·ru un·daa

What time is checkout?
రూము ఎన్ని గంటలకి ఖాళీ చేయాలి? — roo·mu en·nee gan·ţa·la·ki k'aa·ļee chay·yaa·li

Can I have my ..., please?	నా ... ఇస్తారా?	naa ... is·taa·raa
deposit	డిపాజిట్	đi·paa·jiţ
passport	పాస్పోర్టు	paas·pōhr·ţu
valuables	విలువైన వస్తువులు	vi·lu·vai·na vas·tu·vu·lu

banking & communications

Where's an ATM/a public phone?
ఎటిఎం/పబ్లిక్ ఫోను ఎక్కడ ఉంది? — e·ţi·em/pab·lik p'ōh·nu ek·ka·đa un·di

I'd like to ...	నేను ...	nay·nu ...
arrange a transfer	డబ్బు ట్రాన్స్ఫర్ చేయాలి	đab·bu ţraans·p'a·ru chay·aa·li
change a travellers cheque	ట్రావెలర్సు చెక్కు మార్చుకోవాలి	ţraa·ve·lar·su chek·ku maar·chu·kōh·vaa·li
change money	డబ్బు మార్చుకోవాలి	đab·bu maar·chu·kōh·vaa·li
withdraw money	డబ్బు త్డ్రా చేసుకోవాలి	đab·bu vi·ta·đraa chay·su·kōh·vaa·li

What's the ...?		
charge for that	దానికి ఎంత చార్జీ?	daa·ni·ki en·ta chaar·jee
exchange rate	ఎక్స్చేంజి రేటు ఎంత?	eks·chayn·ji ray·ţu en·ta

Where's the local internet café?
ఇంటర్నెట్ కేఫ్ ఎక్కడ ఉంది? — in·ţar·neţ·ţu kayp' ek·ka·đa un·di

How much is it per hour?
గంటకి ఎంత? — gan·ţa·ki en·ta

I'd like to …

get internet access	ఇంటర్నెట్ కావాలి.	in·ţar·neţ·ţu kaa·vaa·li
use a printer/scanner	నేను ప్రింటరు/స్కానరు వాడుకోవాలి.	nay·nu prin·ţa·ru/skaa·naa·ru vaa·đu·kōh·vaa·li

I'd like a …	… కావాలి.	… kaa·vaa·li
mobile/cell phone for hire	నాకు ఒక సెల్ ఫోను అద్దెకు	naa·ku oh·ka sel p'ōh·nu ad·de·ku
SIM card for your network	మీ నెట్‌వర్కుకి సిమ్ కార్డు	mee neţ·var·ku·ki sim kaar·đu

What are the rates?
రేట్లు ఎంత? — rayţ·lu en·ta

What's your phone number?
మీ ఫోన్ నంబరు ఏంటి? — mee p'ōhn nam·ba·ru ayn·ţi

The number is …
నంబరు … — nam·ba·ru …

I'd like to buy a phonecard.
నేను ఫోన్ కార్డు కొనుక్కుంటాను. — nay·nu p'ōhn kaar·đu koh·nuk·kun·ţa·nu

I want to …	నేను … చేయాలి.	nay·nu … chay·yaa·li
call (Canada)	(కెనడాకు) ఫోన్	(ke·na·đaa·ku) p'ōhn
call collect	కలెక్టు కాలు	ka·lek·ţu kaa·lu

I want to send a fax/parcel.
నేను ఫాక్సు/పార్సెల్ పంపాలి. — nay·nu p'aak·su/paar·sel pam·paa·li

I want to buy a stamp/an envelope.
నేను స్టాంపు/కవరు కొనుక్కోవాలి. — nay·nu sţaam·pu/ka·va·ru koh·nuk·kōh·vaa·li

Please send it to (Australia).
(ఆస్ట్రేలియాకు) పంపించండి. — (aas·ţray·li·yaa·ku) pam·pin·chan·đi

sightseeing

What time does it open/close?
ఎన్ని గంటలకి తెరుస్తారు/మూస్తారు? — en·ni gan·ţa·la·ki te·ru·staa·ru/moos·taa·ru

What's the admission charge?
ప్రవేశ రుసుము ఎంత? — pra·vay·şa ru·su·mu en·ta

Is there a discount for students/children?
విద్యార్థి/పిల్లలకి డిస్కౌంటు ఉందా? — vid·yaar·d'i/pil·la·la·ki đis·kown·ţu un·daa

I'd like to hire a guide.

నాకు ఒక గైడు కావాలి. — naa·ku oh·ka gai·đu kaa·vaa·li

I'd like a catalogue/map.

నాకు క్యాటలాగు/మ్యాపు కావాలి. — naa·ku kyaa·ţa·laa·gu/myaa·pu kaa·vaa·li

I'd like to see ...

... చూపిస్తారా. — ... choo·pis·taa·raa

What's that?

అది ఏంటి? — a·di ayn·ti

Can I take a photo?

నేను ఫోటో తీసుకోవచ్చా? — nay·nu p'ōh·ţōh tee·su·kōh·vach·chaa

I'd like to go somewhere off the beaten track.

నాకు ఎక్కువగా ఎవరూ వెళ్ళని చోటకి వెళ్ళాలని ఉంది. — naa·ku ek·ku·va·gaa e·va·roo veļ·ļa·ni chōh·ţa·ki veļ·ļaa·la·ni un·di

When's the next tour?

తర్వాతి టూరు ఎప్పుడు? — tar·vaa·ti ţoo·ru ep·pu·đu

How long is the tour?

టూరు ఎంత సేపు పడుతుంది? — ţoo·ru en·ta say·pu pa·đu·tun·di

Is ... included?	అది ... కలిపా?	a·di ... ka·li·paa
accommodation	రూము అద్దె	roo·mu ad·de
food	భోజనం ఖర్చు	b'ōh·ja·nam k'ar·chu
transport	ప్రయాణం ఖర్చు	pra·yaa·ņam k'ar·chu

sightseeing		
fort	కోట	kōh·ţa
mosque	మసీదు	ma·see·du
palace	భవనం	b'a·va·nam
ruins	శిథిలాలు	şi·đ'i·laa·lu
temple	గుడి	gu·đi

shopping

Where's a ...?	... ఎక్కడ ఉంది?	... ek·ka·đa un·di
camera shop	కెమేరా దుకాణం	ke·may·raa du·kaa·ņam
market	మార్కెట్టు	maar·keţ·ţu
souvenir shop	హస్తకళల దుకాణం	has·ta·ka·ļa·la du·kaa·ņam

I'm looking for …
నేను ... కోసం చూస్తున్నాను. — nay·nu … kōh·sam chooos·tun·naa·nu

Can I look at it?
నేను దానిని చూడొచ్చా? — nay·nu daa·ni·ni choo·đohch·chaa

Can I have it sent overseas?
నేను దానిని దేశాలకు పంపిచొచ్చా? — nay·nu daa·ni·ni vi·day·şaa·la·ku pam·pi·chohch·chaa

Can I have my (camera) repaired?
నా (కెమేరాని) రిపేరు చేస్తారా? — naa (ke·may·raa·ni) ri·pai·ru chay·staa·raa

It's faulty.
అది పని చేయట్లేదు. — a·di pa·ni chay·yaţ·lay·du

How much is it?
అది ఎంత? — a·di en·ta

Can you write down the price?
దాని ధర రాస్తారా? — daa·ni d'a·ra raas·taa·raa

That's too expensive.
అది చాలా ఖరీదు. — a·di chaa·laa k'a·ree·du

I'll give you (300 rupees).
నేను (మూడు వందలు) ఇస్తాను. — nay·nu (moo·đu van·da·lu) is·taa·nu

There's a mistake in the bill.
బిల్లు లో తప్పు ఉంది. — bil·lu lōh tap·pu un·di

Do you accept …?	మీరు ... తీసుకుంటారా?	mee·ru … tee·su·kun·ţaa·raa
credit cards	క్రెడిట్ కార్డు	kre·điţ kaar·đu
debit cards	డెబిట్ కార్డు	đe·biţ kaar·đu
travellers cheques	ట్రావెలర్సు చెక్కు	ţraa·ve·lar·su chek·ku

I'd like (a) …, please.	నాకు ... కావాలి.	naa·ku … kaa·vaa·li
bag	ఒక సంచి	oh·ka san·chi
my change	నాచిల్లర	chil·la·ra
receipt	రసీదు	ra·see·du
refund	డబ్బు వాపసు	đab·bu vaa·pa·su

Less.	తక్కువ.	tak·ku·va
Enough.	చాలు.	chaa·lu
More.	ఎక్కువ.	ek·ku·va

photography

Can you ...?	... చేస్తారా?	... chay·staa·raa
burn a CD from my memory card/stick	నా మెమరీ కార్డు నించి సిడి	naa me·ma·ree kaar·đu nin·chee si·đi
develop this film	ఈ ఫిల్ము డెవెలప్	ee p'il·mu đe·ve·lap

I need a film for this camera.
ఈ కెమేరాకు ఫిల్ము కావాలి. — ee ke·may·raa·ku p'il·mu kaa·vaa·li

When will it be ready?
అది ఎప్పుడు రెడీ అవుతుంది? — a·di ep·pu·đu re·đee a·vu·tun·di

making conversation

Hello./Goodbye.	నమస్కారం./వెళ్ళొస్తాను.	na·mas·kaa·ram/veļ·ļoh·staa·nu
Good night.	ఉంటాను.	un·ţaa·nu
Mr/Mrs/Miss	శ్రీ/శ్రీమతి/కుమారి	şree/şree·ma·ti/ku·maa·ri
How are you?	ఎట్లా ఉన్నారు?	eţ·laa un·naa·ru
Fine, thanks.	బాగున్నాను.	baa·gun·naa·nu
And you?	మీరు ఎట్లా ఉన్నారు?	mee·ru eţ·laa un·naa·ru
What's your name?	మీపేరేంటి?	mee pay·rayn·ţi
My name is ...	నా పేరు ...	naa pay·ru ...
I'm pleased to meet you.	మిమ్మల్ని కలిసినందుకు సంతోషంగా ఉంది.	mim·mal·ni ka·li·si·nan·du·ku san·tōh·sham·gaa un·di

This is my ...		
brother (older)	ఇతను మా అన్న.	i·ta·nu maa an·na
brother (younger)	ఇతను మా తమ్ముడు.	i·ta·nu maa tam·mu·đu
daughter	ఈమె మా అమ్మాయి.	ee·me maa am·maa·yi
father	ఈయన మా నాన్న.	ee·ya·na maa naan·na
friend	ఇతను నా స్నేహితుడు.	i·ta·nu naa snay·hi·tu·đu m
	ఈమె నా స్నేహితురాలు.	ee·me naa snay·hi·tu·raa·lu f
husband	ఇతను నా భర్త.	i·ta·nu naa b'ar·ta
mother	ఈవిడ మా అమ్మ.	ee·vi·đa maa am·ma
sister (older)	ఈమె మా అక్క.	ee·me maa ak·ka
sister (younger)	ఈమె మా చెల్లి.	ee·me maa chel·li
son	ఇతను మా అబ్బాయి.	i·ta·nu maa ab·baa·yi
wife	ఈమె నా భార్య.	ee·me naa b'ar·ya

Here's my (address).	ఇదిగో, నా (అడ్రస్సు).	**i·di·goh naa (ađ·đras·su)**
What's your (email)?	మీ (ఈ-మెయిలు) ఏంటి?	**mee (i·me·yi·lu) ayn·ţi**
Where are you from?	మీదే ఊరు?	**mee·day voo·ru**
I'm from …	మాది ...	**maa·di …**
Australia	ఆస్ట్రేలియా	**aas·ţray·li·ya**
Canada	కెనడా	**ke·na·đaa**
New Zealand	న్యూజీలాండ్	**nyoo·jee·laanđ**
the UK	బ్రిటన్	**bri·ţan**
the USA	అమెరికా	**a·me·ri·kaa**
What's your occupation?	మీరు ఏం చేస్తారు?	**mee·ru aym chays·taa·ru**
I'm a/an …	నేను ...	**nay·nu …**
businessperson	వ్యాపారిని	**vyaa·paa·ri·ni**
office worker	ఉద్యోగిని	**ud·yōh·gi·ni**
Do you like …?	మీకు ... ఇష్టమా?	**mee·ku … ish·ţa·maa**
I (don't) like …	నాకు ... ఇష్టం (లేదు).	**naa·ku … ish·ţam (lay·du)**
art	కళలు	**ka·ļa·lu**
movies	సినిమాలు	**si·ni·maa·lu**
music	సంగీతం	**san·gee·tam**
reading	చదవటం	**cha·da·va·ţam**
sport	ఆటలు	**aa·ţa·lu**

eating out

Can you recommend a …?	ఏదన్నా ... చెప్తారా?	**ay·dan·naa … chep·taa·raa**
bar	మంచి బారు	**man·chi baa·ru**
dish	మంచి వంటకం	**man·chi van·ţa·kam**
place to eat	తినటానికి మంచి చోటు	**tin·na·ţaa·ni·ki man·chi chōh·ţu**
I'd like (a/the) …, please.	... కావాలి.	**… kaa·vaa·li**
bill	బిల్లు	**bil·lu**
drink list	డ్రింకు లిస్టు	**đrin·ku lis·ţu**
local speciality	ఇక్కడి స్పెషల్	**ik·ka·đi spe·shal**
menu	మెను	**me·nu**
nonsmoking/ smoking section	పొగ తాగని/ తాగే స్థలం	**pōh·ga taa·ga·ni/ taa·gay st'a·lam**
that dish	ఆ ఐటం	**aa ai·ţam**

I'd like a table for (four), please.
(నలుగురికి) టేబుల్ బుక్ చేసుకోవాలి. — (na·lu·gu·ri·ki) ţay·bu·lu buk chay·su·kōh·vaa·li

breakfast	టిఫిను	ţi·p'i·nu
lunch	మీల్సు	meel·su
dinner	భోజనం	b'ōh·ja·nam

(cup of) coffee ...	(కప్పు) కాఫీ ...	(kap·pu) kaa·p'ee ...
(cup of) tea ...	(కప్పు) టీ ...	(kap·pu) ţee ...
with milk	పాలతో	paa·la·tōh
without sugar	పంచదార లేని	pan·cha·daa·ra lay·ni

(orange) juice	(ఆరెంజి) రసం	(aa·ren·ji) ra·sam
lassi	మజ్జిగ	maj·ji·ga
soft drink	కూల్ డ్రింకు	kool đrin·ku

I'll have boiled water.
నేను కాచిన నీళ్ళు తీసుకుంటాను. — nay·nu kaa·chi·na neeḷ·ḷu tee·su·kun·ţaa·nu

I'll have mineral water.
నేను బిస్లరి తీసుకుంటాను. — nay·nu bis·la·ri tee·su·kun·ţaa·nu

I'll buy you a ...
నేను మీకు ... కొంటాను. — nay·nu mee·ku ... kohn·ţaa·nu

What would you like?
మీకు ఏం కావాలి? — mee·ku aym kaa·vaa·li

a bottle of beer	బీరు సీసా	bee·ru see·saa
a glass of beer	గ్లాసు బీరు	glaa·su bee·ru

a bottle of ... wine	... వైను సీసా	... vai·nu see·saa
a glass of ... wine	గ్లాసు ... వైను	glaa·su ... vai·nu
red	ఎర్ర	er·ra
white	తెల్ల	tel·la

special diets & allergies

Do you have ... food?	... ఉందా?	... un·daa
halal	హలాల్ ఆహారం	ha·laal aa·haa·ram
kosher	కోషరు ఆహారం	kōh·sha·ru aa·haa·ram
vegetarian	శాఖాహారం	şaa·ka·haa·ram

I'm allergic to …	నాకు ... పడవు.	naa·ku … pa·đa·vu
almonds	బాదాములు	baa·daa·mu·lu
cashews	జీడి పప్పులు	jee·đi pap·pu·lu
dairy products	పాలు	paa·lu
eggs	గుడ్లు	guđ·lu
seafood	చేపలు	chay·pa·lu

I'm allergic to meat.
నాకు మాంసం పడదు. naa·ku maam·sam pa·đa·du

emergencies

Help!	సహాయం కావాలి!	sa·haa·yam kaa·vaa·li
Stop! (doing something)	ఆపండి!	aa·pan·đi
Stop! (moving)	ఆగండి!	aa·gan·đi
Go away!	వెళ్ళిపో!	veḷ·ḷi·pōh
Thief!	దొంగ!	dohn·ga
Fire!	మంటలు!	man·ţa·lu
Watch out!	జాగ్రత్త!	jaag·rat·ta

Call …!	... పిలవండి!	… pi·la·van·đi
an ambulance	అంబులెన్సుని	aam·bu·len·su·ni
a doctor	డాక్టర్ని	đaak·ţar·ni
the police	పోలీసుల్ని	pōh·lee·sul·ni

Could you help me, please?
దయచేసి నాకు సాయం చేస్తారా? da·ya·chay·see naa·ku saa·yam chay·staa·raa

I have to use the phone.
నేను ఫోను వాడుకోవాలి. nay·nu p'ōh·nu vaa·đu·kōh·vaa·li

I'm lost.
నేను దారి తప్పి పోయాను. nay·nu daa·ri tap·pi pōh·yaa·nu

Where are the toilets?
బాత్రూములు ఎక్కడ ఉన్నాయి? baat·room·lu ek·ka·đa un·naa·yi

Where's the police station?
పోలీసు స్టేషను ఎక్కడ ఉంది? pōh·lee·su sţay·sha·nu ek·ka·đa un·di

I have insurance.
నాకు ఇన్స్యూరెన్సు ఉంది. naa·ku in·shu·ren·su un·di

I want to contact my embassy.
నా ఎంబసీకి ఫోన్ చేయాలి. naa em·ba·see·ki p'ōh·nu chay·yaa·li

I've been …	నన్ను ...	nan·nu …
raped	మాన భంగం చేసారు	maa·na b'an·gam chay·saa·ru
robbed	దోచుకున్నారు	dōh·chu·kun·naa·ru

I've lost my …	నా ... పోయింది.	naa … pōh·yin·di
bag	సంచీ	san·chi
money	డబ్బు	đab·bu
passport	పాస్‌పోర్టు	paas·pōhr·ţu

health

Where's the nearest …?	దగ్గరలో ... ఎక్కడ ఉన్నాడు?	dag·ga·ra·lōh … ek·ka·đa un·naa·đu
dentist	దంత వైద్యుడు	dan·ta vaid·yu·đu
doctor	డాక్టరు	đaak·ţa·ru
pharmacist	మందుల దుకాణం	man·du·la du·kaa·ṇam

Where's the nearest hospital?
దగ్గరలో ఆసుపత్రి ఎక్కడ ఉంది? — dag·ga·ra·lōh aa·su·pat·ri ek·ka·đa un·di

I need a doctor (who speaks English).
నాకు (ఇంగ్లీషు మాట్లాడే) డాక్టరు కావాలి. — naa·ku (ing·lee·shu maaţ·laa·đay) đaak·ţa·ru kaa·vaa·li

Could I see a female doctor?
నేను లేడీ డాక్టరును చూడాలి. — nay·nu lay·đee đaak·ţa·ru·ni choo·đaa·li

I've run out of my medication.
నా మందు అయిపోయింది. — naa man·du a·yi·pōh·yin·di

It hurts here.
ఇక్కడ నెప్పిగా ఉంది. — ik·ka·đa nep·pi·gaa un·di

I have diarrhoea.
నాకు విరోచనాలు అవుతున్నాయి. — naa·ku vi·rōh·cha·naa·lu a·vu·tun·naa·yi

I'm allergic to aspirin/codeine.
నాకు యాస్పిరిన్/కోడీను పడదు. — naa·ku yaas·pi·rin/kōh·đee·nu pa·đa·du

I have (a) …	నాకు ... ఉంది.	naa·ku … un·di
asthma	ఆస్తమా	aas·ta·maa
constipation	విరోచన బద్ధకంగా	vi·rōh·cha·na bad·d'a·kam·gaa
fever	జ్వరంగా	jva·ram·gaa
heart condition	గుండె నొప్పిగా	gun·đe nep·pi·gaa
nausea	కారంగా	vi·kaa·ram·gaa

health – TELUGU

I'm allergic to ...	నాకు ... పడవు.	**naa·ku ... pa·đa·vu**
antibiotics	యాంటిబయాటిక్సు	**yaan·ţi·ba·yaa·ţik·su**
anti-inflammatories	యాంటి-ఇంఫ్లేమటరీలు	**yan·ţee·in·p'lay·ma·ta·ri·lu**
bees	కీటకాలు	**kee·ţa·kaa·lu**

responsible travel

I'd like to learn some Telugu.
నేను కొంచెం తెలుగు నేర్చుకుంటాను.
nay·nu kohn·chem te·lu·gu nayr·chu·kun·ţaa·nu

What's this called in Telugu?
దీనిని తెలుగులో ఏమంటారు?
dee·ni·ni te·lu·gu·lōh aym·an·ţaa·ru

Would you like me to teach you some English?
మీకు ఇంగ్లీషు నేర్పమంటారు?
mee·ku ing·lee·shu nayr·pa·man·ţaa·ru

I didn't mean to do/say anything wrong.
తప్పుగా అనుకోవద్దు.
tap·pu·gaa a·nu·kōh·vad·du

Is this a local or national custom?
ఇది ఇక్కడి ఆచారమా, లేక, ఈ దేశ ఆచారమా?
i·di ik·ka·đi aa·chaa·ra·maa ley·ka ee day·şa aa·chaa·ra·maa

I'd like to stay at a locally run hotel.
ఇక్కడి వాళ్ళ హోటల్లో ఉంటాను.
ik·ka·đi vaaļ·ļa hōh·ţal·lōh un·ţaa·nu

Where can I buy locally produced goods/souvenirs?
ఇక్కడ తయారు చేసిన వస్తువులు ఎక్కడ అమ్ముతారు?
ik·ka·đa ta·yaa·ru chay·si·na vas·tu·vu·lu ek·ka·đa am·mu·taa·ru

What's this made from?
ఇది దేనితో చేసింది?
i·di day·ni·tōh chay·sin·di

Does your company have responsible tourism policies?
మీ కంపెనీలో సరైన టూరిజం పద్ధతులు ఉన్నాయా?
mee kam·pa·nee·lōh sa·rai·na ţoo·ri·jam pad·d'a·tu·lu un·naa·yaa

I'd like to do some volunteer work (for your organisation).
(మీ సంస్థ కోసం) కొంత స్వచ్ఛంద సేవ చేస్తాను.
(mee sam·st'a kōh·sam) kohn·ta svach·ch'an·da say·va chay·staa·nu

I'm an (English teacher). Can I volunteer my skills?
నేను (ఇంగ్లీషు టీచర్ని). నా విద్యని స్వచ్ఛందంగా ఇవ్వొచ్చా?
nay·nu (ing·lee·shu ţee·char·ni) naa vid·ya·ni svach·ch'an·dam·gaa iv·vohch·chaa

english–telugu dictionary

Words in this dictionary are marked as n (noun), a (adjective), v (verb), m (masculine), f (feminine), sg (singular), pl (plural), inf (informal) and pol (polite) where necessary.

A

accident ప్రమాదం pra·maa·dam
accommodation ఉండటానికి గది un·đa·ţaa·ni·ki ga·di
adaptor ఎడాప్టరు e·đaap·ţa·ru
address n అడ్రస్సు ađ·đras·su
after తర్వాత tar·vaa·ta
air-conditioned ఎయిరు కండిషన్డు e·yi·ru kan·đi·shan·đu
airplane విమానం vi·maa·nam
airport విమానాశ్రయం vi·maa·naaş·ra·yam
alcohol సారా saa·raa
all (people/things) అందరు/అన్నీ an·da·ru/an·nee
allergy ఎలర్జీ e·lar·jee
ambulance అంబులెన్సు aam·bu·len·su
and మరియు ma·ri·yu
ankle మడమ ma·đa·ma
antibiotics యాంటిబయాటిక్సు yaan·ţi·ba·yaa·ţik·su
arm చెయ్యి chey·yi
ATM ఎటిఎం e·ţi·em

B

baby బాబు/పాప baa·bu/paa·pa m/f
back (of body) వీపు vee·pu
backpack వీపు సంచి vee·pu san·chi
bad చెడు che·đu
bag సంచి san·chi
baggage claim బ్యాగేజి క్లైము byaa·gay·jee klai·mu
bank బ్యాంకు byaan·ku
bar బారు baa·ru
bathroom బాత్రూము baat·roo·mu
battery బ్యాటరీ byaaţ·ţa·ree
beautiful అందమైన an·da·mai·na
bed (cot) మంచం man·cham
bed (made up) పక్క pak·ka
before ముందు mun·du
behind వెనక ve·na·ka
bicycle సైకిలు sai·ki·lu
big పెద్ద ped·da
bill బిల్లు bil·lu
blanket దుప్పటి dup·pa·ţi
blood group రక్తం గ్రూపు rak·tam groo·pu
boat పడవ pa·đa·va
book (make a reservation) v బుక్ చేసుకోవటం buk chay·su·kōh·vaa·ţam
bottle సీసా see·saa
boy అబ్బాయి ab·baa·yi
brakes (car) బ్రేకులు bray·ku·lu
breakfast టిఫిను ţi·p'i·nu
broken (faulty) పాడైంది paa·đain·di
bus బస్సు bas·su
business వ్యాపారం vyaa·paa·ram
buy v కొనటం kōh·na·ţam

C

camera కెమేరా ke·may·raa
cancel క్యాన్సిలు kyaan·si·lu
car కారు kaa·ru
cash n డబ్బు đab·bu
cash (a cheque) v (చెక్కు) మార్చుకోవటం (chek·ku) maar·chu·kōh·va·ţam
cell phone సెల్‌ఫోను sel p'ōh·nu
centre n సెంటరు sen·ţa·ru
change (money) v (డబ్బు) మార్చుకోవటం (đab·bu) maar·chu·kōh·va·ţam
cheap చౌక chow·ka
check (bill) బిల్లు bil·lu
check-in n చెక్ అవటం chek a·va·ţam
chest (body) ఛాతీ ch'aa·tee
child పిల్లాడు/పిల్ల pil·laa·đu/pil·la m/f
cigarette సిగరెట్టు si·gi·reţ·ţu
city బస్తీ bas·tee
clean a శుభ్రం şub'·ram
closed మూసేసారు moo·say·saa·ru
cold (general) a చల్ల chal·la
cold (weather) a చలి cha·li
collect call కలెక్టు కాలు ka·lek·ţu kaa·lu
come రావటం raa·va·ţam
computer కంప్యూటరు kam·pyu·ţa·ru
condom నిరోధ్ ni·rōhd'
contact lenses కాంటాక్టు లెన్సులు kaan·ţayk·ţu len·su·lu
cook v వండటం van·đa·ţam
cost n ధర d'a·ra
credit card క్రెడిట్ కార్డు kre·điţ kaar·đu
currency exchange ఫారిన్ ఎక్స్చేంజి p'aa·rin eks·chayn·ji
customs (immigration) కస్టమ్స్ kas·ţams

D

dangerous ప్రమాదకరం pra·maa·da·ka·ram
date (time) తేదీ tay·dee

day రోజు rōh·ju
delay n ఆలస్యం aa·las·yam
dentist దంత వైద్యుడు dan·ta vaid·yu·đu
depart వెళ్ళటం veḷ·ḷa·ţam
diaper నాపీలు naa·pee·lu
dinner భోజనం b'ōh·ja·nam
direct a నేరుగా nay·ru·gaa
dirty అపరిశుభ్రం a·pa·ri·şub'·ram
disabled చెడి పోయింది che·đi pōh·yin·di
discount n డిస్కౌంటు đis·kown·ţu
doctor డాక్టరు đaak·ţa·ru
double bed డబల్ బెడ్డు đa·bal beđ·đu
double room డబల్ రూము đa·bal roo·mu
drink n పానీయం paa·nee·yam
drive v నడపటం na·đa·pa·ţam
drug (illicit) మాదక ద్రవ్యం maa·da·ka drav·yam

E

ear చె che·vi
east తూర్పు toor·pu
eat తినటం ti·na·ţam
electricity కరంటు ka·ran·ţu
elevator లిఫ్టు lip'·ţu
email ఈమెయిలు i·me·yi·lu
embassy ఎంబసీ em·ba·see
emergency ఎమర్జెన్సీ e·mar·jen·see
English (language) ఇంగ్లీషు ing·lee·shu
entrance ప్రవేశం pra·vay·şam
evening సాయంత్రం saa·yan·tram
exit n బయటకు వెళ్ళే దారి ba·ya·ţa·ku veḷ·ḷay daa·ri
expensive ఖరీదయిన k'a·ree·da·yi·na
eye కన్ను kan·nu

F

far దూరం doo·ram
fast వేగంగా vay·gam·gaa
father నాన్న naan·na
film (camera) కెమేరా ఫిల్ము ke·may·raa p'il·mu
finger వేలు vay·lu
first-aid kit ప్రథమ చికిత్స పెట్టె
pra·d'a·ma chi·kit·sa peţ·ţe
first class ఫస్టు క్లాసు p'asţ klaa·su
fish n చేపలు chay·pa·lu
food ఆహారం aa·haa·ram
foot పాదం paa·dam
free (of charge) ఫ్రీ p'ree
friend స్నేహితుడు/స్నేహితురాలు
snay·hi·tu·đu/snay·hi·tu·raa·lu m/f
fruit పండు pan·đu
full నిండా nin·đaa

G

gift బహుమతి ba·hu·ma·ti
girl అమ్మాయి am·maa·yi
glass (drinking) గ్లాసు glaa·su
glasses కళ్ళజోడు kaḷ·ḷa jōh·đu
go వెళ్ళటం veḷ·ḷa·ţam
good మంచి man·chi
guide n గైడు gai·đu

H

half n సగం sa·gam
hand చెయ్యి chey·yo
happy సంతోషం san·tōh·sham
have ఉంది un·di
he అతను a·ta·nu
head n తల ta·la
heart గుండె un·đe
heavy బరువు ba·ru·vu
help v సాయం చేయటం saa·yam chay·ya·ţam
here ఇక్కడ ik·ka·da
high ఎత్తైన et·tai·na
highway హైవే hai·vay
hike (climb) v ఎక్కటం ek·ka·ţam
hike (walk) v నడవటం na·đa·pa·ţam
holiday సెలవ రోజు se·la·va rōh·ju
homosexual n&a స్వలింగ సంపర్కం
sva·lin·ga sam·par·ki
hospital ఆసుపత్రి aa·su·pat·ri
hot వేడి vay·đi
hotel హోటలు hōh·ţa·lu
hungry ఆకలి aa·ka·li
husband భర్త b'ar·ta

I

I నేను nay·nu
identification (card) గుర్తింపు పత్రం
gur·tim·pu pat·ram
ill జబ్బుగా jab·bu·gaa
important ముఖ్యం muk'·yam
injury గాయం gaa·yam
insurance ఇన్స్యూరెన్సు in·shu·ren·su
interpreter తర్జుమా చేసే వ్యక్తి
tar·ju·maa chay·say vyak·ti

J

jewellery నగలు na·ga·lu
job ఉద్యోగం ud·yōh·gam

K

key తాళం చె taa·ḷam che·vi
kilogram కిలో ki·lōh
kitchen వంట గది van·ţa ga·di
knife కత్తి kat·ti

L

laundry (place) లాండ్రీ laan·đree
lawyer లాయరు laa·ya·ru
left (direction) ఎడమ పక్క e·đa·ma pak·ka
leg (body) కాలు kaa·lu
lesbian n లెస్బియను les·bi·ya·nu
less తక్కువ tak·ku·va
letter (mail) ఉత్తరం ut·ta·ram
light n వెలుతురు ve·lu·tu·ru
like v ఇష్టం ish·ţam
lock n తాళం taa·ḷam
long పొడుగు pōh·đu·gu
lost పోయింది pōh·yin·di
love v ప్రేమించటం pray·min·cha·ţam
luggage సామాను saa·maa·nu
lunch మీల్సు meel·su

M

mail n పోస్టు pōhs·ţu
man మనిషి ma·ni·shi
map మ్యాపు myaa·pu
market మార్కెట్టు maar·keţ·ţu
matches అగ్గిపెట్టె ag·gi·peţ·ţe
meat మాంసం maam·sam
medicine మందు man·du
message రాయబారం raa·ya·baa·ram
milk పాలు paa·lu
minute నిముషం ni·mu·sham
mobile phone సెల్‌ఫోను sel p'ōh·nu
money డబ్బు đab·bu
month నెల ne·la
morning పొద్దున pōhd·du·na
mother అమ్మ am·ma
motorcycle మోటారు సైకిలు mōh·ţaa·ru sai·ki·lu
mouth నోరు nōh·ru

N

name n పేరు pay·ru
near దగ్గిర dag·gi·ra
neck మెడ me·đa
new కొత్త kot·ta
newspaper వార్తాపత్రిక vaar·taa·pat·ri·ka
night రాత్రి raat·ri
no కాదు kaa·du
noisy గోలగా gōh·la·gaa
nonsmoking పొగ తాగని pōh·ga taa·ga·ni
north ఉత్తరం ut·ta·ram
nose ముక్కు muk·ku
now ఇప్పుడు ip·pu·đu
number నంబరు nam·ba·ru

O

old (people/things) ముసలి/పాత mu·sa·li/paa·ta
one-way ticket వెళ్ళేందుకు టిక్కెట్టు
 veḷ·ḷayn·du·ku ţik·keţ·ţu
open a తీసి ఉంది tee·si un·di
outside బైట bai·ţa

P

passport పాస్‌పోర్టు paas·pōhr·ţu
pay v డబ్బు కట్టటం đab·bu kaţ·ţa·ţam
pharmacy మందుల దుకాణం man·du·la du·kaa·ṇam
phonecard ఫోన్ కార్డు p'ōhn kaar·đu
photo ఫోటో p'ōh·ţōh
police పోలీసు pōh·lee·su
postcard పోస్ట్ కార్డు kaar·đu
post office పోస్టాఫీసు pōhs·ţaa·p'ee·su
pregnant గర్భిణి gar·b'i·ṇi
price n ధర d'a·ra

Q

quiet a నిశ్శబ్దం niş·şab·dam

R

rain n వాన vaa·na
razor రేజరు ray·ja·ru
receipt n రసీదు ra·see·du
refund n డబ్బు వాపసు đab·bu vaa·pa·su
registered mail రిజిష్టరు పోస్టు ri·jis·ţa·ru pōhs·ţu
rent v అద్దెకివ్వటం ad·de·kiv·va·ţam
repair v బాగు చేయటం baa·gu chay·ya·ţam
reservation రిజర్వేషను ri·jar·vay·sha·nu
restaurant రెస్టారెంటు res·ţōh·raan·ţu
return (come back) v తిరిగి రావటం ti·ri·gi raa·va·ţam
return (give back) v తిరిగి ఇవ్వటం ti·ri·gi iv·va·ţam
return ticket రాను-పోను టిక్కెట్టు
 raa·nu·pōh·nu ţik·keţ·ţu
right (direction) కుడి పక్క ku·đi pak·ka
road రోడ్డు rōhđ·đu
room n గది ga·di

S

safe a భద్రం b'ad·ram
seat n సీటు see·ţu
send పంపించటం pam·pin·cha·ţam
sex సెక్సు sek·su
share (a dorm) v పంచుకోవటం panch·kōh·va·ţam
she ఆమె aa·me
sheet (bed) దుప్పటి dup·pa·ţi
shirt చొక్కా chōhk·ka
shoes బూట్లు booţ·lu
shop n దుకాణం du·kaa·ṇam
short పొట్టి pōhţ·ţi
shower n స్నానం snaa·nam
single room సింగిల్ రూము sin·gil roo·mu
skin n చర్మం char·mam
skirt n పరికిణి pa·ri·ki·ṇi
sleep v నిద్ర పోవటం nid·ra pōh·va·ţam
slowly మెల్లిగా mel·li·gaa
small చిన్న chin·na
soap సోపు sōh·pu
some కొంత kōhn·ta
soon త్వరలో tva·ra·lōh
south దక్షిణం dak·shi·ṇam
souvenir shop హస్తకళల దుకాణం has·ta·ka·ḷa·la du·kaa·ṇam
stamp స్టాంపు sţaam·pu
station (train) రైలు స్టేషను rai·lu sţay·sha·nu
stomach కడుపు ka·đu·pu
stop v ఆగటం aa·ga·ţam
stop (bus) n బస్సు స్టాపు bas·su sţaa·pu
street వీధి vee·d'i
student విద్యార్ధి vid·yaar·d'i
sun సూర్యుడు soor·yu·đu
swim v ఈదటం ee·da·ţam

T

tampons టేంపన్లు ţaym·pan·lu
teeth పళ్ళు paḷ·ḷu
telephone n ఫోను p'ōh·nu
temperature (weather) ఉష్ణోగ్రత ush·nōhg·ra·ta
that (one) అది a·di
they వాళ్ళు vaaḷ·ḷu
thirsty దాహం daa·ham
this (one) ఇది i·di
throat గొంతు gōhn·tu
ticket టిక్కెట్టు ţik·keţ·ţu
time టైము ţai·mu
tired అలిసి పోయి a·li·si pōh·yi
tissues టిష్యూలు ţish·yu·lu
today ఇవాళ i·vaa·ḷa
toilet బాత్రూము baat·roo·mu
tomorrow రేపు ray·pu
tonight ఈ రాత్రి ee raat·ri
toothbrush టూత్ బ్రష్ toot bra·shu
toothpaste టూత్ పేస్టు toot pays·ţu
torch (flashlight) టార్చి లైటు ţaar·chi·lai·ţu
tour n టూరు ţoo·ru
tourist office టూరిస్టు ఆఫీసు ţoo·ris·ţu aa·p'ee·su
towel తువ్వాలు tu·vaa·lu
train n రైలు rai·lu
translate v అనువదించటం a·nu·va·din·cha·ţam
trousers ప్యాంటు pyaan·ţu
twin beds జంట మంచాలు jan·ţa man·chaa·lu

U

underwear డ్రాయరు đraa·ya·ru
urgent అత్యవసరం at·ya·va·sa·ram

V

vacant ఖాళీ k'aa·lee
vegetable n కూరగాయ koo·ra·gaa·ya
vegetarian a శాఖాహారి şaa·kaa·haa·ri

W

walk v నడవటం na·đa·va·ţam
wallet పర్సు par·su
wash (something) కడగటం ka·đa·ga·ţam
watch n చూడటం choo·đa·ţam
water n నీళ్ళు neeḷ·ḷu
we (excluding 'you') మేం maym
we (including 'you') మనం ma·nam
weekend శని-ఆది వారాలు şa·ni·aa·di vaa·raa·lu
west పడమర pa·đa·ma·ra
wheelchair కుర్చీ బండి kur·chee·ban·đi
when ఎప్పుడు ep·pu·đu
where ఎక్కడ ek·ka·đa
who ఎవరు e·va·ru
why ఎందుకు en·du·ku
wife భార్య b'ar·ya
window కిటికీ ki·ţi·ki
with తో tōh
without లేకుండా lay·kun·đaa
woman స్త్రీ stree
write v రాయటం raa·ya·ţam

Y

yes అవును a·vu·nu
yesterday నిన్న ni·na
you sg inf నువ్వు nuv·vu
you sg pol&pl మీరు mee·ru

Urdu

alphabet

alphabet					
ا *a*·lif	ب be	پ pe	ت te	ٹ ţe	ث se
ج jim	چ che	ح *ba*·ri he	خ khe	د dal	ڈ đal
ذ zal	ر re	ڑ ṛe	ز ze	ژ zhe	س sin
ش shin	ص svad	ض zad	ط *to*·e	ظ *zo*·e	ع ain
غ ghain	ف fe	ق qaf	ک kaf	گ gaf	ل lam
م mim	ن nun	و *va*·o	ہ *cho*·ti he	ی ye	

numerals									
0	1	2	3	4	5	6	7	8	9
٠	١	٢	٣	٤	٥	٦	٧	٨	٩

URDU

اردو

introduction

Urdu (اردو *ur̤·du*) has around 50 million speakers in India and is one of the official languages of the Indian states of Bihar and Jammu and Kashmir. Urdu and Hindi are generally considered to be one spoken language with two different scripts – as such, they constitute the second most spoken language in the world. Like Hindi, Urdu is an Indo-Aryan language which developed from Classical Sanskrit. When Muslim Turks invaded Punjab in 1027 and took control of Delhi in 1193, they paved the way for the Islamic Mughal Empire, which ruled northern India from the 16th century until the mid-19th century. During this time the Muslim speakers of the language known as 'Hindvi' began to write in Arabic script, creating Urdu. Despite its Sanskrit ancestry, much of Urdu's academic and philosophical vocabulary is of Arabic or Persian origin. In the years leading up to the partition of India and Pakistan in 1947, the question of language was strongly linked to religious and cultural pride. Urdu, seen as a Muslim-only language, was chosen as the national language of Pakistan. Issues of language, religion and culture continue to cause tension within both countries.

urdu

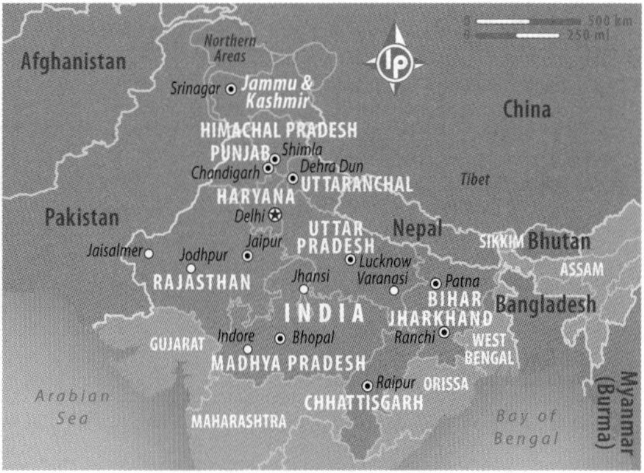

pronunciation

Vowels		Consonants	
Symbol	**English sound**	**Symbol**	**English sound**
a	**run**	b	**bed**
aa	**father**	ch	**cheat**
ai	**aisle**	d	**dog**
ay	**say**	đ	retroflex d
e	**bet**	f	**fun**
ee	**see**	g	**go**
i	**hit**	h	**hat**
o	**pot**	j	**jar**
oh	**note**	k	**kit**
oo	**zoo**	l	**lot**
ow	**how**	m	**man**
u	**put**	n	**not**
		ng	**ring**
		p	**pet**
		r	**run**
		ŗ	retroflex r
		s	**sun**
		sh	**shot**
		t	**top**
		ţ	retroflex t
		v	**very**
		w	**win**
		y	**yes**
		z	**zero**

In this chapter, the Urdu pronunciation is given in green after each phrase.

Aspirated consonants (pronounced with a puff of air after the sound) are represented with an apostrophe after the letter – b', ch', d', đ', g', j', k', p', t' and ţ'. Retroflex consonants (pronounced with the tongue bent backwards) are included in this table.

Each syllable is separated by a dot, and the syllable stressed in each word is italicised. For example:

مہربانی me·har·*baa*·nee

essentials

Yes./No.	جی ہاں۔/جی نہیں۔	jee haang/jee na·*heeng*
Please.	مہربانی کرکے۔	me·har·*baa*·nee kar ke
Thank you.	شکریہ۔	*shuk*·ri·yah
Excuse me. (to get past)	راستہ دے دیجیے۔	*raas*·ţaa de *dee*·ji·ye
Excuse me. (to get attention)	سنئے۔	su·ni·*ye*
Sorry.	معاف کیجئے۔	maaf *kee*·ji·ye

language difficulties

Do you speak English?
کیا آپ کو انگریزی آتی ہے؟ — kyaa aap ko an·*gre*·zee *aa*·ţee hay

Do you understand?
کیا آپ سمجھے؟ — kyaa aap *sam*·j'e

I understand.
میں سمجھ گیا/گئی۔ — mayng sa·*maj'* ga·*yaa*/ga·*yee* **m/f**

I don't understand.
میں نہیں سمجھا/سمجھی۔ — mayng na·*heeng sam*·j'aa/*sam*·j'ee **m/f**

Could you please ...?	مہربانی کرکے ...	me·har·*baa*·nee *kar*·ke ...
repeat that	پھر سے کہئے	p'ir se ka·*hi*·ye
speak more slowly	دھرے بولئے	*d'ee*·re bo·*li*·ye

numbers

0	صفر	*si*·far	20	بیس	bees
1	ایک	ek	30	تیس	ţees
2	دو	do	40	چالیس	*chaa*·lees
3	تین	ţeen	50	پچاس	pa·*chaas*
4	چار	chaar	60	ساٹھ	saat
5	پانچ	paanch	70	ستّر	*saţ*·ţar
6	چھ	ch'ay	80	اسّی	*as*·see
7	سات	saaţ	90	نبّے	*nab*·be
8	آٹھ	aat	100	سو	*so*·oh
9	نو	*no*·oh	1,000	ایک ہزار	ek ha·*zaar*
10	دس	das	100,000	ایک لاکھ	ek laak'

time & dates

What time is it?	ٹائم کیا ہے؟	*taa*·im kyaa hay
It's (ten) o'clock.	(دس) بجے ہیں۔	(das) ba·*je* hayng
Quarter past (ten).	سوا (رس)۔	sa·*vaa* (das)
Half past (ten).	ساڑھے (دس)۔	*saa*·ŗe (das)
Quarter to (ten).	پونے (دس)۔	*poh*·ne (das)
At what time ...?	کتنے بجے ...؟	*kiţ*·ne ba·*je* ...
At 7.57pm.	آٹھ بجنے میں تین منٹ۔	aat ba·*je* meng ţeen mi·*nat*
It's (18 October).	آج (اٹھارہ اکتوبر) ہے۔	aaj (a·*t'aa*·rah ak·*ţoo*·bar) hay

yesterday	کل	kal
today	آج	aaj
tomorrow	کل	kal

Monday	پیر	peer
Tuesday	منگل	*man*·gal
Wednesday	بدھ	bud'
Thursday	جمعرات	ju·*me*·raaţ
Friday	جمع	ju·*maa*
Saturday	ہفتہ	*haf*·ţaa
Sunday	اتوار	*iţ*·vaar

border crossing

I'm in transit.

میی راستے میں ہوں۔	mayng *raas*·ţe meng hoong

I'm on business.

میی کاروبار کرنے آیا/آئ ہوں۔	mayng *kaa*·ro·baar *kar*·ne *aa*·yaa/*aa*·yee hoong **m/f**

I'm on holiday.

میی چھٹی منانے آیا/آئ ہوں۔	mayng *ch'ut*·tee ma·*naa*·ne *aa*·yaa/*aa*·yee hoong **m/f**

I'm here for (three) ...	میں (تین) ... کے لئے آیا/آئ ہوں۔	mayng (ţeen) ... ke li·*ye* *aa*·yaa/*aa*·yee hoong **m/f**
days	دن	din
weeks	ہفتے	*haf*·ţe
months	مہینے	ma·*hee*·ne

I'm going to (Karachi).

میی (کراچی) جا رہا/رہی ہوں۔ — mayng (ka·*raa*·chee) jaa ra·*haa*/ra·*hee* hoong **m/f**

I'm staying at the (Awadh Hotel).

میں (اودھ ہوٹل) میں ٹھرا/ٹھری ہوں۔ — mayng (*a*·wad' ho·*tel*) meng *t'eh*·raa/*t'eh*·ree hoong **m/f**

I have nothing to declare.

کچھ ڈکلیر کرنے کے لئے نہیں ہے۔ — kuch' đik·*ler kar*·ne ke li·*ye* na·*heeng* hay

I have this to declare.

مجھے یہ ڈکلیر کرنا/کرنی ہئے۔ — *mu*·j'e yeh đik·*ler kar*·naa/*kar*·nee haing **m/f**

That's (not) mine.

وہ میرا (نہیں) ہے۔ — voh *me*·raa (na·*heeng*) hay

tickets & luggage

Where do I buy a ticket?

ٹکٹ کہاں ملتا ہے؟ — ti·*kat* ka·*haang mil*·ţaa hay

Do I need to book well in advance?

جانے سے بہت پہلے بکنگ ہونی چاہئے؟ — *jaa*·ne se ba·*huţ peh*·le bu·*king ho*·nee *chaa*·hi·ye

A … ticket to (Kanpur).	(کانپر) کے لئے … ٹکٹ دیجئے۔	(*kaan*·pur) ke li·*ye* … ti·*kat dee*·ji·ye
one-way	ایک طرفہ	ek ţa·ra·*faa*
return	آنے جانے کا	*aa*·ne *jaa*·ne kaa

I'd like to … my ticket, please.	مجھے ٹکٹ … ہے۔	mu·*j'e* ti·*kat* … hay
cancel	کینسل کرانا	*kayn*·sal ka·*raa*·naa
change	بدلنا	ba·*dal*·naa

I'd like a (non)smoking seat.

مجھے (نان) سموکنگ سیٹ چاہئے۔ — mu·*j'e* (naan) *smo*·king seet *chaa*·hi·ye

Is there a toilet/air conditioning?

کیا ٹائلیٹ/اۓ-سی ہے؟ — kyaa *taa*·i·let/e see hay

How long does the trip take?

جانے میں کتنی دیر لگتی ہے؟ — *jaa*·ne meng *kiţ*·nee der *lag*·ţee hay

Is it a direct route?

کیا سیدھے جاتے ہیں؟ — kyaa *see*·d'e *jaa*·ţe hayng

My luggage has been ...	میرا سامان ... گیا ہے۔	*me*·raa *saa*·man ... ga·*yaa* hay
damaged	خراب ہو	k'a·*raab* ho
lost	کھو	k'oh
stolen	چوری ہو	*cho*·ree ho

transport

Where does flight number (12) arrive/depart?
فلائٹ نمبر (بارہ) کہاں اترتی/اڑتی ہے؟
flaa·it *nam*·bar (*baa*·rah) ka·*haang* u·*ţar*·ţee/*uŗ*·ţee hay

Is this the ... to (Agra)?	کیا یہ ... (آگرہ) جاتا ہے؟	kyaa yeh ... (*aag*·raa) *jaa*·ţaa hay
boat	جہاز	ja·*haaz*
bus	بس	bas
plane	ہوائ جہاز	ha·*vaa*·ee ja·*haaz*
train	ٹرین	tren

When's the ... (bus)?	... (بس) کب جاتی ہے؟	... (bas) kab *jaa*·ţee hay
first	پہلی	*peh*·lee
last	آخری	*aa*·k'i·ree
next	اگلی	*ag*·lee

How long will it be delayed?
اسے کتنی دیر ہوئ ہے؟
u·*se kiţ*·nee der hu·*ee* hay

Please tell me when we get to (Islamabad).
جب (اسلاآباد) آتا ہے، مجھے بتائے۔
jab (is·laa·*maa*·baad) *aa*·ţaa hay mu·*j'e* ba·*ţaa*·i·ye

That's my seat.
وہ میری سیٹ ہے۔
voh *me*·ree seet hay

I'd like a taxi ...	مجھے ... ٹیکسی چاہئے۔	mu·*j'e* ... *tayk*·see *chaa*·hi·ye
at (9am)	(صبح نو) بجے	(su·*bah* now) ba·*je*
now	ابھی	a·*b'ee*

How much is it to (Lahore)?
(لاہور) تک کتنے روپیہ لگتے ہیں؟
(*laa*·hor) ţak *kiţ*·ne ru·pa·*ye lag*·ţe hayng

Please put the meter on.
میٹر لگانا۔
mee·tar la·*gaa*·naa

Please take me to …	… لے جائۓ۔	… le *jaa*·i·ye
Please stop here.	یہاں رکۓ۔	ya·*haang* ru·ki·*ye*
Please wait here.	یہاں انتظار کیجۓ۔	ya·*haang* *in*·ţa·zaar *kee*·ji·ye

I'd like to hire a car/4WD (with a driver).
مجھے کار/فور وہیل ڈرایو (ڈرایور کے ساتھ) کرائۓ پر لینا ہے۔ — mu·*j'e* kaar/fohr weel *đraa*·iv (*đraa*·i·var ke saaţ') ki·*raa*·ye par *le*·naa hay

How much for daily hire?
ایک روز کے لۓ کرایا کتنا ہے؟ — ek roz ke li·*ye* ki·*raa*·yaa *kiţ*·naa hay

How much for weekly hire?
ہفتے کے لۓ کرایا کتنا ہے؟ — *haf*·ţe ke li·*ye* ki·*raa*·yaa *kiţ*·naa hay

directions

Where's the …?	… کہاں ہے؟	… ka·*haang* hay
bank	بینک	baynk
foreign currency exchange	فارین ایکسچینج آفس	*faa*·ren *eks*·chenj *aa*·fis
post office	ڈاک خانہ	đaak *k'aa*·naa

Is this the road to (Ajmer)?
کیا یہ (اجمیر) کا راستہ ہے؟ — kyaa yeh (*aj*·meer) kaa *raas*·ţaa hay

Can you show me (on the map)?
(نقشے میں) دکھا سکتے ہیں؟ — (*nak*·she meng) di·*k'aa* *sak*·ţe hayng

What's the address?
پتہ کیا ہے؟ — pa·*ţaa* kyaa hay

How far is it?
وہ کتنی دور ہے؟ — voh *kiţ*·nee door hay

How do I get there?
میں وہاں کیسے جاونگا/جاونگی؟ — mayng *va*·hang *kay*·se *ja*·ung·ga/*ja*·ung·gee **m/f**

Turn left/right.
لیفٹ/رائٹ مڑۓ۔ — left/*raa*·it mu·ŗi·*ye*

It's …	وہ … ہے۔	voh … hay
behind …	… کے پیچھے	… ke *pee*·ch'e
in front of …	… کے سامنے	… ke *saam*·ne
near …	… کے پاس	… ke paas
on the corner	کونے پر	*ko*·ne par
opposite …	… کے سامنے	… ke *saam*·ne
straight ahead	سیدھے	*see*·d'e
there	وہاں	va·*haang*

accommodation

Where's a guesthouse/hotel nearby?
گیسٹہاوس/ہوٹل کہاں ہے؟ gest·*haa*·us/*ho*·tal ka·*haang* hay

Can you recommend somewhere cheap/good?
سستی/اچّھی جگہ کا پتہ دے سکتے ہیں؟ *sas*·tee/*ach'*·ch'ee ja·*gah* kaa pa·*ţaa* de *sak*·ţe hayng

I'd like to book a room, please.
مجھے ایک کمرہ چاہئے۔ mu·*j'e* ek *kam*·raa *chaa*·hi·ye

I have a reservation.
بکنگ تو ہے۔ bu·*king* ţo hay

Do you have a … room?	کیا … کمرہ ہے؟	kyaa … *kam*·raa hay
double	ڈبل	đa·*bal*
single	سنگل	*sin*·gal
twin	ٹوین	*tu*·in

How much is it per night?
ایک رات کے لئے کتنے پیسے لگتے ہیں؟ ek raaţ ke li·*ye* *kiţ*·ne *pay*·se *lag*·ţe hayng

How much is it per person?
ہر شخص کے لئے کتنے پیسے لگتے ہیں؟ har shaks ke li·*ye* *kiţ*·ne *pay*·se *lag*·ţe hayng

For (three) nights.
(تین) دن کے لئے۔ (ţeen) din ke li·*ye*

Can I have my key, please?
چابی دیجئے۔ *chaa*·bee *dee*·ji·ye

Can I get another (blanket)?
کیا ایک اور (کمبل) ملیگا/ملیگی؟ kyaa ek owr (*kam*·bal) mi·*le*·gaa/mi·*le*·gee **m/f**

The (air conditioner) doesn't work.

(اۓ-سی) خراب ہے۔ (e see) k'a·*raab* hay

Is there an elevator/a safe?

کیا یہاں لفٹ/تجوری ہے؟ kyaa ya·*haang* lift/ţi·*jo*·ree hay

What time is checkout?

کتنے بجے کمرہ خالی کرنا ہے ؟ *kiţ*·ne ba·*je kam*·raa *k'aa*·lee *kar*·naa hay

Can I have my ..., please?	... دے دیجئے۔	... de *dee*·ji·ye
deposit	ڈپاسٹ	đi·*paa*·sit
passport	پاسپورٹ	*paas*·port
valuables	بیشقیمتی چیزیں	besh·*keem*·ţee *chee*·zeng

banking & communications

Where's an ATM?

اۓ-ٹی-ایم کہاں ہے؟ e tee em ka·*haang* hay

Where's the nearest public phone?

یہاں پی-سی-او کہاں ہے؟ ya·*haang* pee see o ka·*haang* hay

I'd like to ...	میں ... چاہتا/ چاہتی ہوں۔	mayng ... *chaah*·ţaa/ *chaah*·ţee hoong m/f
arrange a transfer	منتاکل کرنا	*mun*·ta·kil *kar*·naa
change a travellers cheque	ٹریولرس چیک کیش لینا	*tre*·va·lars chek kaysh *kar*·naa
change money	پیسے بدلنا	*pay*·se ba·*dal*·naa
withdraw money	پیسے نکالنا	*pay*·se ni·*kaal*·naa

What's the ...?	... کیا ہۓ؟	... kyaa hay
charge for that	اس کے لۓ چارج	us ke li·*ye* chaarj
exchange rate	ایکسچینج ریٹ	*eks*·chenj ret

Where's the local internet café?

انٹرنیٹ کیفے کہاں ہے؟ in·*tar*·net *kay*·fe ka·*haang* hay

How much is it per hour?

ہر گھنٹے کتنے پیسے لگتے ہیں؟ har *g'an*·te *kiţ*·ne *pay*·se *lag*·ţe hayng

I'd like to ...	مجھے ... ہے۔	mu·*j'e* ... hay
get internet access	انٹرنیٹ دیکھنا	in·*tar*·net *dek'*·naa
use a printer	کاپی نکالنی	*kaa*·pee ni·*kaal*·nee
use a scanner	کچھ سکین کرنا	kuch' skayn *kar*·naa

I'd like a ...	مجھے ... چاہئے۔	mu·*j'e* ... *chaa*·hi·ye
mobile/cell phone for hire	سیل فون کرائے پر	sel fon ki·*raa*·ye par
SIM card for your network	آپ کے نیٹورک کے لئے سم کارڈ	aap ke *net*·vark ke li·*ye* sim kaarđ

What are the rates?
در کیا ہے؟ dar kyaa hay

What's your phone number?
آپ کا نمبر کیا ہے؟ aap kaa *nam*·bar kyaa hay

The number is ...
نمبر ... ہے۔ *nam*·bar ... hay

I'd like to buy a phonecard.
میں فون کارڈ خریدنا چاہتا/چاہتی ہوں۔ mayng *fon*·kaarđ k'a·*reed*·naa *chaah*·ţaa/*chaah*·ţee hoong **m/f**

I want to ...	میں ... چاہتا/چاہتی ہوں۔	mayng ... *chaah*·ţaa/*chaah*·ţee hoong **m/f**
call (Canada)	(کنڈا کو) فون کرنا	(ka·na·*đaa* ko) fon *kar*·naa
call collect	ورس چارجز کرنا	ri·*vars chaar*·jez *kar*·naa

I want to send a fax/parcel.
مجھے فیکس/پارسل بھیجنا ہے۔ mu·*j'e* fayks/*paar*·sal *b'ej*·naa hay

I want to buy a stamp/an envelope.
مجھے ٹکٹ/لفافہ دیجئے۔ mu·*j'e* ti·*kat*/li·*faa*·faa *dee*·ji·ye

Please send it to (Australia).
اسے (آسٹریلیا) کو بھیجئے۔ i·*se* (aas·*tre*·li·yaa) ko *b'e*·ji·ye

sightseeing

What time does it open?
کتنے بجے کھلتا ہے؟ *kiţ*·ne ba·*je k'ul*·ţaa hay

What time does it close?
کتنے بجے بند ہوتا ہے؟ *kiţ*·ne ba·*je* band' *ho*·ţaa hay

What's the admission charge?
اندر جانے کی کیا قیمت لگتی ہے؟ *an*·dar *jaa*·ne kee kyaa *kee*·maţ *lag*·ţee hay

Is there a discount for students?
کیا طالب عام کے لئے خاص چھوٹ ہے؟ kyaa *taa*·li·be ilm ke li·*ye* k'aas ch'oot hay

Is there a discount for children?

کیا بچّوں کے لئے خاص چھوٹ ہے؟	kyaa *bach*·chong ke li·*ye* k'aas ch'oot hay

I'd like to hire a guide.

مجھے گائڈ چاہئے۔	mu·*j'e gaa*·iđ *chaa*·hi·ye

I'd like a catalogue/map.

مجھے کیٹیلاگ/نقشہ چاہئے۔	mu·*j'e* kay·*te*·laag/*nak*·shaa *chaa*·hi·ye

I'd like to see ...

میں ... دیکھنا چہتا/چاہتی ہوں۔	mayng ... *dek'*·naa *chaah*·ţaa/*chaah*·ţee hoong **m/f**

What's that?

وہ کیا ہے؟	voh kyaa hay

Can I take a photo?

کیا میں فوٹو لے سکتا/ سکتی ہوں؟	kyaa mayng *fo*·to le *sak*·ţaa/*sak*·ţee hoong **m/f**

I'd like to go somewhere off the beaten track.

میں کوئ انوکھا جگہ جانا چاہتا/چاہتی ہوں۔	mayng *koh*·ee *aa*·no·k'a *ja*·ga *jaa*·na *chaah*·ţaa/*chaah*·ţee hung **m/f**

When's the next tour?

اگلا ٹور کب ہئے؟	*ag*·laa toor kab hay

How long is the tour?

ٹور کتنی دیر کی ہے؟	toor *kiţ*·nee der kee hay

Is ... included?	کیا ... بھی شامل ہئے؟	kyaa ... b'ee *shaa*·mil hay
accommodation	رہنا	*reh*·naa
admission	اندر جانا	*an*·dar *jaa*·na
food	کھانا	*k'aa*·naa
transport	آنا جانا	*aa*·naa *jaa*·naa

sightseeing

fort	قلعہ	*ki*·la
main square	چوک	*cho*·ok
mosque	مسجد	*mas*·jid
old city	پورانا شہر	*pu*·ra·na *she*·her
palace	مہل	*ma*·hal
ruins	کھنڈہر	*kan*·da·har
temple	مندر	*man*·dir

Where's a ...?	... کہاں ہے؟	... ka·*haang* hay
camera shop	کیمرا شاپ	*kaym*·raa shaap
market	بازار	*baa*·zaar
souvenir shop	نشانیوں کی دکان	ni·*shaa*·ni·yong kee du·*kaan*

I'd like to buy ...
مجھے ... چاہئے۔ mu·*j'e* ... *chaa*·hi·ye

Can I look at it?
دکھائیے۔ di·*k'aa*·i·ye

Can I have it sent overseas?
کیا آپ باہر بھجوا دیں گے/دیں گی؟ kyaa aap *baa*·har *b'ij*·vaa *deng*·ge/*deng*·gee **m/f**

Can I have my (camera) repaired?
یہاں (کیمرا) کی مرمت ہوتی ہے؟ ya·*haang* (*kaym*·raa) kee ma·*ram*·maţ *ho*·ţee hay

It's faulty.
یہ خراب ہے۔ yeh k'a·*raab* hay

How much is it?
کتنے کا ہے؟ *kiţ*·ne kaa hay

Can you write down the price?
دام کاغذ پر لکھئے؟ daam *kaa*·gaz par li·k'i·*ye*

That's too expensive.
یہ بہت مہنگا/مہنگی ہے۔ yeh ba·*huţ* ma·*han*·gaa/ma·*han*·gee hay **m/f**

I'll give you (30 rupees).
میں (تیس روپیہ) دوں گا/دوں گی۔ mayng (ţees ru·pa·*ye*) *doong*·gaa/*doong*·gee **m/f**

There's a mistake in the bill.
بل میں غلطی ہے۔ bil meng *gal*·ţee hay

Do you accept ...?	کیا آپ ... لیتے/لیتی ہیں؟	kyaa aap ... *le*·ţe/*le*·ţee hayng **m/f**
credit cards	کریڈٹ کارڈ	*kre*·đit kaarđ
debit cards	ڈیبٹ کارڈ	*de*·bit kaarđ
travellers cheques	ٹریولرس چیک	*tre*·va·lars chek

Less.	کم۔	kam
Enough.	کافی۔	*kaa*·fee
More.	اور۔	or

I'd like (a) ..., please.	مجھے ... چاہئے۔	mu·*j'e* ... *chaa*·hi·ye
my change	باقی پیسے	*baa*·kee *pay*·se
bag	بیگ	bayg
receipt	رسید	ra·*seed*
refund	پیسے واپس	*pay*·se *vaa*·pas

photography

Can you transfer photos from my camera to CD?
کیا آپ میرے کیمرے کی فوٹو سی ڈی پر لگا سکتے ہیں؟
kyaa aap *me*·re *kaym*·re kee foto see đee par la·*gaa sak*·ţe hayng

Can you develop this film?
کیا آپ یہ ریل دھو سکیے/سکتی ہیں؟
kyaa aap yeh reel d'o *sak*·ţe/*sak*·ţee hayng **m/f**

I need a film for this camera.
مجھے اس کیمرے کے لئے ایک ریل چاہئے۔
mu·*je* is *kaym*·re ke li·*ye* ek reel *chaa*·hi·ye

When will it be ready?
کب تیار ہو گا/ہو گی؟
kab *ţay*·yaar *ho*·gaa/*ho*·gee **m/f**

making conversation

Hello.	السلام عالیکم۔	*as*·sa·laam a·*lay*·kum
Goodbye.	خدا حافظ۔	k'u·*daa haa*·fiz
Good night.	شب بخیر۔	shab·*baa* k'air
Mr	جناب	*saa*·hab
Mrs	صاحبہ	*saa*·hi·baa
Ms/Miss	بیبی	*bee*·bee
How are you?	آپ کیسے/کیسی ہیں؟	aap *kay*·se/*kay*·see hayng **m/f**
Fine.	میں ٹھیک ہوں۔	mayng ţ'eek hoong
And you?	آپ سنائے۔	aap su·*naa*·i·ye
What's your name?	آپ کا نام کیا ہے؟	aap kaa naam kyaa hay
My name is ...	میرا نام ... ہے۔	*me*·raa naam ... hay
I'm pleased to meet you.	آپ سے ملکر بہت خوشی ہوی۔	aap se *mil*·kar ba·*huţ* k'u·*shee* hu·*ee*

This is my …	یہ میرا/میری ... ہے۔	yeh *me*·raa/*me*·ree … hay **m/f**
brother	بھائ	*b'aa*·ee
daughter	بیٹی	*be*·tee
father	والد	*vaa*·lid
friend	دوسپ	dosţ **m&f**
husband	شوہر	*show*·har
mother	امّیجان	*am*·mee·jaan
sister	بہن	be·*han*
son	بیٹا	*be*·taa
wife	بیوی	*bee*·vee

Here's my phone number.
یہ میرا فون نمبر ہے۔ — yeh *me*·raa fon *nam*·bar hay

What's your email address?
آپ کا ایمیل کا پتہ کیا ہے؟ — aap kaa *ee*·mayl kaa pa·*ţaa* kyaa hay

Where are you from?
آپ کہاں کے/کی ہیں؟ — aap ka·*haang* ke/kee hayng **m/f**

I'm from (New Zealand).
میں (نیو زیلینڈ) کا/کی ہوں۔ — mayng (nyoo *zee*·land) kaa/kee hoong **m/f**

What's your occupation?
آپ کیا کرتے/کرتی ہیں؟ — aap kyaa *kar*·te/*kar*·tee hayng **m/f**

I'm a …	میں ... ہوں۔	mayng … hoong
journalist	اخبارنویس	*ak*·baar na·*vees* **m&f**
teacher	ٹیچر	*tee*·char **m&f**

Do you like …?	کیا آپ کو ... پسند ہے؟	kyaa *aap*·ko … pa·*sand* hay
I (don't) like …	مجھے ... پسند (نہیں) ہے۔	mu·*j'e* … pa·*sand* (na·heeng) hay
meditation	دھیان لگانا	d'yaan la·*gaa*·naa
puppetry	پتلیوں کا تماشہ	puţ·li·yong kaa ţa·*maa*·shaa
yoga	یوگاسن	yo·*gaa*·san

eating out

Can you recommend a …?	کیا آپ ... کا نام بتا سکتے/سکتی ہیں؟	kyaa aap … kaa naam ba·*ţaa sak*·ţe/*sak*·ţee hayng **m/f**
bar	بار	baar
dish	کھانا	*k'aa*·naa
place to eat	ڈھابا	*d'aa*·baa

I'd like (a/the) ..., please.	مجھے ... چاہئے۔	mu·*j'e* ... *chaa*·hi·ye
bill	بل	bil
drink list	پینے کا مینیو کارڈ	*pee*·ne kaa *men*·yoo kaarđ
menu	مینیو	*men*·yoo
(non)smoking section	(نان) سموکنگ	(naan) *smo*·king
that dish	وہ کھانا	vo *k'aa*·naa

I'd like to reserve a table for (two) people.
میں (دو) لوگوں کے لئے بکنگ کرنا چاہتا/چاہتی ہوں۔
mayng (do) lo·*gong* ke li·*ye* bu·*king* ka·*raa*·naa *chaah*·ţaa/*chaah*·ţee hoong **m/f**

What's the local speciality?
حاص لوکل چیز کیا ہے؟
k'aas *lo*·kal cheez kyaa hay

breakfast	ناشتہ	*naash*·ţaa **m**
lunch	دن کا کھانا	din kaa *k'aa*·naa **m**
dinner	رات کا کھانا	raaţ kaa *k'aa*·naa **m**
(cup of) coffee ...	(ایک کپ) کافی ...	(ek kap) *kaa*·fee ...
(cup of) tea ...	(ایک کپ) چائے ...	(ek kap) chai ...
with milk	دودھ کے ساتھ	dood' ke saaţ'
without sugar	چینی کے بغیر	*chee*·nee ke ba·*gayr*
(orange) juice	(اورینج) جوس	(*o*·renj) joos **m**
lassi	لسّی	*las*·see **m**
soft drink	سافٹ ڈرنکس	saaft drink **m**
boiled water	ابلا ہوا پانی	*ub*·laa hu·aa *paa*·nee **m**
mineral water	منرل واٹر	*min*·ral *vaa*·tar **m**

I'll buy you a drink.
میں ہی اس کے پیسے دوں‌گا/دوں‌گی۔
mayng hee is drink ke *pay*·se *doong*·gaa/*doong*·gee **m/f**

What would you like?
آپ کیا لیں‌گے/لیں‌گی؟
aap kyaa *leng*·ge/*leng*·gee **m/f**

a bottle of beer	کی بوتل بیر	kee *bo*·ţal bi·*yar*
a glass of beer	کا گلاس بیر	kaa glaas bi·*yar*
a shot of (whisky)	ایک شٹ (ویسکی)	ek shot (*vis*·ki)
a bottle of ... wine	... شراب کی بوتل	... sha·*raab* kee *bo*·ţal
a glass of ... wine	... شراب کا گلاس	... sha·*raab* kaa glaas
red	لال	laal
white	سفید	sa·*fed*

special diets & allergies

Do you have vegetarian food?

کیا آپ کا کھانا سبزی خور کا ہے؟	kyaa aap kaa *k'aa*·naa sab·*zee* k'or kaa hay

I'm allergic to …	مجھے … کی ایرجی ہے۔	mu·*j'e* … kee e·*lar*·jee hay
dairy products	دودھ سے بنی چیزوں	dood' se ba·*nee chee*·zong
eggs	انڈے	*an*·de
nuts	میوے	*me*·ve
seafood	مچھلی	*mach'*·lee

emergencies

Help!	مدد کیجئے!	ma·*dad kee*·ji·ye
Stop that!/Stop there!	بس کرو!/رکو!	bas ka·*ro*/ru·*ko*
Go away!	جاؤ!	*jaa*·o
Thief!	چور!	chor
Fire!	آگ!	aag
Watch out!	خبردار!	k'a·*bar*·daar

Call …!	… کو بلاؤ!	… ko bu·*laa*·o
an ambulance	ایمبلینس	*em*·bu·lens
a doctor	ڈاکٹر	*đaak*·tar
the police	پولیس	pu·*lis*

Could you please help?

مدد کیجئے۔ — ma·*dad kee*·ji·ye

Can I use your phone?

کیا میں فون کر سکتا/سکتی ہوں؟ — kyaa mayng fon kar *sak*·ţaa/*sak*·ţee hoong **m/f**

I'm lost.

میں راستہ بھول گیا/گئی ہوں۔ — mayng *raas*·ţaa b'ool ga·*yaa*/ga·*yee* hoong **m/f**

Where's the toilet?

ٹائلیٹ کہاں ہے؟ — *taa*·i·let ka·*haang* hay

Where's the police station?

تھانا کہاں ہے؟ — *ţ'aa*·naa ka·*haang* hay

I have insurance.

میرے پس بیما ہے۔ — *me*·re paas *bee*·maa hay

I want to contact my embassy.

میں اپنے سفارتخانہ کو فون کرنا چاہتا/چاہتی ہوں۔	mayng *ap*·ne sa·*faa*·raţ *k'aa*·ne ko fon *kar*·naa *chaah*·ţaa/*chaah*·ţee hoong **m/f**

I've been raped.

میری بیعزّتی ہوی۔	*me*·ree be·*iz*·za·ţee hu·*ee*

I've been robbed.

میرا سامان چوری ہوا ہے۔	*me*·raa *saa*·man *cho*·ree hu·*aa* hay

I've lost my …	… کھو گیا/گئ ہے۔	… k'o ga·*yaa*/ga·*yee* hay **m/f**
bags	بیگ	bayg
credit card	کریڈٹ کارڈ	*kre*·đit kaarđ
money	پیسے	*pay*·se
passport	پاسپورٹ	*paas*·port
travellers cheques	ٹریولرس چیکس	*tre*·va·lars cheks

health

Where's the nearest …?	سب سے قریب … کہاں ہے؟	sab se ka·*reeb* … ka·*haang* hay
dentist	ڈینٹسٹ	*đen*·tist
doctor	ڈاکٹر	*đaak*·tar
hospital	ہسپتال	*has*·pa·ţaal
pharmacist	دواخانا	da·vaa·*k'aa*·naa

I need a doctor (who speaks English).

مجھے (انگریزی بولنے والا) ڈاکٹر چاہئے۔	mu·*j'e* (an·*gre*·zee *bol*·ne·*vaa*·laa) *đaak*·tar *chaa*·hi·ye

Could I see a female doctor?

مجھے لیڈی ڈاکٹر چاہئے۔	mu·*j'e le*·dee *đaak*·tar *chaa*·hi·ye

I've run out of my medication.

میری دوا ختم ہوئ ہے۔	*me*·ree da·*vaa* k'atm hu·*ee* hay

It hurts here.

ادھر درد ہو رہا ہے۔	i·*d'ar* dard ho ra·*haa* hay

I have (a/an) …

مجھے … ہے۔	mu·*j'e* … hay

I'm allergic to …

مجھے … کی ایلرجی ہے۔	mu·*j'e* … kee e·*lar*·jee hay

asthma	دمہ	da·*maa* m
constipation	کبض	kabz m
diarrhoea	دست	dasţ m
fever	بخار	bu·*k'aar* m
heart condition	دل کی بیماری	dil kee bee·*maa*·ree f
nausea	الٹی کا احساس	*ul*·tee kaa *eh*·saas m

antibiotics	اینٹیبایوٹکس	*en*·tee·baa·*yo*·tiks m
anti-inflammatories	اینٹی انفلیمٹوریز	*en*·tee in·flay·mi·*to*·rees m
aspirin	اسپرن	*as*·prin m
bees	مدھومکّھی	*ma*·d'u·*mak*·k'ee f
codeine	کوڈین	*ko*·deen m

responsible travel

I'd like to learn some Urdu.
میں کچھ اردو سیکھنا چاہتا/چاہتی ہوں۔
mayng kuch' *uŗ*·du *sik'*·na chaah·ţaa/*chaah*·ţee hoong m/f

Would you like me to teach you some English?
کیا میں اپ کو کچھ انگریزی سکھاوں؟
kya mayng aap ko kuch' *ang*·re·zee *si*·k'a·ung

I didn't mean to do/say anything wrong.
معاف کیجئے، جانبوجھ کر میں نے نہیں کیا/کہا۔
maaf *kee*·ji·ye jaan·*booj'*·kar mayng ne yeh na·*heeng* ki·*yaa*/ka·*haa*

Is this a local or national custom?
کیا یہ لوکل یا قومی روائت ہے؟
kya yeh *lo*·kal yaa *kow*·mee ri·*vaa*·yat hay

I'd like to stay at a locally run hotel.
میں لوکل ہوٹل مے رہنا چاہتا/چاہتی ہوں۔
mayng *lo*·kal *ho*·tal me *reh*·na *chaah*·ţaa/*chaah*·ţee hoong m/f

Where can I buy locally produced goods/souvenirs?
میں لوکل چیزئے خریدنا چاہتا/چاہتی ہوں؟
mayng *lo*·kal *chi*·zeng *k'a*·rid·na *chaah*·ţaa/*chaah*·ţee hoong m/f

What's this made from?
یہ کس چیز سے بنایا ہوا ہئے؟
yeh kis cheez se ba·*na*·ya *hu*·aa hay

I'm (an English teacher). Can I volunteer my skills?
میں (انگریزی ٹیچر) ہوں۔ کیا میں ولنٹری کام کر سکتا/سکتی ہوں؟
mayng (*ang*·re·zi *ti*·char) hoong kya mayng *vo*·lan·ta·ri kam kar *sak*·ţa/*sak*·ţee hoong m/f

english–urdu dictionary

Words in this dictionary are marked as n (noun), a (adjective), v (verb), sg (singular), pl (plural), inf (informal) .and pol (polite) where necessary. Adjectives are given in the masculine form only

A

accident حادثہ *haad*·sah
accommodation رہنے کی جگہ *reh*·ne kee ja·*gah*
adaptor اڈپٹر a·*đap*·tar
address n پتہ pa·*ţaa*
after بعد baad
air conditioner اے-سی e see
airplane ہوائی جہاز ha·*vaa*·ee ja·*haaz*
airport ہوائی اڈّا ha·*vaa*·ee *ađ*·đaa
alcohol شراب sha·*raab*
all سب sab
allergy ایلرجی e·*lar*·jee
ambulance ایمبلینس *em*·bu·lens
and اور owr
ankle ٹکھنا *tak*·naa
antibiotics اینٹبایوٹکس en·ti·baa·*yo*·tiks
arm بازو *baa*·zoo
ATM آئے-ٹی-ایم e tee em

B

baby بچّہ *bach*·chaa
back (body) پیٹھ peet'
backpack بیکپیک *bayk*·payk
bad برا bu·*raa*
bag بیگ bayg
baggage claim بیگیج کلیم *bay*·gayj klaym
bank بینک baynk
bar بار baar
bathroom باتھروم *baaţ*·room
battery سیل sel
beautiful خوبصورت koob·*soo*·raţ
bed پلنگ pa·*lang*
before پہلے *peh*·le
behind پیچھے *pee*·ch'e
bicycle سائکل *saa*·i·kil
big بڑا ba·*ŗaa*
bill بل bil
blanket کمبل *kam*·bal
blood group بلاڈگرپ *blad*·grup
boat جہاز ja·*haaz*
book (make a reservation) v بوکنگ کرانا bu·*king* ka·*raa*·naa
bottle بوتل bo·*ţal*
boy لڑکا *laŗ*·kaa
brakes (car) بریک brek
breakfast ناشتہ *naash*·ţaa
broken (faulty) ٹوٹا *too*·taa
bus بس bas
business کاروبار kaa·*ro*·baar
buy v خریدنا k'a·*reed*·naa

C

camera کیمرا *kaym*·raa
cancel کینسل کرنا *kayn*·sal *kar*·naa
car گاڑی *gaa*·ŗee
cash n نقد na·*kad*
cash (a cheque) v کیش کرنا kaysh *kar*·naa
cell phone سیل فون sel fon
centre n مرکز *mar*·kaz
change (money) v بھونانا b'oo·*naa*·naa
cheap سستہ *sas*·ţaa
check (bill) بل bil
check-in n چیک ان chek in
chest (body) سینہ *see*·naa
child بچّہ *bach*·chaa
cigarette سگریٹ *sig*·ret
city شہر sha·*har*
clean a صاف saaf
closed بند band
cold a ٹھنڈا *t'an*·đa
collect call کلیکٹ کال ka·*lekt* kaal
come آنا *aa*·naa
computer کمپیوٹر kam·*pyoo*·tar
condom کنڈم *kaan*·đam
contact lenses کانٹیکٹ لینس *kaan*·tekt lens
cook v پکانا pa·*kaa*·naa
cost n قیمت *kee*·maţ
credit card کریڈٹ کارڈ *kre*·đit kaarđ
currency exchange کرنسی ایکسچینج ka·*ran*·see *eks*·chenj
customs (immigration) کسٹمس *kas*·tams

D

dangerous خطرناک k'a·*ţar*·naak
date (time) تاریخ *ţaa*·reek'

english–urdu

day روز roz
delay n دیر der
dentist ڈینٹسٹ đ*en*·tist
depart روانہ ہونا ra·*vaa*·nah *ho*·naa
diaper نیپی *nay*·pee
dinner رات کا کھانا raaţ kaa *k'aa*·naa
direct a سیدھا *see*·d'aa
dirty گندہ *gan*·daa
disabled (person) اپاہج a·*paa*·hij
discount n چھوٹ ch'oot
doctor ڈاکٹر *đaak*·tar
double bed ڈبل بیڈ đa·*bal* beđ
double room ڈبل کمرا đa·*bal* *kam*·raa
drink n پینے کی چیزیں *pee*·ne kee *chee*·zeng
drive v چلانا cha·*laa*·naa
drivers licence گاڑی چلانے کا لائسینس *gaa*·ŗee cha·*laa*·ne kaa *laa*·i·sens
drug (illicit) نشیلی دوا na·*shee*·lee da·*vaa*

E

ear کان kaan
east مشرق *mash*·rik
eat کھانا *k'aa*·naa
economy class اکانمی کلاس i·*kaa*·na·mee klaas
electricity بجلی *bij*·lee
elevator لفٹ lift
email ای میل ee mayl
embassy سفارتخانہ sa·*faa*·raţ *k'aa*·naa
emergency امرجینسی i·mar·*jen*·see
English (language) انگریزی an·*gre*·zee
entrance اندر an·*dar*
evening شام shaam
exit n نکاس ni·*kaas*
expensive مہنگا ma·*han*·gaa
eye آنکھ aangk'

F

far دور door
fast جلدی *jal*·dee
father والد *vaa*·lid
film (camera) ریل reel
finger انگلی *ung*·lee
first-aid kit فرسٹ ایڈ کٹ farst ed kit
first-class a اوّل درجہ *av*·val *dar*·jaa
fish n مچھلی *mach'*·lee
food کھانا *k'aa*·naa
foot پیر payr
free (of charge) مفت mufţ
friend دوست dosţ
fruit پھل p'al
full بھرا ہوا b'a·*raa* hu·*aa*

G

gift تحفہ *ţoh*·faa
girl لڑکی *laŗ*·kee
glass (drinking) گلاس glaas
glasses عینک *ay*·nak
go جانا *jaa*·naa
good اَچّھا *ach'*·ch'aa
guide n گائڈ *gaa*·id

H

half آدھا *aa*·d'aa
hand ہاتھ haaţ
happy خوش k'ush
have ہے hay
he وہ voh
head n سر sir
heart دل dil
heavy بھاری *b'aa*·ree
help v مدد کرنا ma·*dad* *kar*·naa
here یہاں ya·*haang*
high اونچا *oon*·chaa
hike n ہائک *haa*·ik
holiday چھٹی *ch'ut*·tee
homosexual a ہمجنس پرست *ham*·jins pa·*rasţ*
hospital ہسپتال *has*·pa·ţaal
hot گرم garm
hotel ہوٹل *ho*·tal
hungry بھوکا *b'oo*·kaa
husband شوہر *show*·har

I

I میں mayng
identification (card) پہچان *peh*·ch'aan
ill بیمار *bee*·maar
important اہم a·*ham*
injury چوٹ choht
insurance بیما *bee*·maa
internet انٹرنیٹ in·*tar*·net
interpreter ترجمان *ţar*·ja·maan

J

jewellery گہنے *geh*·ne
job نوکری *nowk*·ree

K

key چابی *chaa*·bee

kilogram کلوگرام ki·*lo*·graam
kitchen رسوئی ra·*so*·ee
knife چاقو *chaa*·koo

L

laundry (clothes) دھلائی d'u·*laa*·ee
lawyer وکیل va·*keel*
left (direction) لیفٹ left
leg (body) ٹانگ taangg
lesbian n لیزبین *lez*·bi·yan
less کم kam
letter (mail) خط k'aţ
light n روشنی *rosh*·nee
like v پسند کرنا pa·sand *kar*·na
lock n تالا *ţaa*·laa
long لمبا *lam*·baa
lost کھویا ہوا *k'o*·yaa hu·*aa*
love n محبّت mu·*hob*·baţ
luggage سامان *saa*·maan
lunch دن کا کھانا din kaa *k'aa*·naa

M

mail n ڈاک đaak
man آدمی *aad*·mee
map نقشہ *nak*·shaa
market بازار *baa*·zaar
matches ماچس *maa*·chis
meat گوشت gosht
medicine دوا da·*vaa*
message پیغام *pay*·gaam
milk دودھ dood'
minute منٹ mi·*nat*
mobile phone سیل فون sel fon
money پیسے *pay*·se
month مہینہ ma·*hee*·naa
morning سویرا sa·*ve*·raa
mother امّیجان *am*·mee·jaan
motorcycle موٹرسائکل *mo*·tar·*saa*·i·kil
motorway موٹروے mo·*tar*·ve
mouth منہ mung

N

name n نام naam
near پاس paas
neck گردن *gar*·dan
new نیا na·*yaa*
newspaper اخبار *ak'*·baar
night رات raaţ
no نہیں na·*heeng*
noise شورغل *shor*·gul
nonsmoking نان سموکنگ naan *smo*·king
north شمال shu·*maal*
nose ناک naak
now اب ab
number نمبر *nam*·bar

O

old پرانا pu·*raa*·naa
one-way ticket ایک طرفہ ٹکٹ ekţa·ra·*faa*ţi·*kat*
open a کھلا k'u·*laa*
outside باہر *baa*·har

P

passport پاسپورٹ *paas*·port
pay v پیسے دینا *pay*·se *de*·naa
pharmacy دواخانا da·vaa·*k'aa*·naa
phonecard فون کارڈ fon kaarđ
photo فوٹو *fo*·to
police پولیس pu·*lis*
postcard پوسٹکارڈ *post*·kaarđ
post office ڈاک خانہ đaak *k'aa*·naa
pregnant حاملہ *haa*·mi·lah
price n قیمت *kee*·maţ

Q

quiet a خاموش *kaa*·mosh

R

rain n بارش *baa*·rish
razor استرا *us*·ta·raa
receipt n رسید ra·*seed*
refund n رفنڈ ri·*fanđ*
registered mail ریجسٹڈ میل re·*jis*·tađ mayl
rent n کرایا ki·*raa*·yaa
repair v مرمّت کرنا ma·*ram*·maţ *kar*·naa
reservation بکنگ bu·*king*
restaurant ریسٹورینٹ res·*to*·rent
return v واپس آنا *vaa*·pas *aa*·naa
return ticket واپسی ٹکٹ *vaa*·pa·see ti·*kat*
right (direction) داہنہ *daa*·hi·naa
road سڑک sa·*ŗak*
room کمرہ *kam*·raa

S

safe a تجوری ţi·*jo*·ree
sanitary napkin سنیٹری نیپکنس say·*nit*·ree *nayp*·kin

seat n کرسی *kur*·see
send بھیجنا *b'ej*·naa
sex جنس jins
shampoo شیمپو *shaym*·pu
share (a dorm) v ایک ساتھ رہنا ek saaţ' *reh*·naa
she وہ voh
sheet (bed) چادر *chaa*·dar
shirt کرتہ *kur*·ţaa
shoes جوتے *joo*·ţe
shop n دکان du·*kaan*
short چھوٹا *ch'o*·taa
shower n شاور *shaa*·var
single room سنگل کمرہ *sin*·gal *kam*·raa
skin n جلد jild
skirt n لہنگا la·*han*·gaa
sleep n نیند neend
slowly آہستہ aa·*his*·ţaa
small چھوٹا *cho*·taa
soap صابن *saa*·bun
some کچھ kuch'
soon جلدی *jal*·dee
south جنوب ja·*noob*
souvenir shop نشانیوں کی دکان ni·*shaa*·ni·yong kee du·*kaan*
stamp ٹکٹ ti·*kat*
station (train) سٹیشن *ste*·shan
stomach پیٹ pet
stop v ٹھہرنا *ţ'ehr*·naa
stop (bus) n بس اسٹاپ bas *is*·taap
street سڑک sa·*ŗak*
student طالب علم *taa*·li·be ilm
sun سورج *soo*·raj
sunscreen سنبلاک *san*·blaak
swim v تیرنا *ţayr*·naa

T

tampons ٹیمپان *taym*·paan
teeth دانت daanţ
telephone n ٹیلیفون *te*·lee·fohn
temperature (weather) تاپمان *ţaap*·maan
that (one) وہ voh
they وہ voh
thirst پیاس pyaas
this (one) یہ yeh
throat گلا ga·*laa*
ticket ٹکٹ ti·*kat*
time وقت vakţ
tired تھکا ہوا ţ'a·*kaa* hu·*aa*
tissues ٹشیو tish·*yoo*
today آج aaj
toilet ٹئلیٹ *taa*·i·let
tomorrow کل kal
tonight آج رات aaj raaţ
toothbrush برش brush
toothpaste دانت منجن tooţ pest
torch (flashlight) ٹارچ taarch
tour n دورا *dow*·raa
tourist office سیاحوں کا آفس *sai*·yaa·hong kaa *aa*·fis
towel تولیہ *ţow*·li·yaa
train n ٹرین tren
translate ترجمہ کرنا *ţar*·ju·mah *kar*·naa
travel agency ٹریول ایجینٹ *tre*·val *e*·jent
travellers cheque ٹریولرس چیک *tre*·va·lars chek
trousers پینٹ paynt
twin beds ٹون بیڈز tvin beđz

U

underwear کچھا *kach*·ch'aa
urgent ضروری za·*roo*·ree

V

vacant خالی *k'aa*·lee
vegetable n سبزی *sab*·zee
vegetarian a سبزیخور *sab*·zee·*k'or*
visa ویسا *vee*·saa

W

walk v پیدل جانا *pay*·dal *jaa*·naa
wallet بٹوا ba·tu·*aa*
wash (something) دھونا *d'o*·naa
watch n گھڑی g'a·*ŗee*
water n پانی *paa*·nee
we ہم hum
weekend ویک اینڈ veek end
west مغرب *mag*·rib
wheelchair وہیل چئر vheel *chay*·ar
when کب kab
where کہاں ka·*haang*
who کون kown
why کیوں kyong
wife بیوی *bee*·vee
window کھڑکی *k'iŗ*·kee
with کے ساتھ ke saaţ'
without کے بغیر ke ba·*gayr*
woman خاتون *k'aa*·ţoon
write لکھنا *lik'*·naa

Y

yes جی ہاں jee haang
yesterday کل kal
you sg pol&pl آپ aap

Culture

The glory of India is the sheer diversity of its myriad cultures – from rich **histories** and varied **cuisines** to colourful **festivals** and local **languages**, India has it all. Here we present you with a cultural snapshot of the region and give you the tools to communicate and travel in an exciting and respectful way.

history timeline

Take a wander through the rich history of India . . .

3500–2000 BC	The rule of the Indus Valley civilisation known as the Harappan culture, with large cities and a still undeciphered script.
1500–1200 BC	Vedic-Aryan period during which the Hindu sacred scriptures were written and the caste system formalised.
1000 BC	Composition of the Mahabharata, about the exploits of Krishna.
7th century BC	Aryan tribes spread across the Ganges plain.
6th century BC	Jain religion founded by Mahavira.
563 BC	Approximate date of birth of Siddhartha Gautama Buddha.
521–514 BC	Persian king Darius sends an expedition into India, setting the border of the Persian Empire at the Indus River.
364 BC	The Nanda dynasty rules over huge swathes of North India.
326 BC	Alexander the Great advances from Greece, but his troops refuse to go beyond the Beas River (Himachal Pradesh).
321–184 BC	The first great Indian empire, the Mauryan empire, is founded.
3rd century BC	Composition of the Ramayana, probably by the poet Valmiki.
273–232 BC	Emperor Ashoka's rule, characterised by flourishing art and sculpture, and sponsorship of Buddhism as the state religion.
AD 52	St Thomas the Apostle is believed to have arrived in Kerala, accounting for the state's sizable Christian population.
AD 319–510	Golden age of the Gupta empire. Hinduism is the dominant religion.
8th century	Arrival of Islam in India.
850	The Chola empire comes to power in South India.
10th century	Arrival of persecuted Zoroastrians (known as Parsis) from Persia.
1001–25	Reign of Mahmud of Ghazni, including 17 raids into India.
1192	Mohammed of Ghur conquers Delhi and North India comes under Islamic rule.

1336	Foundation of the Vijayanagar empire at Hampi.
1398	Tamerlane invades North India and destroys Delhi.
15th century	Sikh religion founded in Punjab by Guru Nanak.
1498	Vasco da Gama arrives on the coast of modern-day Kerala.
1510	Portuguese forces capture Goa.
1526	Babur becomes the first Mughal emperor by defeating the sultan of Delhi at the Battle of Panipat.
1531	Portuguese forces capture Diu.
1565	Collapse of the Vijayanagar empire.
1600	Britain's Queen Elizabeth I grants first trading charter to the East India Company.
1613	The East India Company establishes its first Indian trading post at Surat (Gujarat).
1631–53	Construction of the Taj Mahal by Mughal emperor Shah Jahan.
1672	The French establish themselves at Pondicherry as the French East India Company.
1739	The Mughal empire's capital, Delhi, is raided by Persia's Nadir Shah.
1750	French East India Company is recalled from Indian soil.
1757	English forces recapture Calcutta (Kolkata) from a local nawab in the Battle of Plassey.
1814	Kumaon and Shimla are annexed to India after battles between Britain and Nepal.
1857	Indian Uprising against British forces at an army barracks in Meerut (Uttar Pradesh).
1858	British government assumes formal control over India.
1869	Birth of Mohandas (Mahatma) Gandhi at Porbandar, Gujarat.
1885	Founding of the Congress Party.
1905	The British make a highly unpopular attempt to partition Bengal.

1909	The so-called Morley-Minto reforms provide for limited Indian participation in government.
1913	Rabindranath Tagore wins the Nobel Prize for Literature.
1919	Massacre of more than 1000 unarmed protesters by British troops at Amritsar (Punjab).
1920–2	Mahatma Gandhi begins anti-British civil disobedience campaign.
1935	Indian women and men are granted the right to vote.
1942	Mahatma Gandhi launches the campaign for Indian independence.
1947	India becomes independent and is divided into two countries: mainly Hindu India and mostly Muslim Pakistan.
1948	Mahatma Gandhi is assassinated in Delhi by a Hindu zealot. First war between India and Pakistan over Kashmir.
1949	UN-brokered ceasefire maintains the separation of India and Pakistan with the Line of Control (LOC).
1950	Chinese take control of Tibet; Tibetan refugees arrive in India.
1951–2	The Congress Party wins India's first post-Independence elections.
1961	Portugal cedes control of Goa and Diu to India.
1962	India loses border war with China over North-East Frontier Area.
1964	Prime Minister Jawaharlal Nehru dies.
1965	Second India–Pakistan war over Kashmir.
1966	Indira Gandhi, Nehru's daughter, becomes prime minister of India.
1971	India–Pakistan war over East Bengal, which subsequently becomes the nation of Bangladesh.
1974	First underground nuclear test is conducted in India.
1975	Indira Gandhi declares state of emergency, known as 'the Emergency', after being found guilty of electoral malpractice.
1984	Indira Gandhi is assassinated by Sikh bodyguards after Indian troops storm Amritsar's Golden Temple. Roop Kanwar commits *sati* (ritual self-immolation) on her husband's funeral pyre.

1987–90	Indian troops are sent as peacekeepers to Sri Lanka.
1989	Conflict in Kashmir begins in earnest, killing 70,000 people between 1989 and 2007. Indian citizen Tenzin Gyatso, His Holiness the Dalai Lama, wins the Nobel Peace Prize.
1991	Rajiv Gandhi is assassinated by a supporter of the Sri Lanka–based Liberation Tigers of Tamil Eelam (LTTE) in Tamil Nadu.
1992	Hindu zealots destroy the Babri Masjid in Ayodhya (Uttar Pradesh), leading to riots across the north of India.
1993	Salman Rushdie is awarded the Booker of Bookers Prize for the 1981 winner *Midnight's Children*.
1997	KR Narayanan becomes India's president, as the first Dalit (member of the Untouchable Hindu caste) to hold the position. Arundhati Roy wins the Booker Prize for *The God of Small Things*.
1998	India conducts nuclear tests, souring relations with Pakistan and attracting sanctions from the international community.
1999	Cyclone devastates the coast of Orissa, killing 10,000 people.
2000	In May, India's population reaches one billion.
2001	Suicide-bomber attacks are launched on the parliament building in New Delhi. 20,000 people are killed by a massive earthquake in Gujarat. VS Naipaul is awarded the Nobel Prize for Literature.
2002	India successfully test-fires its first nuclear-capable submarine-launched missile.
2004	Sikh prime minister, Manmohan Singh, becomes the first member of any religious minority community to hold India's highest elected office. Tamil Nadu and the Andaman and Nicobar Islands are battered by a tsunami and 15,000 people perish.
2005	After 60 years, bus lines are reopened between Pakistani- and Indian-controlled Kashmir.
2006	Kiran Desai wins the Booker Prize for *The Inheritance of Loss*. Bomb blasts on trains in Mumbai (Bombay) leave over 200 people dead.
2007	Scientist Rajendra Kumar Pachauri wins the Nobel Peace Prize (with Al Gore) for his work on climate change.

food

Indian cuisine is known as one of the world's greatest, although it may surprise you to learn that the *tikkas*, *masalas* and *rotis* you're familiar with are in fact the staples of Punjab, a result of the Punjabi diaspora following Partition in 1947. Once you're on the subcontinent, you can really taste true Indian flavours …

Spices are the soul of Indian cookery, utilising a dazzling array of herbs, seeds, berries, rhizomes, flowers, leaves, bark, bulbs and stigmas. No curry would be worth its tang without turmeric, and cardamom pods are prized for coffee and *chai* (tea) alike. *Tulsi* (holy basil) is so sacred to Hindus that it's used in Ayurvedic teas but never in food. Chillies were introduced by the Portuguese over 500 years ago, but their heat has since become synonymous with food from the subcontinent.

Other common features are *dood* (milk) and *dhal* (lentils or other pulses). Over 60 different forms of *dhal* can be prepared, such as *moong dhal* (mung beans), *rajma* (kidney beans) or *lobhia* (black-eyed peas). Milk products are both ubiquitous and delicious. *Ghee* (clarified butter) is used as oil and flavouring, *dahi* (curd or yogurt) helps cool down the most atomic chilli, and a sweet or savoury *lassi* (yogurt drink) is refreshing any time of day.

All meals will be built around a grain, generally rice in the south and wheat in the north. With *basmati* (named after the Hindi 'queen of fragrance') the most famous rice, you'll find it as *pilau* (rice cooked in stock and flavoured with spices) or *biryani* (spiced steamed rice with meat or vegetables). Bread may land on your *thali* (mixed-meal plate) as *roti* or *chapati* (round unleavened bread), *paratha* (flaky bread, often stuffed with cheese), or a thick, teardrop-shaped *naan* cooked in a *tandoor* (clay oven open at the top, fired by charcoal below).

India is a vegetarian's paradise – *sabzi* (vegetables) are served at every meal, cooked either *sukhi* (dry) or *tari* (in a sauce). Inevitable are potatoes, onions and cauliflower – perhaps combined into *koftas* (meatballs), or served in sauce and *paneer* (a kind of cheese). You'll find *baigan* (eggplant/aubergine) fried or curried, sometimes flavoured with different kinds of *saag* (leafy greens). Fresh fruits abound; make sure you sample Maharashtra's *alphonso* mango, the king of all mangoes, not to mention Ladakh's apricots, rosy apples from Himachal Pradesh or the citrus fruits available continentwide. Rarer items include Kerala's red banana *nendraparram*, cooked when still raw, or the *gochian* mushroom, black and beehived, found only in Kashmir. What isn't in season you'll find as pickles, *raita* (yogurt with fruit or vegetables) or *chatni* (chutney). Southern *chatnis* have a coconut base, while northern ones are generally based on mint.

There's also a wide array of meat and seafood dishes to get into. Because of religious taboos associated with Hinduism and Islam (forbidding beef and pork respectively), staple Indian meats are lamb, chicken and goat. Mughlai cuisine prevails in the north, with meat found in *kebabs*, *koftas*, *keema* (spiced mincemeat) and curries.

Authentic *rogan josh* (lamb curry) is yours for the sampling in Jammu and Kashmir, while Goan Christians do a mean pork *vindaloo* (spicy pork curry). Seafood is also not to be missed, especially with 7000km of coastline. Kerala is renowned for its *meen pollichathu* (fish cooked in banana leaves), and the Assamese go weak at the knees for *tenga* (fish stew).

No meal in India is complete without succulent *mithai* (sweets). You'll find orange-coloured *jalebis* everywhere (whorls of deep-fried batter in syrup), as well as delicately flavoured rice pudding (called *kheer* in the north and *payasam* in the south). Desserts fall into categories of *barfi* (fudgelike), *halwa* (with cereals, lentils, nuts, fruit or vegetables), *ladoos* (with lentil flour) and dairy-based (like *rasgulla*, cream-cheese balls flavoured with rose-water).

India's drink of choice is clearly *chai*, served from the Himalayas to the Gulf of Mannar, but you'll also find coffee making inroads. *Masala soda* is a soft drink pepped up with lime and spices, while *lassi* (yogurt drink) and juices also hold their own. Try the refreshing *jal jeera*, made of lime juice, cumin and mint. For local alcohol, do go past *arak*, 'country liquor' distilled from coconut-palm sap, potatoes or rice, and try the safer *mahua* flower brew, toddy (the sap from the palm tree made in Kerala) or rice beer brewed in the east and northeast. In any case, be sensitive to the religion of those around you before planning a Big Night Out.

food on the go

It would be a miracle – and a downright shame – to travel in India without trying the tempting morsels found on streets and platforms across the country. Follow the basics of eating only freshly made delicacies, only where appreciative crowds are gathered, and you needn't miss out on *chaat* (snack food seasoned with spiced fruit and vegetables), *bhajia* (vegetable fritters) or *puri* (deep-fried bread). Fare varies across neighbourhoods, so don't be shy to try food of the *thelas* (carts) that cross your path. Tuck into *aloo tikkas* (potato patties) in the north, *dosas* (rice-flour and lentil crepes) and *idlis* (spongy, round rice cakes) in the south, or *kulfi* (ice cream) on Chowpatty Beach in Mumbai. On a long train trip, nibble on the specialities churned up at particular stations: Lonavla (Maharashtra) is known for *chikki* (nut and jaggery toffee), Agra does *peitha* (crystallised pumpkin) and Dhaund (Uttar Pradesh) serves up *biryani*. The quintessential Indian food-on-the-go must be *paan*, a sweet, spicy and fragrant mix of the slightly narcotic betel nut, lime paste and spices. The addiction of many an Indian, both the *mitha* (sweet) and *saadha* (plain, often with tobacco, or even opium if you have dosh and contacts) versions are traditionally used as a digestive and mouth-freshener after a meal. Chew on a *paan* parcel, and observe the locals spitting red stains onto the road after eating all the good bits.

east indian food

East Indian food is richer in variety than food in the other regions of India, due to its geographical and historical diversity. While Orissa adores fish meals spiced with *ambul* mustard (with mangoes), in Bihar the staple is wholesome *sattu* (roasted chickpea flour) which can be mixed with onion or heated with *ghee* (clarified butter). The Chhath festival in Jharkhand sees an abundance of *thekua* sweets, made of *ghee*, jaggery, flour and aniseed. West Bengalis make short work of spicy *jhaal* (fish with ground mustard seeds and chillies), and top it off with *rasgulla* (cream-cheese balls flavoured with rose-water). The Assamese enjoy sour *kharoli* (fermented mushroom paste) and *khorisa* (fermented bamboo shoots) with rice, while in Manipur the fish diet is supplemented with unusual vegetables like the lotus stem and a bean with an overbearing smell called *yangchok*. The Khasis in Meghalaya make an exquisite *putharo* (fried rice-batter crepe), and the Nagas mash burnt dried fish with *raja mirsh* (an evilly hot chilli) to make pickles. Smoked rats are a dubious delicacy in Mizoram, and in Sikkim you must try *tongba*, a wooden tub of fermented millet seeds onto which you pour boiling water. Arunachal Pradesh has many Tibetan dishes, including *momos* (steamed or fried dumplings) and *churpee* (chewy bits of dried yak cheese).

north indian food

North Indian food might be the most familiar of the regional cuisines – many will know and love the Punjabi classic *baigan bharta* (roasted eggplant fried with onions and tomatoes), for example. Haryana cuisine has largely been taken over by the Punjabi, but traditionally butter (*nooni* or *tindi ghee*) was churned daily there, and given as a gift to new mothers. The traditional Kashmiri *wazwan* (banquet) seats guests in groups of four around an enormous silver platter – each guest's quarter-platter is demarcated by crisscrossing *sheekh* (meat kebabs). Vegetable-poor Rajasthanis rely heavily on grains: *bati* (baked balls of wholemeal flour) combines with *churma* (fried flour balls with sugar and nuts) to make *dhal bati churma*. A refreshing Uttaranchal winter dish is *sani hui muli*, made from radish, lemon, curd and *bhang* (cannabis) seed, while street food in Uttar Pradesh includes *kachoris* (corn or *dhal* puffs) and *nukti ta raita* (curds with droplets of fried gram flour). Madhya Pradesh is famous for *achar gosht* (Hyderabad's picklelike meat dish), and in Delhi, of course, you can sample flavours from the whole of India.

south indian food

South Indian dishes defy easy summary, but rice, *sambar* (*dhal* with cubed vegetables and purée) and *rasam* (*dhal*-based broth with tamarind) are always present. *Idlis* (spongy, round rice cakes) are eaten throughout the region, as are *dosas* (rice-flour and lentil crepes). In Karnataka, this is supplemented with *pallya* (dry vegetables) and *kosambri* (raw salad), or perhaps with *masala* (spiced) rice. Standard sweets are *holige* (rolled *rotis* filled with sweetened lentils) or *Mysore pak* (gram flour cooked in *ghee* and sugar). In Tamil Nadu, *sambar* may be replaced by *vattal kuzhambu* (sun-dried vegetables in tamarind water), while the meat dish can be *kola kozhambu* (spicy meatballs in sour gravy). *Karchikkai* (fried coconut ball) and *pongal* (sweet rice from the first harvest) are special desserts eaten at festival times. The cuisine of Andhra Pradesh mixes Hindu and Muslim influences – main dishes are *pulihora* (spicy vegetable pilau) or spicy kebabs wrapped in thin *roti*. The favourite sweet is *poornam burelu* (fried dumplings with a sweet *dhal* filling). Kerala residents enjoy seafood dishes such as *molee* (seafood cooked in coconut milk and spices). Stew and *appam* (rice pancake) are popular among the Christian population, while the Muslims make a unique *maida paratha* (flaky fried bread), eaten with stew or curry.

west indian food

West Indian cuisine is a riot of flavours and cultural mixing. Thanks to Gujarat's Jain population, vegetable meals are abundant and varied. The standard *thali* is a delight including *kadhi* (sour *dhal*), *farsan* (crunchy snack) and *mithai* (sweets). This is counterbalanced by fried snacks such as *gathia fafda* (fried chickpea-flour sticks), and carnivores will enjoy *siri paya* (goat's head and trotter soup). An after-dinner walk goes well with *kesar-pista* (saffron-pistachio) ice cream. Marathi meals blend north and south, so you can find both butter chicken and *dosas* on the menu. Coastal fare includes *bombil* or Bombay duck, which is actually a small salted fish. On the Deccan plateau you'll find simple *dhals* and a sweet-and-sour curry called *birdha*. *Ladoos* (gram flour and semolina sweetmeats) are highly popular, and you can't leave Mumbai without eating *bhelpuri* – a snack mix which is sweet, sour, hot, soft and crunchy all at once. Goan treats show the mix of local and Portuguese cultures. You'll be served classic Goan dishes like *cafreal* (fried chicken in green *masala* paste) or *caldeen* (fish simmered in coconut milk), then a main course like *assado de bife* (roast beef). Puddings and cakes, like *bathique* (semolina and coconut cake) and *be-binca* (a 40-egg sweet) are specialities of the region.

Desert Festival (Jaisalmer, Rajasthan)

Moustache twirling, snake charming, puppet playing, camel racing, gymnastic leaping, startling local costumes and a Mr Desert competition, all set against the backdrop of the Sam sand dunes of the Rajasthani desert – what more do you need for an exotic experience? Held for three days during full moon in January or February (the cool season), this is Jaisalmer's big moment. Thousands of tourists, both Indians and foreigners, flock to see the festivities, bathing in the moonlight while absorbing the folk music and dance performances which punctuate the evenings. Although the festival has been suspended in previous years because of the Kashmir conflict, the celebration is normally feted as a 'symphony in the golden city' of Jaisalmer. Don't miss out on the turban-tying contest for tourists, or the camel dance!

Durga Puja (Kolkata, West Bengal)

Welcome to one of the most splendid festivals in Bengal – Durga Puja. The Indian lunar calendar month of Asvina (September/October) commemorates the victory of the 10-armed goddess Durga over buffalo-headed demon Mahishasura. Every year thousands of idols of Durga are made out of clay and other materials. Opening with the *tarpan* ritual (offering water to gods and ancestors' souls), the faithful pray to their ancestors at the *ghats* (landings) of the Hooghly River after a program of readings to welcome the goddess, transmitted on All India Radio. After three days of *puja* rituals (offerings or prayers) and displays of the idols, the Durgas (or their reflections in mirrors) are ritually immersed in rivers, tanks and the sea – in a liquid which contains 75 ingredients such as dew collected from lotus pollen and dirt from a prostitute's doorway (for that's where a man leaves his virtue).

Festival of Dance (Khajuraho, Madhya Pradesh)

Best known as home to temples bedizened with Kamasutra carvings, Khajuraho is now enhanced by this classical dance festival held over a seven-day period in February/March. The cream of India's classical dancers perform their art before the illuminated backdrops provided by Chitragupta Temple (dedicated to the sun god Surya) and Vishwanath Temple (dedicated to Lord Shiva). Originally limited to traditional dances – such as the stylised sophistication of Bharata Natyam, Kathak with its detailed footwork, or the dance-drama of Kuchipudi – the festival has recently opened its doors to modern Indian performers. At this time Khajuraho also welcomes pilgrims to the festival of Maha Shivaratri, who come to commemorate the marriage of Shiva.

Ganesh Chaturthi (Mumbai, Maharashtra)

Ganesh Chaturthi is a spirited event held in August/September to celebrate the birth of Lord Ganesh (or Ganpati), god of good fortune. Originally a quiet celebration in the privacy of Indian homes, the festival was converted into a public spectacle during the struggle for independence. The construction of elephant-headed Ganesh statues begins in April, and they range in size from 2cm to over 7.5m. Blessed on the first day of the celebration by a priest wearing a red *dhoti* (long loincloth), the Ganesh idols are worshipped by family and friends for 10 days. Come the 11th day, the Ganpatis (Ganeshas) are paraded through the streets of Mumbai to singing, dancing and jubilation, to be ceremonially immersed in the sea at Chowpatty Beach in the presence of a horde of people chanting 'Oh father Ganesh, come again early next year'.

Holi (Vrindavan, Uttar Pradesh)

Vrindavan is where the young Krishna indulged in pranks such as stealing the clothes of *gopis* (milkmaids) while they bathed in the river. The Holi festival in February/March is usually a time to commemorate the evil demon Holika's sacrifice (in a bonfire) to save the life of her Vishnu-worshipping nephew, and in Vrindavan it's also a celebration of the immortal love of Krishna and Radha. The 'festival of colours' is particularly vibrant here and lasts for 16 days. On the night before Holi massive bonfires are lit, and the next day sees Indians cop a bit of spring fever, hitting the *bhang lassis* (blend of *lassi* and a derivative of marijuana) and throwing coloured water and *gulal* (powder) at anyone within range (clothes you can ditch afterwards are recommended). The powder is made from Ayurvedic herbs to ward off illness caused by the change of season. Vrindavan's special addition to the frenzy are folk dances, songs and processions, with the Bakai-Bihari Temple a focal point for traditional celebrations.

Karthikai Deepam (Tiruvannamalai, Tamil Nadu)

According to legend, Shiva appeared as a column of fire on Mt Arunachala in Tiruvannamalai, thus creating the original *lingam* (phallic symbol). At each November/December full moon (in the Indian lunar calendar month of Kartika), thousands come to worship Shiva's fiery *lingam* in one of South India's oldest rituals. On Mt Arunachala the sacred fire takes the form of a 30m wick burning for up to a week in 2000L of *ghee* (clarified butter) – it can be seen from 35km away! Households also have their own lamps lit in Shiva's honour (an extension of the nationwide Diwali festival), not to mention the bonfires and fireworks which are all part of the spectacle. The thousands of pilgrims who dare to take on the relentless sun climb the mountain in bare feet or walk a 14km lap of its base.

Losar (Dharamsala, Himachal Pradesh)

The Losar festival is the Indian version of Tibetan New Year, with Tibetans across North India welcoming the new year over a period of three days in December/January or February/March, depending on the region. Celebrations include processions, music and dancing, and *chaam* (ritual masked dances), such as the colourful Aji Lhamu dance. On the last day of the year, houses and monasteries are thoroughly cleaned; families drink *changkol* (Tibetan rice wine) and say the auspicious greeting *tashi delek*. His Holiness the Dalai Lama is wished luck in the coming year with the gift of *tseril* (consecrated long-life pills) made from roasted barley dough. New Year's Day is dedicated to secular gatherings with dignitaries, including *dharma* (moral code of behaviour) talks from the Dalai Lama, and on the third day of the festival it's a Tibetan-style singing and dancing party.

Kumbh Mela (Allahabad, Uttar Pradesh)

The Kumbh Mela is the greatest gathering of humanity on earth – close to 100 million people attended the event in 2001, with approximately 15 million people a day taking a sacred bathe at the confluence of the Ganges, the Yamuna and the mythical subterranean Saraswati River. The story goes that gods and demons tussled over a *kumbh* (pitcher) containing the nectar of immortality, with four drops of the nectar landing in the rivers in Allahabad (Uttar Pradesh), Haridwar (Uttarakhand), Ujjain (Madhya Pradesh) and Nasik (Maharashtra). From this auspicious beginning grew the 12-year Kumbh Mela cycle, with pilgrims attending rites every four years in one of the cities. Hindu believers, *sadhus* (holy men) and *nagas* (naked spiritual men) cleanse their souls with a dunk in the Ganges.

Nehru Trophy Snake Boat Race (Alappuzha, Kerala)

The Vembanad Lake in Alappuzha (Alleppey) comes alive on the second Saturday of August each year, when its waters are plied by the giant low-slung *chundan vallams* (snake boats). Each boat is over 30m long and is graced by a raised, serpentine prow (hence the name). The boats are crewed by up to 100 rowers singing in unison, protected by gleaming silk umbrellas as they cover the distance of 1370m. Watched avidly by thousands of cheering spectators on bamboo terraces which are erected for the races, the annual event celebrates the seafaring and martial traditions of ancient Kerala with floats and performing arts. The prize trophy was a gift from Prime Minister Jawaharlal Nehru, who passed through the area in 1952 and was given a resounding welcome and snake-boat escort by the locals.

Procession of All Saints (Old Goa, Goa)

The fifth Monday of Lent (March/April) sees Old Goa remembering its Portuguese past in an event that's one of its kind outside Rome and a relic of the Franciscan order. On the day of the Procession of All Saints, devotees bring 30 brightly dressed, life-sized saint statues out from storage, and hoist them onto their shoulders to be carried in a procession of thousands through the neighbouring villages of Old Goa. As each saint is brought out, a priest recites their life story in Konkani. The whole Goan community turns out for the celebrations, and queues form along the route for people to duck beneath the saints and receive their blessings. Old Goa is converted into a family-friendly fair with stalls, food, and games long into the night. For three days after the procession, the statues are venerated in the Church of St Andrew.

Rath Yatra (Puri, Orissa)

This 'car festival' – where immense chariots are built and hauled by thousands of temple employees – is held on the second day of the bright half of Asadha month (June/July to the uninformed). Commemorating Krishna's journey from Gokul to Mathura, Lord Jagannath (Krishna's Sanskrit name), his brother Balbhadra and sister Subhadra are dragged from Jagannath Mandir to Gundicha Mandir before the eyes of thousands of pilgrims (plus tourists). The largest chariot is 14m high, running on 16 wheels – in previous centuries, worshippers threw themselves under the wheels to die gloriously before their gods. Once at their destination, the three gods take a well-earned break and undertake the return journey a week later. The festivities are concluded by breaking up the *rathas* (cars), with the slats used as firewood in the temple's kitchens or for funeral-pyre fuel.

Tarnetar Mela (Tarnetar, Gujarat)

This three-day wedding fair, where women choose their groom, is held at the Trineteshwar Temple in Tarnetar. Villagers from the region throng Tarnetar in their best attire. Men show their availability by sitting under an embroidered *chhatri* (umbrella), and women indicate their choice by initiating a conversation with one of the suitors. The atmosphere is punctuated by folk songs and dances to the tunes of flutes and drums. Held in August/September, the Mela celebrates the wedding of Arjuna and Draupadi, characters in the Mahabharata. To win Draupadi's hand, Arjuna completed the astounding feat of shooting an arrow through the eye of a rotating fish located at the top of a pole, while balancing on two scales and taking aim from the reflection of the fish in the water below. An indication of how hard it is to get married in Tarnetar?

india's languages

The linguistic array found in India is dazzling, not to mention astounding, bamboozling and utterly overwhelming. At the tip of the iceberg are the 22 languages recognised by the Constitution (Assamese, Bengali, Bodo, Dogri, Gujarati, Hindi, Kannada, Kashmiri, Konkani, Maithili, Malayalam, Manipuri, Marathi, Nepali, Oriya, Punjabi, Sanskrit, Santali, Sindhi, Tamil, Telugu and Urdu). Each state also has official languages – Assam, for example, functions in Assamese and Bodo. Other languages are spoken by large populations, but aren't ranked as 'official'. On the other hand, Hindi, the national language spoken by around 400 million Indians, actually comprises a number of distinct dialects – so what does your Varanasi taxi driver speak? And let's not forget the fact that newspapers and periodicals are produced in 101 languages and dialects, school instruction is conducted in 41 tongues while films are produced in 15, and about 14 scripts are used nationwide. How exactly did a country of one billion people end up speaking over 1600 'mother tongues'?

indo-aryan languages

The two major language families in India are the Indo-Aryan and the Dravidian. The Indo-Aryan family made its appearance in India in about the second millennium BC. It's the most spoken language family in India, now famously incarnated as Hindi and Urdu, with another 200 related variants. Sanskrit is the oldest of these languages and was recorded in the sacred literature of the Vedas, the canon of Hinduism. However, it's considered the 'mother tongue' of only 14,000 Indians, and is granted special status as the classical language of India. While Sanskrit was codified in the 4th century BC by the grammarian Panini, its offshoots, the Prakrits, developed into several literary languages. One famous descendent is Pali, the liturgical language of Theravada Buddhism across Asia, written in various scripts. The Prakrit used to write Jain scriptures – known as *Ardhamagadhi* – was an archaic form of Magadhi (currently spoken by over 10 million people predominantly in Bihar). Maharashtri, probably the most widespread of the Prakrits, was used to write Ancient Indian drama and is the ancestor of Marathi.

The Prakrits, also known as Middle Indic languages, were subsequently transformed by the Muslim invasions between the 13th and 16th centuries. Persian became influential, to be taken over by Urdu as the language of power developed in

Delhi. Simultaneously, Urdu's variant Deccani was born in South India – now known as Dakhni, it's spoken by Muslims on the continent's Deccan plateau. Sindhi, spoken in Gujarat and Rajasthan, was a popular language for Sufi poetry between the 14th and 18th centuries. Sometimes considered a dialect of Punjabi, the Dogri language has two millions speakers in Jammu and Kashmir and surrounding areas and is distinguished by its tones, an unusual trait for a language of this family. Maithili was traditionally the speech of Mithila, a kingdom of Ancient India named in the Ramayana; today it's spoken by 20 million people in Bihar.

dravidian languages

Legends related to Dravidian languages often claim that the language itself originated in a vast, ancient continent far to the south – a theory which sounds as well supported as various attempts by linguists to relate the Dravidian family to Finnish, Japanese or Australian Aboriginal languages. Whatever their history may be, the languages in this group are today mostly spoken in South India. Tamil is the classical Southern Dravidian tongue, with the oldest recorded literature in the Dravidian languages dating from the 3rd century BC. A lesser-known relative is Tulu, spoken by nearly two million people in Karnataka and Kerala – the first language of most of the Dalits (Untouchables) in the region. The Gondi language of Central India, with around two million speakers, has a rich folk literature in the form of both poetry and prose. In the northeastern states, the Kurukh language is spoken by some two million people yet is considered to be endangered because of the low literacy levels of its speakers. Both Gondi and Kurukh are isolated examples of the survival of Dravidian languages in the subcontinent's north. The hybrid Arwi tongue – a combination of Tamil and Arabic which was spoken by the Muslims of Tamil Nadu and Sri Lanka – is considered extinct in India.

austro-asiatic languages

While the majority of India's languages have Indo-Aryan or Dravidian roots, you'll also hear Austro-Asiatic and Tibeto-Burman languages spoken. Austro-Asiatic languages are generally believed to be the original languages of the east of India, subsequently influenced by incoming communities. India's most widely used language from this family is Santali, with official status in the country and around six million speakers in the northeastern states. It belongs to the Munda branch, just like the Korku language, which is spoken by less than 500,000 members of a little-known tribe in Madhya Pradesh and Maharashtra. The Nicobar Islands are home to 20,000 indigenous Nicobarese speakers. The six Nicobarese languages are often considered a separate branch within the Austro-Asiatic language family, although they show similarities with the Mon-Khmer languages of Southeast Asia.

tibeto-burman languages

The original home of the Tibeto-Burman languages seems to have been present-day China. The history of this language family in India is unclear, but around 60 of its languages are spoken today in the northern reaches of Indian territory. Tibetan, spoken by some 120,000 people, is a relative newcomer since the influx of Tibetan refugees which followed China's takeover of their homeland in 1949. Garo, the majority language of the people of the Garo Hills of Meghalaya, is closely related to Bodo, the language of Assam. Unlike most Indian languages, Garo uses the Roman alphabet as it lacks a written tradition of its own. Manipuri (also known as Meitei) is the lingua franca of the northeastern state of Manipuri; among its 1.2 million speakers there's a movement to return to their traditional Meitei Mayek script, instead of the Bengali script currently used. Kok Borok, the state language of Tripura, was first recorded in the Koloma script in the 1st century AD. The Ao language is spoken by some 140,000 residents of Nagaland; it has a rich legacy of folk tales, but with the increase in literacy the oral traditions are dying out. Mizo is the language of more than 500,000 people from the mountainous regions of northwestern India.

other languages

Aside from these major language groups, there are, of course, quirky anomalies. Unexpected but true, the Romani language spoken by the Roma people in Europe is related to Sanskrit, while the nearly extinct Khamyang language spoken by the small tribe of the same name in Assam and Arunachal Pradesh is related to Thai. India can also boast its very own language isolate – the Nihali language, spoken by some 5000 people in Madhya Pradesh and Maharashtra.

The Indian subcontinent was also the birthplace of several pidgins (languages without native speakers, reduced in structure and use) and creoles (pidgins that have become a native language of a community). Some of these are believed to be extinct today (such as a Portuguese-based creole in Goa), while others are still found – for example, the English-based Madras Pidgin in the south, used during the British rule, or the Hindi-based Bazaar Hindustani, spoken in the cities in northern India.

This awesome linguistic richness is just another factor in India's uniqueness. While you'll make an excellent impression by attempting a few words in any of the 15 languages in this phrasebook, bear in mind that most Indians will speak at least one other language – perhaps you can try and ask them about it?

indian english

Indian English is the modern variety of English spoken in India, with native speakers and its own grammar and vocabulary. By some estimates, India now has more speakers of English than any other country in the world, though most speak it as a second language. The origins of Indian English date back to 1600, when Queen Elizabeth I paved the way for the British East India Company's foray into India and over 300 years of trade and conflict. One of the most powerful and lasting legacies of British involvement in India is the language left behind.

English in India today is an official language of government and an important language in business. The first formal effort to spread it was made by Lord Thomas Babington Macaulay during his tenure as a member of the Supreme Council of India. In the 1830s he aimed to create 'a class who may be interpreters between us and the millions whom we govern – a class of persons, Indians in blood and colour, but English in taste, in opinion, in morals and in intellect'. This elite class of Indians took their lessons in the British English typical of the colonial ruling class, with a highly formalised pronunciation and grammar. After India gained independence in 1947, British English continued to be taught as the only proper way to speak English, and even as late as the 1970s, Indians were still learning their English grammar from textbooks half a century out of date. But while the posh-sounding, old-school queen's English was being taught in the classrooms, the variety of English spoken on India's streets was morphing into something else altogether, and over two turbulent centuries the language of the colonial rulers was bent and reformed to better suit its Indian masters.

The influences that shaped Indian English are many and varied. The ancient Indian Sanskrit language and the Portuguese, French and Dutch of the earliest European merchants have all left their mark. It has absorbed words and idioms from many of India's regional languages like Hindi, Gujarati, Marathi and Urdu, which have also influenced its grammar.

While the most widely spoken and understood official language in India is Hindi, it hasn't been universally accepted due to its predominantly northern origins. English lacks any such perceived regional bias, despite its links to the British invaders, and as such it now bridges India's cultural and linguistic divides, linking people from different ends of the country who for centuries had no universal tongue. The following section will take you through the idiosyncracies of Indian English in all its quirks and guises.

pronunciation

The sounds of Indian English are flavoured by the accents of the country's many and varied indigenous languages. Pronunciation will also reflect a person's educational (and therefore class) background – just as it does in Britain, where accents range from the plumb-in-the-mouth Received Pronunciation of the old-school educated elite to the many distinctive regional lilts.

grammar

A common jibe about Indian English has been its use of universally bad grammar but, prejudices aside, this is possibly its most endearing and distinctive quality. Verbs will combine with prepositions in wacky and wonderful ways and prepositions will often be dropped or replaced (*picked* for 'picked on', *return back* for 'return') and the '-ing' form will be often used:

Always, she is singing your praises.
I am driving when the accident is happening.
I went out for a walking.
fooding and lodging

It's also common for 'regular' grammatical principles to be applied to structures that are irregular in standard English, eg *I knowed* for 'I knew', or for adverbs to be created by adding the standard English '-ly', eg *he worked very hardly* for 'he worked very hard'. Constructions like 'a piece of' or 'a bunch of' also change, giving *a chalk piece* and *a key bunch,* and noun plurals might break the 'regular' rules by taking plural '-s' where standard English wouldn't, and vice versa:

a pile of litters	litter
a room full of furnitures	furniture
woods for chopping	wood

Yesterday one of my relative won the lottery.

Indigenous languages come into play in interesting ways, with endings added to standard English nouns to coin new terms. In these examples, the Hindi ending '-ni' is used when talking to (or about) a woman:

daaktarni	female doctor or a doctor's wife
masterni	female school teacher

Word order is also affected, due to the different order that Indian languages employ.

When they are coming?	When are they coming?
My all friends are waiting.	My friends are all waiting.
Your all closets are empty.	Your closets are all empty.

Throughout India, the universal tag question in Indian English is *isn't it?*, a quirk borrowed directly from colloquial Tamil, Kannada and Hindi. It can be used to indicate a genuine question (eg *He is very weak, isn't it?* instead of 'Is he weak?') or to reinforce a statement of fact (*I will be back soon, isn't it?*). Tag questions can be used to convey many different meanings, such as sarcasm (*I am not troubling you, isn't it?*), romance (*I am giving in to him, isn't it?*), bewilderment (*You mean he tried to fly, isn't it?*) and confusion (*I am wrong, right?*).

youngspeak

Teenagers *flip* for the opposite sex, *click* with each other, *bunk* or *cut* (miss) classes to go to the movies, contact *dalals* (brokers) to buy a second-hand motorbike or *PG (paying-guest) digs* (rental accommodation). They say *rubber* for erasers and condoms alike, and tell each other they have *pulled down* (look exhausted) or *gone down* (have lost weight) as they don their *keds* (sneakers) and write in *India ink* (jet-black ink) to their *Miss* (teacher) about how inspired they are by her *love marriage* (as opposed to arranged marriage). Meanwhile, the unpopular kid will find himself labelled a *lech* (lecherous individual) and be regarded by his peers as *shady* and perhaps a bit of a *shiznit* (weirdo).

vocabulary

Acronyms, abbreviations and the use of rhyme are all very popular mechanisms for creating new vocabulary:

ABCD	American Born Confused Desi – young Americans of Indian origin (Hinglish, from Hindi *des* 'country')
BTM	stands for *behanji-turned-mod* – someone trying to be fashionable, but not succeeding (Hinglish, from Hindi *behenji* 'small-town woman')
FOB	Fresh Off the Boat ('immigrant')
MCP	Male Chauvinist Pig
ML	a moral lecture or a mother-in-law
WT	a traveller without a ticket

chai-vai	tea
fighting-writing	wrangling
fundas	fundamentals
ice-cream-fice-cream	ice cream

Colloquialisms, slang and idioms are rife in Indian English. The following are just a few examples:

I got a firing.	I was yelled at, eg *I went to work and I got a firing from the boss.*
cheap and best	good value, eg *That masala was cheap and best, no?*
tell me	a standard greeting when answering the phone, eg *Tell me, how can I help you?*
Hello, what you want?	used to answer the phone, it's meant to be polite but is often perceived as rude by non-Indians
mention not	'you're welcome', used upon being thanked
myself Mita	introductions begin in this manner, eg *Myself Robert. Yourself?*
cooling glasses	sunglasses
dandruff	a person who 'flakes out' and ditches their friends (Indian English)
dingo	a derogatory reference to an Anglo-Indian person (Indian English)
elephant's teeth	something that's largely ornamental or showy (from a Hindi saying 'an elephant has separate teeth for eating and showing')
godown	warehouse
light	electric power
nose cut	humiliation
Peter	a speaker of fluent English (Indian English, used in Tamil Nadu)
stepney	a spare tyre, also slang for a mistress (Indian English, from a brand name of tyres)
swimming dress	swimming costume
two-in-one	boom box

bollywood

Labyrinthine plots, heroic acts by lead actors in the face of tragedy and, of course, song and dance are the key ingredients that keep audiences enthralled. The magic of *Bollywood* cuts across barriers of age, caste and economic status. Past lamentations over the use of any English in Indian films have given way to the *villain* now mouthing exclamations like *dammit*, *bastard* and *bloody fool* – and today, it's not just the villains who freely mouth Indian English; no seduction routine is now complete without the hero with his obligatory *chocolate boy* (seductively appealing) looks uttering *hello baby* and *come on*.

transport

Boarding your chosen mode of transport often hails the inevitable *starting trouble* as your driver waves a hand in the universal sign for *nahi* (no) and heads off in search of a mechanic or a vet. Somewhere along your travels you may well come upon the following words and phrases:

accidented	describes a vehicle involved in an accident, eg 'I accidented my car' (Indian English)
air dash	to take a flight (Indian English)
back up	to reverse (Indian English)
cut	a break in the concrete divider running along the middle of all wide roads to enable motorists to do a U-turn (Indian English)
dickey	the boot of a car, though it might be mistakenly used to refer to the bonnet also (Indian English)
foot over-bridge	a bridge for pedestrians to cross over railway tracks, roads, etc (Indian English)
hill station	a high-altitude village or resort, providing a cool and green holiday escape (Indian English)
Horn OK Please	invites other drivers to announce their presence by tooting
out of station	somewhere in the country (Indian English)
speed-breaker ahead	watch out for speed humps (Indian English)
scootie	two-wheeled vehicle
three-wheeler	an auto-rickshaw
two-wheeler	a motorbike or scooter

food & drink

Given Indian cuisine's incredibly rich and long history, it's not surprising that Indian English has made little headway into its nomenclature. Indeed, most food terminology is firmly rooted in Hindi and other indigenous tongues. While there are examples of Indian English to be found on the menu, such as *Bombay duck* (a small saltwater fish) and *rumble tumble* (spicy scrambled eggs), English is more likely to flavour the kitchens and dining rooms of the country through the classic blend of Hindi and English known as Hinglish – eg *mutton korma* (mutton cooked with a thick spicy gravy). Hinglish also gives us *khaata-peeta type* for a 'foodie' (from Hindi *khaata* 'eating' and *peeta* 'drinking'), but Indian English is clearly at work in *mice running in my tummy* (the literal rendering of the Hindi *pet mein choohe daud rahe hein* for 'I'm starving').

By contrast, the relatively modern influences of alcohol and coffee on Indian culture lend themselves perfectly to the quirky nature of Indian English. On average, Indians consume far less alcohol than their Western counterparts. At trendy clubs and bars serving drinks as fashion statements you can order cocktails and *mocktails* (without alcohol) in tall frosted glasses with cute paper umbrellas. As the image of drinking distances itself from one of debauchery, it's no longer taboo to be *hanged-over*. In hotels and restaurants watch out for the *Bar-Attached* sign, without which liquor can't be served. A drunkard is described as *walking on four legs* (crawling) and *drunken driving* refers to accidents in the wake of inebriation – hopefully less common on *dry days* (national holidays when licensed liquor shops down shutters).

On the nonalcoholic front, H_2O is a no go – drinking *pipe* (tap) water could lay you out with all manner of internal mischief. No such fears with a *cool drink* (any soft drink), *cold juice* (fresh juice) or a *sherbet* (a syrupy drink made from rose essence or almonds). Coffee (pronounced *ko*·fi, *kaa*·pi and *kaa*·fi) is the drink of preference in the south, whereas tea rules in the north. In cities, the traditional *coffee-house* culture, which saw intellectuals gather in murky state-sponsored environs, can be added to India's store of bygone relics, replaced by city cafés serving the growing middle classes with European style decaf, *caffè latte*, double espresso, cappuccino, mocha and Irish coffee. The majority of locals take their coffee either *strong* or *light*. Among the offerings for the coffee-lover are:

black coffee	coffee without milk
cold coffee	iced coffee
decoction	made by brewing freshly ground coffee beans
instant	coffee powder that dissolves instantly in boiled milk
Madras filter coffee	a strong, sweet, milky coffee made from roasted dark coffee beans with the addition of chicory